Professional JMS Programming

Paul Giotta
Scott Grant
Michael Kovacs
Meeraj Kunnumpurath
Silvano Maffeis
K. Scott Morrison
Gopalan Suresh Raj

Wrox Press Ltd. ®

Professional JMS Programming

Published by Wrox Press Ltd,
Arden House, 1102 Warwick Road, Acocks Green,
Birmingham, B27 6BH, UK
Printed in the United States
ISBN 1-861004-93-1

Trademark Acknowledgements

Wrox has endeavored to provide trademark information about all the companies and products mentioned in this book by the appropriate use of capitals. However, Wrox cannot guarantee the accuracy of this information.

Credits

Authors
Paul Giotta
Scott Grant
Michael Kovacs
Meeraj Kunnumpurath
Silvano Maffeis
K. Scott Morrison
Gopalan Suresh Raj

Additional Material
James McGovern

Category Manager
Viv Emery

Technical Architect
Craig A. Berry

Technical Editors
Jim Molony
Matthew Moodie

Author Agent
Emma Batch

Project Administrators
Nicola Phillips
Laura Hall

Technical Reviewers
Carl Burnham
Phil Powers DeGeorge
Matthew Green
Joe Humphrey
Alex Linde
Hemant More
Ron Phillips
Mike Slinn
John Timney
David Whitney

Production Coordinator
Tom Bartlett

Figures
Shabnam Hussain

Cover
Shelley Frazier

Index
Adrian Axinte

Proof Reader
Christopher Smith

About the Authors

Paul Giotta

Paul Giotta holds degrees in electrical engineering from both Rensselaer Polytechnic Institute and the Swiss Federal Institute of Technology. He began his career in the field of R&D for advanced military radar systems at AIL Systems in the US. He later moved to Switzerland and took up work in the development and implementation of financial analytics for the trading of fixed income derivatives at Credit Suisse. Paul ultimately entered the field of software engineering full time when he began work on the architecture and implementation of real-time distributed trading systems (based entirely on Publish/Subscribe messaging) at CS. He later moved on to the development of financial information systems at Olsen & Associates and also worked as an IT consultant for Cambridge Technology Partners. Paul is now chief architect for message servers at Softwired AG in Zurich.

Paul lives in Winterthur, Switzerland, with his wife Andrea and sons Simon and David. In his precious free time he enjoys skiing, snowboarding, hiking, and inline skating.

Paul contributed Chapter 8 and additional material to this book.

Scott Grant

Scott Grant is a Chief Architect with CascadeWorks, Inc., in San Francisco, California, and has over fifteen years of diverse development experience. An independent consultant for many years, he has been a successful founder of two start-up companies, where he has helped to build and shape the engineering teams and environments. A Sun-Certified Java Developer, Scott has published numerous technical articles on Java programming subjects, and enjoys working with emerging Java standards and technologies.

When not programming or writing, he enjoys spending his time with his wife, hiking the trails of Yosemite National Park, and working for Native American causes and charities.

Scott contributed Chapter 7 and additional material to this book.

Michael Kovacs

Michael Kovacs is a Sun-Certified Java 2 Programmer and has been working in Java for the past three years. He has worked on all aspects of web-based software development from the browser to the database. He has recently joined BEA Systems in San Francisco, CA as a Senior Software Engineer working with the WebLogic team. Before joining BEA he relocated last spring from his home in Cleveland, OH to San Francisco to work for Carstation.com, which inspired this book's work. In his previous programming life he was a C programmer who started out writing software for lottery systems. He has a Bachelors degree in Electronic Engineering Technology from The University of Dayton. When not hacking away at his computer he loves playing baseball, football, guitar, and fantasy baseball with his buddies from college, and watching the greatest movie of all time *The Big Lebowski*. Drop him a line at Michael_P_Kovacs@yahoo.com.

Michael contributed Chapter 9 to this book.

To all of my various colleagues with whom I've worked in the past, thank you for your help and friendship.

Meeraj Kunnumpurath

Meeraj Kunnumpurath works as a Senior Information Specialist with Electronic Data Systems, responsible for designing enterprise helpdesk and billing systems mainly using J2EE and XML. He has chosen for personal reasons not to be photographed on the front cover.

Meeraj contributed Chapters 2, 3, and 6, plus additional material to this book.

I would like to dedicate this to God who has given me all I have in this life.

Silvano Maffeis

Silvano Maffeis is CTO at Softwired, a leading vendor of Java messaging middleware for wireline and wireless networks. Silvano holds a Ph.D. in computer science and is the author of numerous publications about Java software development, middleware, and wireless communication.

Silvano contributed Chapter 11 to this book.

K. Scott Morrison

K. Scott Morrison is the Director, Architecture and Technology, for Infowave Software. He is currently leading a number of teams confronting the challenges in opening corporate data stores to an ever-increasing variety of wireless devices. He is a frequent and very popular speaker on topics in XML, Java, and wireless system architectures. Prior to his joining Infowave, Scott was the Senior Architect in the e-business division at IBM's Pacific Development Centre. While at IBM, his focus was on building high-volume, high-transaction rate web systems for travel and transportation, as well as designing and auditing Internet security architectures for government and financial sector clients.

Scott began his career by spending eight years involved in medical imaging research at the University of British Columbia. Here, he worked on Positron Emission Tomography (PET) brain scanner design, produced educational CD-ROMs about Alzheimer's disease for physicians, and conducted original research into neurodegenerative disorders. He has been published extensively in leading journals in medicine and in physics. He has also been a consultant on a number of feature film and television productions. Scott's current research interests lie in enterprise XML messaging architectures, Java/XML integration, and development frameworks for wireless systems.

Scott contributed Chapter 10 plus additional material to this book.

I would like to thank two people who helped me to pull this work together: My wife Liz, for wonderful support even while faced with her own publishing deadlines; and Ali Solehdin, who provided the SOAP and UDDI examples.

Gopalan Suresh Raj

Gopalan Suresh Raj is a senior analyst, software architect, and developer with expertise in multi-tiered systems development, enterprise component architectures, and distributed object computing. He is also an active author, including contributions to *Enterprise Java Computing-Applications and Architecture*, Cambridge University Press, 1999, and *The Awesome Power of JavaBeans*, Manning Publications Co., 1998. His work has been published in numerous technical journals. Visit him at his popular website http://gsraj.tripod.com or mail him at gopalan@gmx.net.

Gopalan contributed Chapters 1, 4 and 5 to this book.

com.sun.jndi...
weblogic.jndi.T3Initial...
weblogic.jms.rtl.Fiorano...
fiorano.jms.runtime.n...
ch.softwired.jms.naming...
com.sun.jndi.ldap.LdapCtxFactory
fiorano.jms.rtl.fscontext.RefFSContextFactory
weblogic.jndi.WLInitialContextFactory
com.sun.jndi.T3InitialContextFactory
weblogic.jms.rtl.FioranoInitialContextFactory
fiorano.jms.runtime.naming.FioranoInitialContextFactory
weblogic.jms.naming.IBusContextFactory
ch.softwired.jms.naming.IBusContextFactory

com.sun.jndi.fscontext.RefFSContextFactory
weblogic.jndi.ldap.LdapCtxFactory
fiorano.jms.rtl.FioranoInitialContextFactory
fiorano.jms.runtime.naming.IBusContextFactory
ch.softwired.jms.naming.IBusContextFactory

Table of Contents

Table of Contents

Table of Contents

Table of Contents

Table of Contents

Table of Contents

Table of Contents

com.sun.jn...
com.sun.jn...
weblogic.jndi.T3Initial Fior...
weblogic.jms.runtime.n...
fiorano.jms.rtl.Fioran...
fiorano.jms.naming...
ch.softwired.fscontext.RefFSContextFactory
com.sun.jndi.ldap.LdapCtxFactory
weblogic.jndi.WLInitialContextFactory
weblogic.jndi.T3InitialContextFactory
fiorano.jms.runtime.naming.FioranoInitialContextFactory
fiorano.jms.rtl.FioranoInitialContextFactory
ch.softwired.jms.naming.IBusContextFactory

Introduction

Message-Oriented Middleware (MOM) has been a vital element for integrating enterprise applications for quite a long time. MOM allows enterprise systems to be composed of self-contained independent entities that are loosely coupled to each other thereby providing flexibility, extensibility, and minimal mutual impact. Products like MSMQ and MQSeries have provided proprietary solutions to meet the various enterprise messaging requirements.

With the emergence of Java as a platform for developing and deploying enterprise applications the need for defining a standard way for Java language programs to participate in enterprise messaging became quite evident. The **Java Message Service (JMS)** defines a standard way for Java language programs to create and exchange enterprise messages. JMS also provides a standard way for Java language programs residing in the various tiers of enterprise applications to access the services of products from traditional MOM vendors.

JMS, like other enterprise Java APIs, specifies a set of interfaces that define the various entities associated with enterprise messaging. **JMS providers** are software products that implement these interfaces and provide enterprise messaging solutions. JMS based enterprise systems typically comprise a set of JMS clients exchanging messages with each other by connecting to a central JMS provider.

Traditional MOM products provided a plethora of proprietary features like message creation, asynchronous and synchronous message delivery, message persistence, guaranteed delivery, message prioritization, message broadcasting, etc. JMS provides the common features provided by all the traditional MOM vendors.

The various messaging features provided by JMS include:

- ❑ Point-to-Point messaging based message queues
- ❑ Publish/Subscribe messaging based on topic hierarchy
- ❑ A set of message interfaces to support different message format requirements
- ❑ Synchronous and asynchronous message delivery
- ❑ Persistent messages
- ❑ Support for transactions

JMS also seamlessly integrates with most of the other enterprise Java APIs like **JDBC (Java Database Connectivity)**, **EJB (Enterprise Java Beans)**, **JTA (Java Transaction API)**, **JTS (Java Transaction Service)**, **JNDI (Java Naming and Directory Interface)**, **JSP (Java Server Pages)**, and **servlets**:

- ❑ JMS clients can demarcate messaging instructions and JDBC calls using the same transaction
- ❑ Servlets and JSPs can use JMS for sending and receiving messages
- ❑ EJB 2.0 specified message-driven beans can respond to asynchronous JMS messages
- ❑ JNDI can be used for storing and retrieving configured JMS objects
- ❑ JMS clients can use JTA to transactionally demarcate the sending and receiving of JMS messages
- ❑ JTS can be used to include JMS messages in distributed transactions along with other JTS-compliant services like database calls

What's Covered in this Book

In this book we will be covering the fundamentals of JMS programming as well as the advanced JMS concepts on interfacing JMS with the other enterprise Java APIs. Specifically we will be looking at:

- ❑ The JMS fundamentals, including the notions of a JMS message, topics, queues, connections, sessions, producers, and consumers
- ❑ The two JMS messaging models: Point-to-Point and Publish/Subscribe
- ❑ Web messaging
- ❑ EJB messaging
- ❑ The use of JMS in clustered architecture
- ❑ Distributed logging using JMS
- ❑ JMS and XML messaging
- ❑ Implementing a wireless JMS system
- ❑ The main JMS providers

Who Should Use this Book

This book is for professional Java developers who need a comprehensive explanation of JMS and how it can be used to solve computing problems. It will also be of interest to developers who have a good working knowledge of Java, and some familiarity with J2EE. It provides developers with core JMS theory alongside practical case studies exemplifying real-world uses of JMS.

What You Need to Use this Book

Various JMS providers are used throughout this book and a comprehensive list of vendors can be found on Sun's web site at: http://java.sun.com/products/jms/vendors.html. However, during the course of this book the following JMS providers are used. You will not need them all but you may need to modify the examples as appropriate for your chosen provider. Appendix A provides details on what will need modifying to run the code on each provider.

JMQ 1.1 (Java Message Queue) from Sun Microsystems

JMQ is a JMS implementation from Sun Microsystems that supports both PTP and Pub/Sub models, and is written in pure Java:

❑ JMQ is available under various "Try & Buy" deals from http://www.sun.com/workshop/jmq

SonicMQ 3.0 from Progress Software

SonicMQ is a complete messaging framework primarily designed for Java applications by Progress Software:

❑ SonicMQ is available for free download from http://www.sonicMQ.com

FioranoMQ 4.6 from Fiorano Software

FioranoMQ is an event-driven communication platform that provides pure Java implementation of JMS, from Fiorano Software:

❑ A 30-day trial version of the software is available for download from http://www.fiorano.com

iBus//MessageServer 4.1 and iBus//Mobile 1.0.0 from Softwired

iBus is a pure Java messaging product family offering the JMS abstraction atop a variety of operating system platforms and transport protocols. Two iBus products will be required for this book, iBus//MessageServer and iBus//Mobile:

❑ iBus products are available for free download from http://www.softwired-inc.com

WebLogic 6.0 from BEA Systems

WebLogic Server is an industry standard application server from BEA Systems. The latest version of WebLogic (v 6.0) implements EJB 2.0 specification (as an optional add-on) and supports message-driven EJBs that are activated by JMS messages:

❑ An evaluation version of WebLogic 6.0 is available from http://www.bea.com

JLog 1.01 from JTrack

In addition to the above JMS providers, the following was used for the logging examples in Chapter 9:

- ❏ JLog 1.01 from http://www.jtrack.com

Software Acknowledgements

The following were used for diagrams in the book:

- ❏ Together 4.2 from TogetherSoft for the sequence diagrams
- ❏ jVision 1.4 from Object Insight, Inc. for the class diagrams

Conventions

We have used a number of different styles of text and layout in this book to help differentiate between the different kinds of information. Here are examples of the styles we use and an explanation of what they mean:

Code has several styles. If it's a word that we're talking about in the text, for example when discussing a Java `StringBuffer` object, it's in this font. If it's a block of code that you can type as a program and run, then it's in a gray box:

```
public void close() throws EJBException, RemoteException
```

Sometimes you'll see code in a mixture of styles, like this:

```
<?xml version 1.0?>
<Invoice>
    <part>
        <name>Widget</name>
        <price>$10.00</price>
    </part>
</invoice>
```

In cases like this, the code with a white background is code we are already familiar with; the line highlighted in grey is a new addition to the code since we last looked at it.

Advice, hints, and background information come in this type of font.

> **Important pieces of information come in boxes like this.**

Bullets appear indented, with each new bullet marked as follows:

- ❏ **Important Words** are in a bold type font
- ❏ Words that appear on the screen, in menus like File or Window, are in a similar font to that you would see on a Windows desktop
- ❏ Keys that you press on the keyboard like *Ctrl* and *Enter*, are in italics

Customer Support

We've tried to make this book as accurate and enjoyable as possible, but what really matters is what the book actually does for you. Please let us know your views, either by returning the reply card in the back of the book, or by contacting us via e-mail at feedback@wrox.com.

Source Code and Updates

As you work through the examples in this book, you may decide that you prefer to type in all the code by hand. Many readers prefer this because it's a good way to get familiar with the coding techniques that are being used.

Whether you want to type the code in or not, we have made all the source code for this book available at our web site at the following address:

http://www.wrox.com/

If you're one of those readers who like to type in the code, you can use our files to check the results you should be getting – they should be your first stop if you think you might have typed in an error. If you're one of those readers who doesn't like typing, then downloading the source code from our web site is a must!

Either way, it'll help you with updates and debugging.

Errata

We've made every effort to make sure that there are no errors in the text or the code. However, to err is human, and as such we recognize the need to keep you informed of any mistakes as they're spotted and corrected. Errata sheets are available for all our books at http://www.wrox.com. If you find an error that hasn't already been reported, please let us know.

Our web site acts as a focus for other information and support, including the code from all our books, sample chapters, previews of forthcoming titles, and articles and opinion on related topics.

P2P Online Forums

Join the mailings lists at http://www.p2p.wrox.com for author and peer support. Be confident that your query is not just being examined by a support professional, but by the many Wrox authors and other industry experts present on our mailing lists.

com.sun.jn...
weblogic.jndi.T3Initia...
fiorano.jms.rtl.Fiorar...
ch.softwired.jms.naming.n...
com.sun.jndi.fscontext.RefFSContextFactory
weblogic.jndi.WLInitialContextFactory
com.sun.jndi.ldap.LdapCtxFactory
fiorano.jms.rtl.FioranoInitialContextFactory
weblogic.jndi.T3InitialContextFactory
fiorano.jms.runtime.naming.FioranoInitialContextFactory
ch.softwired.jms.naming.IBusContextFactory

1

Introduction to Messaging Applications, MOM, and JMS

The task of writing distributed enterprise applications presents us with many significant challenges. Some of these can be overcome by increasing program modularity – composing a unified application from multiple independent modules. This not only allows us to build complex systems using an "assembly-line" approach, but also comes with the benefit of reusability of the modules themselves.

However, it would be helpful if we had a well-defined, reliable framework that would guarantee that our communications would be safely handled between these distributed modules. This is what messaging systems provide for us – a reliable, secure, guaranteed message-delivery mechanism.

In this introductory chapter we will:

- ❑ Define enterprise messaging, clients, destination, domains, and messages
- ❑ Discuss Message-Oriented Middleware (MOM)
- ❑ Look at JMS and the messaging domains supported by JMS
- ❑ Discuss JMS and its relation to other Java technologies
- ❑ Look at the areas that JMS does not address
- ❑ Discuss JMS's role in enterprise applications, application integration, and mobile messaging
- ❑ Finish off this introductory chapter by looking at the various design patterns available for designing MOM applications

Enterprise Messaging

In a lot of enterprise applications, processing of work must be treated as a contractual obligation. Some examples of these can be found in the banking or the telecommunication industries. A customer may request to debit from one account and credit the other, or to buy and sell stock, or to initiate and terminate telephone services. These requests *cannot* be lost. Any enterprise system that is built for these types of processing tasks should ensure that, as long as the request mechanism's preconditions are satisfied, these requests *always* succeed.

Messaging is the best technology for these types of enterprise applications. Other communication models lack the features that make message-based models so resilient to failure. We will be covering alternative ways of communication as we advance through the chapter.

> **Messaging is a system of asynchronous requests, reports, or events that are used by enterprise applications.**

It is an event-driven communications layer that allows enterprise applications – on the same system, the same network, or loosely connected through the Internet – to transfer information as securely as needed and at whatever pace the interacting systems can maintain.

Messages can be written to disk so that they will not be lost if the system fails or goes down. Messages can also be sent or received as part of a transaction. Transactions ensure that messaging operations are coordinated with other work. If a program reads a message but fails before it can complete processing, the message remains to be processed later.

Before we go on, let's identify a few terms that will be important for our messaging discussion:

> **A message is a unit of information or data that is sent from a process running on one computer to other processes running on the same or different computers.**

A message is a lightweight object consisting of a **header** and a **body**. The header contains identification and content-type information. The body contains application data.

> **A destination is the concept that encapsulates the addressing information used by a messaging product to locate the endpoint for message delivery. It is not, in itself, an endpoint.**

The destination in JMS is either a **queue** or a **topic**. We will discuss destinations in more detail when we look at messaging domains later in the chapter. The messaging server, broker, or provider, functions as an intermediary between the requestor and the receiver and acts as the host for the destination.

> **A domain is a logical grouping of related destinations.**

Setting up domains allows us to group related topics or queues. It allows us to use the same topic or queue name over different domains. A single domain can support a combination of both queues and topics.

> **A client is any object, process, or application that makes use of a messaging service.**

In the context of messaging, the term "server" refers to the messaging server, broker or provider. Everything else that interacts with the messaging server and relies on its services is referred to as a messaging client.

The figure below diagrammatically captures the definitions for client, message, destination, and domain:

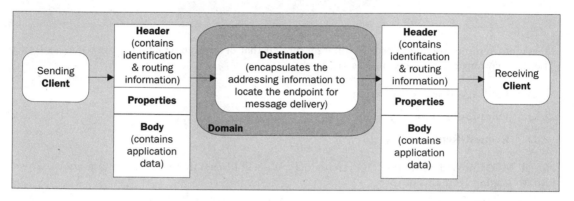

As an example, suppose a distributed component wants to send stock quote information to one or more remotely located distributed components. Rather than having to know the exact clients to which it sends messages containing the stock quote, it can establish a destination, either a message queue or a message topic area with the messaging server, and "post" the stock quote with the server, which then distributes the messages to the appropriately registered receiving clients.

Without the messaging server the sending client would have the burden of monitoring whether or not the receiving client is currently connected, whether or not a network failure occurred during the send operation, and so on. The server plays an important role in transparently handling many network-related issues, including reliable message delivery, which can require transaction processing and/or persistent message storage.

Message-Oriented Middleware

Message-Oriented Middleware (MOM) acts as an intermediary, and provides a common reliable way for programs to create, send, receive, and read messages in any distributed enterprise system. MOM ensures fast, reliable asynchronous electronic communication; and guaranteed message delivery, receipt notification, and transaction control.

The central MOM notion is the concept of a **destination** (a **queue** or a **communication topic**). Messaging clients send messages to the MOM, which in turn *routes* these messages to the appropriate receiver. The figure overleaf shows a couple of enterprise application messaging clients sending messages to each other using the services of a MOM provider:

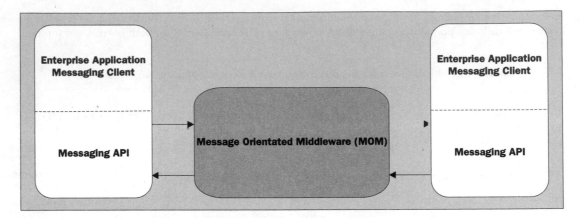

Messaging systems are classified into different models that determine which client receives a message. The most common messaging models are:

❑ **Publish/Subscribe** messaging

❑ **Point-to-Point** messaging

❑ **Request-Reply** messaging

Not all MOM providers support all these models. We will discuss these models in more detail as we get into Messaging Domains in JMS.

Features of MOM

Some of the important features and services provided by MOM are described in the following paragraphs:

❑ **Guaranteed Message Delivery**
Applications sending messages between each other need not even be connected to the network at the same time. MOM guarantees that the messages will be delivered as soon as the network connections are established and the receiving application issues a request for sent messages. You will be able to appreciate this better if you realize that traditional synchronous solutions would require that the two systems be up and accessible to each other *at the same time*.

❑ **Asynchronous Communication**
Once a client application sends out a message to a receiving application, the MOM allows the client application to handle other tasks without waiting for a response from the receiving application.

❑ **Transaction Support**
MOM supports transactions and is also tightly integrated with transaction services. When transaction services are present, they may participate in a MOM transaction.

❑ **One Time, in-Order Delivery**
MOM can provide guarantees that each message will be delivered once and only once, and that the messages are received in the order in which they are sent

❑ **Message Routing Services**
These services give the client application the ability to send messages to their destination using *least-cost* routing. The administrator only needs to define the cost of each route, and the MOM will automatically calculate the most economical path for the message. Moreover, this routing is capable of eliminating single points of failure. Hence, the MOM can reroute around network problems. This is very helpful if you are dealing with unreliable networks such as the Internet.

❑ **Notification Services**
Even though the MOM allows messages to be sent asynchronously freeing up the client application, in some instances, the sending application may want to be notified whether the message was received successfully. So, the MOM also allows the sender the option to review responses, let another application handle them or just completely ignore them. The MOM can also journal messages to provide audit trails.

Advantages of MOM

Message-Oriented Middleware software reduces the complexity involved in developing applications that span multiple operating systems and networking protocols. It achieves this by insulating the application developer from the details of the various operating systems and network interfaces. By providing API (such as JMS) implementations that extend transparently across diverse platforms and networks, MOMs increase the flexibility of an architecture and enable applications to exchange messages with other programs without having to know what platform or processor the other application resides on.

Distributed systems based on the messaging paradigm are relatively easy to modify because event dependencies are resolved through runtime event names, rather than by compilers, linkers or operating systems. Clients of messages operate independently of, and asynchronously from, each other and may change without recompilation. All communication between applications is through messages that are routed through the MOM server. This allows new applications to be added to the distributed system later without recompiling, re-linking or even stopping and restarting any current applications. The messaging paradigm greatly reduces complexity in distributed system design and implementation. Events are published to destinations as they happen; business processes that depend on these events automatically receive them as they occur.

The other advantages of using MOMs are:

❑ **Robustness to Change**
Applications on heterogeneous platforms communicate and interoperate transparently yet each application operates independently of, and asynchronously with, others. Communicating programs remain separately maintained and individually replaceable.

❑ **Time Independence**
Neither the message sender nor the message recipient needs to be online at the same time. The MOM queues messages when their recipients are not available.

❑ **Location Independence**
The message sender, and the message recipient can be migrated from computer to computer at runtime, since both senders and receivers are *decoupled* using destinations (either message queues or communication topics). This enables continuous uninterrupted operation, because software and hardware can be serviced without bringing down the system. Applications can be moved between machines without disrupting other component applications; developers use a logical, consistent naming convention and are completely isolated from low-level details of network programming.

❑ **Latency Hiding**

In traditional synchronous systems, a client is typically suspended while its request is transmitted to the server, and a reply sent back to the client. This makes for hard to design user interfaces, as the application GUI would freeze during a long-running transaction. Making the user-interface responsive in spite of this problem places a heavy demand on the developer. The developer is then forced to work with threads, and potentially has to interrupt pending calling at any time. However, with MOM, the request and reply phases are totally decoupled. Once a request is transmitted, the user-interface can immediately proceed with the next task. This makes for more user-friendly client applications, but still carries a dependency on the developer to cater for the reply phase.

❑ **Scalability**

If you have several clients that generate requests, for example, purchase requests, and one system that processes them, for instance order processing, then you can scale the order processing capacity by adding more machines that look at the same queue. Considering the fact that there is always a limitation on the number of concurrent sockets that a single server machine can keep open, Publish/Subscribe MOM systems scale well in respect to the number of receivers of a particular message.

❑ **Event-driven Systems**

Since events are essentially a form of message, MOMs explicitly support the development of event-driven distributed enterprise applications.

❑ **Simplicity**

MOMs are based on the simple idea of a destination that messages are sent to or received from, which developers can grasp easily and thus quickly become productive.

❑ **Configurable Quality of Service**

With synchronous systems, the Quality of Service is always 100% reliability. Given that, one could easily argue against the need for a different model. However, QoS is a much broader concept than simply reliability, including speed, resilience, latency, and availability. The reality is that sometimes, configurable reliability is preferred, simply because of the cost to speed, resilience, latency, and availability, involved in achieving that 100% reliability.

A MOM-based system can make certain assumptions about the messages it needs to distribute. For example, let us consider that we need to send out a stock quote message to 100,000 clients. As a message carrier, the MOM can decide that since the message is identical for all the 100,000 clients, it will use a more efficient transport protocol than TCP/IP to send the message, like IP Multicast. This means that the message has to be sent only once, irrespective of the number of recipients. In this type of system, let us assume it is adequate if 98% of the clients get the stock quote message. In a synchronous system, to be sure that any client received the message, the system would have to send synchronous messages, in this case, 100,000 of them. This would not only be time-consuming, but also far too expensive for the extra benefit.

However, if MOM clients need reliable and guaranteed delivery I would configure the QoS to be so, such that all my 100,000 clients (100% of them) received the message. Remember, previously we stated that the QoS is configurable. In essence, what we're saying is that MOMs have a choice of QoS as opposed to synchronous systems. It's configurable according to client needs.

The Java Message Service (JMS)

The Java Message Service (JMS) is an API for accessing messaging systems.

The JMS specification defines an interface but does not itself define an *implementation*. JMS provides a standard Java-based interface to the message services of a MOM of some provider. The specification in itself is vendor neutral – it sets requirements but does not dictate how they are implemented. The JMS specification provides Java applications with a common way to create, send, receive, and read an enterprise messaging system's messages.

As shown in the figure below, **JMS Service Providers** implement the JMS interface on top of their messaging services. It is up to the vendor to add facilities, services, or enhancements not included or defined explicitly in the specification. JMS defines queues and topics, but it does not require the provider to implement both. JMS thus tries to maximize portability of the solution with as many features as possible:

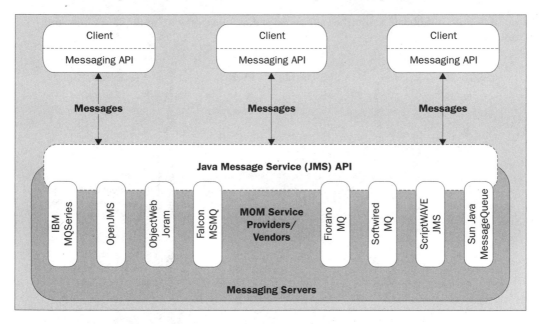

The primary features of JMS are as follows:

❑ **Connection factories** are used in JMS to create connections to a specific JMS provider.

❑ In JMS, Publish/Subscribe messaging and Point-to-Point messaging domains are implemented and defined by separate interfaces so that a provider does not have to support both.

❑ JMS defines the concept of a topic or a queue as the target for a message. Topics are used for Publish/Subscribe messaging. Queues are used for Point-to-Point messaging.

❑ The providers' code is accessed through JMS interfaces, freeing the implementation from the limitations of sub classing.

❑ JMS provides support for distributed transactions and JMS messaging domains.

Messaging systems are classified into different models that determine which client receives a message. The messaging models supported by JMS are:

❑   Publish/Subscribe messaging

❑   Point-to-Point messaging

We describe these models in the following sections.

Publish/Subscribe Messaging

The destination in this paradigm is called a **topic**. This domain allows for **asynchronous** message delivery. When multiple applications need to receive the same messages, Publish/Subscribe messaging is used. The central concept in a Publish/Subscribe messaging system is the topic. This model, as shown in the figure below, is extremely useful when a group of applications want to notify each other of a particular occurrence. A client publishes an event to a topic, and by subscribing, multiple clients are informed of the event.

The point to note in Publish/Subscribe messaging is that, there may be multiple senders and multiple receivers:

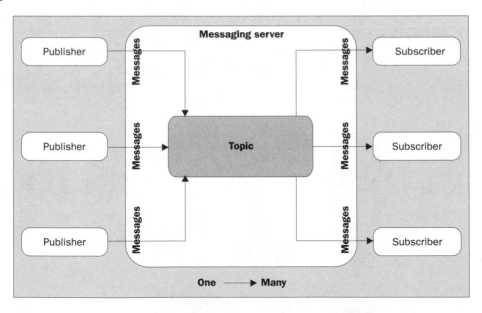

The simple Publish/Subscribe example shown in the above figure contains a single topic and six clients (three publishers and three subscribers). All the subscribers subscribe to the topic and all the publishers publish messages to the topic. The messaging system takes care of distributing messages from the publisher to the subscriber. The characteristic pattern of interaction is as follows:

❑   During the subscriber's initialization, the subscriber registers an instance of a callback (a message handler invoked by the server) with the topic.

❑   The publishing client arrives at a point in its processing when it needs to send out a message. It creates the message and publishes it to the topic.

❏   The messaging system delivers the message to all its subscribers by invoking the respective callbacks that were registered earlier.

❏   Once all the subscribers have been notified, and the appropriate acknowledgements received, the message is removed from the topic.

Durable Subscriptions

When a subscribing client (through its session with the JMS server) requests a durable subscription, the JMS server will, in its persistent store, "save" any messages intended for the subscriber during periods when the subscriber is inactive.

Durability vs. Persistence

Durable versus non-durable relationships exist between a consuming client and the JMS server, which delivers messages. If a particular topic has durable subscribers, the messaging server retains all the messages published on the topic in a database or file for delivery to those subscribers that might be currently disconnected from the server. A message subscription for a client can be placed in a dormant state, halting the delivery of all messages to the client. The messaging server will however, store all the messages for that client until the subscription is awakened. This is really useful for disconnected and mobile users who, even though not always connected to the network, can be assured they will receive all their messages. A message is only deleted from the off-line storage when it has been delivered to all durable subscribers or after the expiration time of the message.

Delivery mode involves a message-level relationship between the producing client and the JMS server, and only indirectly between the producing and consuming clients. The delivery mode field in the message header of every message is set to either persistent message delivery or non-persistent message delivery at the time the message is sent. This is what I refer to as a message-level relationship between the producer and the destination.

A producing client can choose persistent delivery mode for either messaging model – Publish/Subscribe or Point-to-Point. "Durable delivery" is an option for clients that subscribe to topics, not for clients that connect to a queue.

Point-to-Point Messaging

The destination in this paradigm is called a queue. This domain allows for **synchronous** message delivery. When one process needs to send a message to another process, Point-to-Point messaging can be used. However, this may or may not be a one-way relationship. The client to a messaging system may only send messages, only receive messages, or send and receive messages. At the same time, another client can also send and/or receive messages. In the simplest case, one client is the sender of the message and the other client is the receiver of the message.

There are two basic types of Point-to-Point messaging systems. The first one involves a client that directly sends a message to another client. The second and more common implementation is based on the concept of a message queue. Such a system is shown in the figure overleaf:

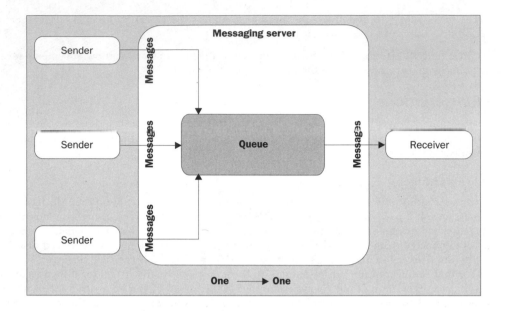

> **The main issue in Point-to-Point messaging is that, even though there may be multiple senders of messages, there is ultimately only a single potential receiver for each message.**

The simple Point-to-Point example shown in the above figure contains a single queue and four clients (three senders and a receiver). The characteristic pattern of interaction in Point-to-Point systems is as follows:

- The sender client arrives at a point in its processing when it's necessary to send out a message. It creates a message and sends it out to the queue. The message is held in the queue.
- The receiver client pauses and checks the queue for messages.
- The message is returned to the receiver client.

Publish/Subscribe vs. Point-to-Point Messaging

When designing messaging applications, design decisions on whether to choose Publish/Subscribe messaging or Point-to-Point messaging have to be based on two fundamental factors:

- The Publish/Subscribe messaging model provides two options not available with Point-to-Point messaging:
  - Clients can produce messages for an unknown, and/or unlimited, number of subscribers: Publish/Subscribe messaging supports **one-to-many** messaging operations
  - Subscribing clients have the choice between durable and non-durable connections to the JMS server
- The Point-to-Point messaging model is designed for **one-to-one** messaging between a producing client and a consuming client

JMS and its Relation to Other J2EE Technologies

The Java platform supports data exchange through a large set of middleware services like databases, asynchronous messaging systems, CORBA ORBs, etc. Java's platform independence and the availability of a large number of middleware services, is turning it into an excellent platform for enterprise solutions. The JMS API has been designed to integrate well with other enterprise Java APIs thus making it an enabling architecture to develop and deploy multi-tier distributed enterprise applications.

JMS and JDBC

JMS clients may use Java Database Connectivity (JDBC) with JMS in the same transaction. It is possible to do this with the Java Transaction API (JTA), but in a lot of cases, this will be achieved automatically by implementing these clients as message-driven EJBs.

JMS and EJB

Unlike other types of Enterprise JavaBeans (EJB), which are synchronously invoked by the EJB container in response to method calls from EJB clients, in the 2.0 version of the EJB specification, the message-driven bean is a type of EJB that is asynchronously invoked by the EJB container when a JMS client sends a message to it. JMS has thus become an important resource that will be available to EJB component developers. It can be used with other resources to implement enterprise services. See Chapter 7 for more details on JMS and EJBs.

JMS and JTA

The Java Transaction API (JTA) provides the transaction developer the requisite API to delimit distributed transactions and an API for accessing a resource's ability to participate in a distributed transaction. A JMS client can therefore use JTA to delimit distributed transactions. This is a function of the transactional environment that the client is running on and not a feature of JMS. However, a JMS provider can choose to support distributed transactions using JTA.

JMS and JTS

JMS along with the Java Transaction Service (JTS) can be used in distributed transactions to combine message sends and receives with database updates and other transaction services. The J2EE-compliant application server should automatically handle this even though it is also possible for JMS clients to code this programmatically.

JMS and JNDI

Configured JMS objects are created on a context accessible through the Java Naming and Directory Interface (JNDI). JMS clients look up these configured JMS objects using JNDI. JMS administrators use provider-specific facilities for creating and configuring these objects. JMS defines connection factories and destinations as administered objects that are configured and placed in a JNDI naming context. This ensures that JMS applications are easy to deploy and highly portable.

JMS and the CORBA Notification Service

The CORBA notification service provides filtering, delivery guarantee semantics, durable connections, and the assembly of event networks on top of the CORBA event service. It gets its delivery guarantee semantics from the CORBA messaging service (which defines asynchronous CORBA method invocation).

Java is already integrated well with CORBA. As of now, Java IDL and COS Naming have been bundled with the JDK since version 1.2. Most uses of COS Naming have been through the JNDI. Similarly, Java already provides RMI over IIOP to integrate seamlessly with CORBA. Most uses of JMS with the CORBA notification service will be through RMI over IIOP. There are a lot of CORBA vendors who are coming out with support for JMS layered on top of CORBA. Instead of competing with the CORBA notification service, JMS will interoperate seamlessly with it and help extend CORBA's reach to Java enterprise platforms.

What Does JMS Not Address?

The JMS specification as of version 1.0.2 does not address the following features, even though some messaging providers add support for these in their product implementations:

❑ **A Wire Protocol for Messaging**
JMS does not specify a wire protocol for messaging. It lets the messaging provider take care of specific protocols used in the implementation.

❑ **A Message Metadata Repository**
JMS does not define a repository for storing message type definitions; neither does it define a language for creating message type definitions.

❑ **Load Balancing Criteria and Fault-tolerant Mechanisms**
A large number of products in the market today provide support for multiple, cooperating clients implementing critical services. The JMS API does not specify how such clients cooperate to appear to be a single, unified service.

❑ **Error Notification**
A number of messaging products define system messages that provide asynchronous notification of problems or system events to client applications. The JMS specification does not attempt to standardize these messages. This means that clients should not be using these messages to ensure that there are no portability problems when moving from one provider to another.

❑ **Administration API**
JMS does not define an API for administering messaging products.

❑ **Security API**
JMS does not define an API for controlling the privacy and integrity of messages. It also does not specify how digital signatures or keys are distributed to clients. Security is supposed to be a provider feature that needs to be implemented by the provider in their own specific way – which severely limits portability and reusability if coding is required to enable this – and security controlled by the administrator without the need for any standard API.

JMS in Enterprise Applications

JMS is an ideal platform for developing and deploying a wide variety of distributed enterprise applications. JMS can also be used as an alternative to traditional synchronous solutions and provides a much better solution than Java/RMI or CORBA (see the section later *"Synchronous vs. Asynchronous Systems"*).

A lot of enterprise scenarios out in the market place today rely on too much overhead from object brokerage and the all-or-nothing resource-intensive transactions. These could be more streamlined using JMS to notify other processes of impending updates.

Some of the areas in which JMS is useful are detailed below:

- ❑ **Enterprise Application Integration (EAI)**
  To achieve a competitive advantage, enterprises have to integrate information stored in multiple databases and applications. Connecting each individual system to each other system takes a lot of time and is also very expensive. JMS, with its platform-independence, asynchronous communication API, guaranteed-message delivery, and fault-tolerance, offers an ideal solution for a number of application integration requirements.

- ❑ **Collaboration**
  Collaborative computing, where users share a wide range of resources, from spreadsheets and presentations to entire web sites, is catching on fast in the corporate world. But successful online collaboration requires workflow automation software to ensure that the shared content is properly managed. Collaboration applications, which require fast, secure exchange of information and data within individual departments and across the enterprise, will find JMS solutions extremely useful. Collaboration solutions based on JMS work across any network, and scale smoothly as new users are added.

- ❑ **Secure and Fault-tolerant Guaranteed Message Delivery**
  For a number of enterprise applications, the critical requirement is not raw speed but absolute reliability and guaranteed delivery under faulty network conditions (which occur for instance over the Internet). JMS provides an ideal base for such systems. Publishers can keep publishing messages to the local destination whether the network is connected or not. When the network comes up again, the local server may automatically forward all pending messages to the remote JMS servers to which it is connected. This automatic store-and-forward mechanism saves developers a lot of time and effort, allowing them to focus more on application requirements rather than on the internal plumbing of the messaging server.

- ❑ **Business-to-Business (B2B) E-Commerce**
  B2B involves two-way exchange of information between businesses. JMS facilitates B2B e-commerce between businesses and suppliers over the Internet. With built-in support for standards-based Publish/Subscribe, queuing, guaranteed message delivery, and automatic message logging, JMS is an ideal platform for developing and deploying such applications.

The human-to-human factor is not to be entirely overlooked either. Workflow architectures that require critical data being propagated to different departments and RDBMS systems can certainly benefit from a JMS-based model. Administrators could for instance monitor some kind of data approval application, and get the latest "messages" on which entries need approval. This notion can be extended to DBA and systems administration in general, for which most notification systems are glorified dialog boxes or e-mails that lack JMS's ability to have interactive application actions and further enterprise responses tied to the message itself, and lack the ability of JMS messages to interact directly with these systems.

Synchronous vs. Asynchronous Systems

RMI or CORBA is for tightly coupled synchronous communications, and JMS is for loosely coupled asynchronous communications.

However, there are other important factors to consider. My point of view is that JMS is a better choice because it offers the flexibility of both models. In any distributed application you will find uses for asynchronous processing if you look hard enough, even if you start out with a bias towards a synchronous design. Using JMS for both synchronous and asynchronous processing gives you a single programming model.

JMS also provides an asynchronous request/reply model, using the `JMSReplyTo` message header. This allows a distributed system to withstand failures and scheduled downtimes of the various nodes in the environment without affecting the health and availability of the system as a whole.

How scalable is the RMI or CORBA solution compared to the JMS solution? If you mix and match the two technologies, your system as a whole is only as strong as its weakest link. Using JMS for pure request/reply interactions buys you some important fault-tolerance advantages:

The traditional client (requestor) and server (replier) are decoupled using a JMS topic or queue. Let's assume it's a topic:

- ❏ You can have more than one replier listening to the same topic for requests.

- ❏ If one of the repliers dies, then you still have other repliers left answering client requests. This N-way-redundancy is transparent to the client: Client requests are "multicast" to all the repliers. Every replier responds, but the client considers only the first arriving response.

Another advantage of request/reply using JMS is preventive maintenance. Assume there is only one replier this time:

- ❏ While your clients are performing requests through a JMS topic, you can move the replier from one machine to another. The client will not throw any exception but transparently start using the new replier machine. No data is ever lost during the transition from one machine to another. That's an important feature if you want to achieve twenty-four seven operation.

All of that is very hard to achieve with a synchronous model like CORBA, DCOM, or RMI. A JMS messaging server, being a Message-Oriented Middleware (much like MSMQ or MQSeries) can buy you much more of a really scalable and fault-tolerant solution.

Loosely Coupled Systems

The term **loosely coupled system** is bound to come up in almost any discussion of JMS-based distributed systems. Loosely coupled systems are typically composed of a group of processes that communicate with each other indirectly. This indirect communication makes it unnecessary for each of these processes to know details about each other: how many there are, where they are located or if they are currently available or not. Indirect communication can be realised by connecting all of the system processes to a Message-Oriented Middleware (MOM) provider rather than connecting them directly to each other.

Since JMS is the standard Java interface to MOM providers, JMS is the most common technology of choice for loosely coupled systems that are implemented in Java. One could argue that systems implemented using JavaSpaces are also loosely coupled, but these two technologies are very similar in any case.

Traditional client/server systems can be considered tightly coupled. The bulk of distributed systems in operation today fall into this category, so before getting into the details of loosely coupled systems, let's have a look at how they differ from tightly coupled systems.

Tightly coupled systems are characterized by connection-oriented communication. Typically, a client opens a connection to a server and then uses this connection to exchange data with that server. The establishment of a connection requires that the server is alive and reachable at the moment that the client tries to contact it. Thus if clients are expected to be able to connect to the server at arbitrary times, then there is a strong high availability requirement on the server.

Connections also require that the client explicitly knows the network address at which the server can be reached. In simple cases where there is a single centralized server and its clients connect only to that server, this does not present a major problem – although there can be a lot of reconfiguration required if the address of the server changes, for example. In more distributed environments, where there are a multitude of servers and each performs a specialized function, keeping track of the address associated with each service, and ensuring that every server is available when each client needs, it becomes more difficult.

Loosely coupled systems use messaging as the means of communication between the system components. Such systems typically are:

- **Asynchronous**
  The code that processes an incoming message is executed when the message arrives. It is not necessary to poll for the availability of a new message, or to block a thread waiting for the arrival of the next message.

- **Temporally Distributed**
  This means that the components of the system that communicate with each other do not all need to be available at the same time. It is not an exception if the intended recipient of a message is not available when the message is sent; processing will continue when the recipient becomes available.

- **Indirectly Addressed**
  It is not necessary for an entity in the system to know the network addresses of the entities with which it exchanges messages. It is not even necessary to know their identities or even how many they are. Message producers address messages to named topics, and consumers of messages independently specify from which topics they want to receive messages.

- **Peer-to-Peer**
  Although the components of a loosely coupled system may request services from each other, the roles of client and server are blurred, or often nonexistent. There are message producers and message consumers, and many components will have both roles at the same time. Since the various system components have equal status, they are referred to as peers.

> **JMS provides the functionality required to realize systems that possess these traits.**

Traditional IT Systems

In order to clearly see the importance that JMS and loosely coupled systems will play in the architectures of J2EE systems, we need to take a look at how distributed systems are evolving. In the past, computer systems have been completely contained within single organizations. Here an organization will often correspond to a single company, but the determining characteristic is that an organization has central control over its IT systems: hardware, software, networking, policies, etc.

In large companies, this could correspond to individual departments rather than the company as a whole. With traditional IT systems, any interaction between the computer systems of two different organizations was actually achieved through the interaction of human representatives from each organization, each with access to the system of their own organization.

For example, the inventory control system of a department store indicates that it is time to reorder a particular item. This results in store employee calling up the distributor of that item and placing an order. The person taking the order then enters it into the order processing system of the distributor.

With the Internet emerging as the common IT platform for commerce, there is a huge movement underway to interconnect businesses directly without requiring human intervention for every transaction. This is giving rise to large-scale distributed systems that span across multiple organizations. "Multiple organizations" does not just mean a handful; an automated business-to-business marketplace may have thousands of participants.

Consider the problems presented by implementing such systems with tightly coupled architectures. Imagine that your company's IT systems have strong dependencies on other systems of other companies over which you have no control. Can you execute distributed transactions that include foreign databases? What guarantees do you have about uptime and responsiveness of the other systems? What about security? Who do you contact to resolve these issues?

The technical aspects of these problems can be solved with enough effort, but the problems are not just technical. The non-technical problems include negotiation, consensus, trust, and standardization among many organizations. Within one company, decisions can be dictated; among many companies, consensus is required, and there is no guarantee that this can always be achieved in a reasonable amount of time. If the technical solutions are extremely complex, staffing problems result. Projects of this magnitude require a large staff of programmers to implement. It is not reasonable to expect to be able to find armies of Java/networking/server gurus, so a simple programming model is required.

Inserting JMS

Inserting JMS as a buffer between the organizations that participate in a large-scale distributed system alleviates many of these problems. Each individual system must have tightly coupled interaction only with the JMS provider. The organization that maintains the JMS server is the central contact for connectivity issues. Security is simplified. The optional JMS support for JTA distributed transactions becomes very important here, as it allows each distributed transaction to be contained within a single organization.

Also important is the fact that JMS presents a simple programming model that facilitates asynchronous communication and concurrent, event-driven processing without requiring programmers to master the subtleties of developing multi-threaded code.

For all of these advantages, JMS introduces its own set of issues and dependencies. JMS relies on a central message server, which some organization must maintain. The interaction between JMS clients and the message server is tightly coupled. This paradox is discussed further below.

The reliability, availability and performance of the server is crucial, otherwise the loose coupling of the other system components is not possible. In many cases, this will mandate that the server is implemented as a cluster that provides load balancing and guarantees high availability, but presents the outward appearance of single JMS-compliant message server (see Chapter 8 for an in depth discussion of this).

Although this discussion has centered around the scenario of large systems that span multiple companies, the usefulness of JMS is not limited to this. Systems that span multiple departments in large companies may represent a similar scenario if the departments have a large degree of autonomy (or simply have difficulty cooperating). In some cases the inter-organizational aspects are not an issue, but a system can still benefit from asynchronous communication.

JMS – Peer-to-Peer or Client/Server?

As you have learned, the JMS API depends heavily on the concepts of connections, clients, and servers. These are the standard concepts of tightly coupled, client/server systems. At this point you might think all of the pontification above about the glory of loosely coupled systems is a bunch of nonsense. But wait, there is an explanation.

There are two different views of a JMS-based, loosely coupled distributed system:

❑ The infrastructure view, in which the messages server is central hub of all communication

❑ The application view, in which the message server does not appear at all

Thus the messaging model is implemented on top of a connection-oriented client/server model. Does this defeat the purpose of messaging? No. Consider these advantages when compared to implementing the distributed system entirely via tightly coupled means:

❑ The whole system has only one well known server address

❑ Only one element of the system (the message server) has a crucial high availability requirement

❑ The most critical part of system is a completely standard, off the shelf product

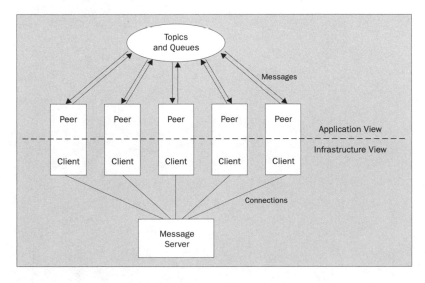

Essentially, the use of a message server as the central hub of an otherwise very decentralized JMS-based system reduces the complexity of the communication infrastructure to that of a simple client/server system with a single server. We will see later that with some limitations of the functionality specified by JMS, multicast networking can be employed to eliminate the central server and bring the connectionless messaging paradigm right down to the network level.

A Distributed System in the PTP Domain

The Point-to-Point example is a business-to-business e-commerce system for delivering flowers worldwide via a network of local flower shops. The example is purely imaginary and would certainly require extensive additional features in order to be acceptable for real business use. Let's walk through the system first, and then enumerate the features that make it interesting from the architectural point of view.

The global flower deliver system allows a customer to order flowers from a fixed list of bouquet types and have them delivered to any address in any country that has affiliated local delivery agents. Customers can order via the World Wide Web, telephone, or in person at a local flower shop. The customer will receive one notification confirming the order, and another one confirming delivery. Notifications may be delivered by e-mail, fax, or ordinary snail mail. The system is centered on a JMS message server, and involves several other generic servers: database, e-mail, and fax.

The application-specific part of the system comprises several functional modules, each of which is either a complete Java application, or a library embedded in a larger Java application. All modules are JMS clients, and in addition, some of the modules are also JDBC clients. These clients execute distributed transactions that include both the JMS connection and the JDBC connection. It is assumed, then, that both of these services provide optional XAResource support so that they can act as resources in a JTA distributed transaction. This also implies that these modules are run within an application server that provides a JTA transaction manager. For simplicity, the application server and transaction manager are not shown explicitly in the diagram:

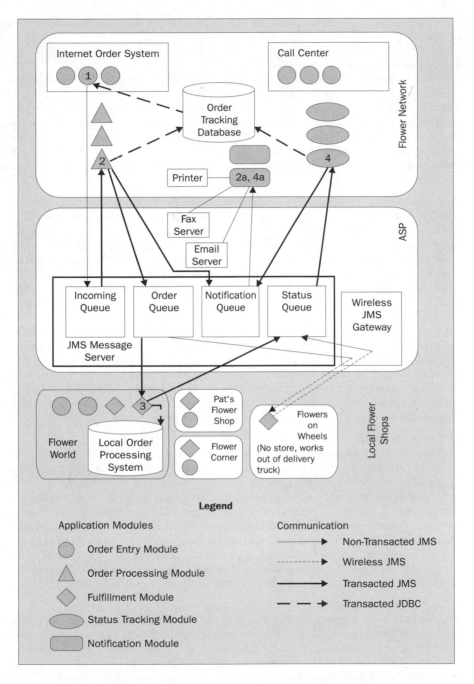

Each type of module is depicted by a different shape in the diagram. Arrows indicating the flow of information are only drawn for selected module instances, in order to keep the diagram comprehensible. In general, each instance of a module of the same type would have the same arrows to and from the JMS server and JDBC server. Note that the arrows only indicate logical message flow and not connections. There need not be more that one connection from a module to the message server.

We will walk through the steps in a normal (exception-free) flower delivery scenario, and explain each module in turn:

❑ **Order Entry Module**
This is the point of contact with individual customers, so variations of this module are embedded in the web system (possibly as an EJB) and the call center application, as well as being available at local flower shops in the form of an application or an applet. Customers interact indirectly with this module to order flowers. The order details (address, bouquet type, delivery date, billing info, etc.) are packed into a JMS message and sent to the incoming queue of the JMS server. This module can also access the order tracking database to allow customers to check the status of their order. Orders can be submitted, though, even when the database is not available.

❑ **Order Processing Module**
This module is a Java application that should run continuously on the systems of the flower network. It receives order messages from the incoming queue and inserts a record in the order tracking database. It then forwards the order message to the order queue. It also sends a message to the notification queue that contains the text of an order confirmation. In step 2a, the notification module receives the message from the notification queue and, depending on the indicated delivery preference, reformats and sends it to the printer, fax server, or e-mail server.

All four interactions – consumption from the incoming queue, producing to the order queue and notification queue, and the insertion of a record into the database – are executed within one distributed transaction so that a failure of this module will not leave these steps partially completed. If an instance of this module fails partway though the processing of an order, the whole transaction will be rolled back, and the order will be effectively "pushed back" onto the incoming queue, as though the failed attempt never happened. It can then be consumed and processed by another instance of the order processing module.

❑ **Fulfilment Module**
This module is a Java application or applet that runs at the various local shops that can fulfill the orders. In the case of an enterprise scale flower delivery service (let's pretend for the sake of the example that such a thing exists) this module could be embedded in the service's own order management system. Each instance of module will subscribe to the order queue using a message selector that selects only messages that lie within the delivery area of the local shop. In more sophisticated shops, this module might be tied into an inventory control system and the messages selector may further restrict the message delivery according to the flowers currently in stock. Another option for the more sophisticated shops is to receive the order and enter it into the local order processing system within a single distributed transaction. When the delivery is complete, a message is sent the status queue confirming this fact.

❑ **Status Tracking Module**
This module has a function similar to that of the order processing module, and it is also a Java application that runs continuously on the systems of the flower network. It consumes messages from the status queue, updates the order tracking database, and sends a delivery confirmation to the notification queue. For each flower delivery, these steps are executed within one distributed transaction. In step 4a, the notification module formats the text from the notification queue and routes it to the appropriate delivery server.

Now that we know how the system works, let's take a look at some of the features that this message-based architecture provides:

❑ Distributed transactions (see Chapter 4 for details) are contained within one organization and never extend beyond the message server. Each distributed transaction is centered on one of the modules. It only involves local databases and the message server. It is never necessary for systems from organizations that otherwise never have direct contact to vote in the same two-phase commit. Thus your transaction will never fail due to a resource that is outside your control.

❑ There is no application-specific code in the message server. None of the system components that contain application code are in the message server, which means that this critical central hub executes exactly the same software that is in use in many other production systems and that was tested by the JMS vendor before shipping. Application-specific code, in contrast, is always new when the system first goes live, and often produced under time pressure. The likelihood of bugs is higher here, so it is advantageous when the system is not crippled by the failure of an application-specific component.

❑ Critical servers, such as the message server, are completely generic and can be maintained by an Application Service Provider (ASP). Thus the maintenance of the message server can be outsourced to an organization that can properly guarantee high availability and back up this guarantee with staff on site 24 hours a day and 7 days a week. Since the server is generic, the ASP does not need to learn how to care for your custom application, but can provide the same service that it may be providing to dozens of other customers. In the case that your application is not big enough to justify its own message server, your queues can coexist on the same server with those of other applications. With proper security configurations, this poses no problem.

❑ There can be any number of instances of each module. Multiple instances of the same module will process orders in parallel. This provides concurrency and load balancing of the application-specific component, without requiring application developers to explicitly program these features. If a module fails, the message that it is currently processing gets rolled back and will be dispatched to another instance automatically by the message server. If no instances of a module are running, the processing gracefully halts and resumes as soon as one or more instances come online. As each new instance comes online and connects to the message server, it begins sharing load automatically, with no additional administrative action required. Thus, the application gets fault tolerance, high availability, load balancing, and concurrency for free.

❑ As an extension of the previous point, new flower shops can be integrated into the system at any time. The only administrative action required is the configuration of access control on the server. Access control is, of course, required to ensure that unauthorized parties do not interfere with the system.

❑ A flower shop can alter the service it provides at any time. If it extends its delivery area, then it need only change the message selector used by its fulfillment module and it will start to receive orders to be delivered in this new area. Perhaps it will only deliver an order outside of its own area if it exceeds a certain amount. This can also be specified with message selectors.

❑ The diagram also shows a case in which a flower delivery truck is tied directly into the system via a wireless gateway. Remember that with JMS, it is not an exception when the recipient of a message is not available when the message is sent. This makes it ideal for a mobile client that could be in a tunnel at any given time (refer to Chapter 11 for disconnected devices).

A Distributed System in the Pub/Sub Domain

In the last example, the messages in the PTP domain corresponded to tasks and it was (effectively) the responsibility of the JMS message server to ensure that each of these tasks was executed exactly once. In contrast, messages in the Pub/Sub domain often contain information that should be distributed to as many interested clients as necessary.

A classic example, and probably one of the most common applications of Pub/Sub messaging, is the distribution of financial data. In this section we will develop an example of a stock price distribution system for a financial trading room. This example draws on elements of several real financial information systems, but is simplified to serve as an architectural example without getting bogged down in too many details.

The initial system will be very skeletal in that it only distributes raw stock prices from market data feeds to traders' desktops as well as middle and back office systems that also require access to live data. We will then demonstrate how the architecture makes it easy to merge in additional services.

The skeletal system is shown in the figure below. The system is fed with price data from several real-time market data services. These may be available via dial-up modem, leased line, satellite feed, Internet, or other means. How each feed is delivered is not important. We will assume that for each feed there is an interface program that is capable of publishing the data to our JMS compliant message server. Let's assume that there are three feeds, and that each covers one of the three major financial regions: North America, Europe, and Asia.

In our trading room, activity is divided up by industry, so the feed interfaces will publish each price to one of the topics dedicated to technology, automotive, or pharmaceutical stock. The diagram also shows a number of subscribers that are consuming the price data. There are two trader desktop systems; each one is only subscribed to the topic containing prices for the industry in which that trader is interested. There are other institutional systems that subscribe to the raw prices. These systems need data from all industries, so they subscribe to all of the topics:

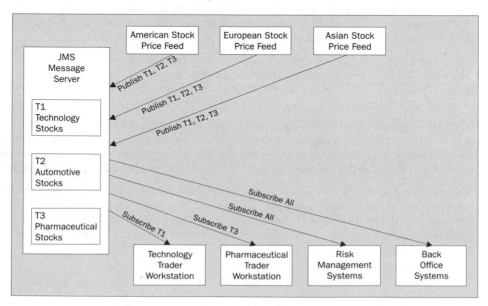

Let us have a look at what we get from the basic system:

❑   Any number of subscribers can have access to the live data.

❑   Asynchronous subscribers get new prices as soon as they are available without wasting time having to poll the price source. Synchronous subscribers (that is those that use the blocking `receive()` call) can also get updates when they occur, but they have to block a thread while waiting for the next one.

❑   Subscribers can restrict the amount of information that is delivered to them by selecting a subset of topics, and additionally by using message selectors. This decreases the amount of unwanted data that is delivered to a particular subscriber.

❑   It is easy to add new subscribers and new price feeds at any time. Adding such a component does not disturb any of the components that are already in place.

Most traders who are watching stock prices are also interested in the volatility of those prices, so we will integrate a volatility calculator into the system. Volatility is a measure of the degree to which a price fluctuates over time, and is the result of a simple statistical calculation on the past stock prices. Our volatility calculator thus needs to subscribe to stock prices as input to the calculation. After performing the calculation, it will publish the results to new topics dedicated to volatility data. When these functions are implemented, the volatility calculator is fully integrated into the system. Other applications can access the calculated volatility data by subscribing to one of the volatility topics.

Now that we have access to volatility data, we would like to calculate theoretical stock option prices. The option price calculation requires stock price and volatility as input. (It actually requires interest rates and few other things also. Providing this additional data requires a hefty bit of infrastructure, so for the purposes of the example we will just assume that it is available by some other means.) The option price calculator is integrated into the system in the same way as the volatility calculator. It subscribes to stock prices and volatilities, and publishes option prices on a new set of topics.

Next we would like to make the calculation engines (for volatility and option prices) redundant in order to increase the reliability of the system. There are a few different possible approaches to this. The most basic approach is just to start a second instance of each engine. Now each time a new stock price is published, two identical volatility updates are published. If one of the volatility calculators fails, then the other still provides a complete set of data. If the subscribers of the calculated data are not adversely affected by receiving redundant updates, then we have already achieved high availability, but not in a particularly efficient way.

Consider this: for each stock price update, there are two identical volatility updates. If the option price calculator calculates a new price each time it receives an update for one of its input values, then each one will calculate three redundant price updates (one new stock price and two redundant volatilities). Two redundant option price calculators will produce a total of six redundant updates for each new stock price. This effect will tend to snowball, so we need to take a more sophisticated approach.

Added Sophistication

One approach is to build a bit more intelligence into update logic of the calculation engines. If the option calculator caches the input values of each calculation, then it can be programmed to calculate a new price only if a volatility price update contains a different value from that used in the last calculation. It might just delay the actual calculation so that several updates of input data that occur within a short time period only trigger one new price calculation. This curbs the snowball effect with minimal effort. The redundant calculators, however, will still produce redundant updates, so if this is not acceptable, we need to move on to the next technique.

The next level of sophistication requires each redundant calculator to subscribe to the topic to which it publishes its results. In this way it has a means to detect the results published by other engines. Each instance of the calculation engine should pause for a small, random delay before actually performing the calculation. If, during this pause, it receives a message from another calculation engine, then it knows that the task has already been performed and it can abort the calculation.

In this scenario, the random delay of the other calculation engine was shorter. This scheme still permits redundant calculations, but they will occur seldom. It is quite effective in providing both increased reliability and load balancing among the different parallel instances of the calculation engines, albeit it is a bit more difficult to implement than in the PTP case.

When a new subscriber is started, it would like to have the most recent price for each stock immediately, rather than wait an unknown amount of time until the stock price changes before seeing the current state of the market. This could be solved with durable subscribers, but durable subscribers, as defined by JMS, will deliver all the price changes that transpired while the subscriber was offline. In most cases, only the current prices are relevant.

To solve this problem, we will add a new service into the system: the MRV (Most Recent Value) service. The MRV service subscribes to all topics and stores the most recent value of each unique item in a database. It then listens for requests for MRVs for specific items on a special destination. It returns the appropriate value from its database to the destination specified in the ReplyTo header of the request. This service is actually best implemented with a queue, as each request is a single task that should be executed by exactly one consumer.

We will add one more useful service to the system. It may be desirable to have the history of all prices and calculations stored in a database for future reference. This can be accomplished by adding a subscriber that listens to all topics and writes all messages into a database. If the JMS and JDBC providers both support distributed transactions then this can be employed to ensure that every message is correctly copied to the database in spite of failures.

The complete system is depicted in this second figure:

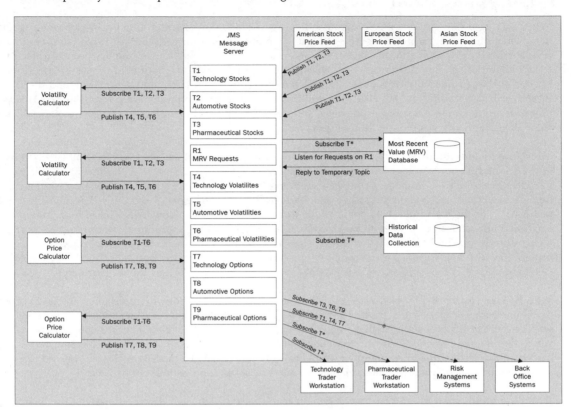

Here are some of the noteworthy aspects of the final system:

- ❏ Each new service could be added without disrupting any of the existing system components

- ❏ Every component can be stopped at any time without triggering exceptions in other system components

- ❏ Each additional subscriber does not add any additional load on the corresponding message producers, only the message server

High availability and load balancing of the individual services are more difficult to implement than in the PTP domain, but nevertheless can be done in the robust fashion described above.
This is still quite advantageous when you consider what it takes to implement these features without leveraging JMS: Your application would need to include a process that knows about all of the calculation engines and can distribute tasks to them. This process should not be the single point of failure – there needs to be a second one that listens to heartbeats from the first one and takes over if it dies (and goes away again if the heartbeats start again). This is complicated stuff if you have to implement it yourself. JMS can make your life easier if you use it right.

JMS in Application Integration

When talking of integration, it is imperative that organizations understand both business processes and data. They must select which processes and data elements require integration. This may involve data-level integration, application interface-level integration, method-level integration and user-interface-level integration. In any business organization, both internal and external integration are related. Unless businesses have some kind of common integration infrastructure that created and maintained the interfaces between different systems, they will find that **Enterprise Application Integration (EAI)** is very labor-intensive. Another issue to consider is web-technologies in the context of enterprise integration since the Internet drives market forces today.

Therefore in addition to EAI, it is also imperative that we talk about **Internet Application Integration (IAI)**. In the first place, a lot of clients are seeking integration in the context of the Internet. This is because the client's e-commerce retail web site has to be integrated with backend systems using a more flexible integration infrastructure rather than hard-coded or even paper-based links. This could use EAI technology, as the web site server could reside within the enterprise. However, a lot of e-business activity is not retail but business-to-business (B2B). This means that operational systems of different corporations must be linked together and this creates a whole new dynamic which sees XML, integration with application servers, and Java becoming more important than EAI. Similarly, vendors like IBM and BEA Systems have strategies that focus on both the EAI and the IAI segments.

With EAI the focus is integrating a set of applications, whether built or bought, inside an enterprise in order to automate an overall business process for that enterprise. With IAI the focus is integrating applications, whether built or bought, across multiple enterprises in order to automate multi-enterprise business processes where the Internet provides the communications backbone. Specific examples are trading groups or associations, virtual companies (components and assembly of a final product are totally out-sourced, the virtual company handles distribution, marketing, and finance) and integrated supply chains.

If you are building an interface between two areas of the company that represent parts of the business you might outsource, externalize to partners, or even offer as part of your service to other companies, then it needs to incorporate open, Internet-based technology. If you don't, the chances are you will have to rebuild the interface in the future when you need to open it up. It's always a trade off, but the thought should be there.

As its name suggests, the distinguishing feature of IAI technology is that it integrates more tightly with Internet technology, particularly Java and application servers. A lot of vendors are working on versions of their message brokers that would run as a task inside a Java application server. There are some good reasons why they would want to do this. Application servers are becoming the focus of a lot of investment because they are highly reliable, transactional, and scalable – capabilities that you want available when you build a message broker. You don't need to build this into your message broker when you can run over an application server. This is important from the customer's point of view too, because if they are building a distributed computing environment as well as an integration infrastructure, both environments need to be integrated with directory, security, and management infrastructure – all complex problems from an installation and management perspective. Why not solve this problem once rather than twice?

Traditionally, there have been a lot of issues surrounding messaging APIs. Many organizations ended up building their own API on top of the original proprietary messaging system API. Clearly, there was some dissatisfaction with the APIs provided by the messaging vendors. Also, the International Middleware Association (IMWA) – formerly Message Oriented Middleware Association (MOMA) – the standards governing body for MOM, never sought to make it their mission to devise a single, industry-standard messaging API.

It is here that JMS could be used as such a messaging API standard. Similarly, with its integration of messaging and message brokers with Java application servers and other Internet-based technology, IAI is an enabler for multi-enterprise e-business processes and will form the majority of integration projects in the future.

JMS is very tightly integrated with Java, meaning that if you are a Java programmer looking at talking to IBM MQSeries, for example, it will be much easier and much more productive to use JMS than the MQSeries API for Java. Each messaging vendor will implement JMS. This means that a Java developer can use JMS with either TIBCO Rendezvous or IBM MQSeries or both.

JavaMail

When first exposed to JMS, many people do not see a big difference between JMS and e-mail. E-mail is, of course, a means for sending and receiving messages. E-mail also has a huge established infrastructure. This infrastructure is ubiquitous, reasonably reliable, and usually someone else's responsibility to maintain.

E-mail is intended for transmitting messages from humans to humans, but by using an API such as JavaMail, it is possible to use e-mail for inter-application messaging. Not only is it possible, but has certainly been done numerous times in the history of distributed programming. In some of these cases e-mail was the best tool for the job, but in others cases JMS may well have been a better choice but may not yet have been available or not well enough understood.

Consider the following example. A company has established, but conventional, retail channels, business processes, and back-office IT systems. This company needs to add the Internet as a new retail channel as soon as possible (or in a matter of weeks, whichever is sooner). The company is not big enough to justify the expenses associated with maintaining a highly available (say 99.9% or better) web site on its own premises, so it outsources this to an ASP. The backend systems must remain on premises for security reasons, but a failure of these systems should not impair the functionality of the web site (a backend failure is costly, but customers do not need to know about it). Thus, the web front end must be able to transmit merchandise orders to the backend system.

Both systems are behind restrictive firewalls, but with enough effort, a secure TCP connection could be tunneled from the web system to the backend. In order to fulfill the requirements, then the web system would need to be able to queue orders and continue processing if the back end is not available. This is possible, but involves re-inventing the (messaging) wheel (remember the time constraints). In this case, encrypted e-mail via JavaMail is used to solve the connectivity problem. The ASP provides access to an SMTP server at no extra cost, and there are almost no firewall issues.

Although e-mail proved to be a quick and effective solution in the example above, there are some shortcomings:

- ❑ **Two Way Communications**
  Although sending messages via an existing e-mail server is trivial, receiving mail requires more effort. A POP or IMAP mailbox, with corresponding address and possibly domain DNS entries, would have to be configured for the web application. In addition, a thread or a process would need to poll the mailbox for new messages. Since the web system had guaranteed uptime, communication in this direction was accomplished using a direct connection instead of e-mail.

❏ **Exception Handling**
If a message cannot be delivered for some reason, for example because of the destination mail server being unavailable for an extended period, the mail system tries to notify the sender via e-mail. Since the web system is not enabled to receive e-mail, it will never get these notifications. The workaround for this was to send a periodic mail containing an order summary. The backend system compares this summary to the received orders and generated an alert if messages were lost. It expects the summaries at regular intervals and will also generate an alert if one does not arrive. This process effectively creates a reliable protocol on top of e-mail.

❏ **Dependency on Third Parties**
This is the downside of using existing infrastructure. The system depends on the availability of the SMTP server. However, the ASP maintains it, most ordinary e-mail services packages do not provide explicit uptime guarantees. Although if necessary one could negotiate a Service Level Agreement (SLA) specifying maximum allowable downtime. E-mail is intended for inter-human messaging and not inter-application messaging. Humans are generally more robust to the failure of a mail server than computer programs are.

In addition to the points mentioned above, there are other shortcomings of using e-mail for inter-application messaging that were not relevant to the example:

❏ **No Transactions**
JMS providers support transactional messaging. This enables the provider to guarantee that messages produced and consumed within one transaction either all succeed or all fail as a single unit. This is important in mission-critical applications, since it means that the failure of the JMS server or of a client will never leave an operation partially completed. E-mail servers do not support transactions.

❏ **Delivery Order**
E-mail systems do not guarantee that messages will be delivered in the order that they were sent. Applications that depend on in-order message delivery would need to implement a custom ordering protocol.

❏ **Binary Data**
E-mail is intended for transmitting human readable text or HTML messages. Minor reformatting, such as the insertion of line breaks is possible. This not critical for the ability of a human to read a message, but could render a message unusable by an application that expects a very rigid format. This is not a showstopper, since it is possible to encode arbitrary binary data as text that can pass through e-mail systems without corruption. The big issue here is efficiency. Encoding binary data using the common base64 algorithm will inflate the size of the data by more than 30% and add the overhead of encoding and decoding each message. In high-volume applications this could be a serious issue.

❏ **Explicit Recipient Identity**
E-mail requires each message recipient to be named explicitly. It does not inherently support the ability to dynamically add subscribers to and remove subscribers from a topic as in JMS. Using aliases on the server can simulate this behavior, but this requires administrative access to the mail server and is not supported by the JavaMail API.

❏ **Load Balancing**
E-mail cannot simulate the ability of JMS to distribute Point-to-Point messages to multiple receivers, with the guarantee that each message is delivered to exactly one receiver.

❑ **Asynchronous Message Delivery**
E-mail systems push messages only as far as a mailbox. Consumers of e-mail messages are required to pull messages from the mailbox. JavaMail does define an event mechanism that will automatically invoke listeners when new mail arrives. However, the incoming part of the underlying mail system is pull-oriented, meaning that the client must explicitly query the mail server to find out if new messages are available. This means that the consumer is required to poll the mailbox in order to cause a "new mail" event to fire.

In summary, despite the JavaMail API, e-mail is intended for the exchange of messages between humans. JMS was designed for inter-application messaging. The fact that both JavaMail and JMS are required components of the Java 2 Platform, Enterprise Edition (as of version 1.3) underscores the fact that they are meant to fulfill different needs. Although the difference between these may not seem dramatic at first glance, the devil is in the details.

JMS provides many features that support the use of messaging in automated, transactional applications. These features would need to be implemented at the application level if JavaMail were to be used in this context. On the other hand, the ability to use JavaMail to cheaply and quickly leverage a huge existing global infrastructure should not be overlooked. Perhaps one day we will see JMS to e-mail gateways, or JMS that uses e-mail as its underlying transport mechanism.

Mobile Messaging

Consider the following scenario. Athul is riding the subway and is viewing stock quotes on his PDA. He suddenly realizes that he wants to buy 100 shares of eCommWare Corporation. He taps his stylus on the item in his portfolio, and enters the quantity and the highest price he wants to pay. He then taps on the 'Buy' button and feels confident that his transaction will be executed exactly once, without any errors. How confident can Athul feel that his transaction will succeed when he knows that there's no reliable network coverage?

In this section we'll see how messaging or information transactions can be carried out with high reliability in spite of the disconnected operation of mobile equipment. We will also see how to deal with the delivery of real-time information to mobile devices. The next generation of message-oriented middleware (MOM) is best suited to support these kinds of applications. We will describe how such applications are implemented using JMS.

Challenges Faced by Mobile Applications

Traditional computing environments are used to having remote access to web pages (HTTP), remote access to files (FTP, NFS), and mail servers (POP3, IMAP, SMTP). These networking requirements are rather rudimentary where communications between devices are limited to a specific application like e-mail or web browsing.

However, multiple devices of a single consumer interacting in a logical way, present a significant challenge to developers of mobile applications (applications that run on a PDA-like mobile device). In these days of volatile market conditions, and world traveling consumers, distributed information systems allow prices to adjust faster to changes in the market place. Decision-making would be a lot easier if people had access to real-time information on mobile devices. When a company's bottom-line totally depends on 'information at your finger-tips', mobile applications have to satisfy some demanding requirements. Sending off a stock purchase request and hoping, wishing, and praying that the transaction succeeded is not an option, so mobile business applications must be reliable, secure, scaleable, robust, and flexible:

❏   Reliability means that a mobile application can reliably transfer messages from one end to the other taking into account unreliable communications and adopting error-recovery mechanisms.

❏   Security means authentication of users; confidentiality; non-repudiation of transactions, etc.

❏   Scalability means that a mobile application may integrate thousands or even millions of users.

❏   Robustness implies that a transaction issued on a mobile device needs to be executed exactly once, in spite of poor network coverage or failures.

❏   Finally, mobile applications ought to be flexible in order to accommodate different bearers (transmission technologies: Short Message Service, Groupe Spécial Mobile, General Packet Radio Service, Universal Mobile Telecommunications System, Bluetooth, Infrared) and interaction styles (synchronous, asynchronous, transactional, one-to-one, or many-to-many).

MOM and Wireless Connectivity

MOMs ensure loose coupling of software components and therefore allow greater flexibility when developing mobile applications. This is because applications communicate with one another indirectly by passing messages through a message service. MOMs will prove even more valuable for developing sophisticated mobile applications because:

❏   MOMs support disconnected operation: application A can send a message to application B, even when B is not available (because it's not running or lacks any network coverage).

❏   MOMs guarantee the delivery of messages: at the middleware level messages are held in databases and forwarded to their recipients as soon as they become available.

❏   MOM libraries can be very lightweight.

❏   MOMs support both transactional interactions and real-time delivery of volatile information.

❏   The MOM model is intuitive and easy to learn. This means that distributed applications can be developed and deployed more quickly.

The Wireless JMS

The JMS messaging server is the sort of "Home Base" of the devices running the JMS client library. It performs activities such as message queuing and forwarding, access control to queues and topics, message encryption, transaction management, and protocol translation. The queue on the server may store a large quantity of messages, and may be able to process hundreds or thousands of messages per second, depending mainly on message size and the speed of the computer hosting it. It may be implemented using a transactional database.

In order to achieve the smallest possible client footprint, the messaging server relieves the client library of most of the work of maintaining JMS state information about open topics and queues, subscriptions, message filters, etc. With this approach, it is possible to reduce the footprint of the applications running on the mobile device aggressively, while maintaining the JMS semantics:

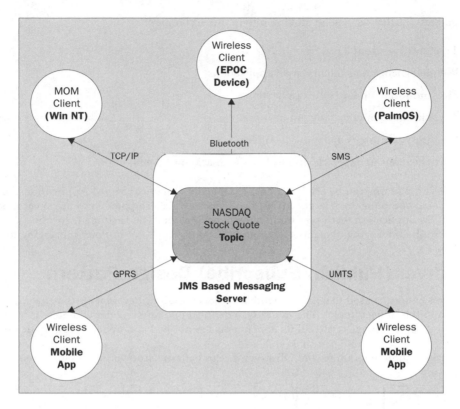

The JMS messaging server should be able to translate and mediate between transport protocols and bearers. This is necessary when, for example, an application running on a Windows NT PC sends a JMS message containing the current stock quote to both a PalmOS device and an EPOC device that have subscribed to the same Publish/Subscribe topic. The PC may transmit the message to the messaging server using TCP/IP over Ethernet, informing the server that the message is to be transmitted to the topic "NASDAQ Stock Quote". The server looks up the subscribers for the topic "NASDAQ Stock Quote", and determines that the PalmOS device is to be contacted using SMS (Short Message Service), while the EPOC device can be reached through Bluetooth. The producer application does not need to know about those bearers, because the message server performs the protocol translation from TCP to SMS and Bluetooth transparently. An application running on an SMS bearer can be changed to use a GPRS (General Packet Radio Service) bearer without modification of the application, because JMS abstracts the bearer.

Design Patterns for MOM Applications

One of the ways of reducing the difficulty of designing MOM-based applications is to employ **design patterns**. These are standard applications scenarios, that are commonly encountered, for which standard design techniques have already been developed. Design patterns sometimes supply the complete solution for an application. If not, they can at least provide a starting point to a more sophisticated design.

Most MOM applications tend to follow a small number of patterns. These patterns allow quick decisions to be made on which product features to use. Without these design patterns, the choice can be overwhelming. These patterns also define how specific messaging errors have to be handled.

The design patterns that we will be looking into in this section are:

- ❏   The Observer design pattern

- ❏   Pseudo-synchronous inquiry-style applications

- ❏   Fire-and-forget update-style applications

- ❏   Asynchronous inquiry-style applications

- ❏   Pseudo-synchronous update-style applications

- ❏   Asynchronous update-style applications with acknowledgement

These six design patterns can be used to create completely functional MOM Applications, or at least major functional components of larger MOM applications. It is also possible to use several patterns in the same MOM application, each providing one major function. The first one is for the Publish/Subscribe messaging domain. The other five are for the Point-to-Point messaging domains.

The Observer (Publish/Subscribe) Design Pattern

The Observer pattern is used to notify dependent observer (subscriber) objects that state information has changed in the subject (topic). The intent is to define a one-to-many dependency between objects so that when one object changes state, all its dependents are notified and updated automatically.

The object interaction diagram for the Observer design pattern is shown in the figure below:

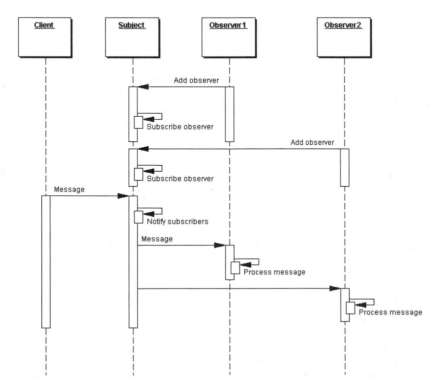

The Observer objects are dependent on the Subject object and therefore should be notified of any change in its state. There's no reason to limit the number of objects to two – there may be any number of Observers for the same subject.

The Observer pattern, also known as the Publish/Subscribe or the Dependents pattern, describes how to establish these relationships. All observers are notified whenever the subject undergoes a change in state. In response, each observer synchronizes its state with the subject's state. The subject is the publisher of notifications. It sends out these notifications without having to know who its observers are. Any number of observers can subscribe to receive notifications.

The Observer design pattern can be used in any of the following situations:

❑ When an abstraction contains two components, one of which needs notification of something, but the other of which doesn't need to know that the notification has been processed. Observing is a process in which the observed doesn't need to know who is observing it, or why. Encapsulating these aspects in separate objects lets you vary and reuse them independently.

❑ When a change to one object requires changing others, and you don't know how many objects need to be changed.

❑ When an object should be able to notify other objects without making assumptions about who these objects are. In other words, you don't want these objects tightly coupled.

Pseudo-Synchronous Inquiry-Style Applications

In any inquiry application, a client program requests information from a server. Often, the client cannot continue until it received the information that it requested. The figure below captures this synchronous request behavior where a sender sends a request to the receiver. On the receiver end, the request message is first read, and then processed before a reply is sent to the original sender. The Sender waits for the reply to come back from the receiver before moving on with other operations and is, in essence, being blocked till the call returns. This is similar to how traditional synchronous RPC calls work. This is therefore a request-reply pattern:

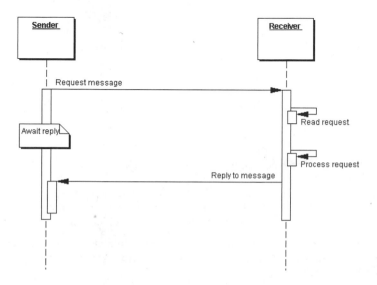

This design pattern has a couple of important characteristics:

❑ Firstly, it is synchronous at the client end. The client-side implementation will not return control until either the result is available, or the operation has failed.

❑ Secondly, this is an inquiry pattern. Data at the server is not affected by running this implementation. The operation can be repeated, as many times as necessary, should it fail. Because inquiries can be repeated, error handling associated with the failure of the operation is simple. There is no need to install complex recovery logic during inquiries.

As this is an inquiry style application, and we do not need recoverability, we can use non-persistent messages both for the inquiry and the reply.

There may be two queues involved in this pattern. Since we do not need recoverability, for requests from the sender to the receiver, we can use a pre-defined queue. For the reply from the receiver to the sender, we can use a temporary queue.

Fire-and-Forget Update-Style Applications

This type of pattern can be used when an application requests changes to data at a server, but does not need to wait for an acknowledgement before proceeding. The figure below shows a client sending a request to a receiver that results in data being updated. There is no reply to acknowledge that the update is successful. By removing the need for immediate synchronous acknowledgement, we can reduce the total load on the server. This is a completely asynchronous, non-blocking, Point-to-Point design pattern:

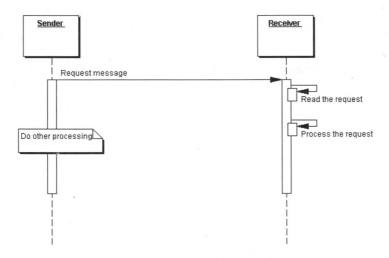

This design pattern has two important characteristics:

❑ Firstly, it is entirely asynchronous. The client sender sends the request and immediately continues other processing. It assumes that the receiver server will process the request sometime in the future. The client sender does not receive any acknowledgement of its request.

❑ Secondly, this is an update pattern. Data will be modified at the receiver server's end. It is therefore very important that the update is not lost. It may also be important not to repeat updates inadvertently.

Unlike inquiries, updates require some form of guaranteed message delivery. The level of guarantee totally depends on the cost associated with re-creation, should the update get lost.

Since some form of guaranteed message delivery is required, use a persistent message queue to hold the update request. Persistent messages are protected from loss even if the server crashes, or the network fails. This kind of message is delivered once, and only once, fulfilling the other criterion for this pattern.

There is only one queue involved in this pattern. You can use a predefined normal queue for the implementation.

Asynchronous Inquiry-Style Applications

This design pattern looks very similar to the pseudo-synchronous inquiry-style application pattern we saw previously. From a message queuing standpoint, many design decisions yield the same results as for the pseudo synchronous case. There is however, one major difference. The client sender does not wait for a reply to its request before continuing to process other things. For this pattern to be applicable the client should have something else to do after it has made the request, even though it may not have received any replies.

As the client sender does not wait for replies to its requests, some other mechanism needs to be employed to receive the replies as they come in. One solution might be to design a multi-threaded client, where one thread is dedicated to waiting for the results to arrive. The other solution is to use an event-based API if it's available.

There are therefore two approaches:

❑ One involves starting a second thread of execution within the application. The thread waits for the arrival of messages. When a message arrives, the thread reads it, and stores the data it contains in the appropriate data structure.

❑ The second approach requires that the chosen message queuing product's API can support asynchronous message receipt.

The figure below shows the asynchronous inquiry-style application design pattern:

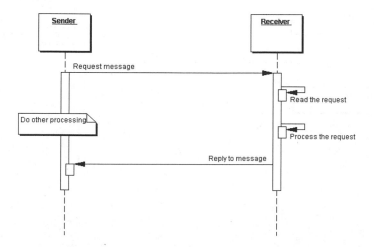

The Asynchronous Inquiry pattern has two important characteristics:

❑ Firstly, it is asynchronous at the client. Once the request has been issued, the client goes on to do other processing without waiting for a reply.

❑ Secondly, the pattern is an inquiry. Data at the server is not affected by running the application and the operation can be repeated as many times as necessary if it should fail. However, the main difference between this inquiry-style and the pseudo-synchronous style pattern is that we don't regard delayed replies as errors.

Since recoverability is not required, as with the pseudo-synchronous inquiry, we can use non-recoverable messages. This means we can use non-persistent messages.

When it comes to a decision on queues, there are a couple of queues involved in this pattern. For results flowing to the client, we can use a temporary dynamic queue. For requests flowing to the server, we can use a normal, pre-defined queue.

Pseudo-Synchronous Update-Style Applications

This is the most tightly coupled design pattern that we will look at. In many respects, it is also the least satisfactory of all the patterns that we will encounter here. Albeit, it is actually the pattern adopted by all client/server applications that do not use messaging, simply because alternative mechanisms offer little else. Every synchronous, blocking RPC call uses this pattern internally.

The next figure shows this pattern. As with the synchronous inquiry pattern, the client cannot continue until it has received a reply from the server:

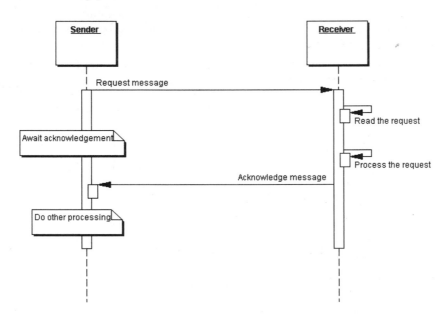

There are two important characteristics of this pattern:

❑   Firstly, it is synchronous. The client sender sends the update request but must wait for the acknowledgement message before proceeding.

❑   Secondly, this is an update. Data will be modified at the server. It is important the data is not lost and that the update request is not repeated inadvertently.

The problem with the pattern is what to do if the client does not receive an acknowledgement. In the case of the inquiry operation, we could just stop waiting and ignore any reply that arrived subsequently. However, we can't do this when an update is being acknowledged. If an acknowledgement is delayed the client waiting for it has absolutely no idea whether or not the server executed the operation correctly. The client probably has to assume that the operation failed, remember the failure, and attempt to resolve the issue by communicating with the server at a later time. All this logic has to be added to the application. The solution to this kind of problem is to use distributed transaction processing and products like BEA Tuxedo or IBM CICS. These systems guarantee that updates occurring on the client and server are all part of the same unit of work that either occurs together or not at all. Using asynchronous update-style applications with acknowledgement design pattern is a better solution to this than using distributed transaction processing products since they tend to be more expensive to buy and operate than message queuing systems.

Since this is an update operation, you are required to use a persistent message delivery mechanism so that you get once and once only delivery of the request and the acknowledgement. Similarly, use a pre-defined normal queue to send messages. For acknowledgements, we need to use a permanent dynamic queue and probably control its deletion.

Asynchronous Update-Style Applications with Acknowledgement

In this pattern, the client sender is interested in the update process, but does not need to wait for it to complete before continuing. The figure below shows an asynchronous update-style application, with acknowledgement required:

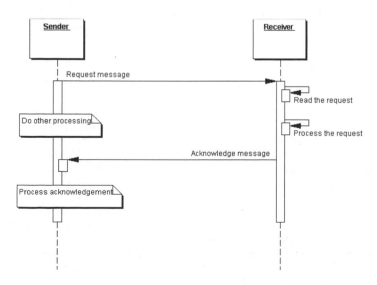

This pattern has a couple of important characteristics:

❑ Firstly, it is entirely asynchronous. The client sender sends an update request and can immediately continue other processing.

❑ Secondly, this is an update. Data will be modified at the server. It is important that the update is not lost and does not repeat inadvertently.

This pattern is very similar to the asynchronous inquiry pattern except for the fact that we cannot lose the request or the acknowledgement. Therefore, we must use persistent messages. The requests and acknowledgements require some kind of message delivery guarantee. The level of guarantee totally depends on the cost associated with re-creation, should the update get lost. Therefore, use persistent messages to hold both the updates and the acknowledgement.

JMS and Available Implementations

As of this writing, the JMS specification is at 1.0.2. A reference implementation (RI) of the Java Message Service API is not available as of yet. However, JavaSoft has promised that it will be part of the reference implementation for the Java 2 Platform, Enterprise Edition 1.3. There are a number of vendors offering JMS implementations or who have pledged support for JMS and the list of those vendors can be obtained at http://java.sun.com/products/jms/vendors.html.

When considering buying a JMS compatible server, it is important to decide whether you are interested in JMS itself, or whether you would like to deploy JMS messaging in the context of other J2EE technologies. J2EE-compatible application servers can deliver a whole host of functions, in addition to the capabilities offered by JMS. If JMS is one of the several items that you're looking for, you can look at a whole host of J2EE Application Server providers like Allaire's JRun, BEA System's WebLogic, Gemstone, Oracle, Orion, etc.

However, if like most developers, you are in search of JMS solution providers specializing in JMS, you have a choice of a dedicated set of vendors that specialize in providing great JMS implementations.

Fiorano Software, Inc. (http://www.fiorano.com) was one of the earliest JMS vendors to enter the market. They provide three products as of this writing – the FioranoMQ Message Server, FioranoMQ InfoBus, and FioranoMQ Bridge. The FioranoMQ server was released in October 1998. FioranoMQ supports both Publish/Subscribe and Point-to-Point messaging domains and can be configured to support either of the topologies. It also supports selective filtering of incoming and outgoing messages and offers XML interoperability that converts JMS messages into external XML messages. They have a very simple and intuitive GUI front-end for their administrative console.

SoftWired (http://www.softwired-inc.com), also one of the earlier JMS vendors, provides three products: The iBus Message Bus which relies heavily on IP Multicast, the iBus Message Server, which is based on the traditional hub-and-spoke architecture and the iBus Mobile for wireless applications. The iBus Messaging server provides support for a variety of transport media in addition to TCP/IP and IP Multicast. These include support for protocols like SMS (Short Message Service) and WAP (Wireless Application Protocol).

The SpiritWAVE JMS framework from SpiritSoft, Inc. (http://www.spirit-soft.com) relies on IP multicast and broadcast technologies to efficiently deliver information to subscribers. It may be of interest to people in the financial industry, as it strongly integrates with traditional financial world middleware products like TIBCO Rendezvous, IBM MQSeries, and Talarian SmartSockets.

Progress Software (http://www.progress.com), is another JMS vendor. As of this writing, SoniqMQ supports both Publish/Subscribe and Point-to-Point messaging domains and can be configured to support either of these topologies. It also supports selective filtering of incoming messages and offers XML interoperability.

Sun released its Java Message Queue (JMQ), in November 1999. Sun however did not write its JMS Server from scratch. Modulus Technologies developed the underlying server. It is generating a lot of interest among Sun and Sun/Netscape Alliance customers.

Appendix A contains more details about some of the most popular JMS Providers available.

Summary

Enterprise messaging is all about asynchronous requests, reports, or events that are used by enterprise applications. Message-Oriented Middleware (MOM) acts as an intermediary, and provides a common and reliable way for programs to create, send, receive, and read messages on any distributed enterprise system. The Java Message Service is an API for accessing such message systems.

The messaging models that are supported by JMS are the Publish/Subscribe messaging model and the Point-to-Point messaging model. In the Publish/Subscribe model, a client publishes a message to a topic, and by subscribing, multiple clients are informed of the message. In the Point-to-Point model, even though there may be multiple senders of messages to a queue, there is ultimately only a single potential receiver for each message.

JMS can be used to develop enterprise applications, in enterprise integration and mobile messaging. Most MOM applications tend to follow a small number of patterns. These patterns allow quick decisions to be made on which product features to use. Without these design patterns, the choice can be overwhelming. These patterns also define how specific messaging errors have to be handled. In the next chapter we will begin with the fundamentals of JMS programming.

```
com.sun.jndi.fscontext.RefFSContextFactory
com.sun.jndi.ldap.LdapCtxFactory
weblogic.jndi.WLInitialContextFactory
fiorano.jms.rtl.FioranoInitialContextFactory
fiorano.jms.runtime.naming.FioranoInitialContextFactory
ch.softwired.jms.naming.IBusContextFactory
```

2

JMS API Fundamentals

The Java Message Service specifies a standard set of interfaces for enabling Java applications to exchange enterprise messages in an efficient and vendor-neutral manner. Various software vendors who provide messaging products implement the interfaces defined in the JMS specification. These software vendors are called **JMS providers** in JMS terminology. Java applications that use JMS for exchanging enterprise messages are called **JMS clients**. JMS clients that don't use any vendor-specific features and use only standard JMS interfaces for implementing their messaging solutions are portable across different JMS providers.

This chapter covers the standard interfaces defined in the JMS specification. These interfaces are defined in a package called `javax.jms` and are available with the standard software distribution for J2EE (Java 2 Platform, Enterprise Edition). The classes and interfaces belonging to the package `javax.jms` are available in the `j2ee.jar` file that can be downloaded with the Java 2 Enterprise Edition 1.2.1.

In this chapter we will cover:

- ❏ JMS architecture
- ❏ Different messaging models
- ❏ JMS Administered objects
- ❏ JMS Connections and sessions
- ❏ Message producers and consumers
- ❏ JMS clients

JMS Architecture

JMS clients normally connect to a central messaging hub supplied by the JMS provider. Clients exchange messages through this messaging hub instead of connecting to each other directly. In addition, clients use the services provided by the JMS provider for sending and receiving enterprise messages. A JMS system is typically composed of the following component parts:

- ❑ JMS providers
- ❑ JMS clients
- ❑ JMS messages
- ❑ Administered objects

> **JMS providers are software vendors who implement the interfaces defined in the JMS specification, and who provide added features like load balancing, clustering, persistence services, etc.**

The examples in this chapter use the **JMQ (Java Message Queue)** implementation from Sun Microsystems. Messaging products either come as standalone products like SonicMQ from Progress Software or as a part of an application server suite like the WebLogic Server from BEA Systems. The open source community also has various JMS implementations, one of which is JBossMQ.

> **JMS clients are Java language applications that exchange JMS messages using the services provided by the JMS provider.**

Portable JMS clients should use only the standard JMS interfaces in their application code and should not use any provider-specific implementation classes.

The JMS specification defines different kinds of messages that can be exchanged by JMS clients. JMS messages can be plain text messages or an entire serialized web of Java objects. The JMS specification defines the following types of message:

- ❑ Messages containing plain text.
- ❑ Messages containing serialized Java objects.
- ❑ Messages containing an un-interpreted stream of bytes.
- ❑ Messages containing a stream of Java primitives and strings.
- ❑ Messages containing a map of Java primitives and strings.
- ❑ Additionally JMS providers may provide their own message extensions. For instance, providers may provide messages that extend plain text messages that can support XML.

JMS providers implement the interfaces defined for the different JMS messages. We will be dealing with JMS messages in more detail in Chapter 3.

> Administered objects are pre-configured objects stored in a namespace by JMS administrators for the use of JMS clients. An administrator is the person responsible for ensuring the proper day-to-day functioning of the JMS system.

Administered objects form the base for writing portable JMS applications. They are normally available for standard JNDI (Java Naming and Directory Interface) lookup even though the JMS specification doesn't make this a requirement. Administered objects can be stored outside the JMS provider in the namespace of any naming and directory service provider.

Connection factories are used for creating **connections** that may represent an open TCP/IP socket to the provider. All configuration information required for creating the connection is stored in the Administered object by the JMS administrators. Connections also act as factories for creating JMS sessions and are explained in further detail in the coming sections.

Sessions are single-threaded contexts for sending and receiving messages, and are used as factories for creating different kind of JMS messages. They are also used for creating objects that send and receive messages. These objects are called **message producers** and **message consumers** respectively.

Message consumers and producers are associated with specific message destinations/sources. A consumer can receive messages only from the message source it is associated with and a producer can send messages only to the message destination it is associated with.

The diagram below depicts the high-level architecture of a JMS system as explained above:

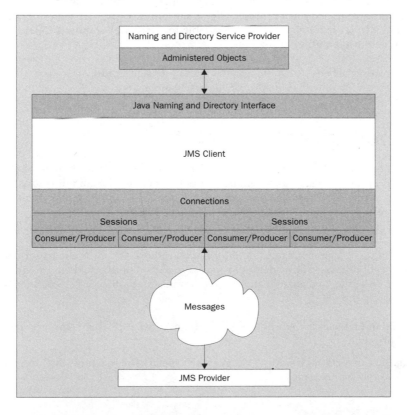

The JMS specification defines interfaces for all the JMS entities explained above. JMS providers provide implementation classes for these interfaces. Portable JMS clients need to be aware of only these interfaces and should not be using the provider-specific implementation classes in the application code. All these objects are explained in further detail in the coming sections.

Messaging Models

JMS specification supports two messaging models:

- **Point-to-Point (PTP)**
  The PTP messaging model is based on **message queues**. JMS clients send messages to and receive messages from specific message queues provided by the JMS provider. In the PTP messaging model, only one client can retrieve a message from the message queue. Once a JMS client has retrieved a message from a message queue, the message is no longer available for any other JMS client accessing the message queue. A message is addressed to a specific message queue and it remains in the queue until a client removes it. Message queues are generally configured and stored in a JNDI namespace and are available for clients by standard JNDI lookup. In the PTP model message producers are called **queue senders** and message consumers are called **queue receivers**.

- **Publish/Subscribe (Pub/Sub)**
  The Pub/Sub messaging model is based on **content hierarchies**. This model enables messages to be addressed to more than one client. In the Pub/Sub model, message producers are called **topic publishers** and message consumers are called **topic subscribers**. Publishers send messages to **topics** to which multiple clients subscribe. Topics are generally configured and stored in a JNDI namespace and are available for clients by standard JNDI lookup. A topic can have multiple publishers as well.

In both messaging models clients can invariantly act as message producers and message consumers. Messaging models are dealt with in further detail in Chapters 4 and 5.

Administered Objects

Administered objects are objects pre-configured and stored by JMS administrators for the use of JMS clients. These objects are normally stored in the namespace of a naming and directory service provider and are available to the JMS clients for standard JNDI lookup. The implementation classes for Administered objects are required to implement `java.io.Serializable` and `javax.naming.Referencable` interfaces so that they can be stored in standard JNDI naming contexts.

Administered objects contain configuration information required by JMS clients for connecting to the JMS provider, local addressing information for message destinations, etc. JMS providers normally provide tools for creating, configuring, and storing administered objects. JMS defines two kinds of administered objects:

- **Connection factories** are administered objects used by JMS clients for creating connections to a JMS provider

- **Destination** objects are used by JMS clients to specify the locations to and from which they send and receive messages

Connection Factories

Connection factories contain configuration information defining the host on which the provider is running, the port on which it is listening, client identifiers for the connections, etc. JMS providers provide vendor-specific tools for configuring connection factories and specifying the different properties associated with connection factories. JMS doesn't define standard ways for defining these properties against connection factories.

Connection factories are defined in JMS using the interface `javax.jms.ConnectionFactory`. This interface doesn't define any methods, but acts as the root interface for the connection factory interfaces specific to the two messaging models.

The interfaces `javax.jms.QueueConnectionFactory` and `javax.jms.TopicConnectionFactory` define the methods required for connection factories used in the PTP messaging model and Pub/Sub messaging model respectively. JMS providers supply the implementation classes for the aforementioned interfaces.

> **Portable JMS clients should be using only the standard JMS interfaces in the application code and should not be using the provider-specific implementation classes. Connection factories form the basis for writing vendor-neutral JMS applications.**

The QueueConnectionFactory Interface

Connections used in the PTP messaging model are called queue connections. Queue connection factories provide factory methods for creating queue connections. The interface `javax.jms.QueueConnectionFactory` defines the methods required for queue connection factories.

This interface defines two methods for creating queue connections. The first method creates a queue connection with the default security credentials for the JMS client:

```
public javax.jms.QueueConnection createQueueConnection() throws
                                JMSException, JMSSecurityException
```

The second method lets the client specify the user name and password when they create the connection:

```
public javax.jms.QueueConnection createQueueConnection(
                java.lang.String user, java.lang.String password)
                        throws JMSException, JMSSecurityException
```

JMS doesn't define the specifics for security authentication. Currently this aspect is very much specific to the JMS provider you use. Both the aforementioned methods throw `javax.jms.JMSException` on any internal server error and `javax.jms.JMSSecurityException` on failing to authenticate the client.

The TopicConnectionFactory Interface

Connections used in the Pub/Sub messaging model are called topic connections. Topic connection factories provide factory methods for creating topic connections. The interface `javax.jms.TopicConnectionFactory` defines the methods required for topic connection factories.

This interface defines two methods for creating topic connections. The first method creates a topic connection with the default security credentials for the JMS client:

```
public javax.jms.TopicConnection createTopicConnection() throws
                              JMSException, JMSSecurityException
```

The second method lets the client specify the user name and password when they create the connection:

```
public javax.jms.TopicConnection createTopicConnection(
                     java.lang.String user, java.lang.String password)
                         throws JMSException, JMSSecurityException
```

JMS doesn't define the specifics for security authentication. Currently this aspect is very much specific to the JMS provider you use. Both the aforementioned methods throw `javax.jms.JMSException` on any internal server error and `javax.jms.JMSSecurityException` on failing to authenticate the client.

Destinations

Destination objects contain the provider-specific addressing information required by the JMS clients for sending and receiving messages. Destination objects are created, configured, and stored in a namespace by JMS administrators for the use of JMS clients. The interface `javax.jms.Destination` is the root interface for different types of Destination objects.

The interfaces `javax.jms.Queue` and `javax.jms.TemporaryQueue` define the methods required for destination objects used in the PTP messaging model and `javax.jms.Topic` and `javax.jms.TemporaryTopic` define those required for the Pub/Sub messaging model. JMS providers supply implementation classes for all the aforementioned interfaces.

Portable JMS clients should never use these provider-specific implementation classes in their application code and should use only the standard JMS interfaces. Destinations should be looked up using standard JNDI method calls and casting the looked up object reference to the required destination interface. For example:

```
InitialContext ctx = new InitialContext();

Queue queue = (Queue)ctx.lookup("myQueue");
```

Queues

Queues are specialized Destination objects used in PTP messaging. Messages sent to a queue obey the classic **FIFO (First-In, First-Out) rule**. Every message in PTP messaging can have one, and only one, receiver. Queues are defined in JMS using the interface `javax.jms.Queue`. JMS providers supply implementation classes for this interface, which can be created, configured, and stored in a namespace by the JMS administrator and can be later looked up by JMS clients. Queues can also be created using queue sessions. Queue sessions are sessions specific to PTP messaging and are covered in detail in Chapter 4.

The interface `javax.jms.Queue` defines two methods. The first one returns the name of the queue:

```
public java.lang.String getQueueName() throws JMSException
```

This method throws a JMSException if the provider fails to return the queue name due to any internal server error.

The second method returns a formatted and printable version of the queue name. This is actually the toString() method defined in the implementation class that overrides the same defined in java.lang.Object:

```
public java.lang.String toString()
```

Temporary Queues

Unlike normal queues that are created for permanent use, temporary queues are dynamic queues that are created only for the lifetime of a queue connection.

Temporary queues can be used for specifying the destination on which a response is expected in a request/response paradigm using PTP messaging. The response destination can be specified using the JMSReplyTo message header when a message is sent. Message headers are explained in detail in the next chapter. Temporary queues that are created using queue sessions can be accessed only by the session that created the queue and all the other sessions belonging to the same connection.

Temporary queues are defined by the JMS interface javax.jms.TemporaryQueue that extends the interface javax.jms.Queue.

The interface javax.jms.TemporaryQueue defines only one method that is used for deleting the temporary queue:

```
public void delete() throws JMSException
```

This method will throw a JMSException if the queue is still in use by senders or receivers.

Topics

Topics are specialized Destination objects used in Pub/Sub messaging. Each message sent to a topic can be shared between different subscribers. Topics are defined in JMS using the interface javax.jms.Topic. JMS providers provide implementation classes for this interface, which can be created, configured, and stored in a namespace by the JMS administrator and can be looked up later by JMS clients. Topics can also be created using topic sessions. Topic sessions are sessions specific to Pub/Sub messaging and are covered in detail in Chapter 5.

The interface javax.jms.Topic defines two methods. The first one returns the name of the topic:

```
public java.lang.String getTopicName() throws JMSException
```

This method throws and a trappable JMSException if the provider fails to return the topic name due to any internal server error.

The second method returns a formatted and printable version of the topic name. This is actually the toString() method defined in the implementation class that overrides the same defined in java.lang.Object:

```
public java.lang.String toString()
```

Temporary Topics

Unlike normal topics that are created for permanent use, temporary topics are dynamic topics that are created only for the life of a topic connection.

Temporary topics can be used for specifying the destination on which a response is expected in a request/response paradigm using Pub/Sub messaging. The response destination can be specified using the JMSReplyTo message header when a message is sent. Temporary topics that are created using topic sessions can be accessed only by the session that created the topic and all the other sessions belonging to the same connection.

Temporary topics are defined by the JMS interface javax.jms.TemporaryTopic, which extends the interface javax.jms.Topic.

The interface javax.jms.TemporaryTopic defines only one method that is used for deleting the temporary topic:

```
public void delete() throws JMSException
```

This method will throw a trappable JMSException if the queue is still in use by publishers or subscribers.

Class Hierarchy

The class hierarchy for JMS destinations is depicted in the class diagram shown below:

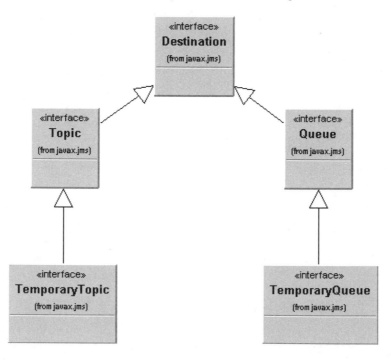

JMS Client to Look up Administered Objects

Now we will write a simple JMS client that will look up connection factories and destinations from a namespace and create a connection to the JMS provider. The client will work with any JMS-compliant provider and has been tested with JMQ 1.1 (Java Message Queue) from Sun Microsystems. JMQ is freely available for development and can be downloaded from http://java.sun.com.

One important step involved in building JMS applications is creating and configuring administered objects. Most of the messaging product vendors provide custom tools for accomplishing this task. In the sample application, we will create and store a queue connection factory, a queue, a topic connection factory, and a topic in the standard Windows NT file system namespace. We will then use JNDI to lookup these objects.

The listing below shows the batch file used for creating, configuring, and storing the required Administered objects for the sample application. Note that all the code in this chapter can be downloaded from the Wrox website at http://www.wrox.com.

The batch file creates a queue called myQueue, a topic called myTopic, a queue connection factory called QCFactory, and a topic connection factory called TCFactory. These objects are stored under the C:\temp directory and are available for standard JNDI lookup using the file system context service provider.

The configuration information for the connection factories specifies that the message provider will be run on localhost and listen on the default port. The -t option is used to specify the type of the Administered object. The -i option specifies the initial context factory. For a complete list of options please refer to the JMQ documentation provided with the installation:

```
@echo off

if "%JMQ_HOME%\lib\jmq.jar" == "\lib\jmq.jar" goto nojmqhome

REM  Create and add the queue
call "%JMQ_HOME%\bin\jmqconfig" -a -t q -n myQueue -o "name=myQueue" -i
"com.sun.jndi.fscontext.RefFSContextFactory" -u "file:C:\temp"

REM  Create and add the topic
call "%JMQ_HOME%\bin\jmqconfig" -a -t t -n myTopic -o "name=myTopic" -i
"com.sun.jndi.fscontext.RefFSContextFactory" -u "file:C:\temp"

REM  Create and add the queue connection factory
call "%JMQ_HOME%\bin\jmqconfig" -a -t qf -n QCFactory -o "host=localhost"
-i "com.sun.jndi.fscontext.RefFSContextFactory" -u "file:C:\temp"

REM  Create and add the topic connection factory
call "%JMQ_HOME%\bin\jmqconfig" -a -t tf -n TCFactory -o "host=localhost"
-i "com.sun.jndi.fscontext.RefFSContextFactory" -u "file:C:\temp"

goto end

:nojmqhome
   echo Please set the JMQ_HOME environment variable.
   goto end
:end
```

Running the above batch file would produce the following output in the command window:

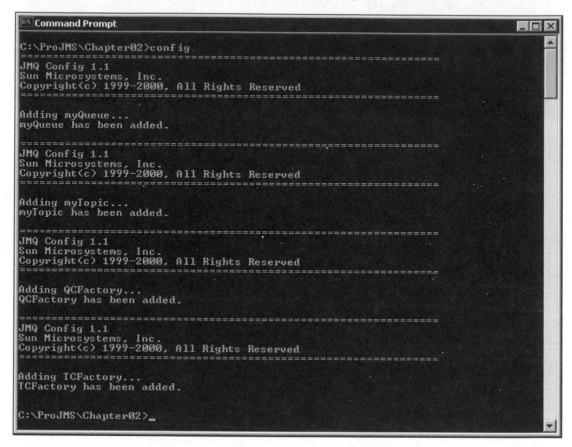

The listing below shows a JMS client using JNDI lookup to retrieve the Administered objects created and stored using the above batch file:

```
import javax.naming.NamingException;
import javax.naming.Context;
import javax.naming.InitialContext;
import java.util.Properties;
import javax.jms.Queue;
import javax.jms.QueueConnectionFactory;
import javax.jms.QueueConnection;
import javax.jms.Topic;
import javax.jms.TopicConnectionFactory;
import javax.jms.TopicConnection;
import javax.jms.JMSException;
```

The JMSLookup class creates the JNDI initial context using the file system initial context factory:

```
public class JMSLookup {

    //Initial context factory
    public static final String CTX_FACT =
                "com.sun.jndi.fscontext.RefFSContextFactory";
    //Provider URL
    public static final String PROV_URL = "file:C:\\temp";
    //JNDI name for the queue connection factory
    public static final String QCF_NAME = "QCFactory";
    //JNDI name for the topic connection factory
    public static final String TCF_NAME = "TCFactory";
    //JNDI name for the queue
    public static final String QUEUE_NAME = "myQueue";
    //JNDI name for the topic
    public static final String TOPIC_NAME = "myTopic";

    public static void main(String args[]) throws Exception {

        //Properties for storing JNDI configuration info
        Properties prop = new Properties();
        //Add the initial context factory
        prop.put(Context.INITIAL_CONTEXT_FACTORY, CTX_FACT);
        //Add the provider URL
        prop.put(Context.PROVIDER_URL, PROV_URL);
        //Create the initial context
        Context ctx = new InitialContext(prop);
```

Instead of passing the JNDI environment properties using Properties objects, they can also be passed as system properties using the –D option when the JVM is invoked. The initial context is then used for looking up the Administered objects stored in the file system namespace:

```
        System.out.println("\nRetrieving: Queue connection factory.");
        QueueConnectionFactory qcf =
            (QueueConnectionFactory)ctx.lookup(QCF_NAME);
        System.out.println("Retrieved: Queue connection factory.");

        System.out.println("Obtaining: Queue connection.");
        QueueConnection qConn = qcf.createQueueConnection();
        System.out.println("Obtained: Queue connection.");

        System.out.println("Retrieving: Topic connection factory.");
        TopicConnectionFactory tcf =
            (TopicConnectionFactory)ctx.lookup(TCF_NAME);
        System.out.println("Retrieved: Topic connection factory.");

        System.out.println("Obtaining: Topic connection.");
        TopicConnection tConn = tcf.createTopicConnection();
        System.out.println("Obtained: Topic connection.");

        System.out.println("Retrieving: Queue.");
        Queue queue = (Queue)ctx.lookup(QUEUE_NAME);
        System.out.println(queue);
        System.out.println("Retrieved: Queue.");

        System.out.println("Retrieving: Topic.");
        Topic topic = (Topic)ctx.lookup(TOPIC_NAME);
        System.out.println(topic);
        System.out.println("Retrieved: Topic.");
```

```
        System.exit(0);

    }
 }
```

When you compile and run the example please make sure you have the required JAR files from the JMQ lib directory in the classpath. These are fscontext.jar, jms.jar, jndi.jar, jmq.jar, and providerutil.jar.

Start the JMQ router by executing the irouter binary. Invoke the Java interpreter on JMSLookup with all the required class files in the classpath. The output is shown below:

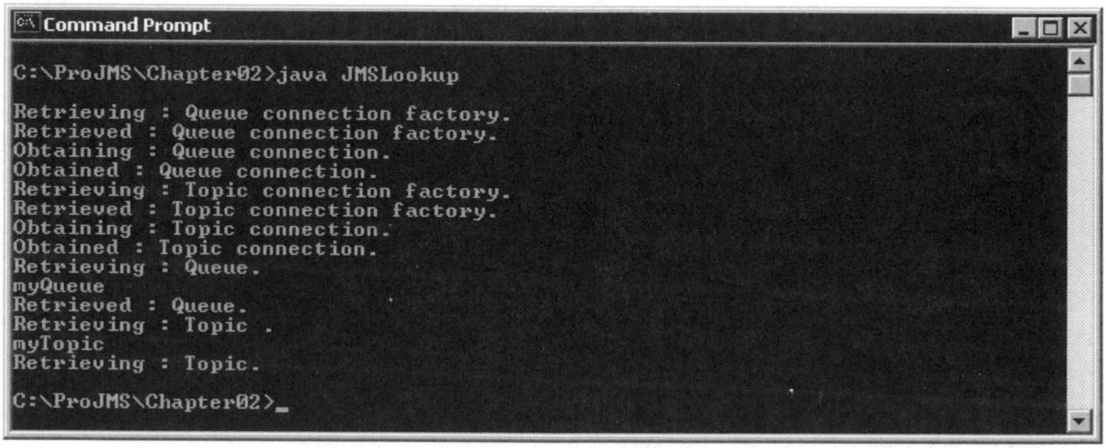

Connections

Connections are created using factory methods provided by the connection factories. The PTP messaging model uses queue connections and the Pub/Sub messaging model uses topic connections. Queue connections are created using queue connection factories and topic connections are created using topic connection factories.

The basic methods used for JMS connections are defined in the interface javax.jms.Connection. Methods specific to the PTP messaging model are defined in the interface javax.jms.QueueConnection, and those specific to the Pub/Sub message model are defined in the interface javax.jms.TopicConnection. JMS providers provide implementation classes for these interfaces. Connections serve various purposes in writing JMS clients:

❑ Connection factories provide client authentication when connections are created

❑ Connection objects act as factories for creating JMS sessions

❑ Connections can be used to define identifiers for JMS clients

❑ Connections provide facilities to the JMS clients to be asynchronously notified by the provider of internal exceptions

Client Authentication

JMS clients are authenticated at the point of creating connections. Connection factories provide two overloaded methods for creating connections. The first one uses the default security credentials for the JMS client thread and the second one provides facility for specifying the user name and password. JMS doesn't define the specifics of security credentials and client authentication. Different JMS providers provide client authentication in vendor-specific manners.

Connection States

A typical JMS client first looks up the required Administered objects (connection factories and destinations) and uses the connection factories to create connections. These connections are used to create sessions and sessions are used to create message consumers and producers. When a connection is created using the connection factory it is created in the *stopped mode*. Even though connections in stopped mode can produce messages, they are not ready to consume messages. To enable message delivery the connection needs to be explicitly started. The interface `javax.jms.Connection` defines the method for starting connections:

```
public void start() throws JMSException
```

This method throws a `JMSException` if the provider fails to start message delivery to this connection due to any internal error.

Connections can be temporarily stopped. When a connection is stopped temporarily, message delivery to this connection is stopped. Calling the method to start the connection discussed above can restart message delivery. JMS clients can still use stopped connections for sending messages, but they can't use stopped connections for receiving messages. The method signature for stopping the connections temporarily is shown below:

```
public void stop() throws JMSException
```

This method doesn't return until the message delivery currently in progress is completed. This method throws a `JMSException` if the JMS provider fails to stop message delivery due to any internal server error.

Connection objects use expensive client-side resources. So it is better to free up these resources when the connection is not in use, by closing the connection. Closing a connection will close all the sessions, producers and consumers associated with the connection. The method signature for stopping the connections temporarily is shown below:

```
public void close() throws JMSException
```

This method doesn't return until all the message delivery currently in progress is completed. This method throws a `JMSException` if the JMS provider fails to close the connection. JMS clients trying to use a closed connection will get an exception.

Client Identifiers

Client identifiers are used for state management at the provider. Providers can use client identifiers to identify the connections and associated objects used by a particular client. There are two ways to assign an identifier to a JMS client. Client identifiers can be used to associate a client connection and related objects to a state maintained by the provider for a client.

The `javax.jms.Connection` interface defines two methods for managing client identifiers. The first method is used to set a client identifier with a connection:

```
public void setClientID(java.lang.String clientID) throws JMSException
```

This method explicitly sets a client identifier to the connection. This method throws a `JMSException` if the provider fails to set the client identifier and an `InvalidClientIDException` if the client ID is invalid or duplicate.

The second method is used for accessing the client identifier associated with a connection:

```
public java.lang.String getClientID() throws JMSException
```

This method throws a `JMSException` if the provider fails to return the client identifier due to any internal server error.

An alternative way of assigning client identifiers is to use client-specific connection factories. Connection factories can be configured such that all the connections created by a connection factory will be assigned a specific client identifier. Configuring connection factories to accomplish this task is specific to JMS providers.

Trying to set the client ID explicitly on a connection created with a pre-configured client ID will throw an `IllegalStateException`.

Exception Listeners

Connections can asynchronously notify JMS clients about internal problems with the provider. This is achieved using exception listeners. The `javax.jms.Connection` interface defines two methods for handling exception listeners with the connection. The first method is used for registering an exception listener with the connection:

```
public void setExceptionListener(ExceptionListener listener)
                                            throws JMSException
```

The second method provides access to the registered exception listener:

```
public ExceptionListener getExceptionListener() throws JMSException
```

javax.jms.ExceptionListener

Exception listeners enable JMS clients to be notified asynchronously about any serious problem with the connection. The implementation classes for exception listeners need to implement the method defined in this interface:

```
public void onException(JMSException ex)
```

Only those exceptions that cannot be notified to the JMS clients otherwise will be notified using this mechanism. For example, if a JMS method call throws a JMSException, the JMS client won't be notified about the exception using this mechanism. The JMS provider will try to resolve the error before the client is notified. This method is specifically useful for connections that only consume messages, as there is no other way to notify the client when its connection fails since the client doesn't make any synchronous method calls.

Specialized Connections

The javax.jms.Connection has specialized sub-interfaces used for different purposes. These specialized sub-interfaces are listed below:

- ❑ javax.jms.QueueConnection
  Queue connections are used in PTP messaging. Queue connections are used as factories to create queue sessions as well as other purposes.

- ❑ javax.jms.TopicConnection
  Topic connections are used in Pub/Sub messaging. Topic connections are used as factories to create topic sessions as well as other purposes.

- ❑ javax.jms.XAQueueConnection
  This interface is used for queue connections that are transacted by definition.

- ❑ javax.jms.XATopicConnection
  This interface is used for topic connections that are transacted by definition.

All the aforementioned interfaces are covered in the appropriate chapter: Chapter 4 for queues and Chapter 5 for topics.

Connection Metadata

The interface javax.jms.Connection provides access to the metadata of the connection. The metadata information includes the JMS and provider versions and JMS properties supported by the connection. JMS properties are covered in detail in Chapter 3. The metadata for the connection is accessed using the interface javax.jms.ConnectionMetaData. The javax.jms.Connection interface provides the method for accessing the metadata interface:

```
public ConnectionMetadata getMetaData()
```

This method throws a JMSException if the provider fails to return the metadata due to any internal error.

javax.jms.ConnectionMetaData

`javax.jms.ConnectionMetaData` interface defines the methods required for accessing the connection's metadata information. The methods defined in this interface are listed below:

Method	Description
`public int getJMSMajorVersion()`	Returns the major version of JMS
`public int getJMSMinorVersion()`	Returns the minor version of JMS
`public String getJMSProviderName()`	Returns the name of the JMS provider
`public String getJMSVersion()`	Returns the version of JMS
`public Enumeration getJMSXPropertyNames()`	Returns an enumeration of the JMS properties supported by the connection
`public int getProviderMajorVersion()`	Returns the major version of JMS provider
`public int getJMSProviderMinorVersion()`	Returns the minor version of JMS provider
`public String getJMSProviderVersion()`	Returns the version of JMS provider

For example, if the returned version is 1.2, then the major version is 1 and the minor version is 2. JMS properties are explained in detail in the next chapter.

Obtaining Metadata Example

The code listing below shows a sample application to print the connection metadata with JMQ. We will be accessing the same Administered objects that we set up in the last example:

```
import javax.naming.NamingException;
import javax.naming.Context;
import javax.naming.InitialContext;
import java.util.Properties;
import javax.jms.Queue;
import javax.jms.QueueConnectionFactory;
import javax.jms.QueueConnection;
import javax.jms.Topic;
import javax.jms.TopicConnectionFactory;
import javax.jms.TopicConnection;
import javax.jms.JMSException;
import javax.jms.ConnectionMetaData;

import java.util.Enumeration;

public class JMSMetaData {

    //Initial context factory
    public static final String CTX_FACT =
        "com.sun.jndi.fscontext.RefFSContextFactory";
    //Provider URL
    public static final String PROV_URL = "file:C:\\temp";
    //JNDI name for the queue connection factory
    public static final String QCF_NAME = "QCFactory";

    public static void main(String args[]) throws Exception {
```

First, a JNDI initial context is created by specifying the initial context factory and the provider URL:

```
//Properties for storing JNDI configuration info
Properties prop = new Properties();
//Add the initial context factory
prop.put(Context.INITIAL_CONTEXT_FACTORY, CTX_FACT);
//Add the provider URL
prop.put(Context.PROVIDER_URL, PROV_URL);
//Create the initial context
Context ctx = new InitialContext(prop);
```

The queue connection factory is looked up and a queue connection is created. Then a reference to the queue connection's metadata is obtained:

```
QueueConnectionFactory qcf =
    (QueueConnectionFactory)ctx.lookup(QCF_NAME);
QueueConnection qConn = qcf.createQueueConnection();
ConnectionMetaData cmd = qConn.getMetaData();
```

Now the metadata for queue connection is printed to the standard output:

```
System.out.println("\nJMS Version: " +
    cmd.getJMSVersion());
System.out.println("JMS Major Version: " +
    cmd.getJMSMajorVersion());
System.out.println("JMS Minor Version: " +
    cmd.getJMSMinorVersion());
System.out.println("Provider Name: " +
    cmd.getJMSProviderName());
System.out.println("Provider Version: " +
    cmd.getProviderVersion());
System.out.println("Provider Major Version: " +
    cmd.getProviderMajorVersion());
System.out.println("Provider Minor Version: " +
    cmd.getProviderMinorVersion());

System.out.println("Supported JMS properties:");
Enumeration enum = cmd.getJMSXPropertyNames();
while(enum.hasMoreElements()) {
    System.out.println("\t" + enum.nextElement());
}

qConn.close();

    }

}
```

Compiling and running the class listed above using JMQ will produce the output shown below:

```
Command Prompt                                                    _ □ ×

C:\ProJMS\Chapter02>java JMSMetaData

JMS Version: 1.0.2
JMS Major Version: 1
JMS Minor Version: 0
Provider Name: Java Message Queue, Sun Microsystems, Inc.
Provider Version: 1.1
Provider Major Version: 1
Provider Minor Version: 1
Supported JMS properties:
        JMSXGroupSeq
        JMSXConsumerTXID
        JMSXGroupID
        JMSXProducerTXID
        JMSXUserID
        JMSXAppID
        JMSXRcvTimestamp

C:\ProJMS\Chapter02>_
```

Sessions

JMS sessions are used for sending and receiving messages. JMS sessions that are created using connections are used for a variety of other purposes as well:

- ❑ Sessions provide an alternative method for creating destinations

- ❑ Sessions are used for creating temporary destinations

- ❑ Sessions are used as factories for creating different types of provider-optimized implementation of JMS messages

- ❑ Sessions are used for creating message producers and consumers

- ❑ Sessions can be used for receiving the messages associated with all the message consumers asynchronously

The basic methods required for JMS sessions are defined in the interface `javax.jms.Session`. This interface has specialized sub-interfaces used for specific purposes. Those interfaces are listed below:

- ❑ `javax.jms.QueueSession`
  Queue sessions are used in PTP messaging.

- ❑ `javax.jms.TopicSession`
  Topic sessions are used in Pub/Sub messaging.

- ❑ `javax.jms.XASession`
  XA sessions are sessions that support JTA (Java Transaction API).

- ❑ `javax.jms.XAQueueSession`
  These sessions are queue sessions that support JTA. These sessions extend the interface of XA sessions.

- ❑ `javax.jms.XATopicSession`
  These sessions are topic sessions that support JTA. These sessions extend the interface of XA sessions.

Creating JMS Messages

Sessions can be used for creating optimized provider implementations of JMS messages. As we have already seen the JMS specification defines interfaces for the different JMS entities like connections, sessions, messages, etc. It is the JMS providers who provide implementation classes for these interfaces. The JMS specification defines different types of message and the interface for JMS sessions defines factory methods for creating all these messages. The signatures for these methods are listed below:

Method	Description
`public BytesMessage createBytesMessage() throws JMSException`	Creates objects of type `BytesMessage`. The interface `BytesMessage` represents message objects holding a stream of uninterpreted bytes.
`public MapMessage createMapMessage() throws JMSException`	Creates objects of type `MapMessage`. The interface `MapMessage` represents message objects holding a map of key/value pairs.
`public ObjectMessage createObjectMessage() throws JMSException`	Creates objects of type `ObjectMessage`. The interface `ObjectMessage` represents message objects holding serialized Java objects.
`public ObjectMessage createObjectMessage(Object obj) throws JMSException`	Creates objects of type `ObjectMessage` pre-populated with the object passed to the method.
`public StreamMessage createStreamMessage() throws JMSException`	Creates objects of type `StreamMessage`. The interface `StreamMessage` represents message objects holding a stream of Java primitives.
`public TextMessage createTextMessage() throws JMSException`	Creates objects of type `TextMessage`. The interface `TextMessage` represents message objects holding plain text.
`public TextMessage createTextMessage(String text) throws JMSException`	Creates objects of type `TextMessage` pre-populated with the text passed to the method.

Destinations and Temporary Destinations

In the section on Administered objects we have seen that one way to get a reference to static destinations stored in a namespace is looking up those objects using JNDI. However, clients can also create destinations when they need to dynamically manipulate the destination identity, using provider-specific names for destinations.

It is worthwhile to note that clients using this functionality may not be portable across different JMS providers. The method used for this purpose is specific to messaging models and is defined in the session interfaces specific to messaging models.

The interfaces `javax.jms.QueueSession` and `javax.jms.TopicSessions` defines the methods for creating destinations for PTP and Pub/Sub messaging model respectively:

Method	Description
`public Queue createQueue(String queueName) throws JMSException`	Creates queues
`public Topic createTopic(String topicName) throws JMSException`	Creates topics
`public TemporaryQueue createTemporaryQueue(String queueName) throws JMSException`	Creates temporary queues
`public TemporaryTopic createTemporaryTopic String topicName) throws JMSException`	Creates temporary topics

The first two methods don't create the destinations physically, but get a handle to the destination stored by the JMS administrator. These methods throw `JMSException` if the provider fails to return a handle to the specified destination.

Creating Message Processors

In JMS terminology objects used for creating messages are called **message producers** and objects receiving messages are called **message consumers**. Message producers and consumers used in the PTP messaging model are called **queue senders** and **queue receivers** and those used in the Pub/Sub model are called **topic publishers** and **topic subscribers** respectively. One of the primary purposes of JMS sessions is the creation of message consumers and producers. In the same way that a JMS connection can have multiple JMS sessions associated with it, a JMS session can have multiple consumers and producers associated with it.

The interface `javax.jms.QueueSession` defines factory methods for creating queue senders and queue receivers:

Method	Description
`public QueueSender createSender(Queue queue) throws JMSException, InvalidDestinationException`	Creates a queue sender for the specified queue that can be used by the session to send messages to this queue.
`public QueueReceiver createReceiver(Queue queue) throws JMSException, InvalidDestinationException`	Creates a queue receiver for the specified queue that can be used by the session to receive messages from this queue.
`public QueueReceiver createReceiver (Queue queue, String selector) throws JMSException, InvalidDestinationException, InvalidSelectorException`	Creates a queue receiver for the specified queue that can be used by the session to receive messages from this queue with the specified message selector.

Message selectors are used for filtering messages and are explained in detail in Chapter 3. A reference for message selector syntax can be found in Appendix B.

All these methods throw JMSException if the provider fails to fulfill the request due to any internal error. In addition they throw InvalidDestinationException if the destination is not valid and InvalidSelectorException if the message selector is not valid.

The interface javax.jms.TopicSession defines factory methods for creating publishers and subscribers:

Method	Description
public TopicPublishercreatePublisher (Topic topic) throws JMSException, TnvalidDestinationException	Creates a topic publisher for the specified topic that can be used by the session to send messages to this topic.
public TopicSubscribercreateSubscriber (Topic topic) throws JMSException, InvalidDestinationException	Creates a topic subscriber for the specified topic that can be used by the session to receive messages from this topic.
public TopicSubscriber createSubscriber (Topic topic, String selector, boolean noLocal) throws JMSException, InvalidDestinationException, InvalidSelectorException	Creates a topic subscriber for the specified topic. The third argument specifies whether the subscriber should receive messages published by publishers belonging to the same connection.

The interface javax.jms.TopicSession also defines methods for creating durable subscribers. JMS clients for receiving messages published even when they are inactive use durable subscribers. There are two methods defined for creating durable subscribers:

```
public TopicSubscriber createDurableSubscriber(Topic topic, String name)
                     throws JMSException, InvalidDestinationException

public TopicSubscriber createDurableSubscriber(Topic topic, String name,
             String selector, boolean noLocal) throws JMSException,
                 InvalidDestinationException, InvalidSelectorException
```

Both of these methods are similar to their non-durable counterparts apart from the fact that they provide an extra argument to specify a name to identify the subscription. JMS clients using durable subscription should use the same client identifier each time they connect to the provider. Durable subscriptions are covered in detail in Chapter 5.

Asynchronous Message Delivery

As we have already seen, messages are delivered to the message consumers associated with a session. Message consumers can receive messages either synchronously or asynchronously. Message consumers are explained in detail in later sections. A JMS session can be set to asynchronously receive the messages for all of its message consumers. This is done using the interface javax.jms.MessageListener that defines a callback method for asynchronous message delivery. The interface javax.jms.Session defines a method for registering message listeners:

```
public void setMessageListener(MessageListener listener) throws JMSException
```

This interface also defines an accessor method for the registered message listener:

```
public MessageListener getMessageListener() throws JMSException
```

javax.jms.MessageListener

This interface defines the callback method for asynchronous message delivery. JMS clients that need asynchronous message delivery should register an implementation of this interface with either the session or the message consumer:

```
public void onMessage(Message msg)
```

The interface javax.jms.Message is the root interface for all the JMS message interfaces. At runtime, the argument will be an implementation class of one of the specific JMS message interfaces.

Transaction Support

JMS sessions can be optionally defined as transaction bound. Transacted sessions can treat a set of messages sent and received as a single atomic unit. This means all the messages in a transaction are either processed completely or not processed at all. The factory methods defined in JMS connection interfaces take an argument to specify whether the created sessions are to be transaction bound or not.

The interface javax.jms.Session interface defines two methods for handling transactions. The first method is used for committing a transaction:

```
public void commit() throws JMSException, TransactionRolledBackException,
                                          IllegalStateException
```

The second method is used for rolling back a transaction:

```
public void rollback() throws JMSException, IllegalStateException
```

Both of these methods complete the current transaction and start a new one.

Acknowledging Messages

Message acknowledgement is automatic for transacted sessions when the transactions are committed. For non-transacted sessions there are three modes of message acknowledgement. Message acknowledgement mode is defined when the sessions are created using the factory methods provided by JMS connections.

These methods take the acknowledgement mode as one of their arguments. The different acknowledgement modes are enumerated as public static member variables in the interface javax.jms.Session.

The different message acknowledgement modes are explained below:

❑   AUTO_ACKNOWLEDGE
    In this mode sessions automatically acknowledge message delivery when the message processing thread returns from the callback method of the message listener for asynchronous delivery or the receive() method of the message consumer for synchronous delivery. Asynchronous message delivery is already covered in a previous section. Synchronous message delivery is covered in the section on message consumers.

❏   CLIENT_ACKNOWLEDGE
In this mode clients explicitly acknowledge messages by calling the `acknowledge()` method on messages.

❏   DUPS_OK_ACKNOWLEDGE
In this mode, sessions lazily acknowledge messages. In this case the provider may deliver a message more than once. This mode should only be used with consumers that are tolerant of duplicate messages. The benefit of using this mode is a reduction in session overhead achieved by minimizing the work the session does to prevent duplicate messages being delivered.

An example of a session that automatically acknowledges message delivery can be seen below:

```
QueueConnection qCon = qcf.createQueueConnection();
QueueSession qSes = qCon.createQueueSession(false, QueueSession.AUTO_ACKNOWLEDGE);
```

Message Producers

Message producers are used for sending messages. Message producers are created using the factory methods provided by sessions. The root interface for all message producers is defined by the interface `javax.jms.MessageProducer`. The interface `javax.jms.QueueSender` defines the message producer for the PTP model and the interface `javax.jms.TopicPublisher` defines the message producer for the Pub/Sub model. Queue sessions provide factory methods for creating queue senders and topic sessions provide factory methods for creating topic publishers.

Message Priority

Message producers can set priorities to all the messages they send, globally as well as individually. This overrides the FIFO behavior of the queue. The range of values is from 0 (lowest) to 9 (highest), with the default priority set to 4. This is defined by the public static member variable `DEFAULT_PRIORITY` in the interface `javax.jms.Message`. The interface `javax.jms.MessageProducer` defines methods for globally setting and getting the priorities for the messages it sends:

```
public void setPriority(int priority) throws JMSException

public int getPriority() throws JMSException
```

Delivery Mode

Message producers let JMS clients globally set the delivery mode for all the messages sent using the message producer. Delivery mode indicates whether the messages are to persist or not. Persistent messages are guaranteed to be delivered once and only once. Persistent messages are only guaranteed not to be lost during transmission, but this doesn't guarantee message persistence and retention at the provider. The interface `javax.jms.MessageProducer` defines methods for setting and getting the delivery mode:

```
public void setDeliveryMode(int mode) throws JMSException

public int getDeliveryMode() throws JMSException
```

javax.jms.DeliveryMode

The interface `javax.jms.DeliveryMode` defines two enumerated public static member variables to define the different delivery modes:

❑   `PERSISTENT` – This defines the persistent delivery mode.

❑   `NON_PERSISTENT` – This defines the non-persistent delivery mode.

Message Time-to-Live

JMS clients can use message producers to globally define the number of milliseconds the message will be retained by the messaging system after the messages are sent. If the time-to-live is set to zero the message never expires:

```
public void setTimeToLive(long time) throws JMSException

public long getimeToLive() throws JMSException
```

Disabling Message Properties

Message producers provide methods for globally disabling the automatic setting of some of the properties for all the messages sent by the producer. The signatures of these methods are listed below:

Method	Description
`public boolean getDisableMessageID()` `throws JMSException`	Returns True if the setting of message ID is disabled.
`public void setDisableMessageID(boolean val) throws JMSException`	Used for disabling/enabling the setting of message ID.
`public boolean getDisableMessageTimestamp()` `throws JMSException`	Returns True if the setting of message timestamp is disabled.
`public void setDisableMessageTimestamp (boolean val) throws JMSException`	Used for disabling/enabling the setting of message timestamp.

Sending Messages

The methods used for sending messages are defined in the messaging-model-specific sub-interfaces of the interface `javax.jms.MessageProducer`. The interface `javax.jms.QueueSender` defines methods for sending messages in the PTP messaging model and `javax.jms.TopicPublisher` defines methods for sending messages in the Pub/Sub messaging model. Both these interfaces define a plethora of overloaded send/publish methods that can be used for overriding the global properties like delivery mode, time to live, priority, etc., set at the message producer level.

The send() methods for javax.jms.QueueSender are listed below:

Method	Description
public void send(Message msg) throws JMSException, MessageFormatException, InvalidDestinationException	Sends the message to the associated queue.
public void send(Message msg, int mode, int priority, long timetolive) throws JMSException, MessageFormatException, InvalidDestinationException	Sends the message to the associated queue. This method lets JMS clients override the globally set message properties.
public void send(Queue queue, Message msg) throws JMSException, MessageFormatException, InvalidDestinationException	Sends the message to the specified queue for unidentified message producers. Unidentified message producers need to specify the destination each time they send a message.
public void send(Queue queue, Message msg, int mode, int priority, long timetolive) throws JMSException, MessageFormatException, InvalidDestinationException	Sends the message to the specified queue. This method lets JMS clients override the globally set message properties.

The methods defined in javax.jms.TopicPublisher for publishing messages are listed below:

Method	Description
public void publish(Message msg) throws JMSException, MessageFormatException, InvalidDestinationException	Sends the message to the associated topic.
public void publish(Message msg, int mode, int priority, long timetolive) throws JMSException, MessageFormatException, InvalidDestinationException	Sends the message to the associated topic. This method lets JMS clients override the globally set message properties.
public void publish (Topic topic, Message msg) throws JMSException, MessageFormatException, InvalidDestinationException	Sends the message to the specified topic for unidentified publishers.
public void publish (Topic topic, Message msg, int mode, int priority, long timetolive) throws JMSException, MessageFormatException, InvalidDestinationException	Sends the message to the specified topic. This method lets JMS clients override the globally set message properties.

All the aforementioned methods throw JMSException if JMS fails to send the message due to some internal server error, MessageFormatException if the specified message is not valid, and InvalidDestinationException if the destination associated with the message producer is not valid.

Message Consumers

Message consumers are entities used by JMS clients for receiving messages. Message consumers used in PTP messaging are called queue receivers and those used in Pub/Sub model are called topic subscribers. JMS sessions act as factories for creating message consumers. Queue sessions are used for creating queue receivers and topic sessions are used for creating topic subscribers.

Message consumers can receive messages both synchronously asynchronously. The interface for message consumers is defined by `javax.jms.MessageConsumer`. The interface `javax.jms.QueueReceiver` defines the methods for PTP message consumers and the interface `javax.jms.TopicSubscriber` defines the methods for Pub/Sub message consumers.

Asynchronous Message Delivery

Message consumers can receive messages asynchronously by registering message listeners. All the message consumers associated with a single session can have different message listeners, but message delivery to these listeners is serialized. If a message listener is registered globally for the session as described in one of the earlier sections, messages intended for all the session's consumers are handled by the session itself. The interface `javax.jms.MessageConsumer` defines methods for setting and getting message listeners:

```
public void setMessageListener(MessageListener listener) throws JMSException

public MessageListener getMessageListener() throws JMSException
```

Synchronous Message Delivery

Message consumers achieve synchronous message delivery by making blocking method calls to the receive methods defined in the interface `javax.jms.MessageConsumer`. A call made to this method will block the thread until a message is available in the destination associated with the consumer:

```
public Message receive() throws JMSException
```

The next method is the same as the one above except for the fact that the client thread is blocked until a message is available or the number of milliseconds specified in the argument, whichever is the earliest:

```
public Message receive(long timeout) throws JMSException
```

The final receive method defined in `javax.jms.MessageConsumer` retrieves a message if one is immediately available:

```
public Message receiveNoWait() throws JMSException
```

All the above methods throw `JMSException` if the provider encounters any internal error. These methods don't throw an exception if there are no messages available to be delivered.

JMS Clients

This section explains the different steps involved in writing normal JMS clients. We will cover only the concepts explained in this chapter. We will not cover advanced concepts like XA sessions, session pools, connection consumers, etc.

Sending Messages

The sequence diagram shown below depicts the basic steps involved in writing a basic JMS client for sending messages:

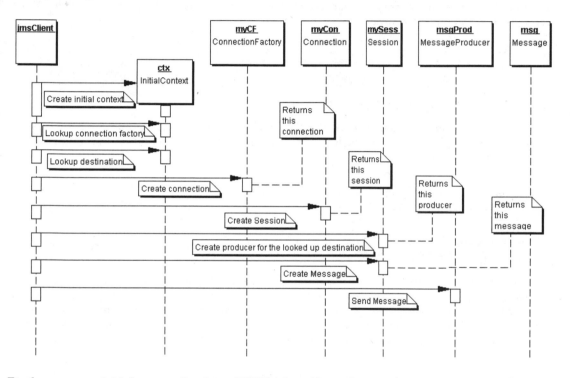

Firstly, create an initial context for doing JNDI lookup. Depending on the service provider the constructor for initializing the initial context may take an instance of java.util.Properties holding the provider URL, name of the initial context factory, etc. Even though the code for creating the initial context is similar for different JNDI service providers, the value passed for the initial context factory and the provider URL vary. For details on provider specific lookups, see Appendix A:

```
Properties prop = new Properties();
prop.put(Context.INITIAL_CONTEXT_FACTORY,
    "com.sun.jndi.fscontext.RefFSContextFactory");
prop.put(Context.PROVIDER_URL, "file:C:\\temp");
Context ctx = new InitialContext(prop);
```

Next, look up the required administered objects. In the PTP model the administered objects are generally queues and queue connection factories whereas in the Pub/Sub they are topics and topic connection factories:

```
//PTP
Queue queue = (Queue)ctx.lookup("myQueue");
QueueConnectionFactory qcf = (QueueConnectionFactory)ctx.lookup("myQCF");

//Pub/Sub
Topic topic = (Topic)ctx.lookup("myTopic");
TopicConnectionFactory tcf = (TopicConnectionFactory)ctx.lookup("myTCF");
```

Then use the connection factory to create connections. Connections can be queue connections for PTP and topic connections for Pub/Sub:

```
//PTP
QueueConnection qCon = qcf.createQueueConnection();

//Pub/Sub
TopicConnection tCon = tcf.createTopicConnection();
```

Use these connections to create sessions. The PTP model uses queue sessions and the Pub/Sub model uses topic sessions. Message acknowledgement mode and transaction support for the sessions can be specified here:

```
//PTP
QueueSession qSes = qCon.createQueueSession(false,
        Session.AUTO_ACKNOWLEDGE);

//Pub/Sub
TopicSession tSes = tCon.createTopicSession(false,
        Session.AUTO_ACKNOWLEDGE);
```

Create message producers for the session and the destination. For the PTP model queue senders are created using queue sessions that are associated to specific queues and in the Pub/Sub model topic publishers are created using topic sessions that are associated to specific topics. You can set different properties, in other words, message time-to-live, message priority, etc. for all the messages sent by this message producer using the various methods discussed in the section on message producers:

```
//PTP
QueueSender sender = qSes.createSender(queue);

//Pub/Sub
TopicPublisher publisher = tSes.createPublisher(topic);
```

Create appropriate messages using the sessions and send them using the required methods defined in the message producer. You can use different versions of send/publish methods defined in the queue sender/topic publisher to override the global values set in the message producer for properties like message time-to-live, message priority, etc.:

```
//PTP
TextMessage msg = qSes.createTextMessage("Hi there");
sender.send(msg);

//Pub/Sub
TextMessage msg = tSes.createTextMessage("Hi there");
publisher.publish(msg);
```

Receiving Messages

The sequence diagram shown below depicts the various steps involved in writing a typical JMS client for receiving messages asynchronously. For synchronous message delivery clients will be using the `receive()` method on the message consumer in a blocking thread:

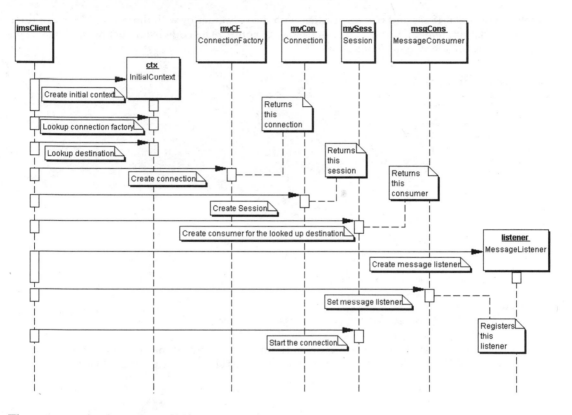

The steps involved in writing JMS clients for receiving messages are listed below. The following steps are common to writing JMS clients for sending and receiving messages:

- ❑ Creating a JNDI initial context
- ❑ Looking up destinations and connection factories
- ❑ Creating connections
- ❑ Creating sessions

Please refer to the last section on writing JMS clients for sending messages for a detailed coverage of writing the aforementioned steps.

Create message consumers using the session for the looked up destination. For the PTP model, queue receivers are created using queue sessions that are associated to specific queues and in the Pub/Sub model topic subscribers are created using topic sessions that are associated to specific topics:

```
//PTP
QueueReceiver receiver = qSes.createReceiver(queue);

//Pub/Sub
TopicSubscriber subscriber = tSes.createSubscriber(topic);
```

Create a message listener and register it either with the consumer or with the session. Message listeners are classes that implement `javax.jms.MessageListener`. The code listing below implements the interface using an anonymous inner class:

```
MessageListener listener = new MessageListener(){
   public void onMessage(Message msg) {

      //Process Message
      try{

      }catch(JMSException e) {
            e.printStackTrace();
            throw new RuntimeException(e.getMessage());
      }

   }
};

//PTP
receiver.setMessageListener(listener);

//Pub/Sub
subscriber.setMessageListener (listener);
```

Connections when created afresh are created in stopped mode and connections in stopped mode can't receive messages. To enable message reception connections should be started explicitly:

```
//PTP
qCon.start();

//Pub/Sub
tCon.start();
```

Multi-threading

Not all objects and methods in JMS support concurrent access by multiple client threads. Destinations, connections, and connection factories support concurrent access whereas sessions, producers, and consumers don't support concurrent access.

One main reason for sessions not supporting concurrent access is that sessions may support transactions, and multiple threads sending and receiving messages over transacted sessions can over-complicate things. The same explanation holds true for consumers and producers since they are created by sessions. The provider always serializes message delivery to all the consumers associated with a session set up for asynchronous operation.

JMS Exceptions

All the exceptions in JMS are sub-classed from the exception `javax.jms.JMSException`. `JMSException` provide exception chaining so that they provide a reference to the parent exception that caused the current exception. They also provide provider-specific error messages and error codes.

The standard exceptions used in JMS are documented in the JavaDoc for JMS, which is available as a download from http://java.sun.com/products/jms/docs.html. The list below shows a few of the standard JMS exceptions and their purpose. Please refer to the documentation for an exhaustive list:

- ❏ `java.lang.IllegalStateException`
  This is thrown whenever a method is invoked at an inappropriate time. An example for this is setting the client ID for a connection created using a connection factory with pre-configured client ID.

- ❏ `javax.jms.JMSSecurityException`
  This is thrown at the point of creating connections on failure of client authentication.

- ❏ `javax.jms.InvalidClientIDException`
  This is thrown if the client tries to assign an invalid client ID to a connection.

- ❏ `javax.jms.MessageNotReadableException`
  This is thrown if a client tries to read a write-only message. Messages are covered in more detail in the next chapter.

- ❏ `javax.jms.MessageNotWritableException`
  This is thrown at if a client tries to write a read-only message.

A Chat Application Using JMS

The sample chat application explained in this section uses most of the concepts explained in this chapter. This application was tested against JMQ from Sun Microsystems, but it should run against any other JMS-compliant provider.

Architecture

The chat application uses the JMS Pub/Sub messaging model. The chat clients are Swing-based applications that take the user name as a command-line argument. All the chat clients subscribe to a common topic to which they publish messages. The Administered objects are stored in the standard WinNT file system namespace and are looked up using the standard JNDI file system context SPI (Service Provider Interface) provided by Sun Microsystems. The Administered objects can be stored in any other standard naming and directory service like LDAP and looked up using JNDI, provided there is an SPI available for the service.

The object model for this application is depicted in the diagram shown below:

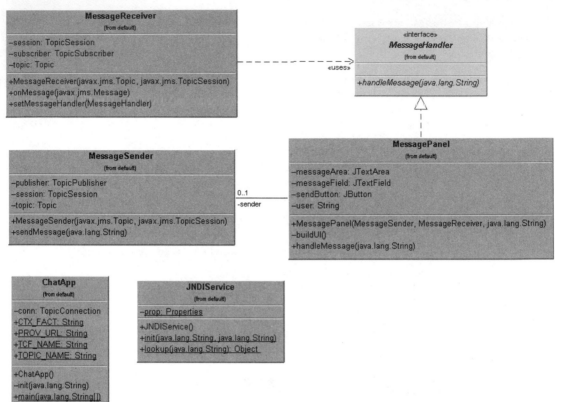

Configuring Administered Objects

The config.bat script described earlier in the chapter can be used for storing a topic named myTopic and a topic connection factory called TCFactory. These are required to run the sample application.

The JNDIService Class

This class is a generic utility class for looking up objects stored in a JNDI namespace:

```java
import javax.naming.NamingException;
import javax.naming.Context;
import javax.naming.InitialContext;
import java.util.Properties;

public class JNDIService {

    private static Properties prop;
```

The class has a static initialization method for setting the provider URL and initial context factory:

```
public static void init(String contextFactory, String providerURL) {

   prop = new Properties();

   if(contextFactory != null) {
      prop.put(Context.INITIAL_CONTEXT_FACTORY, contextFactory);
   }

   if(providerURL != null) {
      prop.put(Context.PROVIDER_URL, providerURL);
   }

}
```

In addition it defines a method for returning the home interface:

```
public static Object lookup(String jndiName) throws NamingException {

   Context ctx = new InitialContext(prop);
   Object obj = ctx.lookup(jndiName);
   ctx.close();
   return obj;

}

}
```

The MessageSender Class

This class is used for sending messages to a given topic using a given topic session:

```
import javax.jms.Topic;
import javax.jms.TopicSession;
import javax.jms.JMSException;
import javax.jms.TextMessage;
import javax.jms.TopicPublisher;

public class MessageSender {

   private Topic topic;
   private TopicSession session;
   private TopicPublisher publisher;
```

Both the topic and the topic session are passed to the class in the constructor:

```
public MessageSender(Topic topic, TopicSession session)
        throws JMSException {

   this.topic = topic;
   this.session = session;
   publisher = session.createPublisher(topic);

}
```

This class also provides a method to send messages to the topic passed in the constructor:

```
public void sendMessage(String message) throws JMSException {

    TextMessage outMsg = session.createTextMessage();
    outMsg.setText(message);
    publisher.publish(outMsg);

}

}
```

The MessageReceiver Class

This class is used for handling asynchronous message delivery:

```
import javax.jms.Topic;
import javax.jms.TopicSession;
import javax.jms.JMSException;
import javax.jms.TextMessage;
import javax.jms.TopicSubscriber;
import javax.jms.MessageListener;

public class MessageReceiver implements MessageListener {

    private Topic topic;
    private TopicSession session;
    private TopicSubscriber subscriber;
    private MessageHandler messageHandler;
```

Similar to `MessageSender` this class is also initialized with a topic and a topic session. A subscriber is created for the passed session and a message listener for asynchronous message delivery is implemented:

```
//Initialize topic and session
public MessageReceiver(Topic topic,TopicSession session)
        throws JMSException {

    this.topic = topic;
    this.session = session;
    subscriber = session.createSubscriber(topic);
    subscriber.setMessageListener(this);

}
//Register the message handler
public void setMessageHandler(MessageHandler messageHandler) {
    this.messageHandler = messageHandler;
}
```

The callback method of the message listener interface will notify the MessageHandler interface that is registered to the MessageReceiver. The MessageHandler is explained in the next section:

```
//Callback method for message listener
public synchronized void onMessage(javax.jms.Message message) {

   try {
      TextMessage inMsg = (TextMessage)message;
      if(messageHandler != null) {
         messageHandler.handleMessage(inMsg.getText());
      }
   } catch(JMSException ignore) {
      ignore.printStackTrace();
   }

}
```

The MessageHandler Class

This interface defines a single callback method called handleMessage() that takes an argument of type String. Classes that want to be notified by the MessageReceiver on an asynchronous message delivery create an implementation of this interface and register it with the MessageReceiver using the setMessageHandler() method of MessageReceiver:

```
public interface MessageHandler {

   //Use my asynchronous message handler for notification
   public void handleMessage(String message);

}
```

The MessagePanel Class

This class extends javax.swing.JPanel and provides the users with facilities for sending and viewing messages:

```
import javax.swing.JTextArea;
import javax.swing.JTextField;
import javax.swing.JButton;
import javax.swing.JPanel;
import javax.swing.JScrollPane;

import java.awt.FlowLayout;
import java.awt.BorderLayout;

import java.awt.event.ActionEvent;
import java.awt.event.ActionListener;

import javax.jms.JMSException;
```

This class implements the `MessageHandler` interface and is initialized with instances of a `MessageSender`, a `MessageReceiver`, and the name of the user who is currently using the application:

```
public class MessagePanel extends JPanel implements MessageHandler {

    private JTextArea messageArea;
    private JTextField messageField;
    private JButton sendButton;
    private MessageSender sender;
    private String user;

    public MessagePanel(MessageSender sender,
        MessageReceiver receiver, String user) {
```

The class registers itself as the `MessageHandler` for the `MessageReceiver` and the `MessageReceiver` will call this class's `handleMessage()` callback method whenever it receives a message asynchronously. The callback method will update the display with the newly received message:

```
        receiver.setMessageHandler(this);
        this.sender = sender;
        this.user = user;
        buildUI();

    }

    //Callback method for asynchronous message delivery
    public void handleMessage(String message) {
        messageArea.append("\r\n" + message);
    }
```

This panel has a non-editable text area for displaying the messages and a text field for typing the messages to be sent. The panel also provides a send button for sending the messages:

```
    private void buildUI() {
```

Create a text area to display the incoming messages and set it to non-editable:

```
        messageArea = new JTextArea(25,25);
        messageArea.setEditable(false);
```

Create a text field to enter outgoing messages:

```
        messageField = new JTextField(50);
```

Create a button to send the message:

```
        sendButton = new JButton("send");
```

Create an instance of `javax.swing.JPanel` and set the layout to `FlowLayout` where the components are laid on the panel from right to left. Add the text field and button to the panel:

```
JPanel bottomPanel = new JPanel();
bottomPanel.setLayout(new FlowLayout(FlowLayout.RIGHT));
bottomPanel.add(messageField);
bottomPanel.add(sendButton);
```

Set the layout of the root panel to `BorderLayout` and add the panel created in the last step to the bottom of the root panel. Add the text area to a scroll-pane so that it can be scrolled and add the scroll-pane to the center of the root panel:

```
setLayout(new BorderLayout());
add(bottomPanel, BorderLayout.SOUTH);
add(new JScrollPane(messageArea), BorderLayout.CENTER);
```

The send button has an anonymous inner class as its action listener and whenever the button is clicked it will append the message in the text area to the name of the user and send the message using the `MessageSender`:

```
sendButton.addActionListener(
    new ActionListener() {
        public void actionPerformed(ActionEvent e) {
            if(!messageField.getText().equals("")) {
                try {
                    sender.sendMessage(user + ": " +
                        messageField.getText());
                } catch(JMSException ex) {
                    ex.printStackTrace();
                    throw new RuntimeException(ex.getMessage());
                }
            }
        }
    }
);

}

}
```

The ChatApp Class

This is the main class for the application:

```
import javax.swing.JFrame;
import javax.jms.Topic;
import javax.jms.TopicConnectionFactory;
import javax.jms.TopicConnection;
import javax.jms.TopicSession;
import javax.jms.JMSException;
import javax.naming.NamingException;
import java.awt.event.WindowAdapter;
import java.awt.event.WindowEvent;
```

```
public class ChatApp {

    public static final String CTX_FACT =
        "com.sun.jndi.fscontext.RefFSContextFactory";
    public static final String PROV_URL = "file:C:\\temp";
    public static final String TCF_NAME = "TCFactory";
    public static final String TOPIC_NAME = "myTopic";

    private TopicConnection conn;
```

If no user name is given at the command line, "Anonymous" is used instead:

```
public static void main(String args[]) {

    try {
        String user = "Anonymous";
        if(args.length > 0) {
            user = args[0];
        }
        new ChatApp().init(user);
    } catch(NamingException e) {
        e.printStackTrace();
        System.exit(0);
    } catch(JMSException e) {
        e.printStackTrace();
        System.exit(0);
    }

}
```

This class looks up the topic connection factory and topic using JNDIService and creates a topic connection and a topic session:

```
private void init(String user) throws NamingException, JMSException {

    JNDIService.init(CTX_FACT,PROV_URL);
    TopicConnectionFactory tcf =
        (TopicConnectionFactory)JNDIService.lookup(TCF_NAME);
    Topic topic = (Topic)JNDIService.lookup(TOPIC_NAME);

    conn = tcf.createTopicConnection();
    TopicSession sess = conn.createTopicSession(false,
            TopicSession.AUTO_ACKNOWLEDGE);
```

The topic and topic session are used to initialize instances of MessageSender and MessageReceiver:

```
MessageSender sender = new MessageSender(topic, sess);
MessageReceiver receiver = new MessageReceiver(topic, sess);
```

A new instance of a `javax.swing.JFrame` is created:

```
JFrame frame = new JFrame("Chat: " + user);
frame.addWindowListener(
    new WindowAdapter() {
        public void windowClosing(WindowEvent e) {
            try {
                conn.close();
            } catch(JMSException ex) {
                ex.printStackTrace();
            } finally {
                System.exit(0);
            }
        }
    }
);
```

The instances of `MessageSender` and `MessageReceiver` along with the user name passed in as a command-line argument are used to initialize an instance of `MessagePanel`. The instance of `MessagePanel` is added to the `JFrame` and the frame is made visible:

```
MessagePanel panel = new MessagePanel(sender, receiver, user);
frame.getContentPane().add(panel);
frame.setSize(300,300);
frame.pack();
frame.show();
conn.start();
}

}
```

Running the Application

To run the application, compile all the classes with the required JAR files in the classpath. All the classes can be compiled without any errors using the `j2ee.jar` file in the classpath. Run the configuration script to store the required administered objects and start the JMQ router. Invoke the JVM on `ChatApp.class`, passing a user name as a command-line argument with the following files in the classpath:

❑   `jmq.jar` – this can be found in the lib directory of the JMQ installation.

❑   `providerutil.jar` and `fscontext.jar` – these files can also be found in the lib directory of the JMQ installation. These files contain the JNDI SPI classes.

❑   `j2ee.jar`

The screenshots below shows Fred and Barney chatting using our chat application:

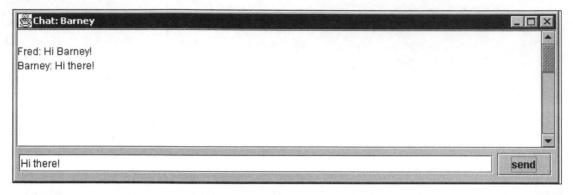

Summary

In this chapter we covered the fundamentals of JMS. First of all we looked at the JMS architecture. We defined JMS providers as software vendors who implement the interfaces defined in the JMS specification and JMS clients as Java language applications that exchange JMS messages using the services provided by the JMS provider.

Note that portable JMS clients should use only the standard JMS interfaces in application code and should not use any of the provider-specific implementation classes. Throughout the chapter we used standard JMS interfaces, and demonstrated them with a few basic examples.

Next we considered the two types of Administered objects. These are pre-configured objects stored in a namespace by JMS administrators for the use of JMS clients. Connection factories are Administered objects used by JMS clients for creating connections to a JMS provider. Destination objects are used by JMS clients to specify the locations to and from which they send and receive messages. The two types of destination, queue and topic, were described in detail.

We also looked at the two message models employed by JMS. Point-to-Point messaging invokes the notion of a queue, where the First-In, First-Out rule is applied. In Publish/Subscribe messaging topics are used. When a message is published on a topic, it is sent to every subscriber of that topic.

The final example in the chapter demonstrated the use of message producers, message consumers, and message clients. A simple chat application was set up, and messages were sent between two users running separate JMS clients.

Although JMS messages were covered briefly, we will consider them in greater detail in the next chapter.

com.sun.jn...
com.sun.jn...
weblogic.jndi.T3Initial...
fiorano.jms.rtl.Fioran...
weblogic.jms.naming.n...
ch.softwired.jms.runtime.nam...
com.sun.jndi.fscontext.RefFSContextFactory
com.sun.jndi.ldap.LdapCtxFactory
weblogic.jndi.T3InitialContextFactory
fiorano.jms.rtl.FioranoInitialContextFactory
weblogic.jms.naming.FioranoInitialContextFactory
fiorano.jms.runtime.naming.FioranoInitialContextFactory
ch.softwired.jms.naming.IBusContextFactory

3

JMS Messages

JMS messages define a unified interface for creating enterprise messages that can hold different content models. JMS defines a set of interfaces to represent the different JMS messages that are implemented by the JMS providers. This chapter deals with JMS messages in detail. We will be covering:

❑   Message headers

❑   Message bodies

❑   Message properties

❑   Message selectors

The JMS Message Model

The main design goals of the JMS message model as defined in the specification are:

❑   A single unified interface for messaging

❑   An interface for creating messages that match the format used by existing non-JMS applications

❑   An interface that supports heterogeneous applications that span across operating systems and machine architectures

❑   An interface that supports the creation of messages that can hold Java objects in their content

❑   An interface that supports the creation of messages that can hold data in their content

Message Structure

JMS defines a set of interfaces that represent the different types of messages classified by the type of content they can have. These interfaces extend the interface `javax.jms.Message`. The structure of a typical JMS message is depicted in the figure shown below:

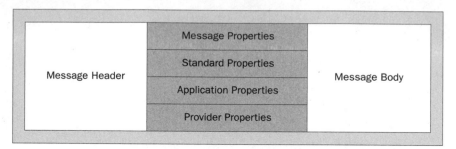

Regardless of the type of the message, all JMS messages are composed of the three basic components shown above: the message header, message properties, and the message body.

Message Header

Message headers contain a set of standard fields defined by the JMS specification. JMS providers are required to provide access to all these header fields in their implementation classes. The values in the header fields are used for proper routing and processing of the messages. JMS header fields identify properties like message destination, message ID, delivery mode, priority, etc. Message headers are covered in detail in the coming sections.

Message Properties

Message properties are used in JMS for adding optional header fields to messages. JMS property values can be any of the Java primitive types, `java.lang.String`, or Java objects. The only Java objects supported are of wrapper types defined for the Java primitives like `java.lang.Boolean`, `java.lang.Byte`, etc. The interface `javax.jms.Message` defines methods for the different types of JMS properties. JMS defines three types of property:

❑ **Standard Properties** are the same as the header fields apart from the fact that they are optional. Standard properties have '`JMSX`' as the property name prefix.

❑ **Application Properties** are custom properties that can be used by JMS clients for implementing application-specific logic.

❑ **Provider Properties** may be useful for the integration of JMS clients with the providers' non-JMS native clients. These properties are all defined by the JMS providers.

JMS properties are covered in detail in the coming sections.

Message Body

JMS defines messages that can support different messaging styles. JMS messages are categorized depending on the type of content they can have in the message body. JMS defines standard interfaces for these messages that extend the interface `javax.jms.Message`. The standard messages supported by JMS are listed below:

- ❑ `BytesMessage`
  Bytes messages are used for exchanging messages containing a stream of uninterpreted bytes, which can often be useful in integrating JMS clients with the provider's native messaging clients. The interface `javax.jms.BytesMessage` defines the methods for bytes messages.

- ❑ `TextMessage`
  Text messages are used for exchanging plain text. Text messages are very useful in exchanging XML documents. The interface `javax.jms.TextMessage` defines the methods for text messages.

- ❑ `ObjectMessage`
  Object messages are used for exchanging serialized Java objects. The interface `javax.jms.ObjectMessage` defines the methods for object messages.

- ❑ `StreamMessage`
  Stream messages are used for exchanging a stream of Java primitives, strings, and objects of types Java primitive wrapper classes. The interface `javax.jms.StreamMessage` defines the methods for stream messages.

- ❑ `MapMessage`
  Map messages are used for exchanging a map of name-value pairs. Names are always strings and values can be Java primitives, strings or objects of types Java primitive wrapper classes. The interface `javax.jms.MapMessage` defines the methods for map messages.

The interface `javax.jms.Session` defines various factory methods (see below) for creating optimized provider implementation of all the aforementioned interfaces. These methods were discussed in detail in the last chapter. The different types of JMS messages are covered in detail in the coming sections. Factory methods define an abstract interface for creating objects, and let the concrete implementation implement the real code for creating objects.

> *The Factory Method pattern is a special case of the Template Method pattern. In this pattern the factory method defines an interface for creating an object. However, it lets subclasses decide which class to instantiate. The Factory Method pattern, in addition to its more general Template Method pattern, is very common in framework design.*

Message Header

JMS header fields are used for the proper routing and processing of JMS messages. The JMS specification defines a set of standard JMS headers. These fields can be set by the client, by the implementation class of the message, or by the JMS provider.

> **Those header fields set by the `send()` method can also be set by the client, but the `send()` method always ignores a field set in this manner and uses its own value. However, message recipients are able to change the header fields of a message after it arrives.**

Message producers and `send()`/`publish()` methods were discussed in detail in the previous chapter. This section covers the standard JMS header fields in detail. Tables of message header `getJMSXXX()` and `setJMSXXX()` methods can be found at the end of this section.

JMSDestination

The `JMSDestination` header field contains the destination to which the message was sent. The value of this field is available for the message sender only after the message is sent and for message recipients soon after the message is received. As explained in the previous chapter, destinations are specified either when the message producer is created using the session or in the send() method of the message producer for unidentified message producers.

JMSDeliveryMode

The value of `JMSDeliveryMode` indicates the delivery mode used when the message was sent. Delivery mode can be set for each individual message a message consumer sends or can be set globally for all the messages sent by the message producer. This field is set by the send() method.

The delivery mode specified in the send() method takes precedence over the one specified globally. If the delivery mode is not specified the default delivery mode, in other words, NON_PERSISTENT, is used. This means that the most efficient delivery mode is used, but message delivery is not guaranteed.

JMSPriority

The value of `JMSPriority` indicates the message priority used when the message was sent. This field is set by the send() method. Message priority can be set for each individual message a message producer sends or can be set globally for all the messages sent by the message producer. JMS defines ten levels of priority from 0 to 9 (the default priority for messages is 4). The value of this field is available for the message sender only after the message is sent and for message recipients soon after the message is received.

The send() method uses either the priority globally specified for the message producer or the priority specified in the send() method. The message priority specified in the send() method takes precedence over the one specified globally. If the message priority is not specified it uses the default global priority.

JMSExpiration

The value of `JMSExpiration` indicates the sum of message time-to-live used when the message was sent and the current time in GMT. Message time-to-live can be set for each individual message a message producer sends or can be set globally for all the messages sent by the message producer. This field is set by the send() method. The value of this field is available for the message sender only after the message is sent and for message recipients soon after the message is received.

The send() method uses the sum of either the message time-to-live globally specified for the message producer or the message time-to-live specified in the send() method and the current time in GMT. The message time-to-live specified in the send() method takes precedence over the one specified globally. If the message time-to-live is not specified it uses the default message time-to-live which is 0. If the message time-to-live is 0 then the expiration is also 0, which means the message will never expire. Most of the JMS providers provide administration tools for monitoring and removing messages from destinations.

JMSMessageID

The JMS providers use the `JMSMessageID` header field to uniquely identify messages. The JMS specification mandates the uniqueness of message IDs for a given provider implementation, but it doesn't mandate uniqueness across multiple implementations. The values of this field are required to be prefixed with the string `'ID:'`.

This field is set by the `send()` method and JMS clients can disable the setting of this field using the `setDisableMessageID()` method defined in the interface `javax.jms.MessageProducer`. However, providers can always ignore this and continue to assign message IDs for the messages sent by the producer.

Assigning unique message IDs to messages requires extra effort from the JMS provider and also increases the size of the message. Hence clients can use this method to notify the provider that they don't depend on the unique message IDs. Then the provider can set the message ID to null. But the provider can also ignore this hint and continue to produce the message IDs. This is entirely up to the discretion of the JMS provider. The value of this field is available for the message sender only after the message is sent and for message recipients soon after the message is received.

JMSCorrelationID

JMS clients can use the header field `JMSCorrelationID` for linking messages. This field is extremely useful for JMS clients working in request/response mode. We have already seen that the message IDs are unique for a given provider implementation.

JMS clients sending a message in response to a request message can set the correlation ID of the response message to the message ID of the request message. This allows the JMS client that initiated the request to easily link the response it received to the request it sent. The example application explained later uses correlation ID to implement a pseudo-duplex messaging system. The correlation ID may also be set to a provider-native byte array. JMS clients normally set the value for correlation ID.

JMSReplyTo

JMS clients can use the header field `JMSReplyTo` for specifying the destination to which the reply messages are to be sent. JMS clients receiving the messages can ignore the value of this field if they want. This field is also extremely useful for JMS clients working in a request/response mode. JMS clients normally set the value for this field.

JMSTimestamp

The value for `JMSTimestamp` indicates the time at which the provider sent the message. This need not be the same as the time at which the message was transmitted to the provider because the provider may delay the sending if the message participates in a transaction.

This field is set by the `send()` method and JMS clients can disable the setting of this field using the `setDisableMessageTimestamp()` method defined in the interface `javax.jms.MessageProducer`. Providers can always ignore this and continue to set the timestamp.

Assigning timestamps has the same kind of overhead associated with it as assigning message IDs. Telling the provider to disable them would cause them to be set to a default value of zero, unless the provider wishes to assign them anyway. The actual implementation is up to the provider.

JMSRedelivered

This is the only header field whose value is directly set by the provider. The provider sets the value of this field to True if it is has already delivered this message once. A message can get redelivered due to number of reasons, for example, the client fails to acknowledge the message or a runtime exception is thrown in the callback method of the asynchronous message listener.

JMSType

Providers that maintain a repository of application-specific message types use the JMSType header field. An example of an application-specific message is SonicMQ's XMLMessage type. This message has a setDocument() method that accepts an org.w3c.dom.Document as a parameter, removing the need for explicit casts and thus saving processor overhead. The JMS client sets this header.

Message Header Methods

The header fields described above each have getJMSXXX() and setJMSXXX() methods, which can be used to manipulate their contents. These methods are defined by the javax.jms.Message interface and are listed below. Note that all these methods are all public.

The getJMSXXX() Methods

Method	Description
Destination getJMSDestination() throws JMSException	Returns the destination of the message.
int getJMSDeliveryMode() throws JMSException	Returns the delivery mode.
int getJMSPriority() throws JMSException	Returns the message priority.
long getJMSExpiration() throws JMSException	Returns the message expiration time as number of milliseconds since 1st of Jan 1970.
String getJMSMessageID() throws JMSException	Returns the message ID.
String getJMSCorrelationID() throws JMSException	Returns the correlation ID as a string.
byte[] getJMSCorrelationIDAsBytes() throws JMSException	Returns the correlation ID as a byte array. The use of this method is not portable across different providers.
Destination getJMSReplyTo() throws JMSException	Returns the destination to which the reply messages are to be sent.
long getJMSTimestamp() throws JMSException	Returns the timestamp as number of milliseconds since 1st of Jan 1970.
boolean getJMSRedelivered() throws JMSException	Returns the redelivered flag.
String getJMSType() throws JMSException	Returns the JMSType set by the JMS client.

The setJMSXXX() Methods

For each `getXXX()` method in the table above, there is a corresponding set method. Below is a selection, and those that are missing can be extrapolated from the methods already described:

Method	Description
`void setJMSDestination(Destination dest)` `throws JMSException`	Sets the destination of the message
`void setJMSDeliveryMode(int deliveryMode)` `throws JMSException`	Sets the delivery mode
`void setJMSPriority(int priority) throws` `JMSException`	Sets the message priority

Using JMS in a Request/Response Paradigm

The sample application illustrates the use of different JMS header fields and shows how the different fields can be accessed and mutated. It also illustrates the use of `JMSCorrelationID` and `JMSReplyTo` header fields to build a pseudo-duplex messaging system where one application sends a request message and another application receives the request and sends a response to the request.

Architecture

The system uses a client and a server application communicating using the Point-to-Point (PTP) messaging model. Both the applications use a request queue and a response queue, which are stored as Administered objects in the standard `WinNT` file system namespace.

This example also illustrates the setting of different JMS headers by the `send()` method. We achieve this by printing the message headers before and after the message is sent.

The various actions performed by the client application are listed below:

❑   Looks up the request queue, response queue, and queue connection factory.

❑   Creates a connection using the connection factory.

❑   Creates a non-transacted session in the auto-acknowledge mode using the connection.

❑   Creates a queue sender for the request queue using the session.

❑   Creates a text message with the message body as the current time and sets the `JMSReplyTo` header to the response queue and prints the JMS header of the message.

❑   Sends the message and prints the JMS header fields of the sent message again.

❑   Creates a queue receiver to the response queue and receives messages using the queue receiver in an infinite loop. If the `JMSCorrelationID` of the received message is the same as the `JMSMessageID` of the sent message, it breaks out of the loop.

❑   Prints the message text of the sent and received messages and the message header of the response message.

The sequence diagram shown below further illustrates the sequence of actions performed by the client:

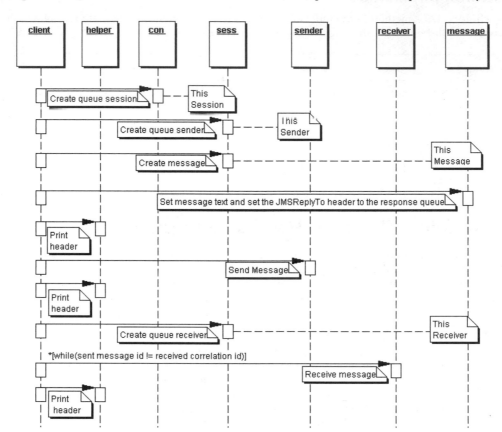

The various actions performed by the server application on startup and on message reception are listed below:

- Looks up the request queue and queue connection factory
- Creates a connection and a session
- Creates a queue receiver for the request queue using the session and registers an asynchronous message listener for the queue receiver
- Prints the body as well as the header fields of received messages
- Creates a new message for every received message and sets the body of the new message to the body of the received message appended with the current date and time
- Sets the JMSCorrelationID header of the new message to the JMSMessageID header of the received message
- Creates a queue sender for the destination specified by the JMSReplyTo header of the received message
- Prints the JMS header fields for the new message before sending
- Sends the message and prints the JMS header fields for the sent message

The sequence diagram shown below depicts the sequence of actions performed by the server at startup and on asynchronous message delivery:

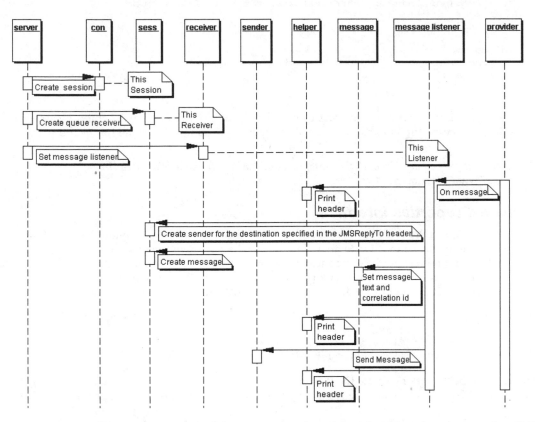

This example was tested against JMQ from Sun Microsystems, but should work with any other JMS-compliant provider. See Appendix A for details on porting code between providers.

Configuring Administered Objects

The sample application uses three Administered objects: a queue connection factory and two queues. The script shown below creates the required Administered objects and stores them in the standard WinNT file system namespace using the `jmqconfig` tool provided by JMQ. This script is specific to JMQ and may vary across different providers:

```
@echo off

if "%JMQ_HOME%\lib\jmq.jar" == "\lib\jmq.jar" goto nojmqhome

REM  Create and add the request queue
call "%JMQ_HOME%\bin\jmqconfig" -a -t q -n requestQueue -o "name=requestQueue" -i
"com.sun.jndi.fscontext.RefFSContextFactory" -u "file:C:\temp"

REM  Create and add the request queue
call "%JMQ_HOME%\bin\jmqconfig" -a -t q -n responseQueue -o "name=responseQueue" -
i "com.sun.jndi.fscontext.RefFSContextFactory" -u "file:C:\temp"
```

```
REM  Create and add the queue connection factory
call "%JMQ_HOME%\bin\jmqconfig" -a -t qf -n QCFactory -o "host=localhost" -i
"com.sun.jndi.fscontext.RefFSContextFactory" -u "file:C:\temp"

goto end

:nojmqhome
    echo Please set the JMQ_HOME environment variable.
    goto end
:end
```

The command-line options for `jmqconfig` were briefly discussed in the last chapter. Please refer to the JMQ documentation for an exhaustive list of command-line options available for `jmqconfig`.

Note that you can download all the examples in this chapter from the Wrox web site: http://www.wrox.com.

The DuplexProperties Interface

This interface holds the constants that specify the initial context factory, provider URL and the names of the queues and queue connection factory. In a practical scenario you may store these properties in some sort of configuration file and read then using a resource bundle. The variables CTX_FACT and PROV_URL hold the name of the initial context factory and the provider URL respectively. These values are used for JNDI lookup. Remember to change the value of PROV_URL to suit your installation directory:

```
public interface DuplexProperties {
    public static final String CTX_FACT =
        "com.sun.jndi.fscontext.RefFSContextFactory";
    public static final String PROV_URL = "file:C:\\temp";
```

The variable QCF_NAME holds the JNDI name of the queue connection factory used for creating the queue connections. Both the client and the server applications use this for looking up the connection factory:

```
    public static final String QCF_NAME = "QCFactory";
```

The variables REQUEST_QUEUE and RESPONSE_QUEUE hold the JNDI names of the request and response queues respectively. The client application looks up both request and response queues whereas the server application looks up only the request queue. The server application sends the response to the queue specified by the client application using the JMSReplyTo header field of the message:

```
    public static final String REQUEST_QUEUE = "requestQueue";
    public static final String RESPONSE_QUEUE = "responseQueue";
}
```

The JNDIService Class

This is a utility class used by both the client and the server for performing JNDI lookup:

```
import javax.naming.NamingException;
import javax.naming.Context;
import javax.naming.InitialContext;
import java.util.Properties;

public class JNDIService {

    private static Properties prop;
```

This class has a static initialization method to initialize the provider URL and initial context factory:

```
public static void init(String contextFactory, String providerURL) {

    prop = new Properties();

    if(contextFactory != null) {
        prop.put(Context.INITIAL_CONTEXT_FACTORY, contextFactory);
    }

    if(providerURL != null) {
        prop.put(Context.PROVIDER_URL, providerURL);
    }

}
```

This class also provides a static utility method for performing JNDI lookup, which accepts the JNDI name as an argument and returns the looked up object:

```
public static Object lookup(String jndiName) throws NamingException {

    Context ctx = new InitialContext(prop);
    Object obj = ctx.lookup(jndiName);
    ctx.close();
    return obj;
    }
}
```

The DuplexHelper Class

This is a utility class used by both the client and server classes for printing the different message header values for the incoming and outgoing messages:

```
import javax.jms.Message;
import javax.jms.JMSException;
import javax.jms.Destination;
import javax.jms.DeliveryMode;

public class DuplexHelper {
```

This class has a static method to print the values of all ten standard JMS message header fields. This method takes the Message object whose header values are to be printed as an argument. Its first action is to print the value of the JMSDestination header field. If the value of this header field is not null it prints the name of the destination, otherwise it prints the string Not set:

```
public static void printHeader(Message msg) throws JMSException {

    //Print JMSDestination Header
    Destination dest = msg.getJMSDestination();
    if(dest != null) {
        System.out.print("\tDestination: " + dest);
    } else {
        System.out.print("\tDestination: Not set");
    }
```

The JMSDeliveryMode header field is compared against the static member variables of the interface javax.jms.DeliveryMode and the delivery mode is printed. Then the value of the JMSExpiration header field is printed:

```
//Print JMSDeliveryMode Header
int deliveryMode = msg.getJMSDeliveryMode();
switch(deliveryMode) {

   case DeliveryMode.PERSISTENT:
      System.out.print("|Delivery Mode: Persistent");
      break;

   case DeliveryMode.NON_PERSISTENT:
      System.out.print("|Delivery Mode: Non-Persistent");
      break;

   default:
      System.out.print("|Delivery Mode: Not set");
      break;
}

//Print JMSExpiration Header
System.out.println("|Expiration: " + msg.getJMSExpiration());
```

If the value of the JMSPriority header field is not -1 the value is printed, otherwise the string Not set is printed. The value of the JMSTimestamp header field is then printed:

```
//Print JMSPriority Header
int prior = msg.getJMSPriority();
if(prior != -1) {
   System.out.print("\tPriority: " + prior);
} else {
   System.out.print("\tPriority: Not set");
}
//Print JMSTimestamp Header
System.out.print("|Timestamp: " + msg.getJMSTimestamp());
```

If the value of the JMSReplyTo header field is not null the name of the destination to which the reply messages are expected to be sent is printed, otherwise the string "Not set" is printed. Then the value of the JMSRedelivered header field is printed:

```
//Print JMSReplyTo Header
Destination replyTo = msg.getJMSReplyTo();
if(replyTo != null) {
   System.out.println("|Reply To: " + replyTo);
} else {
   System.out.println("|Reply To: Not set");
}

//Print JMSRedelivered Header
System.out.print("\tRedelivered: " + msg.getJMSRedelivered());
```

If the JMSType field is set the value of the message type is printed, otherwise the string "Not set" is printed:

```
//Print JMSType Header
String type = msg.getJMSType();
if(type != null) {
    System.out.println("|Type: " + type);
} else {
    System.out.println("|Type: Not set");
}
```

If the header fields for JMSMessageID and JMSCorrelationID are set their values are printed, otherwise the string "Not set" is printed:

```
//Print JMSMessageID Header
String msgId = msg.getJMSMessageID();
if(msgId != null) {
    System.out.println("\tMessage ID: " + msgId);
} else {
    System.out.println("\tMessage ID: Not set");
}

//Print JMSCorrelationID Header
String corId = msg.getJMSCorrelationID();
if(corId != null) {
    System.out.println("\tCorrelation ID: " + corId);
} else {
    System.out.println("\tCorrelation ID: Not set");
}

    }
}
```

The DuplexClient Class

The duplex client is a Java application with a main() method. The class is initialized in the main() method and the start() method is called on the instance of the DuplexClient class. The start() method does all the processing, in other words, sending the message, printing the message header, and receiving the response message:

```
import javax.jms.*;
import java.util.Date;

public class DuplexClient implements DuplexProperties {

    public static void main(String args[]) throws Exception {
        DuplexClient client = new DuplexClient();
        client.start();
    }
```

The start() method first initializes the JNDI lookup service class with the provider URL and the initial context factory and looks up the request queue, response queue, and the queue connection factory:

```
public void start() throws Exception {

    JNDIService.init(CTX_FACT, PROV_URL);
    Queue requestQueue = (Queue)JNDIService.lookup(REQUEST_QUEUE);
    Queue responseQueue = (Queue)JNDIService.lookup(RESPONSE_QUEUE);
    QueueConnectionFactory qcf =
        (QueueConnectionFactory)JNDIService.lookup(QCF_NAME);
```

A queue connection is then created using the queue connection factory and a non-transacted queue session is created using this queue connection. A queue sender is created using the queue session that is attached to the request queue:

```
QueueConnection qCon = qcf.createQueueConnection();
QueueSession qSes =
    qCon.createQueueSession(false, QueueSession.AUTO_ACKNOWLEDGE);
QueueSender sender = qSes.createSender(requestQueue);
```

A text message is created using the queue session, its message body is set to the current date-time, and the JMSReplyTo header is set to the response queue:

```
TextMessage reqMsg = qSes.createTextMessage();
reqMsg.setText("Message sent at " + new java.util.Date());
reqMsg.setJMSReplyTo(responseQueue);
```

The message header fields for the message are printed using the DuplexHelper class and the message is sent. The message headers are printed once again after the message is sent:

```
System.out.println("Request message header before send.");
DuplexHelper.printHeader(reqMsg);
sender.send(reqMsg);
System.out.println("Request message header after send.");
DuplexHelper.printHeader(reqMsg);
```

A queue receiver that is attached to the response queue is created using the queue session and the queue connection is started so that the receiver can start accepting incoming messages:

```
QueueReceiver receiver = qSes.createReceiver(responseQueue);
qCon.start();
```

The queue receiver sits in an infinite loop and receives messages. If the JMSCorrelationID of the received message is the same as the JMSMessageID of the sent message the message texts for the received and sent messages are printed. In addition, the message header fields of the received message are printed and the method breaks out of the infinite loop:

```
while(true) {
    TextMessage resMsg = (TextMessage)receiver.receive();
    String msgId = reqMsg.getJMSMessageID();
    String corId = resMsg.getJMSCorrelationID();
```

```
        if(msgId.equals(corId)) {
            System.out.println("Response received.");
            System.out.println("Request Message: ");
            System.out.println(reqMsg.getText());
            System.out.println("Response Message: ");
            System.out.println(resMsg.getText());
            System.out.println("Response message properties.");
            DuplexHelper.printHeader(resMsg);
            qCon.close();
            return;
        }
    }
  }
}
```

The DuplexServer Class

The duplex server looks up the request queue and the queue connection factory. It creates a queue connection to the provider using the queue connection factory and uses the queue connection to create a non-transacted queue session in the auto-acknowledge mode. A queue receiver is created for the request queue and a message listener is attached to the queue receiver that asynchronously listens for messages. The queue connection is started so that it can accept incoming messages.

When the message listener receives a request message it creates a new response message using the queue session and sets the JMSCorrelationID header of the response message to the JMSMessageID header of the request message. The message listener then creates a queue sender using the queue session that is attached to the destination specified in the JMSReplyTo header of the request message and sends the message:

```
import javax.jms.*;
import java.util.Date;

public class DuplexServer implements DuplexProperties{
```

The class is initialized in the main() method and the start() method is called on the instance of the DuplexServer class. The start() method does all the processing, in other words, starting the connection and setting a message listener for asynchronous message delivery:

```
public static void main(String args[]) throws Exception {
    DuplexServer server = new DuplexServer();
    server.start();
}
```

The start method first initializes the JNDI lookup service class with the provider URL and the initial context factory and looks up the request queue and the queue connection factory:

```
public void start() throws Exception {

    JNDIService.init(CTX_FACT,PROV_URL);
    Queue requestQueue = (Queue)JNDIService.lookup(REQUEST_QUEUE);
    QueueConnectionFactory qcf =
        (QueueConnectionFactory)JNDIService.lookup(QCF_NAME);
```

Then it creates a queue connection using the queue connection factory and a non-transacted queue session using the queue connection:

```
final QueueConnection qCon = qcf.createQueueConnection();
final QueueSession qSes = qCon.createQueueSession(false,
    QueueSession.AUTO_ACKNOWLEDGE);
QueueReceiver receiver = qSes.createReceiver(requestQueue);
```

A message listener is created as an inner class and registered to the queue receiver. The server uses the callback method of the message listener to receive the request messages sent by clients:

```
receiver.setMessageListener(new MessageListener() {
    public void onMessage(Message msg) {
        try {
            TextMessage reqMsg = (TextMessage)msg;
            System.out.println("Request received.");
            System.out.println("Request Message: " +
                reqMsg.getText());
            System.out.println("Request message header.");
            DuplexHelper.printHeader(reqMsg);
```

The message listener then creates a queue sender using the queue session that is attached to the destination specified in the JMSReplyTo header of the request message. The server creates a new message from the same session:

```
Queue responseQueue = (Queue)reqMsg.getJMSReplyTo();
QueueSender sender = qSes.createSender(responseQueue);
TextMessage resMsg = qSes.createTextMessage();
resMsg.setText(reqMsg.getText() + "\r\nProcessed at "
                                    + new Date());
```

It then sets the JMSCorrelationID header of the response message to the JMSMessageID header of the request message:

```
resMsg.setJMSCorrelationID(reqMsg.getJMSMessageID());
System.out.println("Response message header before send.");
DuplexHelper.printHeader(resMsg);
```

The final step is to send the response to the destination specified in the JMSReplyTo header of the request message. Finally the server starts the queue connection so that it can start processing the request messages:

```
            sender.send(resMsg);
            System.out.println("Response message header after send.");
            DuplexHelper.printHeader(resMsg);
        } catch(Exception ex) {
            throw new RuntimeException(ex.getMessage());
        }
    }
});
qCon.start();
    }
}
```

Running the Application

Before you start the application, first run the configuration script from above (`DuplexConfig.bat` from the download) to store the required Administered objects and then start the `irouter` binary that comes with JMQ.

Start the server by invoking the Java interpreter on `DuplexServer` class and start the client by invoking the Java interpreter on the `DuplexClient` class. When you compile and run the example please make sure you have the required JAR files from the JMQ `lib` directory in the class path. The relevant files are `fscontext.jar`, `jms.jar`, `jndi.jar`, `jmq.jar`, and `providerutil.jar`.

The output from the client is shown below:

```
Command Prompt

C:\ProJMS\Chapter03>java DuplexClient

Request message header before send.
        Destination: Not set|Delivery Mode: Not set|Expiration: 0
        Priority: Not set|Timestamp: 0|Reply To: responseQueue
        Redelivered: false|Type: Not set
        Message ID: Not set
        Correlation ID: Not set
Request message header after send.
        Destination: requestQueue|Delivery Mode: Persistent|Expiration: 0
        Priority: 4|Timestamp: 980248358350|Reply To: responseQueue
        Redelivered: false|Type: Not set
        Message ID: ID:PHYSICAL:D8KM500J/DEF_CLASS:[79489910, 0][79489911, 1]
        Correlation ID: Not set
Response received.
Request Message:
Message sent at Tue Jan 23 11:12:38 GMT+00:00 2001
Response Message:
Message sent at Tue Jan 23 11:12:38 GMT+00:00 2001
Processed at Tue Jan 23 11:12:55 GMT+00:00 2001
Response message properties.
        Destination: responseQueue|Delivery Mode: Persistent|Expiration: 0
        Priority: 4|Timestamp: 980248375765|Reply To: Not set
        Redelivered: false|Type: Not set
        Message ID: ID:PHYSICAL:D8KM500J/DEF_CLASS:[79507625, 0][79507626, 1]
        Correlation ID: ID:PHYSICAL:D8KM500J/DEF_CLASS:[79489910, 0][79489911, 1
]

C:\ProJMS\Chapter03>_
```

The output from the server is shown below:

```
Command Prompt - java DuplexServer

C:\ProJMS\Chapter03>java DuplexServer

Request received.
Request Message: Message sent at Tue Jan 23 11:12:38 GMT+00:00 2001
Request message header.
        Destination: requestQueue|Delivery Mode: Persistent|Expiration: 0
        Priority: 4|Timestamp: 980248358350|Reply To: responseQueue
        Redelivered: true|Type: Not set
        Message ID: ID:PHYSICAL:D8KM500J/DEF_CLASS:[79489910, 0][79489911, 1]
        Correlation ID: Not set
Response message header before send.
        Destination: Not set|Delivery Mode: Not set|Expiration: 0
        Priority: Not set|Timestamp: 0|Reply To: Not set
        Redelivered: false|Type: Not set
        Message ID: Not set
        Correlation ID: ID:PHYSICAL:D8KM500J/DEF_CLASS:[79489910, 0][79489911, 1
]
Response message header after send.
        Destination: responseQueue|Delivery Mode: Persistent|Expiration: 0
        Priority: 4|Timestamp: 980248375765|Reply To: Not set
        Redelivered: false|Type: Not set
        Message ID: ID:PHYSICAL:D8KM500J/DEF_CLASS:[79507625, 0][79507626, 1]
        Correlation ID: ID:PHYSICAL:D8KM500J/DEF_CLASS:[79489910, 0][79489911, 1
]
_
```

If you compare the message headers for a given message before and after it is sent, you can see that the headers JMSDestination, JMSDeliveryMode, JMSExpiration, JMSPriority, JMSTimestamp, and JMSMessageID are set by the send() method whereas the JMS client sets the values for the headers JMSReplyTo, JMSCorrelationID, and JMSType. The provider always sets the JMSRedelivered header.

Message Body

JMS messages are categorized depending on the type of content that the messages can have in their body. Accordingly the JMS specification defines five different types of messages that cover most of the enterprise messaging requirements. The JMS specification defines interfaces to represent all these message types and these interfaces extend the interface javax.jms.Message. This interface defines the common methods required for all the messages. These methods can be categorized into two broad categories:

- ❑ Methods for handling the different message header fields
- ❑ Methods for handling the message properties

In addition to the aforementioned methods the interface defines two extra methods. The first one is for explicitly acknowledging the message if the session is created in CLIENT_ACKNOWLEDGE mode:

```
public void acknowledge() throws JMSException, IllegalStateException
```

Acknowledging a message will acknowledge all the previously unacknowledged messages, including the redelivered ones.

The second method is used for clearing the body contents of a message. This will clear only the message body and doesn't alter the message header and message properties:

```
public void clearBody() throws JMSException
```

The interface javax.jms.Session defines factory methods for creating different types of JMS messages. These methods were discussed in detail in the previous chapter. The class diagram shown below depicts the class hierarchy for different types of JMS messages:

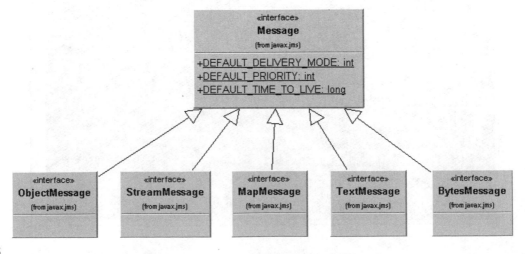

Bytes Messages

Bytes messages are used for exchanging messages carrying a stream of uninterpreted bytes in the message body. Bytes messages are extremely useful in integrating JMS messages with the provider's native messages. It is the responsibility of the message recipient to interpret the stream of bytes into a decipherable message.

Bytes messages can be used in conjunction with the JMSType header to define a repository of custom messages. The message sender will populate the byte stream and the JMSType header. The message recipient can interrogate the JMSType header and use the decoding algorithm specific to the message type to interpret the byte stream. Decoding the uninterpreted stream of bytes in a bytes message is explained in the example towards the end of the section.

The interface javax.jms.Session defines a factory method for creating bytes messages:

```
public BytesMessage createBytesMessage() throws JMSException
```

JMS defines bytes messages using the interface javax.jms.BytesMessage. This interface defines basic methods for sequentially writing and reading Java primitives, strings, and Java primitive wrapper objects. It also provides methods for sequentially writing and reading unsigned bytes in and out of the stream.

readXXX() Methods

Note that all the methods listed below are public. Unless otherwise stated the read methods only read a value from the byte stream if enough bits are left in the stream from the current pointer that can be read and interpreted as the appropriate Java primitive:

Method	Description
boolean readBoolean() throws JMSException, MessageNotReadableException, MessageEOFException	Reads a boolean value from the byte stream.
byte readByte()	Reads a signed byte value from the byte stream.
int readBytes(byte[] bytes) throws JMSException, MessageNotReadableException, MessageEOFException	Reads an array of bytes into the byte array passed as the argument. The number of bytes read is either the length of the array passed or the number of bytes left in the stream whichever is less. The method returns the number of bytes read.
int readBytes(byte[] bytes, int length) throws JMSException, MessageNotReadableException, MessageEOFException	Reads either the number of bytes specified by the length argument or the number of bytes remaining in the stream whichever is less. This method also returns the number of bytes read.
char readChar() throws JMSException, MessageNotReadableException, MessageEOFException	Reads a unicode character value from the byte stream.

Table continued on following page

Method	Description
`double readDouble() throws JMSException, MessageNotReadableException, MessageEOFException`	Reads a 64-bit signed double value from the byte stream.
`float readFloat() throws JMSException, MessageNotReadableException, MessageEOFException`	Reads a 32-bit signed float value from the byte stream.
`int readInt() throws JMSException, MessageNotReadableException, MessageEOFException`	Reads a 32-bit signed integer value from the byte stream.
`long readLong() throws JMSException, MessageNotReadableException, MessageEOFException`	Reads a 64-bit signed long value from the byte stream.
`short readShort() throws JMSException, MessageNotReadableException, MessageEOFException`	Reads a 16-bit signed short value from the byte stream.
`String readUTF() throws JMSException, MessageNotReadableException, MessageEOFException`	Reads a UTF-encoded string from the byte stream.
`int readUnsignedByte() throws JMSException, MessageNotReadableException, MessageEOFException`	Reads the next available 8 bits from the byte stream as an unsigned integer, if enough bits are left in the stream from the current stream pointer.
`int readUnsignedShort() throws JMSException, MessageNotReadableException, MessageEOFException`	Reads the next available 16 bits from the byte stream as an unsigned integer, if enough bits are left in the stream from the current stream pointer.

The readXXX() methods throw a MessageNotReadableException if the message is in write-only mode. A message is in write-only mode the first time it is created or immediately after the method clearBody() is invoked on the message. The readXXX() methods also throw MessageEOFException if not enough bytes are available in the stream to be read.

writeXXX() Methods

For each readXXX() method in the table above, there is a corresponding writeXXX() method. Below is a selection, and those that are missing can be extrapolated from the methods already described:

Method	Description
`void writeBoolean(boolean value) throws MessageNotWritableException, JMSException`	Writes the specified boolean value into the stream.
`void writeByte(byte value) throws MessageNotWritableException, JMSException`	Writes the specified byte value into the stream.

Method	Description
`void writeBytes(byte[] bytes) throws MessageNotWritableException, JMSException`	Writes the contents of the byte array into the stream.
`void writeBytes(byte[] bytes, int offset, int length) throws MessageNotWritableException, JMSException`	Writes the number of bytes specified by the `length` argument starting from the offset specified by the `offset` argument from the byte array into the stream.
`void reset()`	Puts the message in read-only mode and resets the stream pointer to the beginning of the stream.

The `writeXXX()` methods throw a `MessageNotWritableException` if the message is in read-only mode. A message is in read-only mode immediately after the `reset()` method is invoked on the message. The `reset()` method can be either invoked manually or invoked by the `send()` method.

Both the `readXXX()` and `writeXXX()` methods throws `JMSException` if the method call fails due to some internal error.

Text Messages

Text messages contain plain text as the content of their message body. Text messages are very useful for exchanging XML documents between applications. JMS defines text messages using the interface `javax.jms.TextMessage`.

The interface `javax.jms.Session` defines two methods for creating text messages. The first one creates a text message with an empty message body and the second one creates a text message pre-populated with the text passed as an argument to the method:

```
public TextMessage createTextMessage() throws JMSException
public TextMessage createTextMessage(String text) throws JMSException
```

The methods defined in the interface `javax.jms.TextMessage` are explained below:

Method	Description
`String getText() throws JMSException`	Returns the text stored in the message body
`void setText(String text) throws JMSException, MessageNotWritableException`	Sets the body content of the message to the specified text

The first method throws a `JMSException` if it fails to return the message text due to some internal error. The second method throws a `MessageNotWritableException` if the message is in read-only mode and `JMSException` if it fails to set the message text due to some internal error. A message is read-only after it is delivered to a client.

Object Messages

Object messages are used for exchanging serialized Java objects using JMS messages. JMS defines object messages using the interface `javax.jms.ObjectMessage`.

The interface `javax.jms.Session` defines two methods for creating object messages. The first one creates an object message with an empty message body and the second one creates an object message pre-populated with the object passed as an argument to the method:

```
public ObjectMessage createObjectMessage() throws JMSException
public ObjectMessage createObjectMessage(Serializable object)
                                                throws JMSException
```

The methods defined in the interface `javax.jms.ObjectMessage` are explained below:

Method	Description
`Object getObject() throws JMSException, MessageFormatException`	Returns the object stored in the body of the message
`void setObject(Serializable object) throws JMSException, MessageFormatException, MessageNotWritableException`	Sets the body content of the message to the passed object

The first method throws a `JMSException` if it fails to return the message object due to some internal error. The second method throws a `MessageNotWritableException` if the message is read-only and `JMSException` if it fails to set the message object due to some internal error. A message is read-only after it is delivered to a client. Both methods throw a `MessageFormatException` if object deserialization fails.

Stream Messages

Stream messages are used for exchanging a sequential stream of Java primitives, objects, and strings using JMS messages. The only objects supported are types of Java primitive wrapper classes like `java.lang.Integer`, `java.lang.Long`, etc. JMS defines stream messages using the interface `javax.jms.StreamMessage`.

The interface `javax.jms.Session` defines a method for creating stream messages:

```
public StreamMessage createStreamMessage() throws JMSException
```

The interface `javax.jms.StreamMessage` defines all the methods defined in the interface `javax.jms.BytesMessage` except for those for reading unsigned bytes and shorts and those for reading and writing UTF-encoded strings. However, this interface defines extra methods for reading and writing Java objects and unicode strings:

Method	Description
`Object readObject() throws JMSException, MessageNotReadableException, MessageEOFException`	Reads a serialized object from the stream
`void writeObject(Object obj) throws JMSException, MessageNotWritableException`	Writes the specified serializable object to the stream
`String readString() throws JMSException, MessageNotReadableException, MessageEOFException, MessageFormatException`	Reads a Java unicode string object from the stream
`void writeString(String value) throws JMSException, MessageNotWritableException`	Writes the specified string in unicode format into the stream

The `writeXXX()` methods throw a `MessageNotWritableException` if the message is in read-only mode. A message is in read-only mode after the `reset()` method is in invoked on the message. The `reset()` method can be either invoked manually or is invoked by the `send()` method. Both the `readXXX()` and `writeXXX()` methods throw a `JMSException` if the method call fails due to some internal error.

Map Messages

Map messages are used for exchanging a map of Java primitives, strings, and objects of type Java primitive wrapper classes as key/value pairs. Keys are always defined as strings whereas values can be any of the aforementioned types. JMS defines map messages using the interface `javax.jms.MapMessage`.

The interface `javax.jms.Session` defines a method for creating map messages. The signature of the method is shown below:

```
public MapMessage createMapMessage() throws JMSException
```

The various methods defined in the interface `javax.jms.MapMessage` are explained below.

The getXXX() Methods

All the `getXXX()` methods defined by the `javax.jms.MapMessage` return a value that is stored in the map against the key name specified by the argument name:

Method	Description
`boolean getBoolean(String name) throws JMSException, MessageFormatException`	Gets a boolean value from the map
`byte getByte(String name) throws JMSException, MessageFormatException`	Gets a byte value from the map
`byte[] getBytes(String name) throws JMSException, MessageFormatException`	Gets a byte array from the map

Table continued on following page

Method	Description
`char getChar(String name) throws JMSException, MessageFormatException`	Gets a char value from the map
`double getDouble(String name) throws JMSException, MessageFormatException`	Gets a double value from the map
`float getFloat(String name) throws JMSException, MessageFormatException`	Gets a float value from the map
`int getInt(String name) throws JMSException, MessageFormatException`	Gets an int value from the map
`long getLong(String name) throws JMSException, MessageFormatException`	Gets a long value from the map
`short getShort(String name) throws JMSException, MessageFormatException`	Gets a short value from the map
`String getString(String name) throws JMSException, MessageFormatException`	Gets a unicode string value from the map

The `readXXX()` methods throw a `MessageFormatException` if the value stored in the map is not convertible to the specified type. For example calling a `getInt()` for a value stored as a long will throw this exception.

The setXXX() Methods

All the `setXXX()` methods defined by `javax.jms.MapMessage` store the input arguments as a name/value pair in the message map. For each `getXXX()` method in the table above, there is a corresponding `setXXX()` method. Below is a selection, and those that are missing can be extrapolated from those already described:

Method	Description
`void setBoolean(String name, boolean value) throws JMSException, MessageNotWritableException`	Stores a boolean specified by the argument value against a key name specified by the argument name.
`void setByte(String name, byte value) throws JMSException, MessageNotWritableException`	Stores a byte specified by the argument value against a key name specified by the argument name.
`void setBytes(String name, byte[] value) throws JMSException, MessageNotWritableException`	Stores a byte array specified by the argument value against a key name specified by the argument name.

The `writeXXX()` methods throw a `MessageNotWritableException` if the message is in read-only mode. A message is in read-only mode immediately after it is delivered to a client.

Miscellaneous Methods

Method	Description
`void setBytes(String name, byte[] value, int offset, int length) throws JMSException, MessageNotWritableException`	Stores a portion of the byte array specified by the argument `value` starting at the index specified by the argument `offset` and of length as specified by the argument `length` against a key name specified by the argument `name`.
`boolean itemExists(String name) throws JMSException`	Checks whether the specified key name exists in the map.
`Enumeration getMapNames() throws JMSException`	Returns an enumeration of all the key names stored in the map.

Message Encoding/Decoding Application

In this section we will be writing two JMS clients. The first client will randomly generate messages of different formats that carry the same information, and send them to a message queue. The second client will read the message from the queue and retrieve the information from the message by interrogating the message type.

The MessageFactory Class

This class acts as a factory for creating different types of JMS messages:

```
import javax.jms.Message;
import javax.jms.TextMessage;
import javax.jms.BytesMessage;
import javax.jms.StreamMessage;
import javax.jms.ObjectMessage;
import javax.jms.MapMessage;
import javax.jms.Session;
import javax.jms.JMSException;

public class MessageFactory {
```

The class first declares enumerated constants for defining the different message types:

```
public static final int TEXT_MESSAGE = 0;
public static final int BYTES_MESSAGE = 1;
public static final int STREAM_MESSAGE = 2;
public static final int OBJECT_MESSAGE = 3;
public static final int MAP_MESSAGE = 4;
```

A factory method is provided for creating different types of JMS messages. Depending on the value passed for the argument `messageType` this method calls specific private methods to create the appropriate type of JMS message using the `Session` object passed to the method, encapsulating the information defined by the argument `message`. This method also prints the type of the message that is created:

```
public Message createMessage(int messageType,Session session,
       String message) throws JMSException {

    Message msg;

    switch(messageType) {

        case TEXT_MESSAGE:
            System.out.println("Sending text message.");
            msg = createTextMessage(session,message);
            break;

        case BYTES_MESSAGE:
            System.out.println("Sending bytes message.");
            msg = createBytesMessage(session,message);
            break;

        case STREAM_MESSAGE:
            System.out.println("Sending stream message.");
            msg = createStreamMessage(session,message);
            break;

        case OBJECT_MESSAGE:
            System.out.println("Sending object message.");
            msg = createObjectMessage(session,message);
            break;

        case MAP_MESSAGE:
            System.out.println("Sending map message.");
            msg = createMapMessage(session,message);
            break;

        default:
            throw new IllegalArgumentException("Invalid message.");

    }

    return msg;

}
```

This method returns an object of type TextMessage encapsulating the information specified by the argument message:

```
private TextMessage createTextMessage(Session session,String message)
       throws JMSException {

    return session.createTextMessage(message);

}
```

This method returns an object of type `BytesMessage` encapsulating the information specified by the argument `message` as a platform-dependent string:

```
private BytesMessage createBytesMessage(Session session,String message)
    throws JMSException {

  BytesMessage msg = session.createBytesMessage();
  msg.writeUTF(message);
  return msg;

}
```

This method returns an object of type `StreamMessage` encapsulating the information specified by the argument `message` as a stream of bytes:

```
private StreamMessage createStreamMessage(Session session,
    String message) throws JMSException {

  StreamMessage msg = session.createStreamMessage();
  msg.writeString(message);
  return msg;

}
```

This method returns an object of type `ObjectMessage` encapsulating the information specified by the argument `message` as an object of type `java.lang.String`:

```
private ObjectMessage createObjectMessage(Session session,
    String message) throws JMSException {

  return session.createObjectMessage(message);

}
```

This method returns an object of type `MapMessage` encapsulating the information specified by the argument `message`:

```
private MapMessage createMapMessage(Session session,String message)
    throws JMSException {

  MapMessage msg = session.createMapMessage();
  msg.setString("message",message);
  return msg;

}

}
```

The MessageClient Class

This class randomly produces messages of different types carrying the same information and sends them to a message queue:

```
import javax.jms.Queue;
import javax.jms.QueueConnection;
import javax.jms.QueueSession;
import javax.jms.QueueSender;
import javax.jms.QueueConnectionFactory;
import javax.jms.JMSException;

import java.util.Random;
```

The class declares static constants for JNDI initial context factory, provider URL, and JNDI names for the queue connection factory and queue. It also declares a string message that will be sent using different message types and a queue connection:

```
public class MessageClient {

    public static final String CTX_FACT =
        "com.sun.jndi.fscontext.RefFSContextFactory";
    public static final String PROV_URL = "file:C:\\temp";
    public static final String QCF_NAME = "QCFactory";
    public static final String QUEUE_NAME = "myQueue";

    public static final String message =
        "Peace sells, but who is buying?";

    private QueueConnection qCon;
```

In the `main()` method an instance of the class `MessageClient` is instantiated:

```
    public static void main(String args[]) throws Exception {

        final MessageClient client = new MessageClient();
```

A shutdown hook is added to call the `finalize()` method. Shutdown hooks are a feature in JDK 1.3 for adding any code that needs to be executed on program termination, regardless of how the program is terminated:

```
        Runtime.getRuntime().addShutdownHook(new Thread() {
            public void run() {
                client.finalize();
            }
        });
```

The method `sendMessage()` is called on the instance of the class:

```
        client.sendMessage();
    }
```

The queue connection is closed in the `finalize()` method which is called from the shutdown hook:

```
public void finalize() {

    try {
        System.out.println("\nClosing the connection.\n");
        qCon.close();
    } catch(JMSException ignore) {
        ignore.printStackTrace();
    }

}
```

In the `sendMessage()` method the `JNDIService` class is initialized and the queue and queue connection factory are looked up. A queue connection is created and then a queue session is created. The queue session is then used to create a queue sender:

```
public void sendMessage() throws Exception {

    JNDIService.init(CTX_FACT,PROV_URL);

    Queue queue = (Queue)JNDIService.lookup(QUEUE_NAME);
    QueueConnectionFactory qcf =
        (QueueConnectionFactory)JNDIService.lookup(QCF_NAME);

    qCon = qcf.createQueueConnection();
    QueueSession qSes = qCon.createQueueSession(false,
        QueueSession.AUTO_ACKNOWLEDGE);
    QueueSender sender = qSes.createSender(queue);
```

An instance of the class `MessageFactory` is created. A random number generator is used to generate numbers from 0 to 4. The random number is then passed to the `MessageFactory` instance in an infinite loop to create a JMS message that is sent to the message queue:

```
    Random rand = new Random();
    MessageFactory factory = new MessageFactory();

    System.out.println();

    while(true) {
        //Create a random number from 0-4
        int type = rand.nextInt(5);
        sender.send(factory.createMessage(type,qSes,message));
        Thread.sleep(1000);
    }

  }

}
```

The MessageProcessor Class

This class is used to decode JMS messages by interrogating the type of the message and printing the information stored in the message:

```
import javax.jms.Message;
import javax.jms.TextMessage;
import javax.jms.BytesMessage;
import javax.jms.StreamMessage;
import javax.jms.ObjectMessage;
import javax.jms.MapMessage;
import javax.jms.Session;
import javax.jms.JMSException;
```

This class defines a single method for decoding JMS messages:

```
public class MessageProcessor {

    public void processMessage(Message message) throws JMSException {

        Object msg = null;
```

If the message is of type `TextMessage` the message type is printed and the message is cast to a text message. The message body is then retrieved using the `getText()` method:

```
        if(message instanceof TextMessage) {

            System.out.print("Text Message: ");
            TextMessage textMessage = (TextMessage)message;
            msg = textMessage.getText();
```

If the message is of type `BytesMessage` the message type is printed and the message is cast to a bytes message. The message body is then retrieved using the `readUTF()` method:

```
        }else if(message instanceof BytesMessage) {

            System.out.print("Bytes Message: ");
            BytesMessage bytesMessage = (BytesMessage)message;
            msg = bytesMessage.readUTF();
```

If the message is of type `StreamMessage` the message type is printed and the message is cast to a stream message. The message body is then retrieved using the `readString()` method:

```
        } else if(message instanceof StreamMessage) {

            System.out.print("Stream Message: ");
            StreamMessage streamMessage = (StreamMessage)message;
            msg = streamMessage.readString();
```

If the message is of type `ObjectMessage` the message type is printed and the message is cast to an object message. The message body is then retrieved using the `readObject()` method:

```
    } else if(message instanceof ObjectMessage) {

        System.out.print("Object Message: ");
        ObjectMessage objectMessage = (ObjectMessage)message;
        msg = objectMessage.getObject();
```

If the message is of type `MapMessage` the message type is printed and the message is cast to a map message. The message body is then retrieved using the `getString()` method:

```
    } else if(message instanceof MapMessage) {

        System.out.print("Map Message: ");
        MapMessage mapMessage = (MapMessage)message;
        msg = mapMessage.getString("message");

    }
```

Finally the information stored in the message body is printed:

```
        System.out.println(msg);

    }
}
```

The MessageServer Class

This is a JMS client that receives a message from a message queue and uses the `MessageProcessor` class to decode the message:

```
import javax.jms.Queue;
import javax.jms.QueueConnection;
import javax.jms.QueueSession;
import javax.jms.QueueReceiver;
import javax.jms.QueueConnectionFactory;
import javax.jms.MessageListener;
import javax.jms.Message;

import javax.jms.JMSException;

import java.util.Random;
```

The class declares static constants for JNDI initial context factory, provider URL, and JNDI names for the queue connection factory and queue:

```
public class MessageServer {

    public static final String CTX_FACT =
        "com.sun.jndi.fscontext.RefFSContextFactory";
```

```
public static final String PROV_URL = "file:C:\\temp";
public static final String QCF_NAME = "QCFactory";
public static final String QUEUE_NAME = "myQueue";

private QueueConnection qCon;
```

In the `main()` method an instance of the class `MessageServer` is instantiated:

```
public static void main(String args[]) throws Exception {

    final MessageServer server = new MessageServer();
```

A shutdown hook is added to call the `finalize()` method:

```
Runtime.getRuntime().addShutdownHook(new Thread() {
    public void run() {
        server.finalize();
    }
});
```

The method `receiveMessage()` is called on the instance of the class:

```
    server.receiveMessage();
}
```

In the `finalize()` method, which is called from the shutdown hook, the queue connection is closed:

```
public void finalize() {
    try {
        System.out.println("\nClosing the connection.\n");
        qCon.close();
    } catch(JMSException ignore) {
        ignore.printStackTrace();
    }
}
```

In the `receiveMessage()` method the `JNDIService` class is initialized and the queue and queue connection factory are looked up. A queue connection is created and then a queue session is created. The queue session is then used to create a queue receiver:

```
public void receiveMessage() throws Exception {

    JNDIService.init(CTX_FACT, PROV_URL);

    Queue queue = (Queue)JNDIService.lookup(QUEUE_NAME);
    QueueConnectionFactory qcf =
        (QueueConnectionFactory)JNDIService.lookup(QCF_NAME);

    qCon = qcf.createQueueConnection();
    QueueSession qSes = qCon.createQueueSession(false,
                    QueueSession.AUTO_ACKNOWLEDGE);
    QueueReceiver receiver = qSes.createReceiver(queue);
```

An instance of the class `MessageProcessor` is created:

```
final MessageProcessor processor = new MessageProcessor();

System.out.println();
```

A message listener is registered with the queue receiver to handle asynchronous message delivery. In the `onMessage()` callback method the `MessageProcessor` instance is used to decode and print the message:

```
receiver.setMessageListener(new MessageListener() {
    public void onMessage(Message message) {
        try {
            processor.processMessage(message);
        }catch(JMSException ignore) {
            ignore.printStackTrace();
        }
    }
});

qCon.start();

    }
}
```

Running the Application

Start JMQ and run the configuration script to store the required administered objects. Compile all the classes and run the `MessageClient` and `MessageServer` classes in different command windows with the required JAR files in the classpath. The JAR files required are `jmq.jar`, `providerutil.jar`, and `fscontext.jar` that can be found in the `lib` directory under JMQ installation, and `j2ee.jar` that can be found in the `lib` directory under J2EE installation. The figures below show the screenshots of the client and the server running:

```
C:\WINNT\System32\cmd.exe

C:\ProJMS\Chapter03>java MessageClient

Sending object message.
Sending bytes message.
Sending map message.
Sending map message.
Sending map message.
Sending map message.
Sending object message.
Sending bytes message.
Sending map message.
Sending bytes message.
Sending object message.
Sending bytes message.
Sending bytes message.

Closing the connection.

C:\ProJMS\Chapter03>_
```

```
C:\WINNT\System32\cmd.exe                                              _ □ ×

C:\ProJMS\Chapter03>java MessageServer
Object Message: Peace sells, but who is buying?
Bytes Message: Peace sells, but who is buying?
Map Message: Peace sells, but who is buying?
Map Message: Peace sells, but who is buying?
Map Message: Peace sells, but who is buying?
Map Message: Peace sells, but who is buying?
Object Message: Peace sells, but who is buying?
Bytes Message: Peace sells, but who is buying?
Map Message: Peace sells, but who is buying?
Bytes Message: Peace sells, but who is buying?
Object Message: Peace sells, but who is buying?
Bytes Message: Peace sells, but who is buying?
Bytes Message: Peace sells, but who is buying?

Closing the connection.

C:\ProJMS\Chapter03>_
```

Message Properties

Message properties are similar to message headers apart from the fact that message properties are optional whereas message headers are always available. Message properties provide a way of adding application-specific header values to the messages. Message properties are also useful for JMS clients to filter out the messages they receive using message selectors. Message selectors are explained in detail later in this chapter and a reference is provided in Appendix B. Message properties can be of any of the Java primitives or Java string type.

JMS defines three types of properties:

❑ **Application specific properties**
Application specific properties can be set by JMS clients for implementing application specific logic.

❑ **Standard properties**
Standard properties define a set of standard properties, and property names starting with the string 'JMSX' are reserved for standard properties. These properties are almost the same as the header fields apart from the fact that these properties are optional. As we have already seen in the last chapter you can use the connection metadata to get a list of standard properties supported by the provider. Standard properties are explained in detail later.

❑ **Provider properties**
Provider properties are normally used for integrating JMS clients with the provider's non-JMS clients. Property names starting with the string JMS_vendor_name are reserved for provider properties where vendor_name is specific to the provider.

The interface javax.jms.Message defines a set of methods for setting and getting properties of different types as well as methods for iterating through the property names and clearing the set properties.

The getXXXProperty() Methods

All the `getXXXProperty()` methods defined by `javax.jms.Message` return a property as a value, only if the value can be converted into the appropriate primitive:

Method	Description
`boolean getBooleanProperty(String name) throws JMSException, MessageFormatException`	Returns the property whose name is specified by the argument name, as a `boolean`
`byte getByteProperty(String name) throws JMSException, MessageFormatException`	Returns the property whose name is specified by the argument name, as a `byte`
`double getDoubleProperty(String name) throws JMSException, MessageFormatException`	Returns the property whose name is specified by the argument name, as a `double`
`float getFloatProperty(String name) throws JMSException, MessageFormatException`	Returns the property whose name is specified by the argument name, as a `float`
`int getIntProperty(String name) throws JMSException, MessageFormatException`	Returns the property whose name is specified by the argument name, as an `integer`
`long getLongProperty(String name) throws JMSException, MessageFormatException`	Returns the property whose name is specified by the argument name, as a `long`
`short getShortProperty(String name) throws JMSException, MessageFormatException`	Returns the property whose name is specified by the argument name, as a `short`
`String getStringProperty(String name) throws JMSException, MessageFormatException`	Returns the property whose name is specified by the argument name, as a `String`
`Object getObjectProperty(String name) throws JMSException, MessageFormatException`	The only objects that can be set are of types Java primitive wrapper classes like `java.lang.Integer`, `java.lang.Short`, etc

These methods may throw a `MessageFormatException` if the value is not convertible to the appropriate Java primitive or a `JMSException` if the method call fails due to some internal error.

The setXXXProperty() Methods

For each `getXXXProperty()` method in the table above, there is a corresponding `setXXXProperty()` method. Below is a selection, and those that are missing can be extrapolated from the methods already described:

Method	Description
`void setBooleanProperty(String name, boolean value) throws JMSException, MessageNotWritableException`	Sets a Boolean property by the name specified by the argument name and value specified by the argument value

Table continued on following page

Method	Description
`void setByteProperty(String name, byte value) throws JMSException, MessageNotWritableException`	Sets a byte property by the name specified by the argument name and value specified by the argument value
`void setDoubleProperty(String name, double value) throws JMSException, MessageNotWritableException`	Sets a double property by the name specified by the argument name and value specified by the argument value

These methods may throw a `MessageNotWritableException` if the property is read-only. When a client receives a message, its properties are in read-only mode. A `JMSException` is thrown if the method call fails due to some internal error.

Miscellaneous Methods

Method	Description
`public void clearProperties()throws JMSException`	Clears all the properties set for the message
`public Enumeration getPropertyNames(String name) throws JMSException`	Returns an enumeration of available property names
`public boolean propertyExists(String name) throws JMSException`	Checks whether the message contains the specified property

All these methods throw `JMSException` if they fail to return due to some internal error.

Standard JMS Properties

JMS defines a set of standard properties. The property names starting with the string 'JMSX' are reserved for standard JMS properties. The providers need not implement all the standard JMS properties and JMS clients can find the supported JMSX properties using the connection's metadata. The providers set most of the JMSX properties and the JMS clients set a couple of them. The table below explains the different JMS standard properties:

Property	Type	Set by	Description
JMSXUserID	String	Provider	Identifies the user who sent the message.
JMSXAppID	String	Provider	Identifies the application that sent the message.
JMSXDeliveryCount	int	Provider	Indicates the number of times the message has been delivered.

Property	Type	Set by	Description
JMSXGroupID	String	Client	Identifies a custom message group.
JMSXGroupSeq	int	Client	Identifies the sequence number of the message in the current group.
JMSXProducerTXID	String	Provider	Identifies the transaction in which the message was produced.
JMSXConsumerTXID	String	Provider	Identifies the transaction in which the message was consumed.
JMSXRcvTimestamp	long	Provider	Identifies the time at which the message was delivered to the client. The time is defined as the number of milliseconds since the 1st of January 1970.

Message Selectors

Message selectors are strings that conform to the standard ANSI SQL-92 syntax (found at www.ansi.org) after the WHERE criterion, and are used by JMS clients for filtering the messages delivered to them. They are evaluated using JMS properties and standard headers and can be specified using both standard and application-specific properties. Message selectors are specified when the message consumer is created. However, because the provider handles the filtering, the client itself is more efficient, and the messaging traffic imposes less bandwidth use.

The interface javax.jms.QueueSession defines a method to create a queue receiver with a specified message selector:

```
public QueueReceiver createReceiver(Queue queue, String selector)
                throws JMSException,  InvalidDestinationException,
                                        InvalidSelectorException
```

The interface javax.jms.QueueSession defines a method to create a queue receiver with a specified message selector:

```
public TopicSubscriber createSubscriber(Topic topic, String selector,
        boolean noLocal) throws JMSException, InvalidDestinationException,
                                        InvalidSelectorException
```

Example Selectors

This section explains a few examples for JMS message selectors. For a more in depth look at message selectors please refer to Appendix B.

A message consumer with the message selector below will be delivered only those messages having a string property named manager with the value as Vialli:

```
manager = 'Vialli'
```

125

A message consumer with the message selector below will be delivered only those messages having a string property named gender with the value as M AND a numeric property named salary with a value greater than 100:

```
gender = 'M' AND salary > 100
```

A message consumer with the message selector below will be delivered only those messages having a string property named gender with the value as M OR a numeric property named salary with a value greater than 100:

```
gender = 'M' OR salary > 100
```

A message consumer with the message selector below will be delivered only those messages having a string property named name with the value as either all or Dick:

```
name in ('all','Dick')
```

A message consumer with the message selector below will be delivered only those messages having a string property named name with values not starting with the letter J:

```
name NOT LIKE 'J%'
```

A message consumer with the message selector below will be delivered only those messages having the JMSType header set to the string XYZ:

```
JMSType = 'XYZ'
```

JMS message selectors support all the ANSI SQL-92 compliant combinations. Please refer to an ANSI SQL reference for an exhaustive list.

Message Selector Example

The sample application illustrates the use of message selectors. It is the same chat application discussed in the previous chapter with a bit of modified functionality. Some of you might have been to Internet chat rooms that provide the facility to post messages marked private to any of the members participating in the chat. These messages get displayed only on the screens of the members they are addressed to. We will try to achieve this functionality by modifying some of the classes discussed in the previous chapter.

The message panel provides an extra section of user interface for marking a message as private and specifying its intended recipient. All the messages carry a property named addressedTo with default value as all. Whenever a message is marked private the value of this property is changed to the intended recipient's name. The topic subscriber is created with the following message selector:

```
addressedTo in ('all','<user_name>')
```

The <user_name> is the name of the current user. This means that only those messages with the property addressedTo set as either all or the name of the user using a particular instance of the chat application will be delivered to that instance. Hence the users can see only the messages addressed to all users and those specifically addressed to them.

The different class files used in the application are shown below. All of them are modified examples of those described the previous chapter with the modified lines of code highlighted. Only the changes are explained, so please refer to the previous chapter for an exhaustive explanation of the source listings. You will also need all the unmodified files from the previous chapter.

The MessagePanel Class

The user interface now provides facilities to mark a message as private and specify its intended recipient. A checkbox is used to indicate whether a message is private and a text field ID used to specify the name of the intended recipient. All the lines of code listed below should be added to the original MessagePanel.java:

```
import javax.swing.JCheckBox;
import javax.swing.JLabel;

private JCheckBox sendPrivate;
private JTextField recipientField;

recipientField = new JTextField(10);
messageField = new JTextField(30);

bottomPanel.add(new JLabel("Private"));
bottomPanel.add(sendPrivate);
bottomPanel.add(recipientField);
```

In the inner class for the action listener, before sending the message, depending on whether the sendPrivate checkbox is checked, either the string 'all' or the contents of the recipientField text field is passed to the message sender:

```
sendButton.addActionListener(new ActionListener() {
    public void actionPerformed(ActionEvent e) {
        if(!messageField.getText().equals("")) {
            try {
                String recAddr = sendPrivate.isSelected() ?
                    recipientField.getText():"all";
                sender.sendMessage(user + ": " +
                    messageField.getText(),
                        recAddr);
            } catch(JMSException ex) {ex.printStackTrace();
                throw new RuntimeException(ex.getMessage());
            }
        }
    }
  }
);
```

The MessageSender Class

The signature of the sendMessage() method is modified to take an extra argument to specify the intended recipient of the message. This can either be all users or a specific user name depending on whether the message is marked private or not. The method also sets a message property by the name addressedTo whose value is set to that of the argument recpAddr. The message receiver for implementing the message selector will use this property:

```
    public void sendMessage(String message,String recpAddr)
        throws JMSException {
      TextMessage outMsg = session.createTextMessage();
      outMsg.setStringProperty("addressedTo",recpAddr);
      outMsg.setText(message);
      publisher.publish(outMsg);
    }

  }
```

The MessageReceiver Class

The constructor of this class is changed to accept the name of the user using the current instance of the chat application. This value is used to define the message selector for the topic subscriber.

If the name of the user is Tom the selector will be evaluated to:

```
addressedTo in ('all', 'Tom')
```

This means the topic subscriber can receive only those messages having a property named addressedTo whose value is either Tom or all:

```
    public MessageReceiver(Topic topic,TopicSession session,String user)
        throws JMSException {

      this.topic = topic;
      this.session = session;
      String selector = "addressedTo in ('all','" + user + "')";
      subscriber = session.createSubscriber(topic,selector,false);
      subscriber.setMessageListener(this);

    }
```

The ChatApp Class

The only change made to this class is the modified call to the message receiver's constructor:

```
      MessageReceiver receiver = new MessageReceiver(topic, sess, user);
```

Running the Application

Run the configuration script from the previous chapter (config.bat from the download) to store the required Administered objects. Invoke the Java interpreter on the class ChatApp with all the required classes in the classpath.

The screen shots opposite show three users named Tom, Dick, and Harry using different instances of the chat application. Harry sends the message 'Hi all' to all, which is displayed on everyone's screen, whereas Tom sends the message 'Hi Dick' marked private to Dick, which is displayed only on Dick's screen:

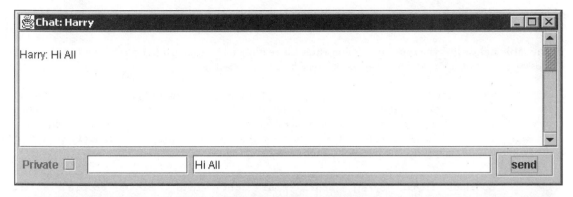

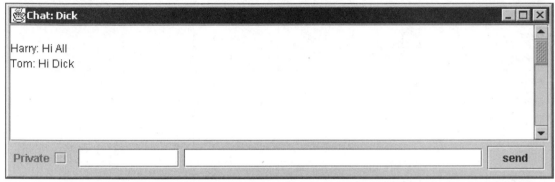

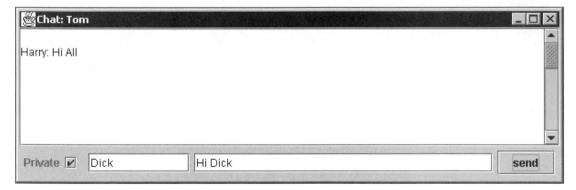

Message Mutability

Message senders can change the message header, body, and properties even after they have sent the message and can even resend the same message. However, the provider will treat this as a new message.

Message receivers can only change the message header of a received message because the body and message properties are always in read-only mode. An attempt to mutate the message body or properties of a read-only message will throw `MessageNotWritableException`.

Type Conversion Rules

The table below lists the type conversion rules for reading a message property or a field from the message body of message types MapMessage and StreamMessage.

Any message property, map message key value or byte message field written as one of the types in the row can be read out as one of the types of the columns for which the cells are marked as Y. All the other cases will throw a JMSException. Please note that the cases for char and byte[] are not applicable for message properties. When a string is read as one of the primitives if the string value cannot be converted to the required type an appropriate instance of NumberFormatException will be thrown:

	boolean	byte	byte[]	short	char	int	long	float	double	String
boolen	Y									Y
byte		Y		Y		Y	Y			Y
byte[]	Y									
short				Y		Y	Y			Y
char					Y					Y
int						Y	Y			Y
long							Y			Y
float								Y	Y	Y
double									Y	Y
String	Y	Y		Y		Y	Y	Y	Y	Y

Summary

In this chapter we have covered JMS messages in detail. We began by detailing the design goals defined in the JMS specification. These goals allow JMS to capture as wide a range of enterprise messaging models as possible.

The bulk of the chapter, however, was devoted to the structure of JMS messages. We learned how every message is split into three parts: the header, the message properties, and the message body. Message headers contain a set of standard fields defined by the JMS specification. The values in the header fields are used for proper routing and processing of the messages. We also saw a sample application illustrating the use of different JMS header fields and how the different fields can be accessed and mutated.

Message properties are similar to message headers. However, unlike message headers, message properties are optional. We saw that message properties provide a way of adding application-specific header values to the messages and that they are also used by JMS clients to filter out the messages they receive using message selectors. The final example we looked at implemented message selectors and application-specific properties using a simple chat application.

JMS messages are categorized depending on the type of content that the messages can have in their body. Accordingly the JMS specification defines five different types of messages that cover most of the enterprise messaging requirements. We looked at an example that demonstrated each of these method types by selecting one at random and sending it to a queue. A message client was set up to consume these messages and process them dynamically.

In the next two chapters we will be covering the two messaging models in detail.

```
com.sun.jndi.fscontext.RefFSContextFactory
com.sun.jndi.ldap.LdapCtxFactory
weblogic.jndi.WLInitialContextFactory
weblogic.jndi.T3InitialContextFactory
fiorano.jms.rtl.FioranoInitialContextFactory
fiorano.jms.runtime.naming.FioranoInitialContextFactory
ch.softwired.jms.naming.IBusContextFactory
```

4

Point-to-Point Messaging

In this the first of two chapters looking at the different messaging models, we will look at the **Point-to-Point (PTP) messaging domain**. This model is based on message queues, whereby a message producer sends messages to a specific queue, and the message consumer receives the messages from that same queue. However, an individual message can only be received by one receiver. If multiple receivers are listening to messages on the queue, the messaging server determines which one will receive the next message based on the routing information available in the message header. If no receivers are listening to the queue, the messages remain in the queue until a receiver attaches to the queue.

In this chapter we will:

❑   Discuss message queues

❑   See how to set up our software environment to start coding PTP applications

❑   Look at transactions and their relation to JMS with code samples

❑   Develop an online banking application, which provides ample opportunities for us to explore PTP messaging and transactions; this application will provide a tutorial on many of the features of PTP messaging

Message Queues

The messaging server administrator explicitly creates queues so that messages are sequentially cached for their receivers. As was mentioned earlier, the producer in the PTP model is called the **sender** and the consumer in the PTP model is called the **receiver**. The sender sends messages to a queue and declares the Quality of Service (QoS) – the delivery mode, time-to-live, and priority – as well as whether any reply is requested from the receiver.

The sender sets headers, properties, and body content for each message before sending it off to the queue on the messaging server. The messaging server (or broker, or provider), records the message in its log, acknowledges receipt of the message to the sender, and immediately distributes the message to the appropriate listening receiver. While only one receiver can consume the latest message, several receivers may be reading the queue, taking turns to consume messages. If the delivery mode of the message is PERSISTENT, any undelivered messages are placed in the messaging server's persistent message store database.

The figure below shows a typical PTP connection topology with several message producers sending messages to queues and message consumers receiving these messages by connecting to the appropriate queues:

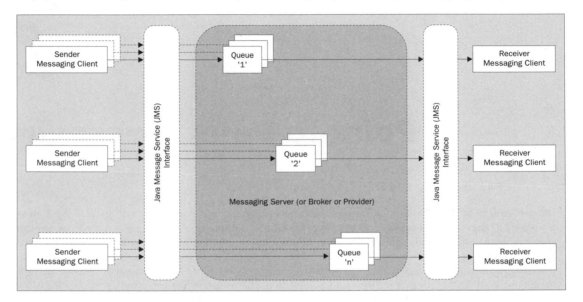

Some of the important characteristics of the PTP messaging domain are as follows:

❑   A queue adheres to the **First-In, First-Out (FIFO)** technique for message delivery. The first message received is the first message delivered. If there are no receivers listening to the queue, the messages are persisted. Durability and persistence are essential to the successful operation of this type of messaging domain.

❑   Even when there are multiple receivers listening for messages from a single queue, there is absolutely one and only one receiver for any given message. Even while many prospective receivers balance the load by listening for messages on the same queue, only one of them takes delivery of a message.

❑   As soon as a message is acknowledged as delivered by the receiver, it is immediately removed from the queue permanently. After this, no one else can either see it or get it.

However, authorized users of the **queue browser** – a mechanism that allows examination of queues without removing messages from them – can scan messages without destroying them by taking advantage of the durability that these sequential queues offer. While many prospective receivers could be listening to, or even browsing the queue, when a receiver elects to accept a queued message, the message is considered delivered. No other receiver will thereafter be able to access that message. Thus, PTP messaging is a one-to-one form of communication.

Software

To work with the JMS samples here, you have to have installed the Java JDK compiler and runtime, a browser capable of running Java, and a JMS 1.0.2 or higher compatible messaging server (broker or provider).

JMS Server and Client Software

You should be able to run the following code samples on any JMS 1.0.2 or higher compatible messaging server. However, in this chapter we will use the freely downloadable Developer Edition of FioranoMQ (from http://www.fiorano.com). Please refer to Appendix A for the simple procedures required to interchange providers in client code, tips on installing FioranoMQ, and full details of administered object configuration.

> *There are a number of other vendors offering JMS implementations or who have pledged support for JMS and the list of those vendors and their corporate URLs can be obtained at http://java.sun.com/products/jms/vendors.html. You can download any messaging server of your choice and set it up according to the instructions that come with your particular JMS messaging server software.*

Queue Management

As mentioned earlier, a queue has to be initially set up on the messaging server by an administrator before it can be used for any coding. The first step is to create a queue connection factory and the queues that we will use while developing our JMS code samples. Detailed instructions on administered object configuration can be found in Appendix A.

Start up the FioranoMQ messaging server by invoking the server startup script `runkrnl.bat`. This script is usually found in the `%FMP_DIR%\shell\` directory. Then, invoke the Fiorano admin console by executing the `runAdmin.bat` batch file. It is usually found in the `%FMP_DIR%\AdminTool` directory in Fiorano MQ 4.6 and in the `%FMP_DIR%\shell\` directory in FioranoMQ 5.0. The screenshot below shows the login screen of the Fiorano administrator console. Log on as the administrator by typing in the appropriate password. In my case the password is "`passwd`":

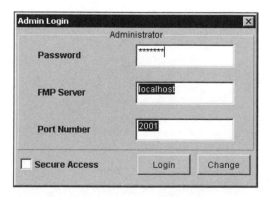

> The FioranoMQ server administrator console is case-insensitive. It ignores case for user names, passwords, destinations, and connection factory names. Please be aware of this when administering and using the FioranoMQ administrator console.

First, we need to set up a queue connection factory called `bank:qcf`. Below is a screenshot showing the FioranoMQ's administrative console, where the `bank:qcf` object is installed by using the **Create** button. The **Queue CFs** tab shows the connection factories currently administered by the server. This object can now be accessed by our messaging client applications through JNDI:

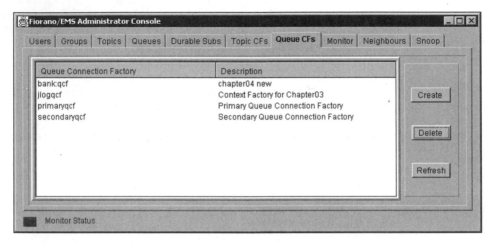

In the same manner, we need a couple of queue objects called `bank:accounts` and `bank:clearing_house`. The screen below shows Fiorano's **Queues** tab, showing the queues `bank:accounts` and `bank:clearing_house` installed. Any messaging client can now access these queues through JNDI lookup:

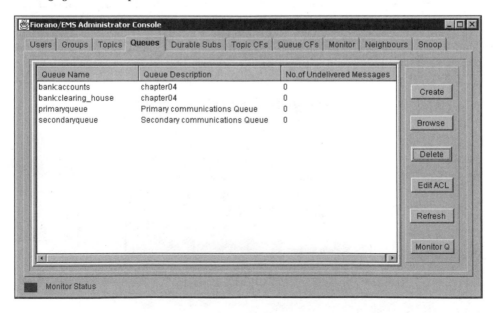

Now we create a couple of users called `athul` and `gopalan`, with password `raj`. Below we see the Users tab, showing the new users in place:

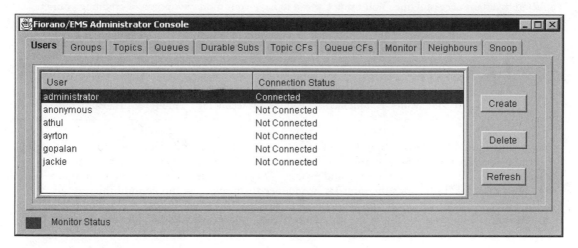

Programming Using the PTP Model

Every PTP messaging application follows the same basic pattern to connect to a queue, send or receive messages from the queue, and to close the queue connections. The basic PTP messaging client program development, as seen in earlier chapters, is as follows:

❑   Obtain a queue connection factory through JNDI lookup

❑   Obtain a queue through JNDI lookup

❑   Create a queue connection from the queue connection factory

❑   Use the queue connection to create the queue session

❑   Decide whether to create a queue sender or a queue receiver

❑   Start the queue connection

❑   Send or receive messages

❑   Close the queue session and queue connection

As we have covered the basics of PTP programming in Chapters 2 and 3, in this section, we will see how to implement a real-world messaging application using the PTP messaging model.

Transactions

A transaction is the most important concept you should be aware of when dealing with enterprise applications. To a user, a transaction is a single change event that either happens or doesn't happen. To system implementers, a transaction is a programming style that enables them to code modules that can participate in distributed computations.

To illustrate this concept, assume you want to transfer money from a savings account into a checking account. In this scenario, it is critical that both accounts are changed by a successful transaction and neither account is affected by an unsuccessful one. You cannot afford to have your money vaporize if crediting your checking account fails for any reason after the debit on your savings account succeeds. Although this may sound like a fairly straightforward request, making this work in a distributed system without deploying some form of transaction control is hard – computers can fail and messages can easily get lost.

> **Transactions are essential for distributed applications. Further, transactions provide modular execution, which complements a component technology's modular programming.**

Transactions provide a way to bundle a set of operations into an atomic execution unit. This atomic, all-or-nothing property is not new: it appears throughout life. For example, a minister conducting a marriage ceremony first asks the bride and groom, "Do you take this person to be your spouse?" Only if they both respond "I do" does the minister pronounce them married and **commit** the transaction. In short, within any transaction, several independent entities must agree before the deal is done. If any party disagrees, the deal is off and the independent entities are reverted back to their original state. In transactions, this is known as a **rollback** operation.

Two-phase Commits

The **two-phase commit protocol** ensures all the resource managers either **commit** a transaction or **abort** it. In the first phase, the transaction service asks each resource manager if it is prepared to commit. If all the participants affirm, then, in the second phase, the transaction service broadcasts a commit message to all of them. If any part of the transaction fails, in other words, if a resource manager fails to respond to the prepare request or if a resource manager responds negatively, then the transaction service notifies all the resource managers and the transaction is aborted. This is the essence of the two-phase commit protocol.

The ACID Properties

All transactions subscribe to the following "ACID" properties:

Atomicity

A transaction either commits or rollbacks. If a transaction commits, all its effects remain. If it rollbacks, then all its effects are undone. In other words, each part of a transaction must complete successfully for the transaction to commit. For example, in renaming an object, both the new name is created and the old name is deleted (commit), or nothing changes (rollback).

Consistency

A transaction always leads to a correct transformation of the system state by preserving the state invariance. For example, within a transaction adding an element to a doubly linked list, all four forward and backward pointers are updated, thus maintaining a consistent state.

Isolation

Concurrent transactions are isolated from the updates of other incomplete transactions. This property is also often called **serializability**. For example, a second transaction traversing a doubly linked list already undergoing modification by a first transaction will see only completed changes and is isolated from any non-committed changes of the first transaction. Note that a transaction should not be dependent on another to prevent deadlocks, in other words, two processes that are sharing some resource (such as read access to a table) both decide to wait for exclusive (write) access.

Durability

If a transaction commits, its effects will be permanent after the transaction commits. In fact, the effects remain even in the face of system failures.

The application must decide what consistency is and bracket its computation to delimit these consistent transformations. The job of the transactional resource managers is to provide consistent, isolated, and durable transformations of the objects they manage. If the transactions are distributed among multiple computers, the two-phase commit protocol is used to make these transactions atomic and durable.

Transactions and JMS

JMS uses the **Java Transaction Service (JTS)** to support transactions.

> **A series of incoming and outgoing messages can be grouped together into an atomic unit of work/transaction.**

There are several ways to use transactions with JMS. If you are using only JMS in your transactions, you can create and use a transacted JMS session. However, if you plan on mixing other operations, such as Enterprise JavaBeans (EJB) with JMS transactions, you are better off using the JTS `javax.transaction.UserTransaction` class in a non-transacted JMS session. This allows you more control over your transactional code while you develop the program since you may need to incorporate specific functionality in your programs based on your requirements to coordinate between JMS and other non-JMS transactional systems like EJB.

Transacted JMS Sessions

In JMS, transacted sessions are generally chained. That means, whenever a commit or rollback occurs in a transaction, the next transaction automatically begins.

The JTS UserTransaction Class

If you are using other transactional resources like EJBs along with JMS, or you have already created a `javax.jts.UserTransaction` object in an EJB, the EJB server will coordinate your transactions. If you create a JMS transacted session when you already have an existing `javax.jts.UserTransaction` object, a `javax.jts.NotSupportedException` should be thrown when you call any other transacted methods on the JMS Session object. The transaction manager throws this exception when a calling thread attempts to start a new transaction when the thread is already associated with a transaction because nested transactions are not supported in EJB.

When combining JMS and EJB operations in a single transaction, you can start the transaction from an EJB automatically, or you can create a `javax.jts.UserTransaction` object on your own. The `javax.jts.UserTransaction.setTransactionTimeout()` method takes an integer `TransactionTimeout` value that specifies how long a transaction can run before it times out. If a transaction times out, it is rolled back. If you have very long running transactions that exceeds this limit, you will need to increase this value to allow transactions to complete.

The pseudo-code for this will be similar to the following, but may vary depending on the J2EE application server you are using:

```
// Create a Transaction object, or look it up using JNDI
javax.jts.UserTransaction userTransaction = new javax.jts.UserTransaction();

// Timeout the transaction if takes longer than specified
userTransaction.setTransactionTimeout (36000);

try {
   // Start the transaction
   userTransaction.begin();

   // Perform JMS and EJB operations

   // Commit the transaction
   userTransaction.commit();

} catch (Exception e) {
   userTransaction.rollback();
   e.printStackTrace();
}
```

Distributed Transactions

The JMS specification does not require that users have to support distributed transactions. This is because, even though it is possible for JMS clients to handle transactions directly, it is believed that not many clients will need to do this. However, JMS specifies that if the user were to provide support for distributed transactions, it should be done through the **Java Transaction API (JTA)** `javax.transaction.xa.XAResource`. Similarly, if a JMS provider is also a distributed transaction monitor, it should provide control of the transaction through JTA. Support for JTA in JMS is however targeted at vendors who integrate JMS into their application server products.

JMS Transaction Examples

When a session is created as transacted, transactions are created. A transacted session is created by the first parameter passed in to the `createQueueSession()` method:

```
QueueSession session = connection.createQueueSession(true,
                                        Session.AUTO_ACKNOWLEDGE);
```

A value of `true` for the first parameter makes this a transacted session. Any message sent on a transacted session starts off a transaction. All messages sent on that session then become part of this transaction, until a `QueueSession.commit()` or a `QueueSession.rollback()` call is invoked.

As soon as a commit call is invoked, all the messages sent until that point are packaged into a transaction and are sent out to the server. The following figure depicts this scenario diagrammatically:

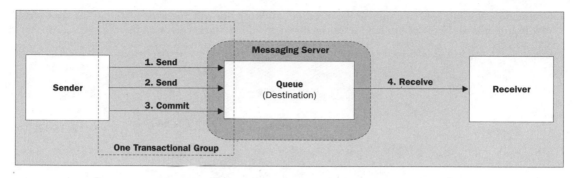

However, if the transaction were rolled back, all sent messages are destroyed, and all the consumed messages are automatically recovered. A commit or rollback call signifies the end of the current transaction and automatically starts off the next transaction.

In the following code sample, assume that we have obtained a reference to a transacted session object called senderSession and we have created a sender object called sender:

```
TextMessage textMessage1 = senderSession.createTextMessage();
TextMessage textMessage2 = senderSession.createTextMessage();

textMessage1.setText(stringData);
textMessage2.setText(stringData);

sender.send(textMessage1);
sender.send(textMessage2);
```

In the code above, the messages textMessage1 and textMessage2 are not sent off immediately as soon as the send() method is invoked on the sender object. Instead they are buffered in an internal storage of the provider's client runtime until either a commit() or a rollback() operation is invoked. The transaction is committed as follows:

```
senderSession.commit();
```

As soon as the commit is called, both the messages (textMessage1 and textMessage2) are sent to the JMS messaging server as a single packaged unit.

On the other hand if a rollback is called at this point then both the messages (textMessage1 and textMessage2) would be discarded:

```
senderSession.rollback();
```

As such, a commit() or a rollback() invocation signifies the end of the current transaction and all subsequent operations on the session automatically become part of the next transaction. In essence, a transacted session always has a current transaction within which its work is done. For example, when working with a purchase order, if the order transaction is successful, the system commits it and moves on to the next transaction. However, if it is a failure, the system rollbacks the transaction and starts working with the next order. At any time the system is always processing some order and always has a current purchase request order on which work is done.

Transactions are not confined only to the message producer side of a messaging system. As shown in the next figure, it is also possible to have a transactional grouping that receives on the message consumer side:

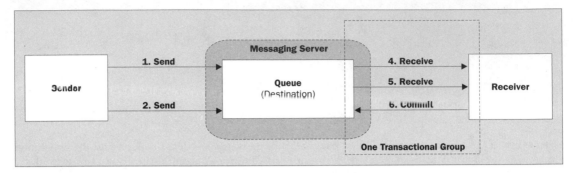

The following code snippet illustrates such a scenario:

```
QueueSession session = null;
session = connection.createQueueSession(true, Session.AUTO_ACKNOWLEDGE);

QueueReceiver receiver = session.createReceiver(queue);
TextMessage request1 = (TextMessage) receiver.receive();
TextMessage request2 = (TextMessage) receiver.receive();
session.commit();
```

In the above scenario, if the transaction successfully commits, a new transaction is started for the subsequent receive operation. If however, something were to fail and the receiver were to rollback, all the messages that were received within this transaction, would be thrown back into the queue and the system would be taken to the state it was in before receiving messages on this transaction.

In such a scenario, the messages now become available to the next receiver as long as their expiration time has not been reached. The next receiver can them pick these messages up and start processing them if it wants to. The JMSRedelivered property is set for these types of messages. Any receiver can examine the property with a call to getJMSRedelivered() and decide whether to process the message or not.

In as similar fashion, it is also possible to group sends and receives together in one transactional group as shown here:

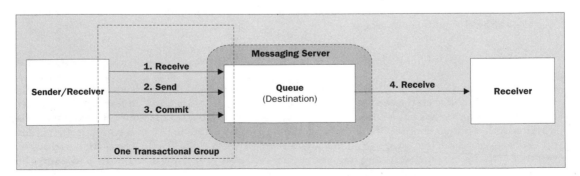

The following code snippet illustrates such a scenario:

```
QueueSession session = null;
session = connection.createQueueSession(true, Session.AUTO_ACKNOWLEDGE);

QueueReceiver receiver = session.createReceiver(queue);
TextMessage request = (TextMessage) receiver.receive();

QueueSender sender = session.createSender(queue);
TextMessage textMessage = session.createTextMessage();
textMessage.setText(stringData);
sender.send(textMessage);

session.commit();
```

We will be looking at how to use the `javax.jts.UserTransaction` class to co-ordinate transactions between JMS and other transactional resources like Enterprise JavaBeans when we look at EJB Messaging in Chapter 7.

In the rest of this chapter we are going to see how to develop an online banking application. There are a number of examples using JMS transactions in this application.

The Online Banking Application

To illustrate the PTP programming model, let us implement an online banking application. Before we start, please be aware that the intention here is to present as many JMS features as possible in order to demonstrate the array of options available to you when developing JMS applications. A lot of error checking has been removed to present relevant information and keep the discussions pertinent to JMS, so that we don't digress from the topic at hand.

Specification

eCommWare Corporation provides online banking services to its customers. This service allows its online customers to connect to any of their accounts in other banks and perform day-to-day banking operations. We will be looking at three different operations that customers can perform on their bank accounts online:

- ❑ Transactional transfer of funds from one account to another
- ❑ Stopping payment instructions from an account
- ❑ Browsing pending instructions for a particular account

The figure below illustrates our online banking solution:

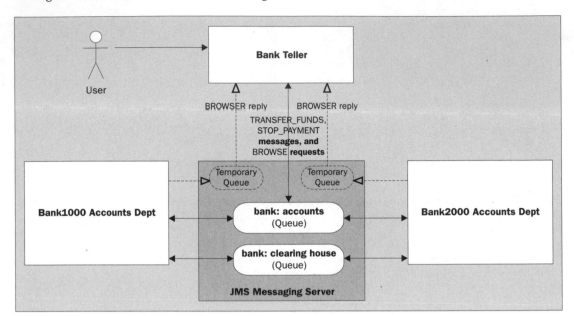

The teller application is the front-end GUI that the users of the application will see. The user is initially asked to logon to the system when they request the services of the bank teller application. The user is prompted to enter the bank they want to connect to (the bank's routing number has to be specified), their name, their account number, and their password. The system then authenticates and authorizes the user to perform operations on their accounts through their bank's accounts department.

Transferring Funds

To transfer funds from one account to another, the user will have to specify the payee bank's routing number, the payee information like their name, account number, and the amount of money they are going to transfer and click on the Submit button.

As soon as the user has specified the instruction, a transactional message is sent to the `bank:accounts` queue to transfer the amount. The bank's accounts department module that is listening to this queue gets this message.

This module in turn checks its books to verify that the user has sufficient funds in their account, debits the specified amount, and sends a message to the `bank:clearing_house` queue stating the amount involved in the transaction. The payee accounts department's liability to the account holder goes down by that much. Both operations are part of one transactional grouping. The payee bank's account department module that is listening to the `bank:clearing_house` queue receives the message transactionally and credits the payee's account.

The sequence of operations of what we just discussed above is shown diagrammatically in the figure below:

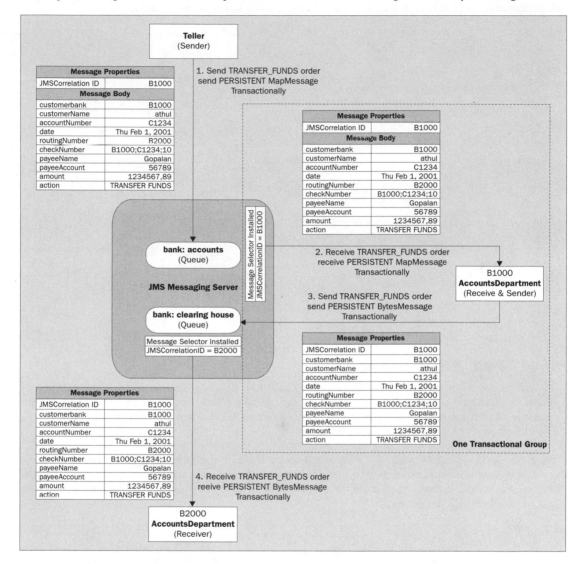

Stop Payments

Similarly, when the account holder needs to send a stop payment instruction to their bank, they construct the stop payment message by filling in the check number, the payee's name, and the amount of the check and send it off to their bank transactionally as a highest priority message.

The scenario diagram for sending stop payment messages from the teller to the bank's accounts department as discussed above is shown diagrammatically in the figure below:

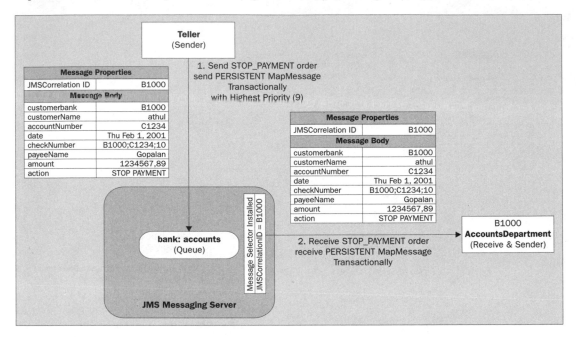

Browse Pending Instructions

It is also possible for the account holder to browse all their pending operations from the various queues. When that option is selected, they are returned a vector of all their operations that are pending to be executed. A temporary queue is created and is used to pass this information along between the accounts department and the teller module.

The figure below diagrammatically illustrates a scenario where the pending messages for a particular account are browsed and passed on to the teller module through the temporary queue that the teller has created dynamically. Once again note that the accounts department's send and receive operations are part of one transactional group:

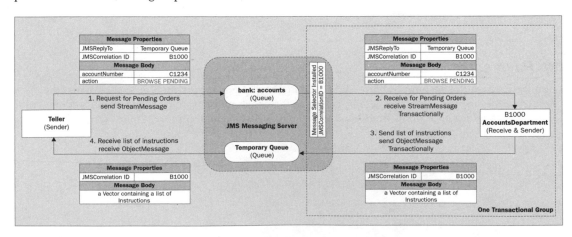

Let us now examine how to program the major modules.

The teller module consists of the `Teller` class, the `TellerPanel` class, and the `Login` class. The accounts department module consists of the `AccountsDepartment` class, the `AccountingPanel` class and the `DisplayHandler` interface. All the modules of this application to exchange instructions use the `Constants` class and the `Instruction` class. At the end of each module, we will show how to compile and execute the samples.

The Constants Class

All the modules in the system use the `Constants` class to retrieve static constant values:

```
package ptp.onlinebanking;

public class Constants {

  static final String PROVIDER_URL =
    "http://localhost:2001";            // For FioranoMQ version 4.6

// "http://localhost:1856";            // For FioranoMQ version 5.0

  static final String USER_NAME = "athul";
  static final String PASSWORD = "raj";

  static final String FACTORY =
    "fiorano.jms.rtl.FioranoInitialContextFactory";        // for FMQ 4.6

// "fiorano.jms.runtime.naming.FioranoInitialContextFactory"; // for FMQ 5.0

  static final String QCF = "bank:qcf";
  static final String ACCOUNTS_QUEUE = "bank:accounts";
  static final String CLEARING_QUEUE = "bank:clearing_house";

  static final String TRANSFER_FUNDS = "Transfer Funds";
  static final String STOP_PAYMENT = "Stop Payment";
  static final String BROWSE_PENDING_REQUESTS = "Browse Pending Requests";

  static final String ECOMMWARE_BANK_NO = "BANK1000";
  static final String HERITAGE_BANK_NO = "BANK2000";
  static final String RAJ_BANK_NO = "BANK3000";

  // A static string denoting a FAILURE of instruction
  static final int FAILED = -1;

  // A static string denoting a REJECTED instruction
  static final int REJECTED = 0;

  // A static string denoting an APPROVED instruction
  static final int APPROVED = 1;

  static final int HIGHEST_PRIORITY_MESSAGE = 9;

}
```

The Instruction Class

All the modules in the system use the `Instruction` class to exchange instructional information. The `Instruction` class implements the `java.io.Serializable` interface and has getter/setter methods to retrieve its elements:

```java
package ptp.onlinebanking;

public class Instruction implements java.io.Serializable {

    protected String customerBank;
    protected String accountNumber;
    protected String customerName;
    protected String date;
    protected String checkNumber;
    protected String routingNumber;
    protected String payeeAccount;
    protected String payeeName;
    protected double amount;
    protected String action;

    public Instruction() {}

    public Instruction(String bank, String account, String name,
                       String time, String check, String routing,
                       String payeeAcct, String payee, double money,
                       String command) {
        this.customerBank = bank;
        this.accountNumber = account;
        this.customerName = name;
        this.date = time;
        this.checkNumber = check;
        this.routingNumber = routing;
        this.payeeAccount = payeeAcct;
        this.payeeName = payee;
        this.amount = money;
        this.action = command;
    }

    public String getCustomerBank() {
        return customerBank;
    }
    public String getAccountNumber() {
        return accountNumber;
    }
    public String getCustomerName() {
        return customerName;
    }
    public String getDate() {
        return date;
    }
    public String getCheckNumber() {
        return checkNumber;
    }
```

```java
    public String getRoutingNumber() {
      return routingNumber;
    }
    public String getPayeeAccount() {
      return payeeAccount;
    }
    public String getPayeeName() {
      return payeeName;
    }
    public double getAmount() {
      return amount;
    }
    public String getAction() {
      return action;
    }

    public void setCustomerBank(String bank) {
      customerBank = bank;
    }
    public void setAccountNumber(String accountNo) {
      accountNumber = accountNo;
    }
    public void setCustomerName(String name) {
      customerName = name;
    }
    public void setDate(String time) {
      date = time;
    }
    public void setCheckNumber(String orderNo) {
      checkNumber = orderNo;
    }
    public void setRoutingNumber(String routingNo) {
      routingNumber = routingNo;
    }
    public void setPayeeAccount(String accountNo) {
      payeeAccount = accountNo;
    }
    public void setPayeeName(String name) {
      payeeName = name;
    }
    public void setAmount(double money) {
      amount = money;
    }
    public void setAction(String command) {
      action = command;
    }

    public void print() {
      System.out.println("\nAccount Number : " + accountNumber);
      System.out.println("Customer Name : " + customerName);
      System.out.println("Date : " + date);
      System.out.println("Check Number : " + checkNumber);
      System.out.println("Routing Number : " + routingNumber);
      System.out.println("Payee Account : " + payeeAccount);
      System.out.println("Payee Name : " + payeeName);
      System.out.println("Amount : $" + amount);
      System.out.println("Action : " + action + "\n");
    }

}
```

The Teller Class

The `Teller` class is used to send out account information on the `bank:accounts` queue:

```
package ptp.onlinebanking;

import javax.jms.*;
import javax.naming.*;
import Common.*;
import java.util.*;

public class Teller {

  private QueueConnectionFactory factory;
  private QueueConnection connection;
  private Queue queue;
  private QueueSession session, transactSession;
  private QueueSender sender;
  private QueueRequestor requestor;

  private String hostName;
  private String userID;
  private String password;

  private static final String CONTEXT_FACTORY = Constants.FACTORY;
  private static final String CONNECTION_FACTORY = Constants.QCF;
  private static final String SENDER_QUEUE = Constants.ACCOUNTS_QUEUE;
```

There are a couple of constructors for the `Teller` class. One of them is the default constructor that does not take any parameters. The other constructor takes in multiple parameters. In these are the hostname or IP:Port of the remote JMS server to connect to, and the username and password of a valid user for the JMS server:

```
public Teller(String host, String user, String passwd) {
  this.hostName = host;
  this.userID = user;
  this.password = passwd;
}

public Teller() {
  this.hostName = Constants.PROVIDER_URL;
  this.userID = Constants.USER_NAME;
  this.password = Constants.PASSWORD;
}
```

User Identification and Authentication

The `createConnections()` method creates and starts connections and sessions. The sample also demonstrates how to connect to JMS messaging servers that run remotely. Typically, this is done by specifying the hostname or the IP:Port address combination on the JNDI server with the `PROVIDER_URL` property. The `JNDIService.init(CONTEXT_FACTORY, hostName)` method of our `common.JNDIService` class does this for us. If you want to examine the relevant code for the `JNDIService` class, go to Chapter 3 where it was introduced. However, please update `JNDIService.java` to specify that it is in the package `common`:

```
public void createConnections() {
  try {
    JNDIService.init(CONTEXT_FACTORY, hostName);

    // Retrieve the connection factory object
    factory = (QueueConnectionFactory) JNDIService
                .lookup(CONNECTION_FACTORY);
    queue = (Queue) JNDIService.lookup(Teller.SENDER_QUEUE);
```

A JMS client can supply its credentials as a name and password combination when creating a connection with the JMS messaging server. If no credentials are supplied, the JMS specification says that the current client thread's credentials are used.

> At the time of writing, the JDK does not define the concept of a thread's default credentials (in this case we're talking about the client thread trying to connect to the JMS server). However, this concept may be defined in the near future. Until then, if a client supplies no credentials, the identity of the user should be taken as the one under which the JMS client is running.

User identification and authentication in JMS-based messaging servers generally works as follows. The system administrator initially sets up all the users in the system using an administration tool or other configuration system that comes with the provider.

A client application connects to the JMS server with the following code:

```
QueueConnection connection = null;
connection = connectionFactory.createQueueConnection("athul", "raj");
```

The provider runtime on the client machine sends a connection request with the username and password to the messaging server. If the authentication succeeds, the connection requested is established and a valid connection object reference is returned to the client. However, if it does not match, the connection is rejected and this causes the provider runtime present on the client to throw a `javax.jms.JMSSecurityException` exception.

Similarly, if the user name sent in the login packet is not found in the repository, the messaging server will reject the connection, and cause the client run-time to throw a `javax.jms.JMSSecurityException` exception. The following code creates the connection in `createConnections()` using identification and authentication:

```
connection = factory.createQueueConnection(userID, password);
connection.setExceptionListener(new ExceptionHandler());
session =
  connection.createQueueSession(false,
                                Session.AUTO_ACKNOWLEDGE);
transactSession = connection.createQueueSession(true,
        Session.AUTO_ACKNOWLEDGE);
connection.start();
} catch (Exception e) {
  e.printStackTrace();
}
}
```

Releasing Resources

It is very important to clean up resources as soon as they are no longer needed. This improves both the scalability and the efficiency of the application. The sender, sessions, and connection are closed and all resources are released before the program terminates. JMS messaging providers typically allocate significant resources outside the JVM on behalf of a connection. Therefore, clients should close connections when they are no longer required.

According to the JMS specification, "Relying on the garbage collector to reclaim these resources is not timely enough". A close() terminates all pending messages received on the connection's receivers. At the time of closing, these receivers may return with a message or not depending on whether there were any more messages available for them.

The closeConnections() method cleans up all the resources:

```
public void closeConnections() {
  try {
    if (sender != null) {
      sender.close();
    }
    if (session != null) {
      session.close();
    }
    if (transactSession != null) {
      transactSession.close();
    }
    if (connection != null) {
      connection.close();
    }
  } catch (Exception e) {
    e.printStackTrace();
  }
}
```

There are three operations that the user can perform. They are:

❑ Transfer funds from one account to another

❑ Stop payments from an account

❑ Browse pending instructions on an account

Depending on the choice that the user makes, the appropriate method is invoked. If the action specified in the instruction object is Constants.BROWSE_PENDING_REQUESTS, then a request is sent to the bank:accounts queue to browse pending instructions of the user's account by invoking the browsePendingRequests() method. For anything else, the sendInstructions() method is invoked:

```
public int execute(Instruction instruction) {
  int result = Constants.APPROVED;
  try {
    if (instruction.getAction()
            .equals(Constants.BROWSE_PENDING_REQUESTS)) {
      result = browsePendingRequests(instruction);
    } else {
```

```
      result = sendInstructions(instruction);
    }
  } catch (Exception e) {
    e.printStackTrace();
  }
  return result;
}
```

The figure below shows the `Teller` class sending out a message to the `bank:accounts` queue transactionally:

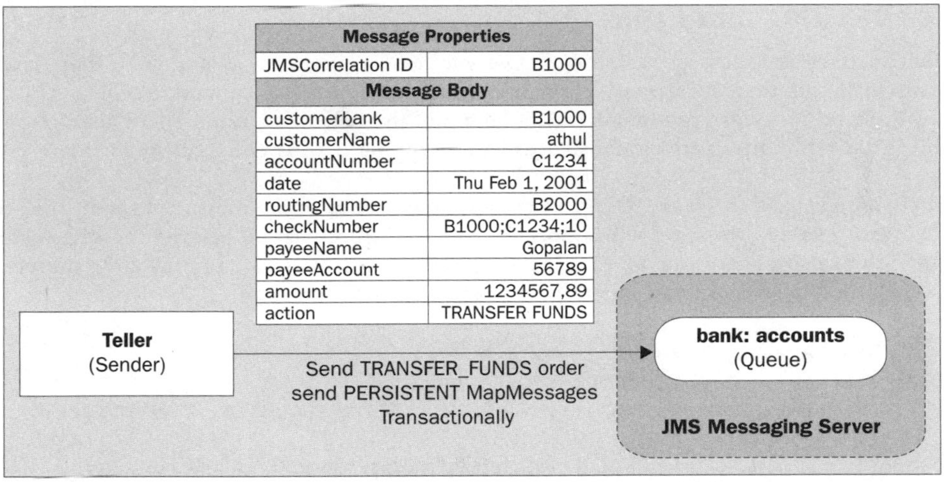

A map message is created and populated with the information that needs to be sent (see Chapter 3). This message is then sent to its destination using a message sender (or producer). The `sender` object is then used to send out the message by invoking its `send()` method with a delivery mode of `PERSISTENT`, a message priority of `Message.DEFAULT_PRIORITY`, and a time-to-live of `Message.DEFAULT_TIME_TO_LIVE`:

```
int sendInstructions(Instruction instruction) throws JMSException {
  int result = Constants.APPROVED;
  try {

    // Create a Sender if one does not exist
    if (sender == null) {
      sender = transactSession.createSender(queue);
    }

    // Create a Map Message
    MapMessage mapMessage = transactSession.createMapMessage();

    // set message properties
    mapMessage.setString("customerBank",
                          instruction.getCustomerBank());
    mapMessage.setString("accountNumber",
                          instruction.getAccountNumber());
```

```
        mapMessage.setString("customerName",
                          instruction.getCustomerName());
        mapMessage.setString("date", instruction.getDate());
        mapMessage.setString("checkNumber",
                          instruction.getCheckNumber());
        mapMessage.setString("payeeName", instruction.getPayeeName());
        mapMessage.setDouble("amount", instruction.getAmount());
        mapMessage.setString("action", instruction.getAction());

        mapMessage.setJMSCorrelationID(instruction.getCustomerBank());
```

Message Priorities and Expiration

When there are several messages awaiting delivery at the receiver end, it is useful if there is a mechanism available that specifies which messages are more important than the others. This way the highest prioritized messages can be moved to the top of the FIFO list. While there are circumstances when this is desirable, there are circumstances when keeping the FIFO list flowing is more preferable.

An integer value is used to set the JMSPriority property field in the message header. JMS defines a ten-level priority value. Messages with priorities from 0 to 4 are **normal** priority messages. However, messages with priorities set from 5-9 should be **expedited**. As is illustrated in the code snippet below, message priorities can be assigned when the message is sent as follows:

```
public static final int PRIORITY = 2;
public static final int TIMETOLIVE = 360000;
sender.send(textMessage, DeliveryMode.PERSISTENT, PRIORITY, TIMETOLIVE);
```

The TIMETOLIVE integer value is added to the GMT time at the client when the message is sent to determine the JMSExpiration date and time of the message. If the TIMETOLIVE is 0, the expiration time is also 0, an indication that the message is intended never to expire. Servers should therefore all have the correct time, and have some sort of mechanism to synchronize their clocks. If time-to-live is quite short, then clock jitter and network latency become problems.

The time-to-live feature ensures that the message is eventually delivered, but can result in out-of-date deliveries when queues are not purged. The JMS specification states that even though clients should not receive messages that have expired, there is no guarantee that this will not happen:

```
        // Send the message
    if (instruction.getAction().equals(Constants.STOP_PAYMENT)) {

      // If it's a Stop Payment, send message of highest priority
      sender.send(mapMessage, DeliveryMode.PERSISTENT,
                  Constants.HIGHEST_PRIORITY_MESSAGE,   // value of 9
      Message.DEFAULT_TIME_TO_LIVE);
    } else {
      mapMessage.setString("routingNumber",
                          instruction.getRoutingNumber());
      mapMessage.setString("payeeAccount",
                          instruction.getPayeeAccount());

      // If it's a Fund Transfer, send message of normal priority
      sender.send(mapMessage, DeliveryMode.PERSISTENT,
```

```
                    Message.DEFAULT_PRIORITY,
                    Message.DEFAULT_TIME_TO_LIVE);
    }

    // Commit the transaction
    transactSession.commit();
    System.out.println(instruction.getAction() + " for Check No: "
                    + instruction.getCheckNumber()
                    + " message, sent for "
                    + instruction.getCustomerBank()
                    + " through the Queue "
                    + queue.getQueueName());
} catch (Exception e) {
    transactSession.rollback();
    System.out.println(instruction.getAction() + " for Check No: "
                    + instruction.getCheckNumber()
                    + " message, could not be sent for "
                    + instruction.getCustomerBank());
    e.printStackTrace();
    result = Constants.FAILED;
}
return result;
}
```

Message Delivery Modes

As was discussed in earlier chapters, JMS supports two different modes of message delivery, `DeliveryMode.NON_PERSISTENT` and `DeliveryMode.PERSISTENT`:

❑ The `DeliveryMode.NON_PERSISTENT` mode has the lowest overhead, as it does not require that a message be logged into the messaging server's persistent store. Therefore, any failure at the JMS provider end can cause the message to get lost. A provider must deliver this type of message **at-most-once**. This means, that a JMS server can lose the message, but it must not deliver it twice. For example, in an application that tracks the location of a radio beacon, it's acceptable to miss the occasional message.

❑ The `DeliveryMode.PERSISTENT` mode instructs the JMS provider to take care to insure that a message is not lost in transit due to a fault at the JMS provider end. The JMS broker should deliver this type of message **once-and-only-once**. This means that any failure at the JMS broker end should not cause it to lose the message and the message should not be delivered twice. However, you should note that the use of this flag does not automatically guarantee that all messages are delivered to every eligible consumer. A good example of this is in an application that posts sell orders on a trading floor.

Request/Reply

When an application sends a message and expects to receive a message in return, **request/reply** messaging can be used. This is essentially standard synchronous messaging. This messaging model is often defined as a subset of one of the other two messaging models. JMS does not support request/reply messaging as a model, though it allows it in the context of the other two messaging models.

JMS Request/Reply

The `browsePendingRequests()` method below illustrates how to simulate blocking request/reply messaging in a MOM scenario. The requestor sends a message to the replier and remains blocked until it receives a reply from the other end. This demonstrates the use of the `request()` API and the `QueueRequestor` class found in the `javax.jms` package.

The `browsePendingRequests()` method sets up a `requestor` object if one does not already exist. The method then creates a temporary queue. The method creates a stream message as a request, specifies the temporary queue reference in the `replyTo` property of the message, sets the `JMSCorrelationID` property with the customer's bank routing number, populates the body, sends it off on the `bank:accounts` queue, and waits for a response from the other end. The program stays blocked until a response comes back. As soon as it receives a reply from the other end, it retrieves the message from the reply.

The figure below shows the `Teller` class requesting and receiving request/reply messages on the temporary queue:

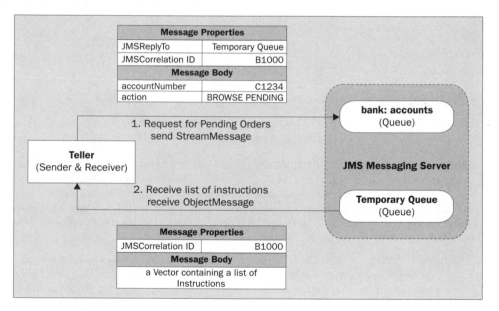

The JMSCorrelationID Field

JMS provides the `JMSCorrelationID` message property field so that any replier can reference the original message request. The `JMSCorrelationID` field can be set by the requestor using the message's `setJMSCorrelationID()` method. Similarly, repliers can access this header field using the message's `getJMSCorrelationID()` method as shown in the code sample below. A messaging client can use this field to link one message with the other. It is generally used to link a response message with its request message. This field can hold any of the following values:

❑ A provider-specific message ID

❑ An application-specific `string`

❑ A provider-native `byte[]` value

As each message sent by a JMS provider is assigned a `JMSMessageID`, it is convenient to link messages through their IDs. All message ID values must start with the `ID:` prefix:

```java
private int browsePendingRequests(Instruction instruction) {
  int size = 0;

  try {

    // Create a requestor object if one does not exist
    if (requestor == null) {
      requestor = new QueueRequestor(session, queue);
    }

    // Create Stream Message
    StreamMessage streamMessage = session.createStreamMessage();

    // Create a Temporary Queue
    TemporaryQueue temporaryQueue = session.createTemporaryQueue();

    // Set message properties
    streamMessage.setJMSReplyTo(temporaryQueue);
    String name = instruction.getCustomerBank();

    // Set message properties and message body
    streamMessage.setJMSCorrelationID(name);
    streamMessage.writeString(instruction.getAccountNumber());
    streamMessage.writeString(instruction.getAction());

    // Request and receive a Object Message
    ObjectMessage objectMessage =
      (ObjectMessage) requestor.request(streamMessage);

    // Get the JMSCorrelationID property
    String correlationID = objectMessage.getJMSCorrelationID();

    // Read the message body
    Vector list = (Vector) objectMessage.getObject();
    size = list.size();
    System.out.println("Received a list of " + size
                      + " messages from Accounting ...");

    // Delete the Temporary Queue
    temporaryQueue.delete();
  } catch (Exception e) {
    e.printStackTrace();
  }
  return size;
}
```

Temporary Queues

Sessions are used to create temporary destinations for convenience. The scope of a temporary queue holds good for the entire connection. According to the JMS specification, "A temporary queue is a unique queue object created for the duration of a queue connection. It is a system defined queue that can only be consumed by the queue connection that created it". Therefore, by implication, its lifetime persists for the duration of the connection if it is not deleted before that. Any of the connection's sessions are allowed to create message consumers for them.

Temporary destinations can be used in conjunction with the JMSReplyTo message property as shown in the code below. The JMSReplyTo message property makes it possible for a requestor to create a temporary queue, and send a message to the replier with the queue reference set in the message using the JMSReplyTo property. The replier uses the reference and sends back the reply on that destination. It is therefore possible for the original requestor to get back a reply to the message, on the temporary queue that it had originally created:

```
Queue temporaryQueue = (Queue) textMessage.getJMSReplyTo();
TextMessage reply = session.createTextMessage();
reply.setText("Re: " + request.getText());
replier.send(temporaryQueue, reply);
```

The temporary queue here is used to service requests. Each temporary destination is unique and cannot be copied. Since temporary destinations may allocate resources outside the JVM, they should be deleted if they are no longer needed. Even if they are not explicitly deleted, they will however, be killed when a connection is closed. Another way they can be deleted is during garbage collection.

The ExceptionHandler Class

The ExceptionHandler class is the handler installed with the Teller class to take care of un-handled JMS errors.

Installing Exception Handers

The Teller class above sets an exception listener. Just like message listeners, exception listeners have a callback mechanism. It has an onException() method that is called by the provider with the JMSException passed in. The exception listener is required to implement the onException() method of the ExceptionListener interface. The provider invokes this method when a JMSException that has nowhere else to go is thrown on the connection with the JMS server. Note that the exception listener is registered with the provider through the Connection object by a call to its setExceptionListener() method.

When a JMS provider detects a problem with a connection, it will inform the connection's exception listener if one has been registered. The JMSException object that is passed to the onException() method contains a description of the problem thus allowing the client to be asynchronously notified of the problem.

The connection serializes executions of its exception listener. All exceptions delivered to the exception listener are exceptions that have no other place to go to be reported. According to the JMS specification, if an exception is thrown on a JMS call it must not be delivered to an exception listener by default. In essence, an exception listener is not for the purpose of monitoring all exceptions thrown by a connection – only for those that aren't handled elsewhere.

The class ExceptionHandler below, implements the onException() callback method:

```
class ExceptionHandler implements ExceptionListener {

  public void onException(JMSException exception) {
    exception.printStackTrace();
    }
  }
}
```

The TellerPanel Class

Now that we have the `Teller` class ready, we need to write a GUI component that will allow the user to interact with our system. The GUI component that we're going to write will be generic enough that it could be used both as an applet and a standalone Java application.

Since the `Applet` class extends the `Panel` class, we will create our `TellerPanel` class to extend `Applet`. That way we can use the same front-end component both as an applet and as a standalone Java application:

```
package ptp.onlinebanking;

import java.awt.*;
import java.awt.event.*;
import java.applet.*;
import java.util.*;
import java.text.*;

public class TellerPanel extends Applet implements ItemListener,
        ActionListener {

  Teller teller;

  String customerBankNumber;
  String customerAccountNumber;
  String customerUserName;

  Label customerBankField;
  Label customerUserField;
  Label customerAccountField;
  Label dateFieldLabel;

  long orderNumber;

  Label actionLabel;
  Label checkLabel;
  Label routingLabel;
  Label accountLabel;
  Label nameLabel;
  Label amountLabel;

  Choice actionChoice;
  TextField checkNumberField;
  Choice routingNumberChoice;
  TextField accountField;
  TextField nameField;
  TextField amountField;

  Button submitButton;
  Button closeButton;

  Instruction instruction;
```

The `getLoginInfo()` method is used to retrieve information about a user's name, their password, the bank that they want to connect to, their account number with the bank, etc. To do this it uses the services of the `Login` class, which we will see later:

```
void getLoginInfo() {
  Login loginFrame = new Login(this);
  loginFrame.setSize(250, 250);
  loginFrame.setLocation(300, 200);
  loginFrame.pack();
  loginFrame.show();
}
```

The `init()` method is used to create a new instance of the `Teller` class and also layout the GUI for our application:

```
public void init() {
  teller = new Teller(Constants.PROVIDER_URL, Constants.USER_NAME,
                      Constants.PASSWORD);

  GridLayout layout = new GridLayout(0, 2, 10, 10);
  layout.setRows(10);

  this.setLayout(layout);

  customerBankField = new Label("Customer Bank: ");
  customerUserField = new Label("Customer Name: ");
  customerAccountField = new Label("Account Number");
  dateFieldLabel = new Label("Date :");

  actionLabel = new Label("Select Action to be performed");
  checkLabel = new Label("Enter Check Number");
  routingLabel = new Label("Select Payee Routing Number");
  accountLabel = new Label("Enter Payee Account Number");
  nameLabel = new Label("Enter Payee's Name");
  amountLabel = new Label("Enter amount in US Dollars");

  actionChoice = new Choice();
  actionChoice.addItem(Constants.TRANSFER_FUNDS);
  actionChoice.addItem(Constants.STOP_PAYMENT);
  actionChoice.addItem(Constants.BROWSE_PENDING_REQUESTS);

  checkNumberField =
    new TextField((new Long(++orderNumber)).toString());

  routingNumberChoice = new Choice();
  routingNumberChoice.addItem(Constants.ECOMMWARE_BANK_NO);
  routingNumberChoice.addItem(Constants.HERITAGE_BANK_NO);
  routingNumberChoice.addItem(Constants.RAJ_BANK_NO);

  accountField = new TextField("S200089820");
  nameField = new TextField("Gopalan");
  amountField = new TextField("1234567.89");
  submitButton = new Button("Submit");
  closeButton = new Button("Close Connections");

  add(customerUserField);
  add(customerBankField);
  add(customerAccountField);
  add(dateFieldLabel);
```

```
        add(actionLabel);
        add(actionChoice);
        add(checkLabel);
        add(checkNumberField);
        add(routingLabel);
        add(routingNumberChoice);
        add(accountLabel);
        add(accountField);
        add(nameLabel);
        add(nameField);
        add(amountLabel);
        add(amountField);
        add(submitButton);
        add(closeButton);

        actionChoice.addItemListener(this);
        routingNumberChoice.addItemListener(this);
        submitButton.addActionListener(this);
        closeButton.addActionListener(this);

        disableCheckField();
        this.setEnabled(false);
    }
```

The getDate() method retrieves the current date in a displayable format to display the current date on screen:

```
String getDate () {
  Date date = new GregorianCalendar().getTime ();
  String time = new SimpleDateFormat("EEE, MMM dd, yyyy").format(date);
  return time;
}
```

The updateFields() method is invoked by the Login class with the customer's name, account number and their bank's routing number:

```
    synchronized void updateFields(String bank, String name,
                                   String account) {
      customerBankNumber = bank;
      customerAccountNumber = account;
      customerUserName = name;

      customerBankField.setText("Customer Bank: " + customerBankNumber);
      customerUserField.setText("Customer Name: " + customerUserName);
      customerAccountField.setText("Account Number: "
                                   + customerAccountNumber);
      dateFieldLabel.setText(getDate());
      this.setEnabled(true);
      invalidate();
    }
```

The start() method is called to retrieve initial information from the user and also initiate the Teller object to create its connections. When running as an applet, the browser invokes this method initially to start off the applet:

```
public void start () {
  getLoginInfo();
  teller.createConnections();
}
```

The `stop()` method actually makes the `teller` object close any open connections that it has and invokes the object's `closeConnections()` method. When running as an applet, the browser invokes this method to stop the applet:

```
public void stop () {
  teller.closeConnections();
}
```

The `TellerPanel` class implements the `ItemListener` interface and its `itemStateChanged()` method so that whenever the user changes the options between transferring funds, stopping payments, and browsing queues, the system responds by recording the choice made and disabling or enabling the appropriate fields:

```
public void itemStateChanged(ItemEvent itemEvent) {

  String choice = (String) itemEvent.getItem();
  if ((choice.equalsIgnoreCase(Constants.STOP_PAYMENT) == true)
        || (actionChoice.getSelectedItem()
            .equalsIgnoreCase(Constants.STOP_PAYMENT))) {
    enableCheckField();
  } else {
    disableCheckField();
  }
}
```

The `TellerPanel` class implements the `ActionListener` interface and its `actionPerformed()` method so that whenever the user clicks on the **Submit** button, the application responds by invoking the `teller` object's `execute()` method with the `instruction` object as a parameter populated with instructions given out by the user. Similarly, when the **Close Connections** button is pressed, the system closes all connections and exits the program. The call to `System.exit()` has no effect when running as an applet inside a browser:

```
public void actionPerformed(ActionEvent actionEvent) {

  Instruction instruction = null;

  if (actionEvent.getSource() == submitButton) {
    instruction = new Instruction();
    instruction.setCustomerBank(customerBankNumber);
    instruction.setAccountNumber(customerAccountNumber);
    instruction.setCustomerName(customerUserName);
    instruction.setDate(dateFieldLabel.getText());
    instruction.setCheckNumber(customerBankNumber + ":"
                        + customerAccountNumber + ":"
                        + checkNumberField.getText());
    instruction.setAction(actionChoice.getSelectedItem());
    instruction
      .setAmount((new Double(amountField.getText())).doubleValue());
    instruction.setPayeeName(nameField.getText());
```

```
        if (actionChoice.getSelectedItem()
                .equalsIgnoreCase(Constants.TRANSFER_FUNDS) == true) {
          instruction
            .setRoutingNumber(routingNumberChoice.getSelectedItem());
          instruction.setPayeeAccount(accountField.getText());
          checkNumberField
            .setText((new Long(++orderNumber)).toString());
        }
        instruction.print();
        teller.execute(instruction);
    }

    if (actionEvent.getSource() == closeButton) {
      stop();
      System.exit(0);
    }
}
```

Check numbers are automatically generated by the system instead of requiring the user to enter them when transferring funds. The `disableCheckField()` method is used to disable the check field so that the user does not edit the check values:

```
void disableCheckField () {
  routingLabel.setVisible(true);
  accountLabel.setVisible(true);
  routingNumberChoice.setVisible(true);
  accountField.setVisible(true);
  checkNumberField.setText((new Long(orderNumber)).toString());
  checkNumberField.setEnabled(false);
  invalidate();
}
```

While performing stop payment operations, the check number has to be keyed in to identify the check. Therefore we use the `enableCheckField()` method to enable this field:

```
void enableCheckField () {
  routingLabel.setVisible(false);
  accountLabel.setVisible(false);
  routingNumberChoice.setVisible(false);
  accountField.setVisible(false);
  checkNumberField.setEnabled(true);
  invalidate();
}
```

The `main()` method is used when trying to run `TellerPanel` as a standalone Java application:

```
public static void main(String[] args) {
  TellerPanel panel = new TellerPanel();
  panel.init();
  Frame frame = new Frame("Bank Teller");
  frame.add(panel, BorderLayout.CENTER);
  frame.setSize(250, 250);
```

```
      frame.setLocation(300, 200);
      frame.pack();
      frame.show();
      panel.start();
   }
}
```

The Login Class

The `TellerPanel` class for authorization and authentication uses the `Login` class. The `Login` class is also used to obtain information such as the client's name, the bank they're connecting to, their account number, and other such information and update the `TellerPanel` with it.

```java
package ptp.onlinebanking;

import java.awt.*;
import java.awt.event.*;

public class Login extends Frame implements ActionListener {

  TellerPanel parent;

  Choice routingNumberChoice;
  TextField accountField;
  TextField nameField;
  TextField passwordField;
  Button submitButton;

  public Login(TellerPanel panel) {

    super("Bank Teller Login Screen ...");
    parent = panel;

    Label bankLabel = new Label("Select Bank Number");
    Label accountLabel = new Label("Enter Account Number");
    Label customerLabel = new Label("Enter Customer User name");
    Label passwordLabel = new Label("Enter Password");

    routingNumberChoice = new Choice();
    routingNumberChoice.addItem(Constants.ECOMMWARE_BANK_NO);
    routingNumberChoice.addItem(Constants.HERITAGE_BANK_NO);
    routingNumberChoice.addItem(Constants.RAJ_BANK_NO);

    accountField = new TextField("C10003365");
    nameField = new TextField("athul");
    passwordField = new TextField("raj");
    passwordField.setEchoChar('*');

    submitButton = new Button("Submit");

    GridLayout layout = new GridLayout(0, 2, 10, 10);
    layout.setRows(5);
```

```
        this.setLayout(layout);
        add(bankLabel);
        add(routingNumberChoice);
        add(accountLabel);
        add(accountField);
        add(customerLabel);
        add(nameField);
        add(passwordLabel);
        add(passwordField);
        add(submitButton);

        submitButton.addActionListener(this);
    }

    public void actionPerformed(ActionEvent actionEvent) {

        if (actionEvent.getSource() == submitButton) {
```

Update the `TellerPanel` with the information obtained from the user through the login pop-up box:

```
        parent.updateFields(routingNumberChoice.getSelectedItem(),
                            nameField.getText(),
                            accountField.getText());
        setVisible(false);
        dispose();
        }
    }
}
```

The screenshot below shows the `Login` class while in execution:

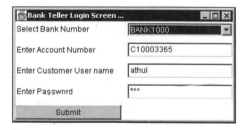

Using the Teller Module

Before doing anything else, make sure the FioranoMQ server (or other messaging server) is up and is ready to send and receive messages. Realize that if the server is not up, we may not be able to either send or receive messages. We can now compile all the files and run the teller module.

> For FioranoMQ users, the CLASSPATH should contain **fmprtl.zip**, and **jndi.jar**. These files can be found in the **%FMP_DIR%\lib** directory, where **%FMP_DIR%** refers to directory file path where you have installed your FioranoMQ Server.

The screenshot below shows the command prompt console while compiling and executing the teller module:

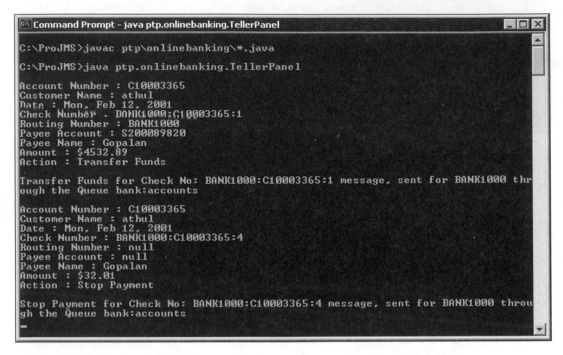

The login screen is the first GUI frame that appears as the teller panel is executed. You cannot do anything without clearing this screen. Therefore, enter any values in the boxes or use the defaults and press the Submit button.

As soon as the login screen is cleared, the teller panel frame will be enabled. You can change the values and click on the Submit button to perform the operation or click on the Close Connections button to close all open resources and exit the program.

The screenshot below shows the `TellerPanel` class while executing the teller module:

Exercise the **Transfer Funds** and the **Stop Payment** choices by entering different values for the different fields. While **Stop Payment** is selected, you will be able to change the check number, but this will be disabled at other times. All the operations you perform on the GUI can be seen executing by looking at the information printed on the console box.

However, please do not execute the **Browse Pending Requests** option as the sender will be blocked on the request call and the receiver, the accounts department module, is only developed in the next section.

The AccountsDepartment Class

The `AccountsDepartment` class is used to receive account information on the `bank:accounts` queue and send out instructions on either the `bank:clearing_house` queue, or any other temporary queue on which the requestor wants it to reply:

```
package ptp.onlinebanking;

import javax.jms.*;
import common.*;
import java.util.*;

public class AccountsDepartment {

  private String bankNumber;
  private QueueConnectionFactory factory;
  private QueueConnection connection;
  private Queue requestQueue, orderQueue;
  private QueueSession session, transactionalSession;
  private QueueReceiver receiver, queueReceiver;
  private QueueSender sender;

  private String hostName;
  private String userID;
  private String password;

  private DisplayHandler parent;

  static final String CONTEXT_FACTORY = Constants.FACTORY;
  static final String CONNECTION_FACTORY = Constants.QCF;
  static final String REQUEST_RECEIVER_QUEUE = Constants.ACCOUNTS_QUEUE;
  static final String ORDER_RECEIVER_QUEUE = Constants.CLEARING_QUEUE;
```

There are a couple of constructors for the `AccountsDepartment` class. One of them is the default constructor that does not take any parameters. The other constructor takes in multiple parameters. In these are the hostname or IP:Port of the remote running JMS server to connect to, and the username and password of a valid user for the JMS server:

```
public AccountsDepartment(String host, String ID, String passwd) {
  this.hostName = host;
  this.userID = ID;
  this.password = passwd;
}

private AccountsDepartment() {
  this.hostName = Constants.PROVIDER_URL;
  this.userID = Constants.USER_NAME;
  this.password = Constants.PASSWORD;
}
```

The `initialize()` method demonstrates how to connect to JMS messaging servers that run remotely. Typically, this is done by specifying the hostname or the IP:Port address combination on the JNDI server with the `PROVIDER_URL` property. The `JNDIService.init(CONTEXT_FACTORY, hostName)` method of our `common.JNDIService` class does this for us. If you want to examine the relevant code for the `JNDIService` class, go to Chapter 3 where it was first introduced:

```
public void initialize() {
  try {
    JNDIService.init(CONTEXT_FACTORY, hostName);
    factory = (QueueConnectionFactory) JNDIService
        .lookup(CONNECTION_FACTORY);
    requestQueue =
      (Queue) JNDIService.lookup(REQUEST_RECEIVER_QUEUE);
    orderQueue = (Queue) JNDIService.lookup(ORDER_RECEIVER_QUEUE);
  } catch (Exception e) {
    e.printStackTrace();
  }
}
```

The `createConnections()` method creates and starts connections and sessions.

Concurrent Delivery of Messages

JMS clients that require concurrent delivery of messages can use multiple sessions. This implies that each session's listener thread runs concurrently. In effect, while the listener on one session is executing, a listener on another session may also be executing concurrently.

In the following `createConnections()` method, a couple of sessions – `session` and `transactionalSession` – are created to illustrate concurrent delivery of messages. In this example, all the listeners created on both the sessions will run concurrently. Each of them may be receiving messages at the same time without affecting the operation of the other:

```
public void createConnections() {
  try {
    connection = factory.createQueueConnection();
    connection.setClientID(bankNumber);

    session =
      connection.createQueueSession(false, Session.AUTO_ACKNOWLEDGE);
    transactionalSession = connection.createQueueSession(true,
        Session.AUTO_ACKNOWLEDGE);
  } catch (Exception e) {
    e.printStackTrace();
  }
}
```

The `closeConnections()` method closes senders, receivers, sessions, and the connection, thus releasing all the resources:

```
public void closeConnections() {
  try {
```

```
            if (sender != null) {
              sender.close();
            }
            if (receiver != null) {
              receiver.close();
            }
            if (queueReceiver != null) {
              queueReceiver.close();
            }
            if (session != null) {
              session.close();
            }
            if (transactionalSession != null) {
              transactionalSession.close();
            }
            if (connection != null) {
              connection.close();
            }
        } catch (Exception e) {
          e.printStackTrace();
        }
    }
```

Message Selectors

While most messaging applications would prefer to get every message sent from a queue, it is possible to reduce the flow of irrelevant messages to a message receiver by using message filters. The JMS specification defines the syntax to allow a receiver to filter and categorize messages by the message header and properties based on specific criteria.

The syntax for creating this filter is based on a subset of the SQL-92 conditional expressions. This may imply that there is an underlying data store that uses SQL-92, but the JMS specification leaves the implementation to JMS vendors. Most vendors use a data store to implement PERSISTENT functionality for messages, while using a temporary cache to store NON_PERSISTENT messages, and it is therefore easy for the vendors to implement a query based retrieval of the messages based on the SQL-92 syntax.

As discussed in Chapter 3, these message filter statements set in the message selector only operate on the content found in the property fields of a message and not on the body of the message. The message receivers to a queue specify the filter criteria, and receivers can use some mechanism to discover what queue attributes are sent (in other words, the names of the properties).

Since the JMS server handles all this work, the application and its communication links are more efficient and consume less bandwidth. It is important to remember that these message selectors do not access the body of the message. They only operate on the content found in the property fields of a message. Also, when using message selectors in JMS, please be aware that although SQL supports arithmetic operations, JMS message selectors do not. Similarly, the JMS specification for message selectors does not support SQL comments either.

For example, the following selector may be placed on a report queue to pull out details of an employee:

```
designation LIKE 'CEO' AND yearlySalary > 10000
```

The fields that you see, like designation, and yearlySalary, are user-defined properties set in the message's property fields by the message sender.

169

The above message selector specifies that the receiver will only process messages that satisfy the following conditions:

❑ The designation attribute should be the string CEO

❑ The yearlySalary should be greater than 10000

As was mentioned earlier, the syntax of the message selector string is based on the SELECT statement of SQL-92 conditional expression syntax.

It is very simple to install a message selector to a queue receiver so that you can receive only the messages that you're looking for. Assuming that we have a valid reference to a queue session, a queue and a string that contains a SQL-92 based conditional expression, installing a message selector while creating the queue receiver is typically done as follows:

```
String messageSelector = "designation LIKE 'CEO' AND yearlySalary > 10000";
QueueReceiver receiver = session.createReceiver(queue, messageSelector);
```

It is also easy for the message sender to set the property fields of the message before sending it off as shown in the following code snippet:

```
TextMessage textMessage = session.createTextMessage();

textMessage.setStringProperty ("employeeName", "Athul S. Raj");
textMessage.setStringProperty ("employeeNumber", "E000000001");
textMessage.setStringProperty ("designation", "CEO");
textMessage.setIntProperty ("yearlySalary", 987654321);

sender.send(textMessage,
            DeliveryMode.PERSISTENT,
            Message.DEFAULT_PRIORITY,
            Message.DEFAULT_TIME_TO_LIVE);
```

The piece of code above illustrates how a message can be set up to hold a set of key-value pairs by the message sender. For example, while employeeName, employeeNumber, and designation are read in as strings, yearlySalary can be read in as an integer. The programmer can refer to these fields by their names such as employeeName, employeeNumber, etc. As the programmer is not required to explicitly format the message, this simplifies code development a lot. Also, the receiving program can access these fields randomly using the name of the appropriate field.

A message selector string can be composed of the following:

❑ **Literals**
    These can be strings or numeric or of Boolean type.

❑ **Identifiers**
    These can be message header field references, JMSX defined properties, JMS provider-specific properties, and application-specific property names.

❑ **Operators**
    These can be logical, comparison, or arithmetic operators.

❑ **Parenthesis**
    These control the evaluation of an expression and can be nested.

❑ **Expressions**
These can be selector, arithmetic, or conditional expressions.

❑ **Comparison tests**
These can be of type IN, LIKE, or null.

❑ **White space**
Horizontals tabs, form feeds, and line terminators are evaluated in the same way as in Java.

Please refer to the JMS specification documentation or Appendix B for more on this.

According to the JMS specification, JMS messaging server providers are required to verify the syntactic correctness of a message selector at the time that it is presented. If the selector presented were wrong a JMS InvalidSelectorException would be thrown.

In the following process() method, a message selector is installed while creating all the queue receivers. The message selector string is as follows:

```
"JMSCorrelationID = '"+ bankNumber +"'"
```

This ensures that these receivers will process only messages with the JMSCorrelationID corresponding to the bank with which the accounts department is associated.

The process() method calls the createConnections() method to establish connections, and then creates the receivers and message listeners for both the requestQueue (bank:accounts) and the orderQueue (bank:clearing_house). It also sets up an exception listener for the AccountsDepartment class:

```java
public void process() {
  try {
    createConnections();

    // Create a Message Selector
    String messageSelector = "JMSCorrelationID = '" + bankNumber + "'";

    // Create a Queue Receiver
    queueReceiver =
      transactionalSession.createReceiver(requestQueue, messageSelector);

    queueReceiver.setMessageListener(new RequestMessageListener(this,
            requestQueue, transactionalSession));

    receiver = transactionalSession.createReceiver(orderQueue,
            messageSelector);
    receiver.setMessageListener(new TransferFundsListener(this,
            orderQueue, transactionalSession));
    connection.setExceptionListener(new ExceptionHandler());
    connection.start();
    System.out.println("Bank No. :" + bankNumber
                        + " up and ready for eCommerce ...");
  } catch (Exception e) {
    e.printStackTrace();
  }
}
```

The `sendTransferFundsMessage()` method is used to send a bytes message containing a `TRANSFER_FUNDS` instruction over to the `bank:clearing_house` queue transactionally.

The figure below shows the `sendTransferFundsMessage()` method sending the `TRANSFER_FUNDS` instruction to the `bank:clearing_house` queue:

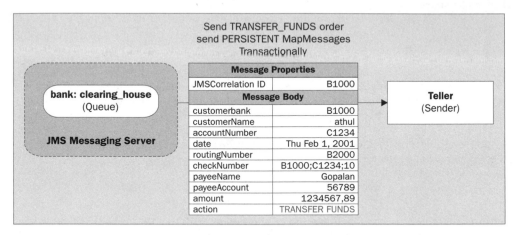

This method is invoked by the `RequestMessageListener` class's `onMessage()` method, which is installed as a message handler for messages arriving on the `bank:accounts` queue. We will be looking at the `RequestMessageListener` class later:

```
boolean sendTransferFundsMessage(Instruction instruction)
        throws Exception {
  boolean result = true;
  if (null == instruction) {
    return false;
  }
  try {

    // Create a Sender if one does not exist
    if (sender == null) {
      sender = transactionalSession.createSender(orderQueue);
    }

    // Create a Bytes Message
    BytesMessage bytesMessage =
      transactionalSession.createBytesMessage();

    // Set message properties
    bytesMessage.setStringProperty("customerBank",
                          instruction.getCustomerBank());
    bytesMessage.setStringProperty("accountNumber",
                          instruction.getAccountNumber());
    bytesMessage.setStringProperty("customerName",
                          instruction.getCustomerName());
    bytesMessage.setStringProperty("date", instruction.getDate());
    bytesMessage.setStringProperty("checkNumber",
                          instruction.getCheckNumber());
    bytesMessage.setStringProperty("payeeName",
```

```
                                    instruction.getPayeeName());
        bytesMessage.setDoubleProperty("amount",
                                    instruction.getAmount());
        bytesMessage.setStringProperty("action",
                                    instruction.getAction());
        bytesMessage.setStringProperty("routingNumber",
                                    instruction.getRoutingNumber());
        bytesMessage.setStringProperty("payeeAccount",
                                    instruction.getPayeeAccount());
        bytesMessage
          .setJMSCorrelationID(instruction.getRoutingNumber());

        // Send the message
        sender.send(bytesMessage, DeliveryMode.PERSISTENT,
                    Message.DEFAULT_PRIORITY,
                    Message.DEFAULT_TIME_TO_LIVE);

        String display = instruction.getAction() + " for Check No: "
                        + instruction.getCheckNumber()
                        + " message, sent for "
                        + instruction.getRoutingNumber()
                        + " through the Queue "
                        + orderQueue.getQueueName();
        System.out.println(display);
        parent.appendData(display);
    } catch (Exception e) {
        String display = instruction.getAction() + " for Check No: "
                        + instruction.getCheckNumber()
                        + " message, could not be sent for "
                        + instruction.getRoutingNumber();
        System.out.println(display);
        parent.appendData(display);
        e.printStackTrace();
        result = false;
        throw e;
    }
    return result;
}
```

Browsing Queue Messages

The QueueBrowser interface defines methods to help client programs browse messages in a queue
without destroying or removing them. This is achieved by retrieving a cursor in the queue at the current
location, forward or backward to the currently adjacent message. As queues are loaded and unloaded
very quickly, browsing is really useful in assessing queue sizes and rates of message growth in a queue.
While browsing queues using a queue browser, instead of retrieving actual data, an enumeration method
is used to return an integer count of the messages in the queue:

```
Vector browseQueueMessages(String accountNumber) {
    QueueBrowser browser = null;
    Enumeration enum = null;
    int count = 0;
    Instruction instruction = null;
    Vector browserList = new Vector();
    try {
```

```
        browser = session.createBrowser(orderQueue);
        enum = browser.getEnumeration();
        while (enum.hasMoreElements() == true) {
          System.out.println("Browser getting Message No. " + ++count);
          BytesMessage msg = (BytesMessage) enum.nextElement();
          if (msg != null) {
            instruction =
              new Instruction(msg.getStringProperty("customerBank"),
                              msg.getStringProperty("accountNumber"),
                              msg.getStringProperty("customerName"),
                              msg.getStringProperty("date"),
                              msg.getStringProperty("checkNumber"),
                              msg.getStringProperty("routingNumber"),
                              msg.getStringProperty("payeeAccount"),
                              msg.getStringProperty("payeeName"),
                              msg.getDoubleProperty("amount"),
                              msg.getStringProperty("action"));
            if (instruction.getCustomerBank().equals(bankNumber)
                  && instruction.getAccountNumber()
                    .equals(accountNumber)) {
              instruction.print();
              browserList.addElement(instruction);
            }
          }
        }
        if (browser != null) {
          browser.close();
        }
      } catch (Exception e) {
        e.printStackTrace();
      }
      return browserList;
    }
```

Other methods like `setRoutingNumber()` to set the bank associated with this `AccountsDepartment` class, `setParent()` to identify the creator of this object, and `appendData()` that's used to update information in the creator of this class are also defined in the following code snippet:

```
public void setRoutingNumber(String routingNumber) {
  bankNumber = routingNumber;
}

public void setParent(DisplayHandler applet) {
  parent = applet;
}

public void appendData(String data) {
  if (parent != null) {
    parent.appendData(data);
  }
}

public static void main(String[] args) {
  AccountsDepartment accounting = new AccountsDepartment();
```

```
        accounting.setRoutingNumber(args[0]);
        accounting.initialize();
        accounting.createConnections();
        accounting.process();
        System.out.println("Accounts Department of Bank " + args[0]
                            + " ... Ready to receive messages.");
    }
```

The ExceptionHandler Class

The `AccountsDepartment` class also sets an exception listener. Note that the exception listener is registered with the provider through the `connection` object by a call to its `setExceptionListener()` method:

```
    class ExceptionHandler implements ExceptionListener {

      public void onException(JMSException exception) {
        exception.printStackTrace();
      }
    }
  }
```

The RequestMessageListener Class

The `RequestMessageListener` class implements the `javax.jms.MessageListener` interface. This is the first requirement for any class aspiring to become an asynchronous message consumer. By implementing the `MessageListener` interface, the class is forced to provide an implementation for the `onMessage()` method. This method is the registered callback method that the provider invokes, when there is a new message available for consumption at the queue.

The `onMessage()` method contains the code for processing the message. Also note that the message listener is registered with the provider through the Receiver object as soon as it is created by a call to its `setMessageListener()` method using the following code snippet:

```
        queueReceiver = transactionalSession.createReceiver(requestQueue,
                                                    messageSelector);
        queueReceiver.setMessageListener(new RequestMessageListener(this,
                                         requestQueue, transactionalSession));
```

The `RequestMessageListener` class serves as the message handler for receiving messages from the `bank:accounts` queue. Also recall that since there is a message selector installed, only messages intended for this receiver will reach this receiver:

```
    package ptp.onlinebanking;

    import javax.jms.*;
    import java.util.*;

    class RequestMessageListener implements MessageListener {

      private QueueSender replier;
      AccountsDepartment parent;
```

```
Queue queue;
QueueSession transactionalSession;

public RequestMessageListener(AccountsDepartment accounting,
                              Queue requestQueue,
                              QueueSession queueSession) {
  this.parent = accounting;
  this.transactionalSession = queueSession;
  this.queue = requestQueue;
}
```

The onMessage() method of the RequestMessageListener class receives all messages intended for a particular bank (as specified in the message selector) from the bank:accounts queue. Depending on the message type of the action field in the instruction received, the accounts department either sends it off to the bank:clearing_house queue, or replies to the message.

The onMessage() method first checks to see if the message received is a stream message. If it is, it invokes the replyToRequest() method. It then checks to see if the message received is a map message. If that is the case, it invokes the processTransactionalMessage() method.

There is really no need to use multiple message types in this application. However they are included to demonstrate their usage:

```
public void onMessage(Message message) {
  try {
    if (message instanceof StreamMessage) {
      replyToRequest((StreamMessage) message);
    }
    if (message instanceof MapMessage) {
      processTransactionalMessage((MapMessage) message);
    }
  } catch (Exception e) {
    e.printStackTrace();
  }
}
```

The figure opposite shows the accounts department receiving a TRANSFER_FUNDS message and sending it off to the bank:clearing_house queue transactionally. Note that the receive and send operations are part of one transactional grouping:

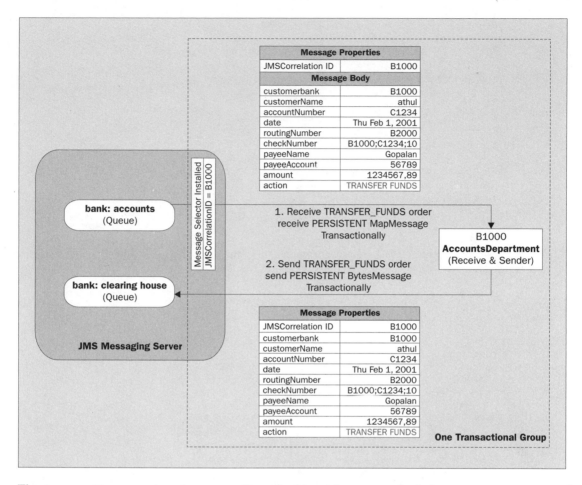

Message Properties	
JMSCorrelation ID	B1000
Message Body	
customerbank	B1000
customerName	athul
accountNumber	C1234
date	Thu Feb 1, 2001
routingNumber	B2000
checkNumber	B1000;C1234;10
payeeName	Gopalan
payeeAccount	56789
amount	1234567,89
action	TRANSFER FUNDS

1. Receive TRANSFER_FUNDS order
receive PERSISTENT MapMessage
Transactionally

2. Send TRANSFER_FUNDS order
send PERSISTENT BytesMessage
Transactionally

Message Selector Installed
JMSCorrelationID = B1000

bank: accounts
(Queue)

bank: clearing house
(Queue)

JMS Messaging Server

B1000
AccountsDepartment
(Receive & Sender)

Message Properties	
JMSCorrelation ID	B1000
customerbank	B1000
customerName	athul
accountNumber	C1234
date	Thu Feb 1, 2001
routingNumber	B2000
checkNumber	B1000;C1234;10
payeeName	Gopalan
payeeAccount	56789
amount	1234567,89
action	TRANSFER FUNDS

One Transactional Group

The `processTransactionalMessage()` method is used to process both the `TRANSFER_FUNDS` and the `STOP_PAYMENT` instructions. There are two options here. If the message contained a `STOP_PAYMENT` instruction, then the accounts department would process it by itself. On the other hand, if the message contained a `TRANSFER_FUNDS` instruction, the class would have to invoke its creator's `sendTransferFundsMessage()` method to send off the instruction to the `bank:clearing_house` queue. The `processTransactionalMessage()` method is also used to commit or rollback the transaction for the transactional group:

```
void processTransactionalMessage(MapMessage message)
      throws Exception {
  try {
    Instruction instruction = receiveNotification(message);
    if ((instruction != null)
          && (instruction.getAction()
            .equals(Constants.TRANSFER_FUNDS))) {

      // Send a message to Clearing house to execute this
      parent.sendTransferFundsMessage(instruction);
    }
```

```
            if ((instruction != null)
                    && (instruction.getAction()
                      .equals(Constants.STOP_PAYMENT))) {

                // It's a STOP_PAYMENT Notification. Process it here ...
            }

            // Commit the transaction
            transactionalSession.commit();
        } catch (Exception e) {

            // Rollback the transaction
            transactionalSession.rollback();
            e.printStackTrace();
        }
    }
```

The `receiveNotification()` method receives the map message and informs everyone concerned that a `TRANSFER_FUNDS` or `STOP_PAYMENT` instruction has arrived:

```
Instruction receiveNotification(MapMessage message)
        throws Exception {
  Instruction instruction = null;
  try {
    instruction =
      new Instruction(message.getString("customerBank"),
                      message.getString("accountNumber"),
                      message.getString("customerName"),
                      message.getString("date"),
                      message.getString("checkNumber"),
                      message.getString("routingNumber"),
                      message.getString("payeeAccount"),
                      message.getString("payeeName"),
                      message.getDouble("amount"),
                      message.getString("action"));

    String display = "Received " + instruction.getAction()
                    + " request for Check No. :"
                    + instruction.getCheckNumber() + " at bank "
                    + instruction.getCustomerBank() + " on "
                    + queue.getQueueName();
    parent.appendData(display);
    System.out.println(display);
  } catch (Exception e) {
    instruction = null;
    e.printStackTrace();
    throw e;
  }
  return instruction;
}
```

If the message received at the `onMessage()` method is a stream message, the message handler invokes the `replyToRequest()` method.

The figure below shows the `replyToRequest()` method replying on a temporary queue as a transactional group:

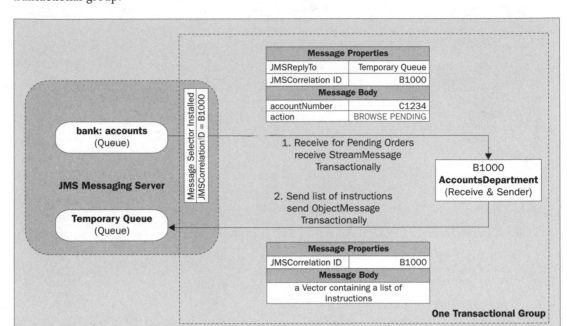

The `replyToRequest()` method informs everyone of the **Browse Pending Instructions** message, and then invokes its creator's `browseQueueMessages()` method and retrieves a list of pending messages from the `bank:clearing_house` queue. It creates an object message and populates its body with the `Vector` object obtained. It then creates a sender on the queue that it was supposed to use (based on the reference obtained from the `ReplyTo` property of the request message) and sends off the message on the specified queue. It then commits the transaction.

If something goes wrong in the process, the transaction is rolled-back and the system goes back to the state it was in before receiving the message. After everything is over, the sender object is closed and resources are released:

```
void replyToRequest(StreamMessage streamMessage)
        throws JMSException {
  try {
    StreamMessage request = (StreamMessage) streamMessage;
    String correlationID = request.getJMSCorrelationID();

    // When a message is received, inform everyone about it
    String display = "Re: Bank No. :" + correlationID;
    parent.appendData(display);
    System.out.println(display);

    // Retrieve a temporary Queue and send back a reply to
    // the message, so that the original requestor receives
    // the reply.
```

```
            Queue temporaryQueue = (Queue) streamMessage.getJMSReplyTo();
            ObjectMessage reply =
              transactionalSession.createObjectMessage();
            reply.setJMSCorrelationID(correlationID);
            String accountNo = streamMessage.readString();
            String command = streamMessage.readString();
            Vector list = null;
            if (command.equals(Constants.BROWSE_PENDING_REQUESTS)) {
              list = parent.browseQueueMessages(accountNo);
            }
            reply.setObject(list);

            if (replier == null) {
              replier = transactionalSession.createSender(queue);
            }

            // Send the reply to the temporary queue
            replier.send(temporaryQueue, reply);

            // commit the transaction
            transactionalSession.commit();
          } catch (Exception exception) {

            // rollback the transaction
            transactionalSession.rollback();
            exception.printStackTrace();
          }
          if (replier != null) {
            replier.close();
            replier = null;
          }
        }
      }
    }
```

The TransferFundsListener Class

The `TransferFundsListener` class implements the `MessageListener` interface and is the message listener installed for all messages received from the `bank:clearing_house` queue. This means that this handler handles all the `TRANSFER_FUNDS` messages transactionally.

The figure below shows the accounts department receiving `TRANSFER_FUNDS` messages transactionally:

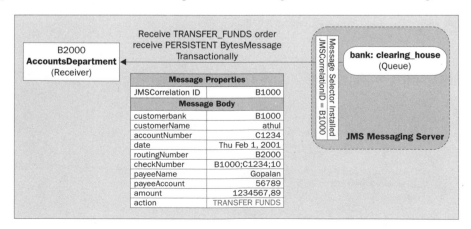

The onMessage() method invokes the receiveTransferFundsNotification() method, which in turn informs everyone of the TRANSFER_FUNDS instruction and processes it. This method also commits the transaction. If something were to go wrong in the processing, the transaction is rolled back and the system goes back to the state that it was before receiving the message:

```java
package ptp.onlinebanking;

import javax.jms.*;

class TransferFundsListener implements MessageListener {

  AccountsDepartment parent;
  Queue queue;
  QueueSession transactionalSession;

  public TransferFundsListener(AccountsDepartment accounting,
                               Queue orderQueue,
                               QueueSession queueSession) {
    this.parent = accounting;
    this.transactionalSession = queueSession;
    this.queue = orderQueue;
  }

  public void onMessage(Message message) {

    if (message instanceof BytesMessage) {
      try {
        receiveTransferFundsNotification((BytesMessage) message);
      } catch (Exception e) {
        e.printStackTrace();
      }
    }
  }

  void receiveTransferFundsNotification(BytesMessage msg)
          throws JMSException {
    try {
      Instruction instruction = null;
      instruction =
        new Instruction(msg.getStringProperty("customerBank"),
                        msg.getStringProperty("accountNumber"),
                        msg.getStringProperty("customerName"),
                        msg.getStringProperty("date"),
                        msg.getStringProperty("checkNumber"),
                        msg.getStringProperty("routingNumber"),
                        msg.getStringProperty("payeeAccount"),
                        msg.getStringProperty("payeeName"),
                        msg.getDoubleProperty("amount"),
                        msg.getStringProperty("action"));

      transactionalSession.commit();

      // Inform everyone about the transfer funds
      String display = "Received " + instruction.getAction()
```

```
                            + " request for Check No. :"
                            + instruction.getCheckNumber() + " from bank "
                            + instruction.getCustomerBank() + " on "
                            + queue.getQueueName();
        System.out.println(display);
        parent.appendData(display);

        // It's a Transfer Funds notification. Process it here ...
      } catch (Exception e) {
        transactionalSession.rollback();
        e.printStackTrace();
      }
    }
  }
}
```

The DisplayHandler Interface

Any class that needs to get notified of changes happening in the `AccountsDepartment` class
implements the `DisplayHandler` interface. The `appendData()` method is invoked by the
`AccountsDepartment` class whenever any changes need to be communicated:

```
package ptp.onlinebanking;

public interface DisplayHandler {
  public void appendData (String data);
}
```

The AccountingPanel Class

Now that we have the `AccountsDepartment` class ready, we need to write a GUI component that will
allow the user to interact with our system. The GUI component that we're going to write will be generic
enough that it could be used both as an applet and a standalone application.

Since `Applet` extends `Panel`, we create our `AccountingPanel` class to extend `Applet`. That way we
can use the same front-end component both as an applet and as a standalone Java application:

```
package ptp.onlinebanking;

import java.awt.*;
import java.awt.event.*;
import java.applet.*;

public class AccountingPanel extends Applet implements ItemListener,
        ActionListener, DisplayHandler {

  Choice routingNumberChoice;
  TextArea displayArea;
  Button quitButton;

  AccountsDepartment accounting;
```

The `init()` method is used to create a new instance of the `AccountsDepartment` class and also layout the GUI for our application:

```
public void init() {

    accounting = new AccountsDepartment(Constants.PROVIDER_URL,
                                        Constants.USER_NAME,
                                        Constants.PASSWORD);
    accounting.setParent(this);

    routingNumberChoice = new Choice();
    routingNumberChoice.addItem(Constants.ECOMMWARE_BANK_NO);
    routingNumberChoice.addItem(Constants.HERITAGE_BANK_NO);
    routingNumberChoice.addItem(Constants.RAJ_BANK_NO);

    displayArea = new TextArea(15, 50);
    displayArea.setEnabled(false);
    displayArea.setText("Before Proceeding, Set up the Receiver:\n"
                        + "Select a Bank from the Choice above ...");

    quitButton = new Button("Close Connections");

    this.setLayout(new BorderLayout());

    add(routingNumberChoice, BorderLayout.NORTH);
    add(displayArea, BorderLayout.CENTER);
    add(quitButton, BorderLayout.SOUTH);

    routingNumberChoice.addItemListener(this);
    quitButton.addActionListener(this);
}
```

The `appendData()` callback method is implemented so that the `AccountsDepartment` can invoke this method to inform the `AccountingPanel` of any changes:

```
public synchronized void appendData (String data) {
    displayArea.append(data + "\n\r");
}
```

The `AccountingPanel` class implements the `ItemListener` interface and its `itemStateChanged()` method so that whenever the user changes between different bank routing numbers, the system responds by recording the new choice and enabling the panel so that the application can be used:

```
public void itemStateChanged(ItemEvent itemEvent) {

    String choice = (String) itemEvent.getItem();
    accounting.setRoutingNumber(choice);
    accounting.initialize();
    accounting.createConnections();
    accounting.process();
    routingNumberChoice.setEnabled(false);
    displayArea.setText("");
}
```

The `AccountingPanel` class implements the `ActionListener` interface and its `actionPerformed()` method so that whenever the user clicks on the **Close Connections** button, the system closes all connections and exits the program. The call to `System.exit(0)` has no effect when running as an applet inside a browser:

```
public void actionPerformed(ActionEvent actionEvent) {

  if (actionEvent.getSource() == quitButton) {
    accounting.closeConnections();
    System.exit(0);
  }
}
```

The `main()` method is used when running an `accounting panel` as a standalone Java application:

```
public static void main(String[] args) {
  AccountingPanel panel = new AccountingPanel();
  panel.init();
  Frame frame = new Frame("Bank Accounting Department");
  frame.add(panel, BorderLayout.CENTER);
  frame.setSize(250, 250);
  frame.setLocation(300, 200);
  frame.pack();
  frame.show();
}
}
```

Using the Accounts Department Module

Before doing anything else, make sure the FioranoMQ server (or other messaging server) is up and is ready to send and receive messages. Realize that if the server is not up, we may not be able to either send or receive messages. We can now compile all the files and run the Teller module.

> For FioranoMQ users, the CLASSPATH should contain `fmprtl.zip`, and `jndi.jar`.
> These files can be found in the `%FMP_DIR%\lib` directory, where `%FMP_DIR%` refers to
> directory file path where you have installed your FioranoMQ Server.

The screenshot below shows the command prompt console while compiling and executing the accounts department module:

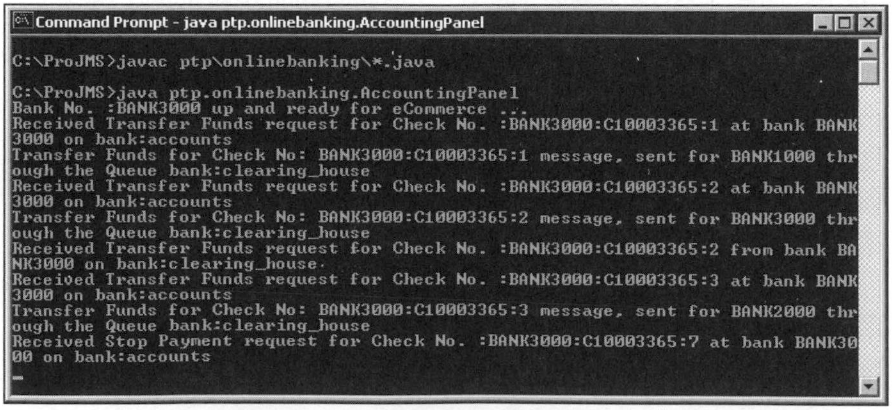

The screenshot below shows the `AccountingPanel` class while executing the accounts department module:

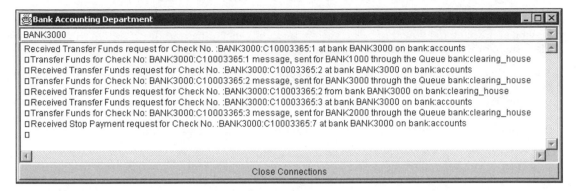

As soon as this frame comes up, select the bank that you want to connect to. If you do not make a choice, nothing will happen. Once the choice is made, the command prompt console will mention that the "**Bank is up and ready for eCommerce ...**". Now if you execute the `TellerPanel` class and log onto the same bank, you will be able to perform all the operations including `TRANSFER_FUNDS`, `STOP_PAYMENT`, and `BROWSE_PENDING_REQUESTS`. When you click on the **Close Connections** button, all open connections for the `AccountsDepartment` class will be closed and the module will terminate execution.

Applets

JMS client applets are written in exactly the same way as normal JMS client applications are written. Browser security restrictions allow unsigned applets to establish connections only with the machine from which the applet is downloaded, in other words, the web server machine. Unlike normal applications (which can connect to a JMS server running on any machine), unsigned applets are allowed to connect only to the machine from which the applet is downloaded.

However, signed applets are allowed to connect to any host to which the web client has authorized access by the certificate provider. The web client can set different levels of permissions for certificates from different certificate vendors and may sometimes deny an applet permission to execute. In such cases, a signed applet carrying a certificate automatically invokes a window on the web client, asking if the user is interested in granting the applet the requisite permissions to execute. Using the advanced security options of popular browsers such as Netscape and Internet Explorer, one can explicitly set security parameters for all certificate holders.

> *We are not going to look at how to develop signed applets as it is tangential to what we're trying to explain here.*

In this section we are going to embed an unsigned applet into a web browser and deploy it on a web server so that client applications can download the page from a web server and execute it from their web browser.

Running the TellerPanel Class as an Applet

Messaging brokers may provide a reduced run-time library for applet support. This run-time library may be architected to allow it to be plugged in by simply including it in the CLASSPATH variable on the file system, or the ARCHIVE tag in a web browser.

The run-time archive used for developing this applet contains all the classes representing FioranoMQ's implementation of JMS. This archive is 100% JMS 1.0.2 compliant. It includes implementation of all the Pub/Sub and PTP functionality. You can therefore modify these applets to work with any other 100% JMS 1.0.2 compliant vendor product. While doing so, make sure that you substitute fmprtl.zip (the client runtime of FioranoMQ) with the client runtime of your specific vendor.

The following listing is for a simple applet demonstrating the usage of JMS APIs from within an applet served from a web server. This applet sends the messages that the user keys in to the queue:

```
<HEAD>
 <BODY>
  <CENTER>
   <OBJECT
    classid="clsid:8AD9C840-044E-11D1-B3E9-00805F499D93"
    WIDTH = 400 HEIGHT = 310
    codebase="http://java.sun.com/products/plugin/1.3/jinstall-13-
win32.cab#Version=1,3,0,0">
    <PARAM NAME = CODE VALUE = "ptp.onlinebanking.TellerPanel.class">
    <PARAM NAME = CODEBASE VALUE = "../../" >
    <PARAM NAME = ARCHIVE VALUE = "fmprtl.zip,jndi.jar" >

    <PARAM NAME="type" VALUE="application/x-java-applet;version=1.3">
    <PARAM NAME="scriptable" VALUE="false">
   </OBJECT>
  </CENTER>
 </BODY>
</HEAD>
```

Before we execute the applet, let's start up a couple of account department modules so that we see everything working together and communicating through the JMS messaging server. The teller module embedded in the applet served out from a web server will be communicating with a couple of accounts department modules from Bank1000 and Bank2000 through the JMS messaging server as shown in the figure below:

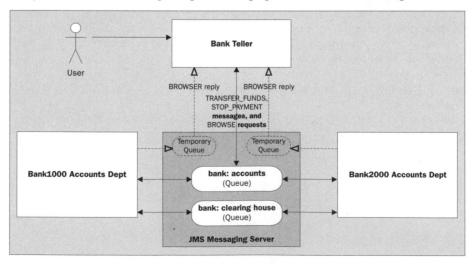

Before doing anything else, make sure the FioranoMQ server (or other messaging server) is up and is ready to send and receive messages. Realize that if the server is not up, we may not be able to either send or receive messages. We can now compile all the files and run the Teller module.

> For FioranoMQ users, the CLASSPATH should contain `fmprtl.zip`, and `jndi.jar`. These files can be found in the `%FMP_DIR%\lib` directory, where `%FMP_DIR%` refers to directory file path where you have installed your FioranoMQ Server.

Deploy the web page containing the `TellerPanel` applet on a web server. Now, start up a couple of accounting panel applications and the web server as shown below:

Once the accounting department panels are up, go to the first accounting panel, click on the Item Choice and select BANK1000. On the other accounting panel, click on the Item Choice and select BANK2000.

The screenshots below show the accounting panels for BANK1000 and BANK2000 running as stand-alone Java applications:

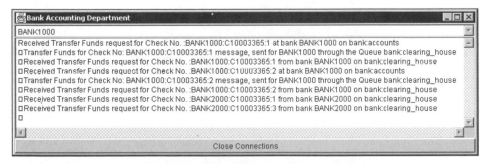

Now bring up the web browser and in its URL, enter the location of the web page containing the `TellerPanel` applet. In my case, it was http://localhost:8080/ptp/onlinebanking/OnlineBanking.html. Once the page comes up, clear the login screen by entering some information and connecting to either the BANK1000 or the BANK2000 accounting department and clicking the Submit button. Exercise all the options available.

The screenshot below shows the page served from a web server running the `TellerPanel` embedded as an applet:

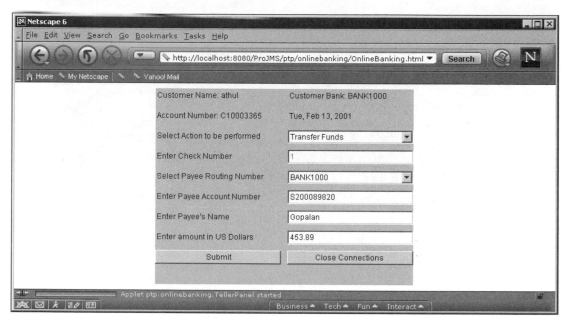

Summary

In this chapter we started off by looking at a general overview of PTP messaging before moving on to discuss message queues and queue management. In order to run the examples later in the chapter we installed our software environment and set up our connection factory, destinations, and users on FioranoMQ.

We then moved on to discuss transactions, noting that transactions are essential for distributed applications, and that transactions provide modular execution, which complements a component technology's modular programming. A series of incoming and outgoing messages can be grouped together into a transaction – a property that JMS can utilize in a number of different ways.

We had an overview of using transactional sessions and saw that you can use the `javax.jts.UserTransaction` class to achieve transactional work coordination between JMS and other transactional systems like EJBs. We then discussed distributed transactions and noted that providers are not required by the JMS specification to implement them. Providers who do want to implement distributed transactions in their servers can do so by using the JTS XA interfaces.

We then moved on to discuss an implementation of an online banking application in which we set up three common banking features – transferring funds from one account to another transactionally, stopping payment instructions from an account holder, and browsing pending instructions for a particular account holder.

While developing this application, we looked at:

- ❑ Providing for user identification, authorization, and remoting
- ❑ Releasing JMS resources
- ❑ Setting message priorities and message expiration
- ❑ Message delivery modes
- ❑ Simulating request/reply messaging in PTP
- ❑ The `JMSCorrelationID` and the `JMSReplyTo` message properties
- ❑ Setting up and using temporary queues
- ❑ Installing exception handlers
- ❑ Concurrent delivery of JMS messages
- ❑ Setting up message listeners
- ❑ Setting up message selectors
- ❑ Browsing queue messages
- ❑ Running JMS applications remotely as applets on a web browser

In the next chapter we will learn about the Publish/Subscribe messaging model by developing a retail stock brokerage application.

```
com.sun.jn...
com.sun.jn...
weblogic.jndi.T3Initial...
weblogic.jms.rtl.Fiorar...
weblogic.jms.runtime.na...
fiorano.jms.rtl.fscontext
com.sun.jndi.ldap.LdapCtxFactory
ch.softwired.jms.naming.RefFSContextFactory
com.sun.jndi.T3InitialContextFactory
fiorano.jms.rtl.WLInitialContextFactory
weblogic.jndi.FioranoInitialContextFactory
fiorano.jms.runtime.naming.FioranoInitialContextFactory
ch.softwired.jms.naming.IBusContextFactory
```

```
com.sun.jndi.fscontext.RefFSContextFactory
com.sun.jndi.ldap.LdapCtxFactory
weblogic.jndi.WLInitialContextFactory
fiorano.jms.rtl.FioranoInitialContextFactory
fiorano.jms.runtime.naming.FioranoInitialContextFactory
ch.softwired.jms.naming.IBusContextFactory
```

Publish/Subscribe Messaging

5

Publish/Subscribe (Pub/Sub) messaging in JMS is based on the concept of topics. The destination in the Pub/Sub domain model is the **topic** and message producers **publish** messages to a specified topic. Message consumers **subscribe** for messages from the topic and receive the messages from the topic when they become available.

Every topic can have multiple publishers (message producers) or subscribers (message consumers) and every message published is received by all the subscribers. Therefore, unlike the Point-to-Point (PTP) messaging model, multiple subscribers will receive the same message that was published to that topic.

These messages can either be persistent or non-persistent. If they are non-persistent, they are not stored in a persistent storage (like a database). This means, they may be lost if the messaging server were to crash. However, persistent messages are not even considered sent before they are stored in the persistent store. The JMS specification dictates that the messaging system guarantees to deliver a persistent message at least once.

What we'll learn in this chapter:

- ❏ We'll start off with a discussion on topics, including a look at Quality of Service in JMS applications.

- ❏ Then we'll move on to see how to set up our software environment to start coding Pub/Sub applications.

- ❏ After configuring our JMS server, we'll move on to developing a retail stock brokerage application, which provides ample opportunities for us to explore Pub/Sub messaging and transactions.

- ❏ While we develop our stock brokerage example, we will also learn about the key JMS Pub/Sub features.

Topics

Messaging server administrators explicitly create topics so that publishers and subscribers can exchange messages. The message producers in this domain model are called publishers and message consumers are referred to as subscribers. Publishers send messages to the topics for subscribers to consume.

The publisher declares the Quality of Service (QoS) while sending the message by setting the delivery mode, the time-to-live, and the message priority. The publisher also specifies whether a reply is requested from the subscriber. The messaging server records these items in its internal buffers, acknowledges receipt of the message to the publisher, and sends off the message to all the registered subscribers of the topic.

Quality of Service (QoS)

JMS supports two types of message delivery:

❑   Reliable message delivery

❑   Guaranteed message delivery

Each of these offers a different level of Quality of Service. The client application configures the type of message delivery when it publishes the message to its destination by specifying the delivery mode as a parameter.

Reliable Messaging

With this type of delivery mode (`DeliveryMode.NON_PERSISTENT`), the messaging server will deliver a message to its subscribing client as long as there are no application or network failures. Delivery would fail if some disruption were to occur. This is referred to as "At-Most-Once-Delivery". The default QoS level in JMS is reliable delivery.

Delivery of `NON_PERSISTENT` messages is attempted only once. If the client does not receive the message for any reason (either the server's internal buffer overflowed, or the client crashed, etc.), these `NON_PERSISTENT` messages are lost as shown in the figure below:

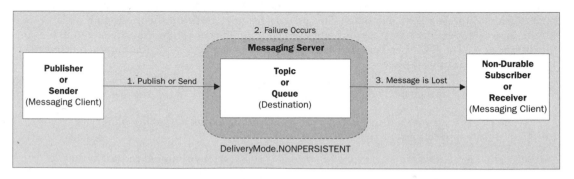

However, in the next scenario, assume that we have a message sent with `NON_PERSISTENT` delivery mode and a durable subscriber/receiver. In this situation, the scenario is as follows and is also represented diagrammatically in the figure below:

❑   The message producer sends or publishes a message to the destination.

❑   An acknowledgement for the message is sent back to the producer.

❑ The messaging server realizes that there are durable subscribers that have not received the message and stores the message in its internal store.

❑ A provider failure occurs – either the server's internal buffer overflowed, or the client crashed, etc.

❑ Since the delivery mode for the message was NON_PERSISTENT, even though there are durable consumers, the message is lost.

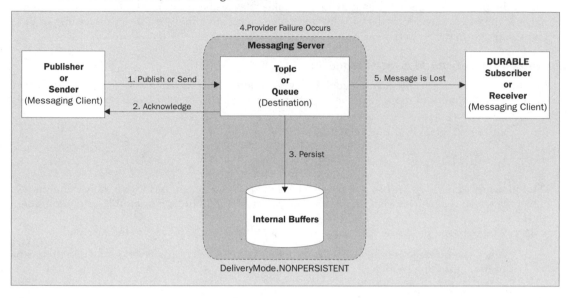

Guaranteed Messaging

With this type of delivery mode (DeliveryMode.PERSISTENT), the messaging server will deliver a message even if there are application or network failures. The messaging server will store the message in its persistent store and then forward the message to its subscribing clients. After the client processes the message, it sends an acknowledgement to the messaging server and verifies the receipt of the message as shown below:

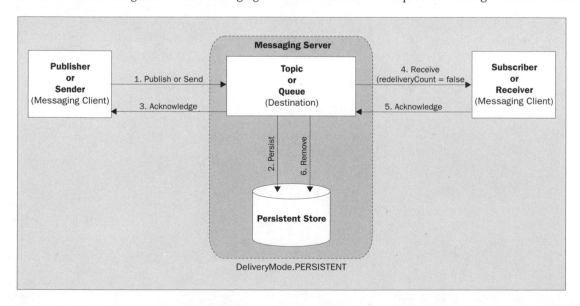

The messaging server will redeliver a message to each client that has not acknowledged receipt of the message. This is referred to as "Once-and-Only-Once-Delivery" since the messaging system ensures that all subscribers get the message just once.

However, if the server cannot deliver the message at all (in other words, the address is bad, the recipient is never awake, the recipent keeps erroring out whenever it tries to receive a message) the message is kept in the persistent store until the time-to-live value is exceeded. As soon as the time-to-live time is reached, the messaging server declares the guaranteed message undeliverable by discarding or deleting the message from the its persistent store.

Guaranteed Delivery for Message Producers

Producer clients can specify guaranteed delivery by sending messages to a topic or queue and specifying PERSISTENT delivery of messages. The code to produce PERSISTENT messages is reproduced below:

```
publisher.publish (bytesMessage,
                   DeliveryMode.PERSISTENT,
                   Message.DEFAULT_PRIORITY, 0);
```

The following scenario describes a situation where the message is sent out with a delivery mode of PERSISTENT, and a provider failure occurs. The consumers may be either durable or non-durable:

❑ The message producer sends or publishes a PERSISTENT message to the destination

❑ Since the message is sent with delivery mode PERSISTENT, it is saved in the persistent store of the messaging provider

❑ An acknowledgement is then sent back to the message producer

❑ At this time, something goes wrong and the server crashes

The figure below also represents this scenario diagrammatically:

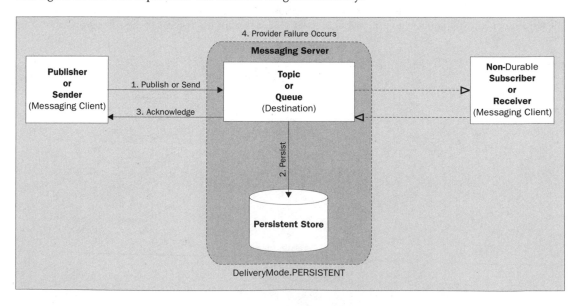

Since the message is declared PERSISTENT, as soon as the messaging server recovers, the delivery is re-attempted. The scenarios are described below:

❑ The messaging server recovers from the failure

❑ It recovers the message that was stored in the persistent store to try to deliver it to all consumers

❑ It sends out the message to all consumers

❑ The consumers respond with an acknowledgement to indicate successful receipt of the message

❑ The messaging server removes the message from its persistent store

The figure below also represents this scenario diagrammatically:

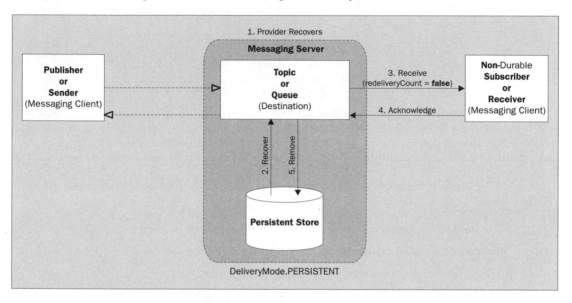

Guaranteed Delivery for Message Consumers

Consuming clients can specify guaranteed delivery by subscribing to a topic or receiving from a queue with a durable subscription. The code to subscribe durably to a destination is detailed below:

```
subscriber = session.createDurableSubscriber(topic,
                                "AccountsDepartment");
```

The following scenario describes a situation where a PERSISTENT message is sent out and a failure happens at a durable subscriber end:

❑ The message producer creates and publishes or sends a PERSISTENT message to the destination.

❑ At the destination, the message is stored in the persistent store.

❑ An acknowledgement for the message is then sent back to the producer.

❑ The server then tries to send the message to all its subscribers.

❑ While acknowledging the message the client durable subscriber crashes.

The scenario is also represented diagrammatically in the figure below:

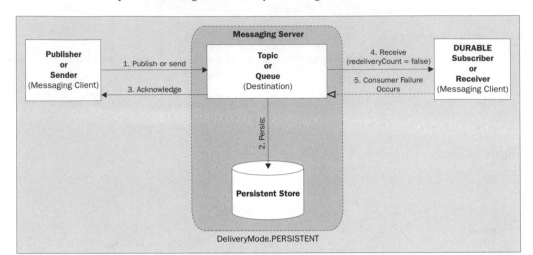

In this scenario, since the message was sent out with a delivery mode of PERSISTENT, the message is safely stored away in the persistent store and is not lost. Therefore, whenever the client comes up, and asks for messages to the destination, the PERSISTENT messages intended for that client can be recovered from the persistent store and sent back to it with the redeliveryCount set to True.

The following scenario describes how the message is redelivered to the durable subscriber in spite of the client failure:

❑   The durable messaging client recovers and asks delivery of messages.

❑   The messaging server retrieves the message from the persistent store.

❑   It redelivers the message with the redeliveryCount set to True.

❑   The subscriber then acknowledges receipt of the message.

The scenario is also represented diagrammatically in the figure below:

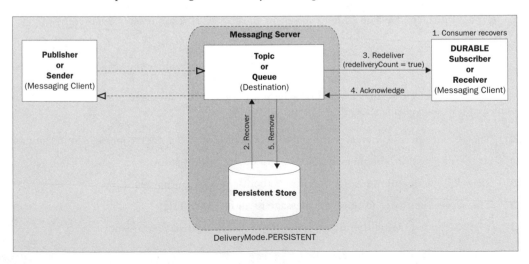

Therefore, if you want to ensure absolutely guaranteed delivery of your messages under all circumstances, your applications should always publish persistent messages with a time-to-live of forever (value of 0), and all your subscriptions should be durable.

Pub/Sub Semantics

The figure below shows message publishers publishing messages by sending them to topics and all the message subscribers who had registered to the topic for messages receiving them as soon as the publisher makes them available at the topic:

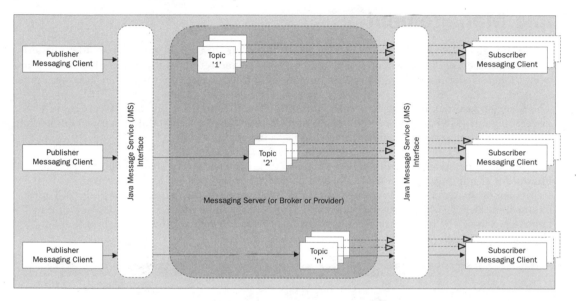

The figure above describes how Pub/Sub semantics work:

❑ Publishers publish messages to specific topics.

❑ The messaging server keeps track of all the messages, and all its current active and durable subscribers, and also provides a secure environment for the messaging system by handling authorization and authentication.

❑ As soon as messages are published on the topic, they are distributed to all its subscribers. Durable subscribers, who were not connected at the time of message delivery, can retrieve the messages if they come up within a specified time.

After the messages have been delivered, the messaging server checks to see if there are any durable subscribers (subscribers who specifically expressed a durable interest in the topic) subscribed to this topic. If, after the initial delivery, any of the durable subscribers did not acknowledge receipt of the message, the message is retained in the messaging server for the period of the expiration time, in the hope that the durable subscribers, if any, will connect to the messaging server and accept delivery of the message.

Every message has an **expiration time** that specifies the maximum amount of time that the Message object can live from the time of its publication in the topic. A message can also be set to live forever, but as soon as all current subscribers and all durable subscribers have received the message, it will be discarded or deleted.

All subscribers are supposed to have a message event listener that takes delivery of the message from the topic and delivers it to the messaging client application for further processing. Subscribers can also filter the messages that they receive by qualifying their subscriptions with a **message selector** as was discussed in Chapters 3 and 4.

Message selectors evaluate a message's headers and properties (not their bodies) with the provided filter expression strings. The expression strings are typically modeled after a SQL-92-based SELECT statement. If there is a match, the message is delivered to the subscriber, if not, the subscriber does not get the message.

Topic Management

As mentioned earlier, a topic has to be set up initially on the messaging server by an administrator before it can be used for any coding. Having downloaded and set up all the required software when we went though Chapter 4, we are now ready to jump into JMS development with Pub/Sub messaging.

The first step as usual, is to create a topic connection factory and the topic that we can use while developing our JMS code samples. Invoke your JMS messaging server's administrative console. Log on to your messaging server's administrative console as the administrator.

Create a topic connection factory called `retailbrokerage:tcf`. The figure below shows the FioranoMQ's administrative console. The Topic CFs tab shows that we have created the `retailbrokerage:tcf` topic connection factory on the messaging server successfully. A Topic Connection Factory object is now created and associated with the name `retailbrokerage:tcf` and is attached to the JNDI tree. This object can now be accessed by all the other messaging client applications through JNDI:

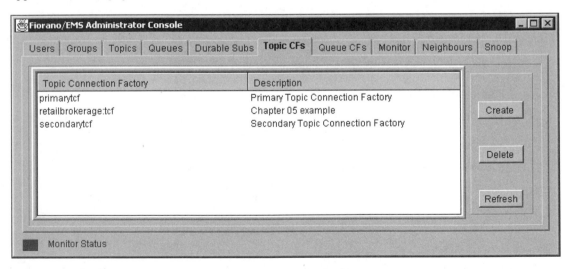

Create topics called `Consumer:Check`, `Equity:Trade`, and `Trade:Price`. The figure below shows the FioranoMQ's administrative console. The Topics tab shows that we have created topics called `Consumer:Check`, `Equity:Trade`, and `Trade:Price` on the messaging server successfully:

Topic Name	Description
consumer:check	This checks risk, compliance, and credit of the stock buyer
equity:trade	This is used to buy or sell stock
trade:price	This is used to inform accounting of the price paid to trade the stock

`Topic` objects are now created and associated with the names `Consumer:Check`, `Equity:Trade`, and `Trade:Price` and are hung off the JNDI tree. These objects can be accessed by all the other messaging client applications through JNDI:

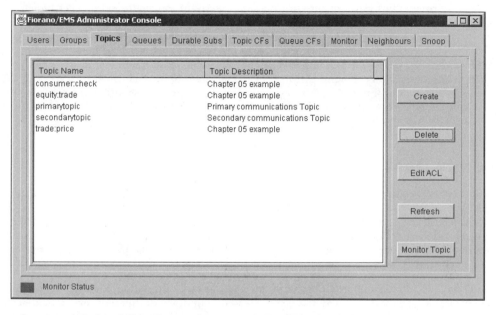

Create the users Athul and Gopalan, with passwords Raj. The figure below shows FioranoMQ's administrative console. The Users tab shows that we have created Athul and Gopalan as users on the messaging server successfully:

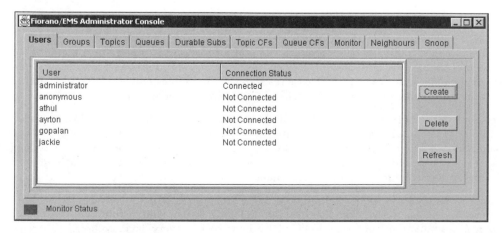

Physical Destinations

Physical destinations are provider-specific entities. Message-Orientated Middleware (MOM) vendors may identify a destination using terminology other than topic or queue. The terms topic and queue are used in JMS to represent destinations that are actually mere abstract representations of the physical destinations provided by the vendor. This is because a vendor may define different messaging behaviors for their product but also provide a JMS interface so as to allow JMS clients and users to interoperate with their MOM software.

One typical example is IBM's MQSeries product (see Appendix A for details). The destinations created by the system administrator through the provider's administrative tool are actually the only way to create these permanent physical queues or topics on the MOM messaging server. Permanent physical destinations are expensive and are usually associated with database tables or files.

> **The JMS 1.0.2 specification explicitly states that the physical creation of destinations (topics and queues) is an administrative task, and is not to be performed by JMS messaging clients. A portable JMS messaging client application should therefore obtain a reference to any administrated object (connection factories and destinations) using a JNDI lookup.**

Temporary Destinations

If you want to create a destination directly from a JMS client, you should use `javax.jms.TopicSession.createTemporaryTopic()` or `javax.jms.QueueSession.createTemporaryQueue()`. These temporary queues and topics have delete methods (`TemporaryTopic.delete()` or `TemporaryQueue.delete()`) and there is never a chance of creating a temporary queue or topic that already exists due to how they are specified. Temporary destinations are the only API defined by the JMS secification that can be created and deleted by JMS messaging clients in a portable fashion.

You don't have to rely on the provider to provide a temporary destination; you can define that on the JMS client-side application. These dynamically created temporary destinations are not expected to survive a sever failure. Dynamic destinations could be lightweight and reside in memory. Again, this depends on the provider's implementation. If you read between the lines of the JMS specification, temporary destinations can only be consumed by sessions of the same connection.

Use of createTopic() and createQueue()

While perusing the interfaces defined in the JMS API for sessions, it appears possible to use `javax.jms.TopicSession.createTopic()` or `javax.jms.QueueSession.createQueue()` to create physical destinations directly. Please realize that JMS defines only the interfaces, not the implementation. These methods are not for creating a physical topic or queue.

The current JMS API is specifically intended not to specify any administration APIs. It was assumed that different JMS providers would have different sets of administration requirements. The creation of a non-temporary queue or non-temporary topic was considered to be a feature provided by the JMS provider's administration facilities. But allowing creation of permanent destinations directly from a JMS client application is definitely not JMS-compliant.

This approach may work well in a small-scale environment, but definitely not in a large-scale enterprise environment. Danger looms when you blend the role of a system administrator with that of a user, for the same reason that you don't want to give DBA privileges to every database user.

Those objects created by `createTopic()` or `createQueue()` are just programming abstractions of the provider-specific destinations. The calls are intended to create identifiers to reference destinations that are maintained by the JMS provider. The physical destinations have to exist already before a JMS client can invoke the corresponding `createTopic()` or `createQueue()` methods.

The JMS 1.0.2 specification explicitly states that these methods are not expected to directly cause a destination to be created in a JMS provider. `createTopic()` and `createQueue()` are only factories to create a destination reference with a provider-specific name. If that destination doesn't already exist physically, the client will receive an `InvalidDestinationException` if it attempts to create a sender on that destination.

The Generic Programming Model

Every Pub/Sub messaging application follows a generic programming template to connect to a topic, publish or subscribe to messages from the topic, and to close the topic connections.

The basic Pub/Sub messaging client program development is as follows:

- ❑ Get (or create) a topic connection factory object.
- ❑ Get (or create) a topic.
- ❑ Use the topic connection factory object to create the Connection object.
- ❑ Use the topic connection object to create the Topic Session object.
- ❑ Decide whether to create a topic publisher or a topic subscriber object. Use the Topic Session and Topic objects to create the message producers (publishers) and message consumers (subscribers).
- ❑ Start the connection.
- ❑ Publish or subscribe to messages.
- ❑ Close the topic session and connection.

The figure below, details the steps that we just described:

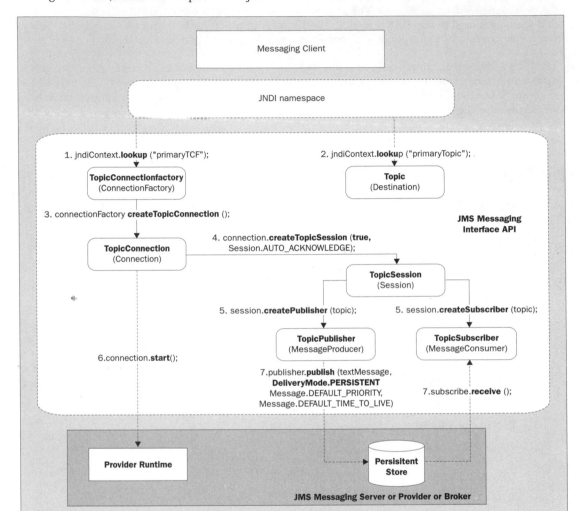

A glance at the figure above will show you how amazingly similar the PTP and the Pub/Sub programming models are. If you were to substitute all the occurrences of queue, sender, and receiver in the PTP API with topic, publisher, and subscriber respectively, you would get the equivalent Pub/Sub API.

Publish/Subscribe via Multicast

A message server is required in order to provide the full set of Pub/Sub functionality defined in the JMS specification. The ability to deliver messages after the publisher is no longer available, and the ability to support transactions and durable subscribers all imply that there must be some process other than that of the publisher and subscribers that stores the messages temporarily. A subset of the JMS Pub/Sub functionality, though, can be supported without a server through the use of IP multicast. The advantages to be gained in return for the sacrifice of functionality are performance, efficiency, and simplified administration.

Consider what happens when publishing stock prices to 100 subscribers over a single LAN segment via a unicast protocol such as TCP/IP. The Network Interface Card (NIC) of the computer of each subscriber "sees" the same message 100 times, but ignores 99 of them because they are addressed to other hosts. In contrast, multicast provides basic Pub/Sub semantics at the network level.

By definition, multicast packets are sent to a multicast address. Unlike unicast addresses, multicast addresses are not associated with a particular host. Any host can subscribe to a multicast address, and as such a multicast address corresponds to a JMS topic. When using multicast-based Pub/Sub, messages travel directly from publisher to subscriber and they must only be transmitted on the network once, no matter how many subscribers there are. This can make a tremendous difference in performance and scalability.

Raw IP multicast is not a reliable protocol, and in contrast to the unicast world, there is no ubiquitous reliable protocol like TCP that is already embedded in every network operating system. There are, however, commercial MOM products, such as Softwired's iBus//MessageBus and FioranoMQ Info Bus, that provide reliable, in-order message delivery over IP multicast via a subset of the JMS API.

The current generation of network routers support routing protocols for multicast packets. This means that, in theory, multicast network traffic could be routed over wide-area networks. In reality this raises concerns in the areas of security and efficiency. Multicast packets contain a time-to-live (not related to the time-to-live of a JMS message) value that is actually an integer that determines how may routers it is permitted to pass through on its way from publisher to subscriber. A large value for the time-to-live implies that publishers and subscribers that are intended to interact are spread over a wide area.

When using multicast over such a wide area, it is difficult to guarantee that publishers and subscribers find each other in an efficient manner. It is also more difficult to ensure that only intended parties have access to the messages being sent; remember that anyone can subscribe to a multicast address through a normal socket interface; it does not even require low-level network access. For these reasons, multicast-based messaging is usually only practical in local area networks and with low time-to-live values.

It is possible, and fairly common, to link together several local multicast LAN's via a unicast bridge. This requires a gateway in each LAN that is a JMS publisher and subscriber. It relays messages to the corresponding gateway of the remote LAN via a unicast connection, where the remote gateway re-publishes them to the same topics in the remote multicast provider.

When is it desirable to use a serverless, multicast-based JMS provider over a server-based one? In cases where it is supported on the underlying network infrastructure and when performance is more important than robustness to failure. The stock price example could be implemented using a multicast-based provider, and this would probably be a better choice for many trading environments. Timely price updates are often critical to traders, whereas if a critical machine fails, or is otherwise not available, the chance to be the first to react to new price information is probably lost anyway.

In contrast, a back-office system keeps the official records of the institution, and absolute reliability is more important that performance, so this type of system would tend to be designed around a transactional server-based provider if it uses JMS.

In general, it is probably advantageous to use multicast JMS when possible: in other words, when it is supported by the network and satisfies the system's design requirements. If a Pub/Sub-based system needs to support the following features, then a server-based JMS is required:

- ❏ Wide Area Network communications
- ❏ Communication through firewalls
- ❏ Secure communication via SSL
- ❏ Transactions
- ❏ Durable subscribers

The Retail Stock Brokerage Application

Let us now look at the different features available in Pub/Sub programming by implementing a real-world JMS application.

Before we start off please be aware that the intention here is to present as many JMS features as possible. This will demonstrate the array of options available to you when developing JMS applications and is not designed to allow you to build fancy applications immediately available for deployment. A lot of error checking has been removed to present relevant information and keep the discussions pertinent to JMS, so that we don't digress from the topic at hand. Similarly, there is really no need to use multiple message types in this application, but they have been included to demonstrate their usage.

Specification

The eCommWare Corporation (from Chapter 4) also provides retail stock brokerage services. Being a typical stock brokerage, they have to handle vast quantities of financial data and needs ten to thousands of instruments (anything of value used as a medium of exchange to buy or sell is an instrument.). This example illustrates event information traveling through the messaging server's event management system at a retail stock brokerage firm. The scenario assumes that the client has already connected to the net and has downloaded the sales order. The main tasks for this application are:

- ❑ **Event generation**
  A consumer discovers a hot technology and places an order with the account representative to buy a certain number of shares of stock.

- ❑ **Information gathering**
  The account representative completes a form in the sales order application.

- ❑ **Evaluating the event's context**
  The sales order application publishes a request-for-reply message on the `Consumer:Check` topic. This message is forwarded to all the clients that have active subscriptions to this topic. In this case, the active subscribers include the accounts department that checks the consumer's accounts and credit line to verify that the required funds are available to support the stock purchase. The accounts department has to reply to the request with an approval. Likewise, the compliance department has to approve the trade, and the risk management department also has to approve the trade. At this point, the business process can move to the next stage.

- ❑ **Notifying the organization**
  The sales order application handles the reply (the credit verification and trade approval) by sending a message to the `Equity:Trade` topic.

- ❑ **Executing the trade**
  The trading application on the exchange floor is the subscriber to the `Equity:Trade` topic. It executes the buy and publishes a message about the purchase to the `Trade:Price` topic.

- ❑ **Propagating information**
  The organization propagates information on the event and takes action for closure. Several applications now receive information on the `Trade:Price` topic. The client management application adjusts the customer's records in the database to reflect the purchase. The accounting application issues an invoice for the stock and logs a receivable. A payroll application adjusts the account representative's commission.

The figure below illustrates this stock brokerage system diagrammatically:

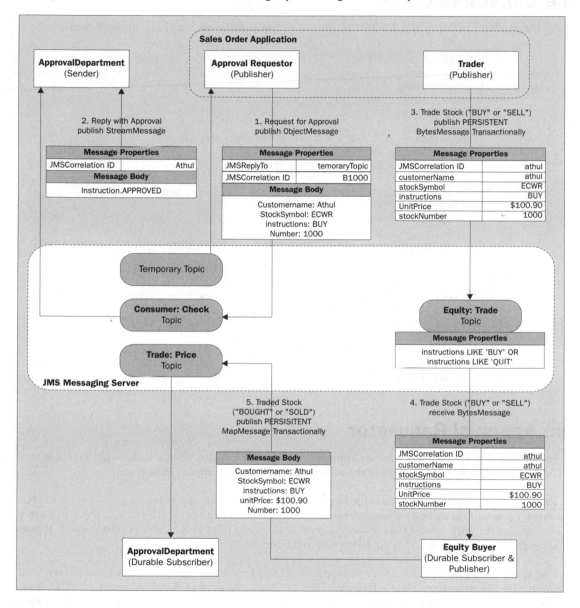

The Constants Class

All the modules in the system use the `Constants` class to retrieve `static` constant values:

```
package pubsub.retailbrokerage;

public class Constants {
    static final String PROVIDER_URL =
     "http://localhost:2001"; // For FioranoMQ version 4.6

    // "http://localhost:1856"; // For FioranoMQ version 5.0
    static final String USER_NAME = "athul";
    static final String PASSWORD = "raj";

    // The initialContextFactory class of the JMS Provider
    static final String FACTORY =
     "fiorano.jms.rtl.FioranoInitialContextFactory";    // FMQ 4.6

    // "fiorano.jms.runtime.naming.FioranoInitialContextFactory"; // FMQ 5.0

    static final String CONNECTION_FACTORY = "retailbrokerage:tcf";
    static final String PRICE_TOPIC = "trade:price";
    static final String CHECK_TOPIC = "consumer:check";
    static final String TRADE_TOPIC = "equity:trade";
    public final static String STOCK_BUY = "BUY";
    public final static String STOCK_SELL = "SELL";
    public final static int APPROVED = 0;
    public final static int REJECTED = 1;
    static final int HIGHEST_PRIORITY_MESSAGE = 9;
}
```

The Approval Requestor

The first step in the solution is for an approval requestor to publish a request-for-reply message on the `Consumer:Check` topic requesting the approval department to approve the trade.

The approval requestor creates a topic requestor and publishes an object message on it. This object message contains in its body a serializable object of class `Instruction`. The `Instruction` class contains all the values required for the approval department to approve or reject the request. It has appropriate get/set methods to access its data members.

The approval requestor also sets some properties of this object message. It creates a temporary topic and passes the temporary topic reference in the `JMSReplyTo` field of the object message. This is to ensure that when the approval department replies to the message, the reply will reach this temporary topic, which can then be deleted as soon as the approval requestor receives the approval message back from the approval department.

Similarly, the `JMSCorrelationID` property is also set for the object message. This field serves to identify the message in question and serves to act as the subject field. The approval requestor sets the `JMSCorrelationID` field with the customer's name. The approval department, while replying back to the request-for-reply message will set this field and send the message back as though it were the regarding subject field.

The reply message is a stream message object. The stream message has a body, which can contain an integer denoting either an `Instruction.APPROVED` value, in which case the trade is approved, or an `Instruction.REJECTED` in which case the permission to trade was denied.

The figure below shows the scenario that has just been described, where the approval requestor sends an object message to the `Consumer:Check` topic requesting permission to trade and gets a response back from the temporary topic with a stream message on whether permission to trade was approved or denied:

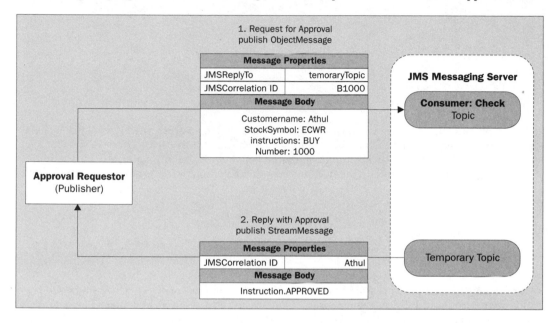

As soon as the approval requestor receives the approval message, the temporary topic is deleted and the integer value containing the permission is passed off to the caller.

The source code for the approval requestor is shown below:

```
package pubsub.retailbrokerage;

import javax.jms.*;
import javax.naming.*;
import common.*;

public class ApprovalRequestor {
    private TopicConnectionFactory connectionFactory;
    private TopicConnection connection;
    private Topic topic;
    private TopicSession session;
    private TopicRequestor requestor;
    private String hostName;
    private String userID;
    private String password;
    private static final String CONTEXT_FACTORY = Constants.FACTORY;
    private static final String CONNECTION_FACTORY =
                                    Constants.CONNECTION_FACTORY;
    private static final String PUBLISHER_TOPIC = Constants.CHECK_TOPIC;
```

The constructor of the `ApprovalRequestor` class takes in multiple parameters. In these are the hostname or IP:Port of the remote-running JMS server to connect to, and the username and password of a valid user for the JMS Server:

```
public ApprovalRequestor(String host, String user,
                      String passwd) throws NamingException {
   hostName = host;
   userID = user;
   password = passwd;

   createConnections();
   }

public void createConnections() throws NamingException {
   try {
```

Recall that we saw the `JNDIService` class in earlier chapters. To refresh your memory, it is a class that retrieves the topic connection factory and the topic. The host name is used to retrieve the Connection Factory object and the destination or topic reference. This way, if the messaging server is running on a remote host, it is possible to specify the host name so that a connection is established with the remote server machine:

```
JNDIService.init(CONTEXT_FACTORY, hostName);
     connectionFactory =
      (TopicConnectionFactory) JNDIService.lookup(CONNECTION_FACTORY);
     topic = (Topic) JNDIService.lookup(PUBLISHER_TOPIC);
```

The username and password are used to authenticate and authorize the user so that only valid users can create a connection to the JMS messaging server and unauthorized access is denied. The code below shows a topic connection being created with the user name and password:

```
connection = connectionFactory.createTopicConnection(userID,
          password);

     connection.setExceptionListener(new ExceptionHandler());
     connection.start();

     session = connection.createTopicSession(false,
                          Session.AUTO_ACKNOWLEDGE);
```

If no credentials are supplied while creating the connection, the JMS specification says that the current thread's credentials are used. However, if the password supplied does not match, the connection is rejected and this causes the provider runtime present on the client to throw a `javax.jms.JMSSecurityException`. Similarly, if the username sent in the login packet is not found in the repository, the messaging server will reject the connection, and cause the client runtime to throw a `javax.jms.JMSSecurityException`:

```
} catch (JMSException exception) {
       exception.printStackTrace();
   }
   }

public void closeConnections() {
```

```
        try {
            if (requestor != null) {
             requestor.close();
            }
            if (session != null) {
             session.close();
            }
            if (connection != null) {
             connection.close();
            }
        } catch (Exception exception) {
            exception.printStackTrace();
        }
    }
```

The method that sends a request-for-reply message stays blocked until it receives a reply, and returns the result:

```
public int getApproval(Instruction instruction) {
    int approval = Constants.REJECTED;

    try {
        // create a requestor object if one does not exist
        if (requestor == null) {
         requestor = new TopicRequestor(session, topic);
        }
        // create Object Message
        ObjectMessage  objectMessage = session.createObjectMessage();
```

A temporary topic is a temporary destination, created for the duration of a topic connection. A `Session` object is used to create a temporary topic:

```
        TemporaryTopic temporaryTopic = session.createTemporaryTopic();
```

Even though a `Session` object is used to create a temporary topic, their lifetime is that of the connection on which they were created.

The `ApprovalRequestor` class uses a temporary topic for receiving replies to its request. Therefore, it sets the temporary topic reference in the object message's `JMSReplyTo` field. This directs the replier to reply to the request on that destination:

```
    objectMessage.setJMSReplyTo(temporaryTopic);

        String name = instruction.getCustomerName();

        objectMessage.setJMSCorrelationID(name);
        objectMessage.setObject((java.io.Serializable) instruction);

        // receive a Stream Message
        StreamMessage streamMessage =
         (StreamMessage) requestor.request(objectMessage);
```

```
        // get the JMSCorrelationID property
        String correlationID = streamMessage.getJMSCorrelationID();

        // read the message body
        approval = streamMessage.readInt();

        if ((approval == Constants.APPROVED)
            && (correlationID.equalsIgnoreCase(name) == true)) {
          System.out.println("Received : Permission to Trade Equity for "
                      + name + " Granted ");
        } else {
          System.out.println("Received : Permission to Trade Equity for "
                      + name + " Denied.");
        }
```

A temporary topic is a unique type of object in that it is the only type of destination that can be created at the client side without requiring that the destination is first pre-created by an administrative tool. A unique feature of this is that its their own connection can be used to create a message consumer for it, which naturally means only sessions of the same connection can consume messages from it too. Each temporary topic is unique and cannot be copied.

It is very important to clean up resources as soon as they are no longer needed. This improves both scalability and efficiency of the application. As these temporary destinations consume resources outside the JVM, it is better to delete them as soon as they are no longer needed. However, the publisher, sessions, and connection are automatically closed and the garbage collector releases all resources when the program terminates:

```
    temporaryTopic.delete();
        } catch (Exception exception) {
            exception.printStackTrace();
        }

    return approval;
    }


    public static void main(String[] args) {
      int approval = Constants.REJECTED;

      if (args.length < 3) {
          System.out.println("\n\tUsage: java "
                      + "pubsub.retailbrokerage.ApprovalRequestor "
                      + "hostName userID password");
          System.out.println("\tExiting Program ...");
          System.exit(-1);
      }

      String hostName = args[0];
      String userID = args[1];
      String password = args[2];

      // create test data and populate the Instruction object
      Instruction instruction = null;
```

```
    instruction = new Instruction("Athul", "ECWR", Constants.STOCK_BUY,
                      100.90, 1000);

    try {

        // create ApprovalRequestor
        ApprovalRequestor requestor = null;

        requestor = new ApprovalRequestor(hostName, userID, password);

        // Request for approval
        approval = requestor.getApproval(instruction);
    } catch (NamingException exception) {
        exception.printStackTrace();
    } catch (Exception exception) {
        exception.printStackTrace();
    }
}
```

If a JMS provider detects a serious problem with a connection this method is invoked passing it a JMSException describing the problem:

```
class ExceptionHandler implements ExceptionListener {

    public void onException(JMSException exception) {
        exception.printStackTrace();
    }

}

}
```

The Instruction Class

While publishing messages to the Consumer:Check topic using an object message, we need to set the body of the object message with a serializable object. The type of information that needed to be encapsulated in this object involved all the relevant information needed to complete a stock trade. This included the customer name, the stock symbol, the instruction to buy or sell stock, the unit price of each stock, and the number of stocks to trade (buy or sell).

The Instruction class is serializable and contains all the relevant information to complete a stock trade. It has get/set methods to retrieve each of its data members. The source code for the Instruction class is listed below.

In the following piece of code, I have used floating point for currency (price). I realize that there are too many opportunities for errors, inaccuracy, and fraud if floating points are used in such cases. Masked decimal is far more accurate. However, since this is a demo, I'm sure you won't mind it:

```
package pubsub.retailbrokerage;

public class Instruction implements java.io.Serializable {
    private String customerName;
    private String stockSymbol;
    private String instruction;
```

```
    private double unitPrice;
    private int numberOfStocks;


    public Instruction() {
     customerName = "";
     stockSymbol = "";
     instruction = Constants.STOCK_BUY;
     unitPrice = 0;
     numberOfStocks = 0;
    }


    public Instruction(String customer, String symbol, String buyOrSell,
                double price, int number) {
     customerName = customer;
     stockSymbol = symbol;
     instruction = buyOrSell;
     unitPrice = price;
     numberOfStocks = number;
    }

    public String getCustomerName() {
     return customerName;
    }
    public String getStockSymbol() {
     return stockSymbol;
    }
    public String getInstructions() {
     return instruction;
    }
    public double getUnitPrice() {
     return unitPrice;
    }
    public int getStockNumber() {
     return numberOfStocks;
    }
    public void setCustomerName(String name) {
     customerName = name;
    }
    public void setStockSymbol(String symbol) {
     stockSymbol = symbol;
    }
    public void setInstructions(String buyOrSell) {
     instruction = buyOrSell;
    }
    public void setUnitPrice(double price) {
     unitPrice = price;
    }
    public void setStockNumber(int number) {
     numberOfStocks = number;
    }
}
```

The Instruction class is used wherever complete information about the stock trade is required in the program.

The Approval Department

The next step in the solution is for the approval department that subscribes to the `Consumer:Check` topic to evaluate the customer's credit, either approve or reject the trade, and inform the requestor about the decision.

The approval department subscribes for messages from the `Consumer:Check` topic, and installs an asynchronous message listener with an overloaded callback function that gets called by the server whenever a new message arrives from the topic.

When an object message is received from the `Consumer:Check` topic, the class retrieves the body from the message to evaluate the request. A stream message that has an integer indicating whether the trade is approved or not is placed in its message body. If the consumer name is "Suresh" and he wants to buy stock, a rejection is recorded in the body probably because he has bad credit, or because he has a criminal record. For all other requests, an approval is granted.

During this time, the `JMSReplyTo` field from the original object message is read and the temporary destination to send the message to is noted. Similarly, the `JMSCorrelationID` property is also noted to set the regarding field.

The stream message's `JMSCorrelationID` is set with the customer name and the body is populated with the approval information and the reply is sent off to the temporary topic.

The figure below shows the scenario that I just described, where the approval department receives an object message from the `Consumer:Check` topic requesting permission to trade. The `JMSReplyTo` field specifies the temporary topic where the `ApprovalDepartment` class has to publish the reply with an approval message (using a stream message):

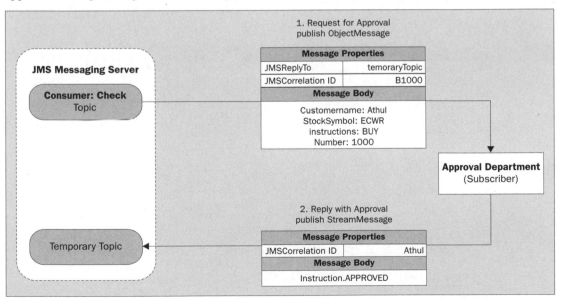

The `ApprovalDepartment` class installs itself as a message handler that receives messages asynchronously for the bound receiver. The `ApprovalDepartment` class implements the `MessageListener` JMS interface. This is the first requirement for any class aspiring to become an asynchronous message consumer.

By implementing the `MessageListener` interface, the class is forced to provide an implementation for the `onMessage()` method. This method is the registered callback method that the JMS server invokes, in case there is a new message available for consumption at the topic:

```
package pubsub.retailbrokerage;

import javax.jms.*;
import javax.naming.*;
import java.io.*;
import java.net *;
import java.util.*;
import common.*;

public class ApprovalDepartment implements MessageListener {
    private TopicConnectionFactory factory;
    private TopicConnection connection;
    private Topic topic;
    private TopicSession session;
    private TopicPublisher replier;
    private String hostName;
    private String userID;
    private String password;
    private ApprovalHandler caller;
    private static final String CONTEXT_FACTORY = Constants.FACTORY;
    private static final String CONNECTION_FACTORY =
     Constants.CONNECTION_FACTORY;
    private static final String SUBSCRIBER_TOPIC = Constants.CHECK_TOPIC;

    public ApprovalDepartment(String host, String ID, String passwd) {
     hostName = host;
     userID = ID;
     password = passwd;

     initialize();
    }

    public ApprovalDepartment(ApprovalHandler callbackImplementor) {
     caller = callbackImplementor;
     hostName = Constants.PROVIDER_URL;
     userID = Constants.USER_NAME;
     password = Constants.PASSWORD;

     initialize();
    }

    // Retrieve the connection factory and the topic references

    private void initialize() {
     try {
        JNDIService.init(CONTEXT_FACTORY, hostName);

        factory =
         (TopicConnectionFactory) JNDIService.lookup(CONNECTION_FACTORY);
        topic = (Topic) JNDIService.lookup(SUBSCRIBER_TOPIC);
     } catch (Exception exception) {
        exception.printStackTrace();
     }
    }
```

The approval department subscribes for messages from the Consumer:Check topic, and installs an asynchronous message listener with an overloaded callback function that gets called by the server whenever a new message arrives from the topic. Note that the message listener is registered with the provider through the Topic Subscriber object as soon as it is created by a call to its setMessageListener() method:

```
public void createConnections() {
    try {

        // Create and start a Topic connection
        connection = factory.createTopicConnection();

        connection.setClientID("ApprovalDepartment");

        // Create a Topic session on this connection
        session = connection.createTopicSession(false,
                          Session.AUTO_ACKNOWLEDGE);

        // Create a Topic Receiver
        TopicSubscriber topicSubscriber = session.createSubscriber(topic);

        // Install an asynchronous listener/callback on the Receiver object
        // just created
        topicSubscriber.setMessageListener(this);
        connection.start();
        System.out.println("Approval Department, up and ready for eCommerce");
    } catch (Exception exception) {
        exception.printStackTrace();
    }
}

// Close all open resources

public void closeConnections() {
  try {
      if (replier != null) {
       replier.close();
      }

      if (session != null) {
       session.close();
      }
      if (connection != null) {
       connection.close();
      }
  } catch (JMSException exception) {
      exception.printStackTrace();
  }
}
```

The `displayUsage()` method gives the user information on how to run the `ApprovalDepartment` class if they did not supply a hostname, a username or a password:

```java
private static void displayUsage() {
   System.out.println("\n\tUsage : java "
                   + "Chapter05.RetailBrokerage.ApprovalDepartment "
                   + "hostName UserName Password");
   System.out.println("\t Terminating Program ...");
   System.exit(-1);
 }

 public static void main(String[] args) {
   if (args.length < 3) {
       ApprovalDepartment.displayUsage();
       System.exit(1);
   }

   String hostName = args[0];
   String userID = args[1];
   String password = args[2];
   ApprovalDepartment approval = new ApprovalDepartment(hostName,
        userID, password);

   approval.createConnections();
 }
```

The `onMessage()` method contains the code for retrieving the properties and the object body:

```java
public void onMessage(Message objectMessage) {
   try {
       ObjectMessage request = (ObjectMessage) objectMessage;
       String correlationID = request.getJMSCorrelationID();

       System.out.print("Re: Customer " + correlationID);

       Instruction instruction = (Instruction) request.getObject();
```

When an application sends a message and expects to receive a message in return, request/reply messaging can be used. This is the standard synchronous object-messaging format. JMS does not explicitly support request-reply messaging, though it allows it in the context of the other two messaging models.

At the approval department end (the subscriber end), a non-transacted session is started on the connection so that messages can be sent to the topic `Consumer:Check`. A subscriber is then created and a message handler is also registered as a callback. When a message is received, the handler uses the `getJMSReplyTo()` method to find to whom to send back a reply. It then retrieves the temporary topic reference from the `JMSReplyTo` property and sends the message on the temporary topic:

```java
Topic temporaryTopic =
       (Topic) objectMessage.getJMSReplyTo();
      StreamMessage reply = session.createStreamMessage();

      reply.setJMSCorrelationID(correlationID);
```

If customer name is "Suresh" and he wants to buy stock, reject it:

```
if ((instruction.getCustomerName().equalsIgnoreCase("Suresh") == true)
        && (instruction.getInstructions().equalsIgnoreCase("BUY")
        == true)) {
    reply.writeInt(Constants.REJECTED);

    if (caller != null) {
```

Invoke the callback function to inform the approval requestor that the request has been denied:

```
caller.processInformation(Constants.REJECTED,
                          instruction);
    }

    System.out.println(". : Insufficient Funds. "
                    + "Sending a Rejection to the Requestor ...");
} else {
reply.writeInt(Constants.APPROVED);

    if (caller != null) {
```

Invoke the callback function to inform the approval requestor that the request has been approved:

```
caller.processInformation(Constants.APPROVED,
                          instruction);
    }

    System.out.println(". : Sending an Approval to the Requestor ...");
    }
```

If there is not a publisher, create one and send the reply to the temporary topic:

```
if (replier == null) {
        replier = session.createPublisher(topic);
    }

    replier.publish(temporaryTopic, reply);
} catch (Throwable exception) {
    exception.printStackTrace();
    }
    }

}
```

The ApprovalHandler Interface

Classes that need to implement a callback for the ApprovalDepartment class use the ApprovalHandler interface. The ApprovalHandler interface has a method called processInformation() that needs to be implemented by whichever class has to be called back when an approval or rejection is sent:

```
package pubsub.retailbrokerage;

public interface ApprovalHandler {

    public void processInformation(int approvedOrDenied,
                        Instruction information);
}
```

We will see more about this interface when we discuss an applet implementation of the retail stock brokerage application.

The Trader

Having received approval to trade from the approval department, the Trader class is used to publish stock trade instructions on what stocks to buy or sell for which customer on the Equity:Trade topic.

The Trader class creates a topic publisher and publishes a persistent bytes message transactionally. There is no particular reason for creating a bytes message here. The Trader class could create a message of any type as long as it is assured that the receiver is capable of handling and interpreting it. Once it creates the bytes message, it fills the message's property values. It sets the JMSCorrelationID property to the name of the customer. Similarly it creates user-defined message properties like customerName, stockSymbol, instructions, unitPrice, and stockNumber, before mapping them to their appropriate values.

There is a very important reason why the instructions are sent in the properties, rather than in the body. You might now be asking, if these instructions are sent as properties in the header, why were they not just header properties all along? Nothing prevents you from embedding the instructions as properties all the time. This is done to illustrate the multiple coding options at your disposal.

The overwhelming reason that the instructions are sent as properties is that the subscriber to the Equity:Trade topic filters messages that it subscribes to and is only interested in looking at certain types of messages.

As we saw in Chapter 4, message selectors do not examine the message body but they examine the message properties and headers to determine if they need to send a message to the subscriber or not. Therefore, the Trader class populates the bytes message properties with relevant information that can be used by the message selectors to filter the message.

Having populated the message property fields with the relevant information, the Trader class publishes the message on the Equity:Trade topic. It then commits the transaction by invoking commit(). The reason transactions are used while publishing messages is that if there were any failure, the system would be brought back to a stable state after the failure.

The bytes message that is sent out by the Trader class is also PERSISTENT. By making it so, the Trader ensures that if something bad happened and the intended receiver did not receive the message, the message would be resent.

The figure below shows the `Trader` class sending a `PERSISTENT` bytes message transactionally to the `Equity:Trade` topic:

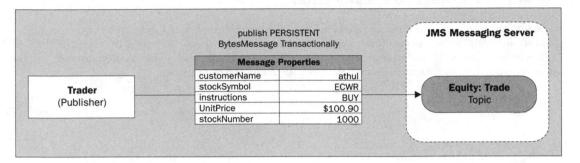

The source code for the `Trader` class is shown below:

```
package pubsub.retailbrokerage;

import javax.jms.*;
import javax.naming.*;
import common.*;

public class Trader {
    private TopicConnectionFactory factory;
    private TopicConnection connection;
    private Topic topic;
    private TopicSession session;
    private TopicPublisher publisher;
    private String hostName;
    private String userID;
    private String password;
    private static final String CONTEXT_FACTORY = Constants.FACTORY;
    private static final String CONNECTION_FACTORY =
     Constants.CONNECTION_FACTORY;
    private static final String PUBLISHER_TOPIC = Constants.TRADE_TOPIC;

    public Trader(String host, String user,
            String passwd) throws NamingException {
     hostName = host;
     userID = user;
     password = passwd;

     createConnections();
    }

    private void createConnections() {
     try {
         JNDIService.init(CONTEXT_FACTORY, hostName);

         // retrieve the connection factory object
         factory =
          (TopicConnectionFactory) JNDIService.lookup(CONNECTION_FACTORY);
         topic = (Topic) JNDIService.lookup(PUBLISHER_TOPIC);
         connection = factory.createTopicConnection(userID, password);

         connection.setExceptionListener(new ExceptionHandler());
```

When a session is created as transacted, unsurprisingly transactions are created. A transacted session is created by the first parameter passed in to the createTopicSession() method. A value of true for the first parameter makes this a transacted session.

The first message sent on a transacted session starts off a new transaction. All subsequent messages sent on that session then become part of this transaction, until a Session.commit() or a Session.rollback() call is invoked. After the call to commit or rollback the next message sent on the connection starts off a new transaction, whose scope continues until the next call to commit or rollback:

```
session = connection.createTopicSession(true,
                            Session.AUTO_ACKNOWLEDGE),

    connection.start();
    System.out.println("Trader, up and ready for eCommerce ...");
} catch (Exception exception) {
    exception.printStackTrace();
}
}

public void performTrade(Instruction instruction) throws Exception {
  try {

    // Create a Publisher if one does not exist
    if (publisher == null) {
     publisher = session.createPublisher(topic);
    }
```

The body of a bytes message contains a stream of uninterpreted bytes. Although nothing prevents us from adding properties to a bytes message, it is typically not done when there is a message body for fear that the inclusion of properties may affect the format of the content in the message body. However, since we are not passing anything in the body of the message, we can add anything we want to its property fields.

A bytes message is generally used for literally copying the body of one of the other four message types. Normal applications, however, use one of the other four message types to perform their operations, and use this message type to transfer raw data from a disk file to a different machine or location. This is a fairly common practice when messages are being reused.

The Trader class uses the bytes message to send information in its property fields that can be retrieved at the other end:

```
System.out.println("Performing Trade for "
                    + instruction.getCustomerName()
                    + " transactionally, Now ...");

    // create a Bytes Message
    BytesMessage bytesMessage = session.createBytesMessage();

    bytesMessage.setJMSCorrelationID(instruction.getCustomerName());

    // set message properties
    bytesMessage.setStringProperty("customerName",
                    instruction.getCustomerName());
    bytesMessage.setStringProperty("stockSymbol",
```

```
                                 instruction.getStockSymbol());
            bytesMessage.setStringProperty("instructions",
                                 instruction.getInstructions());
            bytesMessage.setDoubleProperty("unitPrice",
                                 instruction.getUnitPrice());
            bytesMessage.setIntProperty("stockNumber",
                                 instruction.getStockNumber());
```

In this example the message is said to be of the highest priority because the priority parameter is set to 9. This is a directive to the messaging system to expedite delivery of this message over other messages. If two or more messages are set to the highest priority, the provider's implementation decides which messages are delivered before the others:

```
            // publish the message
            publisher.publish(bytesMessage, DeliveryMode.PERSISTENT,
                        Constants.HIGHEST_PRIORITY_MESSAGE,    // value of 9
            Message.DEFAULT_TIME_TO_LIVE);

            // commit the transaction
            session.commit();
            System.out.println(instruction.getInstructions());
        } catch (Exception exception) {
            session.rollback();
            exception.printStackTrace();
        }
    }

public void closeConnections() {
    try {

        // send a message that I'm going away
        sendQuitMessage();

        if (publisher != null) {
         publisher.close();
        }
        if (session != null) {
         session.close();
        }
        if (connection != null) {
         connection.close();
        }
    } catch (Exception exception) {
        exception.printStackTrace();
    }
}
```

As soon as a `commit()` call is invoked, all the messages sent until that point are packaged into a transaction and are sent out to the server. However, if the transaction is rolled back, all produced messages until that point are destroyed, and all the consumed messages are automatically recovered. A commit or rollback call signifies the end of the current transaction and automatically starts off the next transaction.

In the following code sample, we have obtained a reference to a transacted Session object called `session` and we have created a Publisher object called `publisher`. The message `textMessage` is not sent off immediately as soon as the `publish()` method is invoked on the Publisher object. Instead however, they are buffered in an internal storage of the provider's client run-time library until either a `commit()` or a `rollback()` operation is invoked. If the client dies before committing or rolling back the transaction and the cache is dumped, the transaction fails, and the operation is retried the next time that the client comes up.

As such, `commit()` or a `rollback()` invocation signifies the end of the current transaction and all subsequent operations on the session automatically become part of the next transaction. In essence, a transacted session always has a current transaction within which its work is done:

```java
private void sendQuitMessage() {
    try {

        // create a Text Message
        TextMessage textMessage = session.createTextMessage();

        textMessage.setStringProperty("instructions", "QUIT");
        textMessage.setText("QUIT");

        // publish the message
        publisher.publish(textMessage, DeliveryMode.NON_PERSISTENT,
                Message.DEFAULT_PRIORITY,
                Message.DEFAULT_TIME_TO_LIVE);

        // commit the transaction
        session.commit();
    } catch (Exception exception) {
        exception.printStackTrace();
    }
}
```

The method `doAnother()` asks the user if they want to perform another trade and conveys their response back:

```java
public boolean doAnother() {
    String  another = "yes";
    boolean result = false;

    try {
        java.io.InputStreamReader in =
         new java.io.InputStreamReader(System.in);
        java.io.BufferedReader    stdin = new java.io.BufferedReader(in);

        System.out.print("\nWant to do another Trade? (\"yes\" or \"no\") : ");

        another = stdin.readLine().trim();

        if (another.toLowerCase().startsWith("y") == true) {
         result = true;
        }
    } catch (Exception exception) {
        exception.printStackTrace();
    }
```

```
      return result;
  }

  // Get input from the user regarding the trade (s)he wants to perform

  public Instruction getTradeInput() {

    // Read all standard input and send it as a message.
    String name = "Athul";
    String symbol = "ECWR";
    String direction = "BUY";
    double unitPrice = 100.90;
    String number = "1000";

    try {
        java.io.InputStreamReader in =
         new java.io.InputStreamReader(System.in);
        java.io.BufferedReader stdin = new java.io.BufferedReader(in);

        System.out.print("\nEnter Customer Name : ");

        name = stdin.readLine().trim();

        System.out.print("Enter Stock Symbol : ");

        symbol = stdin.readLine().trim();

        System.out.print("Enter Instruction (\"buy\" or \"sell\") : ");

        direction = stdin.readLine().trim();

        System.out.print("Enter number of stock to trade : ");

        number = stdin.readLine().trim();
    } catch (Exception exception) {
        exception.printStackTrace();
    }

    String command = Constants.STOCK_BUY;

    if (direction.toLowerCase().startsWith("s") == true) {
        command = Constants.STOCK_SELL;
    }

    int value = (new Integer(number)).intValue();
    Instruction instruction = new Instruction(name, symbol, command,
                            unitPrice, value);

    return instruction;
  }

  public static void main(String[] args) {
    if (args.length < 3) {
        displayUsage();
    }
```

```
        String hostName = args[0];
        String userID = args[1];
        String password = args[2];

        try {
            Trader trader = new Trader(hostName, userID, password);
            Instruction instruction = null;
            boolean doAnother = false;

            do {
             instruction = trader.getTradeInput();

             trader.performTrade(instruction);

             doAnother = trader.doAnother();
            } while (doAnother == true);

            trader.closeConnections();
        } catch (NamingException exception) {
            exception.printStackTrace();
        } catch (Exception exception) {
            exception.printStackTrace();
        }
    }
```

The `displayUsage()` method gives the user information on how to run the `Trader` class if they did not supply a hostname, a username, or a password:

```
private static void displayUsage() {
    System.out.println("\n\tUsage : java "
                + "Chapter05.RetailBrokerage.Trader "
                + "hostName UserName Password");
    System.out.println("\t Terminating Program ...");
    System.exit(-1);
}

// The class that implements the callback method

class ExceptionHandler implements ExceptionListener {

  public void onException(JMSException exception) {
      exception.printStackTrace();
  }

  }
}
```

The Sales Order Application

The sales order application gets input from the user, gets the approval to trade from the approval department and uses the trader to send out trade instructions on the `Equity:Trade` topic. In a real-world application, however, the sales order application would not directly post trade requests (for security reasons), but for simplicity, let's assume it does.

The steps that the sales order goes through before sending a message to the `Equity:Trade` topic with a directive to buy or sell stock are as follows:

- ❑ The approval requestor requests the approval department for permission to trade on the `Consumer:Check` topic.

- ❑ The approval department responds with an approval or a rejection.

- ❑ If an approval is obtained, the trader publishes the trade instruction on the `Equity:Trade` topic.

The figure below shows the scenarios that we just discussed:

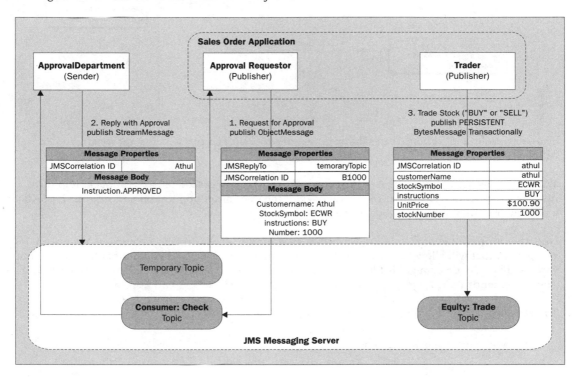

The sales order application gets input from the user, gets the approval to trade from the approval department through the `Consumer:Check` Topic, and uses the trader to send out trade instructions on the `Equity:Trade` topic.

The sales order application implements the `ApprovalHandler` interface. This interface contains a method called `processInformation()` that takes a couple of parameters – an integer that specifies whether the sale was approved or rejected, and an Instruction object containing the details of the trade. The sales order applet creates an implementation for the `processInformation()` method:

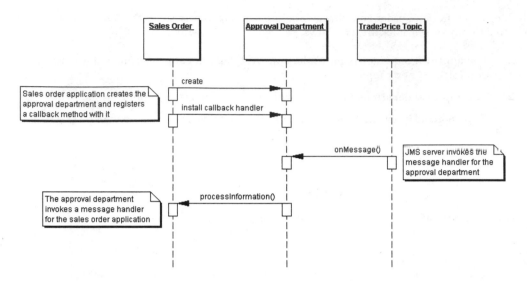

The sales order application creates the approval department and registers the approval handler callback with it.

When the messaging server invokes the approval department's onMessage() callback, it in turn invokes the processInformation() callback of the sales order application and informs it of whether a particular trade was approved or rejected.

Now that we have the ApprovalDepartment and Trader classes ready, we need to write a GUI component that will allow the user to interact with our system. The GUI component that we're going to write will be generic enough that it could be used both as an applet and a standalone application. Since Applet extends Panel, we create our AccountingPanel class to extend Applet.

The source code for the sales order panel is listed below:

```
package pubsub.retailbrokerage;

import java.applet.*;
import java.awt.*;
import java.awt.event.*;

public class SalesOrderPanel extends Applet implements ActionListener,
        ApprovalHandler {
    private TextField nameField;
    private TextField symbolField;
    private TextField numberField;
    private Button buyButton;
    private Button sellButton;
    private Label priceLabel;
    private Label nameLabel;
    private Label symbolLabel;
    private Label unitPriceLabel;
    private Label numberLabel;
    private Label instructionField;
    private Label approvalField;
    private ApprovalRequestor requester;
    private Trader trader;
```

The init() method is used to create a new instance of the SalesOrderPanel class and also layout the GUI for our application:

```
public void init() {
    addComponents();
    initialize();
}

public void stop() {
    if (requester != null) {
        requester.closeConnections();
    }

    if (trader != null) {
        trader.closeConnections();
    }
}

private void addComponents() {
    resize(450, 400);

    GridLayout layout = new GridLayout(0, 2, 10, 10);

    layout.setRows(10);
    this.setLayout(layout);

    nameField = new TextField("Athul");
    symbolField = new TextField("ECWR", 4);
    numberField = new TextField("1000");
    priceLabel = new Label("100.90");
    buyButton = new Button("BUY");
    sellButton = new Button("SELL");
    nameLabel = new Label("Enter the Customer's Name :");
    symbolLabel = new Label("Enter the Stock Symbol :");
    unitPriceLabel = new Label("Unit Price of Scrip (in USD) :");
    numberLabel = new Label("Enter Number of Scrips to trade :");
    instructionField = new Label(".");
    approvalField = new Label(".");

    add(nameLabel);
    add(nameField);
    add(symbolLabel);
    add(symbolField);
    add(numberLabel);
    add(numberField);
    add(unitPriceLabel);
    add(priceLabel);
    add(buyButton);
    add(sellButton);
    add(instructionField);
    add(approvalField);
    buyButton.addActionListener(this);
    sellButton.addActionListener(this);
}
```

```
private void initialize() {
 try {
     requester = new ApprovalRequestor(Constants.PROVIDER_URL,
                           Constants.USER_NAME,
                           Constants.PASSWORD);
     trader = new Trader(Constants.PROVIDER_URL, Constants.USER_NAME,
                 Constants.PASSWORD);
 } catch (Exception exception) {
     exception.printStackTrace();
 }
}

private void getValuesAndProceed(String command) {
 Instruction instruction = null;
 double price = new Double(priceLabel.getText()).doubleValue();
 int number = new Integer(numberField.getText()).intValue();

 instruction = new Instruction(nameField.getText(),
                   symbolField.getText(), command, price,
                   number);

 String data = command + " " + instruction.getStockNumber() + ": "
           + instruction.getStockSymbol() + " @ $"
           + instruction.getUnitPrice() + " -"
           + instruction.getCustomerName();

 instructionField.setText(data);
 instructionField.invalidate();
 System.out.println(data);
 invokeSalesOrder(instruction);
}
```

The `processInformation()` callback method is implemented so that the approval department can invoke this method to inform the sales order panel of any approvals:

```
public synchronized void processInformation(int approve,
                          Instruction instruction) {
  if (approve == Constants.APPROVED) {
      approvalField.setText("  *** APPROVED ***");

      try {

       // invoke Trader methods
       trader.performTrade(instruction);
      } catch (Exception exception) {
       exception.printStackTrace();
      }
  }    // end if APPROVED

  if (approve == Constants.REJECTED) {
      approvalField.setText("  *** REJECTED - No Funds. ***");
  }    // end if REJECTED

  invalidate();
}
```

```
    void invokeSalesOrder(Instruction instruction) {
     int approve = Constants.REJECTED;

     try {
         approve = requester.getApproval(instruction);

         processInformation(approve, instruction);
     } catch (Exception exception) {
         exception.printStackTrace();
     }
    }
```

The SalesOrderPanel class implements the ActionListener interface and its
actionPerformed() method so that whenever the user clicks on the buttons, the system responds:

```
public void actionPerformed(ActionEvent actionEvent) {
    if (actionEvent.getSource() == buyButton) {
        getValuesAndProceed("BUY");
    }

    if (actionEvent.getSource() == sellButton) {
        getValuesAndProceed("SELL");
    }
}
```

The call to System.exit() has no effect when running as an applet inside a browser:

```
    static class CloseAdapter extends WindowAdapter {
        Applet creator;

        public CloseAdapter(Applet parent) {
            creator = parent;
        }

        public void windowClosing(WindowEvent windowEvent) {
            creator.stop();
            System.exit(0);
        }

    }
```

The main() method is used when running sales order panel as a standalone Java application:

```
    public static void main(String[] args) {
        SalesOrderPanel panel = new SalesOrderPanel();

        panel.init();

        Frame frame = new Frame("Retail Brokerage Sales Order");

        frame.add(panel, BorderLayout.CENTER);
        frame.setSize(250, 250);
        frame.setLocation(300, 200);
        frame.pack();
        frame.show();
        frame.addWindowListener(new CloseAdapter(panel));
    }

}
```

Compiling and Running the Examples

Before doing anything else, make sure the JMS messaging server is up and is ready to send and receive messages. If the server is not up, we will not be able to either send or receive messages. The screen text below shows how to compile and run the sample.

Both the programs take the host address of the machine on which the JMS server is running, a valid registered username on the JMS messaging server and the password as their parameters. You can specify the address of your server host in the hostname parameter. If you are running the messaging server locally, you can specify localhost as the address or you can also specify an IP:Port combination like 127.0.0.1:2001. However, if this, or the other two input parameters, are missed out then an error message is printed:

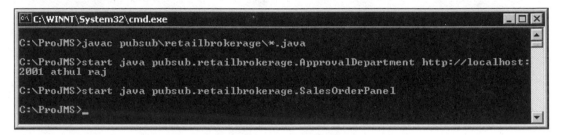

```
C:\ProJMS>javac pubsub\retailbrokerage\*.java

C:\ProJMS>start java pubsub.retailbrokerage.ApprovalDepartment http://localhost:
2001 athul raj

C:\ProJMS>start java pubsub.retailbrokerage.SalesOrderPanel

C:\ProJMS>_
```

The output of the sales order console looks like this:

The output of the approval department console looks like this:

```
Re: Customer Athul. : Sending an Approval to the Requestor ...
Re: Customer Gopalan. : Sending an Approval to the Requestor ...
Re: Customer Raj. : Sending an Approval to the Requestor ...
Re: Customer Suresh. : Insufficient Funds. Sending a Rejection to the Requestor
...
```

The Equity Buyer

The equity buyer subscribes to the Equity:Trade topic. It filters messages so that it only receives buy or quit messages from the topic. After performing the buy, it publishes that information on the Trade:Price topic transactionally.

The equity buyer acts as both a durable subscriber (in other words, it wants to get all messages posted to the topic – not just the ones that occurred while this client was active) for the Equity:Trade topic and a publisher for the Trade:Price topic. Therefore, even while starting off, it creates a couple of connections to each of the topics that it has to interact with.

It then creates a durable subscriber for the Equity:Trade topic giving it the name EquityBuyer and also installs a message selector on the subscriber. This message selector filters messages and delivers to these subscribers only messages with instructions that involve a buy instruction or a quit message.

When a valid message with the trade instruction arrives at the topic, the JMS server passes on the filtered message to the equity buyer's message handler. At that time, the handler distinguishes between a quit message (which is sent as a text message) and a trade instruction message, which is sent as a bytes message.

Once it reads the properties from the bytes message, it reconstructs the instruction, completes the trade and provides the information by publishing the buy information packaged as a map message on the Trade:Price topic. It sends out the map message on a transactional queue and calls the commit() method to force it to go out.

However, if it receives a quit message instead of a trade instruction, it releases all the resources, unsubscribes its durable subscription with the Equity:Trade topic and quits. Before closing its connections, a text message containing the string "QUIT" in its message body is created and published on the Trade:Price topic so that all durable subscribers that see the message will unsubscribe their durable subscriptions at that time.

The equity buyer will not receive sell messages as the equity buyer only processes buy or quit messages. It is not supposed to receive any sell messages, as it is only a buyer. This is the reason for installing a message filter that filters just the buy and quit messages.

The figure overleaf shows the equity buyer class durably subscribed to the Equity:Trade topic with a message selector installed and at the same time, acting as the publisher to the Trade:Price topic, sending out transactional messages:

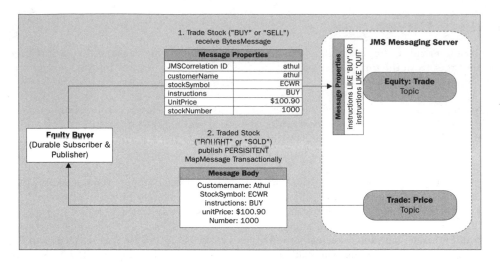

The source code for the EquityBuyer class is listed below:

```
package pubsub.retailbrokerage;

import javax.jms.*;
import javax.naming.*;
import common.*;

public class EquityBuyer implements MessageListener {
    private TopicConnectionFactory factory;
    private TopicConnection publisherConnection;
    private TopicConnection subscriberConnection;
    private Topic topic;
    private TopicSession publisherSession;
    private TopicSession subscriberSession;
    private TopicPublisher publisher;
    private TopicSubscriber subscriber;
    private String hostName;
    private String userID;
    private String password;
    private static final String CONTEXT_FACTORY = Constants.FACTORY;
    private static final String CONNECTION_FACTORY =
     Constants.CONNECTION_FACTORY;
    private static final String SUBSCRIBER_TOPIC = Constants.TRADE_TOPIC;
    private static final String PUBLISHER_TOPIC = Constants.PRICE_TOPIC;

    public EquityBuyer(String host, String user,
                String passwd) throws NamingException {
      hostName = host;
      userID = user;
      password = passwd;

      JNDIService.init(CONTEXT_FACTORY, hostName);

      factory =
          (TopicConnectionFactory) JNDIService.lookup(CONNECTION_FACTORY);

      createConnections();
    }
```

JMS clients that require concurrent delivery of messages can use multiple sessions. This implies that each session's listener thread runs concurrently. In effect, while the listener on one session is executing, a listener on another session may also be executing concurrently:

```java
private void createConnections() {
    try {

        // create and start a topic connection
        subscriberConnection = factory.createTopicConnection();

        subscriberConnection.setClientID(userID);

        // create topic session on the connection just created
        subscriberSession = subscriberConnection.createTopicSession(false,
            Session.AUTO_ACKNOWLEDGE);

        // create and start a topic connection
        publisherConnection = factory.createTopicConnection();

        publisherConnection.setClientID(userID);

        publisherSession = publisherConnection.createTopicSession(true,
            Session.AUTO_ACKNOWLEDGE);

        publisherConnection.start();
        System.out.println("Equity Buyer, up and Ready for eCommerce ...");
    } catch (JMSException exception) {
        exception.printStackTrace();
    }
}

public void closeConnections() {
 try {
    sendQuitMessage();

    if (publisher != null) {
     publisher.close();
    }
    if (subscriber != null) {
     subscriber.close();
    }
    if (publisherSession != null) {
     publisherSession.close();
    }
```

An `unsubscribe()` method is used by the topic session for deleting a durable subscription created by its clients. This deletes the state being maintained on the messaging server on behalf of the subscriber. It is wrong for a client to delete a durable subscription when it has an active topic subscriber for it or while a message received as part of the transaction has not yet been acknowledged:

```java
    if (subscriberSession != null) {
     subscriberSession.unsubscribe("EquityBuyer");
     subscriberSession.close();
    }
    if (subscriberConnection != null) {
     subscriberConnection.close();
    }
    if (publisherConnection != null) {
     publisherConnection.close();
```

```
            }
        } catch (Exception exception) {
            exception.printStackTrace();
        }
    }
```

A text message with QUIT in the body is created and published to the topic to inform all subscribers that the publisher is going away:

```
private void sendQuitMessage() {
    try {

        // create a Bytes Message
        TextMessage textMessage = publisherSession.createTextMessage();

        textMessage.setText("QUIT");

        // publish the message
        publisher.publish(textMessage, DeliveryMode.NON_PERSISTENT,
                    Message.DEFAULT_PRIORITY,
                    Message.DEFAULT_TIME_TO_LIVE);

        // commit the transaction
        publisherSession.commit();
    } catch (Exception exception) {
        exception.printStackTrace();
    }
}
```

Install a durable subscriber with a message filter. Install a message handler and start the connection:

```
public void buyEquities() {
    try {
        topic = (Topic) JNDIService.lookup(SUBSCRIBER_TOPIC);

        // Only select those messages which have the following properties
        String selector =
         "instructions LIKE 'BUY' OR instructions LIKE 'QUIT'";
```

If you want to ensure absolutely guaranteed delivery of your messages under all circumstances, your messaging clients should always publish persistent messages and all your subscriptions should be durable.

Messaging clients should specify a unique name for each durable subscription that they create. The code to create a durable subscriber is reproduced below:

```
        // create a Durable Subscriber on the topic session
        // create the durable subscriber with a given name
        subscriber = subscriberSession.createDurableSubscriber(topic,
                "EquityBuyer", selector, false);

        // install an asynchronous listener/callback on
        // the subscriber object just created
        subscriber.setMessageListener(this);
        subscriberConnection.start();
```

```
        } catch (JMSException exception) {
            exception.printStackTrace();
        } catch (NamingException exception) {
            exception.printStackTrace();
        }
    }

    public static void main(String[] args) {
        if (args.length < 3) {
            displayUsage();
        }

        String hostName = args[0];
        String userID = args[1];
        String password = args[2];
        EquityBuyer buyer = null;

        try {
            buyer = new EquityBuyer(hostName, userID, password);

            buyer.buyEquities();
        } catch (Exception exception) {
            exception.printStackTrace();
        }
    }

    private static void displayUsage() {
        System.out.println("\n\tUsage : java "
                    + "Chapter05.RetailBrokerage.EquityBuyer "
                    + "hostName UserName Password");
        System.out.println("\t Terminating Program ...");
        System.exit(-1);
    }
```

The following function is called by the message handler. It publishes information on the topic informing all subscribers of a buy:

```
    public void informEveryone(Instruction information) {
        try {
            topic = (Topic) JNDIService.lookup(PUBLISHER_TOPIC);

            System.out.println("Creating Topic Publisher");

            // Create a Publisher for this Topic
            publisher = publisherSession.createPublisher(topic);

            // Create a text message for use in the while loop
            MapMessage mapMessage = publisherSession.createMapMessage();

            // Set and Publish the message
            mapMessage.setString("customerName",
                        information.getCustomerName());
            mapMessage.setString("stockSymbol", information.getStockSymbol());
            mapMessage.setString("instructions",
                        information.getInstructions());
```

```
            mapMessage.setDouble("unitPrice", information.getUnitPrice());
            mapMessage.setInt("stockNumber", information.getStockNumber());
            publisher.publish(mapMessage, DeliveryMode.PERSISTENT,
                        Message.DEFAULT_PRIORITY,
                        Message.DEFAULT_TIME_TO_LIVE);
        publisherSession.commit();
    } catch (JMSException exception) {
        exception.printStackTrace();
    } catch (NamingException exception) {
        exception.printStackTrace();
    }
}
```

Here is the message listener that receives messages asynchronously for the bound receiver:

```
public void onMessage(Message message) {
    try {

        // When a message is received, print it out to
        // standard output
        if (message instanceof TextMessage) {
         TextMessage textMessage = (TextMessage) message;
         String stringData = textMessage.getText();

         System.out.println(stringData + " instruction received ...");

         // If "QUIT" instruction received, close everything
         if (stringData.equalsIgnoreCase("quit") == true) {
             closeConnections();
         }
        }

        if (message instanceof BytesMessage) {
         BytesMessage msg = (BytesMessage) message;
         Instruction  instruction = null;

         instruction =
             new Instruction(msg.getStringProperty("customerName"),
                        msg.getStringProperty("stockSymbol"),
                        msg.getStringProperty("instructions"),
                        msg.getDoubleProperty("unitPrice"),
                        msg.getIntProperty("stockNumber"));

         String information = "Bought " + instruction.getStockNumber()
                        + " shares of "
                        + instruction.getStockSymbol()
                        + " at a Price of "
                        + instruction.getUnitPrice()
                        + " in the name of "
                        + instruction.getCustomerName();

         System.out.println(information);

         // pass the information of the "BUY" to all Subscribers
         informEveryone(instruction);
        }
    } catch (JMSException exception) {
        exception.printStackTrace();
    }
}
```

The Accounts Department

The accounts department subscribes durably to the `Trade:Price` topic and receives notification of stocks traded by the trading department.

The `AccountsDepartment` class subscribes durably to the `Trade:Price` topic with the name `AccountsDepartment`. It then installs an asynchronous message handler on this subscriber.

When a message is received on the topic, the server invokes the message handler's callback function with the message passed in. If the message was a map message, the class constructs an Instruction object out of the body retrieved from the message and sends it off to update account details. This in turn invokes all the trade handler interface method `processInformation()` with the Instruction object.

While closing the connections, the class unsubscribes from its durable subscription, before closing other resources.

The figure below shows both the `EquityBuyer` and the `AccountsDepartment` class:

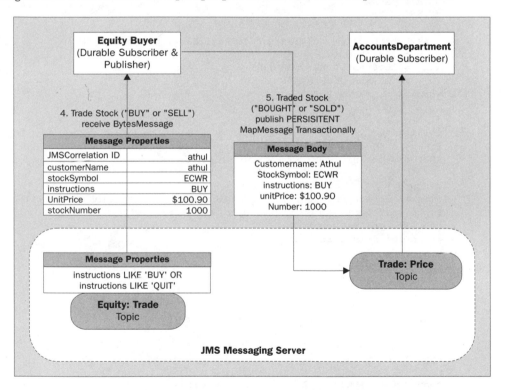

The complete source code for the `AccountsDepartment` class is shown below:

```
package pubsub.retailbrokerage;

import javax.jms.*;
import javax.naming.*;
import java.util.*;
import common.*;
```

```java
public class AccountsDepartment implements MessageListener {
    private TopicConnectionFactory factory;
    private TopicConnection connection;
    private Topic topic;
    private TopicSession session;
    private TopicSubscriber subscriber;
    private String hostName;
    private String userID;
    private String password;
    private TradeHandler caller;
    private static final String CONTEXT_FACTORY = Constants.FACTORY;
    private static final String CONNECTION_FACTORY =
     Constants.CONNECTION_FACTORY;
    private static final String SUBSCRIBER_TOPIC = Constants.PRICE_TOPIC;

    public AccountsDepartment(String host, String ID, String passwd) {
     hostName = host;
     userID = ID;
     password = passwd;
    }

    public AccountsDepartment(TradeHandler callbackImplementor) {
     caller = callbackImplementor;
     hostName = Constants.PROVIDER_URL;
     userID = Constants.USER_NAME;
     password = Constants.PASSWORD;
    }

    void initialize() {
     try {
         JNDIService.init(CONTEXT_FACTORY, hostName);

         factory =
          (TopicConnectionFactory) JNDIService.lookup(CONNECTION_FACTORY);
         topic = (Topic) JNDIService.lookup(SUBSCRIBER_TOPIC);
     } catch (Exception exception) {
         exception.printStackTrace();
     }
    }

    public void createConnections() {
     try {
         initialize();

         // Create and start a Topic connection
         connection = factory.createTopicConnection();

         connection.setClientID("Accounts_Department");

         // Create a Topic session on this connection
         session = connection.createTopicSession(false,
                             Session.AUTO_ACKNOWLEDGE);

         // Create a Durable Subscriber
         subscriber = session.createDurableSubscriber(topic,
             "AccountsDepartment");
```

An asynchronous listener/callback on the Receiver object just created:

```
// Install an asynchronous listener/callback on the Receiver
    // object just created
    subscriber.setMessageListener(this);
    connection.start();
    System.out.println("Accounts Department up and Ready for eCommerce ...");
} catch (Exception exception) {
    exception.printStackTrace();
}
}


private static void displayUsage() {
System.out.println("\n\tUsage : java "
            + "Chapter05.RetailBrokerage.AccountsDepartment "
            + "hostName UserName Password");
System.out.println("\t Terminating Program ...");
System.exit(-1);
}

public void closeConnections() {
try {
    if (subscriber != null) {
     subscriber.close();
    }
    if (session != null) {
     session.unsubscribe("AccountsDepartment");
     session.close();
    }
    if (connection != null) {
     connection.close();
    }
} catch (Exception exception) {
    exception.printStackTrace();
}
}
```

The `updateAccountDetails()` method informs everyone about the buy by printing out the information and invoking the registered callback handler to inform listeners too:

```
public void updateAccountDetails(Instruction information) {
String data = "Bought " + information.getStockNumber()
            + " shares of " + information.getStockSymbol()
            + " at a Price of " + information.getUnitPrice()
            + " in the name of " + information.getCustomerName();

System.out.println(data);

// inform any other registered callback handlers
if (caller != null) {
    caller.processInformation(information);
}
}
```

This is the message listener that receives messages asynchronously for the bound receiver:

```java
public void onMessage(Message message) {
    try {

        // When a message is received, print it out to
        // standard output
        if (message instanceof TextMessage) {
         TextMessage textMessage = (TextMessage) message;
         String stringData = textMessage.getText();

         System.out.println(stringData + " instruction received ...");

         // if a "QUIT" message was received close connections
         if (stringData.equalsIgnoreCase("quit") == true) {
             closeConnections();
         }
        }

        if (message instanceof MapMessage) {
         MapMessage  mapMessage = (MapMessage) message;
         Instruction information = null;

         information =
             new Instruction(mapMessage.getString("customerName"),
                      mapMessage.getString("stockSymbol"),
                      mapMessage.getString("instructions"),
                      mapMessage.getDouble("unitPrice"),
                      mapMessage.getInt("stockNumber"));

         // inform everyone about the stock trade
         updateAccountDetails(information);
        }
    } catch (Throwable exception) {
        exception.printStackTrace();
    }
}

public static void main(String[] args) {
  if (args.length < 3) {
      AccountsDepartment.displayUsage();
  }

  String hostName = args[0];
  String userID = args[1];
  String password = args[2];
  AccountsDepartment accounts = new AccountsDepartment(hostName,
       userID, password);

  accounts.createConnections();
  }

}
```

The TradeHandler Interface

Classes that need to implement a callback for the `AccountsDepartment` class use the `TradeHandler` interface. The `TradeHandler` interface has a method called `processInformation()` that needs to be implemented by whichever class has to be called back when a Trade happens and be informed of its details.

```
package pubsub.retailbrokerage;

public interface TradeHandler {

    public void processInformation(Instruction information);
}
```

We will see more about this interface when we discuss an applet implementation of the retail stock brokerage application.

The AccountingPanel

The `AccountingPanel` applet creates the `EquityBuyer` and the `AccountsDepartment` classes and displays the output of the `AccountsDepartment` class. This class is very similar to the sales order application, in that it can be deployed as both a standalone application and as an applet.

The `AccountingPanel` applet implements the `TradeHandler` interface. This interface contains a method called `processInformation()` that takes an Instruction object containing the details of the trade. The AccountingPanel applet creates an implementation for the `processInformation()` method:

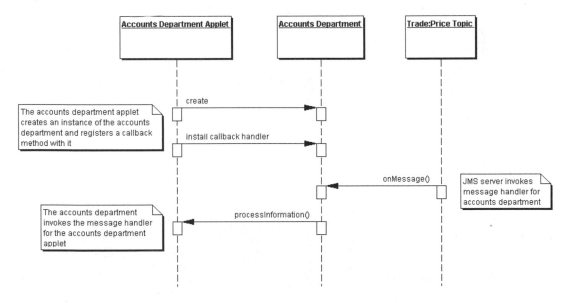

The `AccountingPanel` applet creates an instance of the accounts department and registers the trade handler callback with it. When the messaging server invokes the accounts department's `onMessage()` callback, it in turn invokes the `processInformation()` callback of the accounts department applet and about the details of the trade.

The source code for the `AccountingPanel` applet is as follows:

```
package pubsub.retailbrokerage;

import java.applet.*;
import java.awt.*;
import java.awt.event.*;

public class AccountingPanel extends Applet implements TradeHandler {
    private Label label;
    private TextArea textArea;

    public void init() {
     addComponents();

     String hostName = Constants.PROVIDER_URL;
     String userID = Constants.USER_NAME;
     String password = Constants.PASSWORD;
     EquityBuyer buyer = null;
     AccountsDepartment accounts = null;

     try {
         buyer = new EquityBuyer(hostName, userID, password);

         buyer.buyEquities();

         accounts = new AccountsDepartment(this);

         accounts.createConnections();
     } catch (Exception exception) {
         exception.printStackTrace();
     }
    }

    public synchronized void processInformation(Instruction information) {
     String command = "";

     if (information.getInstructions().equalsIgnoreCase("BUY")) {
         command = "Bought";
     }
     if (information.getInstructions().equalsIgnoreCase("SELL")) {
         command = "Sold";
     }

     String data = command + " " + information.getStockNumber()
                 + " shares of " + information.getStockSymbol()
                 + " at (USD) $" + information.getUnitPrice() + "  for "
                 + information.getCustomerName() + "\n";

     textArea.append(data);
    }

    private void addComponents() {
     resize(450, 400);
     this.setLayout(new BorderLayout());
```

```
        textArea = new TextArea(5, 40);

        textArea.setEnabled(false);

        label = new Label("Retrieving Messages from the "
                    + "Trade:Price Buy Queue");

        add(label, "North");
        add(textArea, "Center");
    }     // end addComponents

    static class CloseAdapter extends WindowAdapter {

     public void windowClosing(WindowEvent windowEvent) {
          System.exit(0);
     }

    }

    public static void main(String[] args) {
     AccountingPanel panel = new AccountingPanel();

     panel.init();

     Frame frame = new Frame("Retail Brokerage Accounting Department");

     frame.add(panel, BorderLayout.CENTER);
     frame.setSize(250, 250);
     frame.setLocation(300, 200);
     frame.pack();
     frame.show();
     frame.addWindowListener(new CloseAdapter());
    }

}
```

Compiling and Running the Accounts Department Example

Before doing anything else, make sure the JMS messaging server is up and is ready to send and receive messages. If the server is not up, we will not be able to either send or receive messages.

Both the programs take the host address of the machine on which the JMS server is running, a valid registered username on the JMS messaging server and the password as their parameters. You can specify the address of your server host in the hostname parameter. If you are running the messaging server locally, you can specify localhost as the address or you can also specify an IP:Port combination like 127.0.0.1:2001.

The results of compiling all the programs and running them are shown below:

```
C:\WINNT\System32\cmd.exe                                          _ □ ×

C:\ProJMS\Chapter05>javac pubsub\retailbrokerage\*.java

C:\ProJMS\Chapter05>start java pubsub.retailbrokerage.ApprovalDepartment http://
localhost:2001 athul raj

C:\ProJMS\Chapter05>start java pubsub.retailbrokerage.SalesOrderPanel

C:\ProJMS\Chapter05>start java pubsub.retailbrokerage.AccountingPanel

C:\ProJMS\Chapter05>_
```

The output of the command console looks like this:

```
C:\WINNT\system32\java.exe                                         _ □ ×
Equity Buyer, up and Ready for eCommerce ...
Accounts Department up and Ready for eCommerce ...
Bought 1000 shares of ECWR at a Price of 100.9 in the name of Athul
Creating Topic Publisher
Bought 1000 shares of ECWR at a Price of 100.9 in the name of Athul
Bought 109 shares of SUNW at a Price of 100.9 in the name of Gopalan
Creating Topic Publisher
Bought 109 shares of SUNW at a Price of 100.9 in the name of Gopalan
Bought 456 shares of MSFT at a Price of 100.9 in the name of Raj
Creating Topic Publisher
Bought 456 shares of MSFT at a Price of 100.9 in the name of Raj
```

The output of the accounts department looks like this:

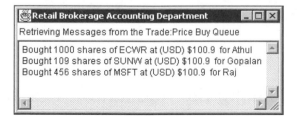

Applets

JMS client applets are written in exactly the same way as normal JMS client applications are written. Browser security restrictions allow uncertified applets to establish connections only with the machine from which the applet is downloaded, in other words, the web server machine. This requires that unlike normal applications (which can connect to a JMS server running on any machine), uncertified applets be allowed to connect only to the machine from which they are downloaded.

However, certified applets are allowed to connect to any host to which the web client has authorized access by the certificate provider. The web client can set different levels of permissions for certificates from different certificate vendors. An applet carrying a certificate automatically invokes a window on web clients that do not allow it requisite permissions, asking if the user is interested in granting the permissions. Using the advanced security options of popular browsers such as Netscape and Internet Explorer, one can explicitly set security parameters for all certificate holders.

The SalesOrder Applet

Messaging brokers provide a reduced run-time library for applet support. The run-time library may be architected to allow new components to be plugged in by simply modifying the classpath to include the additional archive.

The run-time archive used for developing this applet contains all the classes representing FioranoMQ's implementation of JMS. This archive is 100% JMS 1.0.2 compliant. It includes implementation of all the Pub/Sub and PTP functionality. You can therefore modify these applets to work with any other 100% JMS 1.0.2 compliant vendor product. While doing so, make sure that you substitute `fmprtl.zip` (the client runtime of FioranoMQ) with the client runtime of your specific vendor.

The following listing is for a simple web page demonstrating the usage of JMS APIs from within an applet hosted on a web page:

```
<HEAD>
 <BODY>
  <CENTER>
   <OBJECT
    classid="clsid:8AD9C840-044E-11D1-B3E9-00805F499D93"
    WIDTH = 400 HEIGHT = 310
    codebase="http://java.sun.com/products/plugin/1.3/jinstall-13-
win32.cab#Version=1,3,0,0">
    <PARAM NAME = CODE VALUE="pubsub.retailbrokerage.SalesOrderPanel.class">
    <PARAM NAME = CODEBASE VALUE = "../../" >
    <PARAM NAME = ARCHIVE VALUE = "fmprtl.zip, jndi.jar" >
    <PARAM NAME="type" VALUE="application/x-java-applet;version=1.3">
    <PARAM NAME="scriptable" VALUE="false">
   </OBJECT>
  </CENTER>
 </BODY>
</HEAD>
```

Deploying the SalesOrder

Deploy the applet on a web server. Start up the web server and then start up the applications in turn as follows:

```
C:\WINNT\System32\cmd.exe                                          _ □ X

C:\ProJMS>javac pubsub\retailbrokerage\*.java

C:\ProJMS>startup
Starting tomcat in new window
Using classpath: C:\tomcat\classes;C:\tomcat\lib\webserver.jar;C:\tomcat\lib\jas
per.jar;C:\tomcat\lib\xml.jar;C:\tomcat\lib\servlet.jar;C:\jdk1.3\lib\tools.jar;
.;C:\jdk1.3\lib\classes.zip;C:\javamessagequeue\lib\ldap.jar;C:\javamessagequeue
\lib\fscontext.jar;C:\javamessagequeue\lib\jms.jar;C:\javamessagequeue\lib\jndi.
jar;C:\javamessagequeue\lib\jmq.jar;C:\javamessagequeue\lib\providerutil.jar;C:\
Fiorano\lib\fmprtl.zip;C:\Fiorano\bin\jndi.jar;C:\iBusMobile1.0.0\client\j2se\li
b\ibus-mobile.jar;C:\iBusMessageServer\client\lib\msrvClt.jar;C:\MQSeries\java\l
ib\com.ibm.mqjms.jar
C:\ProJMS>start java pubsub.retailbrokerage.AccountsDepartment http://localhost
athul raj

C:\ProJMS>start java pubsub.retailbrokerage.ApprovalDepartment http://localhost
athul raj

C:\ProJMS>start java pubsub.retailbrokerage.EquityBuyer http://localhost athul r
aj

C:\ProJMS>_
```

The screenshot below shows the sales order applet executing in a browser served from a web server:

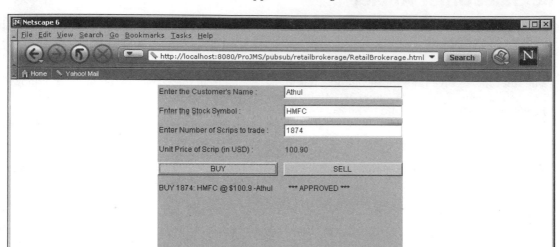

Summary

We started off by looking at a general overview of Pub/Sub messaging. We then moved on to discuss Topics, Quality of Service (QoS) in JMS applications, how to ensure guaranteed messaging in JMS applications, and topic management. We set up our connection factories, destinations and users on our messaging server. We also talked about the differences between the physical destination and those created by client APIs.

We then moved on to look at the generic programming model, which gave us a feel for how similar Pub/Sub programming was to Point-to-Point programming. We started exploring other features of Pub/Sub messaging by developing a retail stock brokerage application.

We first developed the approval requestor. While developing this class we saw how remoting and authentication is handled in Pub/Sub model, and about temporary topics and how to create and get rid of them. We also discussed the TopicRequestor class. We then developed the approval department. While doing so we learnt how to develop an asynchronous message handler, how to simulate request-reply using Pub/Sub messaging, the use of the replyTo() API, and the JMSCorrelationID property. We also learnt how to create, populate and read object messages and stream messages.

We then started the Trader class development. While carrying out this task we learned about the bytes message, and how to program transactions and assign message priorities. We then saw how this all tied into the sales order application. We then developed the EquityBuyer class. While doing this, we learned about durable subscribers and message selectors. We then developed the AccountsDepartment class. We then learned how to develop Pub/Sub-enabled applets and deployed them on the web browser.

6

Web Applications and JMS

In this chapter we will be looking into developing a web application using the standard J2EE web container services and JMS. The application is a browser-based helpdesk ticket system where customers can log cases, and the system users can view the cases. In the application we will be using JMS as the middleware for integrating two separate web-based systems, one for logging the cases and the other for managing the cases, which function in total isolation to each other. The two systems are not aware of the functional details of each other. The case management system sends JMS messages to a message queue when a user raises a case and the messages in the queue are read by the case management system. Similarly when a case status is updated by the case management system a JMS message is sent to a message queue, which is in turn read by the case logging system.

This application assumes basic knowledge of J2EE web containers, Java servlets, JavaServer Pages, custom tags, and of course JMS.

We will be covering the following aspects of JMS and J2EE web components in the case study:

❑   Use of JMS for interfacing two heterogeneous applications functioning in isolation to each other

❑   Asynchronous message delivery

❑   Point-to-Point messaging

❑   Use of JSP custom tags for sending JMS messages

❑   Use of JSP application scope beans as JMS message listeners

❑   J2EE web application paradigm

❑   Use of BEA WebLogic Server 6.0 for deploying JMS-based systems and web applications

JMS on the Web

Message-oriented middleware has been a key element for interfacing distributed applications for quite a long time. JMS, with its support for most of the MOM requirements like PTP messaging, Pub/Sub messaging, synchronous and asynchronous message delivery, can play a vital role in integrating heterogeneous applications functioning in isolation to each other.

One important aspect in web-based e-commerce application development is the asynchronous interchange of electronic data between the participating applications. To make such an application successful, the web-based system should integrate seamlessly with back-office applications, including existing legacy systems. In most of these scenarios the applications interface with each other by sharing data in pre-agreed formats. The interface is more efficient if the applications can interchange data between each other asynchronously. JMS coupled with XML is the most appropriate solution for these scenarios, where XML can take care of the data format issues and JMS the data transport details. We shall see more about JMS and XML in Chapter 10.

The Requirements Analysis

The helpdesk system is to be used by both the customers of ACME Systems and the helpdesk assistants working in the company itself. The quality management group has been trying hard to improve the services provided to its users. They recently decided to implement a browser-based helpdesk system that can be accessed through the Internet.

In the implemented solution described in this chapter, the company's helpdesk assistants can view the cases raised by the users and, as they work on fixing the problems, they can update the status of each case. The progress of the case is visible to the end user in the form of an itemized sequence of tickets. Finally, when the problem is fixed, the helpdesk assistants can close the case, so that the case is no longer visible in the list of pending cases.

After an initial feasibility study and requirements analysis, the business analysts at ACME Systems came up with a list of requirements for the proposed helpdesk system:

- ❏ The customers should be:

  - ❏ Able to access the system from their desktops all over the world
  - ❏ Authenticated before they can use the system
  - ❏ Allocated a case ID for reference when they initiate a new case
  - ❏ Able to track the status of their cases by searching through case IDs

- ❏ The helpdesk assistants should be:

  - ❏ Authenticated before they can use the system
  - ❏ Able to view the list of cases raised by a customer
  - ❏ Able to view further details on individual cases
  - ❏ Able to update the case status and add comments to the case history

Since the system is going to have two very different types of users, it was decided to have the system implemented as two isolated systems loosely coupled to each other to minimize mutual impact and security implications. In modern application development, which can tend to be more about integration than development, an important aspect is integrating applications that are ignorant of each other's functionality. In most cases, it is better to develop enterprise systems as a collection of independent self-contained applications interacting with each other either through exposed APIs or sharing data in pre-agreed formats.

Along with the list of requirements, the business analysts came up with the diagram below depicting all the use cases in the system. Use case diagrams belong to the family of UML diagrams and are used for modeling a system's interaction with external entities. In use case terminology the external entities that interact with the system are called **actors** and the various actions instigated by the **actors** are called **use cases**. A **use case** represents an atomic action as viewed by the external entity, like placing an order or raising a case:

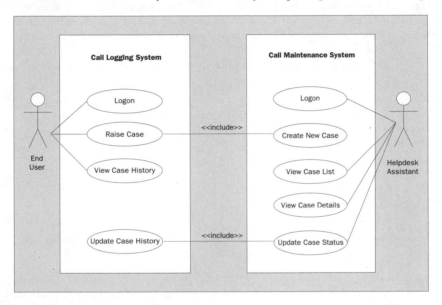

Choosing the Right Technology

The requirements list and the use case diagram were sent to the senior technical architect for a high level proposal on the technology to be used for implementing the system. The technical architect considered the following factors. The proposed technology should:

❑ Support rapid application development to provide a fully functional helpdesk system to the users in a short span of time

❑ Support distributed component architecture for ease of extensibility, support of heterogeneous operating environments, and proper load sharing

❑ Adhere to the corporate policy of not being dependent on a single server vendor

❑ Provide system-level services like transactions, security, and communication, so that the application developers can concentrate on developing the business logic, and make as much use of application server support as possible

❑ Enable easy deployment of the application

Taking all the above factors into consideration a technology based on J2EE was proposed. It was decided to partition the system into two loosely coupled applications, a case logging system and a case management system. Since the relevant users require web access to the applications, it was decided to engineer them as web applications running in J2EE web containers. A MOM solution was proposed to couple the case logging and the case management systems. Due to the support for standards-based solution, JMS was chosen as the preferred MOM solution.

The proposed architecture recommended running the case logging system, the case management system, and the message system in isolation from each other to avoid mutual impact and security implications. It was further recommended to use WebLogic 6.0 for running the web applications and the message broker because of its 100% J2EE compatibility. But it was also suggested that the system be implemented in a vendor-neutral manner, without using any of the value-added features provided the vendor that are not compliant with the J2EE specification, so that switching vendors would not be a complex issue in the future. A fully J2EE compliant implementation would enable the use of three different vendors for the case logging, the case management and the messaging systems.

A high-level diagram depicting the technical architecture of the system is shown below:

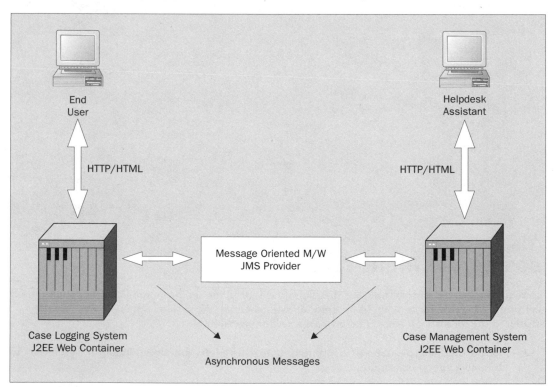

System Design

After the proposed technology was accepted, the technical proposal document and the requirements analysis document were sent to the lead designer in the team for detailed system design.

A high-level design diagram depicting the general dataflow in the system was created:

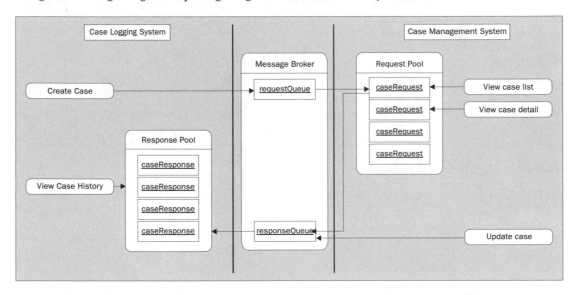

Whenever a customer raises a case, an ID is generated and the case details are wrapped in a JMS message and sent to the message broker's request queue. This message will be delivered to the data repository object `RequestPool` in the case management system, which will be listening asynchronously for messages. On message delivery, the information in the message will be used to create a case request and added into the request pool. An acknowledgement message will be sent back to the message broker's response queue with the case status set to "open". This message will be delivered to a data repository object `ResponsePool` in the case logging system, which will be also be listening asynchronously for messages. On message delivery, the information in the message will be used to create a case response and added into the response pool.

The helpdesk assistants can view the list of cases available in the request pool and expand individual tickets to view case details. They can also add comments and change the status of the cases. All these updates will be sent to the response queue as JMS messages and the message broker will deliver these messages to the response pool. The information in the messages will be used to create case response objects that will be stored in the pool against individual case IDs. When the status is changed to "closed", the case request will be removed from the request pool. The end users can query case history by specifying the case ID and the information will be retrieved from the response pool.

System Interaction Design

It was decided to engineer the system using a JSP presentation tier. The user actions at the browser would be routed to JSP files within the web application. The JSPs were designed with embedded custom tags that implemented the business logic and populated the HTTP Request object with JavaBeans required for rendering the data on the user's browser.

It was decided to identify the sequence of internal system interactions that were triggered by the various use cases and tie them to relevant JSPs, custom tags, and presentation wrapper JavaBeans. Subsequently the lead designer came up with a matrix depicting these relations.

Case Logging System

User/System Action	Description	JSP (.jsp)	Custom Tag	Bean	Scope
Logon	Authenticates the user	logon index	None	ResponsePool	application
Create Case	Creates a case	createcase	createCase	None	N/A
View History	Views case history	case history	viewCase	CaseResponse	request
On Message	Receives response messages from the case mgmt. system	None	N/A	N/A	N/A

Case Management System

User/System Action	Description	JSP (.jsp)	Custom Tag	Bean	Scope
Logon	Authenticates the user	logon index	None	RequestPool	application
List case	Lists all open and pending cases	listcase	listCase	CaseRequest	request
View case	Views case detail	viewcase	viewCase	CaseRequest	request
Update case	Updates case status	updatecase	updateCase	None	N/A
On Message	Receives request messages from the case logging system	None	N/A	N/A	N/A

A series of sequence diagrams were created to illustrate the various internal system interactions triggered by the use cases. The following sections explain those sequence diagrams.

The Case Logging System

This section explains the internal system interactions associated with the case logging system.

Logon

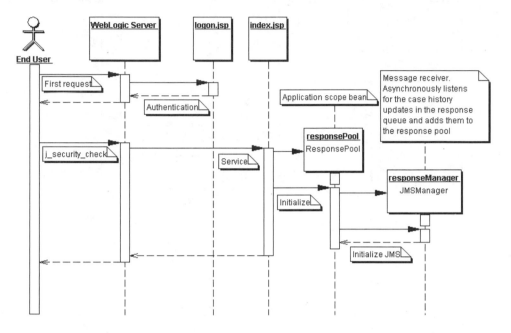

The user authentication for the case logging system was implemented using standard J2EE form-based authentication.

In the configuration file, web.xml, access to the application is restricted to users belonging to the group user. Groups and users were configured within the WebLogic application server (as will be demonstrated later). The user logon action generates the following sequence of events:

❑ The user is presented with the logon form defined in logon.jsp

❑ On successful authentication the user is presented with index.jsp

❑ In index.jsp a ResponsePool object is stored as an application scope bean with name responsePool

❑ The responsePool is initialized by passing in the ServletContext

❑ In the initialization method, responsePool retrieves the JMS configuration information stored in the web.xml file from the servlet context, and initializes an instance of JMSManager named responseManager

❑ The responseManager is used as a message consumer for the case responses sent to the response queue by the case management system

The instance responsePool implements javax.jms.MessageListener to register itself as a message listener with responseManager and on message delivery it creates instances of CaseResponse class and stores them internally.

Create Case

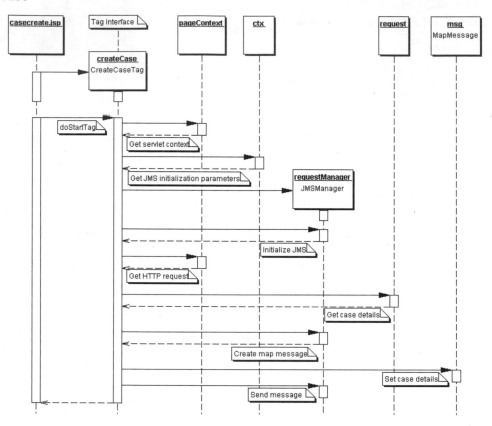

The following sequence of events occurs when the customer raises a case:

- ❏ The request is routed to casecreate.jsp

- ❏ In casecreate.jsp an instance of CaseCreateTag is created

- ❏ The doStartTag() method of the custom tag is called

- ❏ Instances of the servlet context and HTTP request are retrieved from the implicit variable pageContext

- ❏ The JMS configuration information stored in the web.xml file is retrieved from the servlet context

- ❏ This information is used to create and initialize an instance of JMSManager named requestManager, which will act as a message producer to the request queue

- ❏ The case details are retrieved from the HTTP request object and the IDGenerator helper class is used to get the next available case ID

- ❏ The requestManager is used to create a MapMessage and all the case details are stored in the MapMessage

- ❏ The message is the sent to the request queue using requestManager

- ❏ The case ID is stored back in the pageContext to be introduced as a scripting variable to the enclosing JSP, and sent to the user through the output of createcase.jsp for further reference

On Message

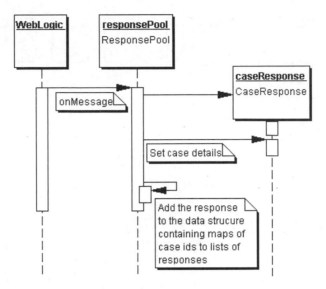

This event occurs when a case status is updated at the case management system. This sends a case response message to the response queue, which is delivered asynchronously to the application scope bean `responsePool` of the case logging system. This message remains in the JMS queue if the case logging system is not running and will be delivered to the system as soon as it is up and running.

The sequence of events is:

❑ The case response details are retrieved from the JMS message

❑ A `CaseResponse` object is created and the attributes are set

❑ The `responsePool` stores responses to a case as an array for that case ID

If the case ID for the response is already there in the pool, the response is added to the end of the list. Otherwise a new map is created for the case ID, and a new list containing the newly arrived response.

View Case History

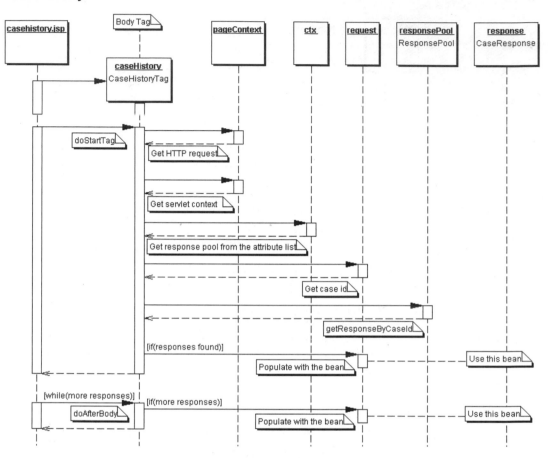

This event occurs when the users enter a case ID and search the case update status. As already mentioned in the previous sections, whenever helpdesk assistants change the status of cases or add comments to cases using the case management system, JMS messages holding the case update information are sent to the response queue. These messages are asynchronously delivered to the application scope bean `responsePool`. These responses are stored by `responsePool` in an internal data structure as a map of case IDs to a list of responses for the case. Whenever users query case statuses by specifying case IDs, this data structure is interrogated and the result is sent back to the user.

The sequence of events is:

❑ The view history request is sent to `casehistory.jsp`.

❑ An instance of tag handler class custom tag `caseHistory`, which implements `BodyTag`, is created within the JSP.

❑ In the `doStartTag()` method of the custom tag, instances of servlet context and HTTP request are retrieved from the implicit variable `pageContext`.

❑ The case ID entered by the user is retrieved from the HTTP request.

- ❑ The application scope bean `responsePool` is retrieved from the servlet context.

- ❑ The instance `responsePool` is queried by passing the case ID to get a list of responses for the case ID.

- ❑ If the returned list is empty `doStartTag()` returns `SKIP_BODY`, which prevents the body of the tag from being evaluated, otherwise the first element in the list, which is of type `CaseResponse`, is stored in the HTTP request and `EVAL_BODY_TAG` is returned.

- ❑ In the `doAfterBody()` method of the tag handler the contents of body content is written to the enclosing writer. If there are more elements in the list retrieved in `doStartTag` the next element is retrieved and stored in the HTTP request and `EVAL_BODY_TAG` is returned. Otherwise `SKIP_BODY` is returned.

- ❑ The JSP declares a request scope bean of type `CaseResponse`, which is populated by the `doStartTag()` and `doAfterBody()` methods of the tag handler. The JSP uses the standard `getProperty` tags of `useBean` to render the data stored in the bean.

The Case Management System

This section explains the internal system interactions associated with the case management system.

Logon

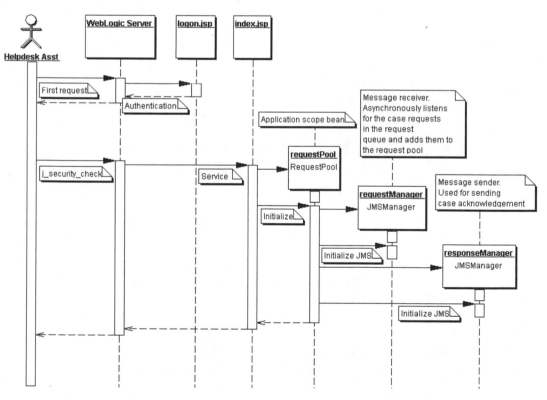

The user authentication for the case management system was implemented using the standard J2EE form-based authentication.

In the configuration file for the web application, web.xml, access to the application is restricted to users belonging to the group system. Groups and users are defined within the WebLogic application server. The user logon action generates the following sequence of events:

❑ The user is presented with the logon form defined in logon.jsp

❑ On successful authentication the user is presented with index.jsp

❑ In index.jsp an instance of RequestPool is stored as an application scope bean named requestPool

❑ The instance requestPool is initialized by passing in the ServletContext

❑ In the initialization method, requestPool retrieves the JMS configuration information stored in the web.xml file and initializes two instances of JMSManager, responseManager and requestManager

❑ The instance requestManager will be used as a message consumer for the case requests sent to the request queue by the case logging system

❑ The instance responseManager is used for sending the initial response with status as "open" to the response queue when a case request arrives afresh

The instance requestPool implements javax.jms.MessageListener too so that it can be registered as a message listener with responseManager. On message delivery it creates instances of CaseRequest class and stores them internally.

On Message

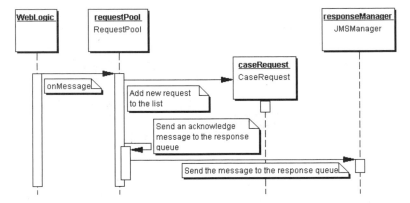

This event occurs when a case request is raised at the case logging system. That will send a case request message to the request queue, which is asynchronously delivered to the application scope bean requestPool at the case management system.

The sequence of events is:

❑ The case request details are retrieved from the JMS message

❑ An instance of CaseRequest is created and the attributes are set

❑ The instance requestPool stores a map of case IDs and case requests, which can later be interrogated to get a list of pending cases or the case details for the specified case ID

❑ When a case request is delivered asynchronously a response message is created using the instance responseManager with status set to "open" and sent to the response pool

Case List

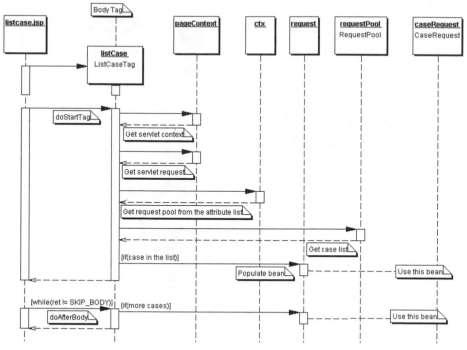

This event occurs when the helpdesk assistant instigates the action to list all pending cases. The case requests are stored in the application scope bean `responsePool` in an internal data structure as a map of case IDs to case requests. Whenever helpdesk assistants query the list of cases, this data structure is interrogated and the result is sent back to the user.

The sequence of events is:

- ❑ The list cases request is sent to `listcase.jsp`.
- ❑ An instance of tag handler class `listCase`, which implements `BodyTag`, is created within the JSP.
- ❑ In the `doStartTag()` method of the custom tag, instances of servlet context and HTTP request are retrieved from `pageContext`.
- ❑ The application scope bean `requestPool` is retrieved from the servlet context.
- ❑ The instance `responsePool` is queried for the list of pending cases.
- ❑ If the returned list is empty `doStartTag()` returns `SKIP_BODY`, which prevents the body of the tag from being evaluated. Otherwise the first element in the list, which is of type `CaseRequest`, is stored in the HTTP request and `EVAL_BODY_TAG` is returned.
- ❑ In the `doAfterBody()` method of the tag handler the body content is written to the enclosing writer. If there are more elements in the list retrieved in `doStartTag()` the next element is retrieved and stored in the HTTP request and `EVAL_BODY_TAG` is returned. Otherwise `SKIP_BODY` is returned.
- ❑ The JSP declares a request scope bean of type `CaseRequest`, which is populated by the `doStartTag()` and `doAfterBody()` methods of the tag handler. The JSP uses the standard `getProperty` tags of `useBean` to render the data stored in the bean to the user's browser.

View Case Details

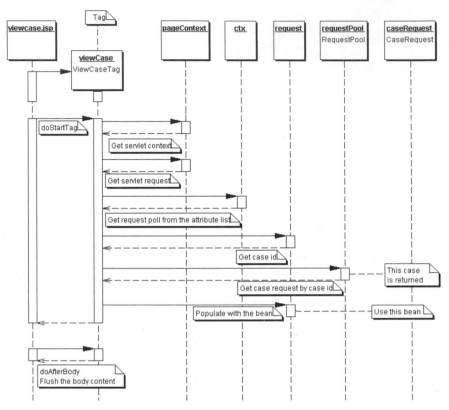

These events occur when the helpdesk assistant opens the case request list to view the details of individual cases.

The sequence of events is:

- ❑ The view case detail request is sent to `viewcase.jsp`.
- ❑ An instance of tag handler class `viewCase`, which implements `BodyTag`, is created within the JSP.
- ❑ In the `doStartTag()` method of the custom tag, instances of servlet context and HTTP request are retrieved from the implicit variable `pageContext`.
- ❑ The application scope bean `requestPool` is retrieved from the servlet context.
- ❑ The instance `responsePool` is queried for case details for the specified case ID.
- ❑ If the requested case is not found, `doStartTag()` returns `SKIP_BODY`, which prevents the body of the tag from being evaluated. Otherwise the returned object of type `CaseRequest` is stored in the HTTP request and `EVAL_BODY_TAG` is returned.
- ❑ In the `doAfterBody()` method of the tag handler the body content is written to the enclosing writer. The enclosing writer for the body content is the instance of `JspWriter` used by the JSP enclosing the tag.
- ❑ The JSP declares a request scope bean of type `CaseRequest`, which is populated by the `doStartTag()` and `doAfterBody()` methods of the tag handler. The JSP uses the standard `getProperty` tags of `useBean` to render the data stored in the bean.

Update Case Status

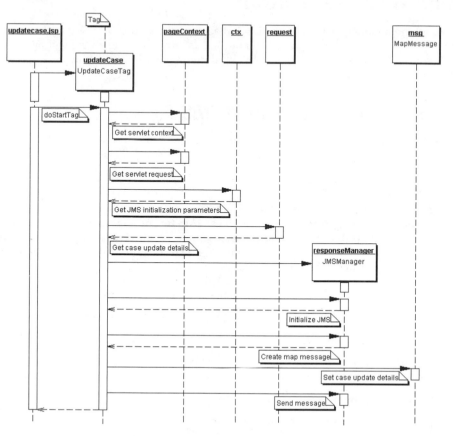

The following sequence of events occurs when the helpdesk assistant updates a case status:

- ❏ The request is routed to `updatecase.jsp`
- ❏ In `updatecase.jsp` an instance of `UpdateCaseTag` is created
- ❏ This class implements the standard JSP `Tag` interface
- ❏ The `doStartTag()` method of the custom tag is called. Instances of servlet context and HTTP request are retrieved from the implicit variable `pageContext`
- ❏ The JMS configuration information stored in the `web.xml` file is retrieved from the servlet context
- ❏ This information is used to create and initialize an instance of `JMSManager` named `responseManager`, which will act as a message producer to the response queue
- ❏ The case update details are retrieved from the HTTP request
- ❏ The instance `responseManager` is used to create a map message and all the case update details are stored into the map message
- ❏ The map message is the sent to the response queue using `responseManager`
- ❏ If the case status is set to "closed", the case request is removed from the `requestPool`

Implementing the System

After doing all the detailed design and the UML diagrams, the system was sent to the development team for implementation. In this section we will get our hands dirty covering all the coding details. Here we will list the source files used in the application and design the internal working details of all the classes and JSPs used in the system.

Implementing and Configuring JMS

This section explains the configuration and implementation details of the helper classes used for JMS messaging.

Common Utilities

The first task in modeling the system was to identify the common entities that would be used by both the systems. Since both the systems were going to use JMS for messaging it was decided to create a service for handling the JMS internals and expose a simple yet efficient API to the application developers for producing and consuming JMS messages. For this the expected functionality for the JMS adapter service was specified. The service should:

❑ Encapsulate the naming and lookup complexities of administered objects

❑ Encapsulate the complexities in creating JMS connections and sessions

❑ Have an adaptable interface that would work with both PTP and Pub/Sub models

❑ Have an interface to produce and consume JMS messages, start and stop JMS connections, and create different JMS messages

❑ Support asynchronous message delivery

❑ Support client IDs and durable subscriptions

❑ Be extendable to support XA connections and sessions

It was also decided to enumerate all the constants in an interface (recall that if a class implements an interface, then the constant declarations are available directly within the class). The following were identified:

❑ Constants to indicate the message model, PTP or Pub/Sub

❑ Constants to indicate the role of the JMS adapter: message producer, message consumer, or both message producer and consumer

The following class diagram depicts the entities used for performing common messaging utilities:

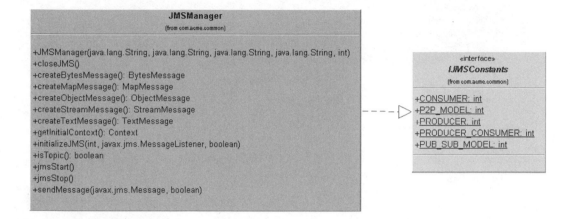

The IJMSConstants Interface

This is an interface used for defining the different constants used in implementing the messaging façade. This interface defines constants to indicate the following:

❑   PTP messaging model

❑   Pub/Sub messaging model

❑   Message producer role

❑   Message consumer role

❑   Both message producer and consumer role

```java
package com.acme.common;

public interface IJMSConstants {

  public static final int PRODUCER = 1;
  public static final int CONSUMER = 2;
  public static final int PRODUCER_CONSUMER = 3;

  public static final int PTP_MODEL = 1;
  public static final int PUB_SUB_MODEL= 2;

}
```

The JMSManager Class

As mentioned earlier this is a façade helper class for handling all the messaging functionality. This class exposes a simple API for initializing the messaging components, creating different JMS messages, and sending and receiving messages. This class can be configured to work with either the PTP model or the Pub/Sub model. It can also be configured to act as a message producer, message consumer, or both message producer and consumer. All the JNDI lookup functionality for administered objects is encapsulated within the class:

```
package com.acme.common;

import javax.naming.*;
import javax.jms.*;
import java.util.Hashtable;

public class JMSManager implements IJMSConstants {

    private ConnectionFactory connFx;
    private Connection conn;
    private Destination dest;
    private Session session;
    private MessageConsumer consumer;
    private MessageProducer producer;

    private int model;

    private String jndiFactory;
    private String url;
    private String jmsFactory;
    private String destName;

    private Context ctx;
```

This class is constructed with the following values:

- ❏ JNDI initial context factory
- ❏ JNDI service provider URL
- ❏ The JNDI name of the JMS destination to be used
- ❏ The JNDI name of the JMS connection factory to be used
- ❏ A constant indicating the message model as specified in the IJMSConstants interface

```
public JMSManager(String ctxFact, String url, String dest,
    String jmsFact, int model) {

    this.jndiFactory = ctxFact;
    this.url = url;
    this.destName = dest;
    this.jmsFactory = jmsFact;
    this.model= model;

}
```

The getInitialContext() method is used for getting the JNDI initial context, using the initial context factory name and the service provider URL passed in the constructor:

```
public Context getInitialContext() throws NamingException {

    Hashtable env = new Hashtable();

    if(jndiFactory != null) {
```

```
            env.put(Context.INITIAL_CONTEXT_FACTORY, jndiFactory);
    }

    if(url != null) {
        env.put(Context.PROVIDER_URL, url);
    }

    Context context = new InitialContext(env);
    return context;

}
```

The class then provides the method initializeJMS() to initialize and start the JMS services for sending and receiving messages. This method expects the following parameters:

❑   A constant defined in the IJMSConstants interface to identify the messaging role: message producer, consumer, or both producer and consumer

❑   A message listener implementation for handling asynchronous message delivery

❑   A Boolean value specifying whether to start the JMS connection implicitly or not

```
public void initializeJMS(int type,MessageListener listener,
    boolean start) throws NamingException, JMSSecurityException,
      JMSException {
```

This method first initializes the JNDI initial context and looks up the connection factory using the name specified in the constructor:

```
if(ctx == null) {
    ctx = getInitialContext();
}

ConnectionFactory connFx = (ConnectionFactory)ctx.lookup(jmsFactory);
```

Then if the message model is Pub/Sub it creates a topic connection and topic session, and looks up the topic:

```
if(model == PUB_SUB_MODEL) {

  conn = ((TopicConnectionFactory)connFx).createTopicConnection();

  session = ((TopicConnection)conn).createTopicSession(
    false,Session.AUTO_ACKNOWLEDGE);

  dest = (Topic)ctx.lookup(destName);
```

If the messaging role is consumer or producer/consumer and the passed message listener is not null a topic subscriber is created and the passed message listener is registered with the topic subscriber:

```
if ((type == CONSUMER || type == PRODUCER_CONSUMER) &&
    listener != null) {

  consumer = ((TopicSession)session).createSubscriber(((Topic)dest));
  consumer.setMessageListener(listener);

}
```

If the messaging role is producer or producer/consumer, a topic publisher is created:

```
if(type == PRODUCER || type == PRODUCER_CONSUMER) {
  producer = ((TopicSession)session).createPublisher(((Topic)dest));
}
```

If the message model is PTP it creates a queue connection and queue session, and looks up the queue:

```
} else if(model == PTP_MODEL) {

  conn = ((QueueConnectionFactory)connFx).createQueueConnection();

  session = ((QueueConnection)conn).createQueueSession(
    false, Session.AUTO_ACKNOWLEDGE);

  dest = (Queue) ctx.lookup(destName);
```

If the messaging role is consumer or producer/consumer and the message listener is not null, a queue receiver is created and the message listener parameter is registered with the queue receiver:

```
if((type == CONSUMER || type == PRODUCER_CONSUMER) &&
    listener != null) {

  consumer = ((QueueSession)session).createReceiver(((Queue)dest));
  consumer.setMessageListener(listener);

}
```

If the messaging role is producer, or producer/consumer, a queue sender is created:

```
if(type == PRODUCER || type == PRODUCER_CONSUMER) {
  producer = ((QueueSession)
    session).createSender(((Queue)dest));
}

}
```

Finally the JMS connection is started depending on the `boolean` value passed to the method:

```
if(start)
  conn.start();

}
```

Various utility and cleanup methods follow. This method starts the JMS connection:

```
public void jmsStart() throws JMSException {
  if(conn != null) {
    conn.start();
  }
}
```

This method temporarily stops the JMS connection:

```
public void jmsStop() throws JMSException {
  if(conn != null) {
    conn.stop();
  }
}
```

This method releases all the JMS resources by closing and stopping the JMS connection:

```
public void closeJMS() {

  if(conn != null) {
    try {
        conn.stop();
        conn.close();
    } catch(JMSException e) {
        System.out.println("JMSManager.closeJMS:");
        e.printStackTrace();
    } catch(Exception e) {
        System.out.println("JMSManager.closeJMS:");
        e.printStackTrace();
    }
  }
}
```

```
public boolean isTopic() {
  return (model == PUB_SUB_MODEL);
}
```

The class provides a method for sending messages that will send or publish the passed messages depending on the configured message model. This method also provides an argument to specify whether the message needs to be persistent or not:

```
public void sendMessage(Message msg,boolean persistent)
    throws JMSException {

  if(persistent) {
    msg.setJMSDeliveryMode(DeliveryMode.PERSISTENT);
  } else {
    msg.setJMSDeliveryMode(DeliveryMode.NON_PERSISTENT);
  }
```

If the configured messaging model is Pub/Sub then publish the message using the Pub/Sub publisher or else send the message using the PTP queue sender:

```
  if(model == PUB_SUB_MODEL) {
    ((TopicPublisher)producer).publish(msg);
  } else if (model == PTP_MODEL) {
    ((QueueSender)producer).send(msg);
  }
}
```

Finally, methods are also provided for creating different types of JMS messages:

```
public MapMessage createMapMessage() throws JMSException {
    return session.createMapMessage();
}
```

```
public TextMessage createTextMessage() throws JMSException {
    return session.createTextMessage();
}
```

```
public ObjectMessage createObjectMessage() throws JMSException {
    return session.createObjectMessage();
}
```

```
public BytesMessage createBytesMessage() throws JMSException {
    return session.createBytesMessage();
}
```

```
public StreamMessage createStreamMessage() throws JMSException {
    return session.createStreamMessage();
}
}
```

Configuring Messaging in the Server

We will now configure the required messaging functionality within the server. Of the following four steps, only the creation of a persistent store for the queue is not covered in Appendix A:

❑   Create a new connection factory `qcFactory`

❑   Create a new JMS server `MyJMSServer`

❑   Create a file system destination store in `C:\temp`

❑   Create a new queue destination `requestQueue` using the above store

Before we begin the configuration, start an instance of WebLogic 6.0 server running and access the administration console through the browser. Assuming you are running the server locally on port 7001, the URL will be as follows, http://localhost:7001/console. This will prompt you for the system user ID and password that you configured on installation.

The Connection Factory

First, create the connection factory by expanding the JMS node and clicking the Connection Factories link under JMS in the left-hand pane and then clicking on the Create a new JMS Connection Factory link in the right-hand pane.

Enter `qcFactory` for the Name and JNDI Name, leave the rest as default, and click on Create:

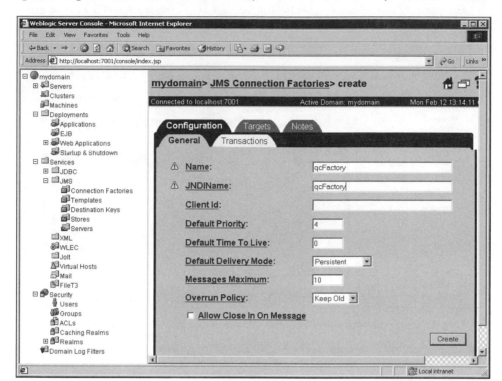

Click on the Targets tab, select myserver in the Available list, move it to the Chosen list, and click Apply.

Destinations

For configuring destinations, first create a store for persistent messages by clicking on the Stores link under the JMS node and click the link Create a new JMSFile Store in the right-hand pane. Give the name as `MyJMSFileStore` and the directory as `C:\temp`. Click on Create:

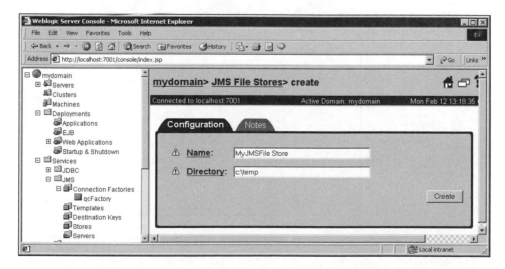

Now click on the **Servers** link under the JMS node and click on the **Create a new JMSServer** link in the right-hand pane. Give the name as **MyJMSServer** and select the store created in the previous step. Leave everything else as default and click **Create**.

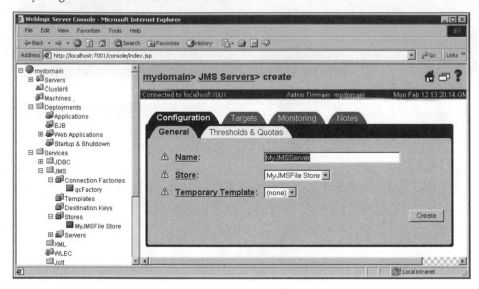

Select the **Targets** tab and move **myserver** from the **Available** list to the **Chosen** list and click **Apply**.

Now click on the **Destinations** node under **MyJMSServer** and click on the link **Create a new JMSQueue** in the right-hand pane. Specify the name and JNDI name as `requestQueue`, leave the rest as default, and click **Create**:

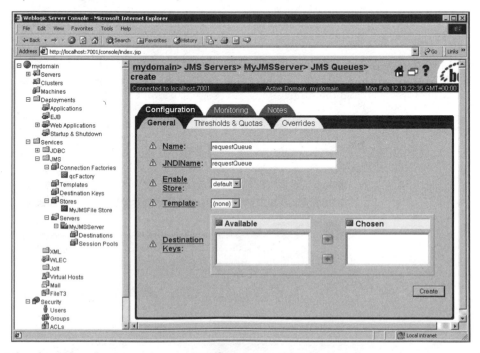

Repeat the above step for a new queue named `responseQueue` as well.

The Case Logging System

This section explains the implementation details of the classes and JSPs used in the case logging system, the customer's view of the application.

The Object Model

The basic entities identified in the case logging system were:

❑   An encapsulation of the details of case responses

❑   A store for the incoming case responses from the message broker

❑   A helper class for generating sequential case IDs

The first entity was called CaseResponse with accessor and mutator methods for the attributes. The following attributes were defined for the CaseResponse entity:

❑   The case ID

❑   The name of the person raising the case

❑   The location of the person

❑   The description of the case

❑   The case status

❑   A comment for the case response

❑   The time at which the response was made

The entity for storing the case requests was called ResponsePool and has the following functionality:

❑   Asynchronously listens to the messages in the response queue

❑   Exposes a method to get the list of case responses for the passed case ID

❑   Exposes a method to get a case request for the specified case ID

❑   Exposes a method to remove a case from the pool for the specified case ID

The helper class for generating case IDs is called IDGenerator with a method for returning the next ID.

The class diagram shown below depicts the entities used in the case logging system:

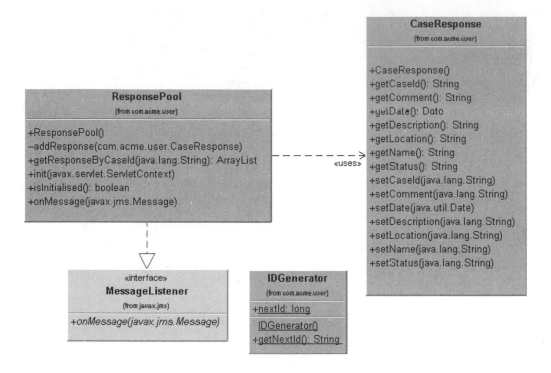

The CaseResponse class follows the basic bean pattern with accessor and mutator methods for the attributes.

The ResponsePool class implements the javax.jms.MessageListener interface to handle asynchronous message delivery, and the java.io.Serializable interface to store the instance of the class in web application session contexts (for replication or persistence). It also defines methods for returning a list of all the case responses for the passed case ID.

Before continuing with the analysis of the web.xml file, which underpins the entire configuration including the security aspects, we'll show how to set up the security details within WebLogic server.

Setting up Security

We need to define the users and groups within the realm of the web container. For our application, we need to create two groups called user and system and users belonging to the groups. For the time being we will create a single user to be added to both the groups. To create a user, click on the Users node under Security in the left-hand pane of the browser-based administration tool, enter the username as tom with an appropriate password, and click on Create.

> Please note that for WebLogic's default security realm the usernames and passwords are case sensitive.

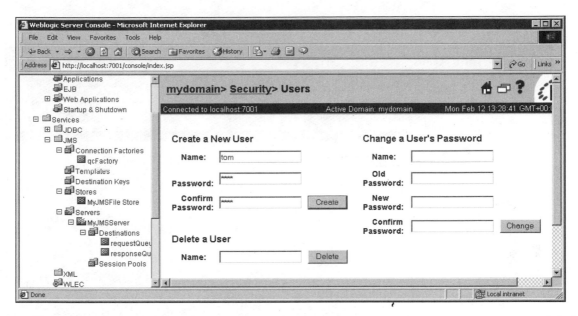

To create a new group click on the Groups node under Security, enter the username as user, and click on Create:

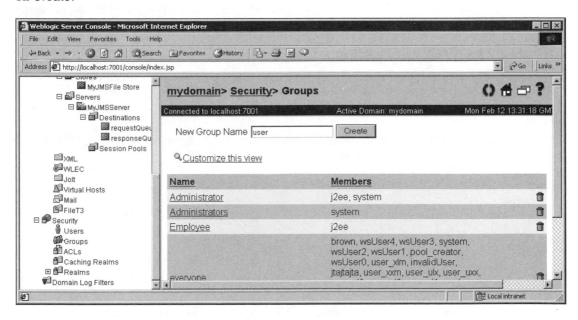

Now to add a user to a group, enter the user `tom` in the following screen:

Repeat the previous steps to create another group called `system` and add the user `tom` to the group `system` as well.

Setting up the Web Application

Now we have configured the necessary security credentials, we get on with implementing the web application itself starting with the all-important `web.xml` file:

web.xml

This is the standard J2EE web application configuration file for declaring servlets/JSPs, URL mapping, security constraints, and initialization arguments:

```
<?xml version="1.0" encoding="Cp1252"?>

<!DOCTYPE web-app PUBLIC "-//Sun Microsystems, Inc.//DTD Web Application 2.2//EN"
"http://java.sun.com/j2ee/dtds/web-app_2_2.dtd">

<web-app>

  <display-name>ACME</display-name>
  <description>ACME Helpdesk System</description>
```

First, we declare the application initialization parameters. These values are available to the application using the `getInitParameter()` method of the servlet context. The initialization parameters declared in the file are the following:

❑ JNDI name of the queue to which case requests are sent

❑ JNDI name of the queue to which case responses are sent

❑ JNDI name of the queue connection factory

❑   JNDI initial context factory name

❑   JNDI service provider URL

```
<context-param>
  <param-name>responseQueue</param-name>
  <param-value>responseQueue</param-value>
</context-param>

<context-param>
  <param-name>requestQueue</param-name>
  <param-value>requestQueue</param-value>
</context-param>

<context-param>
  <param-name>qcFactory</param-name>
  <param-value>qcFactory</param-value>
</context-param>

<context-param>
  <param-name>ctxFactory</param-name>
  <param-value>weblogic.jndi.T3InitialContextFactory</param-value>
</context-param>

<context-param>
  <param-name>provURL</param-name>
  <param-value>t3://localhost:7001</param-value>
</context-param>
```

We then declare the following JSPs:

❑   `newcase.jsp`
This JSP contains the form for submitting a new case

❑   `createcase.jsp`
This JSP does the processing for creating a case and sending JMS messages to the case management system using custom tags

❑   `casehistory.jsp`
This JSP lists the responses received for the case ID entered by the user

```
<servlet>
  <servlet-name>NewCase</servlet-name>
  <jsp-file>newcase.jsp</jsp-file>
</servlet>

<servlet>
  <servlet-name>CreateCase</servlet-name>
  <jsp-file>createcase.jsp</jsp-file>
</servlet>

<servlet>
  <servlet-name>CaseHistory</servlet-name>
  <jsp-file>casehistory.jsp</jsp-file>
</servlet>
```

The following servlet mappings are declared next:

- ❑ The URL `NewCase` is mapped to `newcase.jsp`
- ❑ The URL `CreateCase` is mapped to `createcase.jsp`
- ❑ The URL `CaseHistory` is mapped to `casehistory.jsp`

```
<servlet-mapping>
  <servlet-name>NewCase</servlet-name>
  <url-pattern>NewCase</url-pattern>
</servlet-mapping>

<servlet-mapping>
  <servlet-name>CreateCase</servlet-name>
  <url-pattern>CreateCase</url-pattern>
</servlet-mapping>

<servlet-mapping>
  <servlet-name>CaseHistory</servlet-name>
  <url-pattern>CaseHistory</url-pattern>
</servlet-mapping>
```

The list of welcome files is declared next. The first file displayed after user authentication is `index.jsp`:

```
<welcome-file-list>
  <welcome-file>/index.jsp</welcome-file>
</welcome-file-list>
```

Then the tag library URI is declared. This helps the developers to refer to tag libraries using symbolic URIs rather than specifying relative paths:

```
<taglib>
  <taglib-uri>/user</taglib-uri>
  <taglib-location>/WEB-INF/user.tld</taglib-location>
</taglib>
```

The web application uses standard J2EE web container form-based authentication declared in the `web.xml` file. Access to all the resources in the web application is restricted to the users belonging to the group `user`. The users and groups are to be defined within the realm of the web container in which the web application will be deployed. The configuration file also specifies the page to be presented to the user for authentication as well as the page to be presented when authentication fails. In our case both pages are defined by `logon.jsp`:

```
<security-constraint>

  <web-resource-collection>
    <web-resource-name>user</web-resource-name>
    <url-pattern>/*</url-pattern>
  </web-resource-collection>

  <auth-constraint>
    <description>Helpdesk Users</description>
```

```
            <role-name>user</role-name>
        </auth-constraint>

        <user-data-constraint>
            <transport-guarantee>NONE</transport-guarantee>
        </user-data-constraint>

    </security-constraint>

    <login-config>
        <auth-method>FORM</auth-method>
        <form-login-config>
            <form-login-page>/logon.jsp</form-login-page>
            <form-error-page>/logon.jsp</form-error-page>
        </form-login-config>
    </login-config>

    <security-role>
        <description>Helpdesk Users</description>
        <role-name>user</role-name>
    </security-role>

</web-app>
```

The Logon Screen

This is how our final application will look. For accessing the case logging system, the user would enter the following URL to the browser http://localhost:7001/user. This will prompt them with the screen for entering username and password:

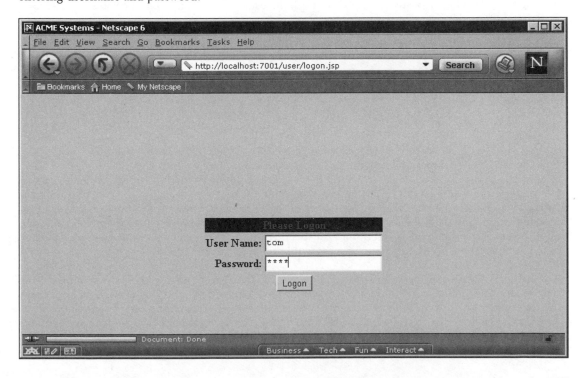

Upon entering valid information and hitting Logon, they will be presented with the index page:

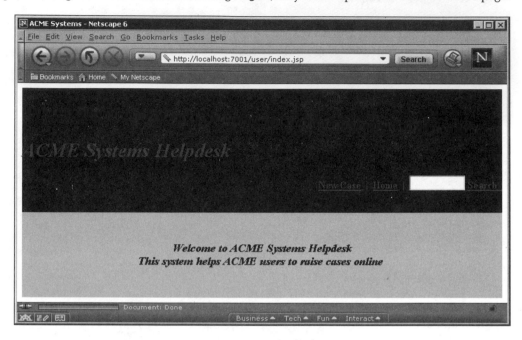

The logon.jsp Page

This JSP is used for authenticating the users. Both case logging and case management systems share the code in this file. This file is also redisplayed when the user authentication fails because of invalid security credentials:

```
<%@ page language="Java" %>

<HTML>

  <HEAD><TITLE>ACME Systems</TITLE></HEAD>

  <BODY BGCOLOR="#CCCCCC" >
    <BR><BR><BR><BR><BR><BR><BR><BR><BR>
```

For standard form-based authentication the login page should have a form with action name j_security_check and two input fields, one named j_username and the other named j_password.

In HTTP form-based authentication, the names of the pages to be presented to the user for security authentication, and on authentication failure, are specified in the deployment descriptor for the web applications. The deployment descriptor also specifies the security group to which the users should belong to be able to access specific resources within the web application.

The real definition of the users and groups, however, is done within the web container. When a user first accesses a resource within the web application the container presents the logon page specified in the deployment descriptor to the user. Once the user fills in the credentials and submits the form, the container uses a resource mapped to the HTTP action j_security_check that does the authentication in a container-specific manner. This resource expects the username and password as HTTP request parameters named j_username and j_password respectively.

If the authentication fails due to invalid security credentials the container presents the user with the error page or else the user is given access to the resources within the web application depending on the access control specified in the deployment descriptor:

```
    <FORM ACTION="j_security_check" METHOD="post">
    <TABLE ALIGN="center">
      <TR>
        <TD COLSPAN="2" ALIGN="center" BGCOLOR="#000000">
          <FONT SIZE="3" COLOR="#0055FF">
            <B>Please Logon</B>
          </FONT>
        </TD>
      </TR>
      <TR><TD ALIGN="right"><B>User Name:</B></TD>
          <TD><INPUT TYPE="text" NAME="j_username"></TD>
      </TR>
      <TR><TD ALIGN="right"><B>Password:</B></TD>
          <TD><INPUT TYPE="password" NAME="j_password"></TD>
      </TR>
      <TR><TD COLSPAN=2 ALIGN="center">
            <INPUT TYPE="submit" value="Logon">
          </TD>
      </TR>
    </TABLE>
    </FORM>
  </BODY>
</HTML>
```

The banner.jsp Page

This JSP is included in all the JSP files in the case logging system and it contains the common menu items and search field to enter case IDs:

```
<%@ page language="Java" %>
<TD VALIGN="center" BGCOLOR="#000000">
  <FONT SIZE="6" COLOR="#0055FF">
    <B><I>ACME Systems Helpdesk</I></B>
  </FONT>
</TD>
<TD VALIGN="bottom" ALIGN="right" BGCOLOR="#000000">
```

The form contains three actions. The first link points to the URL NewCase, which is mapped to newcase.jsp through the web.xml. The second link points to the file index.jsp. The third submits the form named history, which defines an input field for specifying the caseID. The form's action is CaseHistory, which is mapped to casehistory.jsp:

```
    <FORM NAME="history" ACTION="CaseHistory" METHOD="post">

    <A HREF="NewCase">
      <FONT SIZE="3" COLOR="#0055FF">
        <B>New Case</B>
      </FONT>
    </A>
```

```
        <FONT SIZE="3" COLOR="#0055FF">
          <B> | </B>
        </FONT>

        <A HREF="index.jsp">
          <FONT SIZE="3" COLOR="#0055FF">
            <B>Home</B>
          </FONT>
        </A>

        <FONT SIZE="3" COLOR="#0055FF">
          <B> | </B>
        </FONT>

        <INPUT TYPE="TEXT" name="caseId" SIZE="10">
        <A HREF="javascript:history.submit()">
          <FONT SIZE="3" COLOR="#0055FF">
            <B>Search  </B>
          </FONT>
        </A>
      </FORM>
      <BR>

  </TD>
```

The index.jsp Page

This is the first file served to the user after authentication:

```
<%@ page language="Java" %>
```

This JSP initializes an instance of the class `ResponsePool` by passing in the `ServletContext` extracted from `pageContext`. This instance will asynchronously listen to the case responses coming from the case management system through the message broker and acts as a data repository for the case responses:

```
<jsp:useBean id="responsePool" scope="application"
  class="com.acme.user.ResponsePool" />
<%
  if(!responsePool.isInitialized()) {
    responsePool.init(pageContext.getServletContext());
  }
%>
<HTML>
  <HEAD><TITLE>ACME Systems</TITLE></HEAD>

  <BODY>

  <TABLE WIDTH="100%" HEIGHT="100%" CELLPADDING="0" CELLSPACING="0">

    <TR HEIGHT="20%">
      <%@ include file="banner.jsp" %>
    </TR>

    <TR>
```

```
            <TD BGCOLOR="#CCCCCC" COLSPAN="2" ALIGN="center">
            <B><I><FONT SIZE="4" COLOR="#000000">
              Welcome to ACME Systems Helpdesk<BR>
              This system helps ACME users to raise cases online
              <BR>
            </FONT></I></B>
            </TD>
          </TR>

        </TABLE>

      </BODY>

    </HTML>
```

The Business Logic

We now examine the Java code that implements the logic of the customer logging application.

The newcase.jsp Page

This JSP presents the user with a form to enter the initial case details. In the application, the user would first click on **New Case** link on the banner in the welcome page:

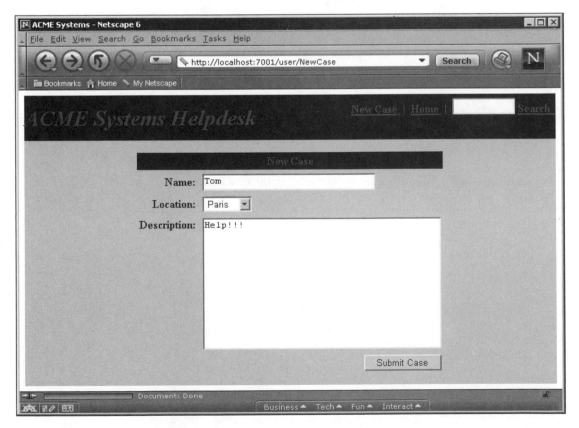

This JSP file contains the form for entering the details for a new case:

```
<%@ page language="Java"%>
<HTML>

  <HEAD><TITLE>ACME Systems</TITLE></HEAD>

  <BODY>

    <TABLE WIDTH="100%" HEIGHT= 100% CELLPADDING "0" CELLSPACING="0">

      <TR HEIGHT="20%">
        <%@ include file="banner.jsp" %>
      </TR>

      <TR>
        <TD BGCOLOR="#CCCCCC" COLSPAN="2" ALIGN="center">
```

The JSP listed above provides a form for entering the details for a new case. The form's action is CreateCase, which is in turn mapped to createcase.jsp:

```
<FORM METHOD="post" ACTION="CreateCase">
  <TABLE CELLPADDING="3" CELLSPACING="3">
    <TR>
      <TD COLSPAN="2" ALIGN="center" BGCOLOR="#000000">
        <FONT SIZE="3" COLOR="#0055FF">
          <B>New Case</B>
        </FONT>
      </TD>
    </TR>
    <TR>
      <TD ALIGN="right">
        <B>Name:</B>
      </TD>
```

The form defines the following controls for entering the case details:

❑ A text control to enter the name of the person

❑ A select control to specify the location

❑ A text area to specify the case description

```
      <TD><INPUT SIZE="30" NAME="name"></TD>
    </TR>
    <TR><TD ALIGN="right">
         <B>Location:</B>
        </TD>
        <TD>
          <SELECT name="location">
            <OPTION>Berlin</OPTION>
            <OPTION>London</OPTION>
            <OPTION>Paris</OPTION>
```

```
            <OPTION>Zurich</OPTION>
         </SELECT>
      </TD>
   </TR>
   <TR><TD VALIGN="top" ALIGN="right">
         <B>Description:</B>
      </TD>
      <TD><TEXTAREA NAME="description" COLS="40"
                    ROWS="10"></TEXTAREA>
      </TD>
   </TR>
   <TR>
     <TD COLSPAN="2" ALIGN="right">
        <INPUT TYPE="submit" value="Submit Case">
     </TD>
   </TR>
  </TABLE>
  </FORM>
 </TD>
 </TR>
 </TABLE>

 </BODY>

</HTML>
```

The createcase.jsp Page

This JSP is called when the user submits a new case. In the New Case page the user would click on
Submit Case:

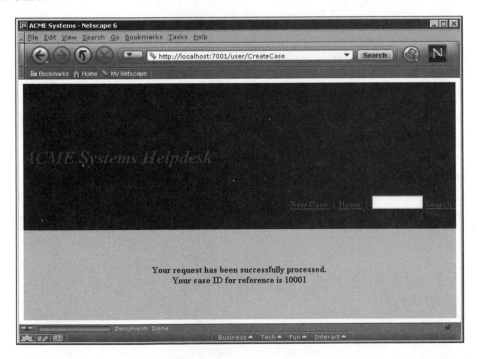

The JSP file declares a tag library with prefix as user and the URI as /user. This URI will be resolved to a tag library descriptor by interrogating the web.xml file. The actual mapping of the file user.tld to the resource /user was done in the deployment descriptor for the web application:

```
<%@ page language="Java"%>
<%@ taglib uri="/user" prefix="user" %>
<HTML>

  <HEAD><TITLE>ACME Systems</TITLE></HEAD>

  <BODY>

    <TABLE WIDTH="100%" HEIGHT="100%" CELLPADDING="0" CELLSPACING="0">

      <TR HEIGHT="20%">
        <%@ include file="banner.jsp" %>
      </TR>


      <TR>
        <TD BGCOLOR="#CCCCCC" COLSPAN="2" ALIGN="center">
```

The JSP file also uses the custom tag createCase, which will invoke the relevant methods in the CreateCaseTag class. The tag handler class will retrieve the case details entered by the user and send a JMS message as explained earlier. It also stores the generated case ID as an HTTP request attribute, which is later retrieved and rendered by the JSP:

```
        <user:createCase/>
        <B>
          Your request has been successfully processed.<br>
          Your case ID for reference is
          <%= caseId %>
        </B>
      </TD>
    </TR>

  </TABLE>

  </BODY>

</HTML>
```

The casehistory.jsp Page

This JSP is invoked when the user searches the case status by specifying the case ID. Note that the full listing shown here will not occur until the helpdesk has responded to the initial enquiry. So if, for example, the user entered the case ID 10001 and clicked on the link Search:

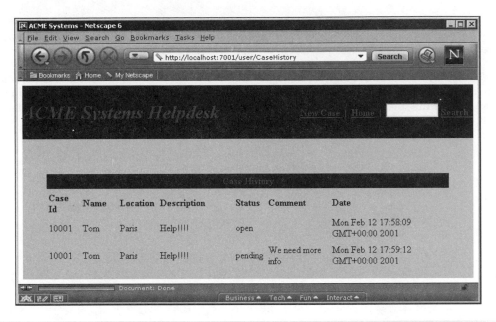

```
<%@ page language="Java"%>
<%@ taglib uri="/user" prefix="user" %>

<HTML>

  <HEAD><TITLE>ACME Systems</TITLE></HEAD>

  <BODY>

    <TABLE WIDTH="100%" HEIGHT="100%" CELLPADDING="0" CELLSPACING="0">

      <TR HEIGHT="20%">
        <%@ include file="banner.jsp" %>
      </TR>

      <TR>
        <TD BGCOLOR="#CCCCCC" COLSPAN="2" ALIGN="center">
          <TABLE CELLPADDING="3" CELLSPACING="3" WIDTH="90%">
            <TR>
              <TD COLSPAN="7" ALIGN="center" BGCOLOR="#000000">
                <FONT SIZE="3" COLOR="#0055FF">
                  <B>Case History</B>
                  </FONT>
                </TD>
              </TR>
            <TR>
                <TD><B>Case Id</B></TD>
                <TD><B>Name</B></TD>
                <TD><B>Location</B></TD>
                <TD><B>Description</B></TD>
                <TD><B>Status</B></TD>
                <TD><B>Comment</B></TD>
                <TD><B>Date</B></TD>
              </TR>
```

The JSP declares the tag library `user`. It uses the custom tag `caseHistory` whose tag handler class is `CaseHistoryTag`. This tag will be executed multiple times depending on the number of items in the case response list for the specified case ID in the application scope bean `responsePool`.

The request scope bean `caseResponse` of type `CaseResponse` is declared with in the aforementioned custom tag. Each time the tag is iterated the tag handler class retrieves the next available item in the response list for the specified case ID and stores it in the HTTP request object. The JSP renders the attributes of the case response object using the standard `getProperty` tag of `useBean`:

```
<user:caseHistory>
  <jsp:useBean id="caseResponse" scope="request"
    class="com.acme.user.CaseResponse" />
  <TR>
  <TD>
  <jsp:getProperty name="caseResponse" property="caseId" />
  </TD>
  <TD>
  <jsp:getProperty name="caseResponse" property="name" />
  </TD>
  <TD>
  <jsp:getProperty name="caseResponse" property="location" />
  </TD>
  <TD>
  <jsp:getProperty name="caseResponse" property="description" />
  </TD>
  <TD>
  <jsp:getProperty name="caseResponse" property="status" />
  </TD>
  <TD>
  <jsp:getProperty name="caseResponse" property="comment" />
  </TD>
  <TD>
  <jsp:getProperty name="caseResponse" property="date" />
  </TD>
  </TR>
</user:caseHistory>
</TABLE>
</TD>
</TR>

</TABLE>

</BODY>

</HTML>
```

The CaseResponse Class

This is the class that models a response received from the case management system. This class has been explained in detail in the section on the object model. This class is used as the type for the request scope bean explained in `casehistory.jsp`:

```
package com.acme.user;

import java.util.Date;
```

```
public class CaseResponse {

  private String caseId;
  private String name;
  private String location;
  private String description;
  private String status;
  private String comment;
  private Date date;

  public CaseResponse() {
  }

  public String getCaseId() {
    return caseId;
  }

  public void setCaseId(String caseId) {
    this.caseId = caseId;
  }

  public String getName() {
    return name;
  }

  public void setName(String name) {
    this.name = name;
  }

  public String getLocation() {
    return location;
  }

  public void setLocation(String location) {
    this.location = location;
  }

  public String getDescription() {
    return description;
  }

  public void setDescription(String description) {
    this.description = description;
  }

  public String getStatus() {
    return status;
  }

  public void setStatus(String status) {
    this.status = status;
  }

  public String getComment() {
    return comment;
```

```
    }

    public void setComment(String comment) {
      this.comment = comment;
    }

    public Date getDate() {
      return date;
    }

    public void setDate(Date date) {
      this.date = date;
    }

  }
```

The ResponsePool Class

An instance of this class works as a data repository for the case responses coming from the case management system. One thing to note here is in real world implementation you may be backing up the data modeled by this class into persistent data storage. The same instance is used as an application scope bean that listens for JMS messages sent to the response pool by the case management system:

```
package com.acme.user;

import java.util.HashMap;
import java.util.ArrayList;
import java.util.Date;
import javax.naming.*;
import javax.jms.*;
import java.io.Serializable;

import javax.servlet.ServletContext;
import com.acme.common.JMSManager;
import com.acme.common.IJMSConstants;
```

This class implements `javax.jms.MessageListener` interface for asynchronously receiving the response messages sent by the case management system to the response queue:

```
public class ResponsePool implements MessageListener, Serializable {
```

The class uses three instance variables:

❑   A `Boolean` to indicate whether the instance of the class is initialized or not. The instances are initialized by calling the `init()` method.

❑   An instance of `JMSManager` that acts a message consumer to the response queue.

❑   An instance of `HashMap` that stores a map of case IDs to list of responses for that case. This data structure is interrogated when the users query case statuses by specifying case IDs.

```
private boolean initialized;
private JMSManager responseManager;
private HashMap responseMap = new HashMap();
```

The init() method takes an instance of ServletContext as the argument. It then queries the web.xml file through the instance of servlet context for the JMS configuration information. This information is then used to create and initialize responseManager and the instance of the class registers itself as a message listener with the responseManager. Finally it sets the value of initialized to true:

```
public void init(ServletContext ctx) throws NamingException,
    JMSException,Exception {

  String responseQueue = ctx.getInitParameter("responseQueue");
  System.out.println("responseQueue: " + responseQueue);

  String qcFactory = ctx.getInitParameter("qcFactory");
  System.out.println("qcFactory: " + qcFactory);

  String ctxFactory = ctx.getInitParameter("ctxFactory");
  System.out.println("ctxFactory: " + ctxFactory);

  String provURL = ctx.getInitParameter("provURL");
  System.out.println("provURL: " + provURL);

  responseManager = new JMSManager(ctxFactory, provURL,
    responseQueue, qcFactory, IJMSConstants.PTP_MODEL);
  responseManager.initializeJMS(IJMSConstants.CONSUMER,
    this, true);

  initialized = true;

}

public boolean isInitialized() {
  return initialized;
}
```

The callback method for asynchronous messages retrieves the case response details from the message and creates an instance of CaseResponse class. If the case ID is already present in the responseMap, the list stored against the case ID is retrieved and the response is added to the list. Otherwise a new list is created, and the response is added to the list and stored in the responseMap against the case ID:

```
public synchronized void onMessage(Message msg) {

  try {

    MapMessage mapMsg = (MapMessage)msg;

    CaseResponse response = new CaseResponse();
    response.setCaseId(mapMsg.getString("caseId"));
    response.setName(mapMsg.getString("name"));
    response.setLocation(mapMsg.getString("location"));
    response.setDescription(mapMsg.getString("description"));
    response.setStatus(mapMsg.getString("status"));
    response.setComment(mapMsg.getString("comment"));
    response.setDate(new Date());

    addResponse(response);
```

```
    } catch(JMSException e) {
      e.printStackTrace();
    }

  }
```

The class also provides a method for retrieving the list of responses for a given case ID:

```
  public synchronized ArrayList getResponseByCaseId(String caseId) {

    ArrayList ls = (ArrayList)responseMap.get(caseId);
    return (ls !=null)?((ArrayList)ls.clone()):(new ArrayList());

  }
```

```
  private void addResponse(CaseResponse response) {

    ArrayList list = (ArrayList)responseMap.get(response.getCaseId());
    if(list == null) {
      list = new ArrayList();
      responseMap.put(response.getCaseId(), list);
    }
    list.add(response);

  }

}
```

The JSP Tag Library

This is the tag library descriptor file `user.tld` that stores the information about the custom tags used in the system:

```
<?xml version="1.0"  ?>
<!DOCTYPE taglib PUBLIC "-//Sun Microsystems, Inc.//DTD JSP Tag Library 1.1//EN"
"web-jsptaglib_1_1.dtd">

<taglib>

  <tlibversion>1.0</tlibversion>
  <jspversion>1.1</jspversion>
  <shortname>User</shortname>
  <info>
    This tag library contains tag extensions
  </info>
```

This file defines two custom tags explained in the previous sections. The custom tag `createCase` is associated with the tag handler class `com.acme.user.CreateCaseTag` and the body content is defined as empty and defines `com.acme.user.CreateCaseTagVariableInfo` as the tag extra info class:

```
  <tag>
    <name>createCase</name>
    <tagclass>com.acme.user.CreateCaseTag</tagclass>
    <teiclass>com.acme.user.CreateCaseTagVariableInfo</teiclass>
    <bodycontent>JSP</bodycontent>
  </tag>
```

The custom tag `caseHistory` is associated with the tag handler class
`com.acme.user.CaseHistoryTag` and the body content is defined as parsable JSP content:

```
<tag>
  <name>caseHistory</name>
  <tagclass>com.acme.user.CaseHistoryTag</tagclass>
  <bodycontent>JSP</bodycontent>
</tag>

</taglib>
```

The CreateCaseTag Class

This is the tag handler class for the custom tag `createCase`:

```
package com.acme.user;

import javax.servlet.jsp.*;
import javax.servlet.jsp.tagext.*;
import javax.servlet.*;
import javax.servlet.http.*;
import javax.jms.*;
import com.acme.common.*;

public class CreateCaseTag extends TagSupport {
```

In the `doStartTag()` method of the tag handler instances of `ServletContext` and
`HttpServletRequest` are retrieved from the implicit variable `pageContext`. The servlet context is
then used to retrieve the JMS configuration information. This information is used to create and initialize
an instance of `JMSManager` that will act as a message producer to the request queue.

The case details are retrieved from the HTTP request object and the next available case ID is retrieved
from `IDGenerator`. These details are stored in a JMS map message and the message is sent to the
request queue using the instance of `JMSManager`. The retrieved case ID is then stored in the HTTP
request object to be retrieved by the enclosing JSP:

```
public int doStartTag() throws JspTagException {

  try {

    ServletContext ctx = pageContext.getServletContext();
    HttpServletRequest req =
      (HttpServletRequest)pageContext.getRequest();

    String requestQueue = ctx.getInitParameter("requestQueue");
    System.out.println("requestQueue: " + requestQueue);

    String qcFactory = ctx.getInitParameter("qcFactory");
    System.out.println("qcFactory: " + qcFactory);

    String ctxFactory = ctx.getInitParameter("ctxFactory");
    System.out.println("ctxFactory: " + ctxFactory);
```

```
        String provURL = ctx.getInitParameter("provURL");
        System.out.println("provURL: " + provURL);

        JMSManager requestManager =
          new JMSManager(ctxFactory, provURL, requestQueue, qcFactory,
            IJMSConstants.PTP_MODEL);
        requestManager.initializeJMS(IJMSConstants.PRODUCER, null, true);

        MapMessage msg = requestManager.createMapMessage();
        String caseId = IDGenerator.getNextId();
        msg.setString("caseId", caseId);
        msg.setString("name", req.getParameter("name"));
        msg.setString("location", req.getParameter("location"));
        msg.setString("description", req.getParameter("description"));

        requestManager.sendMessage(msg,true);
        requestManager.closeJMS();

        pageContext.setAttribute("caseId",caseId);

        return EVAL_BODY_INCLUDE;

    } catch(Exception e) {

        System.out.println("Exception in doStartTag: CreateCaseTag");
        System.out.println(e.getClass());
        System.out.println(e.getMessage());
        e.printStackTrace();
        throw new JspTagException(e.getMessage());

    }

  }

  public int doEndTag() throws JspTagException {
    return EVAL_PAGE;
  }

}
```

The CreateCaseTagVariableInfo Class

This class is used to notify the JSP engine about the scripting variable introduced by the case create tag. Tag extra info classes are used in custom tags for introducing scripting variables in the JSP enclosing the custom tag:

```
package com.acme.user;

import javax.servlet.jsp.tagext.TagExtraInfo;
import javax.servlet.jsp.tagext.VariableInfo;
import javax.servlet.jsp.tagext.TagData;

public class CreateCaseTagVariableInfo extends TagExtraInfo {

  public VariableInfo[] getVariableInfo(TagData data) {

    VariableInfo info[] = new VariableInfo[1];
```

The tag extra info class introduces a variable named `caseId` of type `java.lang.String` that is available from the beginning of the tag to the end of the JSP and is newly declared by the JSP engine. This variable is used in the JSP for displaying the case ID:

```
        info[0] = new VariableInfo("caseId", "java.lang.String",
                    true, VariableInfo.AT_BEGIN);
        return info;
    }
}
```

The CaseHistoryTag Class

This is the tag handler class for the custom tag `caseHistory`:

```
package com.acme.user;

import javax.servlet.jsp.*;
import javax.servlet.jsp.tagext.*;
import javax.servlet.*;
import javax.servlet.http.*;
import javax.jms.*;
import com.acme.common.*;
import java.util.*;

public class CaseHistoryTag extends BodyTagSupport {

    private Iterator it;
```

In the `doStartTag()` method of the tag handler, instances of `ServletContext` and `HttpServletRequest` are retrieved from the implicit variable `pageContext`. The servlet context is then used to retrieve an instance of the application scope bean `responsePool`. The requested case ID is retrieved from the HTTP Request object. The `responsePool` object is then queried to get a list of responses for the specified case ID. If the returned list is empty the method returns `SKIP_BODY`, otherwise an iterator is set to the list, the first object in the list is stored in the HTTP Request object, and `EVAL_BODY_TAG` is returned, which will cause the body of the custom tag to be evaluated:

```
    public int doStartTag() throws JspTagException {

        ServletContext ctx = pageContext.getServletContext();
        HttpServletRequest req =
          (HttpServletRequest)pageContext.getRequest();

        ResponsePool pool = (ResponsePool)ctx.getAttribute("responsePool");
        String caseId = req.getParameter("caseId");
        System.out.println(caseId);

        it = pool.getResponseByCaseId(caseId).iterator();

        if(it.hasNext()) {
            req.setAttribute("caseResponse", it.next());
            return EVAL_BODY_TAG;
        }

        System.out.println("Iterator is empty.");

        return SKIP_BODY;

    }
```

In the doAfterBody() method, the current body content is flushed into the enclosing writer. If the iterator retrieved in the doStartTag() method contains more elements, the next available in the list is stored in the HTTP Request object by the name caseResponse and EVAL_BODY is returned. Otherwise SKIP_BODY is retuned, which will break out of the tag loop:

```
public int doAfterBody(){

  try {
    BodyContent body = getBodyContent();
    if(body != null) {
      getBodyContent().getEnclosingWriter().write(body.getString());
      body.clear();
    }
  } catch(Exception e) {
    new JspTagException(e.getMessage());
  }

  if(it.hasNext()) {
    pageContext.getRequest().setAttribute("caseResponse", it.next());
    return EVAL_BODY_TAG;
  }

  return SKIP_BODY;

}
```

```
public int doEndTag() throws JspTagException {
  return EVAL_PAGE;
}

}
```

The IDGenerator Class

This is a helper class for generating sequential case IDs:

```
package com.acme.user;

public class IDGenerator {

  public static long nextId = 10000;

  public static synchronized String getNextId() {
    return String.valueOf(++nextId);
  }

}
```

The Case Management System

This section explains the implementation details of the classes and JSPs used in the case management system.

The Object Model

The two basic entities identified in the case management system were:

❑ An encapsulation of the details of case requests

❑ A store for the incoming case requests from the message broker

The first entity was called `CaseRequest` with accessor and mutator methods for the attributes. The following attributes were defined for the `CaseRequest` entity:

❑ The case ID

❑ The name of the person raising the case

❑ The location of the person

❑ The description of the case

The entity for storing the case requests was called `RequestPool` and was expected to have the following functionality:

❑ Asynchronously listen to the messages in the request queue

❑ Expose a method to get the case requests currently in the pool

❑ Expose a method to get a case request for the specified case ID

❑ Expose a method to remove a case from the pool for the specified case ID

The class diagram shown below depicts the entities used in the case management system:

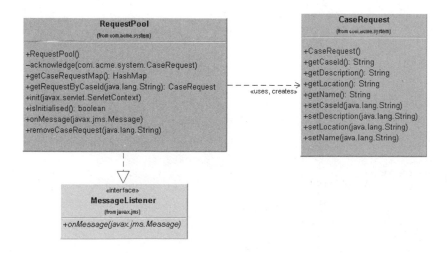

The `CaseRequest` class follows the basic bean pattern with accessor and mutator methods for the attributes.

The `RequestPool` class implements the `javax.jms.MessageListener` interface to handle asynchronous message delivery, and the `java.io.Serializable` interface for cloning and persistence by the web container. It also defines methods to: return a map of all the case IDs to case requests available in the pool; return a case request for the passed case ID; and remove a case request identified by the passed case ID.

Setting up the Security

If you haven't already done so, repeat the previous steps with the WebLogic console to create a group called `system` and add the user `tom` to the group.

Setting up the Web Application

This is the standard J2EE web application configuration file for declaring servlets/JSPs, URL mapping, security constraints, and initialization arguments. It follows the same pattern as for the `web.xml` file of the case logging system, so we will not examine it in detail:

```xml
<?xml version="1.0" encoding="Cp1252"?>

<!DOCTYPE web-app PUBLIC "-//Sun Microsystems, Inc.//DTD Web Application 2.2//EN"
"http://java.sun.com/j2ee/dtds/web-app_2_2.dtd">

<web-app>

  <display-name>ACME</display-name>
  <description>ACME Helpdesk System</description>

  <context-param>
    <param-name>responseQueue</param-name>
    <param-value>responseQueue</param-value>
  </context-param>

  <context-param>
    <param-name>requestQueue</param-name>
    <param-value>requestQueue</param-value>
  </context-param>

  <context-param>
    <param-name>qcFactory</param-name>
    <param-value>qcFactory</param-value>
  </context-param>

  <context-param>
    <param-name>ctxFactory</param-name>
    <param-value>weblogic.jndi.T3InitialContextFactory</param-value>
  </context-param>

  <context-param>
    <param-name>provURL</param-name>
    <param-value>t3://localhost</param-value>
  </context-param>
```

```
<servlet>
  <servlet-name>ListCase</servlet-name>
  <jsp-file>listcase.jsp</jsp-file>
</servlet>

<servlet>
  <servlet-name>ViewCase</servlet-name>
  <jsp-file>viewcase.jsp</jsp-file>
</servlet>

<servlet>
  <servlet-name>UpdateCase</servlet-name>
  <jsp-file>updatecase.jsp</jsp-file>
</servlet>

<servlet-mapping>
  <servlet-name>ListCase</servlet-name>
  <url-pattern>ListCase</url-pattern>
</servlet-mapping>

<servlet-mapping>
  <servlet-name>ViewCase</servlet-name>
  <url-pattern>ViewCase</url-pattern>
</servlet-mapping>

<servlet-mapping>
  <servlet-name>UpdateCase</servlet-name>
  <url-pattern>UpdateCase</url-pattern>
</servlet-mapping>

<welcome-file-list>
  <welcome-file>/index.jsp</welcome-file>
</welcome-file-list>

<taglib>
  <taglib-uri>/system</taglib-uri>
  <taglib-location>/WEB-INF/system.tld</taglib-location>
</taglib>

<security-constraint>

  <web-resource-collection>
    <web-resource-name>system</web-resource-name>
    <url-pattern>/*</url-pattern>
  </web-resource-collection>

  <auth-constraint>
    <description>Helpdesk Assistants</description>
    <role-name>system</role-name>
  </auth-constraint>

  <user-data-constraint>
    <transport-guarantee>NONE</transport-guarantee>
  </user-data-constraint>
```

```
      </security-constraint>

      <login-config>
        <auth-method>FORM</auth-method>
        <form-login-config>
          <form-login-page>/logon.jsp</form-login-page>
          <form-error-page>/logon.jsp</form-error-page>
        </form-login-config>
      </login-config>

      <security-role>
        <description>Helpdesk Assistants</description>
        <role-name>system</role-name>
      </security-role>

    </web-app>
```

The Welcome Screen

In the application we log on to the case management system by entering the URL
http://localhost:7001/system in the browser and entering the system ID and password:

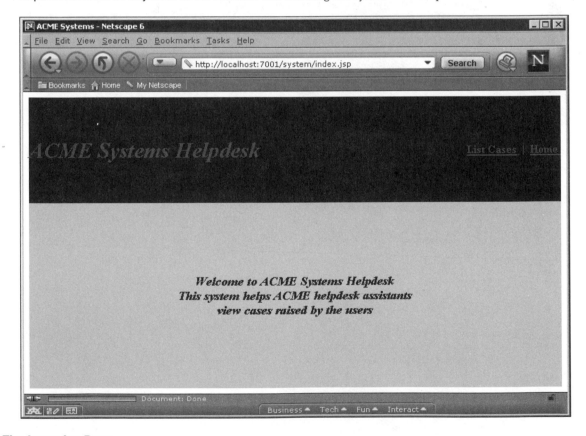

The logon.jsp Page

This is exactly the same as before.

The banner.jsp Page

This JSP is included in all the JSP files in the case management system, and it contains the common menu items. The JSP basically displays two links. The first link points to the URL `ListCase`, which is mapped to `listcase.jsp`. The second link points to the file `index.jsp`:

```
<%@ page language="Java" %>
<TD VALIGN="center" ALIGN="left" BGCOLOR="#000000">
  <FONT SIZE="6" COLOR="#0055FF">
    <B><I>ACME Systems Helpdesk</I></B>
  </FONT>
</TD>

<TD ALIGN="right" BGCOLOR="#000000">
  <A HREF="ListCase">
    <FONT SIZE="3" COLOR="#0055FF">
      <B>List Cases</B>
    </FONT>
  </A>
  <FONT SIZE="3" COLOR="#0055FF">
  <B>  | </B>
  <A HREF="index.jsp">
    <FONT SIZE="3" COLOR="#0055FF">
      <B>Home </B>
    </FONT>
  </A>
</TD>
```

The index.jsp Page

This is the first file served to the user after authentication. This JSP initializes an instance of the class `RequestPool` by passing the implicit variable `pageContext`. This instance will asynchronously listen to the case requests coming from the case logging system through the message broker and acts as a data repository for the case requests:

```
<%@ page language="Java" %>
<jsp:useBean id="requestPool" scope="application"
  class="com.acme.system.RequestPool" />
<%
  if(!requestPool.isInitialized()) {
    requestPool.init(pageContext.getServletContext());
  }
%>

<HTML>

  <HEAD><TITLE>ACME Systems</TITLE></HEAD>

  <BODY>

    <TABLE BORDER="0" WIDTH="100%" HEIGHT="100%"
      CELLPADDING="0" CELLSPACING="0">

      <TR HEIGHT="20%">
        <%@ include file="banner.jsp" %>
```

```
      </TR>

      <TR>
        <TD BGCOLOR="#CCCCCC" COLSPAN="2" ALIGN="center">
          <B><I>
            <FONT SIZE="4" COLOR="#000000">
              Welcome to ACME Systems Helpdesk<BR>
              This system helps ACME helpdesk assistants<BR>
              view cases raised by the users
            </FONT>
          </I></B>
        </TD>
      </TR>

    </TABLE>

  </BODY>

</HTML>
```

The Business Logic

We now examine the Java code that implements the logic of the helpdesk application.

The listcase.jsp Page

This JSP is used for listing all the pending and open cases in the request pool. In the application we would start by clicking on the List Cases link on the banner:

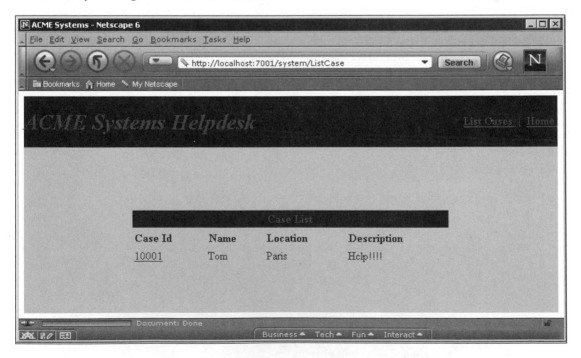

The JSP first declares the tag library. Then it uses the custom tag `listCase` whose tag handler class is `ListCaseTag`:

```
<%@ page language="Java"%>
<%@ taglib uri="/system" prefix="system" %>

<HTML>

  <HEAD><TITLE>ACME Systems</TITLE></HEAD>

  <BODY>

    <TABLE WIDTH="100%" HEIGHT="100%" CELLPADDING="0" CELLSPACING="0">

      <TR HEIGHT="20%">
        <%@ include file="banner.jsp" %>
      </TR>

      <TR>
        <TD BGCOLOR="#CCCCCC" COLSPAN="2" ALIGN="center">
          <TABLE CELLPADDING="3" CELLSPACING="3" WIDTH="60%">
            <TR>
              <TD COLSPAN="4" ALIGN="center" BGCOLOR="#000000">
                <FONT SIZE="3" COLOR="#0055FF">
                  <B>Case List</B>
                </FONT>
              </TD>
            </TR>
            <TR>
              <TD><B>Case Id</B></TD>
              <TD><B>Name</B></TD>
              <TD><B>Location</B></TD>
              <TD><B>Description</B></TD>
            </TR>
```

This tag will be executed multiple times depending on the number of items in the case request list in the application scope bean `requestPool`. The request scope bean `caseRequest` of type `CaseRequest` is declared in the aforementioned custom tag. Each time the tag is iterated the tag handler class retrieves the next available item in the request list and stores it in the HTTP request object. The JSP renders the attributes of the case request object using the standard `getProperty` tag of `useBean` to access the object's attributes:

```
<system:listCase>
  <jsp:useBean id="caseRequest" scope="request"
    class="com.acme.system.CaseRequest" />
  <TR>
  <TD>
  <A href="ViewCase?caseId=<jsp:getProperty name="caseRequest"
    property="caseId" />">
  <jsp:getProperty name="caseRequest" property="caseId" />
  </A>
  </TD>
  <TD>
  <jsp:getProperty name="caseRequest" property="name" />
  </TD>
```

```
          <TD>
          <jsp:getProperty name="caseRequest" property="location" />
          </TD>
          <TD>
          <jsp:getProperty name="caseRequest" property="description" />
          </TD>
          </TR>
       </system:listCase>
     </TABLE>
   </TD>
   </TR>

 </TABLE>

</BODY>

</HTML>
```

The viewcase.jsp Page

This JSP is called when the helpdesk assistant selects a case from the list and requests to view the details. We would view the case details by clicking on the link 10001 in the last screenshot:

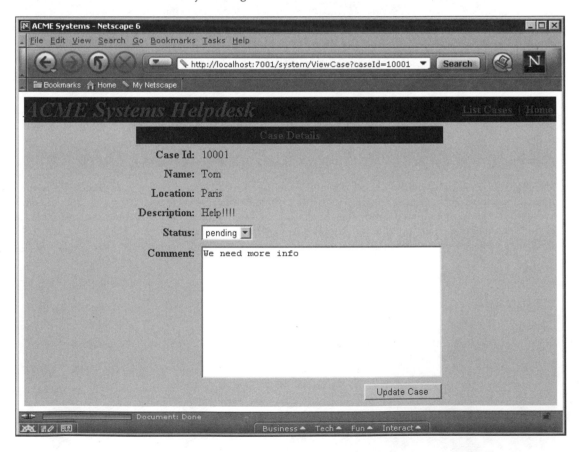

The JSP first declares the tag library. Then it uses the custom tag `viewCase` whose tag handler class is `ViewCaseTag`:

```
<%@ page language="Java"%>
<%@ taglib uri="/system" prefix="system" %>

<HTML>

  <HEAD><TITLE>ACME Systems</TITLE></HEAD>

  <BODY>

    <TABLE WIDTH="100%" HEIGHT="100%" CELLPADDING="0" CELLSPACING="0">

      <TR HEIGHT="20%">
        <%@ include file="banner.jsp" %>
      </TR>

      <TR>
        <TD BGCOLOR="#CCCCCC" COLSPAN="2" ALIGN="center">
```

This tag retrieves the selected case request from the `requestPool`. The request scope bean `caseRequest` of type `CaseRequest` is declared with in the above tag. The JSP renders the attributes of the case request object using the standard `getProperty` tag of `useBean` to access the object's attributes:

```
<system:viewCase>

  <jsp:useBean id="caseRequest" scope="request"
    class="com.acme.system.CaseRequest" />

  <FORM METHOD="post" ACTION="UpdateCase">

  <INPUT NAME="caseId" TYPE="hidden" value=
  "<jsp:getProperty name="caseRequest"
        property="caseId" />">
  <INPUT NAME="name" TYPE="hidden" value=
  "<jsp:getProperty name="caseRequest"
        property="name" />">
  <INPUT NAME="location" TYPE="hidden" value=
  "<jsp:getProperty name="caseRequest"
        property="location" />">
  <INPUT NAME="description" TYPE="hidden" value=
  "<jsp:getProperty name="caseRequest"
        property="description" />">

  <TABLE CELLPADDING="3" CELLSPACING="3">
    <TR>
    <TD COLSPAN="2" ALIGN="center" BGCOLOR="#000000">
        <FONT SIZE="3" COLOR="#0055FF">
          <B>Case Details</B>
        </FONT>
      </TD>
    </TR>
    <TR>
```

```
                    <TD ALIGN="right"><B>Case Id:</B></TD>
                    <TD>
                    <jsp:getProperty name="caseRequest" property="caseId" />
                    </TD>
                  </TR>
                  <TR>
                    <TD ALIGN="right"><B>Name:</B></TD>
                    <TD>
                    <jsp:getProperty name="caseRequest" property="name" />
                    </TD>
                  </TR>
                  <TR>
                    <TD ALIGN="right"><B>Location:</B></TD>
                    <TD>
                    <jsp:getProperty name="caseRequest" property="location" />
                    </TD>
                  </TR>
                  <TR>
                    <TD ALIGN="right"><B>Description:</B></TD>
                    <TD>
                    <jsp:getProperty name="caseRequest" property="description"
                    />
                    </TD>
                  </TR>
                  <TR>
                    <TD ALIGN="right"><B>Status:</B></TD>
                    <TD>
                      <SELECT NAME="status">
                        <OPTION>pending</OPTION>
                        <OPTION>closed</OPTION>
                      </SELECT>
                    </TD>
                  </TR>
                  <TR>
                    <TD VALIGN="top" ALIGN="right"><B>Comment:</B></TD>
                    <TD><TEXTAREA NAME="comment" COLS="40"
                                  ROWS="10"></TEXTAREA>
                    </TD>
                  </TR>
                  <TR><TD COLSPAN="2" ALIGN="right">
                        <INPUT TYPE="submit" value="Update Case">
                      </TD>
                  </TR>
                </TABLE>
              </FORM>
            </system:viewCase>
          </TD>
        </TR>

      </TABLE>

    </BODY>

</HTML>
```

The updatecase.jsp Page

This JSP is called when the helpdesk assistant updates the case status. After adding a comment or solution, click Update Case:

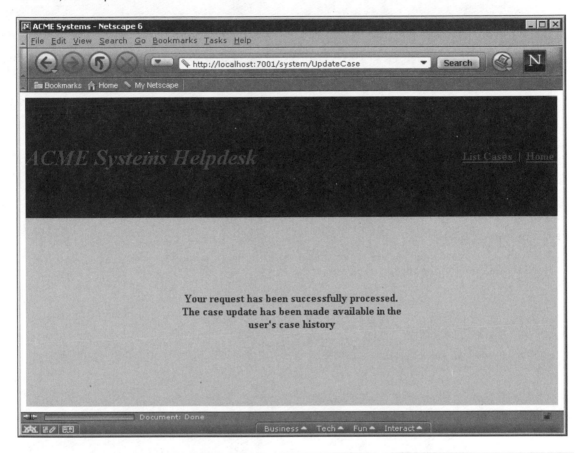

```
<%@ page language="Java"%>
<%@ taglib uri="/system" prefix="system" %>
<HTML>

  <HEAD><TITLE>ACME Systems</TITLE></HEAD>

  <BODY>

    <TABLE BORDER="0" WIDTH="100%" HEIGHT="100%" CELLPADDING="0"
           CELLSPACING="0">

      <TR HEIGHT="20%">
        <%@ include file="banner.jsp" %>
      </TR>

      <TR>
        <TD BGCOLOR="#CCCCCC" COLSPAN="2" ALIGN="center">
```

The JSP file also uses the custom tag `updateCase`, which will invoke the relevant methods in the `UpdateCaseTag` class. The tag handler class will retrieve the case update details entered by the helpdesk assistant and send a JMS message as explained earlier:

```
        <system:updateCase/>
        <B>
          Your request has been successfully processed.<BR>
          The case update has been made available in the<BR>
          user's case history
        </B>

      </TD>
    </TR>

  </TABLE>

</BODY>

</HTML>
```

The CaseRequest Class

This is the class that models a case request received from the case logging system. This class has been explained in detail in the section on the object model:

```java
package com.acme.system;

public class CaseRequest {

  private String caseId;
  private String name;
  private String location;
  private String description;

  public CaseRequest() {}

  public String getCaseId() {
    return caseId;
  }

  public void setCaseId(String caseId) {
    this.caseId = caseId;
  }

  public String getName() {
    return name;
  }

  public void setName(String name) {
    this.name = name;
  }

  public String getLocation() {
    return location;
  }
```

```
  public void setLocation(String location) {
    this.location = location;
  }

  public String getDescription() {
    return description;
  }

  public void setDescription(String description) {
    this.description = description;
  }

}
```

The RequestPool Class

An instance of this class works as a data repository for the case requests coming from the case logging system. The same instance is used as an application scope bean that listens for asynchronous JMS messages sent to the request pool by the case logging system:

```
package com.acme.system;

import java.util.HashMap;
import javax.naming.*;
import javax.jms.*;
import javax.servlet.ServletContext;
import java.io.Serializable;
import com.acme.common.JMSManager;
import com.acme.common.IJMSConstants;
```

This class implements the `javax.jms.MessageListener` interface for asynchronously receiving the request messages sent by the case logging system to the request queue:

```
public class RequestPool implements MessageListener, Serializable {
```

The class uses four instance variables:

- ❑ A `boolean` to indicate whether the instance of the class is initialized or not. The instances are initialized by calling the `init()` method.

- ❑ An instance of `JMSManager` called `requestManager`, that acts as a message consumer to the request queue.

- ❑ An instance of `JMSManager`, called `responseManager` that acts as a message producer to the response queue. This object is used for sending the initial response when a case request first arrives.

- ❑ An instance of `HashMap` that stores a map of case IDs to case requests. This data structure is interrogated when the helpdesk assistants query case request lists and case request details:

```
private boolean initialized;
private JMSManager requestManager;
private JMSManager responseManager;
private HashMap requestMap = new HashMap();
```

The `init()` method takes an instance of `ServletContext` as the argument. It then queries the `web.xml` file through the instance of the servlet context for the JMS configuration information. This information is then used to create and initialize `responseManager` and the instance of the class registers itself as a message listener with the `responseManager`. It also initializes the instance `requestManager`. Finally it sets the value of `initialized` to `true`:

```
public void init(ServletContext ctx) throws NamingException,
    JMSException,Exception {

  String responseQueue = ctx.getInitParameter("responseQueue");
  System.out.println("responseQueue: " + responseQueue);

  String requestQueue = ctx.getInitParameter("requestQueue");
  System.out.println("requestQueue: " + requestQueue);

  String qcFactory = ctx.getInitParameter("qcFactory");
  System.out.println("qcFactory: " + qcFactory);

  String ctxFactory = ctx.getInitParameter("ctxFactory");
  System.out.println("ctxFactory: " + ctxFactory);

  String provURL = ctx.getInitParameter("provURL");
  System.out.println("provURL: " + provURL);

  responseManager = new JMSManager(ctxFactory,provURL,
    responseQueue, qcFactory, IJMSConstants.PTP_MODEL);
  responseManager.initializeJMS(IJMSConstants.PRODUCER,
    null, true);

  requestManager = new JMSManager(ctxFactory,provURL,
    requestQueue,qcFactory,IJMSConstants.PTP_MODEL);
  requestManager.initializeJMS(IJMSConstants.CONSUMER,
    this, true);

  initialized = true;

}

public boolean isInitialized() {
  return initialized;
}
```

The callback method for asynchronous messages retrieves the case request details from the message and creates an instance of `CaseRequest` class. This object is stored against the case ID in the `responseMap`. A response message is then sent to the response pool using `responseManager` with the case status set to "open":

```
public synchronized void onMessage(Message msg) {

  try {

    MapMessage mapMsg = (MapMessage)msg;

    String caseId = mapMsg.getString("caseId");
    String name = mapMsg.getString("name");
```

```
            String location = mapMsg.getString("location");
            String description = mapMsg.getString("description");

            CaseRequest request = new CaseRequest();
            request.setCaseId(caseId);
            request.setName(name);
            request.setLocation(location);
            request.setDescription(description);

            requestMap.put(caseId, request);

            acknowledge(request);

        } catch(JMSException e) {
          e.printStackTrace();
        }

    }
```

Methods are also defined for getting the case request details and removing the case request for the specified case ID:

```
    public synchronized CaseRequest getRequestByCaseId(String caseId) {
      return (CaseRequest)requestMap.get(caseId);
    }
```

```
    public synchronized void removeCaseRequest(String caseId) {
      requestMap.remove(caseId);
    }
```

```
    public synchronized HashMap getCaseRequestMap() {
      return (HashMap)requestMap.clone();
    }
```

```
    private void acknowledge(CaseRequest request) throws JMSException {

      MapMessage mapMsg = responseManager.createMapMessage();
      mapMsg.setString("caseId", request.getCaseId());
      mapMsg.setString("name", request.getName());
      mapMsg.setString("location", request.getLocation());
      mapMsg.setString("description", request.getDescription());
      mapMsg.setString("status", "open ");
      mapMsg.setString("comment", "");

      responseManager.sendMessage(mapMsg, true);

    }

}
```

The JSP Tag Library

This is the tag library descriptor file `system.tld` that stores the information about the custom tags used in the helpdesk system:

```xml
<?xml version="1.0"  ?>
<!DOCTYPE taglib PUBLIC "-//Sun Microsystems, Inc.//DTD JSP Tag Library 1.1//EN"
"web-jsptaglib_1_1.dtd">

<taglib>

  <tlibversion>1.0</tlibversion>
  <jspversion>1.1</jspversion>
  <shortname>System</shortname>
  <info>
    This tag library contains tag extensions
  </info>
```

This file defines three custom tags used in the previous sections. The custom tag `listCase` is associated with the tag handler class `com.acme.system.ListCaseTag` and the body content is defined as parsable JSP content:

```xml
<tag>
  <name>listCase</name>
  <tagclass>com.acme.system.ListCaseTag</tagclass>
  <bodycontent>JSP</bodycontent>
</tag>
```

The custom tag `viewCase` is associated with the tag handler class `com.acme.user.ViewCaseTag` and the body content is defined as parseable JSP content:

```xml
<tag>
  <name>viewCase</name>
  <tagclass>com.acme.system.ViewCaseTag</tagclass>
  <bodycontent>JSP</bodycontent>
</tag>
```

The custom tag `updateCase` is associated with the tag handler class `com.acme.user.UpdateCaseTag` and the body content is defined as parseable JSP content:

```xml
<tag>
  <name>updateCase</name>
  <tagclass>com.acme.system.UpdateCaseTag</tagclass>
  <bodycontent>empty</bodycontent>
</tag>

</taglib>
```

The UpdateCaseTag Class

This is the tag handler class for the custom tag `updateCase`:

```
package com.acme.system;

import javax.servlet.jsp.*;
import javax.servlet.jsp.tagext.*;
import javax.servlet.*;
import javax.servlet.http.*;
import javax.jms.*;
import com.acme.common.*;


public class UpdateCaseTag extends TagSupport {
```

In the `doStartTag()` method of the tag handler instances of `ServletContext` and `HttpServletRequest` are retrieved from the implicit variable `pageContext`. The servlet context is then used to retrieve the JMS configuration information. This information is used to create and initialize an instance of `JMSManager` that will act as a message producer to the response queue. The case update details are retrieved from the HTTP request object. These details are stored in a JMS map message and the message is sent to the response queue using the instance of `JMSManager`. If the case status is "closed" the case request is removed from the case request pool:

```
public int doStartTag() throws JspTagException {

  try {

    ServletContext ctx = pageContext.getServletContext();
    HttpServletRequest req =
      (HttpServletRequest)pageContext.getRequest();
    RequestPool pool =
      (RequestPool)ctx.getAttribute("requestPool");

    String responseQueue = ctx.getInitParameter("responseQueue");
    System.out.println("requestQueue: " + responseQueue);

    String qcFactory = ctx.getInitParameter("qcFactory");
    System.out.println("qcFactory: " + qcFactory);

    String ctxFactory = ctx.getInitParameter("ctxFactory");
    System.out.println("ctxFactory: " + ctxFactory);

    String provURL = ctx.getInitParameter("provURL");
    System.out.println("provURL: " + provURL);

    JMSManager responseManager =
      new JMSManager(ctxFactory, provURL, responseQueue, qcFactory,
        IJMSConstants.PTP_MODEL);
    responseManager.initializeJMS(IJMSConstants.PRODUCER, null, true);

    MapMessage msg = responseManager.createMapMessage();
    msg.setString("caseId", req.getParameter("caseId"));
    msg.setString("name", req.getParameter("name"));
    msg.setString("location", req.getParameter("location"));
    msg.setString("description", req.getParameter("description"));
```

```
      msg.setString("status", req.getParameter("status"));
      msg.setString("comment", req.getParameter("comment"));

      responseManager.sendMessage(msg,true);
      responseManager.closeJMS();

      if(req.getParameter("status").equals("closed")) {
        pool.removeCaseRequest(req.getParameter("caseId"));
      }

      return EVAL_BODY_INCLUDE;

    } catch(Exception e) {

      System.out.println("Exception in doStartTag: CreateCaseTag");
      System.out.println(e.getClass());
      System.out.println(e.getMessage());
      e.printStackTrace();
      throw new JspTagException(e.getMessage());

    }

  }
```

```
  public int doEndTag() throws JspTagException {
    return EVAL_PAGE;
  }

}
```

The ListCaseTag Class

This is the tag handler class for the custom tag `listCase`. This class implements JSP body tag:

```
package com.acme.system;

import javax.servlet.jsp.*;
import javax.servlet.jsp.tagext.*;
import javax.servlet.*;
import javax.servlet.http.*;
import javax.jms.*;
import com.acme.common.*;
import java.util.*;

public class ListCaseTag extends BodyTagSupport {

  private Iterator it;
```

In the `doStartTag()` method of the tag handler, instances of `ServletContext` and `HttpServletRequest` are retrieved from the implicit variable `pageContext`. The servlet context is then used to retrieve an instance of the application scope bean `requestPool`. The `requestPool` object is then queried to get the list of case requests. If the returned list is empty the method returns `SKIP_BODY`, otherwise an `Iterator` is created for the list, the first object in the list is stored in the HTTP request object, and `EVAL_BODY_TAG` is returned, which will cause the body of the custom tag to be evaluated:

```
    public int doStartTag() throws JspTagException {

      ServletContext ctx = pageContext.getServletContext();
      RequestPool pool = (RequestPool)ctx.getAttribute("requestPool");

      it = pool.getCaseRequestMap().values().iterator();

      if(it.hasNext()) {
        pageContext.getRequest().setAttribute("caseRequest", it.next());
        return EVAL_BODY_TAG;
      }

      return SKIP_BODY;

    }
```

```
    public int doAfterBody(){

      try {
        BodyContent body = getBodyContent();
        if(body != null) {
          getBodyContent().getEnclosingWriter().write(body.getString());
          body.clear();
        }
      } catch(Exception e) {
        new JspTagException(e.getMessage());
      }

      if(it.hasNext()) {
        pageContext.getRequest().setAttribute("caseRequest", it.next());
        return EVAL_BODY_TAG;
      }

      return SKIP_BODY;

    }
```

```
    public int doEndTag() throws JspTagException {
      return EVAL_PAGE;
    }

}
```

The ViewCaseTag Class

This is the tag handler class for the custom tag viewCase:

```
package com.acme.system;

import javax.servlet.jsp.*;
import javax.servlet.jsp.tagext.*;
import javax.servlet.*;
import javax.servlet.http.*;
import javax.jms.*;
```

```
import com.acme.common.*;
import java.util.*;

public class ViewCaseTag extends TagSupport {

  private CaseRequest caseReq;

  public int doStartTag() throws JspTagException {
```

In the doStartTag() method the case ID is retrieved from the HTTP request and the application scope bean requestPool is retrieved from the servlet context. The case details are then retrieved from the bean for the specified case is and the case request object is stored in the Request object:

```
ServletContext ctx = pageContext.getServletContext();
HttpServletRequest req =
   (HttpServletRequest)pageContext.getRequest();

RequestPool pool = (RequestPool)ctx.getAttribute("requestPool");
String caseId = req.getParameter("caseId");

caseReq = pool.getRequestByCaseId(caseId);

if(caseId != null) {
  pageContext.getRequest().setAttribute("caseRequest", caseReq);
}

return EVAL_BODY_INCLUDE;

}
```

```
public int doEndTag() throws JspTagException {
  return EVAL_PAGE;
}

}
```

Deploying the System

The system was designed using only standard J2EE features and would support deployment configuration where the two web applications could be run in web containers provided by two different vendors, and the messaging system on a third machine running a JMS provider from a third vendor. But to keep things simple, in this section I'll explain how these three systems can be configured, deployed, and run under the same instance of WebLogic server running on a single machine.

We've been using WebLogic 6.0, which can be downloaded for evaluation from http://www.bea.com.

Compiling the Classes

I recommend that you use the following directory structure:

```
User/
      banner.jsp
      casehistory.jsp
      createcase.jsp
      index.jsp
      login.jsp
      newcase.jsp
      WEB-INF/
              web.xml
              user.tld
              classes/
                      com/
                          acme/
                               common/
                                       IJMSConstants.java
                                       JMSManager.java
                               user/
                                    CaseHistoryTag.java
                                    CaseResponseTag.java
                                    CreateCaseTag.java
                                    CreateCaseTagVariableInfo.java
                                    IDGenerator.java
                                    ResponsePool.java
System/
      banner.jsp
      index.jsp
      listcase.jsp
      login.jsp
      updatecase.jsp
      viewcase.jsp
      WEB-INF/
              web.xml
              system.tld
              classes/
                      com/
                          acme/
                               common/
                                       IJMSConstants.java
                                       JMSManager.java
                               system/
                                      CaseRequest.java
                                      ListCaseTag.java
                                      RequestPool.java
                                      UpdateCaseTag.java
                                      ViewCaseTag.java
```

Compile all the Java classes explained in the previous sections. Make sure that you have
`weblogic.jar` in your classpath.

Creating Web Archive Files

Before the web applications can be deployed into the WebLogic server, we need to create web application archive (WAR) files. This can be done using the JAR utility that comes with JDK software distribution:

```
cd User
jar -cf user.war *
```

```
cd ..\System
jar -cf system.war *
```

Deploying the Web Applications

For deploying the WAR files, first start the WebLogic server. Open the administration console and click on the Web Application link on the left-hand pane navigation tree. This will display the screen shown below:

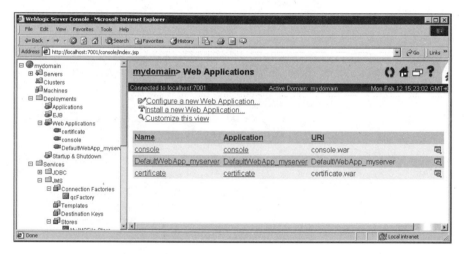

Click on the Install a new Web Application link in the right-hand pane, then browse to the newly created user.war file from the local file system:

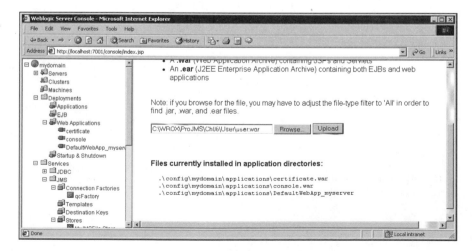

Click on the Upload button:

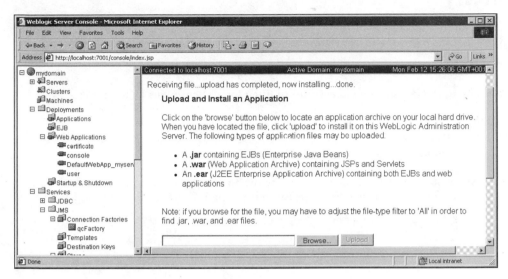

Do the same for `system.war`.

Now expand the **Servers** node in the left-hand pane, and click on the **myserver** node. Now click on the **Deployment** tab displayed on the right-hand pane. Then click on the **Web Applications** tab under the **Deployment** tab. Make sure both web applications are in the **Chosen** list on the right:

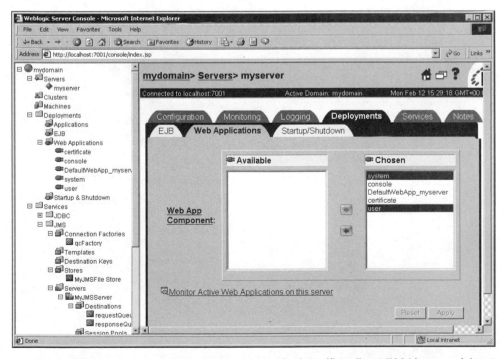

You should be able to run the applications by visiting the http://localhost:7001/user and /system URLs, as we have seen in earlier screenshots.

Summary

In this chapter we have seen a working example of how to integrate JMS with J2EE web containers. We have covered the following in this chapter:

❑ Use of JMS for integrating loosely coupled applications

❑ Use of JSP application scope beans to listen for asynchronous JMS messages

❑ Use of JSP custom tags for sending JSP messages

❑ How PTP messaging can be used for sending messages to external systems that may not be up and running

In the next chapter we will be further enhancing the application by integrating JMS with EJB containers and we will be covering message-driven beans, integrating JMS transactions with EJB transactions.

com.sun.jn...
com.sun.jn...
weblogic.jndi.T3Initia...
fiorano.jms.rtl.Fiorano...
fiorano.jms.runtime.n...
ch.softwired.jms.naming...
com.sun.jndi.fscontext.LdapCtxFactory
com.sun.jndi.ldap.LdapCtxFactory
weblogic.jndi.T3InitialContextFactory
weblogic.jndi.WLInitialContextFactory
fiorano.jms.rtl.FioranoInitialContextFactory
fiorano.jms.runtime.naming.FioranoInitialContextFactory
ch.softwired.jms.naming.IBusContextFactory

com.sun.jndi.fscontext.RefFSContextFactory
com.sun.jndi.ldap.LdapCtxFactory
weblogic.jndi.WLInitialContextFactory
weblogic.jndi.T3InitialContextFactory
fiorano.jms.rtl.FioranoInitialContextFactory
fiorano.jms.runtime.naming.FioranoInitialContextFactory
ch.softwired.jms.naming.IBusContextFactory

IBusContextFactory
RefFSContextFactory
LdapContextFactory
WLInitialContextFactory
FioranoInitialContextFactory
IBusContextFactory

Enterprise JavaBeans and JMS

In this chapter, we will look at the integration of JMS with another J2EE technology, that of **Enterprise JavaBeans (EJB)**. At the time of writing there are two different versions of the EJB specification in use (1.1 and 2.0, which is in proposed-final draft stage), each of which requires a different approach to JMS integration.

We will cover the use of JMS with both EJB 1.1, and EJB 2.0 using the new **message-driven bean** functionality introduced in the EJB 2.0 specification. To do so, we will take the Case Logging application from the previous chapter and extend it to include integration with an EJB. We will modify the application such that messages are published to a topic, where they are picked up by an EJB, which send an e-mail, via JavaMail, to a user of the Case Management system.

In this chapter we will:

❑　Look at the difficulties (prior to EJB 2.0) in using EJBs as JMS consumers

❑　Develop a solution for integrating JMS with EJB 1.1

❑　Replicate this same functionality with an EJB 2.0 message-driven bean to show how the new EJB 2.0 specification simplifies things for us

This chapter assumes that you are familiar with EJB 1.1 development. If you are not, we recommend you take a look at Professional Java Server Programming – J2EE Edition *from Wrox Press ISBN 1-861004-65-6, for a quick tutorial in their use.*

Modifying the Application

The design of our application is going to focus on the problems involved with using EJBs as JMS *consumers*. We will not focus on the use of JMS with EJBs where the EJB acts as a message producer as there is little difference in the process whether an EJB is used or a standard Java class.

> *As this application utilizes much of the same underlying JMS code (the `JMSManager` class, etc.) from the previous chapter, we will not revisit the design specifics of these components but only focus on the EJBs that make up our application, and the design issues faced in using EJBs with JMS. If you are unfamiliar with the `JMSManager` class, and its supporting classes and interfaces, refer back to Chapter 6 for the details.*

We will first focus our discussion on the EJB 1.1 specification and layout the difficulties presented by the lack of any defined integration with JMS, and then present a solution for this in our first EJB code example. Following that we will focus on the new EJB 2.0 specification, which does provide a definition of JMS and EJB integration, and present our same application solution converted to use the new EJB 2.0 specification – and demonstrate the ease with which this specification now allows EJBs to act as JMS consumers.

The application is a simple modification to the Case Logging application from the previous chapter. This time, as well as sending new case logs to a queue we will also publish them to a topic. The EJBs for this application will act as JMS consumers and monitor the topic, picking up submitted entries, and sending e-mail alerts to the user of the Case Management system so that they will know when they have to log on and check the latest submission.

In most applications involving EJBs and JMS, you will use EJBs in just such a fashion; where they act as manager objects that perform asynchronous operations, and delegations based on message types and properties, received from a given destination.

While our application will be fairly straightforward, the concepts presented can be utilized to create some fairly complex systems in which EJBs act as routing managers to asynchronously invoke operations on other EJBs in a "service" framework, for example.

The Help Request

The diagram below demonstrates how the application will work with the inclusion of an EJB:

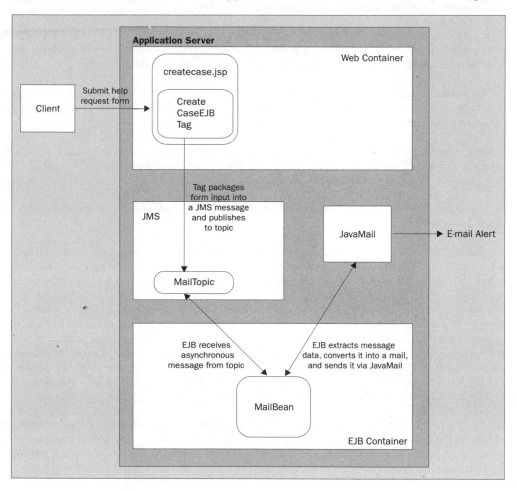

As you can see, the application is a simple one, involving the submission of a "help request" form using many of the same properties utilized by the previous chapter's Case Logging system, and which alerts support personnel via e-mail notifications. A JSP tag packages the help request details into a JMS message and publishes it on our topic.

In the EJB 1.1 example, we will use a WebLogic Startup class to act as a consumer for the topic. When a message is published to the topic, the Startup class will receive the message in its `onMessage()` method, which in turn locates and creates our EJB 1.1 bean, and delegates the message to the EJB for processing. The reasons for using the Startup class to delegate method calls will be explained below, and should become readily apparent.

Our EJB 2.0 example will show how the 2.0 specification simplifies this example even further, and we will modify our architecture to use an EJB 2.0 message-driven bean.

JMS and EJB 1.1

We'll now focus our discussion on the design we presented, and the issues involved in using JMS with EJB 1.1 beans to create the modified Case Logging application.

The EJB 1.1 specification does not provide any integration points for JMS. Due to this, 1.1 EJBs cannot act as direct JMS consumers. The reason for this is that Enterprise JavaBeans are designed to be remotely accessible objects and run within the context of an **EJB container**.

One of the cardinal rules of EJBs is that the client of an EJB never directly accesses the bean class itself. Since this class's lifecycle, and access, is managed by the EJB container, as a client of the bean you are only allowed to access the bean *indirectly* through its **remote interface**.

However, in our application design we want our e-mail EJB 1.1 bean to be able to receive asynchronous JMS messages as a JMS consumer, and the lack of defined integration between the two architectures, as we have discussed, presents us with a design problem.

Before discussing our solution to this problem, let's look at the problem itself, to understand the actual issues involved here.

At first glance, many developers might think the obvious solution to our issue a simple one. It would seem that we should implement the JMS `MessageListener` interface (and its `onMessage()` method) directly in our EJB bean class, along with any of our other business logic methods, and we should be all set.

But this solution will not work. Why? Because it violates the EJB specification's contract for accessing an EJB's bean class. When JMS makes an asynchronous call to our EJB, it must act as an EJB client the same as any other EJB client – meaning it must access the EJB through its remote interface (which implies a series of JNDI lookup operations, as well). So if the bean class were directly implementing the `MessageListener` interface, how would JMS locate the home or remote interfaces, to call the bean's `onMessage()` method? What's more, since the EJB's bean class may not even be instantiated, how would it be registered with JMS, and by what mechanism?

Even assuming that the EJB's bean class was perhaps registered as a `MessageListener` through some other external Java class accessing the EJB as a proper client, and that it may still exist as an instantiated instance in the object pool after the access, there is still no way for JMS to know that it is calling into an EJB when it calls the `onMessage()` method of the bean class asynchronously – and there is no way for JMS to know that it should use a JNDI lookup, and a remote interface to access the EJB.

So what would happen if we were to implement the `MessageListener` interface directly in the EJB's bean class? It is uncertain, since firstly, JMS will not access the EJB bean class through a remote interface but will call directly into the instantiated bean class, thus violating the contract for accessing the bean class only through the remote interface.

Secondly, if the particular bean instance is being reused from the pool, is in the middle of a transaction or some other internal operation, etc., it could be catastrophic. Since the container serializes access to a bean class and its methods, and provides thread safety (an EJB is single-threaded, and as per the EJB spec, must never create its own threads), when JMS calls into the bean instance's `onMessage()` method it has just violated the boundary of the EJB container and the protections it provides. The result could be unforeseen and most likely disastrous if, for example, your EJB is participating in a transaction and JMS suddenly calls directly into the same bean instance (violating the ACID properties of the transaction, that the container helps to guarantee):

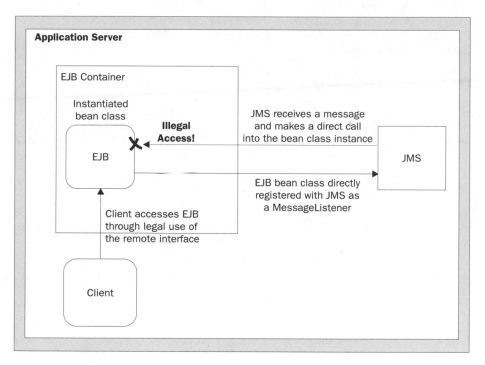

This scenario obviously is not allowed, and therefore we cannot use it. Our next question then becomes, is there any way to allow your EJB to act as a JMS consumer? In EJB 2.0 this answer is yes, but for EJB 1.1 the answer is no.

There is, however, a workaround solution, and this will make up the first code example that we present. The way to solve this problem in EJB 1.1 is to create a **"Delegator"** class.

> *A Delegator class acts as a surrogate for operations to be performed on a delegate class. In our case, for instance, our Delegator class will act as a surrogate for receiving JMS messages through the implementation of the* `MessageListener` *interface, and delegate those messages to our EJB.*

Most application servers provide the ability register and load any number of specified Java class instances upon startup of the server. This allows you to create your own Java classes that can perform any number of operations as the application server is started, and as importantly, which run within the same VM instance as the server.

For our "Delegator" example we will be using the WebLogic 6.0 application server. The WebLogic server provides such a mechanism, called a **Startup class**.

> *It is important to note that the WebLogic Startup class feature is specific to the WebLogic application server only and that this workaround can only be used against the WebLogic Server. However, if you wished to create this same solution in a more platform-neutral manner, you could add the functionality of the WebLogic Startup class to a simple Java application, and run this separately. While this solution would require running a separate VM instance for the Delegator message handler class, it would be a more platform-neutral solution.*

The WebLogic Startup class is nothing more than a Java class which you create that implements a special interface called `WebLogic.common.T3StartupDef`, which contains a couple of methods. The most important method of which is:

```
public String startup(String name, Hashtable args) throws Exception
```

When the WebLogic server starts, any registered Startup classes that are found within the classpath, are instantiated (once instance per Startup class defined) by the WebLogic server and the `startup()` method is called. The `name` and `args` parameters are defined in the WebLogic configuration file (`config.xml`) and can be set through the WebLogic console.

The Startup class can perform any operation it needs to, implement its own methods, etc.

We will use this feature of the WebLogic server (along with the accompanying WebLogic Shutdown class, which is instantiated and its `shutdown()` method invoked upon an initiated shutdown of the WebLogic server) to create a mechanism to delegate JMS messages to our EJB.

> *An initiated shutdown is when the Application Server is shutdown via the WebLogic console, or via the WebLogic* SHUTDOWN *command available via the WebLogic command line utility* weblogic.Admin.

The way the application works is thus: We will create a WebLogic Startup class that will implement the JMS `MessageListener` interface and its associated `onMessage()` method. We will register the class as a JMS subscriber on our e-mail topic, and delegate all of the asynchronously received messages on this topic to our Mail EJB via the proper mechanisms of EJB interface lookup via JNDI, and access of the EJB through its remote interface.

The following diagram shows the conceptual layout of this architecture:

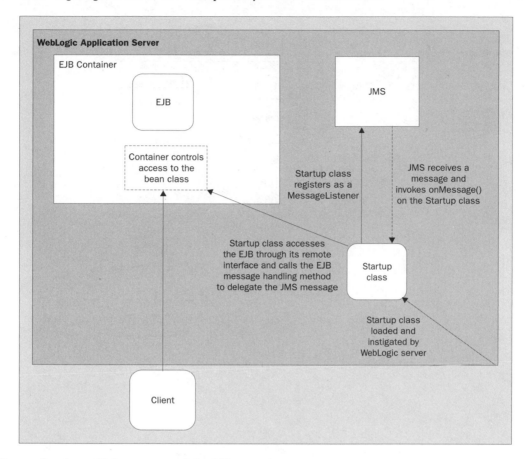

Our application will thus consist of the following components:

❑ A WebLogic Startup class to register as a consumer with JMS and receive asynchronous messages on our "Mail" topic. The Startup class will be coded to delegate incoming JMS messages to our EJB – the "Mail Bean".

❑ A stateless Session EJB – our "Mail Bean" that implements its own method to receive a JMS message and contains all of the code to extract the data from the message and send an e-mail alert via the JavaMail API.

❑ JSPs for displaying and submitting the Help Request input form.

❑ A JSP tag library to handle the POST of the form and to send the request to our topic as a JMS `MapMessage`.

❑ `JMSManager` and the associated support classes used in the previous chapter. We will not cover these classes again, here.

The sequence of events in the application is shown in the following diagram:

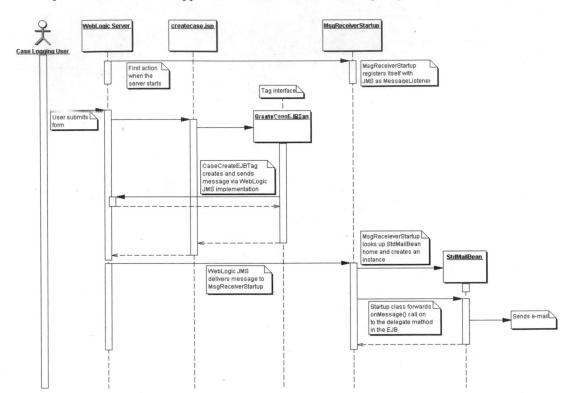

Configuring WebLogic

Before we get into the implementation details as discussed above, we need to set up some additional WebLogic settings.

Configuring JMS

Connection Factories

Create another connection factory by clicking on the Connection Factories node under JMS in the left-hand pane and then clicking on the Create a new JMS Connection Factory link on the right-hand pane.

Enter `mailFactory` for the name and JNDI name, leave the rest as default, and click on **Create**:

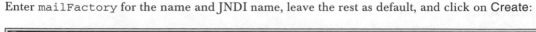

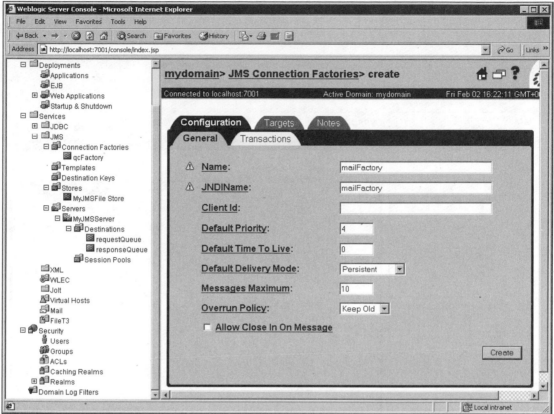

Click on the **Target** tab and select **myserver** in the **Available** list, move it to the **Chosen** list, and click **Apply**.

Destinations

Go to the Destinations node under JMS | Servers | MyJMSServer and click on the link Create a new JMSTopic on the right-hand pane. Specify the name as `MailTopic` and JNDI name as `com.acme.jms.topics.MailTopic`, leave the rest as default, and click Create:

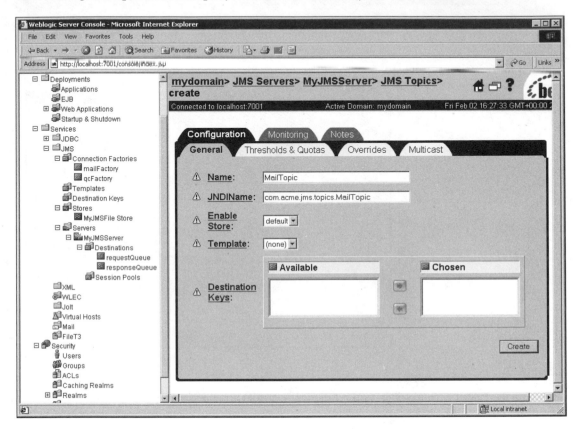

Configuring Startup and Shutdown Classes

We next need to configure our startup and shutdown classes for our EJB 1.1 examples.

Under the Deployments node, click on Startup & Shutdown. Next, in the right-hand pane, click on the Create a new Startup Class link. Enter MsgReceiverStartup for the Name value and com.acme.startup.MsgReceiverStartup as the ClassName value. Click the Create button to create this Startup class entry:

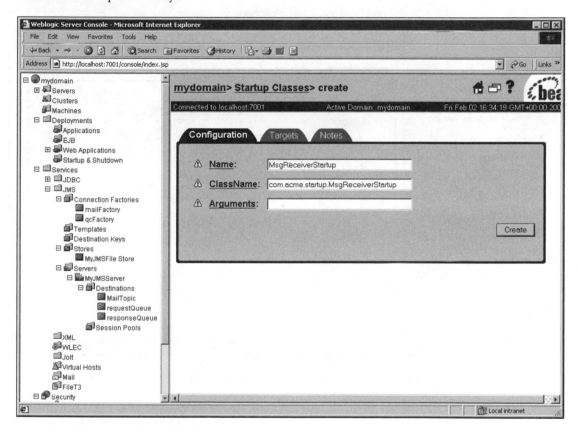

Make sure you go to the Targets tab and add this to the Chosen server selections.

Go back to the **Startup & Shutdown** screen. Click on this to repeat the same process, only choose the link **Create a new Shutdown Class**. Enter `MyShutdownClass` for the **Name** value and `com.acme.startup.MsgReceiverShutdown` for the **ClassName** value. Click the **Create** button to create this Shutdown class entry:

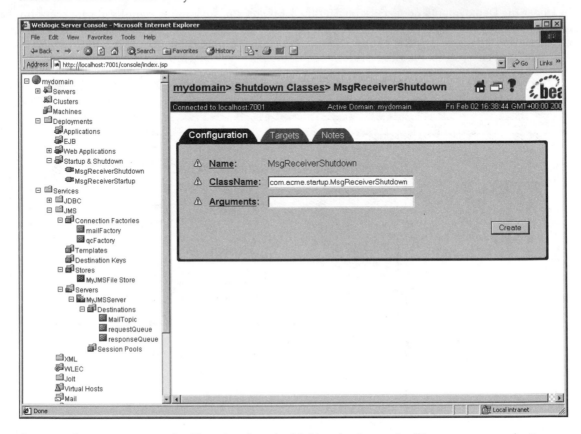

Again, make sure you go to the **Targets** tab and add this selection to the **Chosen** servers selections.

However, in order for WebLogic to be able to load these classes on startup and shutdown, it must be able to find them in its classpath. There are a number of ways to do this but one of the easiest is to edit the `cmd` file that starts WebLogic to lookup a `serverclasses` directory under the WebLogic domain. For example, if your WebLogic domain is `mydomain` then you would edit the following line in `startWebLogic.cmd`:

```
set CLASSPATH=.;\lib\weblogic_sp.jar;.\lib\weblogic.jar;.
\config\mydomain\serverclasses
```

Then you would need to copy the `com.acme.startup` classes (and associated files) into the `serverclasses` directory.

Configuring the Mail Session

The final step in our configuration process is to create a JavaMail mail session in the WebLogic server.

In the left-hand pane of the console application, choose the Mail node. Click on the Create a new Mail Session link. Enter `AcmeMail` for the Name value and `acme/Mail` for the JNDIName value. In the Properties text area, enter the properties as shown. You will need to configure the mail.from and mail.smtp.host values for your own system. Click the Apply button:

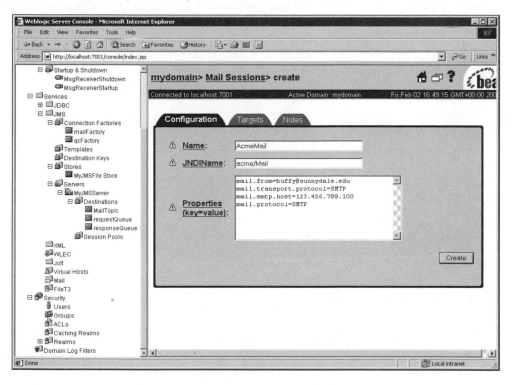

Make sure you go to the Targets tab and add this selection to the Chosen servers selections.

> There is a bug in the current version of the WebLogic 6.0 server (GA) that causes the e-mail example to fail because a transport Provider (SMTP) has not been loaded. The simplest workaround for this is to download the JavaMail package from the Sun website at: http://www.javasoft.com/products/javamila.index.html. Install the JAR file `mail.jar` in your WebLogic `\lib` directory and add the JAR file to your classpath such that it comes before you load the WebLogic JAR files:
>
> set CLASSPATH=.;.\lib\mail.jar;.\lib\weblogic_sp0.jar;.
> \lib\weblogic.jar;.\config\mydomain\serverclasses
>
> If you are running WebLogic from the `startWeblogic.cmd` script, edit this file and change the classapth setting as shown above. Make sure you add the `mail.jar` file *first* in the classpath. This will cause WebLogic to use the class files in the `mail.jar` file instead of the class files packaged with the WebLogic server's `weblogic.jar` file and will load the mail transport providers so that the example application will run successfully.

Implementing the New Case Logging System

The following section describes the classes that make up the implementation of our application.

The MsgReceiverStartup Class

The MsgReceiverStartup class is a WebLogic Startup class that is used to delegate JMS messages to our version 1.1 EJB. The class registers itself as a MessageListener on our JMS topic, within the startup() method code. All incoming messages on this topic will be delivered to the onMessage() implementation of the class.

The class implements three interfaces:

❑ IJMSConstants – Our constants' definitions from the previous chapter

❑ MessageListener – As our class is going to act as a delegate for receiving asynchronous messages on the JMS topic, we implement MessageListener

❑ T3StartupDef – This is a WebLogic-specific proprietary interface that must be implemented by any class that will be registered with WebLogic as a Startup class:

```
package com.acme.startup;

import javax.naming.*;
import javax.jms.*;
import javax.ejb.*;
import java.util.*;
import java.lang.reflect.*;
import java.rmi.RemoteException;

import weblogic.common.*;
import com.acme.common.*;
import com.acme.ejb.mail.*;

public class MsgReceiverStartup implements MessageListener,
                                           IJMSConstants,
                                           T3StartupDef
{
```

We next declare a number of constants for the class:

❑ JNDI_FACTORY – Defines the name of our JNDI context factory.

❑ URL – The location of the WebLogic server (using the "t3" protocol).

❑ JMS_FACTORY – Defines the name of our JMS connection factory, "mailFactory", which we have created in the WebLogic server.

❑ TOPIC – This is the name of our JMS destination.

```
public static final String JNDI_FACTORY =
     "weblogic.jndi.WLInitialContextFactory";
public static final String URL = "t3://localhost:7001";
public static final String JMS_FACTORY = "mailFactory";
public static final String TOPIC = "com.acme.jms.topics.MailTopic";
```

In addition there is a member variable for the `JMSManager` (this is public so it can be called from the Shutdown class that we will see shortly). There is also one private attribute – the `T3ServicesDef` attribute. This is set automatically by the WebLogic server on creation of the Startup class by a call to the `setServices()` method defined in the `T3StartupDef` interface:

```
public static JMSManager mgr;

private T3ServicesDef serv; // Part of WebLogic Start-Up class support

// WebLogic Start-Up Class
public void setServices(T3ServicesDef s) {
   serv = s;
}
```

The `startup()` method is invoked on the class by the WebLogic server upon startup of the application server. As you can see, we create a new instance of `JMSManager` in our constructor. The `startup()` method initializes the `JMSManager` and starts it:

```
public MsgReceiverStartup() {

   mgr = new JMSManager(JNDI_FACTORY, URL, TOPIC, JMS_FACTORY,
                        PUB_SUB_MODEL);
}

public String startup(String name, Hashtable args) throws Exception {

   System.out.println("MsgReceiverStartup called on startup...");

   if (mgr != null) {
      mgr.initializeJMS(CONSUMER, this, true);
   }
   else {
      throw new NamingException("ReceiverStartup - initializeJMS: " +
                                "Naming Exception was thrown");
   }

   return "ok";
}
```

The `onMessage()` method will be invoked upon delivery of a JMS message. The method performs the following tasks:

❑ Gets an initial JNDI context

❑ Uses the JNDI context to "lookup" the home interface

❑ Uses the home interface to retrieve the remote interface

❑ Calls the `onMessage()` method on the remote interface, passing off the JMS message to the EJB for processing

```
    public void onMessage(Message msg) {

      try {
          // Locate the StdMailBean and delegate the JMS Message...
          Context ctx = mgr.getInitialContext();
          StdMailHome mailhome = (StdMailHome) ctx.lookup("StdMailBean");
          StdMail mail = mailhome.create();

          MapMessage m = (MapMessage)msg;
          mail.onMessage(msg);

      } catch(NamingException ex) {
          System.out.println("MsgReceiverStartup.onMessage: " +
                             "NamingException was thrown");
          ex.printStackTrace();
      } catch(RemoteException ex) {
          System.out.println("MsgReceiverStartup.onMessage: " +
                             "RemoteException was thrown");
          ex.printStackTrace();
      } catch(CreateException ex) {
          System.out.println("MsgReceiverStartup.onMessage: " +
                             "CreateException was thrown");
          ex.printStackTrace();
      }
    }
}
```

The MsgReceiverShutdown Class

The MsgReceiverShutdown class is a WebLogic Shutdown class that, as its name implies, and like the Startup class just shown, is called upon shutdown of the WebLogic server. The WebLogic server shutdown operation is typically initiated through the WebLogic console, or via the WebLogic SHUTDOWN command available via the WebLogic command line utility weblogic.Admin, for example:

```
java weblogic.Admin -url t3://localhost:7001 -username system
                    -password password SHUTDOWN
```

This class is self-explanatory. In the same way that the Startup class was implemented, we implement the WebLogic-specific, proprietary interface T3ShutdownDef, and its shutdown() method. When invoked, this method simply calls jmsStop() on the JMSManager static variable of the MsgReceiverStartup class:

```
package com.acme.startup;

import java.util.*;

import weblogic.common.*;

public class MsgReceiverShutdown implements T3ShutdownDef {

  private T3ServicesDef serv; // Part of Weblogic Start-Up class support

  public MsgReceiverShutdown() {}
```

```
    // Weblogic Start-Up Class
    public void setServices(T3ServicesDef s) {
        serv = s;
    }

    public String shutdown(String name, Hashtable args) throws Exception {

        System.out.println("Shutdown - MsgReceiverShutdown class called...");
        if (MsgReceiverStartup.mgr != null)
            MsgReceiverStartup.mgr.jmsStop();

        return "ok";
    }
}
```

Now that we have created our Delegator class we can look at the EJB itself.

The Mail EJB (1.1)

Our Mail EJB 1.1 will be used to send e-mail alerts to a "HelpDesk" e-mail account. This will demonstrate the use of an EJB in concert with our delegator WebLogic Startup class, by allowing our EJB to accept an incoming JMS message from our delegate, extracting the contents of the message, and creating and sending an e-mail message using JavaMail and the parameters from the JMS message.

Our EJB will contain the following files:

- ❑ StdMail.java – This is our remote interface

- ❑ StdMailHome.java – This is our home interface

- ❑ StdMailBean.java – The bean class containing our methods for accepting a JMS message, and for creating and sending an e-mail message using JavaMail

- ❑ ByteArrayDataSource.java – This class is a support class that converts a string into a DataSource

- ❑ ejb-jar.xml – The deployment descriptor file containing our bean's deployment attributes and properties

- ❑ weblogic-ejb-jar.xml – A WebLogic-specific XML file that contains deployment attributes unique and specific to the WebLogic server

The StdMail Interface

This file contains our EJB's remote interface definition. It contains only one method signature, the onMessage() method, which will be called by the WebLogic Startup class to delegate the handling of a JMS message to the EJB (remember, since the EJB itself cannot be called directly by JMS, the WebLogic Startup class will do this for us – receiving the incoming JMS message – but still allowing our EJB to handle the processing of the contents of the JMS message through calls to the onMessage() method defined in the bean's remote interface):

```
package com.acme.ejb.mail;

import javax.ejb.EJBObject;
import javax.jms.Message;
import java.rmi.RemoteException;

public interface StdMail extends EJBObject {

  public boolean onMessage(Message msg) throws RemoteException;

}
```

The StdMailHome Interface

This file contains the EJB home interface. Since this is a stateless session bean, it contains only the create() method:

```
package com.acme.ejb.mail;

import javax.ejb.EJBHome;
import javax.ejb.CreateException;
import java.rmi.RemoteException;

public interface StdMailHome extends EJBHome {

  public StdMail create() throws RemoteException, CreateException;

}
```

The StdMailBean Class

StdMailBean is the bean implementation class, which contains the logic for our EJB. Since it is a stateless session bean, it implements the javax.ejb.SessionBean interface. The EJB has a home interface, StdMailHome, and a remote interface, StdMail, which we saw up above.

This class contains the implementation of our own onMessage() method, and additional, generic, methods for sending an e-mail message. The e-mail in our example is generated by the contents of the message received in onMessage().

Our bean class implements the SessionBean interface, and we also declare a couple of constants to use for defaults:

```
package com.acme.ejb.mail;

import java.io.*;
import java.util.*;
import javax.ejb.*;
import javax.jms.*;
import javax.naming.*;
import javax.activation.DataHandler;
import javax.mail.*;
import javax.mail.internet.*;
import java.rmi.RemoteException;
```

```
public class StdMailBean implements SessionBean {

  private static final boolean VERBOSE = true;
  private static final String MAIL_HOST = "mail.smtp.host";
  private static final String MAIL_SUBJECT = "Help Request";
  private static final String JNDI_MAIL = "acme/Mail";
  private SessionContext context;
  private String message;
```

Then we have a series of standard EJB callback methods, which we won't be implementing:

```
public void ejbCreate () {}
public void ejbRemove() {}
public void ejbActivate(){}
public void ejbPassivate() {}
public void setSessionContext(SessionContext ctx) {
    context = ctx;
}
```

Next we have the `onMessage()` method. As you can see, it accepts a JMS message much like the version of the method defined in `MessageListener`, although ours returns a Boolean result to indicate status.

> *Remember, though, that even though the bean's method is also named `onMessage()` this method is not being called by JMS – it is only a naming convention we have used so that it is familiar.*

First, we check the message type in our `if` block, to make sure it is of type `MapMessage` and then print out some status messages to the console showing the content of our message body values. We extract the values into local variables that we will use in calling our method to send the e-mail:

```
public boolean onMessage(javax.jms.Message msg) {

  if (msg instanceof MapMessage) {

    try {
        System.out.println("Received new message : ");
        MapMessage message = (MapMessage) msg;

        String location = message.getString("location");
        if (location != null)
           System.out.println("   LOCATION = " + location);

        String problem = message.getString("description");
        if (problem != null)
           System.out.println("   PROBLEM = " + problem);

        String name = message.getString("name");
        if (name != null)
           System.out.println("   NAME = " + name);

        String helpdeskEmail = message.getString("helpdesk");
        if (helpdeskEmail != null)
           System.out.println("   HELPDESK EMAIL = " + helpdeskEmail);
```

```
            String caseID = message.getString("caseid");
            if (caseID != null)
               System.out.println("   CASE ID = " + caseID);

            String subject = MAIL_SUBJECT;
```

Next we call a support method createBody() that will format the body of the message for HTML, and then we pass the extracted message body content to the bean's sendMail() method that will create and send our e-mail alert:

```
            String body = createBody(problem, name, location, caseID);

            // Try and send this message via JavaMail...
            boolean val = sendMail(helpdeskEmail, subject,
                                   body, true);

            if (!val)
               System.out.println("StdMailBean.sendMail returned with error");

               return val;

         } catch(JMSException ex) {
            ex.printStackTrace();
         }
      }

      return false;
   }
```

The first thing our sendMail() method does is look up a JavaMail session from the WebLogic server that we configured earlier:

```
   public boolean sendMail(String to, String subject,
                           String body, boolean debug)
   {
      boolean result = false;

      try {
         // Get Mail Session from WebLogic Server...
         InitialContext ctx = new InitialContext();
         javax.mail.Session session = (javax.mail.Session)
             ctx.lookup(JNDI_MAIL);
```

We then call setDebug() on our session, which will display debug messages and output to the WebLogic server standard output – this will allow us to see the operations performed by the JavaMail session, so that we can see what's happening as our e-mail is sent out:

```
         // Set Debug
         session.setDebug(debug);

         // Create new Message
         javax.mail.Message msg =
             new javax.mail.internet.MimeMessage(session);
```

The next set of operations construct our e-mail's header and content – the "To", "From", "Subject", and "Body" fields of the e-mail message. We call one support method, `parseEmailAddress()` to convert our string-based addresses into `javax.mail.internet.InternetAddress` types – the support method will parse multiple, comma separated addresses out of the string, if necessary:

```
if (msg != null)
   System.out.println("Created Message...");

if (to == null || to.trim().equals(""))
  return false;

javax.mail.internet.InternetAddress[] addresses =
      parseEmailAddress(to);
if (addresses != null) {
  System.out.println("TO = " + addresses[0].getAddress());
  msg.setRecipients(javax.mail.Message.RecipientType.TO,
                    addresses);
} else {
  System.out.println("MailBean.sendMail: Error, Invalid " +
                     "\"To\" E-Mail address list\n");
  return result;
}

// Set the message...
if (subject != null) {
  msg.setSubject(subject);
} else {
  msg.setSubject("No Subject");
}

// Set the date...
msg.setSentDate(new Date());

// Set the message body...
if (body == null)
  // Provide simple body 0x20 "space"...
  body = " ";
```

Finally, we set the "header" type of our e-mail – in this case we are creating an HTML mail message so we set the header type to `"sendhtml"`. The next method packages the message content into an HTML template, which supplies the proper tags for wrapping the HTML formatted content of the body (supplying the <HTML></HTML> tags, wrapping the body in a <BODY></BODY> tag set, etc.).

Then the static method `send()` is called on the `Transport` class, which will locate a transport provider (such as SMTP) and send the e-mail message that we have created:

```
msg.setHeader("X-Mailer", "sendhtml");
packageBody(msg, body);

// Now send it;
Transport.send(msg);
```

```
        if (debug)
          System.out.println("Sent email message \"" + subject +
                            "\" to \"". + to + "\"");

        result = true;

    } catch(IOException ex) {
        System.out.println("StdMailBean.sendMail: EMail IOException");
        ex.printStackTrace();
    } catch(NamingException ex) {
        System.out.println("StdMailBean.sendMail: EMail NamingException");
        ex.printStackTrace();
    } catch(MessagingException ex) {
        System.out.println("StdMailBean.sendMail: EMail " +
                            "MessagingException");
        ex.printStackTrace();
    }

    return result;
}
```

The parseEmailAddress() method is used to create an array of InternetAddress types out of our string. If multiple, comma delimited e-mail addresses are supplied, this will convert them to a JavaMail InternetAddress, returning an array of the addresses extracted from the string:

```
public javax.mail.internet.InternetAddress[]
    parseEmailAddress(String addresses) {

javax.mail.internet.InternetAddress[] addr = null;

StringTokenizer tokenizer = new StringTokenizer(addresses, ",", false);
int toks = tokenizer.countTokens();

try {
    if (toks <= 1) {
        System.out.println("Tokens <= 1");
        addr = new javax.mail.internet.InternetAddress[1];
        addr[0] = new javax.mail.internet.InternetAddress(addresses);
    } else {
        System.out.println("Tokens > 1");
        addr = new javax.mail.internet.InternetAddress[toks];
        int index = 0;

        while (tokenizer.hasMoreTokens()) {
            String temp = (String) tokenizer.nextToken();
            temp = temp.trim();
            addr[index++] = new javax.mail.internet.InternetAddress(temp);
        }
    }

} catch(AddressException e) {
    // Log...
    e.printStackTrace();
}

return addr;
}
```

packageBody() wraps the body of our e-mail message in a simple HTML template which supplies the <HTML> and <BODY> tags, and a <TITLE> and then calls setDataHandler(), which supplies a new Data Handler object to the mail Mime message – with the data handler wrapping the Mime message content and type:

```java
protected void packageBody(javax.mail.Message msg, String body)
        throws MessagingException, java.io.IOException {

    String line;
    String subject = msg.getSubject();
    StringBuffer sb = new StringBuffer();
    sb.append("<HTML>\n");
    sb.append("<HEAD>\n");
    sb.append("<TITLE>\n");
    sb.append(subject + "\n");
    sb.append("</TITLE>\n");
    sb.append("</HEAD>\n");

    sb.append("<BODY>\n");

    sb.append(body);
    sb.append("\n");

    sb.append("</BODY>\n");
    sb.append("</HTML>\n");

    msg.setDataHandler(new DataHandler(
        new ByteArrayDataSource(sb.toString(), "text/html")));
}
```

We finish up with the createBody() method. This is another support method that takes the "problem" description of our help request, and formats it in HTML:

```java
protected String createBody(String problem, String name,
                            String location, String caseID) {

    StringBuffer buf = new StringBuffer();
    buf.append("<B>User:</B> \n");
    buf.append(name + "\n");
    buf.append("<BR>\n");
    buf.append("<B>Location: </B>\n");
    buf.append(location + "\n");
    buf.append("<BR>\n");
    buf.append("<B>Case ID: </B>\n");
    buf.append(caseID + "\n");
    buf.append("<HR><BR>\n");
    buf.append("<B>Has submitted the following trouble ticket " +
               "request:</B>\n");
    buf.append("<BR><BR>\n");
    buf.append("     " + problem + "\n");
    buf.append("<BR>\n");
    buf.append("<BR>\n");
    buf.append("This mail is from StdMailBean\n");
    return buf.toString();
}
}
```

The ByteArrayDataSource Class

The ByteArrayDataSource class is a support class with code taken from the example source code provided with the WebLogic server. This is a support class that converts a string into a DataSource:

```
 *
 * $Id: ByteArrayDataSource.java,v 1.6 2000/02/16 00:18:16 brydon Exp $
 * Copyright 1999 Sun Microsystems, Inc. All rights reserved.
 * Copyright 1999 Sun Microsystems, Inc. Tous droits réservés.
 */

package com.acme.ejb.mail;

import java.io.ByteArrayInputStream;
import java.io.InputStream;
import java.io.IOException;
import java.io.OutputStream;
import java.io.UnsupportedEncodingException;
import java.util.Date;

import javax.activation.DataSource;


/**
 * Used to create a DataSource for the mail message.
 */
public class ByteArrayDataSource implements DataSource {
    private byte[] data; // data for mail message
    private String type; // content type/mime type

  /**
   * Create a DataSource from a String
   * @param data is the contents of the mail message
   * @param type is the mime-type such as text/html
   */
    public ByteArrayDataSource(String data, String type) {
        try {
            // Assumption that the string contains only ascii
            // characters ! Else just pass in a charset into this
            // constructor and use it in getBytes()
            this.data = data.getBytes("iso-8859-1");
        } catch (UnsupportedEncodingException uex) { }
        this.type = type;
    }


    //DataSource interface methods

    public InputStream getInputStream() throws IOException {
        if (data == null)
            throw new IOException("no data");
        return new ByteArrayInputStream(data);
    }

    public OutputStream getOutputStream() throws IOException {
        throw new IOException("cannot do this");
    }
```

```
        public String getContentType() {
            return type;
        }

        public String getName() {
            return "dummy";
        }
    }
```

This code is used to help package the string containing our body into a DataSource that we can set as the content of our Mime message in the `sendMail()` method of our `StdMailBean`.

> *The WebLogic server ships with a set of example source code that provides an excellent reference for developing J2EE applications on the WebLogic platform. The sample source for WebLogic 6.0 is available under the standard installation directory at: `%weblogic_install%\samples\`.*

The Deployment Descriptors

The EJB 1.1 and EJB 2.0 specifications require that a deployment descriptor file called `ejb-jar.xml` be packaged with an EJB archive. To properly package our EJB we need to create this deployment descriptor file. As we are using WebLogic, we also have to create the file `weblogic-ejb-jar.xml` for archive. This file is needed by the WebLogic server (this file is a WebLogic construct, and is *not* part of the EJB specification) and contains specific properties for fully configuring and registering the EJB in the WebLogic server environment.

ejb-jar.xml

This file includes information that the server uses to configure the EJB within the server environment; the bean's home interface, the bean's remote interface, the type of EJB (ours is a session bean), transaction information that instructs the EJB container on how the EJB participates in transactions, and references to resources the EJB uses, such as our JavaMail session, etc.:

```xml
<?xml version="1.0" encoding="Cp1252"?>

<!DOCTYPE ejb-jar PUBLIC "-//Sun Microsystems, Inc.//DTD Enterprise JavaBeans
1.1//EN" "http://java.sun.com/j2ee/dtds/ejb-jar_1_1.dtd">

<ejb-jar>

  <enterprise-beans>

    <session>
      <description>EJB 1.1 Mail Bean</description>
      <ejb-name>StdMailBean</ejb-name>
      <home>com.acme.ejb.mail.StdMailHome</home>
      <remote>com.acme.ejb.mail.StdMail</remote>
      <ejb-class>com.acme.ejb.mail.StdMailBean</ejb-class>
      <session-type>Stateless</session-type>
      <transaction-type>Container</transaction-type>
      <resource-ref>
          <description>description</description>
          <res-ref-name>mail/MailSession</res-ref-name>
          <res-type>javax.mail.Session</res-type>
          <res-auth>Container</res-auth>
```

```
        </resource-ref>
      </session>

  </enterprise-beans>

  <assembly-descriptor>
    <container-transaction>
      <method>
         <ejb-name>StdMailBean</ejb-name>
         <method-name>*</method-name>
      </method>
      <trans-attribute>NotSupported</trans-attribute>
    </container-transaction>
  </assembly-descriptor>

</ejb-jar>
```

Let's examine some of the important properties of the file:

❏   The <resource-ref> tag wraps the description of an EJB reference to an external resource, in this case our JavaMail session:

  ❏   <res-ref-name> This is the "name" of the resource manager connection factory.

  ❏   <res-type> This specifies the name of the data source – this is the Java interface or class expected to be implemented by the data source, since this is a JavaMail data source ours is javax.mail.Session.

  ❏   <res-auth> This specifies whether the EJB container signs on to the resource manager on behalf of the EJB or the EJB itself signs on to the resource manager. In our case we set this to "Container" – the other option for this tag is "Application".

weblogic-ejb-jar.xml

Along with the standard deployment descriptor information required by the EJB specification in the ejb-jar.xml file, the WebLogic server also requires its own information for deploying the EJB within the WebLogic server environment. Here is the weblogic-ejb-jar.xml file:

```
<?xml version="1.0"?>

<!DOCTYPE weblogic-ejb-jar PUBLIC "-//BEA Systems, Inc.//DTD WebLogic 6.0.0
EJB//EN" "http://www.bea.com/servers/wls600/dtd/WebLogic-ejb-jar.dtd">

<weblogic-ejb-jar>

  <weblogic-enterprise-bean>
    <ejb-name>StdMailBean</ejb-name>
    <stateless-session-descriptor>
      <pool>
        <max-beans-in-free-pool>200</max-beans-in-free-pool>
        <initial-beans-in-free-pool>20</initial-beans-in-free-pool>
      </pool>
    </stateless-session-descriptor>
    <reference-descriptor>
      <resource-description>
```

```
            <res-ref-name>mail/MailSession</res-ref-name>
            <jndi-name>mail/Session</jndi-name>
        </resource-description>
      </reference-descriptor>
      <jndi-name>StdMailBean</jndi-name>
    </weblogic-enterprise-bean>

  </weblogic-ejb-jar>
```

This file uses the `<ejb-name>` defined name of the `ejb-jar.xml` file (in our case "`StdMailBean`") to configure the bean in the WebLogic server. Again, let's review the important information here:

❑ The `<stateless-session-descriptor>` tag contains configuration settings for a stateless session bean such as information on the object pool settings for our bean:

  ❑ `<max-beans-in-free-pool>` Instructs the EJB container on the maximum number of beans that will be cached in the object free pool.

  ❑ `<initial-beans-in-free-pool>` The number of beans that will be created in the free pool upon initialization.

❑ The `<jndi-name>` tag contains the actual name under which the bean's home interface will be registered in the JNDI directory service. In the case of our bean, the name its home interface will be registered under is `StdMailBean`.

❑ The `<reference-descriptor>` wraps an external reference set up in the `ejb-jar.xml` file.

  ❑ The `<res-ref-name>` is the same name as the resource reference defined in the `<res-ref-name>` tag defined in the `ejb-jar.xml` file.

  ❑ The `<jndi-name>` is the name of the resource as it is registered in JNDI.

The Web Application

For our web application, we're going to add on to our Chapter 6 example application. All we need to do is add a new custom JSP tag and modify the application to use our new tag instead of the old one.

The CreateCaseEJBTag Class

This is the main change in the application. The `CreateCaseEJBTag` is a JSP tag library that receives the data via the `CreateCase.jsp` and uses the `JMSManager` class to send the form data within a `MapMessage` to our JMS topic. This tag will be replacing the `CreateCaseTag` from the previous chapter.

First, it retrieves a number of initialization parameters from the servlet context that are configured in the `web.xml` file:

```
package com.acme.user;

import javax.servlet.jsp.*;
import javax.servlet.jsp.tagext.*;
import javax.servlet.*;
import javax.servlet.http.*;
import javax.jms.*;
import com.acme.common.*;
```

```
public class CreateCaseEJBTag extends TagSupport {

  public int doStartTag() throws JspTagException {

    try {

      ServletContext ctx = pageContext.getServletContext();
      HttpServletRequest req =
          (HttpServletRequest)pageContext.getRequest();

      String jmsFactory = ctx.getInitParameter("jmsFactory");
      System.out.println("jmsFactory: " + jmsFactory);

      String ctxFactory = ctx.getInitParameter("ctxFactory");
      System.out.println("ctxFactory: " + ctxFactory);

      String qcFactory = ctx.getInitParameter("qcFactory");
      System.out.println("qcFactory: " + qcFactory);

      String requestQueue = ctx.getInitParameter("requestQueue");
      System.out.println("requestQueue: " + requestQueue);

      String provURL = ctx.getInitParameter("provURL");
      System.out.println("provURL: " + provURL);

      String topic = ctx.getInitParameter("topic");
      System.out.println("topic: " + topic);

      String helpDeskEmail = ctx.getInitParameter("HelpDesk");
      System.out.println("helpDeskEmail: " + helpDeskEmail);
```

Then we need to create and initialize two JMSManager objects. We need to create two, because unlike the previous chapter we are publishing new messages to a topic and not a queue, however, to make sure that the Case Management system still works we still need to post to the queue:

```
JMSManager topicMgr = new JMSManager(ctxFactory, provURL,
    topic, jmsFactory, IJMSConstants.PUB_SUB_MODEL);
JMSManager queueMgr = new JMSManager(ctxFactory, provURL,
    requestQueue, qcFactory, IJMSConstants.P2P_MODEL);

topicMgr.initializeJMS(IJMSConstants.PRODUCER, null, true);
queueMgr.initializeJMS(IJMSConstants.PRODUCER, null, true);
```

Once we have the Manager objects, we can construct the message from the HTTP request and send it:

```
MapMessage msg = queueMgr.createMapMessage();
String caseId = IDGenerator.getNextId();
msg.setString("caseid", caseId);
msg.setString("name", req.getParameter("name"));
msg.setString("location", req.getParameter("location"));
msg.setString("description", req.getParameter("description"));
msg.setString("helpdesk", helpDeskEmail);
```

```
        topicMgr.sendMessage(msg, true);
        topicMgr.closeJMS();

        queueMgr.sendMessage(msg, true);
        queueMgr.closeJMS();

        pageContext.setAttribute("caseId", caseId);

        return EVAL_BODY_INCLUDE;

    } catch(Exception e) {

        System.out.println("Exception in doStartTag: CreateCaseEJBTag");
        System.out.println(e.getClass());
        System.out.println(e.getMessage());
        e.printStackTrace();
        throw new JspTagException(e.getMessage());

    }

  }

  public int doEndTag() throws JspTagException {
    return EVAL_PAGE;
  }

}
```

The web.xml Descriptor

As you recall from the previous chapter, we add our servlet and JSP configuration information to the standard J2EE web application configuration file web.xml, this contains our application initialization arguments, URL mapping, etc. We need to modify the web.xml file to add look as follows:

```
<?xml version="1.0" encoding="Cp1252"?>

<!DOCTYPE web-app PUBLIC "-//Sun Microsystems, Inc.//DTD Web Application 2.2//EN"
"http://java.sun.com/j2ee/dtds/web-app_2_2.dtd">

<web-app>

  <display-name>ACME</display-name>
  <description>ACME Helpdesk System</description>

    .
    .
    .

  <context-param>
    <param-name>jmsFactory</param-name>
    <param-value>mailFactory</param-value>
  </context-param>
```

```
<context-param>
  <param-name>topic</param-name>
  <param-value>com.acme.jms.topics.MailTopic</param-value>
</context-param>

<context-param>
  <param-name>HelpDesk</param-name>
  <param-value>helpdesk@acme.com</param-value>
</context-param>
```

.
.
.

```
</web-app>
```

> **Be sure to change the HelpDesk parameter to a valid e-mail address of your own.**

We next need to modify our `user.tld` file to add our `CreateCaseEJBTag`.

The user.tld Descriptor

We need to add our `CreateCaseEJBTag` to our tag library definition file `user.tld`. We will modify it as follows:

```
<?xml version="1.0"  ?>
<!DOCTYPE taglib PUBLIC "-//Sun Microsystems, Inc.//DTD JSP Tag Library 1.1//EN"
"web-jsptaglib_1_1.dtd">

<taglib>

  <tlibversion>1.0</tlibversion>
  <jspversion>1.1</jspversion>
  <shortname>User</shortname>
  <info>
    This tag library contains tag extensions
  </info>

  <tag>
    <name>createCase</name>
    <!-- <tagclass>com.acme.user.CreateCaseTag</tagclass> -->
    <tagclass>com.acme.user.CreateCaseEJBTag</tagclass>
    <teiclass>com.acme.user.CreateCaseTagVariableInfo</teiclass>
    <bodycontent>JSP</bodycontent>
  </tag>

  <tag>
    <name>caseHistory</name>
    <tagclass>com.acme.user.CaseHistoryTag</tagclass>
    <bodycontent>JSP</bodycontent>
  </tag>

</taglib>
```

Deploying the System

The application uses both standard J2EE features, and one proprietary feature of the WebLogic application server – the WebLogic Startup class. You could deploy the web application features on one server, JMS on another, and the EJBs on a third, if you so desired. As with the previous chapter, though, we will run ours on the same WebLogic instance using a single Enterprise Application Archive (EAR) file. We'll explain how to build, deploy, and run the applications below.

Compiling the Classes

If you download the source code for this chapter from the Wrox web site (http://www.wrox.com) you will be provided with a series of build scripts that will compile and deploy the application into your WebLogic server. Simply edit them to point to your WebLogic installation and then run `archive11.bat`.

However, a guide to the compilation and deployment process is provided here.

Currently, our application comprises three parts:

❑ The WebLogic Startup classes

❑ The web application

❑ The EJB application

The WebLogic Startup Classes

The Startup classes need the following directory structure:

```
com/
    acme/
        common/
                IJMSConstants.class
                JMSManager.class
        ejb/
            mail/
                StdMail.class
                StdMailBean.class
                StdMailHome.class
        startup/
                MsgReceiverStartup.class
                MsgReceiverShutdown.class
```

We recommend that these files be simply copied into a `serverclasses` subdirectory of your WebLogic domain. In other words:

```
c:\bea\wlserver6.0\config\mydomain\serverclasses\com\...
```

The Web Application

The web application needs the following directory structure:

```
WEB-INF/
        web-xml
        user.tld
        classes/
                com/
                    acme/
                        common/
                                IJMSConstants.class
                                JMSManager.class
                        user/
                            CaseHistoryTag.class
                            CaseResponse.class
                            CreateCaseEJBTag.class
                            CreateCaseTagVariableInfo.class
                            IDGenerator.class
                            ResponsePool.class
banner.jsp
casehistory.jsp
createcase.jsp
index.jsp
login.jsp
newcase.jsp
```

These files should be packaged as a WAR file, called for example, `help.war`.

The EJB Application

The EJB application should have the following directory structure:

```
com/
    acme/
        ejb/
            mail/
                ByteArrayDataSource.class
                StdMail.class
                StdMailBean.class
                StdMailHome.class
META-INF/
        ejb-jar.xml
        weblogic-ejb-jar.xml
```

These files should be packaged together into an EJB JAR file, called for example `std_ejb_mail.jar`.

WebLogic also requires that the various stubs and skeletons be generated for EJBs to be deployed in its container. It provides a utility called **ejbc** in the `weblogic.jar` file for this purpose. A standard example of its use would be:

```
java -classpath c:\bea\wlserver6.0\lib\weblogic.jar weblogic.ejbc
     std_ejb_mail.jar ejb_mail.jar
```

Creating the Enterprise Archive File

The enterprise archive file can simply be created by packaging up the WAR file and the EJB JAR file(s) into a single archive.

This EAR file can then be copied to your WebLogic domain's `applications` directory. Or you can use the WebLogic administration console application to deploy your EAR:

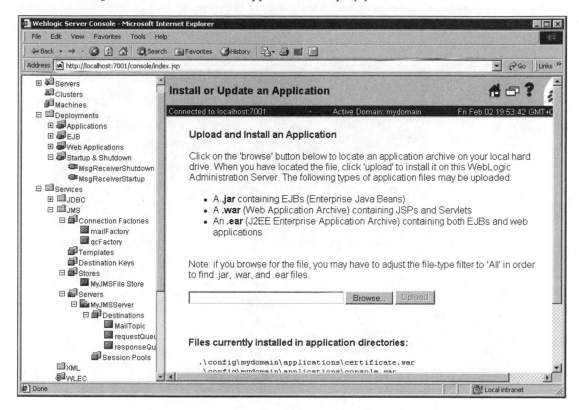

Running the Application

To test out our EJB application, start the WebLogic server running and browse to
http://localhost:7001/help. This will present you with the same web application as we saw in the
previous chapter.

Submit a new case to the system, and watch the output in the server window to see the EJBs in action:

If you check the e-mail account for the helpdesk you should find you have received the corresponding mail:

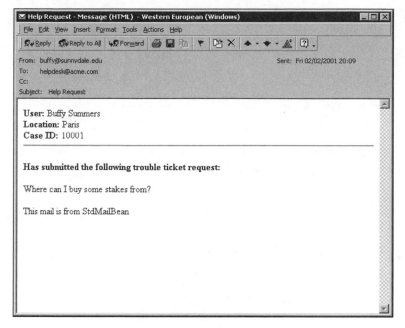

JMS and EJB 2.0

With EJB 2.0 specification Sun introduced a new EJB type, the **message-driven bean**. This bean type was introduced to specifically address the prior lack of integration with JMS that we were forced to work around in our EJB 1.1 example, through the use a delegation model and a WebLogic Startup class.

The EJB 2.0 message-driven bean solves this problem for us. The message-driven bean type now provides a mechanism implemented through the EJB container, for dealing with asynchronous message delivery to an EJB.

In this section we'll show how to create an EJB 2.0 message-driven bean that can be used in place of StdMailBean to achieve the same functionality as demonstrated in the EJB 1.1 example application.

A message-driven bean is stateless (and can only be stateless – there are no other options, though it should be noted that it is not a session bean – a message-driven bean is its own interface type, which only extends the default EJB interface EnterpriseBean), and has these important features:

❑ It implements the MessageDrivenBean interface.

❑ It does not have a home interface (as the developer of a MessageDrivenBean you do not need to create a home interface for the bean). Since this bean type is accessed only by the container in response to JMS messages, there is no home interface for this type of bean.

❑ It does not have a remote interface (as above, as the developer, you don't need to create a remote interface for this type of bean). As above, since this bean type is never accessed remotely by a client, and is only used internally by the EJB container in response to asynchronous JMS message delivery, there is no remote interface.

The following diagram shows the architecture of a message-driven bean:

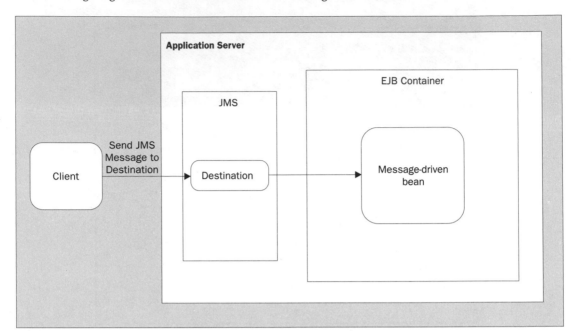

As you can see in the above diagram, a message-driven bean receives JMS messages asynchronously through the EJB container. The deployment descriptor properties for the EJB specify whether the bean is associated with a topic or a queue and whether or not it is a durable subscription. A given message-driven bean can only be associated with one JMS destination. You can change this through the deployment descriptor properties, but once deployed, it may only be associated with a single queue or topic. The WebLogic server's deployment file, `weblogic-ejb-jar.xml` is used to associate a given message-driven bean with a specific topic or queue name – this destination type must exist in the application server.

The Case Logging System with EJB 2.0

Using a message-driven bean, we can simplify our initial application design significantly. Since we no longer need to delegate requests to our bean, we no longer need a WebLogic Startup class. The development of the EJB is simplified as well, since we no longer need to provide the home interface or the remote interface. From the perspective of the client, however, the message-driven bean acts as any other JMS consumer, and the client isn't aware of any difference.

So how does this change the way in which the application works? We will reduce the complexity of our implementation by removing the WebLogic Startup class, and turning our EJB 1.1 stateless session bean into an EJB 2.0 message-driven bean. It's important to note that the same underlying complexity still exists, although now the majority of this will be handled by the EJB container. The EJB container will now intercept the asynchronously delivered JMS message, and locate and invoke the message-driven bean's `onMessage()` method. From an implementation standpoint, though, we have now made things much simpler by creating our message-driven bean. The following sequence diagram shows the changes:

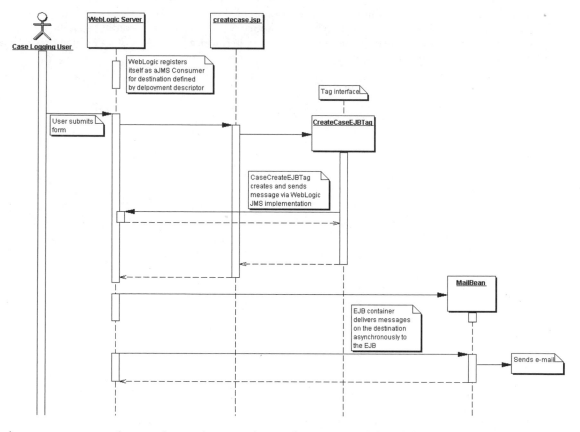

As you can see, our front end stays the same, but we have removed the WebLogic Startup class and consolidated our functionality into a message-driven bean called `MailBean` that will perform the same functions as our EJB 1.1 bean.

Implementing the EJB 2.0 MailBean

We will now present the source code that contains the changes to our application. Since the JSPs are unchanged, we will focus only on the message-driven bean. We will create a new Java package called `com.acme.ejb.messagedriven` and create a new bean class implementation under this package called `MailBean.java`.

Next, we will create two new deployment XML files, `ejb-jar.xml` and `weblogic-ejb-jar.xml`, for deploying our EJB 2.0 bean. By building and deploying this new bean to the server we can demonstrate the new functionality through application since this bean also acts as a durable subscriber on the same `MailTopic` that we used in our first example.

The MailBean Class

The `MailBean` class implements the `MessageDrivenBean` interface. As you can see, the rest of the bean is for the most part identical to the `StdMailBean`'s bean implementation class. One important point, though, is that it also implements the JMS `MessageListener` interface. Whereas 1.1 EJBs cannot implement the `MessageListener` interface directly, the new `MessageDrivenBean` type *must* implement the `MessageListener` interface.

Since our message-driven bean implements almost identical code to our `StdMailBean`, we will only show the differences between the two. First, you'll notice we jump straight into the bean class description. This is because our EJB home and remote interfaces are not part of a message-driven bean. Our class implements two interfaces:

❑ `MessageDrivenBean` – Our bean type.

❑ `Messagelistener` – A message-driven bean class must implement the JMS `MessageListener` interface and its `onMessage()` method.

```
package com.acme.ejb.messagedriven;

import java.io.IOException;

import java.util.*;
import javax.ejb.*;
import javax.jms.*;
import javax.naming.*;
import javax.activation.DataHandler;
import javax.mail.*;
import javax.mail.internet.*;
import java.rmi.RemoteException;

public class MailBean implements MessageDrivenBean, MessageListener {

  private static final boolean VERBOSE = true;
  private static final String MAIL_HOST = "mail.smtp.host";
  private static final String MAIL_SUBJECT = "Help Request";
  private static final String JNDI_MAIL = "acme/Mail";

  private MessageDrivenContext context;
  private String message;

  public void ejbRemove() {}
  public void ejbCreate () throws CreateException {}
```

We implement the `setMessageDrivenContext()` method that is part of the `MessageDrivenBean` interface. We also create an attribute of type `MessageDrivenContext` and set it. This is where you can retrieve the bean's `EJBContext` information.

```
public void setMessageDrivenContext(MessageDrivenContext ctx) {
    context = ctx;
}
```

Finally, you can see that we implement the `onMessage()` method of the `MessageListener` interface directly in the bean class. This will be called whenever an asynchronous JMS message is delivered to our EJB. The code in this method is nearly the same, as the code in `StdMailBean`. The only difference is that the method returns `void` instead of `boolean`. The bean will extract the message body content, and create and send an e-mail alert message:

```
    public void onMessage(javax.jms.Message msg) {
      .
      .
      .
    }

    public boolean sendMail(String to, String subject,
                            String body, boolean debug) {
      .
      .
      .
    }

    public javax.mail.internet.InternetAddress[]
        parseEmailAddress(String addresses) {
      .
      .
      .
    }

    private void packageBody(javax.mail.Message msg, String body)
        throws MessagingException, java.io.IOException {
      .
      .
      .
    }

    private String createBody(String problem, String name, String location)
    {
      .
      .
    buf.append("This mail is from MailBean\n");
    }
```

We will also need the `ByteArrayDataSource` class again, but be sure to update the package directive.

The Deployment Descriptors

To properly package our EJB we again need to create the bean's deployment descriptor file. The `ejb-jar.xml` file contains the EJB specification's deployment descriptor tags, and references the EJB 2.0 DTD. We also have to create the file `weblogic-ejb-jar.xml` for archive. This file contains specific properties for fully configuring and registering the EJB in the WebLogic server environment.

ejb-jar.xml

The `ejb-jar.xml` file is much the same as our previous example. It uses the EJB 2.0 DTD, as you can see in the `<!DOCTYPE ...>` reference, and includes support for a new message-driven bean tag:

```
<?xml version="1.0" encoding="Cp1252"?>
```

```
<!DOCTYPE ejb-jar PUBLIC "-//Sun Microsystems, Inc.//DTD Enterprise JavaBeans
2.0//EN" "http://java.sun.com/dtd/ejb-jar_2_0.dtd">
```

```
<ejb-jar>

   <enterprise-beans>
      <message-driven>
        <ejb-name>MailBean</ejb-name>
        <ejb-class>com.acme.ejb.messagedriven.MailBean</ejb-class>
        <transaction-type>Container</transaction-type>
        <message-driven-destination>
          <jms-destination-type>javax.jms.Topic</jms-destination-type>
          <subscription-durability>durable</subscription-durability>
        </message-driven-destination>
        <resource-ref>
           <description>description</description>
           <res-ref-name>mail/MailSession</res-ref-name>
           <res-type>javax.mail.Session</res-type>
           <res-auth>Container</res-auth>
        </resource-ref>
      </message-driven>
   </enterprise-beans>

   <assembly-descriptor>
     <container-transaction>
       <method>
         <ejb-name>MailBean</ejb-name>
         <method-name>*</method-name>
       </method>
       <trans-attribute>NotSupported</trans-attribute>
     </container-transaction>
   </assembly-descriptor>

</ejb-jar>
```

The tags to note here are:

❑   The <message-driven> tag begins the description of a message-driven bean and its properties

❑   The <message-driven-destination> tag wraps the properties of the type of destination the bean is associated with

❑   The <jms-destination-type> tag contains the type of destination the bean is associated with, either javax.jms.Topic or javax.jms.Queue

❑   The <subscription-durability> tag specifies whether or not the subscription is durable or non-durable

The weblogic-ejb-jar.xml Descriptor

Recall that along with the standard deployment descriptor information required by the EJB specification in the ejb-jar.xml file, the WebLogic server also requires its own information for deploying the EJB within the WebLogic server environment. The weblogic-ejb-jar.xml file for our Message-driven bean implementation looks as follows:

```xml
<?xml version="1.0" encoding="Cp1252"?>

<!DOCTYPE weblogic-ejb-jar PUBLIC "-//BEA Systems, Inc.//DTD WebLogic 6.0.0
EJB//EN" "http://www.bea.com/servers/wls600/dtd/WebLogic-ejb-jar.dtd">

<weblogic-ejb-jar>

    <weblogic-enterprise-bean>
      <ejb-name>MailBean</ejb-name>
      <message-driven-descriptor>
        <pool>
          <max-beans-in-free-pool>200</max-beans-in-free-pool>
          <initial-beans-in-free-pool>20</initial-beans-in-free-pool>
        </pool>
        <destination-jndi-name>
            com.acme.jms.topics.MailTopic
        </destination-jndi-name>
      </message-driven-descriptor>
      <reference-descriptor>
          <resource-description>
              <res-ref-name>mail/MailSession</res-ref-name>
              <jndi-name>mail/Session</jndi-name>
          </resource-description>
      </reference-descriptor>
      <jndi-name>MailBean</jndi-name>
    </weblogic-enterprise-bean>

</weblogic-ejb-jar>
```

This file contains one tag of importance as far as we're concerned, in regard to our message-driven bean:

❑   The `<destination-jndi-name>` tag is used to associate the bean with a named destination. This is the name of the queue or topic that you have created in the WebLogic server for your destination.

Deploying the EJB 2.0 Application

The process is nearly identical to that of the EJB 1.1 version. This time however, the directory structure need only be:

```
com/
    acme/
          ejb/
               messagedriven/
                              ByteArrayDataSource.class
                              StdMail.class
                              StdMailBean.class
                              StdMailHome.class
META-INF/
          ejb-jar.xml
          weblogic-ejb-jar.xml
```

Again package these files into an EJB JAR and run `weblogic.ejbc` on them.

Before you can run the EJB 2.0 example, you must install the EJB 2.0 beta patch for WebLogic 6.0. At the time of writing, EJB 2.0 is only in a proposed-final draft stage so WebLogic must be manually updated with a new JAR file that can be downloaded from the WebLogic website.

Now, when you run the application again you should receive two mails, one from each bean version.

Summary

In this chapter we showed a working example demonstrating how to use EJBs with JMS. We examined the issues involved in using EJBs as JMS consumers for both EJB 1.1 and EJB 2.0. We modified the Case Logging application from the previous chapter so that it demonstrated a delegation solution using a specialized WebLogic Startup class for EJB 1.1, and then showed how the EJB 2.0 message-driven bean simplifies the use of EJBs with JMS when acting as asynchronous consumers of a JMS destination through the integration of the EJB container with JMS.

In the next chapter we will take a more theoretical look at the role of JMS in a clustering architecture.

com.sun.jn...
com.sun.jn...
weblogic.jndi.T3Initi...
weblogic.jms.rtl.Fiorar...
fiorano.jms.naming.Context.ReffSContextFactory
ch.softwired.fscontext.LdapCtxFactory
com.sun.jndi.ldap.WLInitialContextFactory
weblogic.jndi.WLInitialContext
fiorano.jms.rtl.FioranoInitialContext
fiorano.jms.runtime.naming.FioranoInitialContextFactory
ch.softwired.jms.naming.IBusContextFactory

com.sun.jndi.fscontext.ReffSContextFactory
weblogic.jndi.WLInitialContextFactory
weblogic.jndi.T3InitialContextFactory
fiorano.jms.rtl.FioranoInitialContextFactory
fiorano.jms.runtime.naming.FioranoInitialContextFactory
ch.softwired.jms.naming.IBusContextFactory

8

JMS and Clustering

When a JMS message server is used as the basis of a distributed system, the result is a "loose coupling" of the components that compose that system. This decoupling reduces the need for the individual applications to be available at all times. Indeed, the consumer of a message need not have been implemented at the time that the corresponding producer sends it. It is also not necessary for the producers and consumers of messages to know each other's identity. Consumers can be added, removed, and replaced without any need for the producers to be aware of these occurrences.

These features make a new style of distributed architecture possible, where the developers of each element of the system have only limited knowledge and influence over the other elements of the system. This new architecture is required to circumvent the technical and organizational obstacles to the next generation of global, distributed systems. These are systems that span many companies and organizations, and it will not be possible for all parties involved to agree on the countless details required to work together in a tightly coupled fashion.

The two major aspects of loosely coupled systems described above – reduced demands on the availability of messaging participants and reduced awareness of messaging counter parties – cause very high demands to be placed on the message server that connects the system together. Namely, the message server must be available at all times, and all possible producers and consumers of messages that could potentially interact at any time in the future must connect to the same logical server.

We can expect that in very many messaging systems the central logical server will be required to provide a level of reliability and throughput that cannot be fulfilled by one single process running on one physical machine. In short, enterprise message servers will need to be able to combine the resources of multiple computers to create the external appearance of one highly capable central server. This is called **clustering**.

So you just need to run down to the local software store and pick up a cluster, right? Unfortunately, it is not so simple. There is a lot of complexity behind the elegant, all encompassing definition of clustering that I gave above. There's a large number of individual technical problems that can be overcome through clustering, and for a given application, some of these will be more important than others.

Furthermore, there is not just one way to build a cluster, there are an unlimited number of ways to architect a cluster, and each of these will solve some problems better than others. Fortunately, most clusters that you encounter in the marketplace will resemble at least one of the major architecture "themes" that we'll see in this chapter. So if your messaging-based distributed system requires a clustered JMS provider, read on.

This chapter will explain the concepts and issues involved in using clustering to provide scalable messaging services to JMS clients. The material in this chapter is aimed at helping system architects to be better able to:

❑ Understand what clustering is in the context of JMS

❑ Know what to expect from clustering

❑ Know what not to expect from clustering

❑ Define their particular requirements for clustering

❑ Assess how a JMS provider meets these requirements

> *This chapter focuses on clustering as it relates to JMS. Much of the material, however, is relevant to clustering in general. This general material is a necessary prerequisite to understanding the JMS-specific issues. I would even go as far as to say that clustering is particularly important in the world of messaging. By their very nature, distributed architectures that rely on server-based messaging put very heavy demands on the capacity and reliability of a centralized server. This leads to clustering being necessary for JMS providers even more often than for many other type of server application.*

What is a Cluster?

The introduction described clustering and the basic philosophy behind it. Before getting into the details, though, let's set the scene by stating an explicit definition of clustering, and examining the benefits that we can expect from it.

Definitions

> **For the purposes of this chapter, clustering is the use of multiple physical computers to provide a single logical service with more capacity and reliability than would be possible with a single physical computer.**

The concept of providing more of something is central to the definition. If you are not getting more of something you need, be it connections, storage, throughput, or reliability, then all you have done is spend a lot of money on extra hardware that brings no value-added benefit. This can be restated as the requirement that the cluster provide some degree of scalability, since scalability is the measure of how much additional service is provided by each additional machine.

The term **scalable** is often mistakenly interpreted as being synonymous with "high capacity." Actually, scalability together with efficiency determines total capacity. Efficiency refers to how much capacity you get for a given amount of resource, while scalability is the guarantee that you keep getting this efficiency as you add more resources.

Let's look at a concrete example using that most important of benchmarks, message throughput. Suppose two imaginary JMS providers can achieve the throughputs in the table below for clusters of two machines and clusters of ten machines. Provider A is more efficient because it has higher throughput for small clusters than Provider B. Provider B on the other hand is more scalable, because the throughput per machine does not decrease with a large cluster. Which is better? It depends on your needs. If you have a limited hardware budget, and 300 messages per second is sufficient throughput, then Provider A is a good deal. If you absolutely need 1000 messages per second, then Provider B is clearly the only one that can deliver:

Cluster Size	Throughput of JMS Provider A	Throughput of JMS Provider B
2	300 mg/s	200 mg/s
10	600 mg/s	1000mg/s

Most clusters belong to one of two general categories, which I call **service clusters** and **parallel computation clusters**. Although these both fit the above definition of cluster, in practice there is a very dramatic difference in what they are used for, where they are used, and their architecture. Rather than try to define these categories precisely, the following table contrasts their basic characteristics:

Cluster Type	Applications	Provides	Used by	Nodes	Examples
Service Cluster	Data storage and retrieval, data transmission (for example JMS), implementing business logic	Services to clients	Business, service providers	< 10	Oracle Parallel Server, most application servers, many message servers
Parallel Computation	Mathematical computation, modeling, simulation	Results of numerical calculations	Research institutions, military (modeling atomic decay), weather bureau, oceanographers	< 1000	Linux Beowulf, PVM

> **Clustered JMS providers fall cleanly into the category of service cluster, and in the remainder of this chapter the word cluster will be used to refer to this type of cluster exclusively.**

There are other ways to divide clusters into subcategories. One subcategorization that I feel is also important to point out is the one between application and system-level clustering:

❑ In **application-level clustering**, clustering is an integral part of the application and does not make any assumptions about cluster support in the underlying operating system. The various application processes in the cluster communicate directly with each other via a network, or assume that they can share the same disk, or both. (Example: Oracle Parallel Server.)

❑ In **system-level clustering**, the operating system, or a cluster enabling toolkit (which sits above the OS but below the application) provides generic functionality to support clustering. This is intended to make it easier to develop clustered servers, and even to adapt existing monolithic servers to act as a cluster. (Example: Microsoft Windows Cluster Server.)

I would tend to expect that pure Java JMS providers use application-level clustering, as this provides maximum portability. There is no requirement that the server part of a JMS provider be implemented in Java, and in the case that the server is tied to a specific platform, the provider might opt for system-level clustering.

System-level clustering tends to use shared disk architectures. We will look at the pros and cons of this later in the chapter.

The following terms will be used to mean very specific things in the remainder of this chapter. For clarity, they are defined here:

❑ **Node**
This is one element of a cluster. Typically this is used to refer to one machine in the cluster, but sometimes it is more precise to say that it refers to one process. With application-level clustering, the term node should refer to the process, as this is the basic unit of the cluster. It may be desirable to have multiple node processes on one machine, but these different nodes will usually interact in the same way whether they are on the same or different machines. In the case of system-level clustering (particularly at the OS level), one machine may host several different types of server, with redundant instances of those servers existing on other machines. In this case the term node would more often be used to refer to the machine, and not one of the processes. In the rest of this chapter, the term node will generally refer to a process node. When the distinction is important, I will use one the specific terms **process node** or **hardware node**.

There are known to be cases when multiple Java virtual machines sharing the resources of one physical machine perform better than a single virtual machine that tries to use the full resources of the machine. Thus, a cluster that allows multiple process nodes to coexist on one physical machine can take advantage of this performance boost, in addition to the other advantages of clustering discussed in this chapter.

❑ **Monolithic server**
This refers to a server that can only exist on one physical machine. That is to say that a monolithic server is a server that is not clustered.

❑ **Single logical server**
I use this term to refer to a server that appears to the client as though it were monolithic server, even though it could actually be either a cluster or a monolithic server. In this case, the client is indifferent as to which type of server it is, as long as it acts like a monolithic server.

❑ **RAID (Redundant Array of Inexpensive Disks)**
This is clustering for disks. It is a general technique for combining multiple physical disks to provide the outward appearance of one disk that has more capacity, performance, and reliability than the individual disks that compose it.

❑ **LAN (Local Area Network)**
A data network that is confined to a small area, such as a single data center. This usually implies high bandwidth and "cheap" communication.

❑ **WAN (Wide Area Network)**
A data network that spans a large geographic region, or even the whole world. When communicating over a WAN it is often not possible to assume large bandwidth between two arbitrary hosts. There may also be more "costs" (monetary or otherwise) incurred by communicating over a WAN.

Why Clustering?

There are three main reasons for using a cluster instead of monolithic server. Let's look at each of them in detail.

Increased Capacity

Increasing server capacity through clustering is commonly referred to as **load balancing**. By spreading the load over multiple machines, a cluster should be able to accommodate some combination of more messages per second, more bytes per second, more persistent storage, more non-persistent storage, more simultaneous connections, and more active subscriptions. Not all clustering solutions balance all of these – indeed providing more persistent storage is usually a direct tradeoff against another important benefit of clustering, redundant storage (see "High Availability" below). If a JMS message server must accommodate huge numbers of clients, or clients that produce huge message volume, any of the above mentioned parameters could become a bottleneck.

The balancing part of load balancing is also critical. After all, it does no good to provide extra machines if there is no mechanism to guarantee that the load is distributed fairly. If all machines have the same capabilities, then "fairly" means "evenly", but the machines in the cluster are dissimilar, then it takes a more sophisticated scheme to assure fairness.

Load balancing is usually done at the connection level, as each client is typically connected to one and only one node of the cluster. Other schemes are possible, but since the number of active connections is often one of the first limits reached, we'll omit any approaches that require multiple connections per client. A round-robin load-balancing scheme just assigns each new connection to the next node in list. More sophisticated schemes monitor the load of each node and assign new connections to those with the least load. **Static load balancing** schemes apply the balancing criteria only once per new connection. **Dynamic load balancing** schemes reevaluate the balancing criteria for existing connections and will redistribute live connections in order to better utilize lightly loaded machines.

Clusters that intend to provide increased storage capacity must balance message storage. This may be done with a simple approach. For example, each producer's messages are stored only on the machine to which that publisher is connected. This will go a long way toward spreading out the message storage over the cluster, but some publishers may produce much more volume than others, so an even better storage balancing scheme would be independent of the connection-balancing scheme.

It is important to note that clustered JMS servers that use a separate database server for persistent storage (via JDBC) will not provide increased storage capacity just because the number of message server (hardware) nodes increases. If all of those nodes access the same database server, then the total storage capacity of the cluster is the same no matter how many message server nodes there are. In this case clustering could only increase storage capacity if additional database servers are added along with each additional message server node, or if the database itself is clustered independently of the JMS server. All of the configurations described here are described in more detail later in the chapter.

High Availability

High availability is an important theme for message servers. One of the reasons for using inter-application messaging is to obviate the need for message producers to be concerned with whether the corresponding message consumers are available at a particular time. This is only possible when the message server is available at all times. This leads to the need to use clustering to guarantee continuous server availability even in cases where a monolithic server could satisfy the capacity requirements.

The terms high availability and fault tolerance are commonly used to mean the same thing. It is more precise, though, to use these to refer to two separate aspects of reliability:

> **A system is fault tolerant if unexpected failures never lead to lost or corrupt data, but this says nothing about the frequency of failures or the amount of time required to recover. High availability means that there is a guaranteed maximum amount of downtime that will not be exceeded.**

Thus, high availability is not an absolute service level, but a spectrum of service levels. A system's availability is usually specified by the percent uptime it guarantees. 99.0% uptime is generally one of the least demanding values that one would see specified in practice, with each increasing level adding another 9 to the end of the decimal. This is illustrated in the following table:

Guaranteed Uptime	Average Downtime	Typical Implications
95%	8 hours/week	System may be offline 1 hour each night for backup. No need to respond to failures until next business day.
99%	1.5 hours/week	System may be offline 1 hour each week for backup or maintenance. Need to respond to failures within 1 hour (technician must be on call 24 hours).
99.9%	40 mins/month	Backups are done while online. Technician/Sys Admin required on premises 24 hours x 7 days.
99.99%	4 mins/month	All persistent storage on RAID devices. Cold standby machine can be connected to RAID and booted within minutes.
99.999%	5 mins/year	Full hardware redundancy with automatic fail-over. Hot standby has OS booted and backup application running at all times. All data replicated to hot standby machine(s) in real time.

An implication of the table above is that the cost of maintaining a highly available system increases significantly as the guaranteed uptime increases. The actual costs depend on very many site-specific parameters, but one generalization is easy to make: the higher levels of availability are more cost effective for large installations than for small ones. Economies of scale come into play here.

The primary factor is the costs associated with having a system administrator on site nights and weekends. An installation of 100 machines may only require one person on site during off hours, but since we cannot divide people into parts, an installation of two machines requires the same amount of off-hours staffing. For large companies that have their own data centers, the cost effectiveness issue is not a big deal. Small companies that require very high availability, however, must often have their systems located at an application service provider (ASP) where such costs can be spread over the many other customers of the ASP.

Geographical Distribution

When I think of clustering, my first thought is generally of several computers sitting in the same rack, connected with a high speed LAN, and providing high availability and load balancing. Another variation, which fits the definition of a cluster above, is the case where nodes are located in different geographical regions and are connected by a WAN. This configuration can provide better service to local clients in each region than could be provided with a centralized cluster. It can provide higher availability because the local clients will still be able to connect to the local server, even when the WAN connection is broken. It can provide better performance because it will generally be optimized to transfer the least possible amount of data over WAN connections. It can also potentially protect your messaging system from the effects of regional power outages or natural disasters, which could cause the simultaneous failure of all of the nodes in a given region.

In theory, you could take a cluster designed to provide high availability and load balancing over a LAN and just move the nodes to different cities. In practice this would not be a good idea. WAN connections are usually slower and more costly that LAN connections, so you want to be smart about sending messages between servers. In particular, you want to avoid sending messages to a remote server, unless you are sure that they will be consumed there. For this reason I prefer to refer to this case as **message routing**. The term clustering may or may not include the aspect of message routing depending on the context in which it is used.

In Point-to-Point Messaging

In the case of Point-to-Point (PTP) messaging, described in Chapter 4, each message will be consumed by at most one receiver. If multiple copies of a queue message are sent to different local servers, it becomes very difficult to ensure that only one of these copies will be sent to a receiver. The message routing logic will usually not send a queue message to a remote server unless it is certain that it will be consumed there. When possible, the logic will try to favor a receiver connected to the same node to which the message sender is connected, in order to be sure that the message does not travel over a WAN unnecessarily.

In Publish/Subscribe Messaging

For Publish/Subscribe (Pub/Sub) messaging, described in Chapter 5, the message routing logic will be a bit different. There is always some efficiency to gain because at most one copy of each message must be moved to each local server, no matter how many subscribers are actually connected. It may be desirable to unconditionally send every message to every remote server, so that any subscriber has instant access to it as soon as it connects. It may be more efficient to send a message to a remote server only if you know in advance that there is a subscriber connected, or a durable subscriber registered, for the topic to which the message was published.

To some extent, a message routing configuration could provide load balancing and high availability as described above. This is not always a good idea though. Load balancing would mean that if a server were to be too heavily loaded to accept an additional local client, then that client could connect, via a WAN, to a remote server. This would work but would not be particularly efficient. A client might also connect directly to a remote server if the local server crashes. In this case it is difficult to guarantee that all of the messages that would have been available on the local server are available on the remote one. The message routing logic may just not have sent all the messages to the remote server.

In contrast, if the message routing logic tried to insure full redundancy by guaranteeing that every message were copied to every machine before the message was considered to have been sent, the result would be a distributed server that is very slow. The point here is that if a wide area message routing cluster needs load balancing and high availability, then each of the local services should be implemented as a highly available, load-balanced cluster.

What Clustering Cannot Do

In addition to mentioning the reasons for using clustering, it is important to be very clear about the following aspects of performance and reliability that cannot be improved through clustering.

Latency

You might notice that I consistently refer to messaging performance in this chapter in terms of throughput. This is intended to place emphasis on the most important performance scenario: large numbers of messages traveling from many producers to many consumers. Latency, in contrast, can be best described as the minimum time it takes for one message to travel from producer to consumer in a system that otherwise has no load. Clustering cannot decrease latency. In fact clustering will usually increase latency since messages must typically visit several nodes in the process of being delivered. The performance benefits of clustering should result in latencies that do not increase significantly when message throughput becomes very high.

As long as the latency of a message system is reasonable, there is seldom much benefit to be had by trying to decrease it. A securities trading application would usually require latencies to be much less than a second, but many messaging applications could actually tolerate quite high latencies. The important point to remember is that a latency of 1 second does not correspond to a throughput of one message per second; this is because the system does not need to wait for one message to be consumed before the next message may be produced. When writing benchmark programs to measure the performance of a messaging system, it is important to design the benchmark to measure throughput and not latency, as measuring latency will not be a good indicator of how the system performs under heavy load.

Systematic Failures

A cluster is often used to increase the reliability of a system. This reliability come in the form of redundant nodes, so that when one node fails, another node can take over in its place. This provides protection from errors such as hardware failure that tend to occur at random times and are completely independent from one node to another. Systematic failures, on the other hand, are deterministic and reproducible. They are typically the result of programming errors or the failure to safeguard against unexpected occurrences. Clustering cannot provide protection against this type of failure.

Consider what happens if a node fails because it runs out of memory. A backup node could take over, but if the backup node has been mirroring the actions of the primary node that it replaces (and we assume it has the same amount of memory), then we can count on it running out of memory right away also. Sure, there should be some means in place (other than clustering) to prevent the memory overflow. The point here is that clustering cannot compensate for programming deficiencies.

Byzantine Failures

Byzantine failures result when some process on the network runs amok and starts sending corrupt data throughout the system, or worse yet, when some agent maliciously tries to disrupt your system. The rule for systematic failure above holds here also: if one node in a cluster is susceptible to this type of failure, it is likely that all the nodes are, so the redundancy in the cluster will not provide much protection against this.

Aspects of Scalability

Scalability is the measure of how effective a cluster is. In fact, I would go as far as to say that it is the measure of whether or not a group of machines is, effectively, a cluster or not. These statements may sound a bit bold, but my definition of scalability below is quite broad and can be interpreted to encompass everything that has to do with combining multiple computers into a cluster.

In a nutshell, if a cluster of four machines does not provide more of anything (including reliability) that the corresponding monolithic server supplies, the cluster has achieved nothing; you may just as well leave machines two through four switched off. If that cluster of four machines provides four times the capability of a monolithic server, then the cluster scales very well. In fact such ideal scalability is generally impossible to achieve in practice; the challenge is to see how close a cluster can get to this case.

Defining Scalability

The term scalability is used in many different contexts, and depending on context one can probably find quite a few different definitions. In terms of a message server, let's use the following definition:

> **Scalability is the degree to which some aspect of the messaging service is enhanced by adding more resources.**

Specifically in the case of clustering, let's limit the discussion to an even more specific definition: scalability is the degree to which some aspect of the service is enhanced as more physical machines are added to the cluster.

In some cases scalability can be measured quantitatively. For instance, if you have a benchmark that measures the number of messages per second that your cluster can process, you can run it for a cluster of two machines and a cluster of four machines and compare the results. If doubling the number machines doubles the message rate, then the scalability is **linear**, because a plot of message rate versus machine will form a straight line, as shown in the diagram overleaf.

We can be even more quantitative and divide the percent improvement in the benchmark by the percent increase in the number of machines to get a numerical value for the scalability:

> **Scalability = % improvement divided by % increase in number of machines.**

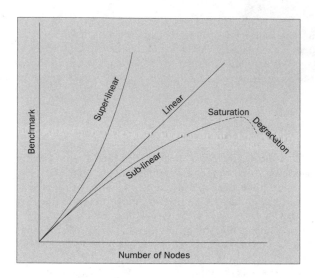

A value of 1 corresponds to linear scalability. A value less than 1 indicates **sublinear** scalability, and a value greater than 1 indicates **superlinear** scalability. Superlinear scalability corresponds to a condition commonly called synergy, in which the whole is greater than the sum of its parts.

Synergy is generally considered to be the result of good teamwork, but in the world of server clustering, it doesn't happen. I will therefore stick to the rule that linear scalability is the best that one can hope to achieve in the world of clustering, and that superlinear scalability is impossible. In practical situations, scalability will always be somewhat less than linear because there is inevitably some extra overhead incurred when increasing the size of a cluster.

Scalability will seldom be constant as the number of nodes in a cluster increases. A very common scenario is that scalability will be close to linear for the first few nodes, and then become sublinear very quickly. At some point the scalability will saturate, or become 0, corresponding to the point where the extra overhead of communication within the cluster equals the gains brought by each extra machine. It is entirely possible that beyond some point, the scalability becomes negative and total capability of the cluster degrades as more machines are added.

A prerequisite to quantitatively measuring scalability is the ability to measure the feature that you are trying to scale. If this is performance, then you will need a quantitative performance benchmark before you can measure the effect of adding nodes. Benchmarking is very much a black art. It is common for two different benchmarks to show very different results for the same server. This is because a message server, like any complex software system, has many different potential performance bottlenecks. The limits imposed by each of these may behave very differently as the load and the number of nodes is increased.

> It is very easy for two different benchmark programs to encounter different bottlenecks and thus show very different scalability behavior. As always, you need to understand what you are measuring. All the caveats that apply to performance benchmarking apply even more so to the quantitative measurement of scalability.

Scalability of Connections

There are many resource limits in a message server that could ultimately lead to scalability concerns. Foremost among them are CPU capacity, memory, and persistent storage (disk) space. It might seem strange to some that the number of client connections might receive more attention than things like message volume and storage capacity addressed below, but connections are a limited resource.

Some operating systems use file descriptors as the interface that gives applications access to network connections. This makes them look like files, even though they are not. Operating systems place a fixed limit on how many open file descriptors a process may have. If a server is implemented in Java, then the problem of connection limits is even more acute, as described below. Message servers by their very nature maintain a lot of client connections, and this is very often the first scalability limit encountered on a monolithic server.

As mentioned above, servers implemented in Java are limited to a number of connections less than that imposed by the file descriptor limit. The explanation for this is somewhat detailed, but since the issue of limited connections very often leads to the need for clustering, it may be worthwhile to understand the background.

The Java I/O API does not provide any means of doing non-blocking I/O. This means that the only way to determine if there is data available to read from a network socket is to actually try to read it. If the read() method call does not return then there is no data available. This, of course, presents a problem if you want your program to do something else until there is data to be read from the socket. Creating a separate thread dedicated to waiting to read from each socket easily solves this problem. If a server has thousands of open connections, though, then it needs thousands of threads that do nothing except wait for incoming data.

Sun clearly designed the Java I/O libraries with the assumption that threads are "cheap". They are in terms of CPU cycles: a thread that is blocked waiting to read data does not consume any CPU, but it does use memory. Java reserves a fixed amount of memory for the call stack of each thread, regardless of how much it actually uses. This is not the same the heap space reserved for allocating objects; it is in addition to the heap. Java VM's generally let you configure the actual stack size. For example, the default stack allocation for Sun's Java 1.3 on Solaris is 512KB, and can be changed by using -Xss command-line option with the java command.

The ultimate problem is that there is a limit to how much memory a single process can use. On 32-bit processors, a pointer cannot address more than 4GB of memory, so it is impossible for a process to use more than this, even if the machine has more than 4GB of total virtual memory. (Total virtual memory is the sum of the amount of real memory and swap space.) When the combined memory of the heap, all the thread stacks, the program code, and the virtual machine itself reaches this limit, then the process is out of memory. 4GB is actually a best case for 32-bit operating systems. Some operating systems do not make the make the maximum possible memory space available to the application: Windows NT gives 2GB, Linux 3GB, and Solaris gives all 4GB.

With 64-bit processors and operating systems, this should cease to be a problem. More importantly, Sun is working on the introduction of non-blocking I/O in future versions of Java. (This is detailed in Java Specification Request #000051: New I/O APIs for the Java Platform.) This will alleviate the need to reserve massive amounts of memory for threads that perform a trivial function.

Keep in mind, that if a program is using a large number of threads for purposes other than blocking connections, this will further reduce the total number of connections that are possible. The actual number of connections that a Java based serve can handle depends, in the end, on the actual Java VM implementation, the OS, and the default stack size. In practice, the limit usually falls somewhere in the range of 1000 to 5000 connections per process.

See the Volano report (http://www.volano.com/report.html) for more details on this.

Connections are a rare case in which we can make some sweeping generalizations, with numbers even, that apply to all Java-based message server clusters:

❑   If you need to support more than 1000 simultaneous client connections, you should plan on using some kind of clustering solution. Most JVMs can support at least this number of connections, if the server does not require many more threads in addition to those associated with connections.

❑   Any cluster should provide, as a minimum, good connection scalability.

Note that the limit on the number of connections, whether it is due to the thread limit or the file descriptor limit, is per process. This means that clustering could be used to alleviate the connection limit even with all of the process nodes running on the same machine. In most cases though, if you have a cluster you will probably want to take advantage of the ability to spread out the load over multiple machines.

Fortunately, it is relatively easy to ensure near linear scalability for connections. Since the connection limit is almost fixed per VM, then each additional VM on an additional physical machine should provide the same number of additional connections. If all other parameters do not scale negatively, then the cluster should be able to handle any number of connections by simply adding machines.

Scalability of Message Throughput

Message throughput is the parameter that most people mean when referring to the performance of a message server. This means, specifically, the total number of messages per second that can be produced and consumed. When people refer to load balancing in a cluster, this is the primary factor that they are seeking to improve. It is clear that message throughput could never scale linearly; in addition to moving messages from producer to the server, and from server to consumer, there is the extra overhead of moving messages among the nodes of the cluster.

The actual scalability of message throughput will depend heavily on the architecture of the particular cluster. It is almost guaranteed to be different for topics and queues, even for the same JMS provider. Clusters that require every message to be unconditionally copied to every node will probably not scale well here, although they will be bound to get good scores for high availability. Shared disk and shared database (more details on these later) are also unlikely to have scaleable throughput as all messages must be written to the same central store, regardless of the number of nodes in the cluster.

The extent to which throughput scales depends on the degree to which message processing can be performed in parallel, and the degree to which unnecessary message copying between nodes can be avoided. In the Pub/Sub domain, messages must be transferred to each node that has subscribers interested in that message. This depends a lot on the actual distribution of the producers and consumers, but in a worst case, when every node has at least one subscriber that is interested in every message, then it will be difficult for any architecture to scale.

The best-case scenario is when all publishers and subscribers for a particular topic are attached to the same node. This case scales well, but if a cluster requires this, then it need not really be a cluster, just a group of isolated monolithic servers and a repository where the clients can look up the location of each server. One implication of such a system is that if the all of the clients needed to access all destinations, then each client would need to be connected to all of the servers. This would mean that this "cluster" also did not solve the problem of a limited number of connections.

In the PTP domain it is hardly useful to copy every message to every node. In fact this would make it difficult to ensure that each message is only delivered to one receiver. If the nodes share information about their receivers, then it is possible to determine on which node the message will be consumed, and transfer it only to that node. If the network communication does not immediately become a bottleneck, then it is possible to get a reasonable amount of parallelism for queues.

In summary, it is safe to say that realizing a high degree of scalability for message throughput in a JMS message server cluster is not trivial.

Scalability of Storage Capacity

In both the PTP and Pub/Sub domains, JMS providers need to be able to store messages until consumers for those messages become available. The primary purpose of a message system is to move messages from producers to consumers, but message storage is also an important part of the loose coupling paradigm. This is what allows producers to send messages at any time, without being concerned about whether the consumer is ready to accept them or not. If message volume is large and the consumers are offline much of the time, the storage capacity of the message server can be quickly exhausted.

Flow Control

Flow control is essential to ensure that producers are stopped before the server's storage capacity is exceeded. It guarantees a graceful degradation of services instead of message loss, but it also detracts from the loose coupling of the system by forcing producers to block until consumers are ready (or messages expire). It is, of course, more desirable when enough storage capacity is available to accommodate the maximum amount of messages that the server will ever need to store.

A natural result of all of this is to use clustering to scale the storage capacity of the server. Each additional machine in the cluster brings additional disk space. In addition these disks can operate in parallel and potentially increase the performance of the server.

Storage Algorithm

Realizing these benefits is not easy though. It means that the cluster must use some algorithm to decide on which node each message should be stored. If redundancy is desired for high availability, then each message must be stored on multiple hardware nodes, but it may not be stored on all nodes, as this would eliminate any chance for scalability. This also introduces complexity in distribution because the cluster must match up each message with a corresponding consumer no matter which node the message is stored on and which node the consumer is connected to.

One possible scheme designates a home node for each destination and all messages produced for a destination are stored on the destination's home node before distribution. This detracts from performance because each message must be moved between as many as three different nodes of the cluster: the node that the producer is connected to, the node that is the destination's home, and the node that the consumer is connected to.

Improving the Algorithm

A possible improvement on this scheme is to always store a message on the node that the producer of the message is connected to. This eliminates one of the "hops" in the previous scheme, but introduces a new twist: the messages for one destination are not all stored on the same node. This could make it difficult to guarantee that the messages are distributed in the order that they arrive.

Fortunately, the JMS specification does not require a provider to guarantee anything about the relative ordering of messages from different producers, only that messages from one producer arrive in the order in which they were sent. This scheme does not, as described here, provide any redundancy for high availability. In general, scalability of storage capacity is a direct tradeoff against redundant storage; for a given number of hardware nodes, the more redundancy there is, the less the effective storage capacity.

As with throughput, cluster architectures that require all messages to be stored on all machines, as well as shared disk and shared database architectures, will not scale with respect to storage. It is important to note, though, that shared disk clusters may (and often do) use a RAID as the shared disk.

RAID subsystems provide the ability to scale storage independently of the server cluster by adding additional physical disks. Likewise, database servers often provide their own clustering implementations that can scale storage capacity over multiple machines without requiring the message server cluster to provide this. In these cases, the RAID controller or the database connections may ultimately limit the message throughput. A cleverly designed message server cluster has the potential to scale storage capacity without such bottlenecks, but realizing this potential is not an easy task.

Scalability of Storage Redundancy

Redundant message storage is necessary in order to provide high availability. It means that each message must be stored on at least two different hardware nodes of the cluster, so that if one of them fails, the message will not be lost. This is one of the most common reasons for employing clustering. Since I take the view that scalability is the ultimate measure of cluster effectiveness, I like to look at storage redundancy from this point of view also. Some may consider this to be stretching the scalability concept too far, but bear with me.

If we make the assumption that only one node of a cluster will fail at one time, then redundancy is a binary factor, you have it or you don't. If we loosen the assumption and look at the possibility of multiple nodes failing simultaneously, or additional nodes failing before the first failed node is replaced, then providing sufficient redundancy is more complex.

There are a number of reasons why multiple nodes could fail at one time. Natural disasters and long term regional power outages will almost certainly take all machines at a site out of service. (Battery powered uninterruptible power supplies (USP) provide protections from short term power outages, but their capacity is limited. True safety only comes with a local power generation plant.) A blown fuse or a broken USP could cause the failure of a subset of machines at one site. Multiple hardware nodes of a cluster should only draw power from the same circuit if the cluster can survive the simultaneous loss of all of these nodes.

A network failure can cause several nodes of the cluster to become unreachable at one time. This situation can be particularly difficult to deal with, since the nodes that are unreachable continue to operate and it appears to them as the rest of the cluster has failed. The implications of this will be discussed below under "Network Partitioning."

Availability of a System Administrator

Another case that is often overlooked in clustering is two or more unrelated node failures that overlap. By "overlap", I mean that the nodes do not necessarily need to fail at exactly the same time, but if one node fails, say due to disk failure, and is not replaced promptly, then another could fail, say due to an OS crash, before the first failed disk in the first node is replaced. We hope that our cluster nodes are reliable, so the likelihood of this happening is extremely small. But how small is it? An important factor here is the time required to replace hardware after it has failed. No matter how automated the system may be, this step requires human intervention.

For example, suppose a data center is unmanned on weekends. If a cluster node bursts into flames and burns up on Friday evening, a backup node should spring into action and take over. The backup has switched over to be primary, but if there were no additional backups for this node, then the new primary runs without a backup until Monday morning when a human is available to cleanup the burnt remains of the failed node and replace it with new hardware and configure it to be the new backup node.

For two days, then, the cluster runs with compromised reliability. It is unlikely that the new primary node fails during this time, but the actual risk should be assessed. If it is too high, then system responsible should consider manning the data center over weekends, or adopting a cluster architecture that supports multiple backup nodes per primary.

Time Required to Restore the Node

After a new hardware node is brought online to replace the failed one, all of the data that should be stored on it must be replaced. It is not enough to restore data from a backup tape, or to match the state of the node that it is replacing. This is because there may be a constant stream of new messages being published that need to be stored on the node that is being replaced.

When the original node failed, a backup node presumably took over its responsibilities, in other words, the backup node became the new primary and took on the job of storing and distributing those messages that the failed node would have been responsible for. The new primary node is now the one that contains the current set of messages. The new replacement node must copy all of the messages and associated state data from the new primary, while the new primary is also handling new incoming messages. If there are Gigabytes of messages stored on the node, this will take some time. Furthermore, the act of copying data from the new primary to the new backup will slow down the performance of the new primary.

If handling new messages has a higher priority than restoring the state of the new backup node, then the restore operation will take even longer. If you are using a shared disk architecture, then there is no data copying required when replacing a failed node. However, shared disk architectures should use a RAID, and after a failed RAID disk is replaced, the same factors come in to play: it takes a non-trivial amount of time to rebuild the contents of the replaced disk.

Additional Node Failure

The point here is there are some situations in which it could take hours to restore a cluster with a failed hardware node back to its full complement of nodes. What happens if another node fails during this period? Things could get ugly. Still we often expect cluster nodes to run for months at a time without a problem, so the chance of two nodes failing within a time interval of several hours is still small. It is important, though, to estimate the actually likelihood of this occurrence and decide if it is acceptable or not. If it is not acceptable, then you need to stop thinking about storage redundancy as a binary "all or nothing" factor, and start thinking about it in terms of scalability.

> **Having a cluster that can keep operating after a node fails is not the end of the story. Any complete high availability scheme requires monitoring, a recovery plan and spare hardware. This is especially true in the case that the cluster can survive one node failure, but not two. This means that after a node has failed, the cluster will have lower availability than a monolithic server, not higher.**

Consider the following unlikely, but enlightening, example: you have a cluster of 365 hardware nodes and hardware failures occur, on average, once per year per node. A little math will show that you can expect a failure once per day on average (including weekends). If your cluster can tolerate exactly one node failure, then you are OK for the first day, but if you do not replace the node right away, a complete cluster failure is only one more day away.

Compare this to the single node case, where you will have no problems for roughly a year (statistically speaking). In fact, with the cluster described above, you will never be able to just sit back and enjoy the reliability of your cluster; you should count on replacing nodes every day. And you had better have plenty of extra hardware in stock.

Scalability Criteria

To come up with a scalability criterion, we actually have to look at how the probability of irreplaceably losing data changes as more nodes are added to the cluster. This probability asymptotically approaches zero as the number of redundant copies of data increases. So in order to be consistent with the other measures of scalability and have a value of 1 corresponding to linear scalability, I would have to come up with some complex function based on the probability of losing data. I could present such a formula, but it would probably not be particularly enlightening for most people, so instead I will present examples of clustering schemes that illustrate the extremes of the scalability range.

The first example is the trivial case of a cluster that provides no redundant message storage. This clearly corresponds to a scalability value of 0, since adding additional nodes to the cluster yields no increase in safety. This would be true of a cluster that is only intended to increase performance through load balancing or to provide message routing. In practice, reliability is one of the primary reasons for clustering, so this type of cluster is not so common.

Primary Backup Configuration

The most basic form of redundant storage in a cluster is a simple primary/backup scheme, where each node that is actively providing services (a primary node) has one corresponding backup node that should be a perfect replica of the primary at all times, at least in terms of the data that it stores. The backup must be able to detect the failure of the primary and take over in its place immediately.

Synchronization of the primary and backup may occur in several ways: they may share a common disk (which introduces a single point of failure; more on this later), the backup may perform all functions identically to the primary and just not produce output, or the primary may send messages directly to the backup that synchronize its data store. Although it is theoretically possible to have more than one backup for each primary, this is not common in practice.

The reasons for this vary from simple cost effectiveness (the extra safety of multiple backups does not justify the extra hardware expense) to practical limitations such as limitations on how many nodes can be connected to a single disk, network bandwidth limitations, or the complexity involved in ensuring that exactly one of the backups takes over after a primary failure.

A cluster that allows only one backup per primary node will show near linear scalability of redundancy when increasing the cluster from 0 backups per primary to 1 backup per primary, as this represents a near ideal increase in reliability. The addition of a second or third backup will yield a further scalability of zero since, in this example, we are assuming the cluster is incapable of utilizing these extra nodes as live backups.

The other extreme is the case of full replication (described below), where every node in the cluster stores every single message. This would correspond to consistent near linear scalability with increasing number of nodes. This type of cluster provides the best possible safety, because even if only one node of the cluster survives, no messages are lost. This comes at the price of poor scalability for throughput and storage capacity.

Network Partitioning

Earlier I mentioned that network failures within the cluster present special problems. A failed or malfunctioning network component (or sometimes even a broken network cable) can cause the cluster to be split into two parts, where each part is still functional. This is referred to **network partitioning**. The most fundamental part of the problem is that it is often impossible for the cluster nodes to detect the difference between network partitioning and the failure of a group of nodes.

When partitioning occurs, it appears to each partition that the nodes in the other partition have failed and each partition tries to keep operating. Each partition will have a different set of clients, and will see different messages. When the network partition is repaired, the nodes in the different partitions will have inconsistent states that are difficult or impossible to reconcile. Assuming that the cluster can detect that a partition has occurred (again this by itself is not trivial) the most basic solution is to force all but one of the partitions to shut down. It is difficult to automate this, since the partitions cannot communicate with each other to come to an agreement.

The most logical action is to kill off all partitions that do not contain a majority of nodes, but the cluster may be split evenly, or it may be split three ways and there is no majority. The common solution for this is to designate one node as the "tiebreaker" when the cluster is started. In the case of partitioning, all partitions that do not contain the tiebreaker shut down.

This is all very complicated and any workable solution depends very much on the characteristics of the particular cluster and exactly how the nodes get partitioned. I will present a trivial example with two message server nodes in primary-backup configuration to demonstrate why this is such a difficult topic for cluster designers. The diagram shows the various stages of failure and recovery:

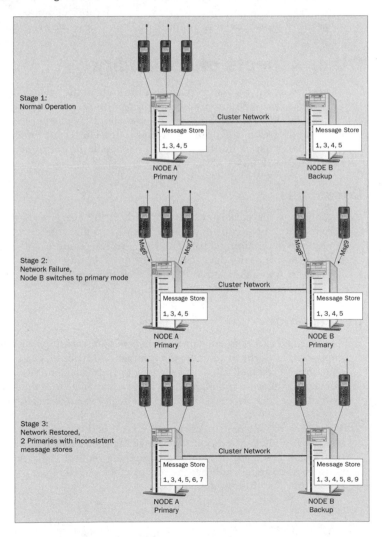

Stage 1 shows normal operation where all clients connect to node A, the primary, to produce and consume messages.

In Stage 2, the network connection between the machines is broken and node B, the backup, switches to primary mode and accepts client connections. Node A is also still primary and has its own clients. Each node handles different messages from this point onward.

In Stage 3, the network connection is restored. Now the two primary nodes can "see" each other, and each contains different messages. If one just shuts down, then messages will be lost. The only way to properly recover from this is to devise a process for the two nodes to reconcile their message stores, transfer all clients to one node and revert the other node to backup mode. The nodes must also ensure that all topic subscribers received all messages that they might have missed while the network connection was down.

It is not possible to rule out out-of-order message delivery. It suffices to say, that if the cluster contains more than two nodes, reconciliation is much more complex. If you need your JMS cluster to be resilient to network partitions, it is important to know how your JMS provider behaves in this scenario.

Other Aspects of Scalability

There are many factors that can lead to limits in the scalability of a cluster. As a rule, a cluster that is designed to provide unlimited scalability with respect to some capacity will still saturate at some point with scalability approaching zero. As scalability is pushed to extremes, even such trivial things as a list of the addresses of the other machines in the cluster become impossible to maintain. Examples of some of the places where bottlenecks can arise are at the consumer, as a result of concurrency, and because of lack of network bandwidth.

Consumers

If a message-server cluster tries to avoid storing every message on every node, then it needs to have a way to match up a consumer on one node to a message stored on another node. Often this will lead to each node maintaining a list of all the consumers interested in messages stored in the topics on that node. The size of the data structure for one consumer may be small, but if there are to be thousands of consumers for each destination then even this can cause the cluster to saturate due to the fact that the nodes run out of room to store consumer info.

Concurrency

As described earlier in the context of connection scalability, each thread consumes a certain amount of memory. This leads to a limit to the number of threads that can exist in a process. There are other ways that concurrency can be limited, though. The operating system may place a limit on the number of threads that can actually execute simultaneously. Software architectures that require excessive thread synchronization can exhibit poor concurrency even though enough resources might otherwise be available.

The effect of poor concurrency on a cluster is that one overloaded node in the cluster can cause other, less heavily loaded nodes to slow down. This happens because the nodes must interact, and if that interaction it accomplished using a blocking request/reply protocol, then a node initiating a request to another node relies on other threads to make effective use of CPU while one thread is waiting for a reply from the other node.

The same node that is waiting for a reply is relying on a sufficient amount of concurrency in the other node to allow it to service the request in a timely manner. Insufficient concurrency on the target node will mean that the reply is delayed because some other action on the target node, which has nothing to do with the reply, has to complete before the request can be serviced. Poor concurrency is characterized by low CPU usage on the nodes that are actively processing messages, despite poorer than expected overall performance.

Network Bandwidth

As we will see below, many cluster architectures rely exclusively on a LAN for inter-node communication. LANs have significantly less bandwidth than the various data conduits within an individual computer. For this reason, the network can easily become a performance bottleneck. Much can be achieved by using high-speed networks and active network components (switches, routers) to interconnect the node cluster. Cluster architectures that permit nodes to communicate over multiple independent networks have an advantage here.

Cluster Architecture

By the architecture of a cluster, I mean the node topology and the techniques employed for achieving scalability. Even for the end user of a clustered JMS messaging system, it is beneficial to understand the architecture used within the cluster, as this will have a big impact on the cluster's capabilities. Some architectures are inherently good at providing certain aspects of scalability, and inherently poor at others, regardless of the actual implementation details.

There is no limit to the number of different possible cluster architectures, but the variety presented in this chapter should be a good representation of the ones most commonly used in practice. In addition, I will discuss a number of clustering issues that must be considered in any architecture. At this point in the chapter, it is important to make the distinction between the two main types of cluster architecture: **shared storage** (**shared disk** or **shared database**) and **private storage** (often referred to by the term **shared nothing**) in which each hardware node maintains its own storage.

Shared storage eliminates many complications involved in cluster design, but creates others. The complications introduced by shared storage are relatively generic and not specific to the requirements of JMS. For this reason, shared storage will be discussed in its own section, and all other sections of this chapter will assume the private storage case unless explicitly stated otherwise.

The Pub/Sub and PTP messaging domains represent, in many ways, two completely different types of messaging. This distinction is particularly true with clustering, as certain architectures provide much better scalability for one domain than the other. For this reason I will begin by pointing out the issues particular to each domain, and then move on to discuss particular aspects of cluster architectures.

Clustering in the Publish/Subscribe Domain

In the Pub/Sub domain, a copy of every message in a topic is sent to every subscriber that is interested in that topic. This allows more possibilities for parallel processing than in the PTP domain, where the cluster must guarantee that a message is not delivered to more than one receiver. With Pub/Sub, every message can be replicated to each cluster node. Each node can forward the message to each subscriber that it knows about with no need to be concerned about the subscribers on other nodes. If a node has no subscribers, it may just discard the message. Since the basic clustering scenario for Pub/Sub is simple, some vendors only provide clustering in this domain.

In reality, of course, clustering in this domain is not quite as simple as this description would lead you to believe. There are a number of factors that add complications, namely durable subscribers, transactions, and failure recovery. Durable subscribers themselves are described in more detail in Chapter 2.

Durable Subscribers

In order to support durable subscribers, messages must be stored somewhere in the cluster. There are two basic approaches to this: **full replication**, in which every message is stored on every node, or **topic home**, in which one node is designated as the "home" for a particular topic and all messages for that topic are stored there. The latter option could be extended to include one or more backup nodes that could store messages in addition to the topic home, and provide redundant storage in case the topic home fails. I will ignore this case for the moment to keep the discussion simple.

Full Replication

Full replication requires the least coordination among the cluster nodes. Each message is replicated to every node and the nodes can otherwise operate quite independently. Not only does this simplify the architecture, it provides superb redundancy. Since every node stores every message, any number of nodes may fail at once without losing messages – as long as at least one survives. The diagram below shows the topology of full replication supporting durable subscribers:

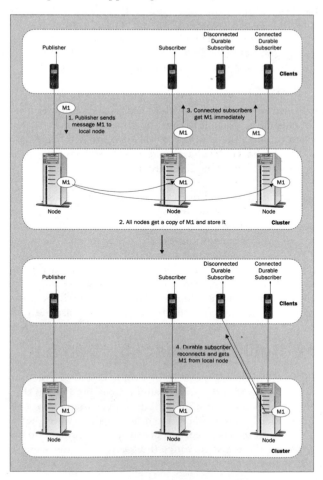

The price for this superb redundancy is poor storage scalability: adding nodes to the cluster will not increase the total storage capacity of the cluster. Moreover, if one node has less storage capacity than the others (it has less hard disk capacity or shares this capacity with other applications), then the entire storage capacity of the cluster is limited to the capacity of that one node.

There are other complications in the case of full replication. I mentioned above that the nodes could operate independently once the messages are copied. This is largely true if all nodes will unconditionally store every message until it expires. To gain more efficiency though, a server will often not store messages in which no durable subscriber is interested. Additionally, the server will usually try to delete messages that have been consumed by all known durable subscribers.

This is not a problem if a durable subscriber will always reconnect to the same node, but this can seldom be guaranteed. Since the durable subscriber may reconnect to any node, this node must have all of the messages in which the durable subscriber is interested. This requires that the nodes share information about durable subscribers: subscription, message selector, subscription termination, and message acknowledgment. Propagating each message acknowledgement to every node could lead to a lot of communication traffic.

Since it is actually not essential to delete each message immediately after the last durable subscriber has acknowledged it, it would be sufficient to send periodic summaries of the acknowledgments, or employ some other protocol between the nodes that enables them to agree on which messages may be removed from storage. A problem arises here when a durable subscriber disconnects and immediately reconnects to another node. That node may not be aware of the most recent message acknowledgments that that subscriber has made, and try to deliver the most recent messages again. Thus, extra logic would be required to handle reconnections properly.

Another shortcoming of full replication, which can offset the benefit of the independence of the nodes, is that it can require substantial network bandwidth. This is a major factor in any architecture, but in full replication, it will become a performance bottleneck quite quickly. If unicast communication is used to interconnect the nodes (as is often the case), then a cluster of n nodes must copy each message n-1 times over the network. This can be reduced to copying each message only once if multicast communication is employed within the cluster.

> *Progress SonicMQ and FioranoMQ are examples of JMS providers that use full replication to provide clustering in the Pub/Sub domain.*

Topic Home

The topic home approach allows scalability of storage space by distributing the responsibility for storing messages in different topics over different nodes. More advanced schemes could potentially distribute message storage for one topic over multiple nodes, but I will not discuss these here in the interest of keeping things simple.

There are two basic variations of the topic home, which are shown as "version 1" and "version 2" in the diagrams overleaf. In version 1, all messages are distributed to all nodes, and the node that is the topic home stores the message, in addition to distributing it to any connected subscribers. In version 2, all messages are sent directly to the topic home, and then the topic home distributes them to those nodes that have subscribers:

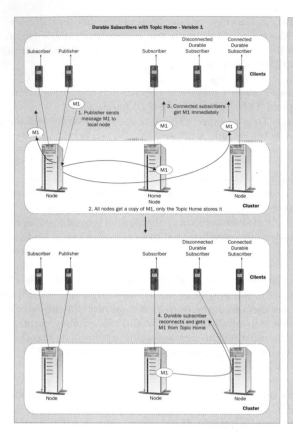 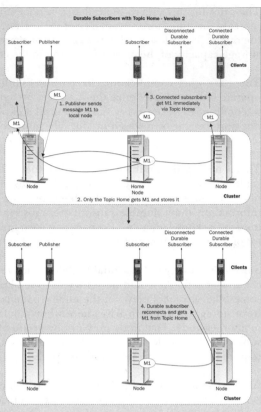

Using unicast communication between the nodes can potentially save network bandwidth. When using multicast, bandwidth would actually need to increase as every message must be sent twice over the network instead of once. When a durable subscriber reconnects to a node, that node must contact the topic home and retrieve all messages that were stored while that durable subscriber was offline. This gives rise to a large potential increase in bandwidth usage compared to full replication – if multiple durable subscribers with interest in the same messages reconnect to the same node at different times, then the same messages must be transferred to that node from the topic home several times.

Topic home solves another potential problem with durable subscribers. Since they can reconnect at any time, and they can potentially reconnect to any node, every node must offer the same "view" of the topic state at the same time. Although one would expect durables to disconnect for longer periods of time, there is nothing to stop them from disconnecting and reconnecting immediately to another node. In the case of the topic home, everything is coordinated from a central point, and the reconnecting subscriber will receive all messages, as it should. As mentioned above, this guarantee is more difficult to achieve with full replication.

*In the PTP domain the corresponding concept is called **queue home**. Later in this chapter I will use the term **destination home** to generically refer to both of these.*

Transactions

The general implications of clustering on **transacted** messages will be presented in a separate section below. Here I will briefly comment on some of the implications relevant to the immediate discussion. Transactions give rise to another situation, besides durable subscribers, in which published messages must be stored. This is because a transacted message cannot be distributed until it is committed, and the commit could occur some time after the message is published.

The simplest variant is to temporarily store the message on the node to which the publisher is connected. When the transaction is committed, processing continues largely as described in the last section. If the producer reconnects to another node before committing, then the transaction must be aborted. If the transaction is large, then a correspondingly large amount of network traffic is generated immediately upon commit.

More refined schemes will try to move the uncommitted messages to other nodes as soon as they are published. If a topic home is used, then version 2 in the diagram above is the natural choice, as the message can be forwarded to the topic home and the topic home can take care that it is not distributed further until committed. In the other schemes, where all messages are sent directly to all other nodes for immediate distribution to currently connected subscribers, extra logic is required to guarantee that the transacted messages are stored and not distributed until the commit comes. This fully distributed case make the atomic properties of the transaction more difficult to guarantee.

Failure Recovery

Failure recovery scenarios tend to complicate operations that are quite simple under normal circumstances. We already looked at the case of a durable subscriber reconnecting above. If the cluster provides support for clients reconnecting after losing their connection to the server, possibly due to failed node, then the complications that arose for durables could apply to normal subscribers as well. In this case it may not even be possible for the cluster to recover the state of the subscriber without the subscriber's help, as the failed node may not have had a chance to report the most recent acknowledgements to the rest of the cluster. This implies that all subscribers need to be treated like durable subscribers, since they can briefly disconnect and reconnect at any time.

Another point to keep in mind is that after a node fails it must sooner or later be replaced. The replacement node must get copies of all messages to store from other nodes before it can be integrated into the cluster. In the case of full replication, this includes all messages for all durable subscribers, which could amount to a huge volume of data. In the case of topic homes, the volume of data for a single node should be much smaller, but recovery is only possible if there was a second node acting as a backup for the node that failed. Remember we did not discuss the implications of this in detail.

Despite all the different tradeoffs involved in the selection of a Pub/Sub clustering architecture, full replication is a clear favorite, since it solves both connection load balancing and high availability with one elegant concept. It does very little for other aspects of scalability, but in practice the two aspects that it does address are the most common reasons for employing clustering. As we shall see next, there is no corresponding single favorite in the PTP domain.

Clustering in the Point-to-Point Domain

If the PTP domain were truly PTP for a queue as a whole, then it would behave like Pub/Sub with only one subscriber permitted for each topic. This would make clustering actually simpler than in the Pub/Sub domain. In reality, JMS allows a PTP queue to have any number of receivers. The PTP aspect applies to individual messages and not to destinations. This makes message distribution more complex in a clustered sever.

Since the same message may never be delivered to multiple receivers, the decision as to which receiver should be able to consume a particular message must be coordinated throughout the cluster. PTP messages must be stored if they cannot be consumed right away. In many ways a queue resembles a topic that has exactly one durable subscriber: a message must be stored until it is consumed once, and then it is safe to delete it immediately. If it were not for the fact that multiple receivers can be connected simultaneously, a queue could actually be modeled as a special case of a topic.

Distribution and Storage

The simplest way to coordinate the distribution of messages is to centralize all distribution logic on one node. This gives rise to the notion of a queue home node for distribution. In other words, for each queue there is one node that has the responsibility for comparing the queue's messages to the list of known receivers and their message selectors, and determining which message should be delivered to which receiver. Since PTP messages must be stored, this concept can be combined with the notion of a queue home for storage, similar to the topic home concept discussed for the Pub/Sub domain.

In theory, each node could contain logic for distributing messages and then employ some form of protocol for reaching consensus with the other nodes before actually sending a message to a receiver. This would add quite a bit of complexity to the cluster. In addition to requiring some form of voting algorithm to determine which node is permitted to distribute a message, the cluster also needs to be able to determine whether message delivery was successful. This is important in the case that the selected node fails, because if it failed before delivery was complete then the voting process must be reinitiated. On the other hand, this scheme could also provide more overall robustness in the case of node failure.

Many voting algorithms require only a majority of nodes to agree on a decision. This means that if a minority of nodes are not reachable, processing can continue without the need to first determine if the nodes have failed and without having to wait for any fail-over processes to complete. The effectiveness of this must be compared to the complexity involved in making the queue home concept provide high availability with a queue home backup.

Full Replication

Even though the PTP domain tends to be better served by centralized distribution logic, the storage need not necessarily be centralized. For example, a full replication scheme, as described above for topics, could be employed. This would provide full redundancy and enhance high availability. It would also ensure that a particular message is readily available on the node on which it will be consumed, even though the decision as to which receiver should consume it is made elsewhere.

A full replication scheme for queues could be quite inefficient, since it requires all messages to be sent to all nodes, even though it is known in advance that it will only be consumed on one of them. The degree to which this is inefficient depends on the cost of distributing a message to multiple nodes, which is high when unicast networking is used, and low when multicast is used.

Queue Homes

The concept of a queue home for storage is more palatable here than it is with topics. Since the logic of queue homes for distribution will probably be incorporated anyway, the additional effort in implementing queue homes for storage, along with backup nodes for high availability, is less in this case. The advantage to be gained by doing this is an additional dimension of scalability, namely scalability of storage capacity as described in the section on scalability above.

Message Routing

An alternative to the concept of queue homes is to employ a message routing scheme. In this scheme, each node keeps a list of which other nodes have receivers for a certain queue. As each message is published, the node to which the publisher is connected routes the message directly to one of the nodes that has receivers for that message. This scheme can allow more parallelism between the nodes and reduce inter-node communication compared to other architectures.

This comes at a price of course. A message routing cluster does not provide the outward appearance of a single monolithic server, but appears more like a loosely associated group of cooperating, but separate message servers. This has implications in terms of fairness and the order of message delivery. For Point-to-Point messaging, the fairness issue means that receivers subscribed to same queue, but connected to different nodes cannot expect to receive messages at the same rate (see "Starvation" below). For Pub/Sub messaging it means that subscribers connected to different nodes cannot all expect to receive a given message at the same time. For both types of messaging, it is difficult to guarantee in-order message delivery across the whole cluster.

Each node in a message routing cluster only stores messages that are destined for consumption on that node, so it can make these local distribution decisions autonomously and in parallel with the other nodes.

Starvation

Message routing is desirable for nodes that are geographically distributed and require more independence from each other due to the relatively high cost and latency of inter-node communication. This can, however, easily lead to receiver **starvation**, where some nodes have a long queue of messages waiting to be delivered to local receivers, while another node has no messages even though it has idle receivers that could consume them. This could happen if one node has very slow receivers, or if a new receiver connects (or an existing receiver reconnects) to a node that previously had no receivers for that particular queue.

Delivery Order

A problem related to starvation is delivery order. Although one of the tenets of JMS is guaranteed in-order delivery, it is impossible to guarantee absolute ordering of messages across multiple receivers unless a message is not delivered until the previous message is acknowledged. This would have dramatic performance implications, and would prevent multiple receivers from processing messages in parallel.

The actual guarantee made by JMS is that all messages consumed by one receiver that originate from the same publisher will be consumed in the order in which the publisher sent them. Despite this, the concept of a message queue is global first in, first out ordering. JMS providers are expected to maintain a global ordering reasonably well across multiple receivers.

Unreasonably Late Delivery

The same conditions that lead to starvation could lead to unreasonably late delivery. This is best illustrated with an example: A publisher sends two messages, A and B, in that order to the same queue. A gets routed to a node that has a large number of undelivered messages for that queue and a very slow receiver. B gets routed to a node that has no undelivered messages for that queue, and is consumed immediately. The messages A and B get consumed out of order. It might be tolerable for them to be out of order by a few seconds, but in an extreme case, message A may be delayed by minutes or hours. Some applications that depend on the "in order" delivery of messages would have trouble functioning correctly in this case.

This problem can be even more acute in the case that the receiver on the node where message A is stored closes before A is consumed. In order to avoid having the message sit indefinately on that node, the only reasonable action is to reroute the message to a node that still has receivers. Consider what happens if the only other receiver in the cluster is the one that already consumed message B. Now it is impossible to deliver the message without violating the strong in-order requirements imposed by JMS. Message routing increases the risk of out of order delivery during normal operation.

> *In all fairness to message routing, I should mention that there are other scenarios in which messages can be delivered out of order even when message routing is not used. These are usually failure scenarios that should occur infrequently.*

The use of a flow control scheme within the cluster could significantly reduce the likelihood of receiver starvation and out of order delivery. This would involve storing each sent message at the node of the publisher until one or more nodes that have potential receivers of that message indicate that they are likely to be able to distribute messages to those receivers with little or no delay. This indication could take the form of flow start and flow stop messages that are sent to all other nodes in the cluster depending on how many undelivered messages that node has for a particular queue.

As with the queue home concept, message routing does not address redundancy and high availability. Thus backup nodes and fail-over logic must be implemented separately.

Failure Recovery

As with the Pub/Sub domain, there are some failure scenarios that cause particular difficulty in the PTP domain. One of these is the case of a node failing and its receivers reconnecting to another node. In the case of full replication and queue home schemes described above, this presents very little difficulty. Since message distribution must either be centralized or well coordinated throughout the cluster, there is very little danger of the new node presenting a different view of the state of the message queue. Not so with message routing; this scheme falls short here too. In this case the receiver finds a completely different set of messages on the new node, some of which may be older than other messages that it already consumed.

Another failure scenario that causes problems for PTP messaging is the case of a receiver failing before it has acknowledged all of the messages that it has received. This case is not specific to clustering, but it is worth mentioning in the context of the current discussion. From the point of view of the JMS provider, if a message has not been acknowledged, it has not been consumed. Any messages that were distributed to the now dead receiver, which this receiver did not acknowledge before failing, must be deliver to another receiver. Remember that JMS guarantees exactly once delivery for persistent messages. By the time that the server detects the failure of the first receiver, all other receivers for the same queue may have already consumed later messages from the same sender. In this case it is not possible to deliver the messages without violating the strict JMS requirements for in-order delivery.

Balancing Load

When using a cluster to increase server capacity, whether for connections, throughput or storage, there must be some mechanism in place to ensure that these resources are fairly utilized across all the nodes of the cluster. This is the balancing aspect that should be inherent in load balancing. If the capacity of the whole cluster is reduced just because one machine is overloaded, then the cluster is not scalable.

When people talk about load balancing in the context of a clustered JMS message server, they are mostly referring to connection load balancing. As mentioned previously, the connection limit of a Java VM is often the first scalability limit encountered in a messaging system. Given that the cluster has no way to know how much message volume each connection will generate in the future, balancing connections among the nodes is often the best means available for balancing overall load. (More advanced schemes for getting around this will be discussed below.)

In the case where a cluster stores messages on the node to which the publisher is connected (instead of having central storage for each destination), connection balancing will effectively determine the balancing of message storage across the nodes. For clusters, the aim of achieving scalable storage capacity, and of balancing the storage across nodes is a highly relevant issue.

Firstly, we'll define some of the terminology needed to discuss load balancing, and the then move on to discuss some common techniques for implementing it.

Note that I prefer the use of the term "fair" to "even", as an evenly balanced load may not be desired, especially when machines with different capabilities are mixed in the same cluster.

Load Monitoring

This is a very important concept in conjunction with any load-balancing scheme. The most effective decisions about distributing load (connections, storage) can be made only if the current load for all nodes is known. The first step here, of course, is to define "load" appropriately. This may be simplistic in that it measures just the number of connections per node, or it may be a complex function that takes many factors into account, such as CPU utilization, memory usage, and I/O volume.

All of the individual system parameters that contribute to this load calculation must be monitored by each node and periodically sent to the entities (other nodes, connection brokers) that are responsible for distributing load fairly. The definition of fair may also be non-trivial if the nodes in the cluster do not have identical hardware capacities. In this case it may be necessary for each node to distribute information about its basic capabilities in addition to load parameters.

Remember though, pure Java programs have difficulty obtaining basic system information like free memory and free disk space. Java-based cluster nodes must interact with native code (either via JNI or a separate process) to get access to all possible system parameters. Static parameters such as total available memory or disk space can be passed to the node as configuration parameters.

Static Load Balancing

This means a critical decision about how to balance load is made once and then never changed. Specifically, the decision of which node a client should connect to is made at the time of connection, and then the client cannot change nodes later, even if the load across the nodes becomes unbalanced. For message storage, this might mean that the home node for a destination is determined when the destination is created, and cannot be changed later.

Static load balancing schemes that distribute load automatically must make simplistic assumptions about load distributions. These assumptions are that all connections generate the same message volume, and that all destinations will handle the same message volume and require the same amount of storage. The cluster cannot automatically predict how connections and destinations will be used at the time that they are created.

The only way around this is to force the system administrator to pre-configure the anticipated load generated by each client and handled by each destination, or worse yet, that the system administrator be required to pre-configure the location of each destination (in the case of destination homes) and pre-configure the node to which each client should connect.

Dynamic Load Balancing

This means the load can be rebalanced at any time. This makes most sense when done in conjunction with load monitoring. If the load becomes unbalanced then it will be corrected, for example by transferring connections to other nodes, or moving destination storage. When this is implemented properly, it provides the most effective load balancing with the least amount of administrative work. There is no need to pre-configure anticipated loads in order to get optimum balancing. However, redistributing connections and storage incurs a lot of overhead, so there is still benefit to getting the load distribution done right on the first try.

Balancing Connections

As mentioned above, load balancing is usually a mater of balancing client connections among the cluster nodes. Any scheme that attempts to balance load independently of connections will almost certainly require clients to connect to multiple servers. This is not practical, as connections are often one of the scarcest resources.

The simplest connection-balancing scheme is to statically connect each new client to another node in round-robin fashion. This assumes that, on average, there will end up being roughly the same number of connections per node, and the same throughput per connection. This can be achieved externally to the cluster by employing a load balancing Domain Name Server (DNS), which translates each new request for the same host name into a different IP address, where each IP address is that of a different cluster node.

Although new connections are spread evenly throughout the cluster, if many connections are closed, and these closed connections are primarily from only a few nodes, the cluster can get unbalanced (unless the DNS is tied into a load monitoring scheme).

IP Redirection

The next step up in sophistication is the use of IP redirection. In this case, a redirector is situated between clients and the cluster, and all connections must go through that redirector. The redirector can be a dedicated computer or a specialized hardware device. It assigns each connection to a different node. It then routes the low-level network packets for each connection to the correct node. Thus it is transparent to both server and client and minimizes the effort required to cluster-enable a server.

These devices tend to be quite sophisticated in that they can direct SSL encrypted connections and they can be configured to ensure that subsequent connections from the same client are always directed to the same node. Hardware redirectors are available from Cisco and F5, among others. Red Hat offers a software solution based on a specially configured Linux kernel.

More sophisticated redirectors can even monitor the load of the individual nodes to perform more effective balancing. This approach has some disadvantages. Since all connections must pass through the redirector, then the questions of scalability and reliability extend to the redirector too. This means that the redirector must also be scalable and highly available if it is not to become the bottleneck of the whole system. It is also difficult to implement dynamic load balancing with redirectors, as a JMS connection is stateful, and a reconnection cannot occur without additional action on the part of the server and client. If the cluster is fault tolerant, then the redirector could be permitted to abruptly break connections to an overloaded node and rely on the client to automatically reconnect.

In general, redirectors are best suited to clustering web servers, where the client and server themselves do not contain any explicit support for clustering, but the connections are stateless and short lived. The diagram below depicts the topology of a system employing connection balancing with packet redirection:

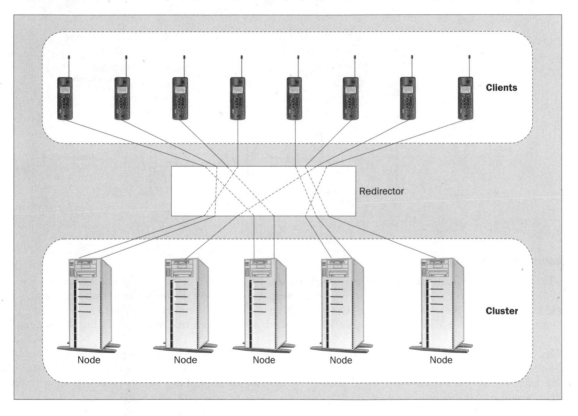

Connection Brokers

As the level of sophistication increases, the amount of cluster support built into the JMS client increases. An example of this is the connection broker. In this scheme, one node of the cluster is designated as the connection broker. All new connections are first directed to this broker. The broker then instructs the client as to which other node it should ultimately connect to.

The broker may assign nodes in a round-robin fashion, or it may use load monitoring to make intelligent assignments. It is inherently static, since the client has no more contact with the broker after the initial connection is made. In contrast to the redirector, the broker cannot introduce a performance bottleneck, and it does not introduce a single point of failure for existing connections.

If the broker fails, then new connections cannot be made, so it is still worthwhile to have a fail-over scheme for the broker when high availability is important. The diagram below shows the topology of a system employing connection balancing with a connection broker:

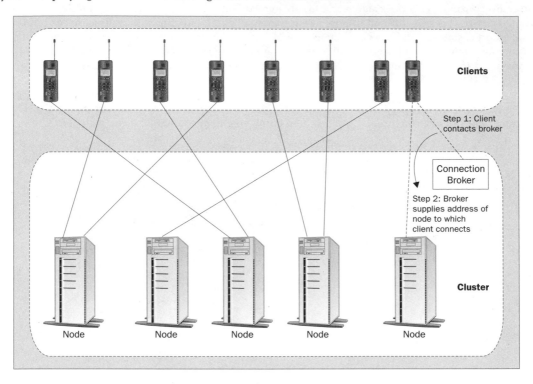

Dynamic Load Balancing

The connection balancing schemes discussed so far are all static. They do not attempt to rebalance connections if some nodes become overloaded compared to others. Dynamic load balancing can ultimately ensure fairer load sharing. Even though an intelligent connection broker can add new connections in such a way that the cluster is balanced, it has no control over the closing of connections.

It could be that all the clients connected to one node close their connections, and that node is suddenly underutilized compared to the others. Dynamic load balancing implies that the cluster has the ability to transfer connections from overloaded nodes to underutilized ones. This can be done with or without the cooperation of the client.

In the case that the client server connection is fault tolerant, a node can abruptly close a connection and rely on the client to reconnect to another node. It is of course more efficient to explicitly instruct the client to reconnect. It could be that the client is in the process of sending a large message or has open transactions. It would be better for it to be able to complete these before reconnecting.

Dynamic connection balancing can benefit from increased monitoring. In addition to knowing the number of connections open on each node, CPU and memory usage, and the average data throughput of each connection monitoring can be used to determine when it would be beneficial to rebalance connections. The act of transferring a connection itself consumes resources, so it is also important not to rebalance excessively.

Balancing Storage

Balancing message storage across nodes can be done independently of connection balancing in some cases. In a full replication scheme, balancing is irrelevant since every message must be stored on every node. If messages are stored on the node to which the publisher is connected, then storage cannot be balanced independently of connections. Of the storage strategies previously described, the destination home (queue home or topic home) schemes are the most relevant to storage load balancing.

The idea of a destination home is that each destination is assigned to one particular node. The assignment of a destination to a node could be done according to hashing algorithm, it could be based on the storage available to the nodes when the destination is created, or it could be pre-configured by an administrator. The last option could create a lot of administrative overhead if there are many destinations, but it allows an important degree of flexibility since the administrator may know in advance that some destinations will require more storage space than others and distribute node assignment accordingly.

Storage balancing could, in theory, be done dynamically. This would require the ability to move the home of a destination from one hardware node to another. This could be done according to load monitoring or as an explicit administrative action. In any case, transferring the storage of a destination involves copying all the stored data across the network. This could lead to so much additional system load that it becomes counterproductive. If a cluster does implement dynamic storage rebalancing, I would not expect it to be invoked very often.

Interconnecting the Cluster

Another critical aspect of the internal architecture of a cluster is the means used to interconnect the nodes. Most of this chapter has implicitly assumed the case of a shared nothing cluster and unicast networking. Shared storage simplifies cluster design considerably, almost to the point that there are no architectural issues to discuss. I argue below, though that shared storage is not very appropriate for message servers, and thus have not given it much treatment so far.

Unicast networking is mature, ubiquitous, and free (or more accurately, bundled with every operating system). As such it is a common first choice for all networking chores. Multicast networking has more limited deployment possibilities (much of the public Internet does not route multicast traffic), but I maintain below that it can provide big advantages when used in cluster architecture.

Shared Storage

In shared storage architecture, all nodes use a common persistent storage medium. Each node can read and write to the shared storage, and thus it provides not only a means for the node to persistently store data but also to share data. The most common realizations of this are shared disk and shared database architectures. Most of the issues and implications of shared storage are the same regardless of whether the sharing is done at the level of the disk controller or the database server, so we'll present the shared disk case for the general discussion and mention some of the differences of the database case afterward.

In shared disk architecture, multiple nodes all use the same disk for persistent storage. This is made possible through special hardware, such as a multi-ported SCSI bus. The hardware solution must include, or be combined with software that provides, disk locking that prevents different machines from writing to the same disk areas at the same time. Beyond this, the interface to the shared disk is pretty much the same as that to an ordinary disk:

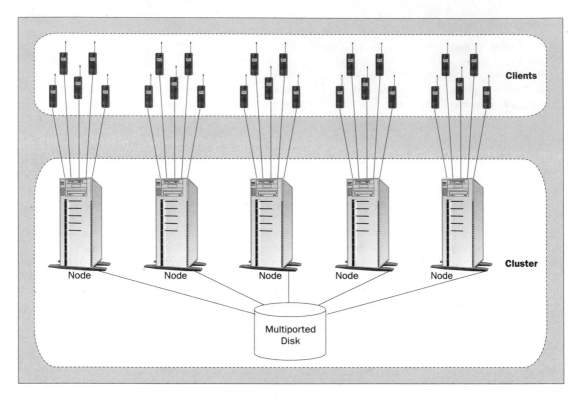

In the simplest case, one node acts as a primary and is the only one that may write to the disk. If that node fails then another one takes over control of the disk and continues providing services. In this way any server that writes to a disk in a transactional manner could be adapted for high availability, even if it was not originally deigned to provide such.

Many OS-level clustering products use this means to cluster enable arbitrary servers. In this case the OS provides the extra functionality required to detect the failed node and activate the backup. An ordinary disk may be used to implement a special case of this in which the disk is manually disconnected from a failed machine and connected to a cold standby machine.

Problems with Shared Disk

The first problem with a shared disk scheme is that disks are the component of a computer system most prone to failure, and they are inherently slow. This means that a shared disk architecture makes the most sense when the disk is a RAID array. There are many types of RAID configuration, but the most suitable ones for use in this situation provides both high availability (one disk can fail without loosing data) and increased speed by accessing disks in parallel. In this sense, the RAID itself is a cluster for disk services.

> *The majority of RAID levels fit this description. RAID 5 seems to be the most commonly used. See* http://www.acnc.com/04_00.html *for a good overview of the various RAID levels.*

Despite the capabilities offered by using RAID, a shared disk always implies a single point of failure – the RAID controller and the multi-ported SCSI bus. It also presents a limit to scalability for a message server, since all messages, even non-persistent ones, must be written to disk before they can be distributed.

Disks are generally faster than data networks (SCSI bus transfer rates are up to 160Mb per second), so a shared disk may be faster for small clusters. However, mutually exclusive disk access and the seek time associated with physically moving disk heads to different parts of the disk will become prohibitive for larger clusters. The use of high speed networking (fiber optic, ATM, Gigabit Ethernet), switched networks, or multicast can ultimately provide more scalability.

In my opinion, shared disks make less sense for message servers than for other types of server. They are appropriate for a database, where the primary purpose of the server is to provide persistent storage and not data transmission. This is most true for data warehousing and data mining applications where the processing power of the hardware node is usually a bigger limitation than the speed of disk access.

Shared Database

The situation is largely the same when all the nodes of a cluster use a common database server for common storage. A database server offers some advantages, though. This is largely a result of the fact that databases servers are designed and optimized for concurrent use by many clients. Database servers can maintain a cache, which will result in far fewer actual disk accesses when multiple nodes access the same data within a short timeframe.

In order to avoid having the database server itself become a single point of failure, the database itself must be implemented as some form of cluster. The usage of a shared database actually translates into an exercise of offloading most of the work of a cluster implementation to the database vendor. The benefit in this is that database clusters are more mature and are currently more widely used than message-server clusters. The downside is that database clusters are designed to support transactional data storage applications and not messaging. My experience and instinct says always use caution when using tools to solve problems that they were not designed to solve.

Misuse of Persistent Storage

The next point may go a bit far in the direction of personal philosophy, but I feel it is worth stating all the same. The whole concept of shared storage clustering is an exercise in misusing persistent storage as distributed inter-process communication. Don't misunderstand this; there are certainly cases where shared storage is the optimum clustering architecture. I believe, though, that very often system designers are much too quick to use disk storage simply because they are most familiar with it.

Distributed Shared Memory

One more side comment before closing this section: shared storage is actually a special case of a more generic concept called **Distributed Shared Memory (DSM)**. This includes any distributed computing technique where multiple processes can access a common memory space, persistent or not. The JavaSpaces API provides DSM services and a JavaSpaces implementation could be used to interconnect the nodes of a cluster. A closer look reveals that despite differences in API and terminology, JavaSpaces provides roughly the same functionality as a message queue. Thus this idea comes dangerously close to the self-defeating concept of using a message queue to implement a message queue.

Shared Nothing

Shared nothing refers to the case when all storage, and all other resources except network communications, are private to each hardware node. This concept is inherently more distributed than shared storage, and is also somewhat more complex to implement. Shared nothing has been the implicit assumption for most of the discussion in this chapter, and thus most of the architectural issues involved have already been covered. This section will be primarily concerned with the lower-level issues of interconnecting the nodes of a cluster when no shared storage medium is used.

In the shared-nothing world, all communication between nodes goes over a network. This may or may not be the same network that clients use to connect to the cluster. There are two types of data that must be exchanged between nodes:

❑   JMS data including messages and possibly other domain-specific data such as information about consumers and destinations.

❑   Cluster internal data consisting of information about nodes joining and leaving the cluster and possibly configuration and administrative data. Some of this data is sent strictly point-to-point, from one node to another, and some must be distributed to many nodes at the same time.

In a shared-nothing cluster, node interaction consists primarily of passing messages between nodes. Here I mean messages in the generic sense: discrete packets of data. These carry a whole host of information that nodes must exchange, including the JMS messages that the cluster is transferring on behalf of a client. This is most commonly accomplished with TCP based unicast networking.

In this section, we will make two basic points: one is that serverless Message-Oriented Middleware (MOM) provides the ideal means of exchanging data throughout a cluster. The other is that multicast communication often provides significant benefits in clustering compared to the more commonly used unicast networking. These two points are related, since multicast is inherently message-oriented, and IP multicast provides a good basis for implementing serverless MOM.

MOM Communication

The first point to make is that JMS defines a standard Java interface to MOM providers. Using MOM to implement a JMS provider may sound like circular logic, but this can actually make sense. What I am actually describing here is a MOM interface to IP Multicast, which can effectively provide non-durable, non-transactional Pub/Sub messaging without a server. Not surprisingly, some multicast-based MOM products, such as those from Softwired and Fiorano, present a subset of the JMS API to the application.

Remember that the purpose of JMS is to provide standard behavior across the products of multiple vendors. If it is important to remain vendor neutral, then it is good to use a JMS-compliant serverless MOM provider for this purpose. When using MOM products to interconnect the relatively closely coupled nodes of a cluster, it may be necessary to rely on the particular behavior of one product, or the extra features not covered by JMS, such as group membership services.

The following features of MOM make it well suited for inter-node communication:

❑   **Discrete Messages**
Most of the information that must be exchanged between cluster nodes represents discrete events – a new message, a new publisher, a session closure, etc. When the messages that carry this information are transmitted over a stream-oriented data channel, then the receiver has the extra work of delimiting and extracting the individual messages from the channel. In practice, this is not very difficult and may actually be done transparently by a mechanism such as RMI sitting on top of the data stream. The point here is that the natural form of data transfer is message oriented and it is convenient to use an abstraction that presents data to the node in this form.

❑   **Subject-Based Addressing**
This is a more indirect means of addressing the other nodes in the cluster. Without this, each node must maintain a table of the IP addresses of all of the other nodes in the cluster, along with information such as the role of each node if relevant. This level of indirection is of prime benefit when a node fails and is replaced by a backup. The backup can take over listening to messages on the same subject, without requiring all of the other nodes to explicitly learn the new IP address and update their tables.

400

❑ **Pub/Sub**
It is very often the case that identical information must be sent to multiple nodes. It is naturally easier to do this as one single operation.

❑ **Group Membership Services**
This is the generic service keeping track of what participants are communicating on a particular subject. In terms of a cluster, this means keeping track of the other nodes, and providing notifications of nodes that join or leave the group, or nodes that fail unexpectedly. This functionality is required in clustering, and using a MOM product that provides these group membership services, like Softwired's iBus//MessageBus, alleviates the need to implement them yourself.

These are many of the same reasons that make MOM useful in general (not just for clusters), and this serves to emphasize the point that MOM will play a big role in the future of distributed systems. These features of MOM go hand-in-hand with the use of multicast networking as the underlying transport: discrete messaging is a must as stream abstractions are not suitable for group communications; subject-based addressing allows groups of machines to be addressed at one time, and Pub/Sub can be efficiently implemented without a server by using multicast.

The features of MOM that are not relevant are message storage and transactions. These are precisely the features that require a server, and thus cannot be used to implement a message server. Basically all nodes in the cluster must be reachable at all times, and any transactional aspects of inter-node communication must be implemented above the MOM layer.

Multicast Networking

In the Internet world, unicast communication is synonymous with the TCP protocol. This is the most ubiquitous protocol in use on the net. This is not surprising, since it is available at no extra cost on virtually every computing platform in use today. It provides reliable, efficient communication and presents an easy to use, stream-based interface. Why use anything else?

> **The features of unicast protocols come at a price: you lose access to the broadcast capability inherent in the hardware layers of most networks. While TCP makes sense for efficient long-distance communication, it can be counterproductive to use it for group communication on local networks.**

Consider this example: a cluster of 10 nodes is interconnected with a single network segment. Each node has, at the hardware layer, access to all packets that are transmitted on that segment. If one node wants to send the same message to all other nodes using TCP, then it must send the message nine times. The network interface of each hardware node "sees" all nine copies of message going by but only passes one of those copies up to the operating system level of its machine. A lot of potential efficiency is lost here. This loss is significant, as for some existing clustering solutions, this is the ultimate limit of scalability, and this limit can be reached with a small number of nodes.

IP multicast provides the necessary alternative to unicast protocols. Multicast packets are sent to class D IP addresses. Unlike the other classes of IP address, a class D address is not associated with a particular host. Instead, any host can instruct its network interface to accept data sent to any number of such addresses.

There are efficiency considerations here. Most network interface cards can handle a dozen or so class D addresses in hardware. Beyond this, they start passing all multicast packets up to the network driver to be filtered in software.

Thus multicast provides the subject-based addressing and publish/subscribe abstractions right at the network layer. However, raw multicast is not reliable, and there is no ubiquitous reliable protocol layer on top of raw IP multicast that fills a role corresponding to the role filled by TCP in the unicast world. There are a number of commercial products that provide a reliable protocol on top of IP multicast, such as the JMS-compliant products mentioned above. Cisco and TIBCO have developed a protocol called **PGM (Pragmatic General Multicast)**, which is proposed as a standard, but if you want to use it now you will still need to buy and deploy a product such as TIBCO's Rendezvous or Talarian's SmartPGM.

Although multicast packets can, in theory, be routed over wide-area networks, it is difficult to guarantee that this is done efficiently. Many Internet providers do not permit routing of multicast packets, and there is almost certainly no firewall that is open for multicast traffic. This means that multicast will seldom be a suitable means of connecting clients to a server, or to interconnect servers separated by an arbitrary distance in a message routing configuration. It is an ideal means for interconnecting the nodes of a tight cluster in a local environment.

How beneficial is multicast communication for a shared-nothing cluster? Let's look at some of the fundamental considerations of clustering. Any architecture that provides high availability must store all persistent data on at least two different nodes. Pub/Sub messages must potentially be sent to all nodes. Group membership functions require messages, especially heartbeat messages that confirm that a node is still alive, to be sent to all nodes. In short clusters require a large percentage of all messages sent between nodes to be distributed to more than one destination node. This means that the use of multicast communication provides a dramatic increase in the efficiency of network utilization compared to unicast communication:

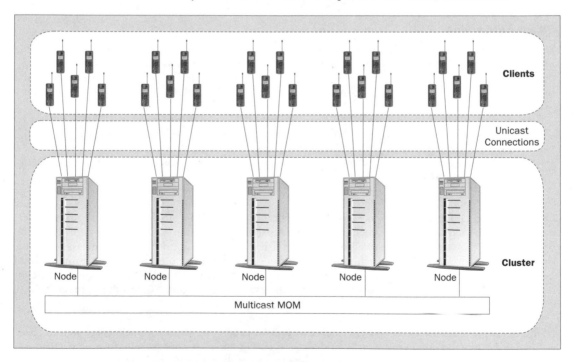

Implications for Transactions

Compared to a monolithic server, the processing of transacted JMS sessions takes on a new dimension in a cluster. The most critical aspect of transacted JMS sessions is that the consumption and production of all messages in the same transaction must succeed or fail in an atomic fashion. Of course all actions are supposed to succeed all the time, but situations do arise when things go wrong: disks fill up, destinations are deleted, etc. The important guarantee in a transacted session is that if any one message fails, then the entire transaction is null and void and the entire transaction must be rolled back as though it never happened.

This is not a complex issue in a monolithic server, but when transaction processing involves multiple nodes, extra coordination is required. It is not permissible to commit part of the transaction on one node, if the commit of another part of the transaction on another node fails. It is also not possible for every node to wait to see if all other nodes succeed before performing the commit itself. This dilemma is usually solved with a **two-phase commit** protocol (which we met in Chapter 4). In the first phase all participating nodes must give a guarantee that they are capable of committing successfully, and in the second phase the nodes are allowed to commit in parallel. Transactions that require a two-phase commit are called **distributed transactions**.

The implication of clustering on transacted message delivery is that every transaction requires a two-phase commit within the cluster. This causes the implementation of the cluster to become more complex, but this should be entirely transparent to the user of the JMS API. The biggest implication for the end user of the JMS messaging system is performance. The extra communication between nodes costs time, and the entire transaction cannot complete until all nodes have reported their individual results. Much of the parallelism that might be expected from load balancing among multiple nodes is lost during a transaction commit. In general, the speed of message delivery for transacted sessions will not scale as well as that for non-transacted sessions.

The degree to which transactions have an effect on performance depends largely on how many nodes are involved in the transaction. This will vary between one and all of nodes in the cluster depending on where the messages are stored. The successful commit of a produced message means that the cluster has securely stored the messages (persistently or non-persistently, depending on delivery mode) and will guarantee delivery with no further action from the client, even in the case of node failures.

A commit must occur after a message is published and before it can be delivered, so some form of storage is always required for transacted messages. When a cluster employs the concept of destination homes, the number of nodes involved actually depends on the number of destinations involved in the transaction and how those destinations are distributed among the nodes.

The redundancy scheme employed, if any, also plays a big role in determining the number of nodes involved in a transaction. If the cluster guarantees that committed messages will ultimately be delivered in spite of node failures, then a successful commit must also imply that redundant copies of the messages are stored on different nodes.

Consider a full replication scheme. In this case all nodes must participate in every transaction. This means that with every commit a session must always wait on the slowest node in the cluster. Thus, with transactions the problem of an overloaded node slowing down the whole cluster becomes more acute. Clusters that have a high degree of redundancy might benefit from only requiring a majority of the backup or redundant nodes to commit successfully before declaring the commit a success to the client. The feasibility of this approach depends on the exact redundancy scheme employed. A node that does not successfully commit will not have a complete set of messages. With a full redundancy scheme, all nodes are active, so a node that was not successful during the original commit must catch up soon by committing the transaction afterward, or the cluster must declared the node as failed and shut it down.

With a primary/backup scheme, the primary must always commit successfully in order for the transaction to succeed, but if any of the backups do not commit successfully, this does not become a problem until a fail-over occurs, which means that the backup potentially has more time to catch up. Thus, with primary/backup, a "lazy commit" policy for the backup nodes, although riskier, might be acceptable in return for better performance.

Other Issues

So far in this chapter, we have seen the major implications of using a clustered JMS message server. Before closing, we'll briefly visit a number of additional aspects that are less important from an architectural standpoint, but are important nevertheless.

Administration

Although the JMS specification clearly defines the external behavior of a message system, it says nothing about administration. This is an area where there are bound to be big differences between JMS vendors, and with clustering this is the case even more so. Most clustering schemes will maintain the outward appearance of a single monolithic server, which means that there is no difference in programming a JMS client for the clustered and non-clustered cases.

This will not be the case for administration. For the administrative functions common to monolithic servers and clusters, it may make sense to present the cluster to the administrator as though it were monolithic. Clustering brings a host of additional administrative functions, though. Such actions as adding a node to or removing a node from the cluster, configuring backup nodes, assigning destination homes and configuring routing, if necessary, require explicit knowledge of each node. Individual cluster implementations will vary as to how many of these functions are required, and which can be performed automatically and which require administer intervention.

Additionally, implementations will vary as to whether such administrative functions can be performed while the cluster is online, or whether it must be shut down. Downtime for administrative actions is not as critical as downtime due to failures, as administration can usually be planned for low usage periods (typically evenings and weekends), insofar as these exist . If your cluster is expected to provide availability of 99.9% or better (refer to the availability table earlier in this chapter), you are pretty much required to perform all administrative and reconfiguration tasks online.

Configuration

Clustering also adds complexity to the task of maintaining consistent configuration data for the server. Some configuration parameters must be the same for all nodes (especially communication parameters required for the nodes to communicate with each other), and some parameters will need to have a certain consistency across the cluster (two nodes should not be home for the same destination, for example).

It is easier to avoid inconsistencies if there is a central repository for all parameters, such as a configuration server file in a shared directory. This introduces a central point of failure, but not a very serious one, unless the nodes need to continuously access the central configuration data. If the nodes only access the configuration data once at startup time, then a failure of the configuration repository will only prevent new nodes from starting, not affect running nodes.

This scheme still creates difficulty if the configuration data is updated while some nodes are online. Nodes that are added after the change will have a configuration that is inconsistent with the existing nodes. It is important for a cluster to have a systematic scheme for ensuring the consistency of node configuration. It is also helpful if the cluster can automatically detect and report an inconsistency, as this can lead to problems that are difficult to diagnose.

Keep in mind that there will always be some bootstrap parameters that are local to each node. Even if there is a central repository, each node will need to be given some parameters in order to find the repository. In the optimal case the parameters should be minimal: a host address and port, a multicast address, or a filename.

After guaranteeing that nodes can start up with a consistent set of parameters, the next issue is parameter updates. If necessary, can parameters be changed while the cluster is online? If so, the cluster must ensure the changes are carried out consistently over all nodes. This is more easily accomplished if all nodes access a common repository. If each node stores its configuration locally after startup, it may be necessary to signal the nodes to reread the central configuration. A more distributed solution is to handle parameter updates in the same fashion as other data that must be exchanged between nodes, and propagate them through the cluster using message passing.

Intra-Node Security

Intra-node security refers to authenticating the nodes that join the cluster or more generally, to restricting access by any process that tries to impersonate a node. For clusters where all nodes are located together in the same data center, this is seldom an issue, as the network itself can be sufficiently isolated that there is no risk of contact with computers that are controlled by other parties.

Intra-node security is more likely to be important in message routing, where the nodes are separated by larger distances and could easily be reached by processes not associated with the messaging system. In this case it is often prudent to employ security measures between nodes similar to those typically employed between client and server. This could include basic connection level authentication, passing authentication tokens with every message exchange, or stronger security in the form of SSL connections.

If reliability is important, then the cluster should employ basic measures against Byzantine failures, in which a process, even if not intentionally malicious, runs amok and starts distributing invalid messages on the cluster network.

A second aspect of cluster security is closely related to configuration. Authentication and access control data must be consistent across the cluster for it to be meaningful. It does little good to deny a user access to a particular destination if that user can gain access to it anyway by just reconnecting to another node. Here again, the security configuration must be stored centrally, or the update mechanism must ensure that changes are propagated to all nodes in a timely manner.

Backup

Typical computer installations will perform nightly backup of all data to tape archives. Such a backup represents a "snapshot" of the state of the system at one point in time. Performing this type of backup of the message store of a message server makes little sense due to the transient nature of the queued messages. The general concept behind a message server is to store messages for the shortest amount of time possible. If you do need to perform such a backup for some reason, then it is difficult to get a consistent snapshot of the whole cluster without shutting the whole system down during the backup. (This is particularly true if the nodes are geographically dispersed.)

If there is a constant flow of messages in and out of the server, then restoring a server from a backup that is several hours old will probably not be very useful. In fact this would almost certainly lead to both message loss and multiple deliveries. This is one of the reasons that the extra reliability provided by clustering is more important for message servers than for many other types of server.

Consider the following two cases in which uncoordinated backups are done while a message is in the process of being routed between two nodes. If a backup of one node is done after the message leaves it, and the backup of the other node is done before the message arrives, then the message will not appear in any of the backups. Alternatively, if the backup of one node is done before the message leaves it, and the backup of the other node is done after the message arrives, then the message appears twice. In this case it could be delivered twice if the whole cluster were restored from the backups.

In general, it is better not to rely on snapshot-style backups for the message store. The only type of backup that makes sense is one that recodes every message store update continuously, as it happens. This actually describes a backup node in a primary/backup redundancy scheme more than a tape archiving procedure.

It is of course useful to backup configuration files and other cluster metadata, but unlike the message store, this does not present special problems.

Summary

Clustering is a world of tradeoffs. Performance, capabilities, scalability, reliability, and complexity are just some of the factors that tend to work against each other. If this were not the case, then there would be one best cluster architecture and this chapter would be very short. In addition to the many possible cluster architectures, there are a variety of problems that can be solved by clustering. Any particular JMS-based distributed system may only face some of these problems; hence you need to define your need before shopping around for a JMS cluster. If this chapter has achieved its purpose, then you should be well prepared to do this.

Examples of JMS providers that support some of the clustering concepts described in this chapter are: FioranoMQ, IBM MQSeries, Progress Sonic MQ, SwiftMQ, and the JMS provider included with BEA WebLogic. Softwired will also release a clustered version of iBus//MessageServer in the near future.

After reading this chapter you should be well equipped to ask the right questions and find out what you need to know about JMS clustering. It should also serve to provide a common set of terminology to help avoid misunderstanding.

In the next chapter, we'll look at one particular use of JMS in a clustered architecture, that of distributed logging.

Distributed Logging Using JMS

9

It is a challenging problem to provide an integrated logging mechanism for Java enterprise applications. These applications may consist of a variety of components such as EJBs, servlets, and JSPs, which run on various possible configurations of hardware. We looked at the clustering issues in JMS development in the previous chapter.

A real-world example where distributed application logging would come in handy would be the problem of logging client sessions in a dynamically load-balanced system. Having a centralized location where this information is logged is very important in tracking session failures.

This chapter will explore the use of JMS messaging to implement a distributed logging service. The logging service will exist within a basic application "framework" of services. The idea of the framework is that it implements basic functionality that is inherent in any enterprise application software development, such as JNDI lookups, configuration information retrieval, and application logging, among others. This framework can then be deployed to the application server and initialized for enterprise application software to use.

In this chapter we will:

- ❏ Discuss the challenges associated with logging within a distributed application
- ❏ Discuss why JMS is a good choice for implementing a distributed logging system
- ❏ Investigate JLog, a specific logging package providing support for a JMS based logging implementation
- ❏ Provide an example of how JLog can be used in conjunction with JMS
- ❏ Discuss the inclusion of a "LogService" within the application framework to wrap the logging service
- ❏ Provide an example servlet and EJB demonstrating the use of the LogService

Logging in a Distributed Environment

This distribution of components presents a difficulty. For example, while there exists a mechanism in the Java Servlet API to log directly to the servlet container's log, in practice it is no more flexible than using the old programmer standby `System.out.println()`. A solution is needed that can accommodate distributed logging requirements by creating a distributed logging mechanism that allows you to receive application log messages from many machines, and not simply log to the local machine as the above solution does.

The need to run in a distributed environment is now a feature of nearly all software applications. While it may not be readily apparent when developing an application on a single development machine, there will be some different challenges when it comes round to addressing the issue of a system that will scale to many clients, and many server machines.

Most commercial grade application servers provide scalability using server clustering. Clustering is a mechanism where two or more application servers run together and share the load of executing the business application software. For example, say a business is experiencing tremendous growth and its hardware infrastructure is not going to be able to support the number of users expected in the coming months. Rather than having to re-architect the software to run in a distributed environment, all that should need to be done is to add another server to the cluster.

Even if a logging utility is used, the largest problem of distributed application logging is that each application server will be logging messages within its respective environment. Since this is now a clustered environment, and load balancing is used by the servers, there is often no way we can know which application server a specific software component is executing on.

For example, say a client error occurs and it is determined that, based on the type of error, the problem must reside within a specific type of servlet. Even if we had the foresight of using a logging package and we are logging error messages judiciously, we must now figure out which application server is executing the servlet instance and then inspect the log file that resides on that particular system. In a cluster of two machines this is a small inconvenience, but imagine a clustered environment of ten application servers. Finding the machine that is executing that particular software component could be a tedious job.

This is a typical situation where the use of a distributed logging mechanism becomes vital, and where JMS is a prudent choice to solve this problem.

Choosing a Platform

There are many packages available for application logging, but not many that support distributed logging by any method other than direct socket connection. This is OK, but for a more elegant, flexible solution we can turn to JMS.

JMS provides several advantages over using custom direct socket connections for logging:

❑ It supports transacted and persistent messages, which the system guarantees to deliver. More software would need to be developed for a socket-based solution to provide this functionality.

❑ It supports the notion of topics, which allow you to manage your log message destinations simply by publishing to a topic created specifically for that message type. If you were to require that in a socket-based solution you would need to filter the messages yourself by creating software that acts in a similar manner.

Obtaining a JMS provider is the first step in creating a JMS logging tool. For our purposes here we will be working with BEA WebLogic Server 6.0, which provides an implementation of Sun's JMS API. The software included with this chapter should work with little modification with other JMS providers. Appendix A gives some guidelines for configuring code for different JMS providers.

Having identified our environment, we must either create or obtain a logging tool that uses JMS for the purpose of logging application messages. When determining whether to buy or build a logging solution, we must look at what tools are available in the marketplace and assess how they fit our needs, both from a requirements standpoint and from a budget standpoint.

JLog

I began investigating many of the various logging implementations that can be found around the Internet, and was fairly certain that I'd have to create JMS logging support myself until I ran across a logging implementation that seemed to fulfill my needs. The tool I ended up selecting is a tool called JLog from a company called JTrack (http://www.jtrack.com).

JLog is designed specifically to be used for distributed application logging. We have selected JLog as our logging implementation, but we still need to do some work to create a configurable logging service that can wrap (in the sense of the Façade pattern below) the functionality of JLog and provide an interface to application developers that will allow us to change logging implementations in the future should we need to.

> *From* "Design Patterns" *by Gamma, et al., 1995 ISBN 0-201633-61-2:* "*The Façade pattern provides a unified interface to a set of interfaces in a subsystem. This unified interface decouples the subsystem implementation from anyone using the façade.*"

To obtain the JLog package visit http://www.jtrack.com and download the latest JLog implementation. After downloading the package unzip the package to a chosen directory. The package will contain a JAR file with the JLog implementation, JavaDocs for the classes, and interfaces in the implementation, and another JAR file containing examples of how to use the package. Some of the examples contained with the JLog package are the basis for some of the examples contained within this chapter.

Overview of Basic JLog Concepts

The JLog package makes heavy use of the Observer pattern (see below) and is quite flexible because of the decoupling between objects that is achieved when using this pattern. Many observers can be created to observe a particular log instance without the log instance caring about how many observers there are. This lends great flexibility in the routing of messages to many destinations, perhaps to be interpreted in different formats.

> *From* "Design Patterns" *by Erich Gamma, et al., 1995:* "*The Observer pattern defines a one-to-many dependency between objects so that when one object changes state, all its dependents are notified and updated automatically. The objects being notified are called the observers and the object that is being observed is called the subject.*"

Additionally, observer filters can be created to observe a particular log, and only messages that match the filter's criteria are received. This is a very powerful mechanism to have at your disposal when creating a logging system.

Interfaces

The JLog package Observer pattern implementation contains two main interfaces:

❑ ILogEventProducer – This is the **subject** being observed. Classes implementing ILogEventListener register with classes implementing this interface.

❑ ILogEventListener – This is the **observer** that will register with, and observe the subject implementing the ILogEventProducer interface.

There are many other interfaces and classes in the package that extend or implement these two interfaces. The following class diagram illustrates the main interface relationships:

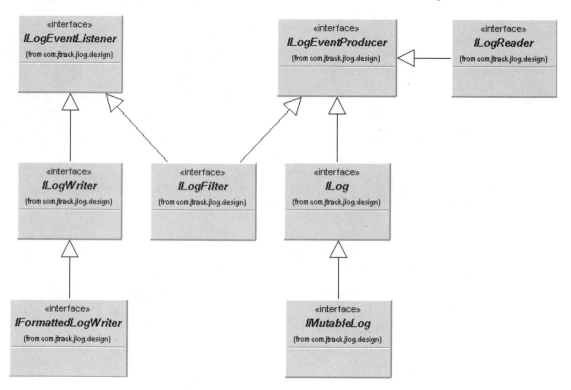

As you can see from the above diagram there are four main subinterfaces extending the basic event producing and listening interfaces, and two subsidiary ones.

Some of the basic component types implementing these interfaces are given below:

❑ **Writers** – which implement ILogWriter – used to write log messages to a specified medium

❑ **Readers** – which implement ILogReader – used to read log messages to a specified medium

❑ **Logs** – which implement ILog – used for recording log messages

❑ **Filters** – which implement ILogFilter – used for filtering messages based on a certain criteria

Additionally there are two more interfaces that extend the functionality of these interfaces:

❑ `IFormattedLogWriter` – Implemented by a writer intended to write messages in a specific format

❑ `IMutableLog` – Extends the `ILog` interface and defines how log messages can be removed from a log instance

Any writer, reader, log, or filter created with the logging package implements one or both of the two event interfaces, or one of their subinterfaces.

Examples Using JLog

Now that we've covered the basic concepts, it's time to demonstrate them with some examples. Since we have a lot of configuration detail to deal with, we have chosen to use the Ant build utility to run all our tasks. This way, we can set all necessary system, compilation, location, classpath, and run-time properties once and for all, and illustrate how to build the examples using simple calls to Ant. We will show here all the necessary target commands within a single `build.xml` script that enable us to build and run the examples. All operating system specifics should be abstracted into the `build.xml` file.

> *Ant is a Java program that automates the process of compiling and manipulating source code structures. To use these scripts, as well as the framework itself, you must obtain a copy of Ant from the Jakarta Apache Project (http://jakarta.apache.org/ant/index.html).*

The first example shows how a `LogEventListener` implementation (`LogWriter`) is created and used in connection with a `LogEventProducer`, in this case, a `Log` object.

Before proceeding, download and install the code distribution for this chapter. To obtain the code distribution visit http://www.wrox.com. After installing the code you're ready to proceed and build the example.

Setting Build Properties

After installing Ant there are a couple of steps that are needed to use it with the build script `build.xml` included in the chapter. You need to change the `<property>` variable tags to match the appropriate settings and directories for your machine.

Our base directory will be `C:\ProJMS\Chapter09`, but the actual value of this is irrelevant, since everything we do will be relative to this base directory:

```
<project name="jms_logging" default="framework" basedir=".">
```

We will give the full set of properties here for the chapter. First we assign some values for the WebLogic server that we'll be using later:

```
<property name="appserver" value="C:/bea/wlserver6.0/config/mydomain"/>
<property name="apphome" value="${appserver}/applications" />
<property name="confighome" value="${appserver}/logconfig" />
<property name="serverclasses" value="${appserver}/serverclasses"/>
<property name="docs" value="./docs" />
```

Note how previous values can be substituted into new values. These are our principle directories:

```
<property name="framework_build" value="./build" />
<property name="framework_src" value="./src/framework" />
<property name="jlog_examples_src" value="./src/examples/jlogexamples"/>
<property name="jlog_examples_build" value="./build" />
<property name="framework_servlet_src"
    value="./src/examples/frameworkServlet" />
<property name="framework_servlet_build" value="./servletbuild" />
<property name="framework_ejb_src" value="./src/examples/frameworkejb"/>
<property name="framework_ejb_build" value="./ejbbuild" />
<property name="descriptorhome" value="./src" />
```

Now we set up the classpaths used for compiling and running the examples. You will need to check the values carefully corresponding to the location of the appropriate JAR files on your machine:

```
<property name="jdbcpath" value="C:/Oracle/Ora81/jdbc/classes111.zip"/>
<property name="xmlparser"
    value="C:/jaxp-1.1ea2/jaxp.jar;C:/jaxp-1.1ea2/crimson.jar"/>
<property name="jlogpath" value="C:/jlog/jlog_1_01.jar" />
<property name="antpath" value="C:/ant/lib/ant.jar"/>
<property name="weblogicjar" value="C:/bea/wlserver6.0/lib/weblogic.jar"/>

<property name="framework_classpath"
    value="${xmlparser};${jlogpath};${weblogicjar};${jdbcpath}" />
<property name="framework_examples_classpath"
    value="${framework_build};${framework_classpath}" />
<property name="framework_servlet_classpath"
    value="${framework_build};${framework_classpath}" />
<property name="framework_ejb_classpath"
    value="${framework_build};${framework_classpath}" />
```

You will need a recent copy of the JAXP release obtainable from http://java.sun.com/xml, which contains the jaxp.jar and crimson.jar libraries for XML parsing. Note that we are using Oracle database driver classes here. This is not essential. If you substitute the classpath for another suitable JDBC driver, you will be able to run the database logging service later, but the use of a database is an incidental part of the chapter, and merely illustrates further uses of the logging service.

We will continue showing sections of the build.xml script as we need them.

Now let's take a look at the source code for a simple logging example:

```
package examples.jlogexamples.simple;

import com.jtrack.examples.AbstractExample;
import com.jtrack.jlog.implementation.Log;
import com.jtrack.jlog.implementation.LogOutputStream;
import com.jtrack.jlog.implementation.LongLogFormatter;
/**
 * This example shows how to log to System.out using
 * a LogOutputStream and the Log class.
 */
public class SimpleLogExample {

  public static void main(String[] args) {
    new SimpleLogExample().runExample();
  }
```

Use the static global log provided by the `Log` class to log messages and add a `LogOutputStream` to the global log so log messages are printed out to `System.out`:

```
protected void runExample() {
    // create a LogOutputStream which listens to the global
    // log and prints out to System.out in a long format

    LogOutputStream logListener = new LogOutputStream(
        Log.global, System.out, new LongLogFormatter());
    // log a few messages
    Log.global.debug( "A debug message", "From SimpleLogExample" );
    Log.global.warn( "A warning message", "From SimpleLogExample" );
    Log.global.trace( "A trace message", "From SimpleLogExample" );
    }
}
```

Looking at the `runExample()` method, the first thing we do is to create a new `LogOutputStream`, which is our listener, and also a type of `LogWriter`. There are three arguments we need to pass to the `LogOutputStream` constructor. The first parameter we pass is our `LogEventProducer`, in this instance `Log.global`.

`Log.global` is a globally available static `Log` instance that can be used for logging. It is for convenience and we will use it in our example so that we don't need to create a `Log` instance ourselves, although there is nothing stopping you from creating a `Log` instance yourself and using it. This `LogWriter` implementation is one that is used to write to output streams, so the next parameter we pass is an output stream, `System.out`, for it to log messages to. Finally a Formatter object is needed so that `LogOutputStream` knows how to format the messages when it logs them to the output stream.

There are a few different types of formats that you can choose from when logging messages; in our example we will use the "Long" format that is part of the JLog package. If you desire a format that doesn't exist within JLog you can create a formatter of your own simply by implementing the `ILogFormatter` interface. For more information about the types of formats that are available, refer to the JLog JavaDocs.

Compiling and Running

To run the code, we first need to compile it. The following dependency chain of `<target>` commands achieves this. First we create the necessary target directories for the compiled code:

```
<target name="frameworkprepare">
  <mkdir dir="${framework_build}" />
  <mkdir dir="${framework_servlet_build}" />
  <mkdir dir="${framework_ejb_build}" />
  <mkdir dir="${confighome}" />
  <copy todir="${confighome}">
    <fileset dir="config"/>
  </copy>
</target>
```

Now we compile the source code for the logging framework into the `build` directory:

```
<target name="framework" depends="frameworkprepare">
  <javac
    srcdir="${framework_src}"
    destdir="${framework_build}"
    classpath="${framework_classpath}"
  />
</target>
```

Note the classpath we specified above in the attributes of the compile instruction. This will compile our example classes into the `build\examples` directory:

```
<target name="examples" depends="framework">
  <javac
    srcdir="${jlog_examples_src}"
    destdir="${jlog_examples_build}"
    classpath="${framework_classpath}"
  />
</target>
```

Finally, we can run the `SimpleLogExample` class:

```
<target name="SimpleLogExample" depends="examples">
  <java
    classname="examples.jlogexamples.simple.SimpleLogExample"
    fork="yes"
    classpath="${framework_examples_classpath}"
  />
</target>
```

Bring up a command window, set your current directory to base of the code installation, and execute `ant SimpleLogExample`. You should see an output similar to that below:

As you can see, the simple example printed out three separate log messages to `System.out`. Each log entry contains the `Log name` (Global System Log), `Entry name` (none), `Timestamp` for the message, `Severity` (Debug, Warning, or Trace in this example), `Title`, executing thread (main), the `Source` code line that logged the message, and the text contents of the message.

Going Further into JLog

The simple example above only demonstrates a small portion of what is available with the JLog package. Returning to the premise that there are two main types of components in a JLog implementation, event listeners and producers, the following two sections will cover in a little more detail some other options available when configuring an application log like the one in the last example.

JLog LogEventListeners

The following class diagram illustrates the relationships that exist between some of the various writers and filters that implement the `ILogEventListener` interface. It is by no means exhaustive; for more types refer to the JLog JavaDoc.

Looking at the diagram, an important thing to note is that all of the log writers implement the `ILogEventListener` interface, which means that all of these writers can be added to an object implementing `ILogEventProducer`, such as the log, reader, and filter classes:

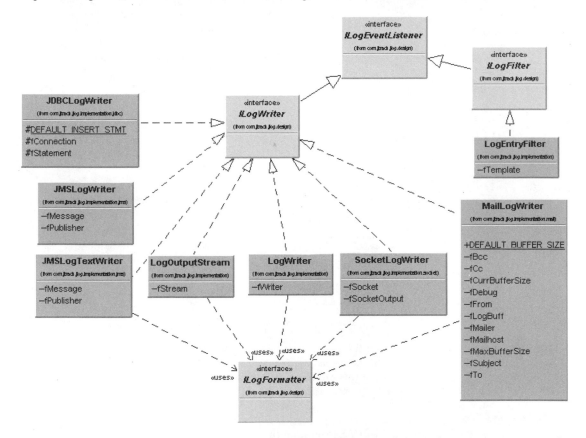

As you can see from the diagram above, all of the Writer objects implement the `ILogWriter` interface, which extends the `ILogEventListener` interface. Any of these components can be added as a listener to the log event producers covered in the next section. In our last example `LogOutputStream` was an event listener that was listening for events from the event producer `Log.global`.

This diagram also contains an `ILogFormatter` interface, which is used by some of the `LogWriter` objects. Objects that implement the `ILogFormatter` interface are intended to perform message formatting for the writer instance that uses them. There are two types of writer objects (JMS, JDBC) that do not use this interface and the reason for that is because they do not require formatted text log messages.

Other than log writers, the other type of interface to extend the `ILogEventListener` interface is the `ILogFilter` interface. Classes that implement the `ILogFilter` interface are event listeners as well as event producers, so you will see them in this diagram and in the next section's diagram as well. Filters act as readers and writers in one. They are a kind of message mediator, because they monitor event producers for a specific type of message and then they themselves produce an event when the specified message type is observed. For more information about log filters please refer to the JavaDoc and example code that come with JLog.

JLog LogEventProducers

The following class diagram shows all of the various `ILogEventProducer` objects such as the `Log` object, and various readers, and filters. In our example above, the `LogEventProducer` was the object `Log.global`. Again, any `LogEventListener` can be registered with a `LogEventProducer`:

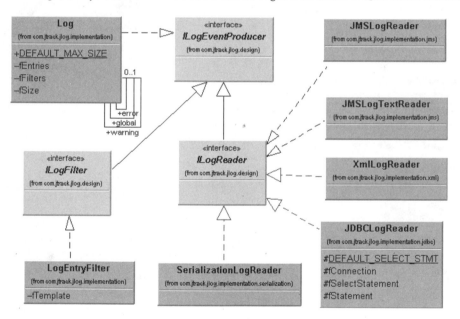

Looking at the diagram, we see that there are two interfaces that extend `ILogEventProducer`, namely `ILogFilter` and `ILogReader`. Since we have already covered `ILogFilter`, we'll focus on `ILogReader`. Classes implementing this interface are event producers that can have event listeners observing them. For example, a `JMSLogReader` can be observed by a `LogWriter`.

The `LogWriter` would be in a position to process log messages that the `JMSLogReader` reads. We will cover in more detail the specifics of JMS logging in the next section. The final thing to note about this diagram is the `Log` object. The `Log` object is the heart of the logging package. You add log messages to `Log` instances, whether you create an instance of your own or use a globally available `Log` instance, which we talked about earlier (`Log.global`), to perform all of the actual logging. The `Log` object is what the various writers and filters listen to for messages.

JLog JMS Implementation

Now that we've covered the basics of what the JLog package has to offer, let's narrow our focus a bit. Since our interests lie mostly with distributed logging using JMS, let's look specifically at the JMSLogWriter and JMSLogReader class diagram:

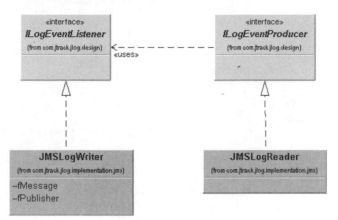

As you can see from the class diagram, the JMSLogReader is a LogEventProducer and the JMSLogWriter is a LogEventListener. You might be thinking to yourself: shouldn't the JMSLogWriter be the producer and the JMSLogReader be the listener? The answer to that question is that each of these two components is both a listener and a producer. The following diagram illustrates this point:

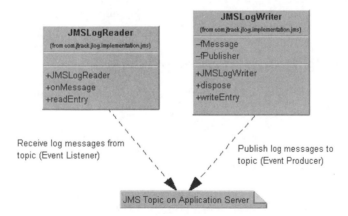

As the above diagram shows, the JMSLogWriter is an **event producer** in that it publishes log messages to a specified JMS topic. The JMSLogReader is an **event listener** in that it subscribes to a specified JMS topic and receives messages. So taking the previous class diagram and combining it with the diagram above, the next diagram illustrates the entire picture as it relates to the roles of log readers and log writers:

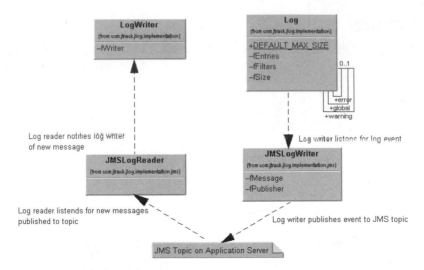

Looking at the above diagram we can see in Step 1 that the JMSLogWriter is an **event listener** listening to the Log object. Then once a Log event occurs the JMSLogWriter turns into an **event producer** because it publishes the new log event to a JMS topic. In Step 3 the JMSLogReader is an **event listener** listening to the topic to which the JMSLogWriter published a message. Once the JMSLogReader has been notified of a new message published to the topic Step 4 occurs where the JMSLogReader acts as an **event producer** informing a log writer that a new message is to be logged.

The use of JLog and JMS together is a very natural fit because they are both based on the same Publish/Subscribe mechanism, which is a very flexible, low-coupling way to piece together event-logging systems.

Logging Example Using JLog and JMS

Now that we've covered how JLog and JMS fit together it's time for an example to illustrate how an implementation works.

> **For this and the rest of the examples throughout the chapter you will need to have BEA's Weblogic 6.0 installed (http://www.bea.com).**

In the following example, the JMSLogExample program performs the following tasks:

- ❏ It connects to the application server's naming service to retrieve a JMS TopicConnectionFactory
- ❏ It retrieves a JMS Topic for publishers and subscribers to use
- ❏ It creates a publisher or subscriber based on the run-time parameters passed in as command-line arguments
- ❏ It publishes messages to the topic if publisher is the selected mode, or subscribes to the topic if subscriber is the selected mode

In this example we have a subscriber, who will be subscribing to a JMS topic to receive messages from, and a publisher, who will be producing the messages. This example code can be run as either the subscriber or the publisher role. Two separate application instances will be needed to execute this example, either in two different windows on the same machine or different windows on different machines.

The example shows how to use `JMSLogWriter` to publish log entries to JMS and how to use `JMSLogReader` to receive log entries from JMS. Let's take a look at the code listing:

```
package examples.jlogexamples.jms;

import com.jtrack.jlog.implementation.*;
import com.jtrack.jlog.implementation.jms.*;
import javax.jms.*;
import javax.naming.*;
import java.util.Hashtable;

public class JMSLogExample {

    //IntialContextFactory that's used to retrieve the JMS factory
    private String JNDI_FACTORY;

    //Factory used to create JMS topic connections
    private String JMS_FACTORY;

    //JMS topic used in this example to publish/subscribe log messages
    private String TOPIC;

    private String HOST;

    private static boolean client;

    protected TopicSession topicSession = null;
    protected TopicConnection topicConnection = null;
    private  InitialContext ctx;
    private LogWriter logWriter;
```

A URL pointing to the JMS provider, and the mode of operation (publisher or subscriber) are needed:

```
public static void main(String[] args) {
    try {
        JMSLogExample example = new JMSLogExample(args);
        example.runExample(client);
        example.shutdown();
    }
    catch(JMSException e) {
        e.printStackTrace();
    }
}
```

In the constructor we use JNDI to get the initial context as well as to process the input arguments. Using the initial context, we retrieve the `TopicConnectionFactory` used to create a `TopicConnection`. That `TopicConnection` is then used to create a `TopicSession`, which could be used later to create a topic in the event that it doesn't already exist. In fact, we will look up an existing administered topic. This can be configured either using a WebLogic startup property or by using the administration console, as we'll see later. After we create an instance of the `JMSLogExample` class we call `runExample()` passing a parameter `client` to indicate what mode of operation this example should run in:

```
    private JMSLogExample(String[] args) {
        super();
        if (args.length != 5) {
            System.out.println("Usage: java " +
                "framework.test.jmstest.JMSLogExample {URL} {context} " +
                "{topic} {JMSfactory} {(subscriber|publisher)}\n");
            System.out.println("e.g. t3://localhost:7001 " +
                "weblogic.jndi.WLInitialContextFactory exampleTopic " +
                "javax.jms.TopicConnectionFactory subscriber ");
            System.exit(1);
        }
        HOST        = args[0];
        JNDI_FACTORY = args[1];
        TOPIC        = args[2];
        JMS_FACTORY = args[3];

        if(args[4].equalsIgnoreCase("subscriber")) {
            client = true;
        }

        try {
            ctx = getInitialContext(HOST);
        }
        catch(NamingException e) {
            System.out.println(e.getMessage());
            System.exit(1);
        }

        try {
            System.out.println("Creating topic connection.");
            topicConnection = getConnectionFactory().createTopicConnection();

            topicConnection.start();
            System.out.println("Creating topic session.");
            topicSession = topicConnection.createTopicSession(false,
                Session.AUTO_ACKNOWLEDGE );
        }
        catch (JMSException e) {
            e.printStackTrace();
        }
    }

    private InitialContext getInitialContext(String url)
        throws NamingException  {
        Hashtable env = new Hashtable();
        env.put(Context.INITIAL_CONTEXT_FACTORY, JNDI_FACTORY);
        env.put(Context.PROVIDER_URL, url);
        return new InitialContext(env);
    }
```

Create a `TopicConnectionFactory` needed to work with JMS:

```
    private TopicConnectionFactory getConnectionFactory() {
        TopicConnectionFactory factory = null;
        try {
            factory = (TopicConnectionFactory)ctx.lookup(JMS_FACTORY);
        }
        catch(NamingException e) {
            System.out.println(e.getMessage());
        }
        return factory;
    }
```

Based on whether it's run as a publisher or subscriber, we'll execute different methods:

```
private void runExample(boolean subscriber) throws JMSException {
    Topic topic = null;
    try {
        topic = (Topic)ctx.lookup(TOPIC);
    }
    catch(NamingException e) {
        System.out.println(e.getMessage());
        System.out.println("Topic lookup failed. Using createTopic().");
        topic = topicSession.createTopic(TOPIC);
        try {
            ctx.bind(TOPIC, topic);
        }
        catch(NamingException ex) {
            System.out.println("Error binding topic: " + e.getMessage());
            System.exit(1);
        }
    }

    if(subscriber) {
        runSubscriber(topic);
        try {
            System.out.println("Waiting for messages to be published " +
                "to topic: " + TOPIC + "\n");
            synchronized(this) {
                wait();
            }
        }
        catch(InterruptedException e) {
            System.out.println(e.getMessage());
        }
    }
    else {
        runPublisher(topic);
    }
}
```

If the example is run in publisher mode we will create a JMS TopicPublisher and pass that as an argument to JMSLogWriter's constructor, along with a message object. Once the writer is created, we add it as a listener to the global log:

```
private void runPublisher(Topic topic) throws JMSException {
```

Create the TopicPublisher and ObjectMessage needed for creating a JMSLogWriter and then create the actual JMSLogWriter:

```
System.out.println("Creating topic publisher");
TopicPublisher topicPub = topicSession.createPublisher( topic );
ObjectMessage message = topicSession.createObjectMessage();
JMSLogWriter logWriter = new JMSLogWriter(topicPub, message );
```

Add the log writer to the global log listeners:

```
        Log.global.addLogEventListener(logWriter);
```

Write some log entries to the global log, which are then published on JMS by the `JMSLogWriter` listening to the global log. They are received by the `JMSLogReader`, which forwards them to a `LogOutputStream`, which finally prints the log message:

```
        Log.global.trace( "A trace message",
          "This is a trace message from the JMSLogExample." );
        Log.global.debug( "A debug message",
          "This is a debug message from the JMSLogExample." );
        Log.global.warn( "A warning message",
          "This is a warning message from the JMSLogExample." );
        System.out.println("published 3 messages to topic: " + TOPIC);
    }
```

If the example is run in subscriber mode, we will create a JMS `TopicSubscriber` and pass that as an argument to the `JMSLogReader`'s constructor. Once we create the `JMSLogReader` we need to create a `LogWriter` to listen to the `JMSLogReader` and to log messages received by the reader. In this case, we'll be logging messages to `System.out`:

```
    private void runSubscriber(Topic topic)    throws JMSException {
        System.out.println("Creating topic subscriber");
        TopicSubscriber topicSubscriber =
            topicSession.createSubscriber( topic );
        JMSLogReader subscriber =
            new JMSLogReader("A Log Subscriber", topicSubscriber );
```

Create a log writer to log to console all messages received by the `JMSLogReader`:

```
        new LogOutputStream( subscriber, System.out, new LongLogFormatter());
    }
```

```
    private void shutdown() {
        try {
            topicSession.close();
            topicConnection.close();
        }
        catch (JMSException e) {
            e.printStackTrace();
        }
    }
}
```

This example demonstrates a simple implementation of logging using JMS but if we look closer we can see that there's a lot of overhead associated with the creation of Log objects. For example, performing JNDI lookups, creating JMS components, and setting up log readers and log writers would be extremely tedious if every single application that wanted to implement logging had to perform these tasks itself. Later, we solve this problem by providing a "logging service" that can be used to abstract the details of initializing and configuring logging so that an application developer can easily implement logging within their applications by using this service.

Compiling and Running the Example

Going back to how we ran our first example, it is very similar for this one. We have already set up all the machinery to compile and deploy the classes, but we need to set up the administered JMS objects at both the client and server ends.

Configure JMS objects in WebLogic

Firstly, configure a topic and a topic connection factory in WebLogic. This is carried out using exactly the same procedure as described in Appendix A. Choose the names `TCFactory` and `myTopic` for the factory and topic respectively. Ensure that both the JMS server and the connection factory are targeted to a live server (you can use the one called `myserver` in the default installation):

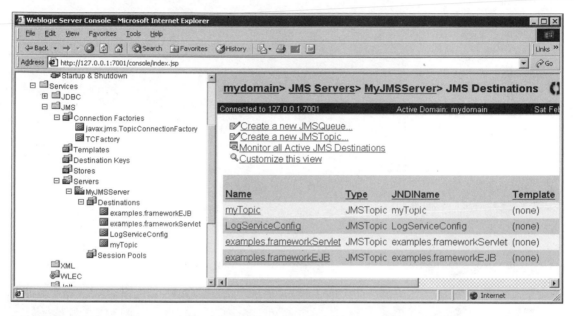

While you are doing this, you may as well set up the other administered objects that we will need later in the chapter, although we'll remind you again about these. Create three more topics `examples.frameworkServlet`, `examples.frameworkEJB`, and `LogServiceConfig`, and create a topic connection factory `javax.jms.TopicConnectionFactory`. Remember to assign the connection factories to the `myserver` target.

Next, we need to set some more properties at the client end. These are the values the clients need to get a reference to the administered JMS objects:

```
<property name="host" value="t3://localhost:7001"/>
<property name="topic" value="myTopic"/>
<property name="initctx" value="weblogic.jndi.T3InitialContextFactory"/>
<property name="connfac" value="TCFactory"/>
```

Now we can run the program as a publisher or subscriber using the Ant targets:

```xml
<target name="JMSLogExample.sub" depends="examples">
  <java
      classname="examples.jlogexamples.jms.JMSLogExample"
      fork="yes"
      classpath="${framework_examples_classpath}"
  >
    <arg value="${host}"/>
    <arg value="${initctx}"/>
    <arg value="${topic}"/>
    <arg value="${connfac}"/>
    <arg value="subscriber" />
  </java>
</target>


<target name="JMSLogExample.pub" depends="examples">
  <java
      classname="examples.jlogexamples.jms.JMSLogExample"
      fork="yes"
      classpath="${framework_examples_classpath}"
  >
    <arg value="${host}"/>
    <arg value="${initctx}"/>
    <arg value="${topic}"/>
    <arg value="${connfac}"/>
    <arg value="publisher" />
  </java>
</target>
```

To get the program running as a subscriber, type ant JMSLogExample.sub:

```
Command Prompt - ant JMSLogExample.sub

C:\ProJMS\Chapter09>ant JMSLogExample.sub
Searching for build.xml ...
Buildfile: C:\ProJMS\Chapter09\build.xml

frameworkprepare:

framework:
    [javac] Compiling 21 source files to C:\ProJMS\Chapter09\build

examples:
    [javac] Compiling 2 source files to C:\ProJMS\Chapter09\build

JMSLogExample.sub:
    [java] Creating topic connection.
    [java] Creating topic session.
    [java] Creating topic subscriber
    [java]
    [java] Waiting for messages to be published to topic: myTopic
    [java]
```

Then start up the publisher in a new window by typing ant `JMSLogExample.pub`:

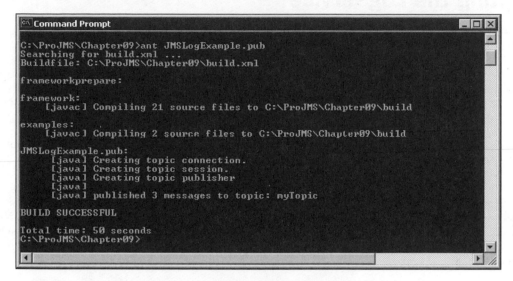

Then go back to the previous screen, and you will see the logging output come through:

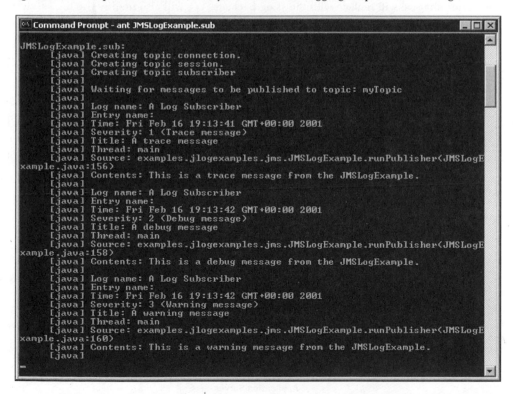

Our logging system has informed us that three messages were published to the topic `myTopic`.

Creating the LogService

In order to make a logging package useful it needs to be easy and convenient for developers to configure and use. This can be accomplished by providing a logging service within a server-side application framework that will abstract out a lot of the configuration and setup issues related to providing a logging service.

For our purposes here I have chosen to use and extend a lightweight, vendor-independent framework for abstracting out server-side development problems.

The system used here adds to an implementation authored by Humphrey Sheil in an article published in the September 2000 issue of *JavaWorld*. The relevant article can be found at http://www.javaworld.com/javaworld/jw-09-2000/jw-0929-ejbframe.html.

Its purpose is to locate and initialize basic service components that exist as tools for enterprise application developers. Some examples of services provided by the basic implementation are: JNDI lookup, database connection manager, configuration service, and of course a logging service. Each service uses a specific configuration file for initialization. `LogService` will use a configuration file called `LogService.properties`.

The logging service within the original implementation is a very simple and non-distributed implementation that we will replace with the JLog package. We will also modify the log service component so that it can handle the added complexity of configuring and managing distributed application logs and the various logging options that we want to implement.

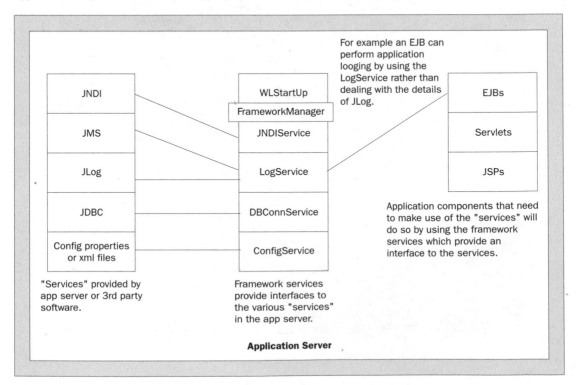

The above diagram gives a high level overview of how the framework fits into the overall picture of an application server and the service it provides to Java enterprise software components. It's important to understand in this relationship that the framework services are available to all applications running within the application server's Java virtual machine, and the "framework manager" is responsible for initializing these services. It does this by "discovering" the services through the use of the Java Reflection API.

For more information regarding the specifics of how the core framework is designed please reference Humphrey Sheil's JavaWorld article.

The following class diagram provides an overall view of the relationships that exist within the framework:

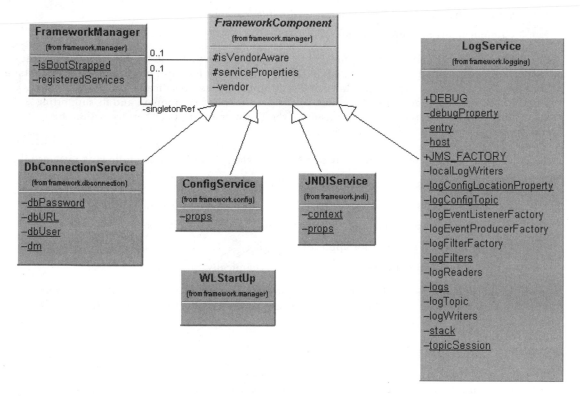

As you can see from the above diagram, each service class extends a base `FrameworkComponent` class that the `FrameworkManager` is responsible for initializing. The `FrameworkManager` class uses the Singleton pattern (see below) in that there is only ever one instance of it.

From "Design Patterns" by Gamma, et al., 1995: "Singletons ensure a class only has one instance, and provide a global point of access to it."

The only class left in the diagram is the `WLStartUp` class. This is a WebLogic Startup class that the application server can call at startup that will initialize the entire framework.

For the rest of the chapter our main focus will be on the `LogService` component of this framework, although we will use the `JNDIService` component to accomplish some of what we need to do in building a configurable `LogService`.

429

The Requirements

The first thing we should do to is to determine what our `LogService` must do. Our previous JMS logging example will help us to determine some of what our new functionality should be. In our example there were many tasks that the example had to undertake before it could begin any actual logging. Examples of these tasks include:

❑   Use of JNDI to lookup objects

❑   Initialization of JMS objects

❑   Specification of a logging topic

❑   Configuring JLog component output media (file, console)

❑   Configuring JLog output formats (XML, HTML, LONG)

None of the above tasks need to be performed by all applications that wish to utilize logging. So the above tasks are abstracted into services. All JNDI services (object lookups, object binding) are contained within the `JNDIService` component. Initialization of JMS objects, specification of a logging topic, and configuring JLog components are all handled by the `LogService` component and its supporting classes. This goes back to our earlier discussion of the Façade pattern. Each service within this framework is an implementation of that pattern.

After some analysis we determine that our `LogService` class should have the following responsibilities:

❑   Retrieve configuration information for itself and for log instances

❑   Initialize JMS components for use with JLog's `JMSLog` components

❑   Create JLog components (readers, writers, filters) via factory classes

❑   Provide interface methods for application logging

❑   Allow modification of the service properties dynamically

Looking at the first item on our list, we need a way to retrieve configuration information for our `LogService` as well as for the different log instances that the `LogService` will create for applications to use for logging messages.

LogService Configuration

For each service that exists within the application framework there is a properties file used to hold configuration information for each respective service. For the `LogService` there are two properties within its `logservice.properties` file:

❑   `debug`
    The global DEBUG flag for the LogService. This provides its initial value upon startup. It can be toggled through JMS as we'll see later.

❑   `logconfiglocation`
    The location of the XML log configuration file. This file contains configuration information detailing what kind of application logs should be created by the LogService upon initialization. We will look more closely at this file in the next section.

Here is a sample configuration for `logservice.properties`:

```
logconfiglocation=config\\mydomain\\logconfig\\logconfig.xml
debug=true
```

XML Configuration File

We tell the `LogService` what types of application logs we'd like with an XML configuration file. Let's take a quick look at a sample XML configuration file and then we'll go over the options available to you when configuring a log instance:

```
<?xml version="1.0"?>

<!DOCTYPE doctype SYSTEM "logconfig.dtd">

<LOGSERVICE>
  <LOG name-"testlog" usefilter="true">
    <DISTRIBUTED datatype="object">
      <READ>
        <MEDIA>
          <CONSOLE format="XML"/>
        </MEDIA>
      </READ>
      <WRITE/>
    </DISTRIBUTED>
  </LOG>

</LOGSERVICE>
```

Let's step through each element in the above configuration:

❑ `<LOGSERVICE>`
Always the root element.

❑ `<LOG name="testlog" usefilter="true">`
The `LOG` element indicates a log to be created by LogService. We give it a name that applications will know it by (`testlog`), and indicate that we'd like this log to work as a filter on the `Log.global` log instance, meaning that all log messages sent to the global log with the title `testlog` will be filtered to this log instance.

❑ `<DISTRIBUTED datatype="object">`
This tag indicates that we wish this to be a distributed log, meaning that we'll use JMS for logging messages. We also indicate what the data type will be of the messages (`object`) since JMS supports different types. (This data type needs to match the data type of the corresponding distributed writer.)

❑ `<READ>`
This tag indicates that this LogService should set up a distributed log in read mode to read incoming messages from a JMS topic of the same name as this log instance.

❑ `<MEDIA>`
We must select a media type for the incoming messages to be sent to, along with a format. In this case we're logging in XML format to the console

❑ `<CONSOLE format="XML"/>`
Log output to be in XML.

❑ `<WRITE/>`
This tag indicates that this LogService should set up a distributed log in write mode to send outgoing messages to a JMS topic of the same name as this log instance.

What this log configuration says:

> *Create a filter on the global log for all messages entitled testlog. Make a distributed log reader (meaning that it subscribes to a JMS topic named after this log filter's name) that logs messages to the console in XML format. Also, create a writer that publishes messages to this log topic.*

After all this is interpreted and performed by the `LogService` what we have is a distributed read/write log filter on the global log for messages entitled `testlog`. It is a bit unorthodox to have a distributed log in read/write mode because ideally in a distributed environment one machine would be writing messages to the log while another machine processes those messages. We have created a read/write distributed log just for the sake of demonstration.

Now let's take a look at all the tags that can be used to configure a `LogService`. The simplest way is through looking at the DTD for the XML configuration:

```
<!ELEMENT LOGSERVICE (LOG+)>
```

The `<LOG>` tag represents a single `Log` configuration, and uses the following attributes:

❑ name
Required. This option is used to indicate the name of the log instance.

❑ usefilter
`true` or `false`. This option is used to indicate whether this log instance is to be created as a separate log object or simply as a filter on the global log that will filter messages sent to the global log with a title matching this log's name. The major difference between the two configurations is that using a filter is simply indicating that we're going to use the global log to log messages and that messages logged to the global log with this log's name will be filtered and sent to a different log destination.

❑ global(optional)
`true` or `false`. This option is used to indicate that we wish to simply use the global log for this log instead of creating a new log instance or a filter.

```
<!ELEMENT LOG   (DISTRIBUTED | NONDISTRIBUTED )>
<!ATTLIST LOG  name      CDATA     #REQUIRED
               usefilter CDATA     #IMPLIED
               global    CDATA     #IMPLIED
               a-dtype   NMTOKENS  'usefilter boolean
                                    global    boolean' >
```

The `<DISTRIBUTED>` tag indicates that this log instance will be a distributed `log`. Again this means that a log instance will be created that will make use of JMS either for reading messages from a topic or publishing messages to a topic based on the configuration options described below. When this tag is used one of three configuration options are available as far as READ/WRITE goes:

❑ READ
A log instance will be created that reads messages from a JMS topic

❑ WRITE
A log instance will be created that writes messages to a JMS topic

❑ READ/WRITE
A log instance will be created and both a reader and a writer will be available for this log instance.

```
<!ELEMENT DISTRIBUTED (READ? , WRITE? )>
<!ATTLIST DISTRIBUTED
  datatype (OBJECT | TEXT ) #REQUIRED
>
```

```
<!ELEMENT NONDISTRIBUTED (READ , WRITE )>
```

```
<!ELEMENT READ (MEDIA )>
<!ELEMENT WRITE EMPTY>
```

The following tags are used in conjunction with the <MEDIA> tag. All of the following tags also must have the following mandatory attribute:

```
format (XML, LONG, MEDIUM, SHORT, HTMLLONG, HTMLTABLE) #REQUIRED
```

This option is used to indicate what format all messages will be logged in:

```
<!ELEMENT MEDIA (FILE | CONSOLE)>
<!ELEMENT DATABASE EMPTY>
<!ATTLIST DATABASE table CDATA #REQUIRED
  format (XML | LONG | SHORT | MEDIUM | HTMLLONG | HTMLTABLE ) #REQUIRED
>
```

```
<!ELEMENT FILE EMPTY>
<!ATTLIST FILE
  usedate (true | false) #REQUIRED
  path CDATA #REQUIRED
  format (XML | LONG | SHORT | MEDIUM | HTMLLONG | HTMLTABLE) #REQUIRED
>
```

```
<!ELEMENT CONSOLE EMPTY>
<!ATTLIST CONSOLE
  format (XML | LONG | SHORT | MEDIUM | HTMLLONG | HTMLTABLE ) #REQUIRED
>
```

```
<!ELEMENT NAME EMPTY>
<!ENTITY % true "">
```

Initializing LogService

Now that we've talked about how to set up log instances within the `LogService`'s XML configuration file, the next item on our list is the initialization of the JLog components performed during `LogService`'s initialization. Upon initialization, the `FrameworkManager` will call `LogService`'s constructor. The `LogService` will perform a few tasks within its constructor:

❑ Call the parent `FrameworkComponent` constructor which will load the `logservice.properties` file for this service.

❑ Retrieve references to three different JLog factory objects which we'll talk more about later.

❑ Retrieve the initial value for the DEBUG setting for the LogService, a global toggle switch that can be activated through JMS.

❑ Retrieve the name and location of the logconfig.xml file containing the descriptions of log instances to be created, which we talked about earlier.

❑ Process each log entry contained within the XML configuration file and initialize JLog components accordingly.

❑ Set up the LogService's dynamic configuration ability, which will allow run-time configuration of the service itself. We'll talk more about this dynamic configuration later.

Now let's look at the code for the constructor of the framework.logging.LogService component:

```
public LogService(String inConfigFileName) throws InitializeException {
    // superclass is framework.manager.FrameworkComponent
    super(inConfigFileName);
```

Initialize each of the factory objects used by this service to create various log components:

```
logEventProducerFactory = LogEventProducerFactory.getInstance();
logEventListenerFactory = LogEventListenerFactory.getInstance();
logFilterFactory        = LogFilterFactory.getInstance();
```

Set the global debug initial value:

```
String debug = serviceProperties.getProperty(debugProperty);
DEBUG = Boolean.valueOf(debug).booleanValue();
```

Get the XML log configuration file location:

```
String logConfigFile =
    serviceProperties.getProperty(logConfigLocationProperty);
```

Parse the XML configuration file and receive array of LogProperties, one for each <LOG> object:

```
LogProperties logConfigs[] = parseXmlConfig(logConfigFile);
```

Initialize JMS for distributed logs:

```
initJMS();
```

Process all log configuration entries and create log instances:

```
for(int i = 0; i < logConfigs.length; i++) {
    BootLogger.logDebug(logConfigs[i].toString());
    if (logConfigs[i].isDistributedLog()) {
        setupJMSLog(logConfigs[i]);
    }
    else {
        setupLocalLog(logConfigs[i]);
    }
    BootLogger.logDebug("Log successfully created: " +
      logConfigs[i].getLogName());
}
```

This LogServiceConfig service is a message-driven mechanism for making changes to the service while it's running, which we'll look at towards the end of the chapter:

```
        setupLogServiceConfig(logConfigTopic);
        BootLogger.logDebug("Initialized LogService Config subscriber");
    }
}
```

Looking at the code above there's a couple of things that need to be discussed. First let's talk about the three "factory" objects that are retrieved. As we talked about earlier, the JLog package contains two major interface types: event producers and event listeners. The factory objects `LogEventProducerFactory` and `LogEventListenerFactory` are used by the `LogService` to create objects that implement these interfaces. The third factory is the `LogFilterFactory` that creates objects that implement the `ILogFilter` interface. If you recall our earlier diagram, the `ILogFilter` interface was special in that it extended both the event listener and event producer interfaces, thus we need a factory to create this type of component.

The second item to talk about is the `LogProperties` class. When we parse the log XML configuration file, each Log entry in the file is represented by a `LogProperties` object. So in the `LogService` constructor a method is called to parse the XML configuration and an array of `LogProperties` objects representing each log entry in the configuration file is returned. These `LogProperties` objects are then used in the creation of log components.

The following class diagram shows the `LogService` class with its supporting classes. Additionally, the JLog interfaces that are created by the supporting factory classes are shown to help tie together the relationship between `LogService` and the JLog package:

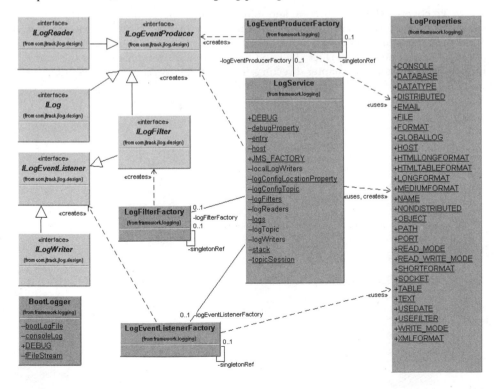

Looking at the diagram above, we can see the `LogService` class that we've been talking about, along with the other classes also that are used to help the `LogService` initialize the various JLog components. As we stated earlier, the `LogService` class contains references to three factory objects. The `LogEventProducerFactory` creates objects that implement the `ILogEventProducer` interface. Examples of classes implementing the `ILogEventProducer` interface are: log readers, logs, and log filters. However, log filters are a bit different, and have a factory dedicated to creating instances of them.

The `LogEventListenerFactory` creates objects that implement the `ILogEventListener` interface. Currently `LogWriter` objects are the only type of class created by this factory.

The final factory class is the `LogFilterFactory`, which is used for creating LogFilter objects implementing the `ILogFilter` interface. Filter objects are special because they implement both the `ILogEventProducer` and `ILogEventListener` interfaces, and are to be thought of more as conduit connecting various other logging components. For example a filter is used to capture log messages meeting specific criteria being sent to a `LogEventProducer` and in turn sending them to a `LogEventListener` desiring those filtered messages.

The final supporting class is the `LogProperties` class. As we stated earlier, it is used to hold the various options available for the creation and configuration of a log instance. The `LogService` class creates and populates instances of `LogProperties` objects on startup. For each entry in the `LogService` XML log configuration, a `LogProperties` object is created and populated with that log's configuration information. Once created, a `LogProperties` object is used in the creation of the various logging components performed by the various factories.

LogService API

Now that we've covered the configuration and initialization of the `LogService` it's time to discuss what interface methods the `LogService` provides for application logging. This is easily accomplished by either inspecting the source code, or browsing the JavaDoc documentation for the framework package. First we need to generate the JavaDocs. To build the JavaDoc documentation for the framework return to a command window and the chapter directory. To build the JavaDoc documentation, we execute the command ant docs for the following target:

```
<target name="docs">
  <mkdir dir="${docs}" />
  <javadoc packagenames="framework.*"
     sourcepath="src"
     destdir="${docs}"
     author="true"
     version="true"
     use="true"
     windowtitle="Enterprise Java Framework"
  />
</target>
```

The documentation is generated and placed into a directory called docs relative to our base directory.

Open the index file and click on the link for the `LogService` class to view the methods that are available for this class.

The important methods to note here as far as an application programmer goes are the various `logXXX()` methods that are available. There are four different levels of severity:

- Trace
- Debug
- Warning
- Error

The other methods provided won't be of much interest to most application programmers but are useful concerning types of log available in the `LogService`. There is also the ability to directly retrieve a `Log` instance and use it, but this would tie anyone using the `Log` instance directly to the JLog package, rather than to our LogService façade, so it's not recommended.

Servlet Example

Now that we've covered what the `LogService` has to offer in the way of functionality let's go through an example of how an Enterprise Java component, in this case a servlet, can use the service.

Let's take a look at the code for the servlet:

```
package examples.frameworkServlet;

import javax.servlet.http.HttpServlet;
import javax.servlet.http.HttpServletRequest;
import javax.servlet.http.HttpServletResponse;
import java.io.PrintWriter;
import java.io.IOException;

import framework.logging.LogService;

public class LoggingServletExample extends HttpServlet {
    int count = 0;

    public void doGet(HttpServletRequest request,
        HttpServletResponse response) {
        LogService.logDebug("examples.frameworkServlet",
            "Entered doGet()");
```

The number of times this servlet is accessed is incremented at each invocation:

```
count++;
LogService.log("examples.frameworkServlet",
    "examplelogservlet accessed " + count + " times.");

try {
    PrintWriter out = response.getWriter();
    out.println("examplelogservlet accessed " + count +
        " times.");
    out.flush();
    out.close();
```

```
        }
        catch(IOException e) {
            LogService.logError("examples.frameworkServlet",
                "Error getting output writer: " + e.getMessage());
        }

        LogService.logDebug("examples.frameworkServlet",
            "Exited doGet()");
    }
}
```

The code for the servlet is very simple and is meant as a simple demonstration of how to use the LogService within a Java application container. You can see that each call to the LogService logXXX() methods pass two parameters; the first is the title of the message, the second the message to be logged. The key thing to note is the title of the message. The title is what's being used to filter messages to the logs for this example. Let's take a look at the XML configuration entries for this example:

```
<LOG name="examples.frameworkServlet" usefilter="true">
  <NONDISTRIBUTED>
    <READ>
      <MEDIA>
        <FILE path="c:\" usedate="false" format="LONG"/>
      </MEDIA>
    </READ>
    <WRITE/>
  </NONDISTRIBUTED>
</LOG>
```

Even though the following two entries essentially make this log a distributed read/write on the same machine which could be accomplished within a single Log entry, the next two entries demonstrate how one Log instance could be set up as a distributed read log on one machine while another machine could setup a distributed write log:

```
<LOG name="examples.frameworkServlet" usefilter="true">
  <DISTRIBUTED datatype="OBJECT">
    <READ>
      <MEDIA>
        <FILE path="C:\" usedate="false" format="XML"/>
      </MEDIA>
    </READ>
  </DISTRIBUTED>
</LOG>
```

We could imagine that this entry is in logconfig.xml on another machine:

```
<LOG name="examples.frameworkServlet" usefilter="true">
  <DISTRIBUTED datatype="OBJECT">
    <WRITE/>
  </DISTRIBUTED>
</LOG>
```

Recall that examples.frameworkServlet is also configured as the name of the JMS topic used as the destination for logging messages in this distributed version.

If you chose the latter `logconfig.xml` entries, then the service messages would be handled by JMS. There are a few steps that need to be taken before running the servlet example. We need to install the servlet and the service framework within our application server. For this example we've used the WebLogic 6.0 server, so the setup will be somewhat specific to that application server but with some modifications to the framework, this example could easily be run with any J2EE-compliant application server. Slight differences in deployment settings and classpaths are easily handled by editing the `build.xml` script.

We first need to tell the server how to install the servlet with the following `web.xml` file:

```xml
<?xml version="1.0" encoding="ISO-8859-1"?>
<!DOCTYPE web-app
    PUBLIC "-//Sun Microsystems, Inc.//DTD Web Application 2.2//EN"
    "http://java.sun.com/j2ee/dtds/web-app_2_2.dtd">
<web-app>
  <servlet>
    <servlet-name>
        examplelogservlet
    </servlet-name>
    <servlet-class>
        examples.frameworkServlet.LoggingServletExample
    </servlet-class>
  </servlet>
  <servlet-mapping>
    <servlet-name>
        examplelogservlet
    </servlet-name>
    <url-pattern>
        /examplelogservlet
    </url-pattern>
  </servlet-mapping>
</web-app>
```

This minimal file tells the server to install our servlet and to make it visible at the address `examplelogservlet` relative to our application URL. We store this file in the same directory as the source code for the servlet. Later it will be bundled into the WAR file and deployed to the server.

The deployment targets for the servlet example are as follows. First we compile the servlet code into a build directory (refer to our original settings for these values):

```xml
<target name="servletmake" depends="framework">
  <javac
    srcdir="${framework_servlet_src}"
    destdir="${framework_servlet_build}"
    classpath="${framework_servlet_classpath}"
  />
</target>
```

Next we build the WAR file `logservlet.war` for the servlet using the class file from our build directory. This is a very simple structure, because it merely contains the servlet class and the basic `web.xml` file above:

```xml
<target name="servletwar" depends="servletmake">
  <war warfile="logservlet.war" webxml="${framework_servlet_src}/web.xml">
    <classes dir="${framework_servlet_build}" />
  </war>
</target>
```

The next step is to make a fresh copy of the service framework in the server installation. This target copies the compiled classes to a new directory under the WebLogic installation. These classes are suitable for including in the run-time classpath of the WebLogic instance, rather than as an specific application library, since we may want them to be available to several client applications:

```
<target name="builddeploy" depends="framework">
  <copy todir="${serverclasses}/framework">
    <fileset dir="${framework_build}/framework"/>
  </copy>
</target>
```

The next step is to copy the WAR file to the application deployment directory. In this case, the directory resolves to C:\bea\wlserver6.0\config\mydomain\applications:

```
<target name="servletexample" depends="servletwar,builddeploy">
  <move file="./logservlet.war" todir="${apphome}"/>
</target>
```

If you go back to the frameworkprepare target of our first simple example, you will see that we have already copied over the relevant configuration files from the config folder of the home directory to the logconfig directory below our application server deployment root. These configuration files consist of:

❑ logservice.properties
  Provides the bootstrap information to access the next file

❑ logconfig.xml
  The configuration file for setting up logging services

❑ logconfig.dtd
  The descriptor file for the XML above, which needs to be available when parsing the configuration file

In addition, there are two futher configuration files used by other services within the framework:

❑ jndiservice.properties
  Used with the system to connect to the messaging provider:

```
framework.weblogic.jndi.url=t3://localhost:7001
framework.weblogic.jndi.factory=weblogic.jndi.T3InitialContextFactory
```

❑ dbconnectionservice.properties
  Connection details to test the database service (used in the EJB example later)

```
dbconnection.properties
framework.db.user=scott
framework.db.password=tiger

framework.db.driver=oracle.jdbc.driver.OracleDriver
framework.db.url=jdbc:oracle:thin:@dbserver:1521:database

framework.db.executesanitycheck=false
```

Concerning the database service, this is not essential to us. Providing that you have a suitable database driver in the classpath, and have configured the lookup URL, username, and password as above, then any database will do. The last property is set to `false` which means that no database access check will be attempted when the service is booting up, and so no corresponding errors will occur if you have not configured this service.

All these files are now located at `C:\bea\wlserver6.0\config\mydomain\logconfig`. The remaining task is to edit the WebLogic startup script (in `mydomain\startWebLogic.cmd`) to provide the appropriate system properties for the service, and to set the classpath.

Check that these directories and JAR files (including `"."`) are in the classpath in this order:

```
.
C:\jaxp-1.1ea2\jaxp.jar
.\lib\weblogic_sp.jar
.\lib\weblogic.jar
.\config\mydomain\serverclasses
C:\jlog\jlog_1_01.jar
C:\jaxp-1.1ea2\crimson.jar
C:\ant\lib\ant.jar
C:\Oracle\Ora81\jdbc\classes111.zip
```

The last library should contain the JDBC driver for your database, which we configured in `dbconnectionservice.properties`. Check that the following system properties are set in the main Java command to start the server. They tell the system where the framework code is, where the boot file for the `LogService` configuration details are, whether to set `DEBUG` on bootup, and whether to exit if there is a problem with the service:

```
-Dframework.rootdir=C:\bea\wlserver6.0\config\mydomain\serverclasses
-Dframework.configdir=C:\bea\wlserver6.0\config\mydomain\logconfig
-Dframework.boot.debug=true
-Dframework.exitoniniterror=false
-Dweblogic.Domain=mydomain
-Dweblogic.Name=myserver
-Dbea.home=C:\bea
-Djava.security.policy==C:\bea\wlserver6.0/lib/weblogic.policy"
-Dweblogic.management.password=%WLS_PW%
```

The very last thing to check is that the boot file `logservice.properties` file is pointing to the right configuration directory. This is a little tricky unless you notice that the WebLogic start up script jumps up two directories before executing the Java runtime. So the location of the configuration file as given in the boot file should be relative to this:

```
logconfiglocation=config\\mydomain\\logconfig\\logconfig.xml
debug=true
```

Note that this extra level of redirection is to accommodate the design of the underlying framework, which requires a similar kind of properties file for each service.

Running the Example

If you made any changes to the WebLogic configuration files, be sure to restart the server so that the changes will take effect. Once you've restarted the server we're ready to try to execute our example. Open up a browser window and enter the URL to point to the machine on which your WebLogic server is running with the path to the example servlet appended (http://localhost:7001/logservlet/examplelogservlet). If everything is working you should see a very simple output in the browser like this:

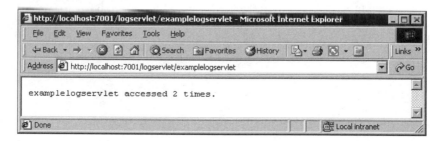

Now let's take a look at the log files generated by running this example. The supplied `logconfig.xml` has two logs setup for this example, a distributed read/write, and a nondistributed log. One of them logs to a file in Long format and the other in XML format. The default setting shipped with the framework creates the files in directory `C:\`.

Examining the contents of the `examples.frameworkServlet.xml` log file, we see the following entries:

```
<LogEntry>
<LogName>examples.frameworkServlet</LogName>
<EntryName></EntryName>
<Time>Thu Feb 15 23:26:20 GMT+00:00 2001</Time>
<Severity>2(Debug message)</Severity>
<Thread>jim1 (192.168.10.75)</Thread>
<Source>examples.frameworkServlet.LoggingServletExample.doGet(LoggingServletExampl
e.java:25)</Source>
<Title>examples.frameworkServlet</Title>
<Contents>Entered doGet()</Contents>
</LogEntry>

<LogEntry>
<LogName>examples.frameworkServlet</LogName>
<EntryName></EntryName>
<Time>Thu Feb 15 23:26:21 GMT+00:00 2001</Time>
<Severity>1(Trace message)</Severity>
<Thread>jim1 (192.168.10.75)</Thread>.
<Source>examples.frameworkServlet.LoggingServletExample.doGet(LoggingServletExampl
e.java:29)</Source>
<Title>examples.frameworkServlet</Title>
<Contents>examplelogservlet accessed 1 times.</Contents>
</LogEntry>

<LogEntry>
<LogName>examples.frameworkServlet</LogName>
<EntryName></EntryName>
<Time>Thu Feb 15 23:26:21 GMT+00:00 2001</Time>
```

```
<Severity>2(Debug message)</Severity>
<Thread>jim1 (192.168.10.75)</Thread>
<Source>examples.frameworkServlet.LoggingServletExample.doGet(LoggingServletExampl
e.java:43)</Source>
<Title>examples.frameworkServlet</Title>
<Contents>Exited doGet()</Contents>
</LogEntry>
```

If you chose a DISTRIBUTED log for the servlet in the logconfig.xml file, then you can check the throughput of messages in the WebLogic console. Navigate to the **Destinations** folder under your JMS Server and select **Monitor all Active JMS Destinations** and you'll see the screen below. You need to have set up the examples.frameworkServlet topic that we mentioned earlier:

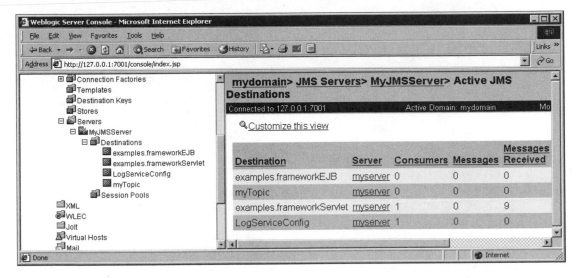

EJB Example

Servlets aren't the only Java enterprise component capable of using the LogService. We'll now look at a simple EJB example that demonstrates how to use the LogService, as well as some of the other services that exist within the framework.

This is the entry in the logconfig.xml for this service:

```
<LOG name="examples.frameworkEJB" usefilter="true">
    <NONDISTRIBUTED>
        <READ>
          <MEDIA>
             <FILE path="C:\" usedate="false" format="LONG"/>
          </MEDIA>
        </READ>
        <WRITE/>
    </NONDISTRIBUTED>
</LOG>
```

Let's take a look at the code for the `FrameworkTesterBean`:

```
package examples.frameworkejb.ejb;

import java.sql.Connection;
import java.sql.ResultSet;
import java.sql.SQLException;
import java.sql.Statement;

import javax.ejb.CreateException;
import javax.ejb.SessionBean;
import javax.ejb.SessionContext;
import javax.naming.InitialContext;
import javax.naming.NamingException;

import framework.dbconnection.DbConnectionService;

import framework.logging.LogService;
import framework.jndi.JNDIService;
import framework.jndi.JNDIServiceLookupException;

public class FrameworkTesterBean implements SessionBean {

    private SessionContext context = null;
```

EJB lifecycle methods:

```
    public void ejbActivate() {}
    public void ejbRemove() {}
    public void ejbPassivate() {}
    public void setSessionContext(SessionContext inContext) {
     this.context = inContext;
    }
```

The following tests the logging, JNDI lookup, and database connectivity within the host application server:

```
    public void ejbCreate() throws CreateException {
        LogService.logDebug("examples.frameworkEJB",
                "FrameworkTesterBean::ejbCreate() ENTRY");

        LogService.logDebug("examples.frameworkEJB",
                "FrameworkTesterBean::ejbCreate() EXIT");
    }
```

This method tests the service availability of the framework from within the EJB:

```
    public void doWork() {
      LogService.logDebug("examples.frameworkEJB",
                "FrameworkTesterBean::doWork ENTRY");
      try {
        FrameworkTesterHome home =
            (FrameworkTesterHome)
                JNDIService.findHome FrameworkTesterHome.JNDI_NAME);
      }
      catch(JNDIServiceLookupException jse) {
        LogService.logError("examples.frameworkEJB",
            "FrameworkTesterBean::ejbCreate(): " +jse);
        jse.printStackTrace();
      }
```

To test the `DBConnectionService` functionality, we look up the database `emp` table:

```
try {
  Statement stmt =
    DbConnectionService.getConnection().createStatement();
  stmt.execute("select * from emp");
  ResultSet rs = stmt.getResultSet();
  while (rs.next()) {
    LogService.logDebug("examples.frameworkEJB",
      rs.getString("empno") + " - " +
      rs.getString("ename")  + " - " +
      rs.getString("deptno"));
  }
}
catch(SQLException se) {
  LogService.logError("examples.frameworkEJB",
    "FrameworkTesterBean::doWork(): " +se);
  se.printStackTrace();
}
LogService.logDebug("examples.frameworkEJB",
    "FrameworkTesterBean::doWork EXIT");
}
}
```

As you can see the implementation is very similar to that of our example servlet as far as the `LogService` is concerned. The only difference between the two examples, in terms of `LogService` use, is the title and contents of the messages we're logging.

To run the following example you need to have successfully set up a database in the `dbconnectionservice.properties` file. We saw an example of this earlier where we assumed an Oracle service available on machine `dbserver` at port 1521, and we use the standard example schema `scott/tiger`, which has an employee table `emp`. If you have a different database available, edit the `dbconnectionservice.properties` file and ensure that the JDBC driver is available in the WebLogic classpath.

To run the EJB example, return to the command-line window at the home directory and execute the command `ant runejbexample`. The targets are executed in the following order. The `ejbmake` target compiles the source code for the EJB:

```
<target name="ejbmake" depends="framework">
  <javac
    srcdir="${framework_ejb_src}"
    destdir="${framework_ejb_build}"
    classpath="${framework_ejb_classpath}"
  />
</target>
```

This depends on the service framework code, which is compiled first. Next, we use Ant's `ejbjar` facility for creating the deployment package. Ant has built-in capability for compiling EJBs for WebLogic (although it uses WebLogic's own EJB compiler):

```
<target name="ejbdeploy" depends="ejbmake, builddeploy">
  <ejbjar srcdir="${framework_ejb_build}" flatdestdir="true"
    descriptordir="${descriptorhome}">
    <weblogic
      destdir="${apphome}"
      classpath="${framework_ejb_classpath}"
    />
    <include name="**/*-ejb-jar.xml"/>
    <exclude name="**/*weblogic*.xml"/>
  </ejbjar>
</target>
```

Note the `destdir` attribute of the `weblogic` tag. This sends the EJB JAR file straight to the server's deployment base where it replaces any previous version and is re-installed automatically by the server. To run the example, we provide command-line arguments to a client test harness `FrameworkTesterMain`, passing in the initial context factory and provider URL:

```
<target name="runejbexample" depends="ejbdeploy">
  <java
    classname="examples.frameworkejb.FrameworkTesterMain"
    fork="yes"
    classpath="${framework_ejb_build};${framework_classpath}"
  >
    <arg value="${host}"/>
    <arg value="${initctx}"/>
  </java>
</target>
```

Note the two arguments consisting of the JNDI parameters necessary to connect to the bean. The output shows the test harness looking up the EJB on WebLogic, and executing a test call:

Recall that the output of the configuration is specified in the `logconfig.xml` file. Here we specified output to a file in `C:\`. Examining the `C:\examples.frameworkEJB.log` file we see a sequence of log outputs like the following. The thread first enters the `ejbCreate()` method of the bean as the container activates the bean instance:

```
Log name: Global System Log
Entry name:
Time: Fri Feb 16 23:50:33 GMT+00:00 2001
Severity: 2 (Debug message)
Title: examples.frameworkEJB
Thread: jim1 (192.168.10.75)
Source: examples.frameworkejb.ejb.FrameworkTesterBean.ejbCreate
    (FrameworkTesterBean.java:62)
Contents: FrameworkTesterBean::ejbCreate() ENTRY

Log name: Global System Log
Entry name:
Time: Fri Feb 16 23:50:33 GMT+00:00 2001
Severity: 2 (Debug message)
Title: examples.frameworkEJB
Thread: jim1 (192.168.10.75)
Source: examples.frameworkejb.ejb.FrameworkTesterBean.ejbCreate
    (FrameworkTesterBean.java:64)
Contents: FrameworkTesterBean::ejbCreate() EXIT
```

Then the test harness calls up the `doWork()` method through the remote handle:

```
Log name: Global System Log
Entry name:
Time: Fri Feb 16 23:50:33 GMT+00:00 2001
Severity: 2 (Debug message)
Title: examples.frameworkEJB
Thread: jim1 (192.168.10.75)
Source: examples.frameworkejb.ejb.FrameworkTesterBean.doWork
    (FrameworkTesterBean.java:73)
Contents: FrameworkTesterBean::doWork ENTRY
```

The database is then queried, and you will get a number of results like these:

```
Log name: Global System Log
Entry name:
Time: Fri Feb 16 23:50:33 GMT+00:00 2001
Severity: 2 (Debug message)
Title: examples.frameworkEJB
Thread: jim1 (192.168.10.75)
Source: examples.frameworkejb.ejb.FrameworkTesterBean.doWork
    (FrameworkTesterBean.java:99)
Contents: 7369 - SMITH - 20

Log name: Global System Log
Entry name:
Time: Fri Feb 16 23:50:33 GMT+00:00 2001
Severity: 2 (Debug message)
Title: examples.frameworkEJB
Thread: jim1 (192.168.10.75)
Source: examples.frameworkejb.ejb.FrameworkTesterBean.doWork
    (FrameworkTesterBean.java:99)
Contents: 7499 - ALLEN - 30
```

447

Finally, the method exits:

```
Log name: Global System Log
Entry name:
Time: Fri Feb 16 23:50:33 GMT+00:00 2001
Severity: 2 (Debug message)
Title: examples.frameworkEJB
Thread: jim1 (192.168.10.75)
Source: examples.frameworkejb.ejb.FrameworkTesterBean.doWork
  (FrameworkTesterBean.java:110)
Contents: FrameworkTesterBean::doWork EXIT
```

If you set up the examples.frameworkEJB topic in WebLogic, then you could run a distributed JMS version of the logging service as we did in the servlet case. Simply edit the logconfig.xml file to define a distributed <LOG> for this service.

So we have seen that once we have done some initial server configuration and installation of the LogService, we can quickly prototype new useful logging services for Java enterprise components.

Using JMS to Enhance the LogService

Now that we have a LogService that is capable of being configured to create application logs, we turn our focus to another problem commonly found in real-world software implementations. It is quite a common occurrence in a production environment that problems are discovered that for one reason or another are difficult or impossible to recreate in a QA or development environment. For this reason it would be convenient if one were able to be given insight into the workings of the production system in a similar fashion to a QA or development environment.

The way to accomplish this is by the use of appropriate debugging or trace statements placed strategically within the software. This is a very common practice when developing software. It is also very common that accompanying statements like these will be a global flag controlling whether or not these statements will be executed. For example:

```
if (LogService.DEBUG) {
    LogService.logDebug("debug statement");
}
```

The variable DEBUG would be a debug flag set somewhere within a class, perhaps by a global DEBUG flag. There are a few different ways in which this flag could be switched within the code. First there is the simple approach, which is "hard-coding" the value to true or false. This method requires code compilation every time debug statements need to be turned on or off. This is not a viable option for software running in a production environment.

The second method is to pass a run-time parameter to the system upon startup, which sets this flag to true or false and remains in that state throughout the life of the application instance. This option is viable in environments where software can be started and stopped without compromising the integrity of an entire system.

The third method is the most advanced method offering the most control. Controlling the flag setting during run time via a configuration tool that can change the value while the software system is up and running without having to restart the entire system. This method is ideal for systems that need to run continuously where it's not convenient to stop the entire system to place it into "debug mode".

The use of JMS will allow us the luxury of dynamically configuring our log service, no matter how many servers we have the service deployed on. All that we need to do is to simply create a JMS topic that our log service will subscribe to and create a tool that can be used to publish configuration settings to this same topic. The following diagram illustrates the concept:

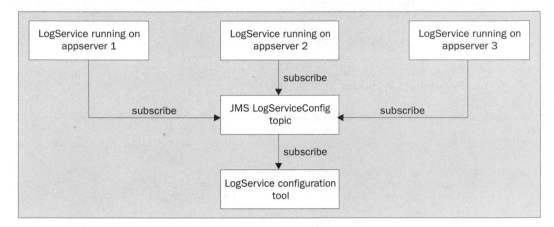

The methods needed to configure the LogService class to accommodate this "dynamic configuration" are shown below. The setupLogServiceConfig() method (contained within the LogService class) is used to set this LogService as a subscriber to the LogServiceConfig JMS topic, which is used to dynamically configure the LogService class:

```
private void setupLogServiceConfig(String topicName)
    throws InitializeException {
```

Set up a subscriber to the LogServiceConfig topic to watch for DEBUG toggle messages:

```
    try {
        Topic topic = getTopic(topicName);
        TopicSubscriber topicSubscriber =
          topicSession.createSubscriber(topic);
        topicSubscriber.setMessageListener(this);
        if(LogService.DEBUG)
           LogService.logDebug("LogService", "successfully initialized " +
             "LogServiceConfig for LogService");
    }
    catch(JMSException e) {
        throw new InitializeException("JMS Error initializing Log " +
          "Service config subscriber", e);
    }
}
```

The above method retrieves the JMS topic and subscribes to it with LogService class being set as the listener. The onMessage() method implements the MessageListener interface and is used to receive configuration messages for this LogService. This object subscribes to a JMS topic that is used to broadcast configuration messages for all LogService objects on all application servers in a cluster:

```
public void onMessage(Message msg) {
    try {
```

Right now we're only implementing one property and we can embed that into the message itself:

```
DEBUG = msg.getBooleanProperty("debug");
LogService.logDebug("LogService",
    "LogService DEBUG set to: " + DEBUG);
if(msg instanceof ObjectMessage) {
```

If we want to use a serialized object to hold configuration info, we implement this in here.

```
    }
    else if (msg instanceof TextMessage) {
```

If we want to use a text message in XML or some other format we implement this here.

```
        }
    }
    catch (JMSException jmse) {
        LogService.logError("LogService", "Error processing " +
        "LogServiceConfig message: " + jmse.getMessage());
    }
}
```

The above method implements the `MessageListener` interface to respond to published messages.

To test your `LogService` and its ability to be configured via JMS messaging, a small GUI tool is included with the framework code for the chapter. Again, we can use Ant to build and run the configurator:

```
<target name="runconfigurator" depends="framework">
  <java
     classname="framework.logging.config.LogServiceConfigurator"
     fork="yes"
     classpath="${framework_build};${framework_classpath}"
  >
    <arg value="${host}"/>
  </java>
</target>
```

Since this is our last `build.xml` entry, we close the `<project>` tag:

```
</project>
```

Note the hostname argument passed to the program; this enables the tool to initialize JMS objects. Remember to add the `LogServiceConfig` topic to WebLogic if you haven't already done so. Start your WebLogic server. Once that is complete, you simply run the test tool by returning to the command window and executing the command `ant runconfigurator`.

After you've run the configuration tool, and it has connected to the WebLogic server, you will be presented a GUI interface like this one:

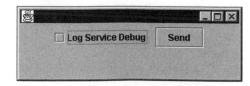

You can now toggle the `LogService` debug mode by simply setting the checkbox and clicking the **Send** button. A log, logging to the console, should have already been set up in the `logconfig.xml` watching the `LogServiceConfig` log. You can see the message confirming the debug setting. However, note that the `LogService` is not actually initialized until the service framework has booted – you'll need to run the EJB or servlet tests to wake it up. The following is sample output from toggling the checkbox and shows the `LogService` receiving the new configuration setting:

```
Log name: Global System Log
Entry name:
Time: Fri Feb 16 03:45:49 GMT+00:00 2001
Severity: 2 (Debug message)
Title: LogService
Thread: jim1 (192.168.10.75)
Source: framework.logging.LogService.onMessage(LogService.java:356)
Contents: LogService DEBUG set to: false

Log name: Global System Log
Entry name:
Time: Fri Feb 16 03:46:05 GMT+00:00 2001
Severity: 2 (Debug message)
Title: LogService
Thread: jim1 (192.168.10.75)
Source: framework.logging.LogService.onMessage(LogService.java:356)
Contents: LogService DEBUG set to: true
```

You are encouraged to investigate and develop the service framework and logging system using the download bundle. Because of restrictions of space, and the complexities involved in integrating all the systems, we have not been able to incorporate all features and possibilities of the logging service in this chapter, but we hope to have provided useful architectural and practical advice on how to set up a distributed logging system.

Summary

There are many logging packages available to be used in application development but when it comes to developing J2EE components in a distributed environment most implementations fall short. The one that we have selected for use in this chapter, JTrack's JLog (http://www.jtrack.com), provides the support needed to implement distributed logging using JMS.

The framework is an attempt to provide enterprise Java application developers a set of useful tools. The `LogService` attempts to enhance the usability of the JLog package, as well as provide a flexible, easily configurable logging tool.

We have met and solved some of the challenges involved in implementing distributed logging service using messaging. In the next chapter we will be looking at how XML can enhance the content and portability of our messaging systems.

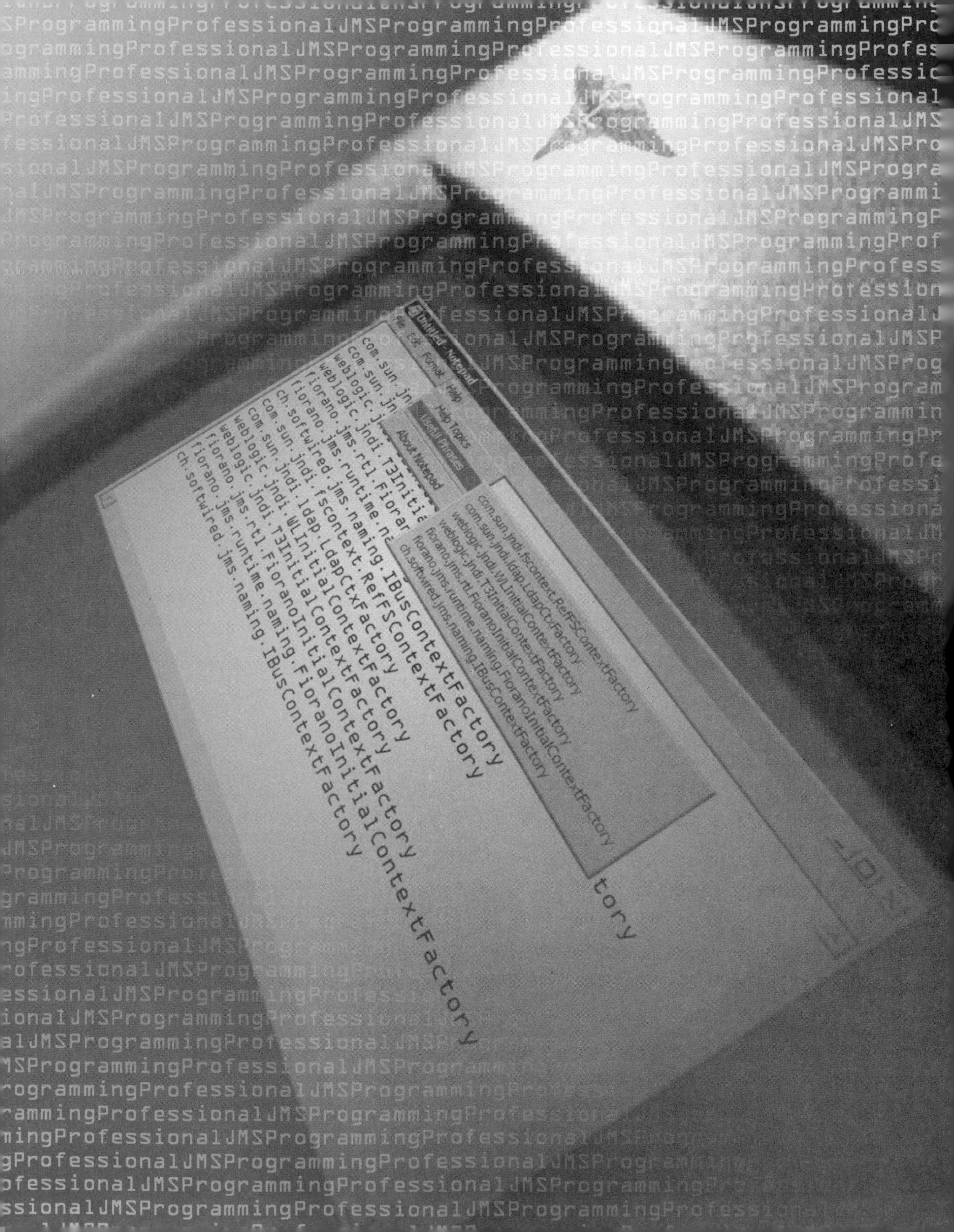

JMSProgrammingProfessional
Untitled - Notepad
File Edit Format Help
Help Topics
Useful Phrases
About Notepad
com.sun.jndi.fscontext.RefFSContextFactory
com.sun.jndi.ldap.LdapCtxFactory
weblogic.jndi.WLInitialContextFactory
weblogic.jndi.T3InitialContextFactory
fiorano.jms.rtl.FioranoInitialContextFactory
fiorano.jms.runtime.naming.FioranoInitialContextFactory
ch.softwired.jms.naming.IBusContextFactory

10

XML Messaging

XML is a hot topic. It seems that every commercial software vendor is announcing support for the **eXtensible Markup Language (XML)** in one form or another. The technology began fairly simply as a means of describing documents, but people quickly realized it had wide application as a generalized way of describing any data. Now, many development organizations are beginning to look to this technology to solve their interoperability problems and provide them with a flexible model for deploying distributed applications. XML is also central to some of the most exciting areas of development on the Internet today, such as the emerging web services arena.

As with any new and rapidly evolving technology, there are a number of design tradeoffs to be made and pitfalls to avoid. The intent of this chapter is to guide newcomers by reviewing the basic concepts behind XML messaging using JMS, and in the process highlight some of the current issues that they should consider when designing JMS applications using XML.

This chapter is broken into four major subsections:

- ❑ *What XML Brings to Messaging:* Here, we will examine the XML value proposition, highlighting why XML is effective as a messaging format, and how it complements JMS by further achieving the goals of this technology.

- ❑ *Parsing and Transformation:* Presents the major parsing paradigms in XML, providing a simple Java example of each using the JAXP API.

- ❑ *XML and JMS:* Looks at the relationship between XML and JMS, and the special considerations that have to be made in bringing these two technologies together.

- ❑ *An XML Router Example:* The example section develops a simple content-based JMS router. This routes and transforms XML messages between queues, based on the value of attributes in an XML message.

XML is a diverse and complex topic, and we really cannot hope to do more than scratch its surface here. For further information on working with XML, we recommend you look at Professional XML ISBN 1-861003-11-0, *also from Wrox Press.*

What XML Brings to Messaging

We have come to recognize the value of XML as a means to manipulate documents, but how can it help in the messaging world and in particular, how can it be applied to a JMS application? Simply put, a message is a document. The advantages of using XML in a simple file-based application apply equally to any messaging application. But there is one even more important quality that is unique to messaging:

> **XML reduces system coupling.**

One of the primary reasons for adopting JMS and the messaging paradigm is to build *loosely coupled* systems that can accommodate the problems associated with networks, availability of other systems, widely changing loads, etc. XML takes this one step further, and reduces coupling in the API.

Coupling Through APIs

The strength of the messaging paradigm is that it has always been highly effective under such constraints as limited system resources or network bandwidth. Messaging, by its nature, promotes a loose coupling between systems, where coupling, in this sense, refers to a number of important characteristics. Messaging, in and of itself, does not always ensure loose coupling; however, it does have a number of qualities – particularly when used in conjunction with XML – that encourage loose coupling.

Systems couple through APIs (here I consider a message *and* its handler to constitute an API). The message is a contract between communicating systems; it defines parameter types and placement, communications overhead, etc. How the handler abstracts the message away affects the degree of coupling. Handlers that are tolerant of minor message changes, such as modifications to versioning information, or the addition of fields to support parametric polymorphism etc., promote loose coupling. Changes made to a server, for example, may not necessitate simultaneous changes on all clients. Loosely coupled APIs typically exploit late binding of message content to the local type system.

> *Late binding of messages refers to when message contents are converted to native types in a language like Java. For example, when you compile a program in Java or C++, the compiler checks to ensure that the types in the call are consistent with at least one of the method signatures. This ensures that simple syntactic typing errors are caught early, but it does comes at the expense a certain amount of flexibility and adaptability to change. A system that exploits late binding is one in which the decision about what content maps to what type is made at run time. Late binding is a double-edged sword; on one hand, you have flexibility to adapt to changing interfaces on the fly; on the other, you must ensure that your program can handle the ambiguous cases.*

In contrast, tightly coupled APIs are intolerant of changes to the contract. These are typically statically type-checked at compile time, which promotes type safety but provides little flexibility and potential for adaptation. Critics charge that such APIs are "brittle" – that is, any change made to the message or to any handler behavior requires that all participants be changed at the same time. This can be very expensive if there are a large number of clients using the interface.

Coupling also refers to the relative independence of the two systems. In a loosely coupled environment, the remote system's hardware, OS, network protocol, or even the language the application is written in should not be important – or indeed even necessary – details of concern to developers.

Coupling also refers to communications style, which is often dictated by the capabilities of the transport layer. Systems that exhibit tight coupling at the communications layer demand that servers be available when a client sends a message to them; if a server is unavailable, then the client must immediately take corrective action. Furthermore, such clients typically expect servers to deliver reply messages synchronously. In contrast, loosely coupled systems can easily tolerate an unavailable server. Messages may be queued for later deliver, when the server becomes available. Clients, if they expect a reply at all, expect asynchronous delivery.

Loose coupling clearly had benefits in a networked world of questionable reliability. Historically, it promoted a much more coarsely grained model of distributed computing and parallelism than we see now; programs tended to be standalone, the communications peer-to-peer rather than client-server. Development of each application-peer was handled independently, and often by different groups.

As networks matured, development tools and programming techniques became more sophisticated, and tight coupling became more prevalent. Developers shifted their focus to client/server systems, where the attention was on distributed processing within network-spanning applications. The entire interaction, client to server and back again, became the singular focus, with end-to-end responsibility often falling to one group.

What is interesting is that the very factors that gave rise to messaging in the first place are what fuel its current resurgence. Business wants to interact with other business across the Internet. Each organization wants to be responsible for administering only its systems. It wants to be flexible to accommodate continuously shifting requirements. It does not necessarily trust its trading partners to be reliable. And it wants to do it over the public Internet, which notwithstanding the phenomenal success of the Web is notoriously unreliable.

XML Refresher

This chapter will assume a prior knowledge of basic XML concepts. However, in the following section, we will briefly review some of the important details of XML that will be needed to understand some of the later examples, including DTDs, schemas, and namespaces.

We will use the following simple profile data as a basis for examining these:

Name	John Smith
Address	123 Main St
Phone	+1 (555) 555-1212
Credit Card #1 Number	1234567890
Credit Card #1 Expiry	12/02
Credit Card #2 Number	9876543210
Credit Card #2 Expiry	06/03

The Document

Our profile data, rendered as a simple XML document, would look like the following:

```xml
<?xml version="1.0" encoding="UTF-8"?>
<Profile>
  <Name>John Smith</Name>
  <Address>123 Main St</Address>
  <Phone>+1 (555) 555-1212</Phone>
  <CreditCardList>
    <Card>
      <Number>1234567890</Number>
      <Expiry>12/02</Expiry>
    </Card>
    <Card>
      <Number>9876543210</Number>
      <Expiry>06/03</Expiry>
    </Card>
  </CreditCardList>
</Profile>
```

Here, we have several levels of structure, including a credit card list with two distinct items. This is a well-formed document, meaning that all opening tags have a corresponding closing tag and there is no tag overlap. This version of the document does not have an associated schema (validation will be reviewed in the next sections), so none of the values have any typing. All data types must be assumed to be strings. The encoding scheme uses Unicode (http://www.unicode.org), the global encoding standard. This makes it a particularly good match for applications written in Java, which uses 16-bit Unicode character encoding (other languages, such as Visual Basic and C++, can of course manipulate Unicode text).

The DTD

A DTD internal subset (that is, a syntactic description embedded in the document) for the profile document looks like the following:

```xml
<?xml version="1.0" encoding="UTF-8"?>
<!DOCTYPE  Profile [
   <!ELEMENT Profile (Name, Address, Phone, CreditCardList)>
   <!ELEMENT Name (#PCDATA)>
   <!ELEMENT Address (#PCDATA)>
   <!ELEMENT Phone (#PCDATA)>
   <!ELEMENT CreditCardList (Card+)>
   <!ELEMENT Card (Number, Expiry)>
   <!ELEMENT Number (#PCDATA)>
   <!ELEMENT Expiry (#PCDATA)>
]>
<Profile>
   <Name>John Smith</Name>
   <Address>123 Main St</Address>
   <Phone>+1 (555) 555-1212</Phone>
   <CreditCardList>
      <Card>
         <Number>1234567890</Number>
         <Expiry>12/02</Expiry>
```

```
        </Card>
        <Card>
           <Number>9876543210</Number>
           <Expiry>06/03</Expiry>
        </Card>
    </CreditCardList>
</Profile>
```

Profile is a pretty simple document, so most of the DTD can be figured out from context. The ELEMENT tag defines the name of each element, and its content. The terminal elements, such as Name, Address, etc. have a content type of parsed character data (#PCDATA) – basically arbitrary text strings. Using DTDs, elements can be empty; they can contain other elements; they can contain PCDATA; or elements can contain a mixed content, meaning that they are composed of other elements and character data. One of the fundamental problems with DTDs is that they do not really add strong typing to XML; everything pretty much remains a string. This problem is solved by XML Schema, which we will touch on briefly in the next section.

Here is an example document demonstrating both entities and attributes in DTDs:

```
<?xml version="1.0" encoding="UTF-8"?>
<!DOCTYPE Document [
    <!ELEMENT Document (#PCDATA)>
    <!ATTLIST Document docVersion CDATA #REQUIRED>
    <!ENTITY insertName "John Smith" >
]>
<Document docVersion="1.23">
    Dear &insertName;,
    It has come to our attention...
</Document>
```

You can load this document into a web browser that will parse the file, check it is well-formed, validate it against the DTD, and display it rendered with a default style sheet. The result will look similar to the following (note that in Internet Explorer, XML is rendered nicely in colour using a default style sheet):

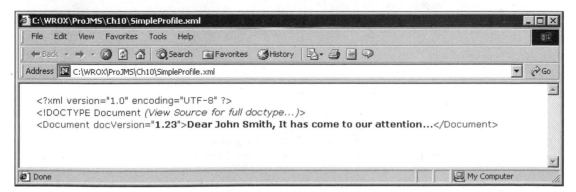

The Schema

We will not delve into the XML Schema specification in detail. To get a sense of what it offers, here is an example of an external schema document for the profile document:

```xml
<?xml version="1.0" encoding="UTF-8" ?>
<!--
W3C Schema generated by XML Spy v3.5 NT (http://www.xmlspy.com)
-->

<xsd:schema xmlns:xsd="http://www.w3.org/2000/10/XMLSchema"
    elementFormDefault="qualified">
  <xsd:element name="Address" type="xsd:string" />
  <xsd:element name="Card">
    <xsd:complexType>
      <xsd:sequence>
        <xsd:element ref="Number" />
        <xsd:element ref="Expiry" />
      </xsd:sequence>
    </xsd:complexType>
  </xsd:element>
  <xsd:element name="CreditCardList">
    <xsd:complexType>
      <xsd:sequence>
        <xsd:element ref="Card" maxOccurs="unbounded" />
      </xsd:sequence>
    </xsd:complexType>
  </xsd:element>
  <xsd:element name="Expiry" type="xsd:string" />
  <xsd:element name="Name" type="xsd:string" />
  <xsd:element name="Number" type="xsd:string" />
  <xsd:element name="Phone" type="xsd:string" />
  <xsd:element name="Profile">
    <xsd:complexType>
      <xsd:sequence>
        <xsd:element ref="Name" />
        <xsd:element ref="Address" />
        <xsd:element ref="Phone" />
        <xsd:element ref="CreditCardList" />
      </xsd:sequence>
    </xsd:complexType>
  </xsd:element>
</xsd:schema>
```

This schema was generated based on an example profile document using XMLSpy (http://www.xmlspy.com), a very popular commercial XML editor. Most of it is self-evident; this clarity is one of the strong points of XML Schema. Notice the use of the namespace `xsd:` preceding all of the elements. Namespaces exist to group and disambiguate elements – though sometimes, as here, they do affect readability. In this example, the `xsd` namespace clearly classifies all elements as being in the Schema namespace (more on namespaces below).

Namespaces

Namespaces were introduced to XML to resolve the ambiguities that naturally occur when you give everyone the flexibility to choose their own tag names: inevitably, people choose very similar names, which can potentially be the cause of confusion. Consider our own profile:

```
<Profile>
    <Name>John Smith</Name>
    <Address>123 Main St</Address>
    <Phone>+1 (555) 555-1212</Phone>
    <CreditCardList>
        <Card>
            <Name>Visa</Name>
            <Number>1234567890</Number>
            <Expiry>12/02</Expiry>
        </Card>
        <Card>
            <Name>MasterCard</Name>
            <Number>9876543210</Number>
            <Expiry>06/03</Expiry>
        </Card>
    </CreditCardList>
</Profile>
```

Here, the credit card name was added in an element Name, a subordinate to Card. Maybe this happened because we tried to reuse a previously defined structure. Unfortunately, we have already made use of the Name tag for the person's name. How can we disambiguate between the two when we are searching for name? (This problem will become more obvious as we look at some simple parsing examples further on.)

Namespaces allow us to resolve this ambiguity by associating tags and attributes with a unique identifier:

```
<Profile xmlns:personal="someURI"
         xmlns:cc="someOtherURI">
    <personal:Name> John Smith </personal:Name>
    <personal:Address> 123 Main St </personal:Address>
    <personal:Phone> +1 (555) 555-1212 </personal:Phone>
    <personal:CreditCardList>
        <cc:Card>
            <cc:Name>Visa</cc:Name>
            <cc:Number>1234567890</cc:Number>
            <cc:Expiry>12/02</cc:Expiry>
        </cc:Card>
        <cc:Card>
            <cc:Name>MasterCard</cc:Name>
            <cc:Number>9876543210</cc:Number>
            <cc:Expiry>06/03</cc:Expiry>
        </cc:Card>
    </personal:CreditCardList>
</Profile>
```

Here, we have used the reserved name xmlns to define two unique namespaces. These are assigned the aliases personal and cc, which can be used to qualify tags and attributes. The namespaces are distinct because they are bound to different URIs. Usually, such URIs take the form of a URL indicating a unique resource on the Internet.

459

*A Uniform Resource Identifier (URI) is a unique name for a resource, where a resource could be an HTML page, a program, a video clip, etc. A **Uniform Resource Locator (URL)** is a URI that explicitly identifies the protocol to access the resource, and a location on the Internet. The W3C defines a Uniform Resource Name as a URI with, "an institutional commitment to persistence, availability, etc.", meaning that while the physical location of a resource may change, it can still be located through the institution. For more information, see the W3C overview of naming and addressing at http://www.w3.org/Addressing.*

Needless to say, being forced to qualify every element can become pretty tiresome. Fortunately, XML provides the concept of a default namespace. Any specific namespace can override this default. For example:

```
<Profile xmlns="someURI"
         xmlns:cc="someOtherURI">
   <Name>John Smith</Name>
   <Address>123 Main St</Address>
   <Phone>+1 (555) 555-1212</Phone>
   <CreditCardList>
      <cc:Card>
         <cc:Name>Visa</cc:Name>
         <cc:Number>1234567890</cc:Number>
         <cc:Expiry>12/02</cc:Expiry>
      </cc:Card>
      <cc:Card>
         <cc:Name>MasterCard</cc:Name>
         <cc:Number>9876543210</cc:Number>
         <cc:Expiry>06/03</cc:Expiry>
      </cc:Card>
   </CreditCardList>
</Profile>
```

The first namespace, previously called `personal` has had its alias removed. This implies it is now the default namespace for all tags not otherwise overridden by the `cc` alias.

Namespaces were introduced after the XML 1.0 specification. There is no support for them in DTDs, but as we have observed, XML Schema is namespace-aware. Some parsers do not acknowledge namespaces, notably those that only support DOM Level 1 or SAX 1. In general, namespaces will not cause these parsers to fail, but you will have to dissect the prefixes on your own.

XHTML

One of the problems with HTML is that while it looks like XML, it actually isn't. There are a number of HTML constructs that are valid from the perspective of the HTML schema, but which result in documents that are not well formed, and thus violate the basic tenet of XML. As a result, much of the emerging technology being built to process XML, including editors, cannot be used to produce and validate HTML. Often, the solution of vendors and standards groups is to treat HTML as a special case – the DOM is a good example of this.

Consider, for example, the HTML `IMG` tag:

```
<IMG SRC="car.jpg" WIDTH="128" HEIGHT="128">
```

This is perfectly valid HTML; however, the missing closing tag for the `IMG` element will cause most XML parsers to reject it.

The W3C has recognized this problem and is defining HTML 5 as valid XML. The result, called XHTML, will enforce the XML well-formedness constraint. For more information, see http://www.w3.org/MarkUp.

The Message as an API

Message formats are a contract, an API, between communicating systems. Formats and business processes associated with them are agreed on through a process of negotiation between stakeholders on each side of the transaction. For example, a stock exchange system might be developed to accept orders sent as messages in the following simple format:

```
Operation    Stock    Number
BuyStock     Wrox     1000
SellStock    Wrox     500
```

Here we are naming a service (in this base `BuyStock` or `SellStock`), and including two parameters required by this service. The result might be a status message:

```
Status
OK
Failed
```

What we have done here is defined a simple API for a stock exchange system. However, as developers we have become accustomed to thinking of an API in terms of objects or procedures. We think about classes, methods, overloading, typing, etc. Therein lies part of the problem: in Java, or other high-level languages, the syntax has been well defined. We do not have to worry how we are going to delimit the parts of the data – we simply use commas in a method call, packaging our parameter list in parenthesis. Syntax and typing are an implicit part of the language, and compilers are great at catching syntax and type errors. In traditional messaging, however, it is up to the developers to define much of this.

The problems with this style of messaging fall into four broad categories:

❑ Structure

❑ Parsing and Validation

❑ Typing and Encoding

❑ Bandwidth and Resource Conservation

Each of these will be examined in the following sections.

Structure

Traditional messaging systems suffered from a lack of standardization defining how structures should be rendered, and even how they should be documented. This often leads to groups developing completely proprietary, idiosyncratic message delimiting schemes. For example, with our simple stock exchange API, we are using commas to delimit parameters. How would we extend our API to accept a variable length list of repeated stocks and numbers? We could simply append them:

```
Operation, Stock, Number, Stock, Number, Stock, Number, ..., Stock, Number
```

Or alternatively use additional special characters to create a list-like structure:

```
Operation, {[Stock, Number], [Stock, Number], ..., [Stock, Number]}
```

Neither of these is particularly elegant. Furthermore, neither lends itself well to applying the principles of object-oriented design. We are overloading the operation interface, but we aren't really encapsulating data effectively.

Sometimes message structure simply directly maps structure from high-level languages. For example, in an exchange between two systems both running C compilers on identical machines (same OS, same word length), the structure may simply be a serialized `struct`. It isn't human readable, but it is recoverable on the other machine.

With no standard means of defining structure in messages, negotiation between groups defining an API will often focus on issues of syntax, rather than the content, which is ultimately quite a bit more important.

Parsing and Validation

If there is no standardization of how messages are structured, then parsers are going to be incompatible, and everyone will generally have to write and maintain their own. This can create a huge maintenance and deployment issue. Consider the case where two businesses are exchanging messages using a pre-defined schema. Generally, these businesses will maintain their own applications; this implies that both have their own parsers that must functionally track each other. As messages evolve, how are they versioned? How do parsers handle versions of messages that they have never encountered?

The code to do message validation is often deeply embedded in parsing code. For example:

```
BuyStock, Wrox, X
BuyStock, Wrox X
```

In the first example, the X here should be numeric according to the rules we have defined. In the second example, the comma delimiter is missing, so the program may be assuming the stock name is "Wrox X". Unfortunately, a large number of programs validate implicitly as they parse, rather than validating against some kind of template that can easily be modified to accommodate changes to the message. Such interfaces are often characterized as brittle because of how susceptible they are to failure if a message is modified.

If we do have such a template, how should it be distributed among parties that need it? Copies could be replicated among all systems processing the message; a central repository could be set up; it could even be embedded in messages. Although each of these is possible, there has been no standard way of implementing any of these strategies.

Typing and Encoding

Character encoding has always been an issue with traditional messaging systems. Many text-based message systems did not support Unicode originally, which made it very difficult to transmit messages containing localized language strings. There have been significant character set issues among systems in the past. Translations from ASCII to IBM's EBCIDC are commonplace in many large messaging environments.

Type binding between languages can be the source of numerous problems. When two systems want to exchange a floating-point value via a message, they must agree on how to render the value in the message so it can be bound into their local type systems. Standards do exist for some simple types. ISO, for example, has defined standard representations for time. However, in general, if you needed a comprehensive type-binding scheme, you had to look at something like CORBA-IDL.

Bandwidth and Resource Conservation

Traditional messaging has always encouraged terseness in messages to accommodate low bandwidth communications links. Although the explosive growth of the Internet has allowed us to become less restrictive in our use of bandwidth, there is still a tendency for message designers to highly optimize messages, densely packing in as much data as possible to maximize information content for the lowest possible bandwidth. This has led to a number of messaging protocols that are machine understandable at the expense of human readability. There are some applications that demand such packaging to sustain real-time-like performance – multi-player game environments come to mind. However, ultimately, this does make it difficult to track problems by inspecting the message flow. Anyone who has tried to track a CORBA message dialog can readily attest to this.

The XML Solution

Using XML as a basis for message formats can eliminate most of these problems, and thus promote loose coupling between systems. There are a number of important reasons for this, which we will expand on in the following sections. These are:

- ❑   XML is language- and platform-independent

- ❑   XML is standards-based

- ❑   XML is extensible

- ❑   XML is flexible

- ❑   XML has rich structures

- ❑   XML uses Unicode

- ❑   XML has a powerful validation model

- ❑   XML is human readable, and machine understandable

On its own, no single point is compelling enough to change how messaging is done. Taken as a whole, though, it is hard to argue against using XML for messaging.

Language and Platform Independence

XML is not tied to any language, operating system, networking protocol, hardware, or – possibly most important of all – vendor. From the beginning, the architects of XML recognized that to be successful, XML would have to be the common means of describing data between vastly different systems.

Of course, vendors will always attempt to differentiate their products by adding features. Furthermore, since the specifications are evolving very rapidly, it is easy to become locked into enhancements or limitations of a particular product. However, the neutrality of the basic recommendations is extremely important.

Standards-Based

The W3C is responsible for the standardization of XML. The word XML actually describes a diverse and evolving family of technologies and standards into which new features and refinements are continuously added. But the core technology is actually very stable and mature. Out of this has come a rich assortment of tooling from vendors and the open source movement. This means that developers do not have to write parsers – production-quality parsers are available in almost every language. Most of these come at no charge and with unrestrictive distribution licenses. Developers do not have to build specialized message editors that are aware of the nuances of their vocabulary because there are many of these already in existence.

With a standard already defined and tools widely available that support it, developers can concentrate on building good APIs and flexible messaging vocabularies to solve the problem at hand, rather than building infrastructure and arguing over message structuring rules. This focuses messaging projects on the content of the transactions, which is ultimately where the challenges are.

> *The similarities between XML and HTML are not coincidental. Both actually derive from a common ancestor, the Standardized General Markup Language (SGML). Like XML, SGML allowed users to add structure to documents independent of presentation. Stylistic transforms could then be applied to add presentation details. SGML saw use in government and technical publishing; however it is very complicated and expensive to support.*

Extensibility

XML places few restrictions on how element tags and attributes are named. Developers are free to give tags meaningful names, so that messages can become self-documenting. It provides much the same freedom that we have in choosing descriptive object and variable names in high-level languages. Parsers are really only interested in structure, so need no modifications to accommodate changes in document organization.

Flexibility

XML applications tend to be very forgiving when changes are made to documents. For example, returning to our profile example, suppose a new element, `City` was introduced, but our application that processes it was not changed:

```
<Profile>
    <Name>John Smith</Name>
    <Address>123 Main St</Address>
    <City>Any Town</City>
    <Phone>+1 (555) 555-1212</Phone>
    <CreditCardList>
        <Card>
            <Number>1234567890</Number>
            <Expiry>12/02</Expiry>
        </Card>
        <Card>
            <Number>9876543210</Number>
            <Expiry>06/03</Expiry>
        </Card>
    </CreditCardList>
</Profile>
```

The document remains well formed, so the parser will not report any exceptions. Depending on how they are constructed, most XML applications will simply use the parser to mine the information they need. In general, a new field will be ignored. This may not be the desired behavior; however, it does demonstrate that the system is more resilient to change. Consider, for example, a Publish/Subscribe application using XML messages. New elements could be added to the messages without breaking subscribers that have not been updated to specifically make use of the new elements.

The message validation process may flag the change, but we can choose to ignore validation errors due to added elements that we intend to ignore.

Rich Structures

XML supports rich structures with deep, hierarchical nesting and a model for containing repeated elements. One of the few demands that XML makes is that documents must be well formed. This simple demand actually greatly simplifies document processing and general legibility: one can infer meaning from inspection of a well-designed XML document. HTML, in contrast, does not have to be well formed, and thus is often difficult to parse, to edit, and too often to follow.

The XML strategy of defining hierarchies that contain data maps elegantly onto the data structures of most languages, making XML a good choice as a serialization format for languages like Java or C++.

Unicode Support

One of XML's most visible benefits is that the documents are plain text. They can be read by humans, and edited with a simple text editor. This has been extremely important for interoperability between systems, as virtually all computers support some kind of text encoding. However, even something like defining the bindings between binary values and characters has been a contentious issue in the computing community. ASCII encoding is popular because of the tremendous success of PCs and UNIX systems; however, alternative coding like IBM's EBCDIC is very common in mainframe and midrange computer environments.

Internationalization has always been an important requirement for XML. Encoding schemes like ASCII are really only appropriate for supporting languages that use the Latin alphabet. Other character sets exist, which support other languages; however, a truly global encoding solution needs to be able to potentially support all characters from a single encoding scheme. XML addresses these issues by adopting Unicode as the base character encoding scheme for text.

Validation Model

XML can solve some difficult problems in message structural and content validation. In particular, it decouples validation from the parser; the implication of this is that changes to the document structure or content do not force changes on the parser, only to an external grammar that defines the rules that a document must follow to be valid. Recompilation and linking of parser modules to accommodate message schema changes is not necessary; instead, XML allows a very late binding between message handlers and validation model. Naturally, this lowers code maintenance costs enormously, but it also provides great flexibility in an environment where message formats can evolve continuously.

DTDs provide a means of describing the structure of an XML document. Most XML parsers can optionally be set to validate a document against a DTD, which may be integrated within the document or stored separately. Actual content validation is more complex. XML inherently is weakly typed; everything in an XML document is a string. Weak typing is not necessarily always a bad thing: virtually every developer has a favorite scripting language they use to get things done quickly. Scripting languages are inherently weakly typed, but they can be used to great advantage in rapid application development. Nevertheless, when moving to enterprise class applications with large teams of developers, weak typing in a language can become a serious liability.

DTDs do little to remedy XML's weak typing, describing no more than structural organization and string content models. XML Schema, however, adds support for simple types, enumerations, ordered lists, and inheritance to messages undergoing validation. This is useful as a contractual basis for type bindings between XML messages and strongly typed, high-level languages like Java and C++. There are already some commercial and open-source tools that automatically generate utility classes for marshaling and unmarshaling between XML messages and the aforementioned object-oriented languages. This will be examined in detail in the section about Java/XML data binding, later in the chapter.

Schema Distribution Model

If you do have a schema language that effectively decouples validation from parsing, how do you distribute the schema? There are three options:

- ❑ Embedded schemas
- ❑ Locally replicated schemas
- ❑ Schema repositories

XML supports all three models. Using DTDs as an example of a schema description, the schema document could embed the schema:

```
<?xml version="1.0" ?>
<!DOCTYPE Profile [
<!ELEMENT Profile (Name, Address, Telephone)>
<!ELEMENT Name (#PCDATA)>
<!ELEMENT Address (#PCDATA)>
<!ELEMENT Telephone (#PCDATA)>
]>
<Profile>
   <Name>John Smith</Name>
   <Address>123 Main St.</Address>
   <Telephone>+1 (555) 555-1212</Telephone>
</Profile>
```

The square brackets define what is called the internal DTD subset. This method of distributing schemas has some obvious advantages. It solves the potential problem of having a handler process a message with an out of date schema, but it comes with a high overhead.

A DTD can also reference an external file containing the schema description. This is done through a URL:

```
<?xml version="1.0" ?>
<!DOCTYPE Profile SYSTEM "http://someServer/profile.dtd">
<Profile>
    <Name>John Smith</Name>
    <Address>123 Main St.</Address>
    <Telephone>+1 (555) 555-1212</Telephone>
</Profile>
```

This is similar to the Java convention for referencing tag descriptor libraries. Either this can point to a local file, or perhaps some centralized repository. The former suffers, like all replication schemes, from the danger of reading stale data. Repositories may also become inaccessible because of firewalls, network outages, etc.

Human Readable, Machine Understandable

One of XML's greatest values is its most obvious: it is human readable. This helps immeasurably when debugging application problems. Dialogs between systems can easily be tracked, captured, played-back for testing, and even modified. For example, a test suite could be based on a series of core XML messages. Technologies such as XSLT, a language for transforming XML from one form to another, could be used to generate all the possible permutations of these messages for exhaustive server testing.

Issues

There are some arguments against using XML as a messaging format. Generally, these surface in discussions about highly resource-constrained devices, such as PDAs, or in environments where network bandwidth is limited. The following sections will examine these issues in detail.

Parser Size and Complexity

Parser size and complexity is becoming a problem. The XML 1.0 specification (2nd Edition) (downloadable from http://www.w3.org/TR/2000/REC-xml-20001006), at 59 pages, is a model of elegance and simplicity. A number of the associated technologies in the XML family, however, are becoming increasingly complex and difficult for vendors to implement efficiently.

A number of the more popular and standards-compliant parsers currently available have a large memory footprints and demand high processing bandwidth. As such, they preclude implementation on resource-constrained devices, such as PDAs or programmable mobile phones. There are some solutions to this problem, including indexing a document with technologies like XMLC. There are also parsers available that work on small devices by compromising support for some standards; however there is no standardization among these, which ultimately causes problems.

Message Overhead

The most common criticism leveled against XML messaging is overhead. Text-based messages structured with markup are not very bandwidth efficient, particularly as messages become large and highly structurally complex. For LAN and WAN messaging, this is not a significant issue; the bandwidth tradeoff is a minor sacrifice measured against the gains listed above. For wireless devices, however, this is often a critical issue.

The WAP forum had to consider this issue when it began defining standards for data services on mobile phones. One component of the WAP standard is an XML-based presentation markup language called Wireless Markup Language (WML). This is analogous to HTML, but optimized for devices with small display real estate, limited entry capability, narrowband communication channels, and severe limitations on processing power.

The WAP forum has addressed the issue of WML verbosity by introducing a binary compression scheme for XML. It relies on lossless substitutions for certain common tags and idioms, and selective filtering of some document content like DTDs (WBXML is described in the *WAP Binary XML Content Format*, Version 4, Nov 99 http://www1.wapforum.org/tech/documents/SPEC-WBXML-19991104.pdt). Usually, this would be implemented as a layer in the transport interface.

The cost of such compression is legibility on the wire. This may not seem like much of a sacrifice, as the data can be trivially decoded; however consider how much web development has benefited from the plain text representation of HTTP and HTML, which permits client/server dialogs to be easily tracked using a basic network sniffer.

Packaging of Non-XML Data

Consider a simple XML messaging scheme like the following:

```
<?xml version="1.0" encoding="UTF-8"?>
<Envelope>
  <Header>
     ...
  </Header>
  <Body>
     ...
  </Body>
</Envelope>
```

The Header contains control information such as identifying a service that the message is targeted for, and message unique identification. The Body element contains the data to be sent to a remote application.

The problem with using XML to package arbitrary data is that some data will result in illegal XML. For example:

```
<Body>
   < Remote parser will reject
</Body>
```

Sometimes this can be solved using entity references, the predefined XML escape sequences:

```
<Body>
   &lt Remote parser will reject
</Body>
```

But there are other cases that cannot be so easily escaped:

```
<Body>
    This data contains an </unbalanced> tag
</Body>
```

In this case, one option is to declare a CDATA section, which effectively declares the area off limits to further parsing. This is sometimes used to transport an existing XML document packaged in an XML envelope. The parser would reject this without the CDATA escape because the XML declaration <?xml> can only occur once in a document, and must be the first token in the document:

```
<?xml version="1.0" encoding="UTF-8"?>
<Envelope>
  <Body>
    <![CDATA[<?xml version="1.0" encoding="UTF-8"?>
      ...
    ]]>
  </Body>
</Envelope>
```

Although this works, it is an inelegant hack. It also does not address the problem of non-textual data, such as binary pictures. For binary data, a standard encoding schema is needed. Most messaging application make use of Base64 as a solution to this.

> *Base64 is described in RFC 2045, titled* Multipurpose Internet Mail Extensions (MIME) Part One: Format of Internet Message Bodies *(http://www.ietf.org/rfc/rfc2045.txt)*.

Binary content can be encoded using Base64 alone:

```
<Body>
<BinaryPicture>
      sdfsd73hd77n4sfYsa9hGY8w9s3 ...
</BinaryPicture>
</Body>
```

Ultimately, this is not a very satisfactory solution. The parser on the receiving system must process this entire document, which means that it will isolate the encoded binary item as a string, holding it in memory in its entirety. This could seriously limit the scalability of a high volume messaging application. It would also be incredibly wasteful of resources if the goal of parsing were simply to get at a header value, perhaps so the message could be relayed to its ultimate destination by an intermediate.

There are also some general design problems with this. Both the sending and receiving parties must be made aware that the BinaryPicture element contains data encoded in Base64 (this could be indicated using some features built into XML Schema). Consider also multiple attachments. What if a picture, a sound file, and a spreadsheet file all had to be transferred?

We could define our own schema defining a container for multiple attachments, with items that have attributes describing metadata about the attachment like their type, encoding, etc. Furthermore, whatever we came up with would be a proprietary solution. Fortunately, this problem has already been addressed in the context of mail, which faced similar challenges a number of years ago.

RFC 2387, The Multipart Internet Mail Extensions (MIME) Multipart/Related Content-type *(http://www.ietf.org/rfc/rfc2387.txt) defines a standard for aggregation of interrelated objects.*

It's not XML, but it can be processed very efficiently, and there are a lot of tools, infrastructure, and general expertise that support it. Several of the XML messaging standardization efforts, which will be described later, have settled on the MIME multipart/related content type to package problematic data. This includes other XML documents, as was alluded to above. In particular, MIME defines mechanisms for not only rendering binary content in Base64, but also packaging raw data, which removes some processing burden from the sender and receiver. This is an important consideration for high volume applications.

MIME is best illustrated with an example:

```
Content-Type: Multipart/Related;
  boundary=boundary_marker;
    start="xml-message1@someURL";
    type=text/xml;

-- boundary_marker
Content-Type: text/xml;
Content-Description: Main XML message envelope
Content-ID: "xml-message1@someURL"

<?xml version="1.0" encoding="UTF-8"?>
<Envelope>
  <Header>
    <Manifest>
      ...
    </Manifest>
  </Header>
  <Body>
   ...
  </Body>
</Envelope>

--boundary_marker
Content-Type: image/jpeg
Content-Description: An encoded binary picture
Content-Transfer-Encoding: base64
Content-ID: "image1.jpg@someURL"

bshOI47KJ64kI6hksdf7gh32fsd87kj3r3
Sdfkj3483jusYioyu8reti34hfs89fsdio
I5h3489hpw
   ...

--boundary_marker--
```

The opening line declares the MIME content type to be multipart/related. MIME defines a number of standard parameters represented as simple attribute-value pairs. MIME supports recursive structures: a MIME body part may contain other MIME entities. This does complicate processing somewhat, but in general, MIME lends itself well to parsing by existing Internet infrastructure, like firewalls, which may not be XML-aware.

The boundary attribute defines a marker delimiting the MIME parts. One of the MIME parts is the root, and may be the logical piece that relates all the other parts. The start attribute, if included, points to the root MIME part's content ID; the first MIME part is the default root if this is not specified. The content type attribute in the main header defines the content type of the root MIME part.

Each MIME part has a distinct header, defining its content type (the content types are defined in the MIME specification RFC 2045), an optional description, an encoding, and a content ID.

Notice here we have included a manifest element in our XML header. It is a common strategy to use manifests when packaging data items, especially if the package can be broken up into multiple components. Java JAR files are a good example. The manifest here might contain references to MIME parts using the unique MIME Content-ID parameter. For example, Microsoft's BizTalk messaging framework, which will be examined later in the chapter, uses manifests to refer to body parts using URIs. The manifest for a BizTalk version of the above message might look like:

```
<manifest>
   <reference>
      <attachment href="CID:image1.jpg@someURL"./>
      <description> Description of JPEG image1 </description>
   </reference>
</manifest>
```

Content ID URLs are described in RFC 2111, *Content-ID and Message-ID Uniform Resource Locators* (http://ietf.org/rfc/rfc2111.txt). Notice that in this example, the Body element remains in the primary MIME part with the headers. Since the body is where XML unfriendly data may appear, it may be better to simply remove this entirely to its own separate MIME part that could be encoded as necessary. If we left it in the primary document with the headers, this entire MIME part may have to be encoded, including the headers. This would impede quick and efficient access to header fields, perhaps by an intermediate. Creation of a separate MIME part for the body is the solution adopted by the ebXML group with its payload (analogous to the body), which is placed in a distinct MIME part.

Parsing and Transformation

In order to explore some of the parsing and transformation options available for XML documents, let us create a sample XML message. The following might be sent to a simple stock trading system, to buy 1000 share of Wrox stock:

```
<?xml version="1.0" encoding="UTF-8"?>
<Envelope>
  <Header>
    <Service name="buy"/>
  </Header>
  <Body>
    <Trade>
      <Stock>
        Wrox
      </Stock>
      <Number>
        1000
      </Number>
    </Trade>
  </Body>
</Envelope>
```

We will store this in the file buy.xml, so it can be used in some examples that follow. As we examine some real messaging standards, it will become apparent how much this is over simplified. It does follow a typical message design pattern and for the purposes we hope to illustrate, it is sufficient. Note that we have a packaged the message in an XML envelope; this implies that any data we intend to transmit must be valid XML or the receiver's message handler will throw an exception. We will not deal with packaging non-XML data here (see the previous section). The envelope contains both header sections, which define the remote service we are targeting, and a body, which contains any parameters to pass to the service. Here, we have essentially created a serialized XML version of the following simple Java class:

```
public class Trade {

  public String stock;
  public int number;

  public Trade(String stock, int number) {
    this.stock = stock;
    this.number = number;
  }
}
```

JAXP

All the parsing examples in this chapter will make use of the **Java API for XML Parsing (JAXP)**. There are in fact a large number of different parsers available. Some of these emphasize speed; others small memory footprint; others conformance to the various parsing specifications that are available. For example, Crimson, the default parser that comes with the distribution, emphasizes a fairly small memory footprint. In contrast, a popular open source parser Xerces (http://xml.apache.org), which also will ultimately be accessible using JAXP, is highly feature rich, but with a larger footprint. The point of JAXP is not to be yet another parser, but to be a pure Java API that can abstract away the implementation details of the common parsers. This way, programmers developing with the JAXP API could later easily substitute in an alterative parser – perhaps to finely tune the balance between performance and resource consumption – without breaking their existing code. Specification of the actual parser instance to instantiate can be made at run time using properties on the Java command line.

JAXP is registered as JSR 000063 in the Java Community Process (it is actually a follow-up to JSR 000005, adding support for newer specifications and technologies). Download the JAXP distribution from http://www.javasoft.com/xml/download.html. As mentioned above, the distribution comes with an implementation of Sun's Crimson parser (previously known as Project-X), which is a small-footprint parser supporting SAX 2.0 and the DOM level 2 core recommendations.

DOM and SAX are the two most popular parsing technologies in the XML community. Each approaches parsing in different way. DOM provides an API to traverse and manipulate an XML document as a tree structure. SAX, in contrast, is an event-driven parser. Developers create event handlers that respond to parsing events such as the start or end of the document, an element, a processing instruction, character data, etc. Each has its strengths and limitations, and some parsing applications will naturally lend themselves to one or the other.

Note that JAXP also supports an abstract transformation interface called TraX. The TraX API allows arbitrary XML transformation engines to be plugged into it. The current version of the JAXP distribution includes the Xalan 2 XSLT parser. XSLT is a transform language for XML. It is extremely powerful, but also a complex language. Wrox has some excellent books covering XSLT.

At the time of writing, we used JAXP 1.1, early access 2, for all the examples in this chapter.

Tree-Based Parsing

The **Document Object Model (DOM)** is an API defined by the W3C to inspect and modify XML and HTML documents in a standardized way. The DOM API is actually platform- and language-neutral; implementations of the DOM exist in Java, C++, Visual Basic, and ECMAScript. Documents can be in XML format, or as a special case of this, traditional HTML. The later allows languages like JavaScript to have a standard API to access and manipulate documents residing in the context of a browser. Information about the DOM can be found at http://www.w3.org/dom. The DOM level 1 became a W3C Recommendation in Oct 1998. The DOM level 2, adding support for namespaces and a stylesheet model, was awarded Recommendation status in November 2000.

DOM parsing involves parsing a textual document into a tree of nodes. All the components of the document, including elements, attributes, values, CDATA sections, etc. are contained in node objects; this entire tree of nodes is kept in memory at all times, so large documents can consume considerable memory space and take a while to parse (the lazy DOM was developed to deal with this, and will be explained later). The DOM provides interfaces to inspect each node, alter its contents, get its child nodes, remove nodes, append nodes, etc. Most DOM implementations require a lot of navigation code to walk through this tree, and as a result can become difficult to understand and maintain.

Here is a node tree for the simple `buy.xml` document described above:

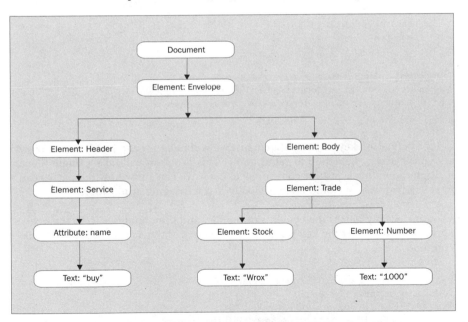

The DOM defines an inheritance hierachy of objects that are used to access nodes in this tree. When a document is parsed using the DOM, the user is returned a root object implementing the `org.w3c.dom.Document` interface. This object can be thought of as the root of the tree, and is represented above by the `Document` node. The document interface provides factory methods to create objects in the tree, such as elements, text nodes, attributes, etc. The interface also provides two important navigation methods: `getDocumentElement()` – a convenience routine that returns the document's root element (in our example, element `Envelope`); and `getElementsByTagName()` – returns a `NodeList`, which is a collection of nodes from anywhere in the node tree matching the tag provided as a parameter. As we will see, this is useful for navigating directly to an element.

The following code shows how we might navigate the tree, using DOM interfaces in the JAXP API from Sun:

```java
import java.io.File;
import java.io.IOException;

// JAXP
import javax.xml.parsers.FactoryConfigurationError;
import javax.xml.parsers.ParserConfigurationException;
import javax.xml.parsers.DocumentBuilderFactory;
import javax.xml.parsers.DocumentBuilder;

// DOM
import org.w3c.dom.Document;
import org.w3c.dom.Node;
import org.w3c.dom.NodeList;

import org.xml.sax.SAXException;
import org.w3c.dom.Element;

public class DOMExample {

  public static void main(String[] args) {
    if (args.length != 1) {
      System.err.println("Usage: java DOMExample [filename]");
      System.exit(1);
    }

    DOMExample domExample = new DOMExample();
    Document document = domExample.parse(args[0]);
    if (document != null) domExample.analyze(document);
  }
```

First of all, let's define the key import statements we will need for the JAXP implementation of a DOM parser, and a basic main() method to get us going. This program will take a single filename as a parameter. Right now, this is just for convenience. Later we can show how the parser can work from a java.lang.String, which would be more likely in a messaging application.

Our main routine simply parses the contents of the file, and then analyses it. In the analysis routine, we will show how we can extract the key serialized parameters of the Trade object. Let's have a look at the parse() method:

```java
  public Document parse(String filename) {
    Document document = null;
    try {
      DocumentBuilderFactory documentBuilderFactory =
        DocumentBuilderFactory.newInstance();

      documentBuilderFactory.setValidating(false);

      DocumentBuilder documentBuilder =
          documentBuilderFactory.newDocumentBuilder();
      document = documentBuilder.parse(new File(filename));
```

```
        } catch (ParserConfigurationException e) {
            System.out.println("Parser does not support feature");
            e.printStackTrace();
        } catch (FactoryConfigurationError e) {
            System.out.println("Error occurred obtaining DocumentBuilderFactory.");
            e.printStackTrace();
        } catch (SAXException e) {
            System.out.println("Caught SAX Exception");
            e.printStackTrace();
        } catch (IOException e) {
            System.out.println("Error opening file: " + filename);
        }
        return document;
    }
```

The `DocumentBuilderFactory` is a JAXP class that abstracts away the instantiation of a parser instance. It allows us to plug in alternative parsers, and choose which parser to instantiate at run time. Right now, we will just take the default parser, which in JAXP 1.1, is Sun's Crimson parser.

Since we have not defined a DTD or schema for our file, we will explicitly turn off validation. The actual parsing is done using the `DocumentBuilder.parse()` method. This routine returns a document, that we in turn pass back to `main()`.

Note that we are providing a `java.io.File` object to parse. This method has other signatures, including `DocumentBuilder.parse(java.io.InputStream)`. For example, a valid alternative would have been:

```
String textInputMsg  = "<?xml version=\"1.0\"?> (The rest of the document)";
StringReader stringReader = new StringReader(textInputMsg);
InputSource inputSource = new InputSource(stringReader);
Document document = documentBuilder.parse(inputSource);
```

Now that we have our `Document` instance, let's have a look at the `analyze()` method, which will navigate this document, extracting some useful data from it. We will do two things: isolate the service name, which is an attribute of the service element, and unserialize the `Trade` object. The correct term for this is "unmarshaling", but more on that in the upcoming section on data binding:

```
public void analyze(Document document) {

    Element rootElement = document.getDocumentElement();
    System.out.println("Root element of document is:" +
        rootElement.getTagName());
```

First, walk through children looking for the `Element` node with name `Header` (bear in mind that XML is case-sensitive):

```
NodeList nodeList = rootElement.getChildNodes();
Node node = null;
Element header = null;
int i = 0;
while (i < nodeList.getLength()) {
    node = nodeList.item(i);
```

```
            if (node.getNodeType() == Node.ELEMENT_NODE) {
                header = (Element) node;
                if (header.getTagName().compareTo("Header") == 0)
                    break;
            }
            i++;
        }
        if (i > nodeList.getLength()) {
          System.err.println("Parse Error: Can't find Header element");
          System.exit(0);
        }
```

Now walk through `Header`'s children looking for the `Element` node with name `Service`:

```
        nodeList = header.getChildNodes();
        Element service = null;
        i = 0;
        while (i < nodeList.getLength()) {
          node = nodeList.item(i);
          if (node.getNodeType() == Node.ELEMENT_NODE) {
              service = (Element) node;
              if (header.getTagName().compareTo("Service") == 0)
                  break;
          }
          i++;
        }
        if (i > nodeList.getLength()) {
            System.err.println("Parse Error: Can't find Service element");
            System.exit(0);
        }

        // Get attribute value from service
        String serviceName = service.getAttribute("name");
        System.out.println("Service name is: " + serviceName);
```

Unmarshal the `Trade` object:

```
        nodeList = document.getElementsByTagName("Trade");
        if (nodeList.getLength() != 1) {
          System.err.println("Parse Error: Can't find trade element or multiple " +
                             "trade elements found");
          System.exit(0);
        }
        Element trade = (Element) nodeList.item(0);

        // Get stock name
        nodeList = trade.getElementsByTagName("Stock");
        if (nodeList.getLength() != 1) {
          System.err.println("Parse Error: Can't find Stock element or " +
                             "multiple Stock elements");
          System.exit(0);
        }
        Node stock = nodeList.item(0);
```

```
        nodeList = stock.getChildNodes();
        if (nodeList.getLength() != 1) {
          System.err.println("Parse Error: Stock element has multiple children");
          System.exit(0);
        }
        Node textNode = nodeList.item(0);
        String stockName = textNode.getNodeValue().trim();
        System.out.println("Stock name is: " + stockName);

        // Get number of shares
        nodeList = trade.getElementsByTagName("Number");
        if (nodeList.getLength() != 1) {
          System.err.println(
              "Parse Error: Can't find Number element or multiple Number elements");
          System.exit(0);
        }
        Node number = nodeList.item(0);
        nodeList = number.getChildNodes();
        if (nodeList.getLength() != 1) {
          System.err.println("Parse Error: Number element has multiple children");
          System.exit(0);
        }
        textNode = nodeList.item(0);
        String numberStr = textNode.getNodeValue().trim();
        int numberValue = (new Integer(numberStr)).intValue();
        System.out.println("Number is: " + numberValue);

        Trade tradeOrder = new Trade(stockName, numberValue);
    }
  }
```

First, the code demonstrates the `Document.getDocumentElement()` convenience routine. Here, we are simply using it so we can gain access of the root element. This is where we will start walking the tree by accessing its children using the method `Node.getChildNodes()` (remember that the `Element` interface, like the document interface, extends `Node`). Tree-walking code is not hard, but it can get a little ugly. In particular, you will quickly discover that our node tree diagram above has been over simplified, and there are a number of additional nodes that complicate the picture, but will still have to be accounted for as we walk the tree. For example, the line feeds and whitespace we added to our `buy.xml` file are processed quite literally by the parser; this means that a typical element node actually looks like this:

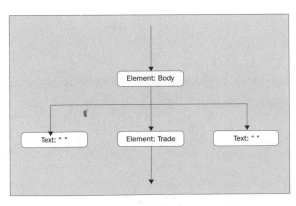

It is up to the application to decide what to do with extra whitespace.

The first part of the code walks down through elements in the order Envelope, Header, Service. Note where we cast a Node into an Element so we can make use of the Element.getTagName() method to make sure we have located the right element. We are casting the service Node to an Element to take advantage of that interface's getAttribute(String) method. Casting may not be an efficient operation in some languages.

> *The DOM acknowledges this with support for two perspectives on interfaces: both an inheritance-based object-oriented view, and a "flattened" view, where everything is represented as a Node. An alterative would have been to use the Node.getAttributes() method, which returns a NamedNodeMap that has a similar query function (as well as functions to examine attributes by index), but it returns the attribute again as a Node, so additional steps are still required.*

Once we have found the service name, we try to unserialize (or reconstitute the object from its representation in XML) the Trade object. This time, rather than tree-walking, we will simplify things by making use of the getElementsByTagName() method on the Document and Element interfaces. These return a NodeList, which is a container holding references to the all nodes underneath the Document or Element that match the tag name. This is both good and bad: while it greatly simplifies navigation, it also means that you may inadvertently pull out unexpected elements from deep within your structure. One of the reasons namespaces were invented was to avoid these kinds of element name collisions. Be careful though, DOM level 1 does not support them (DOM level 2, used here, does). (A better way of querying documents is to use XPath expressions, which we will not cover here. Have a look at http://www.w3.org/TR/xpath.)

Most of the code for unserializing Trade is straightforward, but there are a few things to note. First, we isolate the Trade element from the document root; we then use this new Element root to search deeper in the structure for the Stock and Number elements. The point of this is to demonstrate how we can segment off parts of a tree to minimize the search space and in doing so create a more accurate search. Note that getNodeValue() is returning only strings, which are DOM's fundamental representation of everything, so we must cast where appropriate. It's not apparent here, but if we had any entity references in our document, DOM would have substituted these for their entity values internally during parsing. Thus, you cannot isolate entity references using DOM. For example, if we replaced the string "Wrox" with an entity reference, the value of element Stock would still be Wrox books:

```xml
<?xml version="1.0" encoding="UTF-8"?>
<!DOCTYPE Envelope [
<!ENTITY stockName "Wrox">
]>
<Envelope>
    <Header>
        <Service name="buy"/>
    </Header>
    <Body>
        <Trade xmlns:n="http://www.infowave.com/nameSpaces">
            <Stock>
                &stockName; books
            </Stock>
            <Number>
                1000
            </Number>
        </Trade>
    </Body>
</Envelope>
```

To test the code, copy the `DOMExample.java`, `Trade.java` and `buy.xml` files to the same directory and make sure you have `.`, `jaxp.jar`, and `crimson.jar` in your classpath:

```
C:\WINNT\System32\cmd.exe                                    _ □ ×

C:\WROX\ProJMS\Ch10>java DOMExample buy.xml
Root element of document is:Envelope
Service name is: buy
Stock name is: Wrox
Number is: 1000

C:\WROX\ProJMS\Ch10>
```

Although this code works, and demonstrates two methods of navigating a DOM structure, it has some practical problems. This code is very brittle. Knowledge of the document organization is woven throughout the Java code: if we make any significant structural changes to our document, the code will have to be changed by hand. For example, suppose we added an inner envelope to our document structure:

```xml
<?xml version="1.0" encoding="UTF-8"?>
<Envelope>
  <InnerEnvelope>
    <Header>
      ...
    </Header>
    <Body>
      ...
    </Body>
  </InnerEnvelope>
</Envelope>
```

The first part of our example, where we walk the tree, would fail because it effectively has the previous structure hard-coded into it. The second part, however, which uses queries on the tag name, would still function correctly. Any changes to tag names would break both methods, which unfortunately have these embedded in the code.

This code is also difficult to follow, and contains a number of reoccurring patterns. It is not hard to imagine how difficult the maintenance of such a program would be. This does beg the question of why you would write the code in the first place. Since really the Java code is being driven by the message structure, couldn't we simply automatically generate this code based on knowledge of the message organization? This is the subject of the upcoming section on data binding.

Event-Based Parsing

Although the DOM is very flexible, it does have some drawbacks. We have seen how awkward tree walking code can become. There are also some practical considerations with using the DOM. When you parse a document, the entire structure is built in memory as a tree of nodes. Every node is an object that must be instantiated. This can consume a lot of memory if the document is large. It also isn't very fast. If a node has siblings, children, or a parent, links must be created to articulate these relationships. The DOM uses strings in its interfaces, which is not very efficient in most languages, Java included. DOM processing overhead can be a problem if the goal is to build a highly scalable application that is required to process a high volume of XML messages.

The **Simple API for XML (SAX)** was designed to address some of these issues. SAX is an event-based parser. Rather than creating a parse tree, SAX provides application designers with a callback interface. As the XML document is processed, these interfaces are called; designers can build their own handlers to responds to these events. The design of SAX was actually a collaborative effort by members of the XML-DEV mailing list, coordinated by David Megginson.

There are a few key advantages to parsing with SAX. SAX operates on streams, so does not need to keep a representation of the entire document in memory at one time. For the same reason, it is also very fast because there are no significant objects to initialize and assemble into a tree structure, like DOM. The parser's code typically also has a very small memory footprint, which is advantageous for resource-constrained devices. As we will see, SAX is very well suited for unmarshaling objects that have been serialized in documents. It is not so well suited for applications where you need random access to the document, or you want to modify the document significantly; in this case, use DOM.

SAX defines a number of callbacks, but the most commonly used are:

```
DefaultHandler.startDocument()
DefaultHandler.endDocument()
DefaultHandler.startElement(String uri, String locaName,
     String Qname, Attributes attr)
DefaultHandler.endElement(String uri, String locaName,
     String Qname)
DefaultHandler.characters(char[] ch, int start, int length)
```

SAX provides the `org.xml.sax.helpers.DefaultHandler` class with empty methods. Application designers extend this class, overriding the handlers with their own customized implementation. An instance of this class is then registered with the SAX parser. The SAX parser processes the document as a stream, activating each callback at appropriate times. For example, given our test message, SAX would call methods at the following times (We are only showing a single example call for the `Envelope` element and the `Wrox` character text for clarity – in reality each element and string of character data would result in a call to the appropriate method):

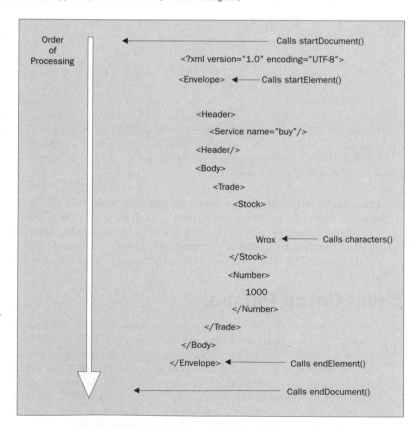

This is all probably best demonstrated with an example. The following uses the SAX 2.0 conventions, which have changed slightly from the previous version, and so may not exactly match other examples you may come across:

```java
import java.io.File;
import java.io.IOException;
import java.net.MalformedURLException;

// SAX related classes
import org.xml.sax.XMLReader;
import org.xml.sax.InputSource;
import org.xml.sax.SAXException;

// JAXP related imports
import javax.xml.parsers.SAXParser;
import javax.xml.parsers.SAXParserFactory;
import javax.xml.parsers.FactoryConfigurationError;
import javax.xml.parsers.ParserConfigurationException;

public class SAXExample {

  public static void main(String args[]) {

    if (args.length != 1) {
      System.err.println("Usage: java SAXExample [filename]");
      System.exit(1);
    }

    SAXExample saxExample = new SAXExample();
    saxExample.parse(args[0]);
  }

  public void parse(String filename) {

    // Create SAXParserFactory based on the JAXP distribution
    SAXParserFactory saxParserFactory = null;
    try {
      saxParserFactory = SAXParserFactory.newInstance();
    }
    catch (FactoryConfigurationError e) {
      System.err.println("Factory does not recognize parser.");
      System.exit(0);
    }

    try {
      // Create SAXParser and XMLReader based on the JAXP distribution
      SAXParser saxParser = saxParserFactory.newSAXParser();
      XMLReader xmlReader = saxParser.getXMLReader();

      SAXExampleHandler saxExampleHandler = new SAXExampleHandler();
      xmlReader.setContentHandler(saxExampleHandler);
      xmlReader.setErrorHandler(saxExampleHandler);

      // Parse file
      try {
```

```
            InputSource inputSource =
                new InputSource((new File(filename)).toURL().toString());
            xmlReader.parse(inputSource);

            Trade tradeOrder = saxExampleHandler.getTrade();
            System.out.println(
                "Trade order for "
                    + tradeOrder.number
                    + " shares of stock "
                    + tradeOrder.stock);

        }
        catch (MalformedURLException e) {
            System.err.println("Bad filename: " + filename);
        }
        catch (IOException e) {
            System.err.println("IO Exception on filename: " + filename);
        }

    }
    catch (ParserConfigurationException e) {
        System.err.println("Error configuring feature in parser.");
    }
    catch (SAXException e) {
        System.err.println("Received SAXException: " + e);
    }
  }
}
```

Like the DOM example, this program takes a file name as argument. The `parse()` method uses the JAXP API to instantiate a SAX parser (once again using Sun's Crimson parser underneath the hood). The code instantiates a `SAXExampleHandler` (which is our implementation of the `DefaultHandler` class) and registers it with the parser. Note that `XMLReader.parse()` method is expecting an `org.xml.sax.InputSource` object. The `InputSource` class allows us to wrap various sources, including a text string. Here, we are giving a string URL. To get this, we are taking advantage of the Java 1.2 modification to the `File` class that provides a `toURL()` method. As an alterative, the `InputSource` can wrap a text string. This would be a more likely scenario for a JMS application. For example:

```
String textInputMsg  = "<?xml version=/"1.0/" ...";
StringReader stringReader = new StringReader(textInputMsg);
try {
    InputSource inputSource = new InputSource(stringReader);
    xmlReader.parse(inputSource);
}
```

As the SAX parser processes the `InputSource`, it calls the methods of the handler. Here is what the handler code looks like:

```
// SAX related classes
import org.xml.sax.Attributes;
import org.xml.sax.helpers.DefaultHandler;

public class SAXExampleHandler extends DefaultHandler {
```

```
    private java.lang.StringBuffer charBuffer = new StringBuffer();
    private int numberValue;
    private java.lang.String serviceName;
    private java.lang.String stockName;
    private Trade tradeOrder;

    public void startDocument (){
      System.out.println("Start document processing...");
    }

    public void endDocument (){
      System.out.println("End document processing");
      // Create our Trade object
      tradeOrder = new Trade(stockName, numberValue);
    }

    public void startElement(String uri, String name,
      String qName, Attributes attributes) {
      if (name.compareTo("Service")==0){
        serviceName=attributes.getValue(uri, "name");
      }
      // Reset char buffer whenever we start a new element
      charBuffer.setLength(0);
    }

    public void endElement(String uri, String name, String qName) {
      // Record any serialized attributes of the Java Trade class
      if (name.compareTo("Stock") == 0) {
        stockName = charBuffer.toString().trim();
        System.out.println("Stock is: " + stockName);
      } else    if (name.compareTo("Number") == 0) {
        numberValue = (new Integer(charBuffer.toString().trim())).intValue();
        System.out.println("Number is: " + numberValue);
      }
    }

    public void characters (char ch[], int start, int length){
      // Append characters to the current char buffer
      charBuffer.append(ch, start, length);
    }

    Trade getTrade() {
      return tradeOrder;
    }
}
```

There are a couple of important things to notice here. SAX does not guarantee that a callback to `characters()` will return all the text between elements in a single call. Although in general you will observe that character data is aggregated in a single callback to `characters()`, SAX makes no promises about how characters could be broken up, or "chunked" by the SAX driver. Furthermore, you may not notice this behavior until the parser encounters a sequential character stream. For example, the following XML fragment:

```
<Stock>
  Wrox books
</Stock>
```

Could potentially result in the following call sequence:

- ❑ startElement() – Called for Stock opening tag
- ❑ characters() – Called for \n\tWrox fragment
- ❑ characters() – Called for books\n fragment
- ❑ endElement() – Called for Stock closing tag

Here, rather than a single call to characters() with the char array \n\tWrox books\n, there are two separate callbacks. This is why we are actually collecting the character strings in the StringBuffer instance charBuffer, which is reset at on each startElement() callback and examined at each endElement() callback. Some newer SAX parsers may provide developers with a feature that can be set that forces aggregation of multiple sequential characters() calls into one.

Note also that we are checking element names in the endElement() callback, and storing the results as Java attributes of our handler class. When we have reached the end of our document, we take the stockName and numberValue elements and construct a Trade object, which is accessible via an accessor method getTrade() in the handler class. Thus, our main routine can get access to this unmarshaled object.

Locating the value of the name attribute in the Service tag is very simple. Here, we simply check the tag name any time the startElement() callback is active. One of the parameters of this method is an Attributes class, which has a number of convenience accessors for examining attributes and their values.

Overall, the code is much simpler and easier to follow – and will be similarly easier to maintain. Since we are targeting elements only by name, we are resilient against most structural changes that could occur in the message. Nevertheless, we still have the problem of potentially running into element naming conflicts. Namespaces offer one answer to this. Another is adding logic to track exactly where we are in the document, based on calls to startElement() and endElement().

Test the code in exactly the same way as before, passing in the buy.xml file as argument, and the output should be the same:

```
C:\WINNT\System32\cmd.exe

C:\WROX\ProJMS\Ch10>java SAXExample buy.xml
Start document processing...
Stock is: Wrox
Number is: 1000
End document processing
Trade order for 1000 shares of stock Wrox

C:\WROX\ProJMS\Ch10>
```

SAX does have its drawbacks. In contrast to DOM, which provides CRUD (Create, Retrieve, Update, and Delete) interfaces for nodes, SAX is fundamentally a read-only technology. It also processes the stream using one pattern, effectively a depth-first search. There is no interface available to provide random access to the document. Furthermore, as documents become more complex, the handler can become elaborate, leaving us again with a difficult-to-maintain piece of code.

Java XML Data Binding

Both DOM and SAX provide flexible means to process XML documents. But as we saw in the last two sections, the Java code that does this can become very tedious. Notice, however, that with both the DOM and SAX implementations, there were many repeated code patterns; once you found one element, you could use the same tricks to find them all. The document structure also drove the code; this meant that the code was highly coupled to the document organization and thus intolerant to change (notwithstanding our opening assertion that XML is flexible under such conditions). It also forces Java programmers to learn about the details of XML, which is predicated on a very different data model from Java.

The key observation to make in the DOM and SAX examples is that the end result is really just to extract a `Trade` object from its serialized form in the XML document. And the steps to do this are quite mechanical, as shown.

Data binding is the process of mapping between objects in a language like Java (or C++, Visual Basic, etc.) and an XML document. It provides for a graph of Java objects to be marshaled into an XML document representation. It also provides for the reverse: to unmarshal an XML document into a graph of Java objects:

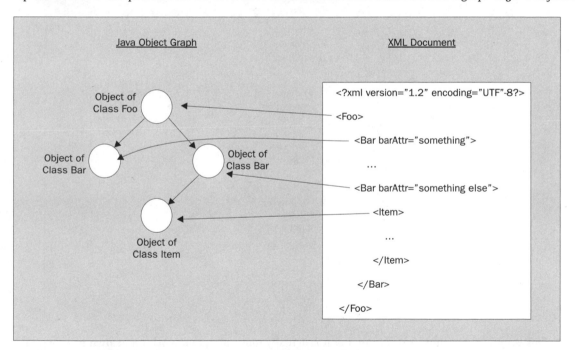

The key observation to make here is that the code needed to apply this is deterministic. The utility functions that affect these transforms (as well as Java code describing the data classes and a representation of the XML document schema) should be able to be automatically generated from a common underlying structural representation. This representation could be an XML Schema or DTD, a predefined set of Java classes, or some kind of generic modeling language, such as XMI, the XML Metadata Interchange. This is an XML language used mainly for exchanging model data between UML modeling tools.

> *The XMI specification is promoted by the Object Management Group (OMG), an industry organization responsible for standardizing object technologies. CORBA and UML are some of its higher profile efforts. Download the XMI specification from: ftp://ftp.omg.org/pub/docs/formal/00-11-02.pdf.*

If this sounds vaguely familiar, you've probably already used similar technology. It has become very common to use code generation to create a binding between Java objects and relational databases. EJB Entity Beans, Java Data Objects, and a host of proprietary vendor solutions do a similar thing: map between Java and SQL type systems. Java programmers simply work with Java objects, which are proxies for data residing in tables in the underlying database.

For more about Java Data Objects, registered as JSR-000012, see http://java.sun.com/aboutJava/communityprocess/jsr/jsr_012_dataobj.html.

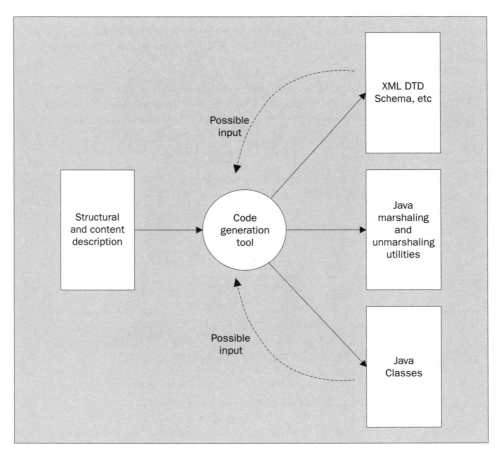

This sounds like a simple operation, but it is actually quite complex. XML on its own is very weakly typed – everything is a string. Once we impose typing on a document using a description like schema, we still have to map between this and the type system of the language we are using. There is not always a clean match. For example, consider enumerations, which exist in XML Schema. Enumerations exist in C/C++ and Visual Basic, but there is no equivalent base type in Java. Furthermore, our Java classes must enforce schema constraints such as minimum and maximum number of items (again assuming XML Schema); otherwise, an object graph may marshal into an invalid document. If constraints exist in preexisting Java code, these too should be mapped into schema equivalents to ensure that the document can be unmarshaled without causing an error.

There are some real benefits to data binding. Some of these make it particularly well suited for messaging applications. Java programmers simply work with Java classes, something to which they are accustomed. The utility classes encapsulate parsing complexity, so programmers really do not need to learn anything about XML. As we have observed, the utility classes should be code generated. This eliminates a significant potential source of errors. We still, of course, have a very tight coupling between document structure and Java code; however at least we can easily regenerate code when changes are mandated.

At present, XML/Java data binding tools are still uncommon. The XML Data Binding Specification also goes by the name Project Adelard. The Castor Project is developing code generation for bindings between XML, Java, and Java Data Objects (JDO). Breeze XML Studio, from The Breeze Factor is a commercial package that is available now that has much of the functionality described. It is anticipated that similar functionality will be made available in upcoming versions of Microsoft Visual Studio in support of its .NET initiative. In the emerging web services arena, toolkits are appearing that create proxy objects for Simple Object Access Protocol (SOAP) accessible web services. These implicitly marshal and unmarshal to SOAP style messages. Microsoft's ROPE – a part of its SOAP toolkit – implements some of these features.

> *For more about Project Adelard, registered as JSR-000031 under the Java Community Process, see* http://java.sun.com/aboutJava/communityprocess/jsr/jsr_031_xmld.html. *For the Castor Project, see* http://castor.exolab.org. *For the Breeze Factor, see* http://www.breezefactor.com.

XML and JMS

The previous sections have looked at XML, and what it has to offer messaging applications in general. In this section, we will examine some of the special considerations associated with bringing JMS and XML together. Most application designers will attempt to decouple the two, because there really should not be any dependencies created between the two technologies. For example, most JMS-related application code should simply operate on the `javax.jms.Message` interface. The application can extract (or insert) text strings as appropriate. These strings may or may not be XML – the handler should encapsulate this so that the system could be easily adapted to accommodate non-XML content, if the need arises. Similarly, the XML code should be logically distinct from the JMS code. This allows reuse of message handlers in non-JMS applications (for example, as a web service handler). We will explore some of these design principles while developing a content-based router using JMS and XML in a later section.

Carrying this idea one step further, consider what happens when you need reliability in your messaging application, but you may not always be able to delegate this to the JMS infrastructure. This might be the case when a message has to transit across multiple intermediates, some of which may not have access to robust messaging software for transport. In these cases, it becomes particularly important to design message format to accommodate the fields needed to support reliable transfer across unreliable transports. Essentially, this means re-implementing some of what we take for granted from JMS providers. We will examine these interesting issues in the following sections.

Of course, there are also times when coupling between XML and JMS is entirely appropriate. In these cases, we should attempt to leverage what each technology does best. The following sections will consider these issues as well.

Requirements of Robust Messaging Systems

As messaging systems become more widely used, greater demands are made of them. Many of these demands need to be anticipated early because they can have a profound effect on message design. A typical requirement a mature messaging architecture must satisfy is for durable message transport. This provides message resilience by ensuring that data in transit is not lost if a system – or even the entire network – fails. How to exchange errors and remote exceptions between the server and the client is another important point of consideration. The need to expose ACID (the transaction properties Atomicity, Consistency, Isolation, and Durability) server transactions to a client is also common. That is, provide a client API – possibly integral to the messaging infrastructure, and potentially interfacing with a downstream XA-protocol interface exported by a data store – to begin, end, monitor, commit, and rollback a distributed transaction. This interface may further coordinate two-phase commits among multiple data stores, thus making the messaging infrastructure into a resource manager. A good example is a bank doing a credit/debit between two partners. Either both operations must succeed or the transaction as a whole must rollback, undoing the changes on both systems.

Reliability is also important: there must be a guarantee that messages will arrive at their destination, even if the receiving system (or any intermediate hop) is currently down. Furthermore, only a single copy of the message must arrive. Imagine a bank system where a single debit message arrived twice. Scalability and fault tolerance are always necessary; previous discussions touched on these issues. Advanced queuing functions that relate to Quality of Service (QoS) need to be considered in a mature and robust messaging environment. Some examples are:

- ❑ Message prioritization
- ❑ Time-to-live; cancellation
- ❑ Globally unique message identification
- ❑ Association linking responses to requests when communication channels are multiplexed

One needs to consider session establishment, maintenance, identification, and teardown on a remote server, as well as distributed naming for remote services (for example, associating a well-known service name with a transport instance, such as a particular message queue). More complicated message flow models (beyond hub-and-spoke and even Publish/Subscribe) begin to become necessary as messaging architectures grow. High-level infrastructure that can choreograph complicated lattice communication flows, where messages fan out and consolidate, becomes crucial as messaging architectures expand in the enterprise. Workflow applications exhibit this kind of behavior.

For example, consider an electronic form that requires several authorizations. Authorizations can be made serially (that is, A gives their approval, followed by B,...); however, if each is independent, they could proceed in parallel. The final step then involves consolidating all the individual authorizations into a completed electronic form. Messaging applications often exhibit similar behavior, and orchestrating these can be extremely complex. This demands complicated, high-level software that coordinates transport infrastructure and applications (such as IBM's MQSeries Workflow).

Application-based vs. MOM-based Robust Messaging

The point of enumerating these issues is to draw attention to a fundamental consideration when designing a messaging framework. Since we know that eventually, the above items will become the requirement list for any rigorous and comprehensive messaging deployment, the question becomes *where* to address them.

One strategy is to push these functions into the application, thereby greatly increasing its complexity and demanding that considerable message handling logic be built into it (a task as daunting as it is unrewarding). To accomplish this, however, the message must have visible fields built in to enable messages to be reliable, traceable, expirable, etc. The message, therefore, becomes quite complex.

This strategy allows the application to make use of a transport that is very fast, simple, and lightweight, such as connection-oriented TCP sockets or connectionless UDP datagrams. XML is effective in such messaging applications because it is flexible enough to readily accommodate the additional fields needed to support implementation of some of the above demands. We will shortly see how to accomplish this when we examine some existing XML message frameworks like BizTalk and ebXML. It is a basic requirement to decouple these messages from transport. Therefore, they must support the message hooks to implement reliability in the application itself.

Alternatively, the messaging infrastructure can assume full responsibility for all these items. This is exactly what robust, Message-Oriented Middleware (MOM) attempts to do: take on the burden – in its role as transport – of all or many of the items listed above. There are a large number of implementations of MOM, including BEA MessageQ, IBM's MQSeries, Microsoft's MSMQ, Progress's SonicMQ. They take the focus of the above items away from the developer, and turn it over to the MOM administrator. This results in much more flexible application code. Changes to systems or network topology become administrative changes, not coding changes. JMS is effective as an interface to messaging systems because it abstracts away the complexity of each different messaging product, helping developers decouple from a particular proprietary implementation.

It may seem like we have two competing agendas here, but in reality, when brought together, XML and JMS are actually very complementary. The next sections look at some of the considerations in making XML and JMS work effectively together.

JMS Headers and Properties

One of the fundamental design considerations when using JMS and XML is what data should go into JMS properties and what should go into the message. Each implementation will have slightly different requirements, and so will have to take different approaches. However, there are some important issues to consider.

Data put into JMS properties can be used for message selection. Fields that identify remote services by logical name are good candidates for inclusion in a JMS property. In the web services arena, it is common to use a URL to identify target services. A JMS equivalent could be a specific topic or queue; however, it is more common to publish multiple services off a single topic or queue. JMS defines a SQL-like syntax for selecting messages based on property contents that is highly efficient (depending on the service provider's implementation). This is available to both the Point-to-Point and Publish/Subscribe messaging domains. Pushing these data into the message will force the handler to examine each message individually. The message would have to be parsed and queried, probably using an XML query language like XPath, which has a very different syntax and query model from the JMS message selection. This forces Java programmers to learn about XML, which may not be a bad thing, but it may also not be an effective allocation of resources. It is also not particularly efficient, particularity for simple routing applications.

On the other hand, using JMS properties couples you to JMS. The JMS specification does not try to define how JMS properties are exposed to non-JMS enabled applications. Thus, in a business-to-business MOM-messaging environment, where not all the applications are using JMS, this could create problems. Furthermore, if messages leave the control of the MOM software, for example, in a multi-hop system where the final hop uses simple HTTP as transport, then the JMS headers will be lost.

It is important to remember that two systems that communicate using messaging may not be directly connected. For example, a message may have to traverse multiple intermediates to get to its destination. The term "multi-hop" refers to these systems. Each hop may use different transports, such as HTTP, or even a MOM system that is not JMS-compliant, and thus may drop JMS headers and properties. The presence of intermediates will have an effect on the choice of what goes into the message proper, and what goes into JMS properties and headers. Some of the messaging frameworks we will examine in Appendix C have very specific rules regarding how intermediates treat headers.

One solution to the problem of preserving JMS headers and properties would be to render these into the XML message for transport to non-JMS clients. This would be particularity appropriate if the messaging format used one of the detailed messaging frameworks like ebXML or BizTalk, which already define XML elements for most of the important JMS properties that implement reliable messaging.

The JMSType header, which is a standard JMS header, has potential use to identify XML message schemas residing in a repository. The JMS specification does not specify how a repository is to be implemented, and warns that service providers may have their own implementation of this header.

What follows is an example, using simple synchronous queuing, of sending a message with an accompanying schema entry:

```
String text  = "<?xml version=\"1.0\"?> ...";
TextMessage textMessage = queueSession.createTextMessage();
textMessage.setText(text);
textMessage.setJMSType("http://someInternetAddress/example.dtd");
queueSender.send(textMessage);
```

On the receiving end:

```
TextMessage textMessage = (TextMessage) queueReceiver.receive();
String text = textMessage.getText();
String schema = textMessage.getJMSType();
```

The receiver would make use of this URI in validation (the URI could identify a DTD, XML Schema, or even some other schema definition language). Of course, the message itself could also contain the URI in the DOCTYPE as well.

JMS Body and XML Documents

XML documents are best transported using the JMS `javax.jms.TextMessage` class. As an example, here is a simple XML text string sent to a queue:

```
String text = "<?xml version=\"1.0\" encoding=\"UTF-8\"?> ... ";
TextMessage textMessage = queueSession.createTextMessage();
textMessage.setText(text);
queueSender.send(textMessage);
```

The synchronous receiver is similar:

```
QueueReceiver queueReceiver = queueSession.createReceiver(queue);
TextMessage textMessage = (TextMessage) queueReceiver.receive();
String text = textMessage.getText();
```

To prepare a message for parsing with DOM and SAX:

```
StringReader stringReader = new StringReader(text);
InputSource inputSource = new InputSource(stringReader);

try {
  Document doc = documentBuilder.parse(inputSource); // Parse with DOM
  xmlReader.parse(inputSource); // or Parse with SAX

} catch (java.io.IOException e) {
    System.err.println("IO Exception" );
} catch (org.xml.sax.SAXException e) {
    System.err.println("IO Exception" );
}
```

Translation from an existing SAX or DOM representation to a text string is quite a bit more complicated. For DOM, it is not too complicated to build a recursive utility method that visits every node in depth-first order, rendering the results into a `java.io.StringWriter`. If you build your own, the `DOMEcho` class, included in the JAXP distribution, is a good place to start. For SAX, consider the `XMLWriter` class from David Megginson's site at http://megginson.com/Software/index.html.

Another consideration is to use the JAXP TRaX API with a null transform, writing into a `StreamResult` object. A strategy similar to this – but with a real XSLT transform – is employed in the router example below.

Another parsing and manipulation technology to keep an eye on is JDOM (http://www.jdom.org). This is a 100% pure Java API that approaches XML from the perspective of the Java programmer and leveraging the features of the language. The focus is to make working with XML simple and intuitive. JDOM greatly simplifies translation of text representations of XML to/from models like DOM and SAX. This will be a hot technology.

JMS and Service Provider Security

XML does not solve messaging security issues on its own. The W3C has a working group studying digital signatures of documents (http:///www.w3.ord/signature). At the time of writing, the group has published candidate recommendations for document signing and canonical representations of XML. At the end of January 2001, the W3C formed an activity to study document encryption (http://www.w3.org/Encryption/2001/Activity). Signing and encryption of XML documents are both complex problems to be solved, but are important for global electronic commerce.

> *People interested in a current approach to the XML signing and encryption problem now may want to look at IBM's XML Security Suite on its AlphaWorks site: http://www.alphaworks.ibm.com/tech/xmlsecuritysuite. It features element-level encryption and signing functions for DOM documents, implemented using Java.*

Documents can be encrypted as a whole; of course, this solution creates a new set of problems. If messages are encrypted, how can a broker in a hub-and-spoke architecture get at routing information embedded in the message? These issues áre similar to those faced when web browsers connect to servers using SSL across intermediate proxies. If the proxy is visible, the solution is to use specific proxy connection methods and dialogs built into the HTTP specification. If the proxy is invisible, such as redirectors that operate at the application protocol level, little can be done. These devices often loose their ability to perform sophisticated redirections because they cannot parse the encrypted message.

End-to-end security could be achieved as a piecemeal collection of secure segments, but this is rarely compatible with corporate security policies. Witness the outcry over the segmented encryption scheme used in WAP to connect mobile devices to the enterprise. From the handset to the carrier's WAP gateway, the messages are encrypted using WTLS. Between the gateway and the enterprise, they are encrypted using SSL. The momentary exposure of the message in plain text as it is converted from one cipher to another – albeit on a secured system – makes a number of large corporations uncomfortable enough to purchase their own gateway and house it in their secure network.

We can alternatively rely on MOM security. Most commercial vendors of MOM products have some kind of encryption solution that works transparently, sometimes available through a business partner. For example, IBM maintains a list of third-party vendors that provide security products that work in conjunction with its MQSeries product at http://www-4.ibm.com/software/ts/mqseries/directory/secprods.html.

To Validate or Not to Validate

XML provides a rich validation model for documents – but should you use it? The problem with validation is that it consumes resources, and so may not be appropriate for high message volume applications. The validation question is really a question of trust. Does your service provider's infrastructure guarantee message integrity? If so, you do not have to validate to catch corruption errors.

More significant is the question of trust surrounding the party who sent the message. If you control the applications on both sides of the message exchange, you probably skip validation because you know the behavior of both parties (after exhaustive testing, naturally). If you don't trust the other party – and this is the case with most business relationships – then you will probably be forced to validate messages to ensure that they honor the contract of the API.

Validation alone, however, does not solve some fundamental security problems. If a party sends you a message with an embedded schema, or even a reference to a schema, can you trust this? One of the problems with this model is that the remote party is both telling you something, and telling you how to interpret it. The more flexible we build our systems, the more susceptible we become to such attacks. Thus, it is important that a schema come either from a trusted repository, or from a remote system that is sufficiently trusted and authenticated.

An XML Router Example

Now let's develop a simple example program to demonstrate some of the concepts we have been looking at. In this example, we will develop a simple XML router, than receives messages on a queue, examines the content of the message, adds a log entry to the message header, and forwards the resulting message on a queue named by the message. We will use the Point-to-Point messaging domain here, but the idea can be very simply extended to Publish/Subscribe. For example:

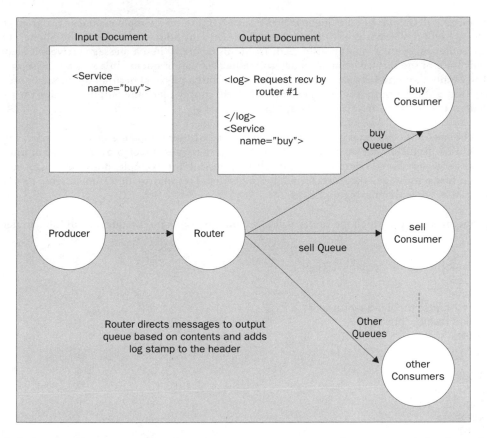

First, let's develop the program based on the input message sent to the router, and the desired output messages that the router produces. As input, we will again use our simple stock buy example (keep this in a file called `simpleMsg.xml` so we can use it later):

```xml
<?xml version="1.0" encoding="UTF-8"?>
<Envelope>
  <Header>
    <Service name="buy"/>
  </Header>
  <Body>
    <Trade>
      <Stock>
        Wrox
      </Stock>
      <Number>
        1000
      </Number>
    </Trade>
  </Body>
</Envelope>
```

This message will be placed on a queue called `routerInput` by a simple producer program (the producer we will develop is really just a test scaffolding to introduce messages to the queue). Our message router program synchronously reads from this queue. When a message arrives, it inspects the name attribute of the service element to determine its destination queue. In a real application, there would be some mapping between a local service name and a physical destination queue name. To simplify things for the purposes of the example, we will simply place the output message on a queue named after the service – in this case, "buyService".

It would be useful if our router entered a log entry in the header indicating that it routed the message. This would be useful so that we could track problems if messages traveled over a series of intermediate routers to get to its ultimate destination. The SMTP protocol, for example, does something similar. Every hop that a message takes is recorded in the header. This information is invaluable to mail administrators when diagnosing problems.

So our output message, which the router will place on the `buyService` queue, will look something like this:

```
<?xml version="1.0" encoding="UTF-8"?>
<Envelope>
  <Header>
   <log> Request received by router#1 </log>
   <Service name="buy"/>
  </Header>
  <Body>
   <Trade>
    <Stock>
     Wrox
    </Stock>
    <Number>
     1000
    </Number>
   </Trade>
  </Body>
</Envelope>
```

Of course, the router should be able to route to any queue named as a service. We will make the simplifying assumption that the router can create any queue it needs. In a real application of course, queues should probably be fixed by a the administrator of the JMS service provider, and any message containing a service name that doesn't map to a physical queue should be logged as an error.

We will try to make a logical separation of our router into two main parts: a dispatcher, which reads from input queues and writes to output queues; and a message handler, which parses and interprets the input XML message, and produces the output XML message containing the log entry.

We will develop the message handler first. Ideally, the dispatcher should simply send the input text message to the handler, and get an output text message back, along with the destination queue name. This way, the dispatcher is shielded from needing to know anything about the details of XML. We will call our message handler class `XmlMsgHandler`. Here is the main code defining the class and its attributes. We look at the individual methods, including the constructor in detail as we develop the logic to the code:

```
package xmlrouter;

import java.io.StringWriter;
import java.io.StringReader;
import java.io.IOException;

// JAXP
import javax.xml.parsers.DocumentBuilderFactory;
import javax.xml.parsers.DocumentBuilder;

// SAX
import org.xml.sax.InputSource;
import org.xml.sax.SAXException;

// DOM
import org.w3c.dom.Document;
import org.w3c.dom.Element;
import org.w3c.dom.Node;
import org.w3c.dom.NodeList;

// TRaX
import javax.xml.transform.TransformerFactory;
import javax.xml.transform.Transformer;
import javax.xml.transform.Templates;
import javax.xml.transform.stream.StreamSource;
import javax.xml.transform.stream.StreamResult;
import javax.xml.transform.dom.DOMSource;

public class XmlMsgHandler {
    private javax.xml.transform.TransformerFactory transformerFactory = null;
    private javax.xml.transform.Transformer transformer = null;
    private javax.xml.parsers.DocumentBuilderFactory documentBuilderFactory = null;
    private javax.xml.parsers.DocumentBuilder documentBuilder = null;
    private final java.lang.String styleSheetFileName = "msgTransform.xsl";
    private javax.xml.transform.Templates templates = null;
```

The imports for JAXP, SAX, and DOM probably look familiar from out earlier examples. The TRaX imports probably will not be familiar.

TRaX is a new addition to the JAXP API to encapsulate XML transformers in a vendor-neutral manner, the same as it does for SAX and DOM. In this case, we will be using TRaX to access the Xerces XSLT processor, which comes with the JAXP distribution. We will not cover XSLT in detail here, but essentially it is a stylesheet language for transforming XML from one form to another. Probably the most common use of XSLT is to transform an XML document containing data into a presentation markup language, like WML or HTML (which XSLT handles as a special case). Here, we will use it simply to add the log entry to the XML message.

It is a trivial example of a very powerful technology, but it does make an interesting point. Once you have a basic dispatcher/handler program written in Java, the actual behavior of the program for different messages can be implemented as a stylesheet. The advantage to this is that additional behavior for new message types can simply be added as new stylesheet that is registered with the application. The Java code never needs to be recompiled. XSLT, although complex, is extremely powerful at transforming XML, and is often much simpler to write than the equivalent Java code.

Furthermore, there are a number of graphic mapping programs becoming available that automatically generate XSLT based on associations created between an input and output DOM. This would allow an administrator with no significant knowledge of XSLT to create transforms between input and output messages. Graphical transform utilities are commonly available for commercial-grade message routers, such as IBM's MQSeries Integrator or Mercator's e-Business Broker.

Let's have a look at the constructor for our message handler:

```
public XmlMsgHandler() throws ParsingException {

    //Initialize message handler object
    transformerFactory = TransformerFactory.newInstance();
    try {
        // Use transformer templates.
        templates = transformerFactory.newTemplates(new
        StreamSource(styleSheetFileName));
    } catch (javax.xml.transform.TransformerException e) {
        throw new ParsingException("\nCaught TransformerException: " + e);
    }
    documentBuilderFactory = DocumentBuilderFactory.newInstance();

    //Turn off validation, and turn off namespaces
    documentBuilderFactory.setValidating(false);
    documentBuilderFactory.setNamespaceAware(false);

    try {
        documentBuilder = documentBuilderFactory.newDocumentBuilder();
    } catch (javax.xml.parsers.ParserConfigurationException e) {
        throw new ParsingException("Caught ParserConfigurationException: " + e);
    }
}
```

The first thing to notice is that it throws a ParsingException. This is a simple new exception we will define later as a catchall for parsing errors. It simply extends java.lang.Exception.

In the above constructor for XmlMsgHandler, most of the code should be fairly familiar setup from the DOM example we did earlier. Note here we are creating a TRaX template from an XSLT style sheet residing in the file msgTransform.xsl (more on this file later). In a real application, we would load a set of different transforms, each for a different message type. To simplify things, here we will just use one. The template is a compiled version of the stylesheet that we will apply to each incoming message. It acts as a thread-safe factory for transformer objects, which we will encounter later, that actually effect the transform.

Now we need a method so that the handler can pass in a text-based input message, and get back an output message and the queue it should be placed in. We need a simple structure DestinationBoundMsg to contain this output, which we'll look at next. Here is the analysis routine, which returns a DestinationBoundMsg object:

```
public DestinationBoundMsg analyzeMsg(String textInputMsg)
    throws ParsingException {

    // Parse document into DOM tree
    StringReader stringReader = new StringReader(textInputMsg);
    InputSource inputSource = new InputSource(stringReader);
    Document document = null;
    try {
```

```
        document = documentBuilder.parse(inputSource);
        document.normalize();
    } catch (IOException e) {
        throw new ParsingException("Caught IOException: " + e);
    } catch (SAXException e) {
      throw new ParsingException("Caught SAXException: " + e);
    }

    //Get destination name based on query of document
    String destinationName = getDestinationName(document);

    //Use XSLT transform to add fields to message and convert into a stream we
    //can easily convert to a string.
    StringWriter buffer = new StringWriter();
    try {
        // Get transformer from templates factory.
        transformer = templates.newTransformer();
    transformer.transform(new DOMSource(document), new StreamResult(buffer));
    } catch (javax.xml.transform.TransformerException e) {
        throw new ParsingException("Caught TransformerException: " + e);
    }

    return new DestinationBoundMsg(destinationName, buffer.toString());
}
```

As you can see, first we create a DOM document object from the input message. We then query this document for the destination name (we will cover this in a moment). Finally, we take our DOM document and apply a transform to it, adding the log entry. Notice that the `transform()` method takes an input `DOMSource` object, and output `StreamResult` object as parameters. TraX also provides a number of wrappers for different input and output types:

❑   `DOMSource`, `DOMResult`

❑   `SAXSource`, `SAXResult`

❑   `StreamSource`, `StreamResult`

These can be mixed and matched in different pairs, such as `SAXSource` in and `DOMSource` out. This provides you with the ability to transform between XML representations. This is very powerful. In the `analyzeMsg()` method, we are exploiting this to render the output as a stream, which we can easily convert to a string reply message and encapsulate in the output `DestinationBoundMsg`.

Here is the code to find the service name:

```
public String getDestinationName(Document document) throws ParsingException {
    //Use XPath-like syntax to get service element
    Element rootElement = document.getDocumentElement();
    XmlUtilities xmlUtilities = new XmlUtilities();
    NodeListImpl nodeList = xmlUtilities.findElementByQuery( rootElement,
        "/Header/Service");
    if (nodeList.getLength() != 1){
        throw new ParsingException("ParsingError: " +
        "Could not find service or found multiple services.");
    }
    Element service = (Element) nodeList.item(0);

    //Get attribute value from service
    String serviceName = service.getAttribute("name");
```

At this point, we would probably use a naming service to map the service attribute to a destination. JNDI would be a good choice, but we could also query a singleton information service that is initialized with an XML properties file. To simplify the example, we will use the `serviceName` directly, and assume it maps directly to a logical queue or topic name:

```
    return serviceName;
  }
}
```

Here is the container class for the returned messages:

```
package xmlrouter;

public class DestinationBoundMsg {
   private String destination = null;
   private String msg = null;

   public DestinationBoundMsg() {
      super();
   }

   public DestinationBoundMsg(String destination, String msg) {
      this.destination = destination;
      this.msg = msg;
   }

   public java.lang.String getDestination() {
      return destination;
   }

   public java.lang.String getMessage() {
      return msg;
   }

   public java.lang.String getMsg() {
      return msg;
   }

   public void setDestination(java.lang.String newDestination) {
      destination = newDestination;
   }

   public void setMsg(java.lang.String newMsg) {
      msg = newMsg;
   }
}
```

For completeness, here is the code for the `ParsingException`:

```
package xmlrouter;

public class ParsingException extends Exception {

   public ParsingException() {
      super();
   }
   public ParsingException(String s) {
      super(s);
   }
}
```

We could simply walk the tree as we saw in the prior DOM examples, but let's try something different. XPath is powerful query syntax for accessing information in XML documents. As we will see later when we examine our stylesheet, it is commonly used in XSLT applications. The simplest form of XPath queries uses a file system like notation to indicate an element. For example, we could isolate the service element in our example using the query: "/Envelope/Header/Service". This simplicity has made XPath a favorite tool among XML developers. XPath actually has very rich query syntax, but we only need to do simple queries like the one above. Rather than use an existing XPath service, we will write our greatly simplified version so that you can become a little more familiar with DOM concepts.

The example above makes a query for the element Service subordinate to Header that in turn is subordinate to the current element (our query is being done from the Envelope element down. Here is the XmlUtilities class. Note that it makes a recursive depth-first search for elements matching the query string. It returns a NodeListImpl, essentially a list of nodes that match the query.

```java
package xmlrouter;

import org.w3c.dom.Node;
import org.w3c.dom.NodeList;

public class XmlUtilities {
```

Return NodeListImpl list of elements matching XPath-like queryString; only supports very simple fully qualified queries like a/b/c:

```java
    public NodeListImpl findElementByQuery(Node parent, String queryString)
        throws ParsingException {
        NodeListImpl nodeListImpl = new NodeListImpl();
        String thisElement;
        String queryTail;
        if (queryString.charAt(0) != '/') {
            throw new ParsingException("Malformed query string: " + queryString);
        }

        boolean queryTerminus;
        int elementEnd = queryString.indexOf("/", 1);
        if (elementEnd == -1) {
            queryTerminus = true;
            thisElement = queryString.substring(1);
            queryTail = null;
        } else {
            queryTerminus = false;
            thisElement = queryString.substring(1, elementEnd);
            queryTail = queryString.substring(elementEnd);
        }

        //Iterate through list of children. Return all children matching query
        NodeList nodeList = parent.getChildNodes();
        for (int i = 0; i < nodeList.getLength(); i++) {
            Node child = nodeList.item(i);
            if (child.getNodeType() == Node.ELEMENT_NODE) {
                if (child.getNodeName().compareTo(thisElement) == 0) {
                    if (queryTerminus) {
                        nodeListImpl.add(child);
```

```
        } else {
            nodeListImpl.add(findElementByQuery(child, queryTail));
        }
    }
  }
}
return nodeListImpl;
}
}
```

The `NodeListImpl` is a concrete implementation of the DOM `NodeList` interface. Every time we find a node that matches the full query, we place it in the list. As we back up through our recursion stack, we also aggregate multiple lists into a `NodeListImpl` that is ultimately returned to the caller. Here is the code for the `NodeListImpl`:

```java
package xmlrouter;

import java.util.ArrayList;

public class NodeListImpl implements org.w3c.dom.NodeList {
    private ArrayList nodes = new ArrayList();

    public NodeListImpl() {
        super();
    }

    public void add(NodeListImpl nodeListImpl) {
        if (nodeListImpl.getLength()>0) {
            nodes.addAll(nodeListImpl.getNodes());
        }
    }

    public void add(org.w3c.dom.Node node) {
        nodes.add(node);
    }

    public int getLength() {
        return nodes.size();
    }

    public ArrayList getNodes() {
        return nodes;
    }

    public org.w3c.dom.Node item(int i) {
        return (org.w3c.dom.Node) nodes.get(i);
    }
}
```

That's it for the `XmlMsgHandler` class itself. Here is the stylesheet. This should be called `msgTransform.xsl`, and should reside in the directory you run the program from:

```
<?xml version="1.0"?>
<xsl:stylesheet xmlns:xsl="http://www.w3.org/1999/XSL/Transform" version="1.0">

<xsl:template><xsl:apply-templates /></xsl:template>

<xsl:template name="/">
   <xsl:copy>
      <xsl:apply-templates />
   </xsl:copy>
</xsl:template>

<xsl:template match="Envelope">
   <xsl:copy>
    <xsl:apply-templates />
   </xsl:copy>
</xsl:template>

<xsl:template match="Header">
   <xsl:copy>
   <log>Request received by router#1
   </log>
    <xsl:apply-templates />
   </xsl:copy>
</xsl:template>

<xsl:template match="Body">
   <xsl:copy>
      <xsl:for-each select="/">

         <xsl:copy />
      </xsl:for-each>
      <xsl:apply-templates />
   </xsl:copy>
</xsl:template>

<xsl:template match="Service">
<xsl:copy>
        <xsl:attribute name="name">
        <xsl:value-of select="@name" />
        </xsl:attribute>
</xsl:copy>
</xsl:template>

</xsl:stylesheet>
```

We will not try to go into detail about XSLT here. Wrox does have some excellent references, such the *XSLT Programmer's Reference* ISBN 1-861003-12-9, if you are interested. The thing to notice is the addition of the log entry, under the template match for the header element. Most of the remainder of the style sheet is responsible for echoing existing structure as is.

Now let's consider the JMS dispatcher. In this example, we will make use or the asynchronous message listener model. Our implementation will be single-threaded; however it is easy to extend the example to work with multiple JMS queueSessions in multiple threads. These could potentially be monitoring one input queue, or multiple input queues.

Here is our dispatcher class, called `MessageRouter`. This is where the `main()` method resides for this program:

```
package xmlrouter;

import javax.jms.QueueSession;
import javax.jms.QueueConnection;
import javax.jms.Queue;
import javax.jms.JMSException;
import java.util.Properties;
import javax.jms.QueueConnectionFactory;

public class MessageRouter {

    private Listener listener = null;
    private QueueConnection queueConnection = null;
    private QueueSession queueSession = null;

    public static void main(String[] args) {
        if (args.length != 1) {
            System.err.println("Usage: java MessageRouter QueueName");
            System.exit(0);
        }
        print("MessageRouter starting...");
        MessageRouter messageRouter = new MessageRouter();
        try {
            messageRouter.init(args);
            messageRouter.monitor();
        } catch (JMSException e) {
            e.printStackTrace();
        } catch (ParsingException e) {
            e.printStackTrace();
        }
        print("MessageRouter done.");
    }

    void init(String[] args) throws JMSException, ParsingException  {
        print("Creating a new connection factory");

        JNDIHelper h = new JNDIHelper();
        QueueConnectionFactory queueConnectionFactory =
            (QueueConnectionFactory) h.getConnectionFactory("qcFactory");

        //Create a connection
        print("Creating a new connection ");
        queueConnection = queueConnectionFactory.createQueueConnection();

        print("Creating a new queue session ");
        queueSession =
            queueConnection.createQueueSession(false,
            QueueSession.CLIENT_ACKNOWLEDGE);

        queueSession.recover();
```

```
        //Create a queue with a Queue Name
        String queueName = args[0];
        print("Creating a new queue: " + queueName);
        Queue queue = queueSession.createQueue(queueName);

        // Initialize listener object. It's onMessage() method will handle
        // incoming messages. This could throw a ParsingException if init fails.
        listener = new Listener(queueSession, queue);

        // Start connection.
        print("Starting connection");
        queueConnection.start();
    }

    public void monitor() {
        // Hang around until termination order appears, then cleanup.
        while (true) {
            try {
                Thread.sleep(1000);
            } catch (Exception e) {
                // Do nothing
            }
            if (listener.terminateFlag) {
                print("Closing down all resources...");
                try {
                    listener.close();
                    queueConnection.close();
                } catch (JMSException jmse) {
                    jmse.printStackTrace();
                }
                break;
            }
        }
    }

    public static void print(String s) {
        System.out.println("MessageRouter \t:"+s);
    }
}
```

Here is our message listener, called `Listener`:

```
package xmlrouter;

import javax.jms.QueueSession;
import javax.jms.Message;
import javax.jms.TextMessage;
import javax.jms.Queue;
import javax.jms.QueueReceiver;
import javax.jms.QueueSender;
import javax.jms.JMSException;
```

```java
public class Listener implements javax.jms.MessageListener {
    private QueueReceiver queueReceiver;
    private QueueSession queueSession;
    public boolean terminateFlag = false;
    private XmlMsgHandler xmlMsgHandler = null;

    public Listener(QueueSession queueSession, Queue queue)
        throws JMSException, ParsingException {
        this.queueSession = queueSession;
        queueReceiver = queueSession.createReceiver(queue);
        queueReceiver.setMessageListener(this);
        xmlMsgHandler = new XmlMsgHandler();
    }

    public void close() throws JMSException {
        //Have to cleanup outside the onMessage() call or things blow up...
        print("Starting cleanup");
        queueReceiver.setMessageListener(null);
        queueSession.close();
    }

    public static void print(String s) {
        System.out.println("Listener \t:"+s);
    }

    public String getInputMsg(Message message) throws javax.jms.JMSException {
        TextMessage textMessage = (TextMessage) message;
        String textInputMsg = textMessage.getText();
        textMessage.acknowledge();
        return textInputMsg;
    }

    public void onMessage(Message message) {

        try {
            // Get text contents of message
            String textInputMsg = getInputMsg(message);
            print("Received: "+textInputMsg);

            // Parse and transform message
            DestinationBoundMsg destinationBoundMsg =
            xmlMsgHandler.analyzeMsg(textInputMsg);
            print("Output Message Destination: " +
                    destinationBoundMsg.getDestination() + "\n");
            print("Output Message:\n" + destinationBoundMsg.getMsg());

            // Send message on its way.
            sendMsg(destinationBoundMsg);

        } catch (ParsingException e) {
            e.printStackTrace();
        } catch (JMSException e) {
            e.printStackTrace();
        }
```

```
            //Program will process until terminateFlag is set to true.
            //This could be done based on some condition noted in a message.
            //if (someCondition)
            //    terminateFlag=true;
    }

    public void sendMsg(DestinationBoundMsg destinationBoundMsg)
        throws javax.jms.JMSException {

        //Send message to indicated destination
        String queueName = destinationBoundMsg.getDestination();
        Queue queue = queueSession.createQueue(queueName);
        QueueSender queueSender = queueSession.createSender(queue);
        TextMessage textMessage = queueSession.createTextMessage();
        textMessage.setText(destinationBoundMsg.getMsg());
        queueSender.send(textMessage);
        queueSender.close();
    }
}
```

Note we have commented out the termination check. You could implement some check based on message contents if desired.

Now all we need is a simple producer and consumer. Here is the producer:

```
package xmlrouter;

import javax.jms.QueueConnectionFactory;
import javax.jms.QueueConnection;
import javax.jms.QueueSession;
import javax.jms.QueueSender;
import javax.jms.Queue;
import javax.jms.TextMessage;
import javax.jms.JMSException;

public class Producer {

    public static void main(String[] args) {

        if (args.length != 2) {
            System.err.println("Usage: java Producer QueueName MsgFileName");
            System.exit(0);
        }

        //This is provider specific
        print("Creating a new connection factory");
        JNDIHelper h = new JNDIHelper();
        QueueConnectionFactory queueConnectionFactory =
          (QueueConnectionFactory) h.getConnectionFactory("qcFactory");

        try {
            print("Creating a new connection ");
            QueueConnection queueConnection =
            queueConnectionFactory.createQueueConnection();
```

```
        print("Creating a new queue session ");
        QueueSession queueSession =
        queueConnection.createQueueSession(false,
                    QueueSession.CLIENT_ACKNOWLEDGE);
        queueSession.recover();

        String queueName = args[0];
        print("Creating queue name: " + queueName);
        Queue queue = queueSession.createQueue(queueName);

        print("Starting connection");
        queueConnection.start();

        String fileName = args[1];
        print("Reading message from file: " + fileName);
        String textInputMsg = FileToString.getDocument(fileName);
        TextMessage textMessage = queueSession.createTextMessage();
        textMessage.setText(textInputMsg);

        print("Sending message... ");
        QueueSender queueSender = queueSession.createSender(queue);
        queueSender.send(textMessage);

        print("Starting cleanup");

        queueSender.close();
        queueSession.close();
        queueConnection.close();

        print("Done.");

    } catch (JMSException e) {
        e.printStackTrace();
    }
}

public static void print(String s) {
    System.out.println("PRODUCER    :"+s);
}
}
```

The producer reads a message from a file as a string using the `FileToString` utility class. The program then writes this string to the named queue and exits.

Here is the `FileToString` utility class:

```
package xmlrouter;

import java.io.*;
public class FileToString {

    public FileToString() {
        super();
    }
```

```
    public static String getDocument(String fileName) {
        File file = new File(fileName);
        StringBuffer fileText = new StringBuffer();
        try {
            FileReader fileReader = new FileReader(file);
            BufferedReader bufferedReader = new BufferedReader(fileReader);

            String line;
            while ((line = bufferedReader.readLine()) != null) {
                fileText.append(line);
                fileText.append("\n");
            }
        } catch (FileNotFoundException e) {
            System.err.println("Could not find file " + fileName);
            System.exit(0);
        } catch (IOException e) {
            System.err.println("IO Exception on file " + fileName);
            System.exit(0);
        }

        return fileText.toString();
    }
}
```

Here is the consumer:

```
package xmlrouter;

import javax.jms.QueueConnectionFactory;
import javax.jms.QueueConnection;
import javax.jms.QueueSession;
import javax.jms.QueueReceiver;
import javax.jms.Queue;
import javax.jms.TextMessage;
import javax.jms.JMSException;

public class Consumer {

    public static void main(String[] args) {
        if (args.length != 1) {
            System.err.println("Usage: java Consumer QueueName");
            System.exit(0);
        }

        //Provider specific for Sun's JMQ
        print("Creating a new connection factory");

        JNDIHelper h = new JNDIHelper();
        QueueConnectionFactory queueConnectionFactory =
            (QueueConnectionFactory) h.getConnectionFactory("qcFactory");

        try {
            print("Creating a new connection ");
            QueueConnection queueConnection =
                queueConnectionFactory.createQueueConnection();
```

```
        print("Creating a new queue session ");
        QueueSession queueSession =
        queueConnection.createQueueSession(false,
                    QueueSession.CLIENT_ACKNOWLEDGE);
        queueSession.recover();

        String queueName = args[0];
        print("Creating a new queue: " + queueName);
        Queue queue = queueSession.createQueue(queueName);

        print("Starting connection");
        queueConnection.start();
        QueueReceiver queueReceiver = queueSession.createReceiver(queue);

        boolean forever = true;
        while (forever) {
            TextMessage textMessage = (TextMessage) queueReceiver.receive();

            String text = textMessage.getText();
            print("Consumer received: " + text);
            textMessage.acknowledge();
        } // While

        print("Starting cleanup");
        queueReceiver.close();
        queueSession.close();
        queueConnection.close();

        print("Done.");

    } catch (JMSException jmse) {
     jmse.printStackTrace();
     }
  }

  public static void print(String s) {
      System.out.println("Consumer \t:"+s);
  }
}
```

The consumer runs forever, echoing what it received to standard output. A last class is a helper class called JNDIHelper. It enables all the programs to access a queue connection factory through JNDI. Here, we've chosen to set up the objects in Fiorano, but you could in theory choose any provider:

```
package xmlrouter;

import javax.naming.Context;
import javax.naming.InitialContext;
import javax.naming.NamingException;
import java.util.Properties;
import javax.jms.ConnectionFactory;
```

```
public class JNDIHelper {

    public static final String ICF="fiorano.jms.rtl.FioranoInitialContextFactory";
    public static final String URL="localhost:2001";


    public static ConnectionFactory getConnectionFactory(String factory) {
        ConnectionFactory cf = null;
        try {
            Properties p = new Properties();
            p.put(Context.INITIAL_CONTEXT_FACTORY, ICF);
            p.put(Context.PROVIDER_URL,URL);
            Context ctx = new InitialContext(p);
            cf = (ConnectionFactory) ctx.lookup(factory);
        }
        catch (NamingException n) {
            n.printStackTrace();
        }
        return cf;
    }
}
```

To run this example, compile all the code in a single directory xmlrouter, ensuring that you have all of the necessary JAR files in your path. You need jms.jar, jndi.jar, and Fiorano's fmprtl.zip for the messaging; jaxp.jar, crimson.jar, and xalan.jar from the JAXP distribution.

We must also set up Administered objects. Set up two queues in the Fiorano administration tool, one called routerInputQueue and one called buy:

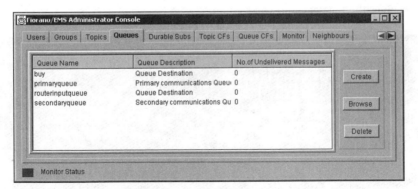

Also, set up a queue connection factory called qcFactory:

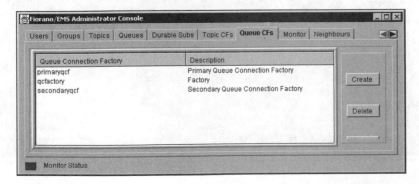

Note that we used Fiorano extensively in Chapters 4 and 5, so refer to these chapters if you have any problems. Make certain `msgTransform.xsl` and `simpleMsg.xml` are in the current directory.

Then, start the router, the consumer, and finally the producer in different windows. The following script would run the system:

```
start java xmlrouter.MessageRouter routerInputQueue
start java xmlrouter.Consumer buy
java xmlrouter.Producer routerInputQueue simpleMsg.xml
```

For example, in reverse order of our starting them up, we see the following outputs. The producer reads the file and sends the message:

```
C:\ProJMS\Chapter10>java xmlrouter.Producer routerInputQueue simpleMsg.xml
PRODUCER        :Creating a new connection factory
PRODUCER        :Creating a new connection
PRODUCER        :Creating a new queue session
PRODUCER        :Creating queue name: routerInputQueue
PRODUCER        :Starting connection
PRODUCER        :Reading message from file: simpleMsg.xml
PRODUCER        :Sending message...
PRODUCER        :Starting cleanup
PRODUCER        :Done.

C:\ProJMS\Chapter10>_
```

The router receives the message and passes it on:

```
C:\ProJMS\Chapter10>java xmlrouter.MessageRouter routerInputQueue
MessageRouter   :MessageRouter starting...
MessageRouter   :Creating a new connection factory
MessageRouter   :Creating a new connection
MessageRouter   :Creating a new queue session
MessageRouter   :Creating a new queue: routerInputQueue
MessageRouter   :Starting connection
Listener        :Received: <?xml version="1.0" encoding="UTF-8"?>
<Envelope>
  <Header>
    <Service name="buy"/>
  </Header>
  <Body>
    <Trade>
      <Stock>
        Wrox
      </Stock>
      <Number>
        1000
      </Number>
    </Trade>
  </Body>
</Envelope>

Listener        :Output Message Destination: buy

Listener        :Output Message:
<?xml version="1.0" encoding="UTF-8"?>
<Envelope> <Header><log>Request received by router#1
    </log> <Service name="buy"/> </Header> <Body>    Wrox    1000    </Body> </
Envelope>
```

The consumer picks up the message:

```
Command Prompt - java xmlrouter.Consumer buy                    _ □ ×
C:\ProJMS\Chapter10>java xmlrouter.Consumer buy
Consumer           :Creating a new connection factory
Consumer           :Creating a new connection
Consumer           :Creating a new queue session
Consumer           :Creating a new queue: buy
Consumer           :Starting connection
Consumer           :Consumer received: <?xml version="1.0" encoding="UTF-8"?>
<Envelope> <Header><log>Request received by router#1
      </log> <Service name="buy"/> </Header> <Body>   Wrox   1000   </Body> </
Envelope>
```

Note that queues are created dynamically here (however in Fiorano, it is necessary to register the queue objects), so you can vary the service names in the message. You may want to start multiple consumers to receive these. The router will print the input message, and the output destination queue and message. The consumer will also print each message it reads.

Emerging Standards

The real power of XML is that it is extensible. Of course, this is also its problem: we could easily be faced with a cacophony of competing, idiosyncratic messaging structures. Fortunately, there are standardization efforts underway. Some of these simply attempt to describe a basic, extensible message structure, others deal with issues such as service discovery, orchestration of message exchanges, distributed repositories, etc.

In Appendix C, we will examine a sample of the efforts now underway. Few of these at present define an explicit model for access using JMS – much of the momentum here is in the emerging web services arena, which emphasizes the use of HTTP as a lightweight transport. However, many of these efforts will ultimately support bindings to Message-Oriented Middleware (MOM) systems, particularly through the JMS API. In the meantime, some of these efforts – particularly those defining basic message formats – are mature enough to serve as the basis for JMS messaging now, with only a few relatively safe assumptions. The point of this section is twofold: to bring your attention to what may be important future protocols in the messaging world; and to serve as an inspiration for your own messaging definitions if you cannot align to the standard immediately. It is always better to take advantage of existing experience that to try to reinvent from nothing.

Summary

We have seen how coupling occurs between systems, based on API, on communication style, and on environment. One of the best reasons to adopt JMS is to build loosely coupled systems that are independent, flexible, and tolerant of changes. We explored how XML can contribute further to building loosely coupled systems. XML brings standards, vendor and system independence, internationalization, and flexibility to messaging systems. Consideration must be given to issues like parsing overhead, bandwidth utilization, and how to effectively package non-XML data. We have considered three different models of accessing the data in XML-based messages: through the DOM, using SAX; and finally using data binding, which is still in its infancy, but promises to greatly simplify how developers work with XML messages.

We then looked at what is involved in writing applications that use both JMS and XML together. This is an area that remains immature, with no real standards to guide developers; however, based on what we know about XML messaging in the web services arena, we can identify some best practices. Using these, we developed a simple XML router that reads messages from an incoming queue, and routes them to an outgoing queue based on the message content. This example also gave us a basic framework for doing simple stylesheet transforms on messages. As graphical XML translation tools mature, allowing automatic generation of stylesheets, message translations like this will become quite common.

In the final chapter, we will look at one area where JMS and messaging could be of considerable potential – mobile messaging.

com.sun.jn...
weblogic.jndi.T3Initial...
fiorano.jms.rtl.fioran...
ch.softwired.jms.naming.n...
com.sun.jndi.LdapCtxFactory
weblogic.jndi.WLInitialContextFactory
com.sun.jndi.fscontext.RefFSContextFactory
fiorano.jms.runtime.FioranoInitialContextFactory
weblogic.jndi.T3InitialContextFactory
fiorano.jms.rtl.fioranoInitialContextFactory
ch.softwired.jms.naming.IBusContextFactory

com.sun.jndi.fscontext.RefFSContextFactory
weblogic.jndi.ldap.LdapCtxFactory
weblogic.jndi.WLInitialContextFactory
fiorano.jms.rtl.T3InitialContextFactory
fiorano.jms.runtime.FioranoInitialContextFactory
ch.softwired.jms.naming.IBusContextFactory

11

JMS for Mobile Applications and Wireless Communication

The emergence of mobile devices and packet-oriented wireless bearers is generating a new mass market that is expected to surpass one billion users this decade. The new **Wireless Net**, connecting mobile devices using wireless bearers, promises exciting new opportunities.

After analysing problems and requirements of next-generation wireless services, we will conclude that JMS, when implemented correctly, offers an ideal middleware solution for such services.

The chapter is structured as follows:

❑ We'll first look at current market trends in the mobile messaging world

❑ We'll give an overview of current-generation and next-generation wireless bearers

❑ We'll then describe the mobile device platforms that are being considered for the new generation of mobile phones and communicators, namely Symbian, Palm OS, and Windows CE

❑ We'll cover some of the technical issues facing mobile applications

❑ By taking those issues as a starting point, we'll derive some requirements for mobile applications middleware

❑ We'll show how JMS can be used for developing wireless applications that are interactive and able to deliver richer content to the user

❑ Finally, we'll give example applications enabled by mobile JMS technology

First of all, however, let's make sure we are on the same page with some definitions of the different technologies in this area.

Terminology

The growth of the mobile applications industry has given rise to a vocabulary of new acronyms and terms, some of which will be familiar, and some not. In this preliminary section we present the main terms used in this chapter for quick reference:

Acronym	Expansion	Description
GSM	Global System for Mobile Communication	A mobile telephone system widely used in Europe
SMS	Short Message Service	A service for sending messages of up to 160 characters to mobile phones that use GSM
AMPS	Advanced Mobile Phone Service	A mobile telephone system widely used in the United States
GPRS	General Packet Radio Service	A packet-based wireless bearer based on the GSM standard
EDGE	Enhanced Data Rates for Global Evolution	A packet-based wireless bearer based on the GSM standard
UMTS	Universal Mobile Telecommunications System	A third-generation wireless bearer
i-mode	–	A mobile telephone system widely used in the United States
WAP	Wireless Application Protocol	A standard to enable users to access Internet services via their cellular phones
GPS	Global Positioning System	GPS-enabled devices are able to compute their geographic location by processing signals received from GPS satellites

Market Trends

The next few years will be characterized by:

- ❏ The appearance of new types of mobile devices or "communicators", unifying the features of cellular phones and PDAs.
- ❏ The appearance of packet-oriented wireless bearers, such as GPRS, EDGE, and UMTS. Such bearers allow a communicator to be "always on", meaning always able to receive e-mail notifications and the like, without requiring the user to dial into the network service.
- ❏ Communicator devices outnumbering personal computers with Internet access.

The Y-axis in the graph opposite shows worldwide mobile Internet subscribers versus fixed Internet subscribers. The numbers are given in millions. Countries such as Finland already have high Internet and mobile device penetration rates and might reach the crossing point earlier than 2004:

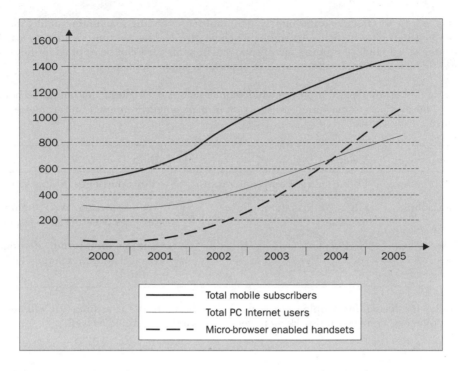

1600
1400
1200
1000
800
600
400
200

2000 2001 2002 2003 2004 2005

———— Total mobile subscribers

———— Total PC Internet users

— — — Micro-browser enabled handsets

For further resources in this area, see The Wireless Internet, *Nomura Equity Research, September* 2000: *http://www.nomura.co.uk.*

Fatter Clients

The accepted wisdom today is that communicator devices will run fatter client applications than earlier realized. With microprocessor power on mobile devices increasing more rapidly than wireless bandwidth, and with mobile users demanding applications such as chat, multimedia messaging, and trading, it makes sense to deploy custom software on the mobile device. This will allow the user to display richer content, and to use a mobile application when the mobile device is temporarily disconnected from the network. Java, XML, and messaging middleware will undoubtedly play important roles in the Wireless Net.

Machine-to-Machine Communication

At the moment, wireless communication is still used predominantly for voice calls (80% of the total traffic), but the traffic generated by data services (Internet surfing, SMS) is growing rapidly. Whereas most of the communication is occurring in human-to-human or human-to-machine forms, machine-to-machine communication is expected to become very important on the Wireless Net. The reasons are the following:

❑ Automobiles, streetcars, vending machines, and other devices are being equipped with powerful CPUs as well as with wireless modems. For example, certain Coca-Cola vending machines allow you to purchase a can by dialing into the machine or by sending an SMS message to it. A can is released immediately and charged to your phone bill.

❑ Embeddable wireless modems are getting cheaper. For example, the Siemens DECT Engines product line consists of wireless transceivers that can be embedded into consumer products and other devices.

❑ It is more cost effective to monitor and administer a vending machine remotely than by sending staff into the field. A vending machine can send an alert notification to a service center shortly before running out of supply. The same idea can be applied to the reading of gas-meters, the remote administration of parking meters, and so on.

The following table provides examples of wireless interactions occurring from human to human, human to machine, and machine to machine. A distinction is made whether interactions are voice-enabled or data-driven:

Type	Voice	Data
Human-Human	Phone calls, phone conferences	Short messages (SMS), Voice-over-IP
Human-Machine	Flight confirmation, phone banking	Web browsing, WAP, i-mode, SMS services (weather, movies, etc.)
Machine-Machine	N/A	Remote monitoring, alerting, remote administration, manufacturing control

In short, today it's normal for people to carry a cellular phone. In the near future, it will become normal for home appliances, vehicles, and parking meters to be wireless-enabled as well.

Location

At the beginning of this chapter, we stated that the combination of mobile devices and packet-oriented wireless bearers enable interesting new applications and services. But there is a third important ingredient, namely **location information**.

Consider what shopping could be like in two to three years from now. Walking along Sixth Avenue, your communicator beeps. You open it up and activate the Buddies application. This application has a radar-sweep interface, in which you see that one of your friends or relatives is located within 200 yards from you. Now both you and your friend receive an alert notification from the nearby Starbucks, offering you a discount on a tall latté in case you decide to meet at that coffee shop within 30 minutes. You can accept or deny the invitation, or simply enter a private chat session with your friend to figure out whether you want to get together or not.

Location information is likely to play an important role in mobile shopping, wireless advertising, entertainment, anti-theft systems, and so forth. Location information enables an application running on a mobile device to obtain position information about the user of the device (if the user allows this), about other users, or about objects of common interest (museums, galleries, restaurants, etc.).

There are two main techniques for providing location information to mobile applications: putting a **GPS (Global Positioning System)** module onto the device, or, in case of a mobile phone, using the geographical location of the nearby base stations to compute the location of the mobile device. Many different solutions are being tested today. They typically differ in:

❑ **Accuracy**
A high-quality positioning system can provide location information with an accuracy of 10 feet.

❑ **Efficiency**
A high-quality positioning system can compute the location of a mobile device in 1 to 2 seconds. However, GPS can incur a substantial computational burden on the mobile device.

❑ **Cost**
GPS-based location systems require the presence of a GPS hardware module on the device. The extra cost can be substantial. Positioning systems relying on base station information are often less accurate than GPS, but do not require any special hardware on the device.

❑ **Power Consumption**
Positioning solutions differ further in their power consumption. Long battery life is an important acceptance criterion for mobile devices, but a GPS module often consumes substantial battery power.

Whatever technique is used, confidentiality remains a key concern for the user of location-based services. Whoever can track your location information can draw conclusions about your shopping patterns or about other personal habits.

Another issue is the lack of application development standards for accessing location information programmatically. For example, there are no standard APIs for requesting location information in a convenient and portable way. Initially, it is expected that location information will be offered to applications via a wireless-messaging bearer, for instance SMS. In this case, a device sends an SMS message containing a special keyword to a service number. A location service sends back a reply message to the application, containing location information of the device itself, or of another device. Eventually, it is expected that APIs will be established for the Java 2 Platform, Micro Edition (J2ME) as well as for other development environments.

Wireless Bearers

Loosely speaking, a **bearer** can be defined as a wireless transport means. Anything that can transport information from one device to another is called a bearer, examples being GSM, AMPS, GPRS, Infrared (IrDA), and Bluetooth. As this book is published, there is much talk of a next-generation bearer called UMTS, and about whether it is worth the telecoms industry spending billions in UMTS licenses and infrastructure upgrades. However, these issues will be discussed later.

Bearers can be characterized as 2G, 2.5G, and 3G. 2G bearers are the so-called connection-oriented bearers, whereas 2.5G and 3G are packet-oriented.

> *G stands for "Generation".*

Connection-Oriented versus Packet-Oriented

A **connection-oriented bearer** requires a sender of information to establish a network connection to a network service provider or ISP, before any data can be sent. This has two disadvantages for mobile applications. First, establishing a connection is a time-consuming process, as users of WAP-over-GSM have experienced. Second, it is not possible to "push" a notification to a mobile device without forcing the device to establish a network connection. With a connection-oriented bearer, users are typically charged for the whole time the connection is open, no matter whether data is transmitted through that connection or not.

On the other hand, with a **packet-oriented bearer**, a device can send and receive packets of information without the need to dial into a network service provider or ISP. Spontaneous networking and communication becomes a reality. The term "always-on communication" is often used to denote that a service can send a data packet to a device, and that the device can respond to the packet immediately by alerting the user, for example. With packet data, users will only pay for the amount of data they actually communicate, and not for idle time.

We can say that packet-oriented bearers are much better suited to the connectionless model of JMS, and that there is an "ideal fit" between the two technologies. This will be further motivated later in the chapter.

Second Generation (2G) Bearers

Second generation bearers are able to transport data reliably from one device to another, although at a rather low speed, examples being GSM, AMPS, and HSCSD. Also, 2G bearers are connection-oriented.

GSM

GSM (Global System for Mobile communication) offers data transmission speeds of up to 9,600 bps. It is a digital mobile telephone system that is widely used in Europe and other parts of the world, and uses a variation of time division multiple access (TDMA). It is currently the most widely used digital wireless telephone technology in the world. According to the GSM Association, GSM has over 120 million users worldwide and is available in 120 countries.

GSM digitizes and compresses data, then sends it down a channel with two other streams of user data, each in its own time slot. It operates at either the 900 MHz or 1,800 MHz frequency band. The choice of frequency is implemented in the mobile device's hardware.

Another interesting feature of GSM is that it includes the SMS wireless messaging solution, which is quickly growing in popularity.

AMPS/DAMPS

Digital-Advanced Mobile Phone Service (D-AMPS), sometimes spelled **DAMPS**, is a digital version of Advanced Mobile Phone Service, the original analog standard for cellular telephone service in the United States. Both DAMPS and AMPS are now used in many countries. Like GSM, DAMPS implements the TDMA standard.

For further information see Second Generation Mobile and Wireless Networks, *Ulysses Black, Prentice Hall 1998, ISBN 0-136212-77-8.*

HSCSD

High-Speed Circuit-Switched Data (HSCSD) is circuit-switched wireless data transmission for mobile users at data rates up to 38.4 kbps, four times faster than the standard data rates of GSM. HSCSD is comparable to the speed of many computer modems that communicate through today's fixed telephone networks.

2.5 Generation (2.5G) Bearers

It's still a long way to go until 3G bearers such as UMTS are both available and cheap. UMTS is not expected to become widely available until 2003. There is a risk that UMTS will not be successful due to the problems mentioned below. For this reason, 2.5G bearers such as GPRS and EDGE are being launched. Those bearers are packet-oriented and provide transmission speeds of up to a few hundred kilobits per second.

GPRS

General Packet Radio Service (GPRS) is a packet-based wireless communication service that, when available in 2001, promises data rates from 56 up to 114kbps and continuous connection to the Internet for mobile phone and computer users. GPRS directly supports the Internet Protocol (IP) and the CCITT X.25 protocol. A mobile GPRS application will typically use the TCP/IP or UDP protocol over GPRS.

Even though the transmission rate of GPRS is still much too low for multimedia and other traffic intensive applications, it provides an important new feature making it very appealing for JMS – GPRS is a packet oriented bearer, as opposed to GSM, AMPS/DAMPS, and HSCSD, which are connection-oriented bearers.

EDGE

Enhanced Data Rates for Global Evolution (EDGE), a faster version of the GSM wireless service, is designed to deliver data at rates up to 384 kbps and enables the delivery of multimedia and other broadband applications to mobile phone and computer users.

EDGE is a packet-oriented bearer delivering much higher speed than GPRS, anticipating the speed advances of UMTS. Also, EDGE does not incur high license cost and does not require a new network infrastructure. It might not be as fast as UMTS, but could well turn out much cheaper.

The EDGE standard is built on the existing GSM standard, using the same frame structure and cell arrangements. Ericsson notes that, when available, its base stations can be updated purely with software, without the need to exchange hardware components. Wireless data services based on EDGE are expected to become widely available during 2002.

See Ericsson's website for more details on EDGE's capabilities: http://www.ericsson.com /wireless/products/mobsys/gsm/subpages/umts_and_3g/edge.shtml

Third Generation (3G) Bearers

Third generation bearers are also packet-oriented but provide data speeds of more than 1 mbps. This makes those bearers appealing for multimedia applications, video conferencing, high-quality real audio, and so forth.

UMTS

Universal Mobile Telecommunications System (UMTS) is the most talked about and controversial broadband bearer. UMTS transmits text, digitized voice, video, and multimedia at data rates up to and possibly higher than 2 megabits per second, offering a consistent set of services to mobile computer and phone users no matter where they are located in the world. UMTS is geared to provide a fast and direct packet switched IP service to the end user.

Endorsed by major standards bodies and manufacturers, UMTS is planned to be the world standard for mobile connectivity by 2003. Once UMTS is fully implemented, mobile computer and phone users can be constantly connected to the Internet as they travel. However, the following concerns are being voiced in respect to the deployment of UMTS:

❑ **High cost of licenses**
European governments are selling UMTS licenses to the highest bidders, through an auctioning mechanism. Some carriers have spent billions acquiring UMTS licenses. The question is: how will the carriers make this investment profitable?

521

❑ **High cost of infrastructure**
UMTS requires new network infrastructure. The investment costs can be several billion dollars, in addition to the already paid license fees. Again, we should ask about the business model, and about how the telecoms industry are working on making that investment profitable, given that UMTS itself will eventually be replaced by an even faster technology.

❑ **Resistance**
Rolling out new base stations is not easy, as the population is becoming more concerned about health risks imposed by electromagnetic radiation. Lawsuits could impose a considerable delay on the rollout of UMTS infrastructure.

❑ **Transmission rates lower than advertised**
UMTS is poised to provide transmission rates higher than 1 mbps. But in reality, such transmission rates will be achieved only in the ideal – and rare – situation where your UMTS base station is underutilized, located nearby, and when you are standing still. Initially, UMTS transmission rates could be as low as 100 kbps, leading to disappointment and maybe even rejection of UMTS technology.

Other Bearers

Wireless LANs have the potential of providing high-speed interconnectivity in metropolitan areas or in buildings, at a low cost. Another bearer to watch is **Bluetooth**, which provides high-speed wireless connections between a variety of devices (phone, headset, PDA, printer) over distances of a few meters.

An intelligent combination of EDGE, wireless LAN technology, and Bluetooth might result in an appealing and cost-effective alternative to UMTS. For example, railway stations, airports, restaurants and other public locations could be equipped with a Wireless LAN or Bluetooth technology. This allows fast Internet access for travelers, as well as mobile access to business data through Virtual Private Networks (VPNs). Outside those locations, EDGE provides the mobile user with sufficient bandwidth for Web surfing and e-mail access.

Wireless LANs, Bluetooth, and EDGE incur much lower license and infrastructure cost than UMTS. Nevertheless, bandwidth of more than 10 megabits per seconds (Wireless LAN) can be offered in airports and other frequently visited locations.

Availability of Wireless Bearers

The following table summarizes the main characteristics of current- and next-generation wireless bearers:

Bearer	Availability	Where	Speed	Features
GSM	Early 1990s	Europe, Asia	9.6 kbps	Connection-oriented, incorporates wireless messaging (SMS)
DAMPS	Early 1990s	USA	13 kbps	Connection-oriented
HSCSD	1999	Europe	38.4 kbps	Connection-oriented, based on GSM

Bearer	Availability	Where	Speed	Features
GPRS	2000/2001	Europe, Asia, USA	115 kbps	Packet-oriented, based on GSM
EDGE	2001/2002	Europe, Asia, USA	384 kbps	Packet-oriented, based on GSM
UMTS	2003 (?)	Worldwide	2 mbps	Packet-oriented, requires new network infrastructure

For further sources in this area, please see Winning in Mobile eMarkets, *Market study by TIMElabs Research Center, 2000,* http://www.timelabs.de.

Wireless Device Platforms

Wireless operating systems also represent a crucial point of control in the emerging market for wireless solutions. The three main contenders are Symbian, Palm OS, and Windows CE. In the author's view, Symbian is the most likely to emerge as the leading technology in this area because it is backed by the telecommunications industry (notably Ericsson, Nokia, and Motorola) and represents the most solid and flexible technology.

In the following sections we will look at Symbian, Palm OS, and Windows CE mostly from the point of view of operating system support for Java applications, and for various communication bearers.

Symbian

Symbian is at the heart of the mobile handset manufacturers' plans to dominate the Wireless Net. Symbian is a UK-based corporation and was established by Ericsson, Motorola, Nokia, and Psion, in December 1998, with Matsushita (Panasonic) joining as a shareholder in May 1999. Symbian is dedicated to working closely with the wireless community in order to enable a mass market for communicator devices. Symbian has established strategic partnerships with the global leaders in the wireless industry, as well as international companies from all areas of the wireless value chain.

The Symbian mobile device platform is based on the EPOC operating system, which was originally designed by the Psion team. The Symbian platform is a multi-threaded, multi-tasking operating system optimized for next-generation mobile devices, such as smart phones and communicators.

Key Features

The key features of the Symbian platform are:

❑ There are three reference designs:

  ❑ Quartz is aimed at communicators with pen based input

  ❑ Crystal is aimed at communicators with a keyboard

  ❑ Pearl is aimed at smart phones

❑ Supported programming languages are C++, Java (PersonalJava and J2ME), and OPL. PersonalJava provides a JDK 1.1.x-compatible execution environment for small devices, and thus supports `java.net` sockets and object serialization, making it an ideal Java platform for implementing JMS. J2ME is a Java execution environment targeted at small devices, but is more restrictive than PersonalJava. For example, J2ME does not support object serialization. Nevertheless, J2ME can be used to implement all of the JMS abstractions, except the `javax.jms.ObjectMessage` type.

❑ Close integration of contact information, messaging, browsing, and wireless telephony (for instance, using the JavaPhone API).

❑ Support for various communication protocols and bearers TCP/IP, WAP, GSM, Bluetooth, IrDA, and serial line.

❑ Full-strength encryption and certificate management, secure communications protocols, as well as certificate-based application installation.

❑ Microkernel 32-bit operating system design, supporting multithreading and "background" services, as well as protected memory.

> **The Symbian platform is ideally suited for running sophisticated, mobile Java applications. Symbian has officially committed to supporting the Java platform and a PersonalJava-compatible JVM is included on the Symbian platform.**

Palm OS

At the time of writing Palm OS owns 70% of the US PDA market. However, the question whether Palm Computing will be able to establish a strong foothold in the emerging communicator market will become clear during the next few years.

The Pilot-connected organizer was invented back in 1995. Before the advent of the Palm platform, Palm Computing was developing software for other handheld devices, working with many hardware manufacturers to have them adopt the vision of those at Palm Computing. This turned out to be a very difficult task and so Palm Computing decided to create its own hardware – and the Palm was born.

The fundamental idea behind its strategy was to grow a large base of customers using the devices as personal organizers, and then to focus on signing up developers to broaden their usefulness. Today the Palm Developer Network has attracted more than 50,000 developers.

Key Features

The Palm OS platform consists of five primary components:

❑ Palm OS software

❑ Reference hardware design

❑ HotSync conduit data synchronization technology for one-button synchronization

❑ Platform component tools including an API that enables developers to write applications

❑ Software interface capabilities to support hardware add-ons

The Palm OS platform architecture is shown diagrammatically below:

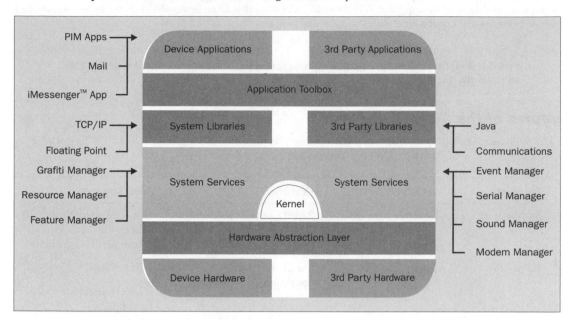

The operating system design of the Palm OS is much more simplistic and less flexible than Symbian. For example, Palm OS supports neither multithreading nor multitasking. Also, the strategy of Palm Computing in respect to Java is unclear. The company has not officially committed to supporting Java on Palm OS. As of today, applications for the Palm are written predominantly in the C programming language and not in Java.

Windows CE

Windows CE is Microsoft's 32-bit operating system for mobile devices and Pocket PCs. Windows CE implements the Windows desktop metaphor popular on PCs and laptops. In spite of a massive marketing effort, Windows CE has grabbed only a relatively small share of the market share to date. One reason might be that the desktop metaphor is appealing for PCs and laptops, but many users find it awkward on mobile devices.

The key features are:

❑ Protected virtual memory increases reliability, since a faulty application cannot damage other running applications or the operating system services

❑ Processes and threads allows Windows CE to execute multiple tasks or applications in parallel

❑ Advanced power management

❑ Advanced user interface services and components

❑ Communications protocols TCP/IP, SSL, Serial, IrDA, Telephony API (TAPI), and SNMP

Although Microsoft does not officially support Java in its development environment for Windows CE, Java execution environments for Windows CE are available from several vendors. Typically, those Java environments are compatible with the PersonalJava standard.

> **Protected virtual memory, 32-bit technology, and native threads make Windows CE an ideal platform for mobile Java applications.**

Features of the Main Platforms

The following table summarizes the main characteristics of Symbian, Palm OS, and Windows CE, from the point of view of running JMS applications on them:

Platform	Availability	Features	Java Support
Symbian	Quartz: Now Crystal: 1Q/2001 Pearl: 2001	32 bit operating system, with low footprint and low resource usage	PersonalJava: Now J2ME: 2001 (Strategic for Symbian)
Palm OS	Now	Simplistic 16 bit operating system design	J2ME: Now (Not strategic for Palm Computing)
Windows CE	Now	32 bit operating system	PersonalJava: Now (Not strategic for Microsoft)

Other Platforms to Watch

Other platforms to watch closely are embeddable variants of the Linux operating system, as well as real-time operating systems such as VxWorks and OS-9.

Mobility Issues

Mobile applications present many challenges for software developers. These challenges are not adequately addressed by data communication techniques such as HTTP, CORBA, or RMI, which were designed for wired environments. At this early stage of experience with wireless systems, mobile applications are typically written to function on one particular type of device or PDA. To work well on another type of device, applications must be rewritten. This is obviously an uneconomical process with the proliferation of device types.

In the wired world, middleware has been used very successfully for almost two decades now to allow applications to run on multiple platforms without need to rewrite them. Therefore it's an appealing idea to also use middleware on mobile devices, to make mobile applications more portable. However, most middleware products on the market today have not been tailored for mobile devices. For example, they require more memory than is available on a PDA and only support communication protocols that were designed for wired networks, notably TCP/IP.

In this section we will look at the very specific issues of developing mobile applications, and derive requirements for mobile messaging middleware. In the next section, we show that JMS provides an ideal platform for hosting mobile applications, if the JMS middleware adequately addresses the needs and restrictions of mobile applications.

Developing applications to run on mobile devices requires developers to deal with issues not present in traditional fixed line systems:

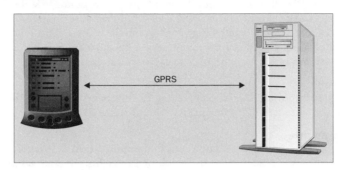

Consider the simple scenario depicted above:

- **Disconnected operation**
  Mobile applications lose and regain network connectivity much more often than non-mobile applications. The developer must be able to cope with intermittent communication links and implement software layers that ensure the delivery of important data between the server and the mobile device.

- **Resource constraints**
  Mobile applications must be optimized aggressively for small ROM and RAM footprints, as well as for low usage of CPU cycles and battery power.

- **Multiple bearers**
  Internet applications only need to support HTTP or TCP/IP. Mobile applications are written against many different bearers: SMS, GPRS, Infrared, Bluetooth, and HTTP. An application written for one bearer typically needs to undergo substantial modifications in order to run on another bearer.

- **Multiple platforms**
  As was pointed out above, it is unclear which operating system will be the winner in the mobile communicator device market, if there is going to be only one winner at all. Palm OS is strong in the PDA market, but Symbian and Windows CE are contenders in the communicator market. Therefore it is advantageous to develop applications in such a way that they can be run on various platforms, without requiring substantial modifications.

- **Security**
  A key concern in a mobile environment. Identification, authentication, and data encryption must be embedded into mobile applications.

- **Deployment and management**
  Deploying a mobile application to a hundred thousand devices and administering its client and server parts is another concern.

Requirements for Mobile Middleware

Building mobile applications using a JMS implementation targeted at mobile devices can solve most of these issues and problems. In this section we elaborate on what features such a special purpose JMS middleware must provide to mobile applications:

❑ **Support for disconnected operation**
The middleware should neither raise communication errors nor lose data when a mobile device loses network coverage. The illusion of a fully reliable communication link between mobile devices and servers is to be provided to the developer. This feature makes the development of mobile applications much easier, because developers can focus on the application services rather than on low-level communication issues.

❑ **Small footprint**
It is particularly important that the messaging client library (stored in the communicator) should have a small memory footprint (ROM and RAM).

❑ **Open bearer models**
The middleware should offer the same set of communication abstractions atop various wireless bearers. This allows applications to be developed once and operate atop various bearers.

❑ **Multi-platform middleware**
This should be pure Java and compatible to Java standards such as J2ME or PersonalJava. This allows applications to be adapted for various platforms more easily.

❑ **Security**
Access control, identification, authentication, and end-to-end data encryption is to be provided by the middleware. This dramatically simplifies the development of secure mobile solutions.

❑ **Deployment and management**
This requirement goes beyond the scope of middleware. Nevertheless, a solution must be provided through appropriate libraries and tools. For example, the JavaPhone API provides APIs and classes supporting the deployment of Java applications to mobile devices.

The JMS Solution

We have outlined the core issues facing developers of mobile applications, and we have established requirements for mobile middleware in order to address those issues. In this section we will argue that a JMS implementation targeted at mobile devices fulfils these requirements and is thus a very appealing platform for advanced mobile solutions.

Motivation

For three decades now, message-oriented middleware (MOM) has been used for the reliable transmission of important information from one system to another. Messaging middleware allows for loose coupling of software components and thus for greater flexibility. Nowadays, JMS is the MOM standard for Java. It allows you to develop distributed applications more quickly, and in a platform-independent "Write Once, Run Anywhere" manner. JMS will prove even more valuable for developing sophisticated mobile applications because of the reasons given below.

Since JMS embodies a message-oriented rather than a connection-oriented model, it is ideally suited for applications that are resilient to intermittent network connectivity and able to operate while disconnected from the server. This is achieved by providing persistent message queues on both the mobile device and the server.

iBus//Mobile

The JMS abstractions can be implemented in a very lightweight manner. The iBus//Mobile product, an implementation of JMS for mobile devices, has shown that the JMS features (notably PTP and Pub/Sub) can be implemented in a Java library of only 70k. At run time, an iBus//Mobile application can live with as little as 50k Java heap space.

The message-oriented paradigm maps nicely into the packet-oriented communication model of SMS, GPRS, EDGE, and UMTS. Furthermore, messaging can also be performed efficiently on both connection-oriented bearers such as GSM, and connection-oriented protocols such as TCP and HTTP. Hence, a JMS implementation can be designed in such way that arbitrary protocols and bearers can be plugged-in.

Another fact proven by iBus//Mobile is that mobile JMS middleware, if designed appropriately, can support multiple mobile OS platforms.

Security needs to be supported at different levels. First, a system administrator can control access to JMS topics and queues for individual mobile devices. Mobile devices (or more exactly, the applications running on them) are identified using userID/password combinations or security certificates. Furthermore, the messages are to be encrypted before transmission via a bearer. In any case you might want to check that your JMS vendor provides flexible access control and data encryption.

Regarding security, iBus//Mobile provides access control to JMS topics and queues, using a userID/password combination. Furthermore, iBus//Mobile will encrypt the traffic between a mobile application and the iBus//Mobile gateway. For that, various third-party encryption libraries can be used, such as Certicom (http://www.certicom.com). iBus//Mobile provides an open API allowing system integrators to extend the product to support other third-party security libraries and key management systems.

Architecture

One possible JMS solution for mobile devices consists of three components: the **JMS provider**, the **mobile JMS gateway**, and the lightweight **JMS client library**. Note that this is the architecture of the iBus mobile messaging middleware. This architecture is particularly suited for wireless portals and wireless ASP solutions:

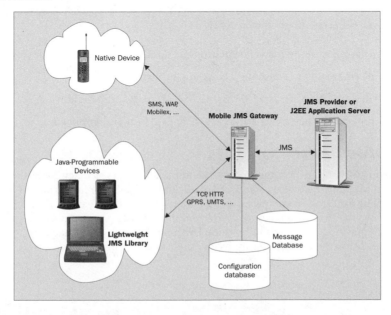

The JMS Provider

This is a JMS message server product running in a data center. It can be either a standalone JMS server, such as Softwired's iBus//MessageServer, or a JMS-enabled application server, such as BEA Weblogic.

The JMS Gateway

This can be seen as the home base to which mobile devices connect through wireless bearers. From the JMS provider's point of view, the gateway is a regular JMS client. From the mobile device's point of view, the gateway is a communications hub and message format translator. Optionally, the gateway can be incorporated into the JMS provider.

The Lightweight JMS Client Library

Applications such as chat rooms, games, financial tickers and m-commerce transaction tools typically require a customized application to be available on the mobile device. We have so far assumed that a JMS-enabled Java application is deployed onto mobile devices. For this type of application, a lightweight JMS client library is provided with the iBus//Mobile package. However, our proposed architecture is more general in that it can also support non-programmable devices such as WAP phones, SMS phones, and pagers. Therefore we will consider the deployment of the lightweight library as optional.

The client-to-gateway protocol is proprietary and optimized for low overhead. All information is transmitted in binary form. A JMS publish operation typically results in an overhead of less than 20 bytes. This makes the iBus//Mobile lightweight JMS library appealing not only for mobile devices but also for Java applets.

JMS Message Flows

This section explains the JMS message flows occurring between backend applications and mobile devices. At this point we assume that all messages (even device-to-device interactions) pass through the gateway. This is to guarantee the delivery of messages, in case a receiving device is temporarily disconnected or turned off.

We will look at four different interaction scenarios:

- ❑ A backend application sends an asynchronous notification to a native device
- ❑ A native device sends a request to a backend application
- ❑ A backend application sends a JMS message to a programmable device
- ❑ A programmable device sends a JMS message to a backend application

Backend to Native Device

Assume a backend JMS application running on the application server machine in the above scenario diagram. The application would like to transmit a stock alert via SMS, to a group of users interested in a particular stock. The application encodes the stock alert into XML, creates a JMS text message and writes the XML into the text message body. Now assume the message is put into a JMS queue called `stock-alerts`. This is all that needs to be done by the developer of the backend application. The following tasks are performed transparently by the mobile JMS infrastructure.

We further assume the gateway is configured to receive messages put into the queue `stock-alerts`. The text message is received by the gateway and the XML information is parsed. Embedded in the XML information, there is the name of a SMS distribution list (for example `stock-alerts-list`) for the alert. The distribution list contains the SMS addresses to which the alert is to be sent. This information is administered by the gateway, to relieve the backend applications from maintaining their own distribution lists.

Now the XML is converted to an SMS text string by the gateway and is sent to all the SMS addresses located in the distribution file.

This also works for other wireless messaging standards besides SMS. For example, WAP-push and paging. WAP-push is part of the WAP 1.2 specification. It provides asynchronous notifications from the WAP gateway to a mobile WAP device.

Native Device to Backend

Imagine a user of an SMS-enabled phone querying their flight departure time. The user creates an SMS message containing the information `LAX SR118` and sends it to a service telephone number. The gateway is configured for receiving the SMS messages sent to that number, either through a GSM modem or through a direct link to an SMS control center.

The SMS is received by the gateway and is parsed. The first token `LAX` denotes a channel that is defined in the gateway configuration database. By looking up the channel in the configuration database, the gateway obtains the name of a JMS queue to which the message should be forwarded.

Next, the SMS (the string `LAX SR118`) is converted to XML and put into a JMS text message. Finally, the JMS message is forwarded to the queue we obtained from the gateway configuration database.

Now a backend JMS application can read the text message, look up the departure time of flight SR118, and send back a response to the user, also via SMS.

Backend to Programmable Device

The message flow occurs slightly differently when the lightweight JMS library is deployed on the mobile device. Assume a Palm PDA or a Symbian communicator running a stock ticker Java application. The ticker uses the JMS Pub/Sub model to subscribe to the topic `quotes`. A backend application receives stock quotes from a financial data feed such as Reuters or Bloomberg, and publishes them on topic `quotes`. The mobile JMS infrastructure performs the necessary steps for transmitting quotes from the backend to one or many mobile devices, in a reliable, efficient, and secure manner. Now let us look at the message flow.

First, the mobile ticker application is started. It creates a JMS topic subscriber on the topic `quotes`. The JMS client library will inform the gateway that it is interested in messages published on `quotes`.

When the backend application publishes a JMS message using a JMS topic publisher, the message is first received by the gateway. Next, the gateway puts the message into a database in case the device has lost network coverage. Then, the gateway transmits the message to the mobile device(s) using a wireless bearer such as GPRS. The client dispatches and acknowledges the message. Finally, the gateway removes the acknowledged message from its database.

Programmable Device to Backend

Imagine an m-commerce application allowing the user to send purchase requests to a backend application. For that we will use a queue entitled `purchases`.

The mobile application creates a queue sender for queue `purchases`. Next, a JMS message detailing a purchase is created and sent to the queue. This results in the JMS message being stored in an embedded database on the device, to ensure the message is not lost if the device loses network coverage. The JMS client library transmits the message from the local database to the gateway. The message is deleted from the on-device storage only when the JMS library knows for sure that the message has arrived at the gateway.

Once the gateway has received the message, it puts it into the queue `purchases` of the JMS provider. The message is now accessible to backend applications.

Configurations

In the simple cases we have looked at, a deployment consists of one JMS provider, one gateway and several mobile devices. For e-business applications, portals, groupware and so on, we envisage a deployment containing at least one message server and one gateway. For certain embedded distributed systems, however, such as an elevator control system, a configuration without message servers might be more appropriate.

The reason for this is that a JMS message server typically requires a server platform based on the Windows or Unix operating system. Such a server component might be just too expensive for an embedded system, especially if only a small number of JMS clients are involved. Rather, the boards could exchange (non-persistent) JMS messages directly among themselves using point-to-point TCP/IP connections or multicast channels. Note, however, that such a configuration typically does not allow for JMS messages to be stored persistently. For that a message server is required.

The figures below depict peer-to-peer and device-to-gateway configurations:

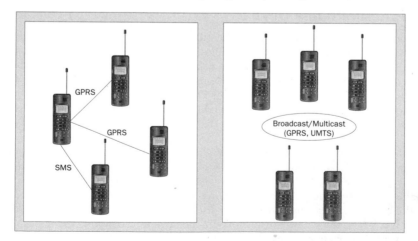

The figure above shows peer-to-peer configuration using Point-to-Point (PTP) communication (left) and multicast communication (right). Below we see a possible device-to-gateway configuration:

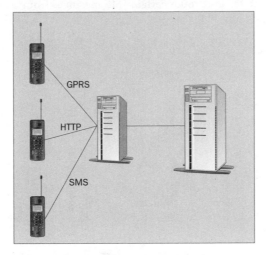

For real scalability, we should consider a configuration with several gateways (below), where each gateway supports hundreds or thousands of mobile devices:

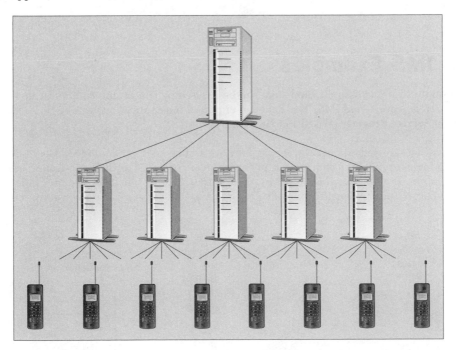

Note that we assume that the JMS provider implements load sharing and fault-tolerance, which is the case in the high-end JMS solutions available on the market today (see Chapter 8 on JMS clustering).

Going further, a business-to-business configuration might then consist of two servers interconnected by SSL or HTTP. For example, the architecture of a highly scalable wireless portal might foresee a data center in each country (or state), and route certain JMS messages from one data center to another using HTTP as a bearer:

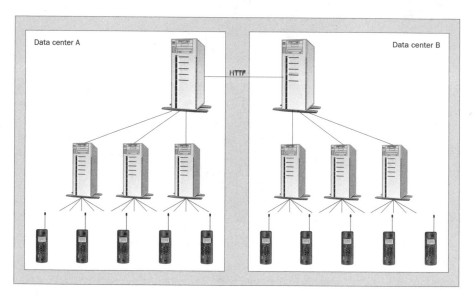

Mobile JMS Examples

This section illustrates two applications that can be realised by combining communicator devices, packet-oriented bearers, and JMS. The data center part of the applications can be hosted by a **Wireless Application Service Provider (WASP)** or by a wireless portal.

Both applications are very similar in the way they are architected and deployed. They both consist of application logic running in a data center, possibly under control of a J2EE application server. The data center further hosts a scalable JMS message server infrastructure, which is either a standalone JMS product or part of the J2EE application server. The data center also hosts one or more mobile gateways:

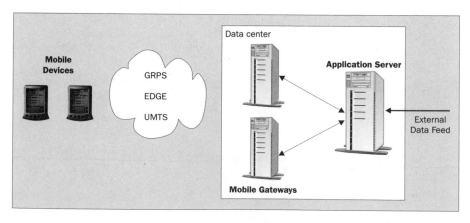

Trading Platform

The trading platform allows you to view stock quotes in real-time, and to trade in a reliable and secure manner. The system guarantees efficient distribution of stock quotes to many subscribers, using a packet-oriented wireless bearer. The system further ensures reliable exactly-once execution of the transactions issued by the user, such as buying or selling stock. This is accomplished using the store-and-forward mechanism outlined in the programmable device to backend scenario above.

The following screenshot was taken using the Symbian Quartz emulator, and exemplifies what the trading application could look like to the end user:

More details on Symbian applications can be found on the Softwired website –
http://www.softwired-inc.com/products/mobile/example.html. Details of running iBus//Mobile
on a Symbian emulator can be found in the online documentation provided with the download.

Message Flow

A simple trading application can be built using one JMS topic called quotes for transmitting stock quotes from the data center to the mobile devices, and one message queue called transactions for transmitting purchase orders from the devices to the data center. The following sequence diagram illustrates the interactions occurring between a mobile device and a JMS server application in the data center. The server application is responsible of publishing stock quotes onto the quotes topic and for executing the orders arriving on the transactions queue:

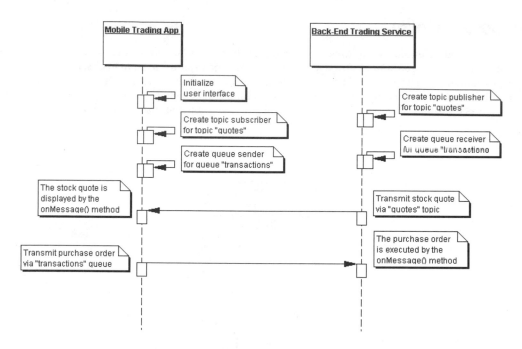

Source Code

We will implement a simplified version of the trading application using the iBus//Mobile JMS middleware product from Softwired. This can be downloaded from http://www.softwired-inc.com/downloads/downloads.html. Be sure to download the full JMS server as the mobile extension works as an extension of this. Another useful application is the iBus//MessageServer AdminTool, which can be used for administering topics and queues.

No graphical user interface is provided, which means all relevant information is logged to a command window. Also, the information transmitted as a quote was simplified as well. For example, we provide only one value field, instead of an asking price and a bid value. All the instructions on how to compile and run the example follow the source code listings.

The example consists of three Java classes:

- ❏ TickerClient.java
  This is a fully functional iBus//Mobile JMS application. It can be run on a PersonalJava-enabled mobile device, such as a Symbian or Windows CE device. It can also be run on a J2SE virtual machine or as an applet. The ticker client uses a UDP communication protocol, optimized for GPRS and UMTS.

- ❏ TickerServer.java
  This is the server-side or backend of the application. The ticker server runs on a server machine, typically in a data center. It uses JMS to interact with the ticker client via the iBus//Mobile gateway.

- ❏ TickerConstants.java
  Constants, which are used by both the client and the server. For instance, queue and topic names.

Features of iBus//Mobile

Before going into the specific aspects of iBus//Mobile, some main product features need to be explained. Although iBus//Mobile implements the standard JMS API for exchanging information between mobile applications and back-end systems, there are product-specific aspects in respect of application initialization, communication protocols, and Quality of Service (QoS). Details are provided in the *iBus//Mobile Programmer's Manual* that accompanies the download.

One distinguishing feature of iBus//Mobile is its ability to provide the JMS abstractions on top of virtually any wireless bearer. In order to run atop a specific bearer, an appropriate iBus//Mobile **protocol stack** is used by the mobile application. Protocol stacks are instantiated by **protocol loaders**. iBus//Mobile ships with a set of protocol loaders for SMS, GPRS, TCP, and HTTP. Developers can implement and use their own stacks and protocols loaders.

Typically, a protocol loader also instantiates protocol objects for adding a certain QoS to the raw bearer. Examples being guaranteed delivery, data compression, and encryption. If guaranteed delivery is required by an application, then protocol objects are loaded that store JMS messages locally on the device. This is to allow a disconnected operation of the device.

Mobile Ticker Client

The mobile JMS ticker client uses a topic (called `quotes`) for receiving quotes from the backend service in real time. It also uses a queue (called `transactions`) for transmitting trade requests to the backend:

```
package mobile.ticker;

// Implementation of javax.jms.*:
import ch.softwired.mobilejms.*;

// Mobile access to JNDI:
import ch.softwired.mobileibus.naming.NameServer;

// For registering iBus//Mobile protocol loaders:
import ch.softwired.mobileibus.qos.ProtocolStackFactory;

import java.util.Random;
import java.util.Hashtable;

public class TickerClient implements MessageListener {
    private final Random random_ = new Random();

    // For issuing trades via a message queue:
    private QueueConnection tradeConnection_;
    private QueueSession tradeSession_;
    private QueueSender tradeSender_;

    // For receiving quotes via a topic:
    private TopicConnection quoteConnection_;
```

When the `main()` method is executed, the client first goes through an initialization step in which an iBus//Mobile protocol stack loader is specified. This allows a developer to choose a particular communication protocol (for example, TCP, HTTP, or UDP) and a particular Quality of Service (QoS) (for example, reliable sliding window, reliable store-and-forward). The protocol and QoS will be used between the mobile device and the gateway application:

```
    // Initializes and starts the ticker client:
    public static void main(String[] args) throws Exception {
        TickerClient client = new TickerClient();

        client.initialize();
        client.subscribe();
        client.start();

        System.err.println("Client is ready.");
        System.err.println();

          // Prevent the main thread from terminating. Otherwise
          // the client might just terminate as well.
          Thread.currentThread().sleep(60000);
    }
```

The client will connect to the gateway located on the same host as the client (localhost). To connect to another gateway, the host name of the gateway can be passed to the registerQos() method. This is described in the *iBus//Mobile Programmer's Manual*. Finally, a topic and a queue connection factory is created:

```
    private void initialize() throws JMSException {
        TopicConnectionFactory quoteConnFactory;
        QueueConnectionFactory tradeConnFactory;

        // Register an iBus//Mobile protocol stack loader.
        // This ticker client can run atop virtually any wireless
        // bearer or communication protocol. It's a matter of defining
        // an appropriate Quality of Service (QoS) loader:

        Hashtable qosParams = new Hashtable();

        qosParams.put("HOSTNAME", TickerConstants.HOSTNAME);
        ProtocolStackFactory.registerQos ("qos-ticker", TickerConstants.QOS_LOADER,

qosParams);

        // Create a JMS Topic- and a QueueConnectionFactory for the
        // aforementioned QoS loader:
        quoteConnFactory = NameServer.lookupTopicConnectionFactory("qos-ticker");
        tradeConnFactory = NameServer.lookupQueueConnectionFactory("qos-ticker");

        // Create a JMS Topic- and a QueueConnection:
        quoteConnection_ = quoteConnFactory.createTopicConnection();
        tradeConnection_ = tradeConnFactory.createQueueConnection();
    }
```

Next, the client application creates a queue sender for the transactions topic, and a topic subscriber for the quotes topic. The topic subscriber is used for receiving quotes published by the backend. The queue sender allows the client to issue a trade to sell or buy a particular item:

```
    private void subscribe() throws JMSException {
        Topic quoteTopic;
        TopicSession quoteSession;
```

```
        TopicSubscriber quoteSubscriber;
        Queue tradeQueue;

        // For receiving quotes from the back-end (see "onMessage()"):
        quoteSession = quoteConnection_.createTopicSession(false,
            Session.AUTO_ACKNOWLEDGE);
        quoteTopic = quoteSession.createTopic(TickerConstants.TOPIC_QUOTES);
        quoteSubscriber = quoteSession.createSubscriber(quoteTopic);
        quoteSubscriber.setMessageListener(this);

        // For transmitting trades to the back-end:
        tradeSession_ = tradeConnection_.createQueueSession(false,
            Session.AUTO_ACKNOWLEDGE);
        tradeQueue = tradeSession_.createQueue(TickerConstants.QUEUE_TRADES);
        tradeSender_ = tradeSession_.createSender(tradeQueue);
    }
```

When a quote is received, onMessage() is invoked by the iBus//Mobile run-time system. The client then uses a random number to decide whether it wants to issue a trade based on the information received in the quote:

```
    public void onMessage(Message msg) {
        final MapMessage quote = (MapMessage)msg;
        int quantity;
        String symbol;
        String value;
        long timeStamp;

        // Extract ticker symbol, current value, and time stamp:
        try {
            symbol = quote.getString(TickerConstants.MAP_KEY_SYMBOL);
            value = quote.getString(TickerConstants.MAP_KEY_VALUE);
            timeStamp = quote.getJMSTimestamp();
        } catch (JMSException je) {
            System.err.println("MapMessage.get<Type> failed: " + je);
            return;
        }

        // Display the quote:
        printQuote(symbol, value, timeStamp);

        // Figure out whether we want to issue a trade:
        if ((quantity = computeQuantity(symbol, value)) > 0) {
            System.out.println("Trading " + quantity + " items of "
                + symbol + "@" + value);

            // Issue a trade:
            try {
                doTrade(symbol, value, quantity);
            } catch (JMSException je) {
                System.err.println("doTrade failed: " + je);
                return;
            }
        } else {
```

```
        System.out.println("No trade for " + symbol + "@" + value);
    }
}
// Starts the JMS connections:
private void start() throws JMSException {
    tradeConnection_.start();
    quoteConnection_.start();
}
```

This illustrative client system uses a random number to decide whether a trade shall be issued for a particular quote:

```
private int computeQuantity(String symbol, String value) {
    final int tradeThreshold = 400;
    final int nextRand = random_.nextInt() % 1000;

    if (nextRand < tradeThreshold) {
        return nextRand;
    } else {
        return 0;
    }
}
```

```
// Sends a trade request to the back-end:
private void doTrade(String symbol, String value, int quantity)
    throws JMSException {
    MapMessage trade = tradeSession_.createMapMessage();

    trade.setString(TickerConstants.MAP_KEY_SYMBOL, symbol);
    trade.setString(TickerConstants.MAP_KEY_VALUE, value);
    trade.setInt(TickerConstants.MAP_KEY_QUANTITY, quantity);

    tradeSender_.send(trade);
}

// Displays a quote:
private void printQuote(String symbol, String value, long timeStamp) {
    System.out.println("---------------------------------");
    System.out.println("Got next quote > ");
    System.out.println("    Symbol: " + symbol);
    System.out.println("    Value: "  + value);
    System.out.println("    Timestamp: "  + timeStamp);
    System.out.flush();
}
```

Back-end Ticker Service

The back-end ticker service is a more conventional JMS application in the sense that it is not run as a mobile application. Whereas the ticker client receives from the quotes topic and sends messages to the transactions queue, the ticker server receives from the transactions queue and publishes quotes to the quotes topic. The class has some of the same structure as the previous one. We start off with a main() method for initialization procedures:

```
package mobile.ticker;

import javax.jms.*;
import javax.naming.*;
import java.util.Hashtable;
import java.util.Random;

public class TickerServer implements MessageListener {
    private final Random random_ = new Random();

    // For receiving trades:
    private QueueConnection tradeConnection_;

    // For publishing quotes:
    private TopicConnection quoteConnection_;
    private TopicSession quoteSession_;
    private TopicPublisher quotePublisher_;

    // Initializes and starts the server application:
    public static void main(String[] args)
        throws JMSException, NamingException {
        TickerServer server = new TickerServer();

        server.initialize();
        server.subscribe();
        server.start();
          server.publishQuotes();

        System.err.println();
    }
```

We then proceed to create and configure the destinations:

```
    private void initialize() throws JMSException, NamingException {
        TopicConnectionFactory quoteConnFactory;
        QueueConnectionFactory tradeConnFactory;
        Context messaging;
        Hashtable env = new Hashtable();

        // Initilize JNDI context:
        env.put(Context.INITIAL_CONTEXT_FACTORY, TickerConstants.JNDI_FACTORY);
        messaging = new InitialContext(env);

        // Look up connection factories through JNDI:
        tradeConnFactory =
          (QueueConnectionFactory)messaging.lookup("QueueConnectionFactory");
        quoteConnFactory =
          (TopicConnectionFactory)messaging.lookup("TopicConnectionFactory");

        // Create a JMS Topic- and a QueueConnection:
        tradeConnection_ = tradeConnFactory.createQueueConnection();
        quoteConnection_ = quoteConnFactory.createTopicConnection();

        tradeConnection_.setClientID("tradeConnection");
        quoteConnection_.setClientID("quoteConnection");

    }
```

```java
// Issues JMS subscriptions:
private void subscribe() throws JMSException {
   Topic quoteTopic;
   Queue tradeQueue;
   QueueSession tradeSession;
   QueueReceiver tradeReceiver;

   // For transmitting quotes:
   tradeSession =
      tradeConnection_.createQueueSession(false, Session.AUTO_ACKNOWLEDGE);
   tradeQueue = tradeSession.createQueue(TickerConstants.QUEUE_TRADES);
   tradeReceiver = tradeSession.createReceiver(tradeQueue);
   tradeReceiver.setMessageListener(this);

   // For receiving trades:
   quoteSession_ = quoteConnection_.createTopicSession(false,
      Session.AUTO_ACKNOWLEDGE);
   quoteTopic = quoteSession_.createTopic(TickerConstants.TOPIC_QUOTES);
   quotePublisher_ = quoteSession_.createPublisher(quoteTopic);

   // Publish quotes in NON_PERSISTENT mode:
   quotePublisher_.setDeliveryMode(DeliveryMode.NON_PERSISTENT);
}
```

```java
// Starts the JMS connections. Starts publishing quotes:
private void start() throws JMSException {
   tradeConnection_.start();
   quoteConnection_.start();
}
```

The message handler is then defined. The handler is called by the JMS run-time system when a trade arrives:

```java
public void onMessage(Message msg) {
   MapMessage trade = (MapMessage)msg;
   String symbol;
   String value;
   int quantity;

   // Extract ticker symbol, current value, and time stamp:
   try {
      symbol = trade.getString(TickerConstants.MAP_KEY_SYMBOL);
      value = trade.getString(TickerConstants.MAP_KEY_VALUE);
      quantity = trade.getInt(TickerConstants.MAP_KEY_QUANTITY);
   } catch (JMSException je) {
      System.err.println("MapMessage.get<Type> failed: " + je);
      return;
   }

   printTrade(symbol, value, quantity);
}
```

The `publishQuotes()` method is in charge of publishing a quote every three seconds:

```
private void publishQuotes() throws JMSException {
    final String SYMBOL = "CSCO";
    final double BASE_VALUE = 35.0;
    MapMessage quote;

    for (;;) {
        final double nextValue = BASE_VALUE + random_.nextDouble();
        quote = quoteSession_.createMapMessage();
        quote.setString(TickerConstants.MAP_KEY_SYMBOL, SYMBOL);
        quote.setString(TickerConstants.MAP_KEY_VALUE, "" + nextValue);

        quotePublisher_.publish(quote);

        try { Thread.currentThread().sleep(3000); }
        catch (InterruptedException ie) {}
    }
}
```

```
// Print a trade:
private void printTrade(String symbol, String value, int quantity) {
    System.out.println("---------------------------------");
    System.out.println("Got trade request > ");
    System.out.println("    Symbol: " + symbol);
    System.out.println("    Value: "  + value);
    System.out.println("    Quantity: "  + quantity);
    System.out.flush();
}
}
```

System Constants

This class stores the constants used in common between client and server:

```
package mobile.ticker;

// Constants used by both TickerClient and Tickerserver.

public class TickerConstants {
    // Keys used within MapMessages:
    public final static String MAP_KEY_SYMBOL   = "Symbol";
    public final static String MAP_KEY_VALUE    = "Value";
    public final static String MAP_KEY_QUANTITY = "Quantity";

    // iBus//Mobile QoS loader for GPRS (UDP): for iBusMobile 2.0
    public final static String QOS_LOADER =
        "ch.softwired.mobileibus.qos.QOS_UDP_RELIABLE_SLIWIN";


    // iBus//Mobile QoS loader for GPRS (UDP): for iBusMobile 1.0

    // public final static String QOS_LOADER =
    //     "ch.softwired.mobileibus.qos.QOS_DEFAULT";
    // Hostname of the machine running the server
    public final static String HOSTNAME = "localhost";

    // Topic name (for the quotes):
    public final static String TOPIC_QUOTES = "quotes";
```

```
        // Queue name (for the trades):
        public final static String QUEUE_TRADES = "transactions";

        // For JNDI initialization:
        public final static String JNDI_FACTORY =
            "ch.softwired.jms.naming.IBusContextFactory";
    }
```

The MAP_KEY constants denote the keys that we use for storing and accessing information in JMS map messages. Both the ticker client and the ticker server access these constants.

The QOS_LOADER constant is used only by the client, it denotes the iBus//Mobile protocol stack loader used by the mobile ticker application. This loader is optimized for pushing JMS messages over GPRS and with high throughput and low latency.

TOPIC_QUOTES and QUEUE_TRADES define the topic and the queue name used by ticker client and server.

Finally, JNDI_FACTORY is used by the ticker server application to initialize the JNDI provider.

Running the Ticker System

These are the steps for running the demo locally on a developer workstation. Make sure that you have ibus-mobile.jar and msrvClt.jar in your classpath. They can be found in the \client\j2se\lib\ directory of iBus\\Mobile and the \client\lib\ directory of iBus\\MessageServer respectively:

❑ Start the iBus//MessageServer. On Windows, the "Start Server" application is selected through the iBus//MessageServer program group.

❑ Start the iBus//Mobile gateway. On Windows, the "Start Gateway" application is selected through the iBus//Mobile program group.

❑ Start the ticker server and ticker client as below:

Possible Enhancements

The trading application can be extended in various ways. For example, a confirmation queue can be added, allowing the backend to transmit a confirmation to the mobile client, after a trade request has been processed.

An alerting function is another interesting extension. A mobile client can specify a ticker symbol along with a threshold value. Whenever the quote of the given instrument changes by more then the given threshold value (over a certain period of time), an alert message is pushed to the client.

Buddies

The Buddies application offers functions similar to AOL Instant Messenger or ICQ, but on a mobile device. The user can create a buddy list, containing name and address of friends and family members. When one of the buddies turns his or her communicator on, you will hear a beep from your communicator to indicate a change on your buddy list. The Buddies user interface shows which of your buddies are online and their location. Thus, the server side of the Buddies application requires location information.

Message Flow

Several message flows are necessary to realize the Buddies service. One flow of information is from the device to the backend, to inform the backend when the user logs in or out. This is accomplished through the JMS queue `login`. There are further flows of messages from the device to the back-end:

❑ If the device is capable of determining its own location through a local GPS module, that information is to be transmitted to the backend at regular time intervals. This is accomplished through the JMS queue `my location`.

❑ When the user modifies the buddy list, an update message is sent to the backend through the JMS queue `updates`.

❑ Also, each device sends a heartbeat message to the backend every now and then, using the JMS queue `heartbeat`. This is to inform the backend that the device is still running. Consider the situation where the Buddies application terminates without publishing a logout message on the `login` queue. The backend has no way of figuring out that the user is no longer online, unless a heartbeat mechanism is provided.

Finally, there is one message flow from the backend to the device to inform the device of events that relate to its buddy list, like a list member logging in or out. This is where our JMS design becomes a bit tricky: the backend needs to be able to send JMS messages to every single device, individually. This can be accomplished in two different ways:

❑ **Use one queue per device**
This means the backend can publish a JMS message on queue `john_smith` to deliver a message only to John Smith's device. This sounds elegant at first, but might result in a huge amount of JMS queues opened by the backend, when our Buddies application becomes very popular. A high-end JMS message server is able to cope with thousands of open JMS destinations, but opening hundred of thousands or millions of destinations concurrently might require a huge amount of resources (notably memory) at the backend.

❑ **Use a JMS message selector as a filter**
In this design there is exactly one queue called `notify` for transmitting information from the backend to a device. When the backend wants to transmit a message to John Smith's device, the JMS header property `USER_NAME` is set to `John Smith`. The client application uses a JMS selector for that property when subscribing to `notify`. This solution allows messages to be routed efficiently by the backend JMS infrastructure, provided JMS selectors are evaluated by the JMS provider and not by the lightweight JMS client library.

The diagram below shows the flow of messages. First, the mobile client transmits a JMS message containing login information to the service. If the device is able to determine its location, it will send a first JMS message containing is location to the service.

Next, assume the user of Buddies adds a new contact to a buddy list. An update message is sent to the service. The service will now update the buddy list of the user, and could even notify the contact that they have been added to that list. If nothing else happens, the client application will periodically send its current location to the service as well as a heartbeat message. For optimization, a JMS message could carry both the heartbeat and the location information.

If a contact on the buddy list changes his or her status, a notification message will be sent from the service to the clients who have that contact on their list. In the diagram this would mean an arrow from the service to the client:

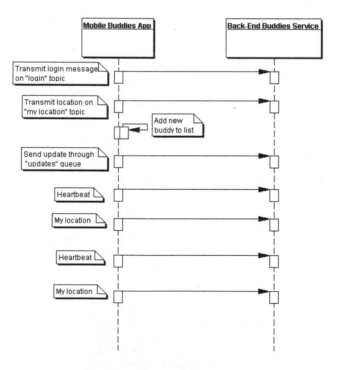

Possible Enhancements

The Buddies application can be enhanced with features allowing the user to establish chat sessions or voice conferences with their buddies, with instant messaging capabilities, or with a radar-like user interface spotting the geographical location of the buddies.

Summary

The JMS messaging paradigm is easy to learn and is a powerful tool. It offers the necessary system-level support for disconnected operation of mobile devices. This chapter described issues facing the developer of mobile applications, and how mobile messaging addresses those issues. Also, we have sketched the architecture and the main features of a JMS solution for wireless information services.

The main conclusion is that wireless applications such as financial data feeds, chat systems, buddy lists, etc. consist of a scalable server infrastructure (the data center) servicing large numbers of mobile devices. We propose to deploy J2EE application server technology at the data center, J2ME technology on the mobile device, and to use a wireless-enabled JMS middleware as the bridge between the mobile world and the data centers.

Untitled - Notepad
File
Edit
Format
Help
Help Topics
Useful Phrases
About Notepad
com.sun.jndi.fscontext.RefFSContextFactory
com.sun.jndi.ldap.LdapCtxFactory
weblogic.jndi.WLInitialContextFactory
weblogic.jndi.T3InitialContextFactory
fiorano.jms.rtl.FioranoInitialContextFactory
fiorano.jms.runtime.naming.FioranoInitialContextFactory
ch.softwired.jms.naming.IBusContextFactory

JMS Providers and JNDI

This appendix provides a brief overview of some of the leading JMS providers. We will also explore ways of exploiting JNDI to construct portable messaging code for the providers. The JMS providers covered in this appendix are:

- ❑ **JMQ 1.1 (Java Message Queue)** from Sun Microsystems

- ❑ **SonicMQ 3.0** from Progress Software

- ❑ **MQSeries JMS** from IBM

- ❑ **FioranoMQ 4.6** from Fiorano Software

- ❑ **iBus//MessageServer 4.1** from Softwired

- ❑ **WebLogic 6.0** from BEA Systems

- ❑ **J2EE 1.3beta Reference Server** from Sun Microsystems

JMQ, SonicMQ, FioranoMQ, and iBus//MessageServer are specialized messaging products compliant with the JMS v1.0.2 specification. MQSeries JMS is a JMS extension of IBM's enterprise messaging system family MQSeries. WebLogic 6.0 is a J2EE compliant application server with full support for JMS. J2EE 1.3beta reference server is a reference implementation from Sun Microsystems of the various J2EE APIs defined in the J2EE 1.3 specification, which includes JMS 1.02.

This appendix is divided into two sections. In the first section we will be writing a simple portable JMS client that accesses any message broker without code changes (there is one exception to this rule). In the second section, we will be covering the main features of the JMS providers, as well as running the portable client on each one.

> We will be looking at a number of JNDI service provider utilities that can be
> downloaded from **http://java.sun.com**. A summary of these is available from
> **http://java.sun.com/products/jndi/serviceproviders.html**. Note that you will find
> many of the required library JAR files already within JMS provider installations.

The Portable JMS Client

The sample application is a simple JMS application that acts as a JMS client that produces and
consumes messages using the Pub/Sub messaging model. The client looks up a topic named myTopic,
and a topic connection factory TCFactory.

The JNDI initial context factory and the provider URL will be passed into the application as command-
line arguments. To explain the various options available the following configuration will be used to
store the Administered objects:

- ❑ For JMQ and MQSeries JMS the Administered objects will be stored in the WinNT file
  system context and looked up using JNDI

- ❑ For SonicMQ the Administered objects will be stored in a standalone LDAP server and
  looked up using JNDI

- ❑ For iBus//MessageServer, FioranoMQ, and WebLogic the Administered objects will be stored
  in their internal JNDI compliant namespace and looked up using JNDI

The client will create appropriate connections, sessions, producers and consumers for producing and
consuming messages. The JNDI provider URL and the name of the initial context factory are passed as
command-line arguments:

```
import javax.jms.Topic;
import javax.jms.TopicConnectionFactory;
import javax.jms.TopicConnection;
import javax.jms.TopicSession;
import javax.jms.TopicPublisher;
import javax.jms.TopicSubscriber;

import javax.jms.JMSException;
import javax.jms.TextMessage;

import javax.naming.Context;
import javax.naming.InitialContext;
import javax.naming.NamingException;

import java.util.Properties;

public class PortableJMSClient {
```

The JNDI names of the Administered objects are stored in two class variables. The topic is called
myTopic and the topic connection factory is called TCFactory:

```
public static final String TOPIC_FACTORY = "TCFactory";
public static final String TOPIC = "myTopic";
```

First an instance of `java.util.Properties` is created and stored with the following JNDI environment values:

- ❑ The JNDI provider URL. This depends on the JNDI service provider implementation used for storing the Administered objects.

- ❑ The JNDI initial context factory:

  - ❑ For JMQ and MQSeries JMS we use Sun's initial context factory for file system context

  - ❑ For SonicMQ we use Sun's LDAP initial context factory

  - ❑ For FioranoMQ and iBus//MessageServer the initial context factory that comes with the server is used

  - ❑ And for WebLogic the T3 initial context factory is used

The two parameters mentioned above are passed to the program as command-line arguments:

```
public static void main(String args[]) throws NamingException,
    JMSException {

  Properties prop = new Properties();

  if(args.length == 2) {
     //Add the initial context factory
     prop.put(Context.INITIAL_CONTEXT_FACTORY, args[0]);
     //Add the provider URL
     prop.put(Context.PROVIDER_URL, args[1]);
  }

  //Create the initial context
  Context ctx = new InitialContext(prop);

  //Create an instance
  PortableJMSClient client = new PortableJMSClient();

  //Publish and subscribe messages using Pub\Sub
  client.doPubSub(ctx);

  //Close initial context
  ctx.close();

}

private void doPubSub(Context ctx) throws NamingException,
     JMSException {

  //Lookup the topic
  Topic topic = (Topic)ctx.lookup(TOPIC);

  //Lookup the topic connection factory
  TopicConnectionFactory tcFactory =
     (TopicConnectionFactory)ctx.lookup(TOPIC_FACTORY);
```

```
        //Create topic connection
        TopicConnection tCon = tcFactory.createTopicConnection();
        //Create topic session
        TopicSession tSes = tCon.createTopicSession(false,
           TopicSession.AUTO_ACKNOWLEDGE);

        //Create topic publisher
        TopicPublisher publisher = tSes.createPublisher(topic);
        //Create topic subscriber
        TopicSubscriber subscriber = tSes.createSubscriber(topic);

        //Start queue connection
        tCon.start();
```

A text message is created using the topic session and is published using the message publisher. The same message is then received by the topic subscriber:

```
        TextMessage msg = tSes.createTextMessage();
        System.out.println("Publishing message on the topic");
        //Send message
        publisher.publish(msg);
        //Receive message
        msg = (TextMessage)subscriber.receive();
        System.out.println("Received message from the topic");

        //Close queue connection
        tCon.close();

    }
}
```

Configuring and Running the Client

There are four main steps in running the client explained above:

- ❑ Compile the class listed in the last section
- ❑ Store the Administered objects myTopic and TCFactory in the namespace of a JNDI service provider implementation
- ❑ Start the message server
- ❑ Run the client

The first step is the same for all the four JMS implementations. The second and third steps are specific to the JMS provider used. Even though the fourth step is also common for all the JMS providers, we will be passing different command-line parameters for the JNDI service provider URL and initial context factory depending on the JNDI service provider implementation used for storing the Administered objects.

Compiling the Client

Apart from the JDK standard edition classes, we need the JMS and JNDI classes. The JNDI classes/interfaces are available in JDK 1.3 standard edition (although it doesn't cover the full implementation of JNDI 1.2.1). The JMS classes/interfaces are available in the j2ee.jar file available with J2EE SDK 1.2.1, but will almost certainly also be available with your provider installation, as will most of the libraries you need to use them.

JMQ (Java Message Queue)

JMQ is a JMS implementation from Sun Microsystems that supports both PTP and Pub/Sub models, and is written in pure Java. JMQ is available under various "Try & Buy" deals from http://www.sun.com/workshop/jmq. There are three forms of this product available:

❑ **Developer Edition**
   This version is available free of cost for development. The software distribution includes the following:

   ❑ JMS implementation classes

   ❑ Client runtime

   ❑ 5-connection router

   ❑ Development license for single router instance

   ❑ Different command-line utilities for configuring Administered objects, administering users, monitoring, etc.

   ❑ Client authentication server for development

   ❑ Sample applications and online documentation

❑ **Business Edition**
   This edition provides unlimited user connection for a single router instance running on a single host as well as all the features available for the developer edition

❑ **Business 10-pack Edition**
   This is same as the business edition, but provides licensing for ten instances of the router either running on the same host or across multiple hosts

Product Features

JMQ provides a simple, powerful, and flexible messaging solution:

❑ JMQ can be run on both Windows (NT and 2000) and Unix (Solaris SPARC) platforms. It can run with JDK 1.1.8 or Java 2 Platform.

❑ JMQ is compliant with JMS 1.02 and supports the following features as specified in the JMS specification:

   ❑ Publish/Subscribe messaging model

   ❑ Point-to-Point messaging model

   ❑ Certified message delivery

❑ JMQ provides access to JMS Administered objects through JNDI (Java Naming and Directory Interface). It supports LDAP (Lightweight Directory Access Protocol) and file system service providers. JMQ comes with a command-line utility for configuring Administered objects.

❑ JMQ supports fully connected multi-router network where routers are connected to each other through a single hub.

❑ JMQ provides utilities for remotely administering the router and provides facilities for debugging, monitoring, administering users, etc.

JMQ Binaries

JMQ comes with a set of binaries for running the router, administering the users, configuring Administered objects, monitoring, etc.

irouter

The `irouter` binary is used for routing the messages delivered by JMS applications to other JMS applications and routers. This can be found in the `bin` directory of the JMQ installation. The screenshot below shows an instance of JMQ router up and running:

```
Router (irouter)                                                    _ □ ✕
Initializing router...

Java(tm) Message Queue          Copyright 1999-2000
Version: 1.1 < Build U-209 >    Sun Microsystems, Inc.
Compile: Sat 05/13/2000         All Rights Reserved
>>>>>>>>>>>>>>>>>>>>>>>>>>>>><<<<<<<<<<<<<<<<<<<<<<<<<<<<
>> Available Router Connections set to 5
<<router ready>>
```

Please refer to the JMQ deployment documentation for the different command-line options available for running the router.

irmon

This utility can be found in the `bin` directory of the JMQ installation and is used for monitoring the debugging information and network output. JMQ provides an exhaustive set of options for debugging and monitoring the router.

ircmd

This utility enables the users to perform administrative tasks on the router. The user can query connection information, control monitor and debug options, etc. The screenshot shows running the `ircmd` with the `help` command executed:

```
Router Command Environment (ircmd)                                    _ □ ✕
Initializing JMQ Command Interface ...

Java(tm) Message Queue            Copyright 1999-2000
Version: 1.1 ( Build U-209 )      Sun Microsystems, Inc.
Compile: Sat 05/13/2000           All Rights Reserved
>>>>>>>>>>>>>>>>>>>>>>>>>>><<<<<<<<<<<<<<<<<<<<<<<<<<


cmd>open localhost
Connected to localhost
cmd>help
Commands by category:

General:
help             Show this page
script           Read commands from a script file
quit             Quit command prompt

Connecting to a host:
open hostname    Opens a connection to the host.
close            Closes the current connection.

Remote Commands:
status           Status of a host
hosts            List of all current hosts
connections      List of all current connections
interests        List of current interest patterns
ping             Ping a particular host
connect          Forces a connection between hosts
set              Sets a configuration parameter
query            Queries a host or application
wait             Set the wait time for responses

Resource Files:
show             Displays various contents of resource files
setpath path     Sets the resource path.
addpath path     Appends the resource path.

For additional information on a specific command,
enter 'help' followed by the command.
Example : 'help show'

cmd>_
```

jmqconfig

This utility can be used for configuring and storing the JMS Administered objects. This can be used for storing, deleting, viewing, and listing the destinations and connection factories in a JNDI namespace. The jmqconfig utility provides various command-line options for specifying the type of the Administered object, the JNDI service provider, initial context factory, etc. The screenshot below shows the use of jmqconfig to store a queue named myQueue in the file system provider context at the location c:\temp:

```
Command Prompt                                                        _ □ ✕
C:\>jmqconfig -a -t q -n myQueue -o "name=myQueue" -i "com.sun.jndi.fscontext.Re
fFSContextFactory" -u "file:C:/temp"
================================================================
JMQ Config 1.1
Sun Microsystems, Inc.
Copyright(c) 1999-2000, All Rights Reserved
================================================================

Adding myQueue...
Warning: myQueue already exists.
Are you sure you want to overwrite this object? (y/n) y
myQueue has been added.


C:\>_
```

jmqadmin

This is used for running the graphical administration console for performing the following tasks:

- ❑ Deleting queues and their persistent messages
- ❑ Administering users
- ❑ Security authentication
- ❑ Managing logs etc.

The utility doesn't let you delete durable topics. JMQ also provides a simple and non-encrypted client authentication server for development that can be administered using the administration console. The figure below shows the main screen for the administration console:

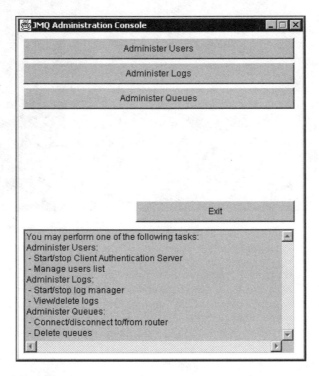

Running the Portable JMS Client

The topic and topic connection factory are stored in the WinNT file system context for JMQ (we could also use LDAP; see jmqconfig earlier in the appendix).

Configuring the Administered Objects

We will be storing the Administered objects under the directory C:\temp in the WinNT file system context for the Java Message Queue. The JMQ implementations for the interfaces for topic and topic connection factory can be created and stored in a JNDI namespace using the jmqconfig tool explained earlier. Run the following command to store the topic myTopic in the WinNT file system context:

```
"%JMQ_HOME%\bin\jmqconfig"  -a -t t -n myTopic -o "name=myTopic" -i
"com.sun.jndi.fscontext.RefFSContextFactory" -u "file:C:/temp"
```

❑ The -a option is for adding an object.

❑ The -t option specifies the type:

    ❑ t – Topic

    ❑ q – Queue

    ❑ tf – Topic connection factory

    ❑ qf – Queue connection factory

❑ The option -n defines the JNDI name of the object.

❑ The option -o is used for specifying different properties specific to destinations and connection factories. In the above example it is used to specify the name of the topic in JMQ. This is different from the JNDI name.

❑ The option -i specifies the JNDI initial context factory.

❑ The option -u specifies the JNDI service provider URL.

The following command can be used for storing the topic connection factory TCFactory:

```
"%JMQ_HOME%\bin\jmqconfig"  -a -t tf -n TCFactory -o "host=localhost" -i
"com.sun.jndi.fscontext.RefFSContextFactory" -u "file:C:/temp"
```

Here the –o option is used to specify the host on which the message broker will be running.

Running the Client

For running the client, first start the JMQ router by running the irouter binary as explained in one of the previous sections. Now invoke the Java interpreter on the class PortableJMSClient with all the required classes in the classpath and passing the JNDI provider URL and the JNDI initial context factory as command-line arguments.

The required JAR files can all be found in the JMQ installation library:

❑ jms.jar

❑ jmq.jar – This JAR file contains JMQ's JMS implementation classes

❑ fscontext.jar and providerutil.jar – These JAR files contain the required SPI classes for the JNDI file system context

The following command-line arguments should be passed to the program for running the client:

❑ com.sun.jndi.fscontext.RefFSContextFactory – This is the initial context factory for the JNDI file system context

❑ file:C:/temp – This is the JNDI service provider URL

> In Java file protocol URLs, the file separator can be forward or backward.

The screenshot below shows the JMS client running against JMQ:

Progress SonicMQ

SonicMQ is a complete messaging framework primarily designed for Java applications by Progress Software. SonicMQ is available for free download from http://www.sonicMQ.com. SonicMQ comes in three flavors:

- ❑ **Developer Edition**
  This version is designed for easy installation. The developer edition restricts the connections from a single IP address and number of connections to 100. Developer edition doesn't provide the advanced security features available in the other editions.

- ❑ **Professional Developer Edition**
  This version supports unlimited client connections, clustering, DRA (Dynamic Routing Architecture) – which is explained later – and security with 40 and 56 bit encryption. But this edition doesn't support application deployment.

- ❑ **E-Business Edition**
  This version provides all the features in the aforementioned editions plus a complete deployment environment.

Product Features

On top of providing the basic messaging infrastructure, SonicMQ provides many other features for enterprise application development. A brief list of the features provided by SonicMQ is shown below:

- ❑ JMS implementation supporting both PTP and Pub/Sub models

- ❑ Support for hierarchical security management

- ❑ Guaranteed message persistence over the Internet

- ❑ High scalability for volume of messages

- ❑ Message security, encryption and security management

- ❑ Built-in integration with XML parsers; also provides an interface called XMLMessage that is a specialized sub-interface of TextMessage

- ❑ Dynamic Routing Architecture (DRA), which let enterprises exchange messages between each other dynamically through a single message server

- ❑ SonicMQ provides clustering of message servers to ensure 7/24 uptime

SonicMQ Binaries

SonicMQ comes with a set of applications for running the message server, administering the server, configuring and storing Administered objects, etc. These applications are available in the Start menu for Windows installation.

startbr

This batch file is used for starting the SonicMQ message broker. For windows installation this batch file is available using the shortcut Start Broker as shown below:

By default, the broker listens on the TCP/IP port 2506. The message broker is responsible for accepting messages from, and delivering messages to, the clients.

The screenshot below shows the SonicMQ message broker up and running:

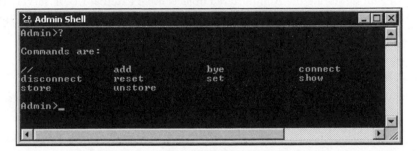

admin

This is a text-based tool for administering the message server or a cluster. For Windows installation, the batch file is available via the shortcut Admin Shell. The screenshot below shows the administration tool running with the `help` command executed:

The admin shell can be used for the following tasks:

❑ Adding and deleting clusters, brokers to clusters, users, groups, queues, queue access control lists, topics, topic access control lists, etc.

❑ Connecting to and disconnecting from the broker

❑ Connecting to and disconnecting from the administered object store

❑ Showing the details about users, destinations, etc.

Please refer to the SonicMQ documentation for further details on the usage of the administration tool.

explorer

This is a graphical tool for performing all the features provided by the admin tool discussed above. For Windows installation the batch file is available by the shortcut Explorer. The screenshot below shows the explorer running with the screen for adding destinations:

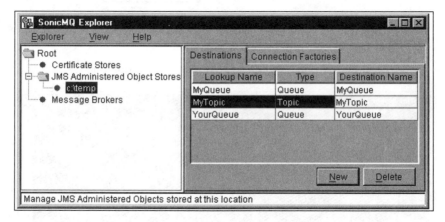

Other Utilities

SonicMQ also provides other utilities for creating and configuring security databases. It also comes with Cloudscape RDBMS and can interface with Oracle and Microsoft SQL Server for running the security databases.

Running the Portable JMS Client

For SonicMQ we will be storing the Administered objects in an external LDAP server. The server I've used here is a standalone LDAP server for WinNT, which is available for download from http://www.eudora.com/free/ldap.html. (For Unix/Linux any one can obtain a copy of the openLDAP server from http://www.openldap.org.)

Configuring and Running the LDAP Server

First extract the contents of the downloaded archive to a directory on your local file system. Let us call the directory <LDAP_HOME> from here onwards:

- ❏ Copy the file `QcSlapd.exe` from the directory `<LDAP_HOME>\binaries` to `<LDAP_HOME>\bin`

- ❏ Copy the files `libdb226.dll` and `libdb226.lib` from the directory `<LDAP_HOME>\lib\Release` to `<LDAP_HOME>\bin`

- ❏ Copy the files `SLAPD.AT.CONF`, `slapd.conf` and `SLAPD.OC.CONF` from the directory `<LDAP_HOME>\conf` to `<LDAP_HOME>\bin`

- ❏ Create two directories named `dbfiles` and `logs` under the directory `<LDAP_HOME>\bin`

- ❏ Edit `slapd.conf` file and make the changes highlighted in the listing below. The prefix `C:/ldap` should be replaced with the value of `<LDAP_HOME>`:

```
#############################################################
#     Global options
#############################################################
include "C:/ldap/bin/slapd.at.conf"
include "C:/ldap/bin/slapd.oc.conf"
schemacheck on
#referral ldap://localhost
#############################################################
#     ldbm database definitions
#############################################################
database    ldbm
index default

suffix ""

rootdn "cn=manager"
rootpw pass
```

Run the executable `QcSlapd.exe` with the `-debug` switch. The screenshot below shows the LDAP server up and running:

Configuring the Administered Objects

We will be storing the Administered objects in the namespace of an LDAP server. For this, first start the LDAP server as explained in the previous section. Then start the SonicMQ explorer by running the `explorer.bat/explorer.sh` file available in the `bin` directory under SonicMQ installation. Click on the **JMS Administered Objects Store** item in the tree on the left panel and then click on the **JNDI** radio button on the right panel. Enter the following text in the text box in the right panel without any line breaks:

```
java.naming.provider.url="ldap://localhost:389"
java.naming.factory.initial="com.sun.jndi.ldap.LdapCtxFactory"
java.naming.security.authentication="simple"
java.naming.security.principal="cn=manager"
java.naming.security.credentials="pass"
```

The text above defines the environment properties required for connecting to the LDAP server. Now click on the **Connect** button:

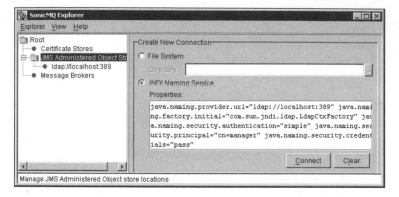

Now click on the ldap://localhost:389 item in the left-hand tree. The panel on the right will show the destination and the connection factory tabs. In the **Destination** tab click on the **New** button and enter the text `myTopic` for lookup name and destination name. Select **Topic** from the destination type pick-list and hit *enter*:

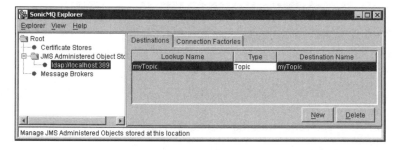

Click on the **Connection Factories** tab and then click on the **New** button. Enter the text `TCFactory` for the lookup name, select the type as **TopicConnectionFactory** and enter the host on which the SonicMQ message broker will be listening as `localhost:2506`. Click on the **Update** button:

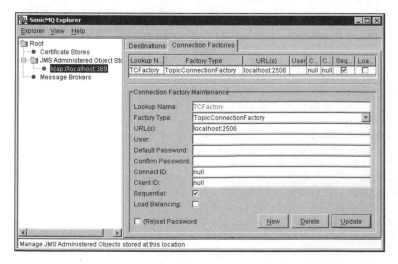

Running the Client

For running the client first start the LDAP server as explained in the last section and the SonicMQ message broker by running the `startbr.bat/startbr.sh` binary as explained in one of the previous sections. Now invoke the Java interpreter on the class `PortableJMSClient` with all the required classes in the classpath and passing the JNDI provider URL and the JNDI initial context factory as command-line arguments.

The required JAR files are:

❑   `jms.jar` – The JMS library.

❑   `client.jar` – This JAR file contains SonicMQ's JMS implementation classes. This file can be found in the `lib` directory under the SonicMQ installation.

❑   `jndi.jar/ldap.jar` – JNDI 1.2.1, or any LDAP provider.

The following command-line arguments should be passed to the program for running the client:

❑   `com.sun.jndi.ldap.LdapCtxFactory` – This is the initial context factory for the JNDI LDAP

❑   `ldap://localhost:389` – This is the JNDI service provider URL

The screen below shows the JMS client running against SonicMQ:

```
C:\ProJMS\AppendixA>echo %classpath%
.;C:\Progress_SonicMQ\lib\jms.jar;C:\Progress_SonicMQ\lib\client.jar;C:\jdk1.3\l
ib\jndi1_2_1\lib\jndi.jar

C:\ProJMS\AppendixA>java PortableJMSClient com.sun.jndi.ldap.LdapCtxFactory ldap
://localhost:389
Publishing message on the topic
Received message from the topic

C:\ProJMS\AppendixA>_
```

IBM MQSeries JMS

The IBM MQSeries range of products provides services that enable applications to communicate with each other using messages and queues. IBM provides support for developing MQSeries applications in Java, through a number of Java-based APIs, which are downloaded separately. A 60-day trial version of the software can be downloaded from http://www-4.ibm.com/software/ts/mqseries/downloads/, while the Java APIs can be found at http://www-4.ibm.com/software/ts/mqseries/api/mqjava.html.

MQSeries JMS Features

MQSeries JMS supports both the PTP and Pub/Sub messaging models. However the latter model requires Service Pac MA0C to be installed on top of the main application:

❑ MQSeries Java enables Java applets, applications, and servlets to issue calls and queries to MQSeries, giving access to mainframe and legacy applications without necessarily having any other MQSeries code on the client machine.

❑ The MQSeries JMS classes add the following over the base MQSeries functions:

❑ Asynchronous message delivery

❑ Message selectors

❑ Support for Pub/Sub messaging

❑ Structured message classes

❑ MQSeries initializes authorization checks that are carried out on each resource, using the tables that are set up and maintained by the MQSeries administrator.

❑ Data integrity is provided via units of work. The synchronization of the start and end of units of work is fully supported as an option on each message get/set method call, allowing the results of the unit of work to be committed or rolled back.

❑ Recovery support is provided by logging all persistent MQSeries updates

MQSeries Binaries

MQSeries comes with binaries for configuring Administered objects and assisting in the running of programs. Once MQSeries has been installed, it will run in the background until told to stop. On Windows platforms the server's status can be checked by examining the MQSeries icon in the system tray. A green arrow signifies that the server is up and running, while a red arrow signifies that it has been stopped. The server can be configured, started, and stopped by right-clicking on this icon.

runjms

MQ JMS includes a utility file, runjms (runjms.bat on Windows NT) to help you to run JMS programs. The Java properties needed for trace and logging are passed in as arguments. The directory names used in the file are suggested defaults that may be altered to suit your particular installation:

```
java -DMQJMS_LOG_DIR="%MQ_JAVA_INSTALL_PATH%"\log -
DMQJMS_TRACE_DIR="%MQ_JAVA_INSTALL_PATH%"\trace -
DMQJMS_TRACE_LEVEL="%MQJMS_TRACE_LEVEL%" %1 %2 %3 %4 %5 %6 %7 %8 %9
```

JMSAdmin

To run the MQ JMS admin tool, execute the JMSAdmin utility file (JMSAdmin.bat on Windows platforms) found in the installation directory.

This admin tool can be used to configure Administered objects or run a batch process. The configuration mode provides a command line where administration commands can be entered. The command to start the tool in batch mode must include the name of a file that contains an administration command script.

In order for the admin tool to function correctly, the `JMSAdmin.config` file must be set up correctly. This file is found in the same directory as the `JMSAdmin` utility file. The following lines must be changed to suit your system's LDAP or file system setup. The # character denotes a comment. If you wish to swap between a file system and LDAP, comment out the file system line and remove the comment from the LDAP line:

```
#PROVIDER_URL=ldap://localhost:389
PROVIDER_URL=file://C:/temp

#INITIAL_CONTEXT_FACTORY=com.sun.jndi.ldap.LdapCtxFactory
INITIAL_CONTEXT_FACTORY=com.sun.jndi.fscontext.RefFSContextFactory
```

`JMSAdmin.config` contains the default settings for the admin console, but you can provide an alternative configuration file at the command prompt by invoking the optional `-cfg` parameter, followed by the alternative filename.

Once the admin tool has been started, Administered objects can be configured using a set of configuration commands of the form VERB [param]*. A full listing of these commands can be found in the MQSeries JMS documentation. Below is an example of a queue connection factory being configured:

```
C:\WINNT\System32\cmd.exe - JMSAdmin

5648-C60 (c) Copyright IBM Corp. 1999. All Rights Reserved.
Starting MQSeries Classes for Java(tm) Message Service Administration

InitCtx> DEFINE QCF(QCFactory)

InitCtx> DISPLAY CTX

  Contents of InitCtx

      .bindings               java.io.File
    a QCFactory               com.ibm.mq.jms.MQQueueConnectionFactory

  2 Object(s)
    0 Context(s)
    2 Binding(s), 1 Administered

InitCtx> _
```

Running the Portable JMS Client

The topic and topic connection factory are stored in the WinNT file system context for MQSeries JMS (we could also use LDAP, see *JMSAdmin* earlier in this section).

Configuring the Administered Objects

We will be storing the Administered objects under the directory `C:\temp` in the WinNT file system context for the MQSeries JMS. The implementations for the interfaces for topic and topic connection factory can be created and stored in a JNDI namespace using the JMSAdmin tool explained earlier. Make sure the `JMSAdmin.config` file contains the following uncommented lines, while all references to LDAP should be commented out:

```
PROVIDER_URL=file://C:/temp
INITIAL_CONTEXT_FACTORY=com.sun.jndi.fscontext.RefFSContextFactory
```

Run the following commands to store the topic `myTopic` and the topic connection factory `TCFactory` in the WinNT file system context. The final command verifies that the process was successful by displaying the contents of the current context:

```
C:\WINNT\System32\cmd.exe - JMSAdmin                              _ □ X

5648-C60 (c) Copyright IBM Corp. 1999. All Rights Reserved.
Starting MQSeries Classes for Java(tm) Message Service Administration

InitCtx> DEFINE T(myTopic)

InitCtx> DEFINE TCF(TCFactory)

InitCtx> DISPLAY CTX

  Contents of InitCtx

      .bindings                  java.io.File
    a TCFactory                  com.ibm.mq.jms.MQTopicConnectionFactory
    a myTopic                    com.ibm.mq.jms.MQTopic

  3 Object(s)
    0 Context(s)
    3 Binding(s), 2 Administered

InitCtx> _
```

Running the Client

In MQSeries, queues are managed by a component called a queue manager. The queue manager provides messaging services for applications and ensures that messages are put on the correct queue or that they are routed to another queue manager. Before applications can send any messages, you must create a queue manager.

The screenshot below shows the process involved in creating a queue manager. Make sure that the MQSeries server is up and running as described above. First check to see if a queue manager is already up and running. The default name for a queue manager is `QM_<host_name>`, but this can be changed at time of installation. If there is no queue manager running, start one up. Finally a number of system queues must be created using the `MQJMS_PSQ.mqsc` script file:

```
C:\WINNT\System32\cmd.exe                                        _ □ X

C:\MQSeries\java\bin>dspmqbrk
MQSeries message broker for queue manager QM_d8km500j not active.

C:\MQSeries\java\bin>strmqbrk
MQSeries message broker started for queue manager QM_d8km500j.

C:\MQSeries\java\bin>runmqsc < MQJMS_PSQ.mqsc_
```

The following files must be specified in the classpath:

- ❏ `com.ibm.mq.jar` – This JAR file contains Java implementations of the MQSeries connection options

- ❏ `com.ibm.mqjms.jar` – This JAR file contains MQSeries' JMS implementation classes

The following command-line arguments should be passed to the program for running the client:

❑ `com.sun.jndi.fscontext.RefFSContextFactory` – This is the initial context factory for the JNDI file system context

❑ `file:C:/temp`: This is the JNDI service provider URL

The screenshot below shows the JMS client running against MQSeries JMS:

```
C:\WINNT\System32\cmd.exe                                           _ □ ×

C:\ProJMS\AppendixA>echo %classpath%
.;C:\MQSeries\java\lib\com.ibm.mq.jar;C:\MQSeries\java\lib\com.ibm.mqjms.jar

C:\ProJMS\AppendixA>java PortableJMSClient com.sun.jndi.fscontext.RefFSContextFa
ctory file:C:/temp
Publishing message on the topic
Received message from the topic

C:\ProJMS\AppendixA>_
```

FioranoMQ

FioranoMQ is an event-driven communication platform that provides a pure Java implementation of JMS, from Fiorano Software. A 30-day trial version of the software is available for download from http://www.fiorano.com.

Fiorano Features

Fiorano supports both PTP and Pub/Sub messaging models. It also supports security, remote administration, guaranteed message delivery, and scalability:

❑ Fiorano provides a C++ run-time library for interoperating with non-JMS clients

❑ Fiorano is available either as a message broker based on hub-and-spoke technology, which is applicable in scenarios where guaranteed message delivery, remote administration, and message transfer over the Internet are important, or as a message bus based on reliable multicast backbone, which is more effective in an intranet-based zero-administration messaging system

❑ Fiorano guarantees high performance, scalability, and fail-over protection by networking multiple Fiorano servers together

❑ Fiorano supports inbuilt SSL support with 128-bit data encryption. It also supports ACL based security and certificate based authentication.

❑ Fiorano provides a robust and lightweight runtime environment

❑ Fiorano supports naming and directory services based on JNDI and LDAP

❑ Fiorano supports remote administration of the messaging system.

❑ Fiorano uses server push technology relieving the clients from the overhead of message polling

Fiorano Installation Tips

Fiorano 5.0 users can skip this section completely. Here are a few tips about installing and working with FioranoMQ 4.6 for first-time users. I would advice you to install the FioranoMQ server into a non-space directory like "C:\FioranoMQ". However if you prefer to install it onto a directory with spaces like "C:\Program Files\Fiorano\FioranoMQ", this section is for you. Users who have installed the Server into a non-space directory can skip this section completely.

Installing FioranoMQ 4.6 on the Windows Platform

On the Windows platform, Fiorano's scripts need modification if you install into a directory with embedded spaces (like "C:\Program Files"). You don't run into any of this if you installed to a non-space directory like "C:\FioranoMQ".

Installing into a directory with embedded spaces (like "C:\Program Files")

If you installed into a directory with embedded spaces, you need to modify the runkrnl.bat (the Fionaro messaging server startup script) and the runAdmin.bat (the Fionaro administrative console startup script) to make sure that the messaging server and the administrator console run fine. The details of what needs to be done are discussed below.

runkrnl.bat

Users have to start the FioranoMQ messaging server by running %FMP_DIR%\shell\runkrnl.bat (usually C:\Program Files\Fiorano\FioranoMQ\shell\runkrnl.bat). The server startup script assumes that the current directory is the Fiorano installation directory, and not many clues are provided to assist people in editing the script to run. The last line in the script needs quotes around most of the program names, as follows (this is supposed to be all on one line):

```
"%FMP_DIR%\bin\java" -cp "%FMP_DIR%\lib\rt.jar;%FMP_DIR%\bin\fmpkrnl.zip;"
COM.Fiorano.fmp.executive.FMP -p "%FMP_DIR%\bin"
```

In addition, the following has to be uncommented:

```
set FMP_DIR=C:\Progra~1\Fiorano\Fioran~1
```

runAdmin.bat

To run the Fiorano admin console, Fiorano's script (C:\Program Files\Fiorano\FioranoMQ\AdminTool\runAdmin.bat) has to be modified as follows.

Uncomment the following line in the script:

```
set FMP_DIR=F:\Progra~1\Fiorano\Fioran~1
```

Add quotes around path names as before (the following is supposed to be all one line):

```
"%JAVA2_VM%\bin\java" -cp
"%JAVA2_VM%\lib\rt.jar;%FMP_DIR%\lib\fmprtl.zip;%FMP_DIR%\lib\swing.jar;%FMP_DIR%\
lib\sfc.jar;%FMP_DIR%\lib\symbeans.jar;%FMP_DIR%\AdminTool\AdminTool.zip;"
fiorano.jms.AdminGUI.AdminTool
```

You are now all set to use the FioranoMQ 4.6 Server and start exploring JMS with it.

Fiorano Binaries

Fiorano comes with a set of binaries for running the router, administering the users, configuring Administered objects, monitoring, etc.

runkrnl

This program is used for starting the Fiorano server, and is available as a batch file for Windows platforms and a shell script for UNIX platforms in the shell directory in the Fiorano installation. This program can take the location of the configuration file that contains the various configuration values set by the server during boot-up as a command-line argument. The list shown below explains some of the parameters that can be configured using this file:

- ❏ The location of the message database directory
- ❏ The default port on which the server listens
- ❏ Restricting anonymous connections
- ❏ Enabling non-SSL connections
- ❏ Setting the server name
- ❏ Setting message pre-fetch size for queues

The listing below shows a sample configuration file:

```
##############################
# Server configuration file  #
##############################
SERVER_NAME=enterprise.department.serverName
PORT=2001
SERVER_ADDRESS=localhost
USE_SSL=false
RESTRICT_ANONYMOUS_LOGIN=TRUE
USE_NAGLES_ALGO=TRUE
CLIENT_MESSAGE_FILTERING=TRUE
ENABLE_LOG=true
USE_OPTIMIZED_CACHE=TRUE
USE_OPTIMIZED_QGMS=TRUE
PPREFETCH_SIZE_PER_QUEUE=128*1024
ENABLE_CRASH_PROTECTION=TRUE
IDLE_TIME=30
LOSE_PERSISTENT_MESSAGES_FOR_SLOW_SUBSCRIBER=false
```

runAdmin

This administration tool can be used to create Administered objects like topics, queues, destinations, etc. It can also be used for creating users. It is also possible to control access to Administered objects by setting access control lists for each topic. This way an administrator can control access to Administered objects by different users.

The administration tool can be invoked on Windows platforms by running runAdmin.bat and on UNIX platforms by running runAdmin.sh scripts. These files can be found in the AdminTool directory in the Fiorano installation. This application is password protected and the default password is normally passwd, though you may find that your network/host login password also works.

Fiorano comes with a few starter destinations. The tool can be also used for monitoring the server, snooping messages, etc. The screenshot shows the administration tool displaying the tab for configuring queues:

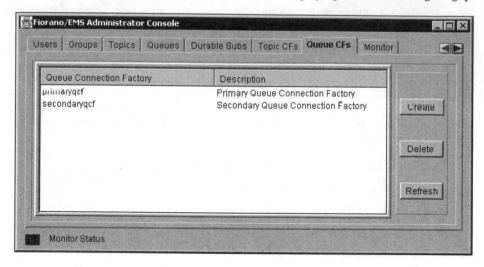

Dispatcher

The dispatcher can be used for maintaining server clusters and servers. The binary for running the dispatcher is available in the `dispatcher` directory under Fiorano installation. The dispatcher can be run on Windows platforms by running the file `runDispatcher.bat` and on UNIX platforms by running `runDispatcher.sh`.

Dispatcher Administration

The FioranoMQ Dispatcher can be administered using a GUI tool provided in the same directory as the `runDispatcher` binary. The Dispatcher Administration tool can be used to administer the server cluster. The tool provides the administrator with the following options:

❑ Add FioranoMQ servers to cluster

❑ Remove FioranoMQ servers from cluster

❑ Check the state and the number of clients on all the FioranoMQ servers in the cluster

❑ Limit the total number of client connections across all servers managed by this dispatcher and the total connections on each server

The figure below shows the tool for administering the dispatcher:

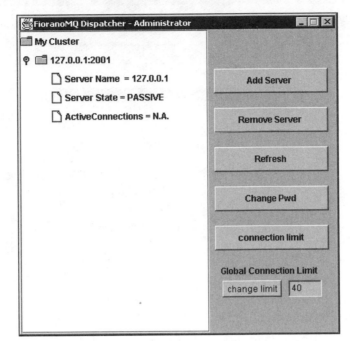

FioranoMQ Router

Used to run the Fiorano Message Router, this application needs to be run before two servers can be connected to each other as "neighbors" using the administration tool. The router can be invoked by running the `runRouter` script available in the `shell` directory under the Fiorano installation.

Running the Portable JMS Client

We will be storing the Administered objects in the internal JNDI namespace provided by the FioranoMQ server and later looking them up using JNDI.

Configuring the Administered Objects

For storing the Administered objects, first start the FioranoMQ JMS server by running the `runkrnl` script available in the `shell` directory under the Fiorano installation. Once the server is running, start the administration tool by running the `runAdmin` under the `AdminTool` directory under the Fiorano installation. This will show a graphical tool with multiple tabs for maintaining users, groups, connection factories, destinations, etc. Click on the Topics tab and then click on the Create button. This will open a response window prompting for the topic name and description. Enter the text `myTopic` for the topic name and click on the button OK:

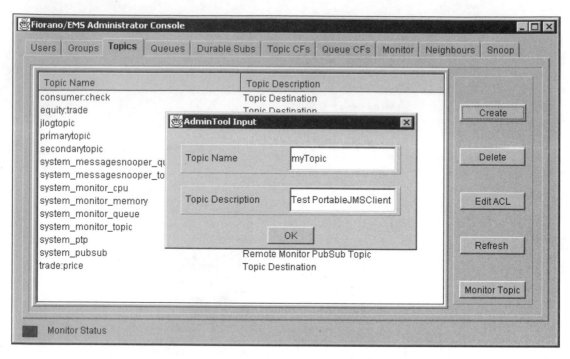

Click on the **Topic CFs** tab and then click on the **Create** button. This will open a response window prompting for the topic connection factory name and description. Enter the text TCFactory for the topic connection factory name and click on the button **OK**:

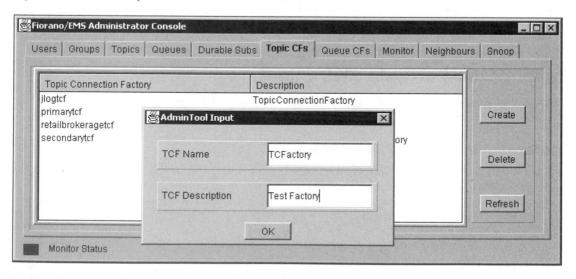

Running the Client

For running the client first start the FioranoMQ message broker by running the runkrnl script as explained earlier. Now invoke the Java interpreter on the class PortableJMSClient with all the required libraries in the classpath, and passing the JNDI provider URL and the JNDI initial context factory as command-line arguments.

The required JAR files are:

❑ `fmprtl.zip` – This ZIP file contains FioramoMQ's JMS implementation classes. It can be found in the `lib` directory under the Fiorano installation.

The following command-line arguments should be passed to the program for running the client:

❑ `fiorano.jms.rtl.FioranoInitialContextFactory` – This is the initial context factory for the JNDI lookup

❑ `localhost:2001` – This is the JNDI service provider URL

The figure below shows the JMS client running against FioranoMQ:

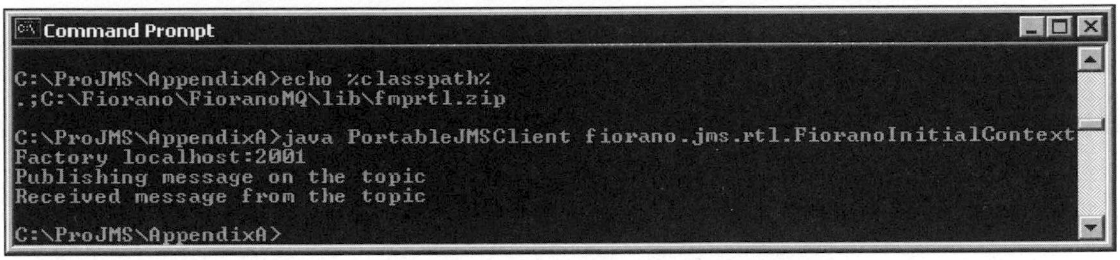

Softwired iBus

iBus is a pure Java messaging product family offering the JMS abstraction atop a variety of operating system platforms and transport protocols. iBus products are available for free download from http://www.softwired-inc.com. iBus consists mainly of three products:

❑ **iBus//MessageServer**
A JMS implementation supporting both the PTP and Pub/Sub model, as well as message persistence, transactions, HTTP tunneling, access control to JMS destinations, and SSL security.

❑ **iBus//MessageBus**
A fully distributed message bus middleware implementing the JMS Pub/Sub model atop reliable IP multicast communication. This product is typically used on trading floors and in data centers.

❑ **iBus//Mobile**
A JMS add-on product allowing the seamless integration of mobile devices into a JMS infrastructure. This product is typically used for wireless portals and wireless ASP (WASP) solutions.

iBus Features

iBus offers an end-to-end JMS platform in that it runs not only on server platforms and workstations, but also on mobile phones, PDAs, and communicator devices. A list of the main features provided by the iBus product family is shown below:

❑ High scalability, performance, and reliability

❑ Hierarchical access control, client authentication, and data encryption

- ❑ Administration GUI and administration API

- ❑ Built-in integration with XML parsers

- ❑ XML message type

- ❑ Built-in integration with LDAP and other JNDI providers

- ❑ JMS message delivery via TCP, HTTP, SSL, and reliable IP multicast

- ❑ JMS message delivery via wireless bearers (GPRS, UMTS, SMS) using an optimized transmission protocol

- ❑ JMS message transformation to and from WML and other formats, using XML Style Sheets

- ❑ Light-weight JMS client library suitable for mobile devices and Applets

- ❑ Run-time library allowing applications written in C and C++ to produce and consume JMS messages

iBus//MessageServer Binaries

iBus//MessageServer comes with a set of applications for running the message server, administering the server, configuring JMS destinations, etc. These applications are available in the Start menu for Windows installations.

startserver

This batch file is used for starting the iBus message server. For Windows installations, a shortcut is provided in the iBus//MessageServer program group:

The message server accepts messages from, and delivers messages to, the JMS client applications. Persistent JMS messages are stored in an embedded database, which is part of the iBus//MessageServer product offering. Optionally, iBus//MessageServer can be configured to store JMS messages in an Oracle database.

The screenshot below shows the iBus//MessageServer server up and running:

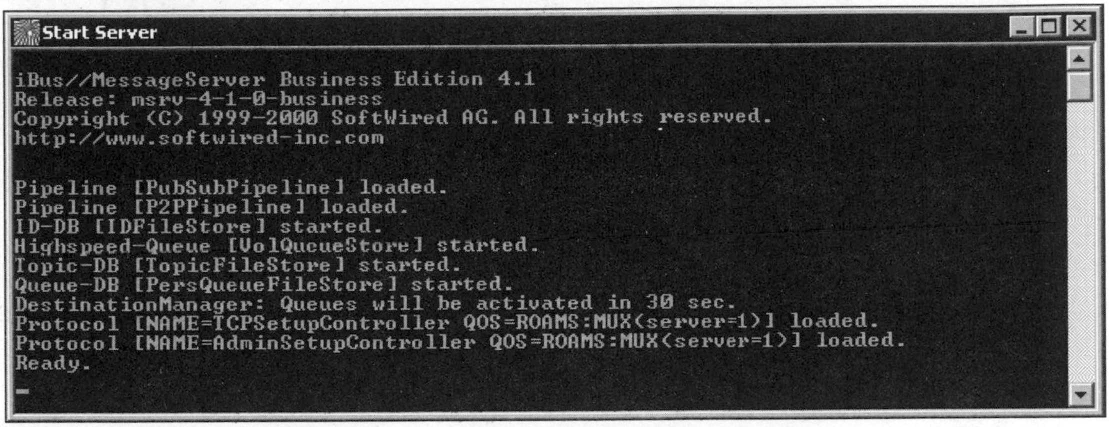

configwizard

iBus//MessageServer can be configured for various transport protocols (notably TCP, HTTP, and SSL), to use an Oracle database instead of the default database that is bundled with iBus//MessageServer, for using thread pools internally, and so on. The Config Wizard allows you to easily create customized configurations of the message server:

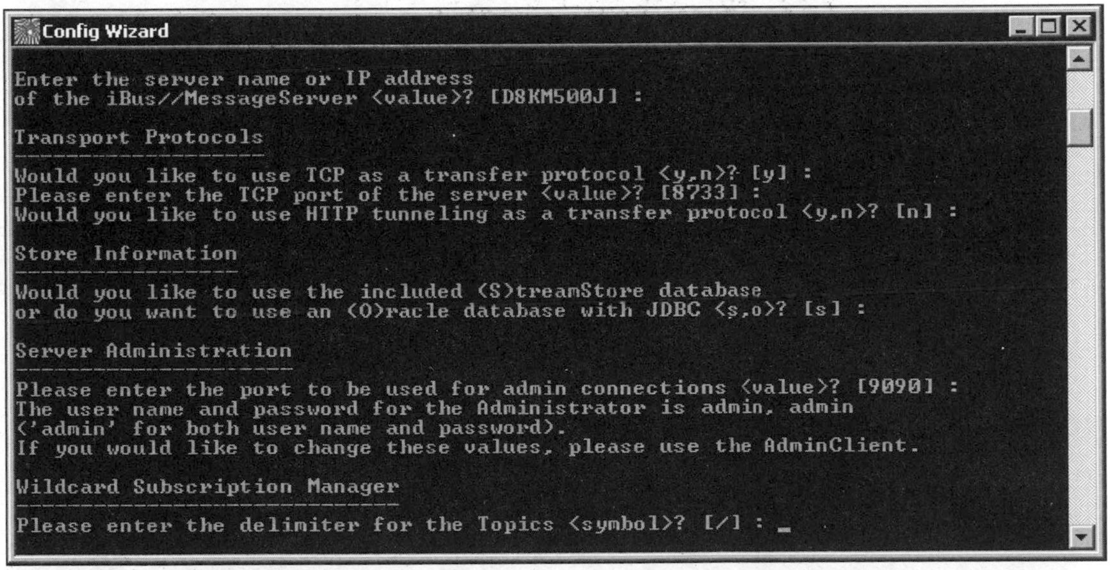

Administration Client

This graphical user interface allows you to create administered topics and queues, to manage access control lists, to track JMS message flows, and to perform other message server administration tasks. Note that this must be downloaded separately from the message server. The screenshot overleaf shows the Administration Client with the screen for monitoring and administering message flows:

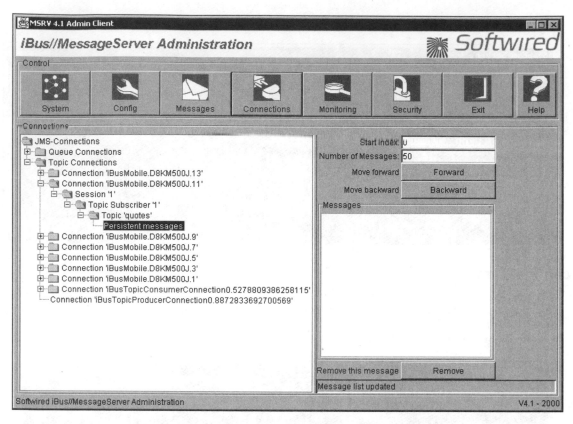

The Administration Client is also provided in a text-based version, allowing message server administration to occur also on console terminals:

Other Utilities

iBus//MessageServer further provides a wizard for configuring an external Oracle database, a Client Shell tool for compiling and running JMS client applications easily, and an administration API for performing iBus//MessageServer administration tasks programmatically in Java.

iBus//MessageServer can be combined with iBus//MessageBus as well as with iBus//Mobile, leading to an end-to-end JMS platform for wired and wireless systems.

Running the Portable JMS Client

We will be storing the administered JMS objects in the internal JNDI namespace provided by iBus//MessageServer and later look them up using JNDI.

Configuring the Administered Objects

First start the iBus//MessageServer by selecting the **Start Server** shortcut located in the iBus//MessageServer program group on Windows, or by executing the `startserver.sh` shell script on Unix. The shell script is located in the `server/bin` subdirectory of the iBus//MessageServer installation.

Next, start the iBus//MessageServer Admin Client by selecting the **Start Admin** shortcut located in the iBus//MessageServer Admin Client program group on Windows, or by executing the `startAdmin.sh` shell script on Unix. The shell script is located in the `adminClient/bin` subdirectory of the Admin Client installation.

Click on the **Messages** button, select **Topics** in the tree panel on the left-hand side. A form appears into which you can enter the topic name, `myTopic`, and click **Create**:

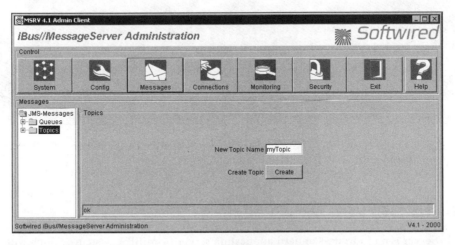

iBus//MessageServer comes configured with a topic and a queue connection factory under the names `TopicConnectionFactory` and `QueueConnectionFactory`. Further factories can be set up and bound by the user using LDAP, but it is very rarely that an iBus//MessageServer user needs to carry out this task. Change the following line in the code to run `PortableJMSClient.java` on iBus//MessageServer:

```
public static final String TOPIC_FACTORY = "TopicConnectionFactory";
```

Running the Client

For running JMS clients, iBus//MessageServer provides a Client Shell tool in the iBus//MessageServer Windows program group. The Client Shell opens a Windows command tool with the Java classpath set up correctly for running iBus//MessageServer clients. So there is no need to include any extra JAR files in the classpath.

The following command-line arguments should be passed to the program for running the client:

❑ `ch.softwired.jms.naming.IBusContextFactory` – This is the initial context factory for the JNDI lookup

❑ `localhost` – This is the JNDI service provider URL

The figure below shows the JMS client running against iBus//MessageServer:

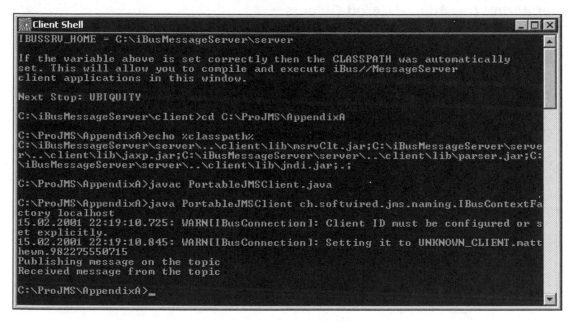

The warnings occur because iBus//MessageServer prefers a client to set a client ID when it creates a topic or queue connection, as we saw in the code in Chapter 11.

WebLogic Server

WebLogic Server is an industry-standard application server from BEA Systems. Along with supporting most of the enterprise Java API like EJBs and JSPs, WebLogic is fully compliant with the JMS 1.0.2 specification. The latest version of WebLogic (v 6.0) implements EJB 2.0 specification (as an optional add-on) and supports message-driven EJBs that are activated by JMS messages. An evaluation version of WebLogic 6.0 is available from http://www.bea.com.

WebLogic JMS Features

WebLogic supports both Pub/Sub and PTP messaging models. WebLogic JMS can work with other WebLogic features like EJBs, JSPs, servlets, JDBC connection pools, JTA, etc. The main WebLogic features related to JMS are listed below:

- WebLogic 6.0 implements JMS 1.0.2.

- JMS configuration properties can be set using the administration console.

- JMS applications can interoperate with other resource managers (primarily databases) using the JTA. JMS applications can participate in transactions with other Java APIs, like EJBs, that use JTA.

- Supports message multi-casting.

- Supports databases and files for persistent message storage.

- Can work with other enterprise APIs such as Enterprise Java Beans (EJB), JDBC connection pools, servlets, and RMI.

- WebLogic also ships with JDBC drivers for all the popular RDBMS vendors. It also supports databases like Cloudscape in which Java objects can be stored directly.

- WebLogic 6.0 implements EJB 2.0 beta and supports message-driven EJBs.

- WebLogic provides server clustering and the following clustering features are available for JMS applications:

  - Load balancing within a cluster

  - Transparent access to destinations from any server in the cluster

- WebLogic also provides custom JMS extensions listed below:

  - Create XML messages

  - A session exception listener similar to the standard JMS connection exception listener

  - A configurable threshold of pre-fetched asynchronous messages allowed on the session

  - Set or display the multicast session overrun policy that is applied when the message maximum is reached

  - Dynamic creation of permanent queues or topics

  - Also supports NO_ACKNOWLEDGE and MULTICAST_NO_ACKNOWLEDGE modes, and extended exceptions

  - Custom destination templates that can be shared by multiple destinations

  - Use of destination keys to set message sort order

WebLogic Server

Running the startWebLogic.cmd file on Windows platforms or the startWebLogic.sh file on UNIX platforms can start WebLogic server. The server reads all the configuration information from the properties file on startup. It initializes the queues, topics, and connection factories defined in the properties file during startup. WebLogic 6.0 server can be started on Windows platforms using the Start Default Server shortcut available on the Start menu.

WebLogic Console

WebLogic Server 6.0 provides a powerful browser-based administration console. The console can be accessed using the URL http://<host:port>/console where the host and port are the host and port on which the server is listening. The default port is 7001. The screenshot below shows the administration console for WebLogic 6.0 with one of the JMS-specific screens open:

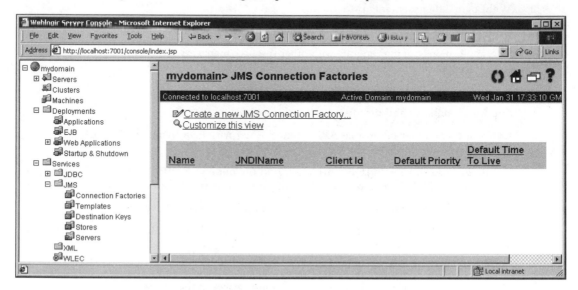

Running the Portable JMS Client

We will be storing the Administered objects in the internal JNDI namespace provided by the WebLogic server and later looking them up using JNDI. We will be using WebLogic 6.0 for this example.

Configuring the Administered Objects

Start the WebLogic server using the short cut available under the Start menu on Windows platforms or the shell-scripts available for UNIX platforms. Once the server is up and running start your browser window and access the URL http://localhost:7001/console assuming the server is running on the local machine and listening on the default port. You will have to enter the password for the system user that you configured at installation.

Expand the JMS node under the Services node in the left-hand tree and click on the Servers node under the JMS node. Now click on the Create a new JMSServer... link on the right-hand panel:

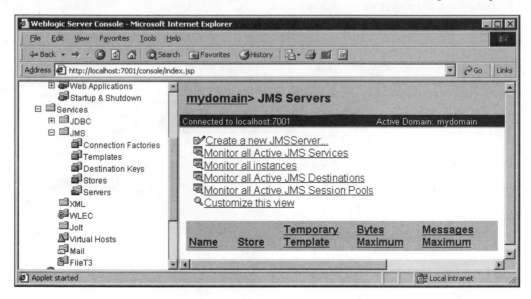

Enter the text MyJMSServer for the server name, leave everything else as default, and click on the Create button:

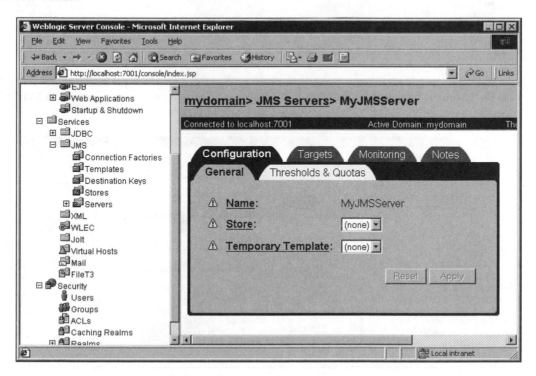

Now click on the **Targets** tab and add the JMS server created in the last step to the required WebLogic server. Here I am using the default server **myserver**. Select the server from the **Available** list and add it to the **Chosen** list. Now click on the **Apply** button:

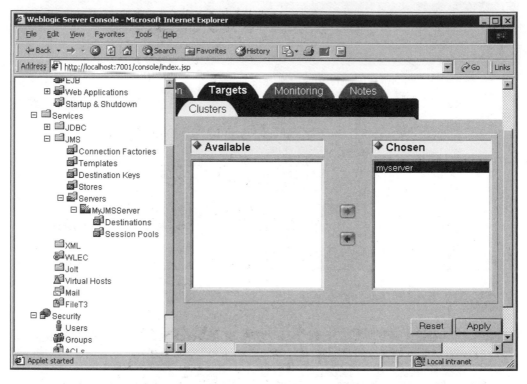

Now expand the node **MyJMSServer** under the **Servers** node and click on the **Destinations** node. Now click on the **Create a new JMSTopic** link on the right-hand panel. Add the topic name and JNDI name as myTopic, leave everything else as default, and click on the **Create** button:

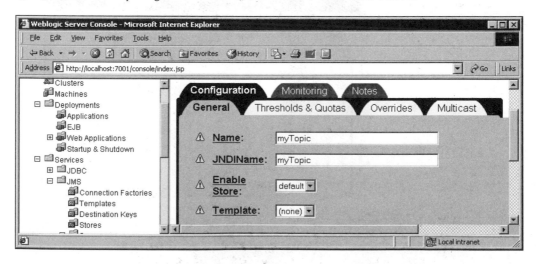

Now click on the Connection Factories node and then click on the Create a new JMSConnectionFactory link on the right-hand panel. Enter the connection factory name and the JNDI name as TCFactory, leave everything else as default, and click on the Create button:

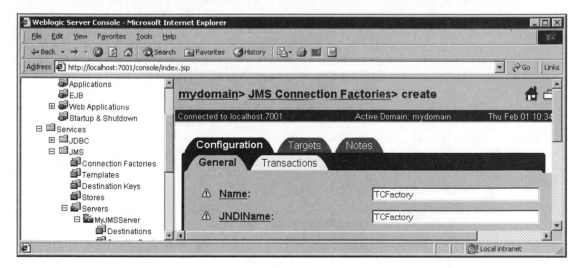

Now click on the Targets tab and make the newly created connection factory available to the required server. Select the server from the Available list and add it to the Chosen list. Now click on the Apply button.

Running the Client

For running the client first start the WebLogic server as explained earlier. Now invoke the Java interpreter on the class PortableJMSClient with all the required classes in the classpath, and passing the JNDI provider URL and the JNDI initial context factory as command-line arguments.

The required JAR files are:

❑   weblogic.jar – This JAR file contains all the required classes for JNDI and JMS. This can be found in the lib directory under the WebLogic installation.

The following command-line arguments should be passed to the program for running the client:

❑   weblogic.jndi.T3InitialContextFactory – This is the initial context factory for the JNDI lookup

❑   t3://localhost:7001: This is the JNDI service provider URL

The figure below shows the JMS client running against WebLogic:

583

J2EE 1.3 Reference Implementation

J2EE 1.3 reference server, which was only available as a beta release at publication of this book, is a reference implementation from Sun Microsystems of the various J2EE APIs defined in the J2EE 1.3 specification. The reference implementation supports EJB 2.0, Servlet 2.3, JSP 1.2, and JMS 1.02 (which is mandatory in this specification). The beta version is available under the early access program and can be downloaded from http://java.sun.com/j2ee. The reference implementation is fully compliant with the JM3 1.02 specification and supports both Pub/Sub and PTP messaging models.

J2EE Server

J2EE server can be started by running the file j2ee.bat or j2ee.sh file available in the bin directory under the J2EE reference implementation installations. Make sure that you have set the environmental variables J2EE_HOME and JAVA_HOME before you start the server. By default, the server listens on the following ports for various services:

- ❑ 8000 – For HTTP connections, which, can be altered by editing the web.properties file in the config directory under the J2EE installation

- ❑ 7000 – For HTTPS connections, which can be altered by editing the web.properties file in the config directory under the J2EE installation

- ❑ 1050 – For JNDI lookups, which can be altered by editing the orb.properties file in the config directory under the J2EE installation

The reference implementation defines two JMS-related properties files in the config directory.

- ❑ jms_client.properties
  This file contains the various properties required by the JMS clients for JNDI lookup, connecting to the server, preferred communication protocol, and logging level.

- ❑ jms_service.properties
  This file defines the various properties required for the JNDI server for implementing durable subscriptions and message redelivery.

Administration Tool

The administration tool is a command-line utility for managing various resources on the server. This tool can be run by using the `j2eeadmin.bat` or `j2eeadmin.sh` file that can be found in the `bin` directory. The tool can be used for:

- ❑ Adding, listing, removing JDBC drivers
- ❑ Adding, listing, removing JDBC data sources
- ❑ Adding, listing, removing JDBC XA data sources
- ❑ Adding, listing, removing JMS destinations
- ❑ Adding, listing, removing JMS connection factories
- ❑ Adding, listing, removing connector factories

We will have a look at some of the commands related to JMS:

Adding a queue named `myQueue`	`j2eeadmin -addJmsDestination myQueue queue`
Adding a topic names `myTopic`	`j2eeadmin -addJmsDestination myTopic topic`
Adding a queue connection factory named `QCFactory`	`j2eeadmin -addJmsFactory QCFactory queue`
Adding a topic connection factory named `TCFactory`	`j2eeadmin -addJmsFactory TCFactory topic`
Listing all the configured JMS destinations	`j2eeadmin -listJmsDestination`
Listing all the configured JMS connection factories	`j2eeadmin -listJmsFactory`
Removing a JMS destination named `myQueue`	`j2eeadmin -removeJmsDestination myQueue`
Removing a JMS connection factory named `QCFactory`	`j2eeadmin -removeJmsFactory QCFactory`

Running the Portable JMS Client

Configuring the Administered Objects

We will be storing the Administered objects in the internal JNDI namespace provided by the J2EE reference implementation.

Type the following commands to add a topic named myTopic and a topic connection factory named TCFactory in the command window:

```
C:\ProJMS\AppendixA> j2eeadmin -addJmsDestination myTopic topic
C:\ProJMS\AppendixA> j2eeadmin -addJmsFactory TCFactory topic
```

Running the Client

For running the client first start the J2EE server as explained earlier. Now invoke the Java interpreter on the class PortableJMSClient with all the required classes in the classpath and passing the location of the JMS client properties file as a system property using the –D option.

The required JAR files are:

❑   j2ee.jar – This JAR file contains all the required classes for JNDI and JMS

The following property should be passed to the program using the –D option for the Java interpreter:

❑   Property name – jms.properties.

❑   Property value – <J2EE_HOME>\config\jms_client.properties. Where <J2EE_HOME> is the directory under which the J2EE reference implementation is installed

The figure below shows the JMS client running against the J2EE reference implementation:

```
C:\ProJMS\AppendixA>echo %classpath%
.;C:\j2sdkee1.3\lib\j2ee.jar

C:\ProJMS\AppendixA>java -Djms.properties=C:\j2sdkee1.3\config\jms_client.proper
ties PortableJMSClient
Java(TM) Message Service 1.0.2 Reference Implementation (build b10)
Publishing message on the topic
Received message from the topic

C:\ProJMS\AppendixA>
```

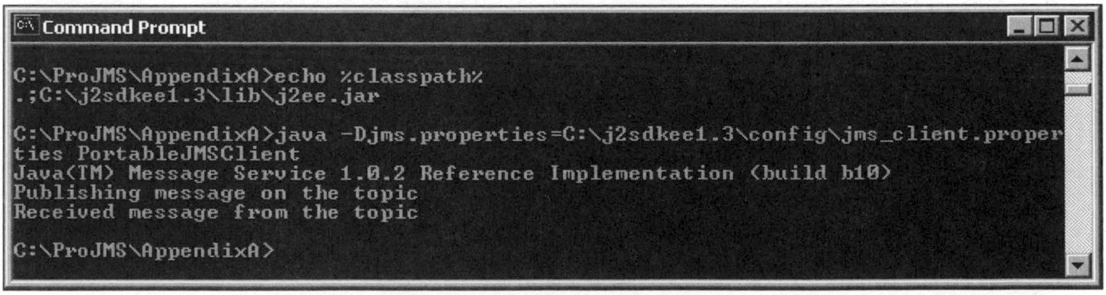

Message Selector Syntax

A message selector is a string expression whose syntax is based on a subset of the SQL-92 conditional expression syntax. The syntax is composed of:

- ❑ Literals
- ❑ Identifiers
- ❑ Whitespace
- ❑ Expressions
- ❑ Logical operators
- ❑ Comparison operators
- ❑ Arithmetic operators

The tables below provide a handy reference of the main components and construction rules. Note that all selector syntax is case-insensitive.

Literals

Element	Syntax and Specifications
String literals	Zero or more characters enclosed in single quotes
Exact numeric literals	Numeric `long` integer values, signed and unsigned
Approximate numeric literals	Numeric `double` values in scientific notation or numeric `double` values with a decimal, signed or unsigned
Boolean literals	`true` or `false`

An example of a numeric `double` value in scientific notation is:

`-30.9E7`

An example of a double value with a decimal:

`-92.8`

Identifiers

Element	Syntax and Specifications	Limitations
Applies to all	A case-sensitive character sequence that must begin with a Java-identifier start character, and all following characters must be Java-identifier part characters	Cannot be `null`, `true`, `false`, `NOT`, `AND`, `OR`, `BETWEEN`, `LIKE`, `IN`, or `IS`
Message header field references	`JMSDeliveryMode` `JMSPriority` `JMSMessageID` `JMSTimestamp` `JMSCorrelationID` `JMSType`	`JMSDeliveryMode` and `JMSPriority` cannot be `null`
`JMSX`-defined property references	`null` when a referenced property does not exist	–
`JMS_provider`-specific property references	`null` when a referenced property does not exist	–
Application specific property name	`null` when a referenced property does not exist	–

Operators

The table below lists the operator and expression syntax in message selectors (based on the SQL-92 SELECT statement syntax):

Element	Syntax and Specifications
Logical	In precedence order: NOT, AND, OR
Comparison	=, >, >=, <, <=, <> (not equal)
Arithmetic	In precedence order: ❑ Unary + or − ❑ Multiplication * or Division / ❑ Addition + or Subtraction −
Arithmetic range between two expressions	expr1 BETWEEN expr2 AND expr3 expr1 NOT BETWEEN expr4 AND expr5

An example of logical operator is usage is:

```
x NOT = true
```

An example of arithmetic operator usage is:

```
y - 64
```

An example of arithmetic range operator usage is:

```
z NOT BETWEEN 19 AND 28
```

Expressions

Element	Syntax and Specifications
Selector	Conditional expression that matches when it evaluates to true.
Arithmetic	Include: ❑ Pure arithmetic expressions ❑ Arithmetic equations ❑ Identifiers with numeric values ❑ Numeric literals

Table continued on following page

Element	Syntax and Specifications
Conditional	Include: ❑ Pure conditional expressions ❑ Comparison operations ❑ Logical operations ❑ Identifiers and Boolean values ❑ Boolean literals (`true` and `false`)

An example of selector expression usage is:

```
((5+5) = (7+3))=true
```

An example of arithmetic expression usage is:

```
90/9
```

An example of conditional expression usage is:

```
x > 10 OR y = true
```

Comparison Operators

The table below lists the Comparison Test syntax that can be used in message selectors (based on the SQL-92 SELECT statement syntax):

Element	Syntax and Specifications
IN	`Identifier IN (str1, str2,...)` `Identifier NOT IN (str1, str2,...)`

LIKE	`Identifier LIKE (str1, str2, ...)`
	 `Identifier NOT LIKE (str1, str2,...)`
	
	 Can be enhanced with pattern values:
	 Underscore (_) stands for any character
	 Percent % stands for any sequence of characters
	 To explicitly defer the special characters _ and %, precede their entry with the Escape character.

NULL	`Identifier IS NULL`
	 `Identifier IS NOT NULL`
	 For:
	 ❑ header field value
	 ❑ property value
	 ❑ existence of a property

An example of IN usage is:

```
country IN ('US','UK','India')
```

An example of LIKE usage is:

```
state LIKE 'TN' is true for 'Athul' 'Aditya' and false for 'Kalyan'
```

An example of null usage is:

```
x IS NULL
```

Example

Below is an example of a message subscriber being created with a message selector. In this case the subscriber will only receive messages whose addressedTo property is all or their own name:

```
String selector = "addressedTo in ('all','" + user + "')";
subscriber = session.createSubscriber(topic,selector,false);
```

Untitled - Notepad
File Edit Format Help
Help Topics
Useful Phrases
About Notepad
com.sun.jndi.fscontext.RefFSContextFactory
com.sun.jndi.ldap.LdapCtxFactory
weblogic.jndi.WLInitialContextFactory
weblogic.jndi.T3InitialContextFactory
fiorano.jms.rtl.FioranoInitialContextFactory
fiorano.jms.runtime.naming.FioranoInitialContextFactory
ch.softwired.jms.naming.IBusContextFactory

Emerging XML Standards

We are going to look at three interesting XML messaging frameworks in detail: **SOAP**, **BizTalk**, and **ebXML**. There are many others, but these have a number of the important characteristics that message wire formats need. They are also interesting to contrast because they try to meet different goals.

Messaging Frameworks

SOAP simply tries to define a basic XML format oriented toward the RPC-style of communications. It is both transport- and platform-neutral. SOAP is deliberately simple so that more complex features, such as those required in business messaging, can be incorporated into it.

Essentially, this is what BizTalk does: it extends SOAP, adding hooks for reliable messaging, service naming, outside transport bindings, etc.

Finally, ebXML looks at business messaging as a whole, including modeling and articulation of the processes behind message exchange. Out of this standard also comes an XML message format that meets the demands of a global market without reliance on a particular transport.

We have also included a brief look at XMSG, published in a W3C Note, and interesting for its straightforward approach some messaging challenges, and some coverage of the W3C's XML Protocol Activity.

> **A word of caution: this is a very fast moving area, and the information presented here is subject to a lot of change.**

SOAP

The **Simple Object Access Protocol (SOAP)** is an XML messaging protocol co-authored by representatives from Microsoft, DevelopMentor, UserLand, IBM, and Lotus and submitted to the W3C. It provides a very simple and straightforward XML framework for defining messages. Of the messages formats we will examine, SOAP has so far generated the most interest from vendors and developers alike. You can download the SOAP specification from http://www.w3.org/TR/SOAP.

Although SOAP is intended to be the wire protocol for a distributed object system, there are a number of basic requirements that it explicitly does not address. These include distributed garbage collection and object references, both of which greatly add to application server complexity.

Similarly, the spec does not attempt to define object lifecycle functions, such as construction, activation, destruction, etc. SOAP does not attempt to define how to batch multiple messages together, a process called "Boxcarring". The spec does not preclude any of these things: a SOAP RPC may reference a remote, stateful object if the particular implementation provides this functionality; it just does not try to state how this might be done.

There is a danger here that we will be inundated with proprietary vendor implementations that do not interoperate (remember CORBA?). Nevertheless, there is considerable excitement around SOAP, and Microsoft has announced that it will be the foundation of its .NET platform.

Message Format

The SOAP message format is interesting to contrast against that of ebXML. The differences stem for the very different objectives of the groups that designed the messages. SOAP really is intended only as a simple and flexible message protocol. Its strength is that it does not try to over define; instead, it provides extensibility so application designers can add the additional functions they need.

Reliable messaging is a good example of SOAP's extensibility. SOAP does not implement reliability; however, Microsoft's BizTalk framework, described below, uses SOAP messages and adds the necessary fields to implement this (as well as a number of other functions). Because of this simplicity, SOAP is a good foundation to base new messages on when some of these features are delegated to infrastructure, such as the case in a number of JMS applications using robust MOM as a service provider:

Messages in SOAP are fundamentally one-way (the send-and-forget model). However, there are semantics for synchronous request/response (that is, the RPC model) defined in the spec, and this will likely be the dominant SOAP interaction model.

SOAP messages must be well formed, but not necessarily validated XML. In contrast to ebXML, described below, SOAP packaging makes use of XML. The spec defines a mandatory, namespace-qualified root element called an envelope, which is a container for both header and body elements:

```
<?xml version="1.0" encoding="UTF-8"?>
<SOAP-ENV:Envelope
 xmlns:SOAP-ENV="http://schemas.xmlsoap.org/soap/envelope/"
 SOAP-ENV:encodingStyle="http://schemas.xmlsoap.org/soap/encoding/"/>

<SOAP-ENV:Header>
</SOAP-ENV:Header>

<SOAP-ENV:Body>
</SOAP-ENV:Body>
</SOAP-ENV:Envelope>
```

The drawback of this is the difficulty in transporting anything that might break an XML parser handling the message. Binary attachments, invalid XML fragments, or even valid XML documents that contain their own root will cause problems. Typically, people will address this by escaping data in CDATA sections, escaping with parameter entities, or encoding with Base64.

Multiple attachments remain a problem; however, there is a W3C note exploring this issue. SOAP Messages with Attachments, released in December 2000, can be downloaded from http://www.w3.org/TR/2000/NOTE-SOAP-attachments-20001211. The note proposed a packaging using MIME multipart/related structure, which is the solution adopted by the ebXML committee.

The SOAP envelope contains an optional, namespace-qualified header. SOAP defines a number of header elements; however, the intent of the header scheme is to be entirely flexible, allowing users to add their own. This is one of the most powerful idioms in XML messaging. Header extension does not require that prior notice be served to a receiving party; the receiver will not consider additional, unrecognized headers an error condition. Header elements can contain two optional attributes:

```
<SOAP-ENV:Header>
  <n:UserDefHeader xmlns:n="..." Actor="..." MustUnderstand="...">
    Header content
  </n:UserDefHeader>
</SOAP-ENV:Header>
```

The actor attribute identifies the application for which the header is intended. Note that SOAP messages can transit intermediaries (that is, they can be multi-hop). Intermediaries must remove headers targeted for them and process the message accordingly before forwarding.

The mustUnderstand attribute indicates whether the actor it identifies must process the header element. This is an interesting requirement brought about because of the flexibility of XML. On one hand, we promote XML as being good for messaging because minor changes to messages rarely break handlers; indeed, most handlers will simply ignore added elements or attributes.

Consider the case, though, where this behavior could lead to problems. What if you wanted to weed out any handlers that had not been updated to accommodate the message changes? This is the problem solved by the mustUnderstand attribute. If this attribute is set to "1", but the handler cannot process the header; it must signal an error.

The body is a mandatory, namespace-qualified container for further XML data. These data items are called body entries. Body entries may be further namespace qualified to disambiguate between schemas. The spec defines a fault element for communicating server problems back to a client. Applications render faults into the body section. There can only be a single Fault element present in the body:

```
<SOAP-ENV:Fault>
  <faultcode> "Fault code" </faultcode>
  <faultstring> "String describing fault" </faultstring>
  <faultactor> "Some URI" </faultactor>
  <detail>
    ...
  </detail>
</SOAP-ENV:Fault>
```

Four general faultcode categories are defined in the spec, categorizing faults as resulting from problems with the initial namespace (which defines SOAP version), problems with the message processor not understanding a part of the message it should, client errors (which include problems with message contents), and server errors (generally processing errors unrelated to the message content).

It is intended that faultcodes be extensible. The faultstring is intended for human consumption, not machine processing. Both the faultcode and the faultstring are mandatory. faultactor is an optional element containing a URI specifying the process where the fault was registered. This is important for messages that traverse multiple intermediaries. Finally, if any problem occurs in processing the contents of a message body, the resulting fault element must contain a detail element. The detail element is a container for detail entries, which further describe the error. Detail entry structure is flexible.

SOAP adopts primitive type definitions (int, float, string, etc.) from XML Schema. The spec is quite detailed on how to render types, including compound types like arrays and structures, which greatly aids in creating deterministic bindings to other languages. For example, consider this simple Java code sample:

```java
public class FamousAuthors {
  String[] author = {"Mark Twain", "Charles Dickens", "George Orwell"};
}

FamousAuthors myWriterList = new FamousAuthors();
```

This could be marshaled into the following document fragment using the SOAP conventions:

```xml
<myWriterList>
<author SOAP-ENC:arrayType="xsd:String[3]">
  <name>Mark Twain</name>
  <name>Charles Dickens</name>
  <name>George Orwell</name>
</author>
</myWriterList>
```

In this case the array is defined in a schema as follows:

```xml
<element name="author" type="SOAP-ENC:Array"/>
```

If a schema is not defined, the above serialization is decomposed into:

```
<myWriterList>
  <SOAP-ENC:Array SOAP-ENC:arrayType="xsd:string[3]">
    <SOAP-ENC:string>Mark Twain</SOAP-ENC:string>
    <SOAP-ENC:string>Charles Dickens</SOAP-ENC:string>
    <SOAP-ENC:string>George Orwell</SOAP-ENC:string>
  </SOAP-ENC:Array>
</myWriterList>
```

Similarly, consider a more complex example:

```
public class Portfolio {

  public String symbol;
  public double value;

  public Portfolio(String symbol, double value) {
    this.symbol = symbol;
    this.value = value;
  }
}

Portfolio[] myPortfolio = new Portfolio[2];

myPortfolio[0]=new Portfolio("WROX",123.45);
myPortfolio[1]=new Portfolio("ABC",987.65);
```

This would be marshaled in a SOAP message as:

```
<SOAP-ENC:Array SOAP-
ENC:arrayType="PortfolioTypeDefSchemaNameSpace:myPortfolio[2]">
  <myPortfolio>
    <symbol>WROX</symbol>
    <value>123.45</value>
  </myPortfolio>
  <myPortfolio>
    <symbol>ABC</symbol>
      <value>987.65</value>
  </myPortfolio>
</SOAP-ENC:Array>
```

Again, the array `myPortfolio` must be defined in a schema that is referenced by the namespace `PortfolioTypeDefSchemaNameSpace`. Interested readers should refer to the SOAP specification for more details.

Transport Binding

A fundamental design goal of SOAP has been to stay simple and flexible, and make use of existing, proven technology, particularly transport infrastructure. The SOAP authors felt that this would actually make it more successful, as SOAP can readily adapt to the wildly varying requirements of different vertical markets. Version 0.9 of the SOAP specification actually explicitly tied it to HTTP. The idea was to create a protocol that could make extensive use of existing infrastructure (and there was a lot of this around), be able to easily traverse firewalls (since most are port 80/443 friendly), and take advantage of the mature HTTP security model.

To ensure that SOAP calls were upfront about their intent – after all, this is an API for remote processing, which will make most security managers nervous – all calls made use of the M-POST method, something provided by the HTTP extensions framework. By SOAP 1.1, the proposal had decoupled from a specific transport binding and made M-POST optional, acknowledging its lack of native support; however, HTTP is still the reference in the specification document, though one could equally use SMTP/POP3/IMAP4, or MOM systems.

Moving to a robust MOM system would provide reliable messaging features, asynchronous messaging, different messaging paradigms like Publish/Subscribe, etc. None of these is accounted for in a SOAP binding to HTTP (although the hooks can be built in, as we will see when we explore BizTalk).

IBM is working on a binding of SOAP to its flagship MOM product, MQSeries. A preview of this technology is available in the IBM Web Services Toolkit, downloadable from http://alphaworks.ibm.com/tech/webservicetoolkit. MQSeries, of course, provides a JMS API; however, this demonstration makes use of the product's proprietary Java API, based on the cross-language MQI specification. Nevertheless, it does serve as an inspiration and a clear indication that SOAP bound to MOM is coming and will be significant in the future.

What if you want to use SOAP as a messaging framework in a JMS application as of now? At present, there are no standard guidelines available that define a JMS binding; however, there are enough clues in the existing HTTP binding to be able to do this in such a way that we will likely align with future standards. The following is a simple SOAP request and response sequence, bound to HTTP. First the SOAP request:

```
POST /soaptest/stocks/listeners/services.asp HTTP/1.0
User-Agent: Mozilla/4.0 (compatible; MSIE 4.01; MS ROPE Engine)
Accept:*/*
Authorization: dXNlcm5hbWU6cGFzc3dvcmQ=
Content-Type: text/xml
Content-Length: 455
SOAPAction:
http://palm.infowave.com/soaptest/stocks/listeners/services.asp#GetStockQuote
Host: palm.infowave.com

<?xml version='1.0'?>
<SOAP-ENV:Envelope
   xmlns:SOAP-ENV='http://schemas.xmlsoap.org/soap/envelope/'
   SOAP-ENV:encodingStyle='http://schemas.xmlsoap.org/soap/encoding/'
   xmlns:xsi='http://www.w3.org/1999/XMLSchema-instance'
   xmlns:xsd='http://www.w3.org/1999/XMLSchema'>
  <SOAP-ENV:Body>
    <GetStockQuote xmlns='http://palm.infowave.com'>
      <Symbol>WROX</Symbol>
    </GetStockQuote>
  </SOAP-ENV:Body>
</SOAP-ENV:Envelope>
```

The SOAP response:

```
HTTP/1.1 200 OK
Server: Microsoft-IIS/4.0
Date: Tue, 06 Feb 2001 18:59:15 GMT
MessageType: CallResponse
Content-Type: text/xml
Expires: Tue, 06 Feb 2001 18:59:15 GMT
Set-Cookie: ASPSESSIONIDGQGQQIGP=BINNEHKDOFDDDJKJFMKNKKFM; path=/
Cache-control: private
```

```
<?xml version='1.0'?>
<SOAP-ENV:Envelope
    xmlns:SOAP-ENV='http://schemas.xmlsoap.org/soap/envelope/'
    SOAP-ENV:encodingStyle='http://schemas.xmlsoap.org/soap/encoding/'
    xmlns:xsi='http://www.w3.org/1999/XMLSchema-instance'
    xmlns:xsd='http://www.w3.org/1999/XMLSchema'>
  <SOAP-ENV:Body>
    <GetStockQuoteResult xmlns='http://palm.infowave.com/'>
       <result>123.45</result>
    </GetStockQuoteResult>
  </SOAP-ENV:Body>
</SOAP-ENV:Envelope>
```

SOAP request messages are contained as data of the HTTP POST method (or alternatively, M-POST for implementations that support it). The HTTP content-type parameter must be set to `text/xml`. In JMS, using the `javax.jms.TextMessage` class can imply this (the JMS spec is quite clear about the intentions of the `TextMessage` class). This should be further qualified using a custom JMS property defining the text as XML (as opposed to unstructured text).

SOAP has also defined a new HTTP header field: `SOAPAction`. `SOAPAction` is a URI indicating the purpose of the message. Usually, this would indicate object and method names in an RPC-style application. Servers will use this field to map the message to an appropriate handler. Pulling this out of the message and placing it into the transport binding is an interesting design decision.

The implication is that message handlers – such as a server, but also any intermediate – only need to be able to parse HTTP, not XML. This makes sense for a number of reasons. Parsing the simple, non-nested attribute:value header items of HTTP is much more efficient than XML; this makes operations like dispatch and routing very efficient.

There is also a wealth of existing Internet infrastructure that is already able to process HTTP headers. For example, the presence of `SOAPAction` as an HTTP header simplifies the task of building service-based filtering rules into firewalls, which may not have XML parsers, but are likely to be HTTP aware. A farm of servers providing web services could be physically partitioned using HTTP load balancers that distribute requests based on the service identified in the `SOAPAction` field.

Note that the URI of the initial HTTP request may also indicate the intent of the message. If this is the case, then set the `SOAPAction` value to an empty string.

`SOAPAction` is an obvious candidate for a JMS message property. This can also be a reasonable substitute for the lack of an easily parameterized URI in JMS applications. Once it is a property, the richness of the JMS message selection features become available to build extremely adaptable applications.

The properties functionality of JMS does provide us with an easy way of mapping the HTTP SOAP header entries. It also means we can leverage its powerful selection features. JMS in general also gives us most of the features we need to implement business messages, such as reliability, unique message identification, and message correlation IDs for request/response messaging over a shared channel. Making use of these does tie us to JMS, though. In the next sections, we will see how some of these features can be integrated directly into the XML messaging framework.

BizTalk

The **BizTalk Framework** is an XML messaging format defined by Microsoft to support business-to-business information exchange. Naturally, it integrates with the company's BizTalk server; however, the framework is intended to support integration between different systems and so is not coupled to this.

BizTalk is particularly intriguing because it shows how a very simple specification like SOAP can be extended to meet the requirements of business-to-business electronic commerce. BizTalk SOAP features reliable messaging, more sophisticated addressing that targets business processes, and transfer of complex data sets.

Like the ebXML committee, the BizTalk designers recognize the need for exchange of non-XML data, so the framework supports attachments using MIME conventions and the multipart/related content type. The MIME root element contains the SOAP envelope. The BizTalk specification calls this the "primary document."

The adoption of MIME, however, permits other data, including other valid or invalid XML documents, to be included as attachments, thus solving a persistent SOAP problem. MIME encoding also opens the possibility of using the secure version of MIME, called S/MIME, to secure attachments, assuming that the transport does not provide security on its own.

> *S/MIME provides security services on top of the original MIME specifications. It supports encryption and digital signing of messages. S/MIME is defined in RFC 2311, available at http://www.ietf.org/rfc/rfc2311.txt.*

Message Format

BizTalk starts with the SOAP 1.1 specification, and then adds additional headers – called BizTags – to implement reliable messaging, routing, and many of the more generalized fields needed to exchange data in a business environment. There is also a diverse set of defined bindings, including HTTP, SMTP, FTP, MSMQ, DCOM, etc. At present, the specification is at version 2.0, which can be downloaded from http://www.microsoft.com/biztalk/techinfo/framework20.htm.

BizTalk introduces two new mandatory header elements to SOAP 1.1 (most namespaces have been removed for clarity – in an actual implementation, these must be included):

```
<SOAP-ENV:Header>
  <endpoints SOAP-ENV:mustUnderstand="1">
    <to>
      <address xsi:type="..."> "Unique business entity ID"
      </address>
    </to>
    <from>
      <address xsi:type="..."> "Unique business entity ID"
      </address>
    </from>
  </endpoints>
  <properties SOAP-ENV:mustUnderstand="1">
    <identity> "Globally unique message ID" </identity>
    <sentAt> "Date time" </sentAt>
    <expiresAt> "Date time" </expiresAt>
    <topic> "Some URI" </topic>
  </properties>
</SOAP-ENV:Header>
```

The `endpoints` element identifies the business parties involved in the information document exchange. Note that any application processing this message must process this header entry; it is an error to ignore it, as signified by the value of the `mustUnderstand` attribute. The `address` element could contain a URI, or alternatively some other unique identifier that both parties recognize. The `xsi:type` attribute must characterize this identifier (the `xsi:type` attribute was introduced with XML Schema as a way of identifying types in instance documents).

The inclusion of source and destination identifiers acknowledges the focus of BizTalk on application-to-application business transactions. Basic SOAP bound to HTTP only provides the `SOAPAction` parameter (or potentially the original POST URL) as a means of identifying the destination application.

BizTalk explicitly supports an addressing model decoupled from transport. Not only is it available (and required) in the header, but the schema puts few restrictions on its form: as long as the applications can understand it, it is valid. Note also that by providing source and destination addresses, dynamic routing of messages across intermediates, which is common in business interactions, becomes possible.

The `identity` element, subordinate to `properties` uniquely identifies this particular document instance. This must be globally unique, and is used to implement request/response semantics, message acknowledgements (described below), and for general logging purposes. The `sentAt` and `expiresAt` elements are necessary for reliable messaging and basic messaging application architecture. For example, most queueing applications will set expiries on messages simply to avoid swamping queues if problems arise with the message receivers.

In Pub/Sub applications, it is common for certain items to be timely (such as a stock price). The `topic` element supports application-level routing decisions, and is really a nod toward messaging paradigms like Pub/Sub.

BizTalk further defines three optional headers: services, manifest, and process. The first of these is as follows (again, namespaces are removed):

```
<SOAP-ENV:Header>
   <!-- Mandatory endpoints and properties elements removed for clarity -->
   <services SOAP-ENV:mustUnderstand="1">
     <deliveryReceiptRequest>
       <sendTo>
         <address> "Some URI" </address>
       </sendTo>
       <sendBy> "Date time" </sendBy>
     </deliveryReceiptRequest>
     <commitmentReceiptRequest>
       <sendTo>
         <address> "Some URI" </address>
       </sendTo>
       <sendBy> "Date time" </sendBy>
     </commitmentReceiptRequest>
   </services>
</SOAP-ENV:Header>
```

BizTalk actually provides a very rich environment for specification of deadlines, allowing developers to bound transport and transaction times. This manifests in the `deliveryReceiptRequest` and `commitmentReceiptRequest` headers, each of which has individually specified deadlines, and the general message `expiresAt` element in the header.

`DeliveryReceiptRequest` is used provide functionality similar to the JMS `Session.AUTO_ACKNOWLEDGE`. When a recipient accepts the message, it must reply to the address by the stated deadline.

`CommitmentReceiptRequest` informs the handler that it must send an acknowledgement when it commits to processing the message, implying that it has parsed and understood the message contents. It is similar to the JMS `javax.jms.Message.acknowledge()` feature under the `Session.CLIENT_ACKNOWLEDGE` option.

The manifest header is used to indicate that this document has multiple related parts. The manifest provides URI references using the SOAP `href` attribute, either to additional information in the SOAP body (called the primary document), in an attachment encoded in a MIME part, or potentially to an external resource outside of the message:

```
<SOAP-ENV:Header>
  <!-- Mandatory endpoints and properties elements removed for clarity -->
  <manifest SOAP-ENV:mustUnderstand="1">
    <reference>
      <attachment href="..."/>
      <description> "String description" </description>
    </reference>
  </manifest>
</SOAP-ENV:Header>
```

There can be multiple references in a manifest. The example shows a reference with an `attachment` tag; references can alternatively contain a document tag, which contains a reference to the primary document. If this reference is to an attachment, it uses a content ID URL (CID) scheme. Content ID URLs are described in RFC 2111 (see http://www.ietf.org/rfc/rfc2111.txt). This provides a URL that points to the MIME part's Content-ID header. The `description` element simply contains additional text describing the reference. This element is optional.

Finally, BizTalk includes an optional header that identifies the business process associated with this document. For example, two airline reservation systems might exchange messages concerning availability of seats on a particular flight segment at a specific time. The business process could be a SeatAvailability. The `process` header uses URI references to identify both the process and a particular instance of the process involved in the communication, as multiple instances could potentially be running and require unique identification to maintain stateful communications. It also provides a detail container that can hold additional application-specific XML data.

```
<SOAP-ENV:Header>
  <!-- Mandatory endpoints and properties elements removed for clarity -->
  <process SOAP-ENV:mustUnderstand="1">
    <type> "Some URI" </type>
    <instance> "Some URI" </instance>
    <detail>
      ...
    </detail>
  </process>
</SOAP-ENV:Header>
```

Note that `instance` provides the basis for providing server-side sessions, much as a cookie does on the Web. The detail element is flexible, and can contain application specific information.

Receipt headers can also be included as responses to a message containing the `deliveryReceiptRequest` or `commitmentReceiptRequest` elements:

```
<SOAP-ENV:Header>
    <!-- Mandatory endpoints and properties elements removed for clarity -->
    <deliveryReceipt SOAP-ENV:mustUnderstand="1">
        <receivedAt> "Date time" </receivedAt>
        <identity> "Some URI" </identity>
    </deliveryReceipt>

    <commitmentReceipt SOAP-ENV:mustUnderstand="1">
        <decidedAt> "Date time" </decidedAt>
        <decision> "Positive or negative" </decision>
        <identity> "Some URI" </identity>
        <commitmentCode> "Specific code" </commitmentCode>
        <commitmentDetail>
            ...
        </commitmentDetail>
    </commitmentReceipt>
</SOAP-ENV:Header>
```

Here, identity refers to the `identity` of the document that requests the receipt. Recall that this is a required element of every document, and can be found in the properties header described previously. The `decision` element is simply positive or negative, declaring whether the process committed or not. The `commitmentCode` field is a qualified name that describes the status more specifically than the simple positive or negative status of the decision element. Applications needing to communicate further details can use the `commitmentDetail` element to contain customized structures.

ebXML

The **Electronic Business XML Initiative (ebXML)** is a joint undertaking between UN/CEFACT (the United Nations Centre for Trade Facilitation and Electronic Business, see http://www.unece.org/cefact) and OASIS (the Organization for the Advancement of Structured Information Standards, see http://www.oasis-open.org).

UN/CEFACT describes itself as responsible for "worldwide policy and technical development in the area of trade facilitation and electronic business". OASIS is "a non-profit, international consortium dedicated solely to product-independent data and content interchange". The ebXML group formed in November 1999, budgeting an 18-month timeframe to define the framework necessary to enable a single, global electronic marketplace. Details on the project are available at http://www.ebxml/org.

Of course, electronic exchange of business data is nothing new: EDI has been available for years as a solution to streamline information exchange and eliminate the need for many business documents. However, the older EDI protocols such as EDIFACT and X12 share the problems of many traditional messaging frameworks: they are extremely complicated and tightly coupled; the systems that support it are expensive to procure and difficult to support. As a result, EDI has seen widespread use only by very large organizations. The Fortune 100 use EDI; the corner store does not.

ebXML has set out to change this. One of its primary goals has been to build a generalized business messaging framework that will accommodate not just the industry giants, but also address the particular needs of developing nations and small to medium-sized businesses. To achieve this, ebXML must be able to run securely over public networks, and make use of inexpensive, commodity technologies. It would also leverage XML as a framework for exchanging business data. The ebXML effort chose XML because of its flexibility, its internationalization capabilities (UTF-8 or UTF-16 are to be used as a character encoding), and the readily available supply of processing technology.

It is an ambitious goal. What makes ebXML particularly compelling is that it goes quite a bit farther than simply defining message formats. It actually defines an entire process for modeling business interactions. It even recommends UML as a common modeling language to document the business relationships between trading partners.

In ebXML, every trading partner is described by a profile. In addition to the typical information like name, address, etc. that one would expect, the profile contains information about services that the organization offers, and a list of its business processes. Business processes – which the committee calls "choreographies" – are a focal point of the ebXML work.

Choreographies describe the messaging dialogs (which really involve an exchange of business documents) necessary to produce a business transaction. Business processes also characterize relationships between organizations doing business, including defining the roles and responsibilities each assumes.

Core components – data such as name, address, etc., and including both atomic types and aggregations of these – have been defined in a syntactically neutral manner; this way, they can be implemented in a diverse assortment of languages and shared between clients and servers. The ebXML committee also intends to describe globally distributed repositories to contain the business processes and profiles of trading partners. Repositories include message schemas, along with the query semantics supporting interface discovery, loading of core business components, etc.

Due to the high profile and ambitious objectives of the group, a number of other independent development efforts have begun to participate. A recent addition to the organization is a working group on trading partner agreements, which is starting with IBM's tpaML as a basis.

The Open Travel Alliance (OTA), which is defining XML-based standards for exchange of travel industry information, has contributed its profile specification. The OTA has defined messages for CRUD operations on remote profile servers (where profiles contain data like name, address, telephone number, etc.). OTA messages are interesting because profile servers can maintain state, and can implement simple row locking functionality that is accounted for in the message. They also define security information in the XML message, including authentication credentials.

The ebXML group met in May 2000 in Brussels and demonstrated a proof-of-concept, in which a small company exchanged OTA-style messages with a large enterprise. Message transfer utilized both HTTP and SMTP as transport protocols. By their August meeting, they were able to offer a dynamic trading network between participating vendors, which demonstrated a number of typical transport models such as point-to-point, hub-and-spoke message brokering, and message distribution across federated servers. In December 2000, the committee announced that it was two months ahead of schedule, and would release a formal specification in March 2001.

Message Format

The ebXML specification as a whole is very detailed and comprehensive in its approach to messaging, and to do it justice would really require a book in itself (and no doubt there will be titles covering this soon). What is most relevant to this section, however, is the ebXML message structure, which should serve as a guide on how to construct generalized wire protocols using XML.

The *ebXML Messaging Service Specification*, published by the Transport, Routing, and Packaging group (see http://www.ebxml.org/project_teams/transport/transport.htm), describes message formats and their relationship to transport. The ebXML committee focused on keeping messages simple, yet still robust even when transported across potentially unreliable channels. It defines the basic functions needed to serve the needs of a global marketplace, but additionally leaves the door open for vendors to add additional fields to realize increased reliability and functionality.

The ebXML proposal is explicitly decoupled from any individual transport. The *Overview and Requirements* document for Transport, Routing and Packaging (available at the same link), still in draft at the time of writing, offers HTTP, SMTP, FTP, CORBA, and commercial MOMs as potential transports. Thus, JMS would be a likely API to access transport, and this is exactly what JAXM, described below, intends to facilitate.

However, to be an effective global electronic business protocol, the authors recognize that reliability and security are essential. Because they cannot simply delegate these to transport infrastructure (impossible when these qualities could not be expected from HTTP or SMTP), they are incorporated into the message. There are facilities – some optional, some not – to account for security, quality of service, message routing, audit trails, restart and recovery, etc.

Message headers can contain timestamps, may have maximum lifetime fields, response addresses, priority fields, references to external documents contained in a manifest, etc. There are extensive requirements for error reporting, and high expectations on acknowledgements. Digital signatures can be applied to payload documents and to message headers. There is also support for ACID transactions. Although most ebXML documents reside still in draft form, overall it is a startlingly comprehensive and well thought out piece of work:

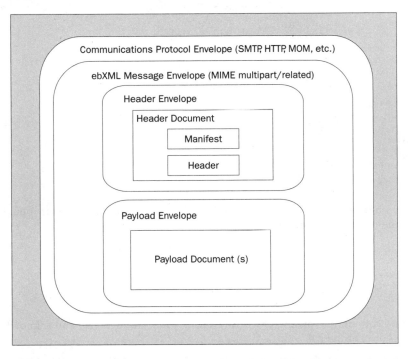

All ebXML messages are contained in an outer envelope defined by the external communications protocol, such as HTTP. Within this container is a message envelope defined as a MIME multipart/related message. This is independent of the transport protocol. MIME was chosen over an XML-based packaging for a number of reasons. There was no widely accepted spec for packaging messages with XML when the committee formed (indeed, at the time of writing, there still is not). In contrast, MIME, although developed for SMTP, is widely accepted for packaging both SMTP and HTTP content – no changes to this specification would be required to support ebXML. In contrast, a strictly XML-based solution would have required all non-XML data to be encoded.

Thus, the spec acknowledges that not all data interactions lend themselves well to XML packaging. By encoding them as MIME messages, non-textual data such as binary picture formats can be encapsulated in well-supported formats, which is often preferable over attempting to embed piecemeal in documents.

In fact, ebXML opens its definition of document as simply "any data that can be represented in a digital form". This includes sets of XML elements, PDF files, any binary format, and document fragments. Encryption and signing was an important consideration. Processing efficiency may also have been a consideration. Transactional EDI implementations often have to process very high message volumes. A general criticism leveled at XML messaging is that parsing into DOM trees may be too processor intensive for some high performance applications, such as a stock exchange. MIME is not structurally complex, so lends itself to very efficient processing.

The message envelope described above contains one or two further structures, which are actually MIME headers followed by content. There is a mandatory header envelope, which further decomposes into an XML header document. There is also an optional payload envelope, which contains the actual payload document, which may or may not be in expressed in XML. The XML header document structure is as follows:

```
<?xml version="1.0" encoding="UTF-8"?>
<ebXMLHeader
    xmlns=http://www.ebxml.org/namespaces/messageHeader Version="0.8"
    MessageType="...">
  <Manifest>
  ...
  </Manifest>
  <Header>
  ...
  </Header>
  <Routing Header>
  ...
  </Routing Header>
</ebXMLHeader>
```

The version number reflects the version available at the time of writing. The attribute `MessageType` must take on one of the following values:

- ❏   `Normal`
- ❏   `Acknowledgement`
- ❏   `Error`

These values indicate (not surprisingly) whether this is a normal message, and acknowledgement, or an error message. For example:

```
<ebXMLHeader
    xmlns=http://www.ebxml.org/namespaces/messageHeader Version="0.8"
    MessageType="Normal">
```

The acknowledgement value is interesting, because it is the first indication that the design of ebXML implements reliable messaging over potentially unreliable transports. At present, the specification defines this only for directly connected applications (that is, they are not using visible intermediates). Future versions will implement reliable messaging across intermediates.

The manifest is a container for URL-based references to documents associated with the message (namespaces and attributes have been removed for clarity):

```
<ebXMLHeader>
  <Manifest>
    <DocumentReference>
      <DocumentLabel>
        "Document description code"
      </DocumentLabel>
      <DocumentId> "Some URL" </DocumentId>
    </DocumentReference>
  </Manifest>
</ebXMLHeader>
```

These associated documents may be contained within a MIME body part elsewhere in this message. They may also be external to the message.

The generic header element (which is a sub-element of the `ebXMLHeader`) contains a number of children:

```
<ebXMLHeader>
  <!-- Mandatory Manifest element removed for clarity -->
  <Header>
    <From>
      <PartyId context="...">
        "Some ID, possibly a URN"
      </PartyId>
    </From>
    <To>
      <PartyId context="...">
        "Some ID, possibly a URN"
      </PartyId>
    </To>
    <TPAInfo>
      ...
    </TPAInfo>
    <MessageData>
      ...
    </MessageData>
    <ReliableMessagingInfo DeliverySemantics="..."/>
  </Header>
</ebXMLHeader>
```

`To` and `From` elements obviously identify the communicating parties, using a subordinate `<PartyId>` element that can use a URN or other identifier that may be more appropriate for the operation. In contrast to BizTalk, this element does not have an `xsi:type` attribute explicitly identified in the specification, but the context attribute is intended to serve the same purpose. `TPAInfo` contains information describing the trading partner agreement. Trading partner agreements may document rules under which trading can occur, locations to report errors, etc. This element includes:

```
<Header>
  <!-- Mandatory From and To elements removed for clarity -->
  <TPAInfo>
    <TPAId> "Some URI" </TPAId>
      <ConversationId> "Some URI" </ConversationId>
      <ServiceInterface>
        "Some service ID, possibly URN"
      </ServiceInterface>
```

```
            <Action>
               "Some process ID within the service interface"
            </Action>
         </TPAInfo>
      </Header>
```

`TPAId` identifies the actual trading partner agreement. In the event of an error, this may be used to determine where to send an error message (or a specific error handler might be identified, as described below). `ServiceInterface` and `Action` ultimately name the service that is to process the message. It is interesting to note how deeply embedded in the structure these data reside, demanding significant parsing to extract. Services may also appear in the payload document. Most implementations will likely map `ServiceInterface` and `Action` to a business object and method.

The `MessageData` element in `Header` contains additional elements to implement the functions commonly provided by message-oriented middleware. JMS provides access to the service provider's equivalents of these through the `javax.jms.Message` class:

```
<Header>
   <!-- Mandatory From, To, and TPAInfo elements removed for clarity -->
   <MessageData>
     <MessageID> "Unique message ID" </MessageID>
     <TimeStamp> "Date time" </TimeStamp>
     <RefToMessageID>
        "Reference to unique message ID"
     </RefToMessageID>
   </MessageData>
</Header>
```

> *MessageID must uniquely identify a message, using the message identification rules outlined in RFC 2392,* Content-ID and Message-ID Uniform Resource Locators, *which can be found at http://www.ietf.org/rfc/rfc2392.txt.*

`RefToMessageID` is a correlation identifier, so that request/response messaging can build on top of the ebXML message framework. The `TimeStamp` here must conform to the Coordinated Universal Time (UTC) format described in ISO-8601 (http://www.iso.ch/markete/8601.pdf). This representation uses the model CCYYMMDDThhmmss.sssZ where T is a time indicator, used here to delimit, and Z is a timezone indicator, also used here to delimit. This works with the XML Schema derived data types for date and time. For example:

```
<MessageData>
   <MessageID>mid:20011231.999999@wrox.com</MessageID>
   <TimeStamp>20011231T235959.999Z</TimeStamp>
   <RefToMessageID></RefToMessageID>
</MessageData>
```

The `ReliableMessagingInfo` child of the `Header` element contains a single attribute, `DeliverySemantics`, which can be set to one of the following values:

- ❑ `OnceAndOnlyOnce`
- ❑ `BestEffort`

If set to the former, additional elements will be required in the message to implement reliable messaging independent of transport:

```
<Header>
    <!-- Mandatory From, To, TPAInfo, and MessageData elements
       removed for clarity -->
<ReliableMessagingInfo DeliverySemantics="..."/>
</Header>
```

The RoutingHeader contains the following subordinate elements:

```
<ebXMLHeader>
   <RoutingHeader>
     <SenderURI> "Some URI" </SenderURI>
     <ReceiverURI> "Some URI" </ReceiverURI>
     <ErrorURI> "Some URI" </ErrorURI>
     <TimeStamp> "Date time" </TimeStamp>
     <SequenceNumber> "Integer sequence no." </SequenceNumber>
   </RoutingHeader>
</ebXMLHeader>
```

SenderURI defines actual message handlers, as opposed to a party identifier defined in the Header described above. Note the identification of a specific error handler. This is quite a bit more flexible than simply having an error flag rendered in the message and assuming that every receiver can process it.

The SequenceNumber is another field used to implement reliable messaging, and is only included if one time delivery has been indicated earlier. The specification describes the actual algorithm to implement and it is well worth reading. Even when working with JMS over a reliable service provider, it is valuable to understand what the service provider actually has to go through to ensure reliability, as this always has performance implications.

The ebXML spec also contains a detailed framework for error reporting. ebXML does not render errors in the header; instead, the MessageType attribute in the ebXMLHeader is set to "Error" and a dedicated XML error document is inserted into the payload. The error document structure is as follows:

```
<?xml version="1.0" encoding="UTF-8"?>
<ebXMLError xmlns=http://www.ebxml.org/namespaces/errorVersion="0.8">
  <ErrorHeader ID='...'>
    ...
  </ErrorHeader>
  <ErrorLocation>
  </ErrorLocation>
</ebXMLError>
```

There can be only a single ErrorHeader, but zero or more ErrorLocation fields. The ErrorHeader contains up to four subordinate elements:

```
<ebXMLError>
  <ErrorHeader ID='...'>
    <ErrorCode> "Error code string" </ErrorCode>
    <Severity> "Warning or Error" </Severity>
    <Description xml:lang='...'>
      "String describing error"
    </Description>
    <SoftwareDetails>
```

```
        "String describing software details"
      </SoftwareDetails>
    </ErrorHeader>
  </ebXMLError>
```

Note that it optionally provides for both localized language text description of the error (which could be output to a user), and more detailed, developer-level error messages. `ErrorCode`'s include one of the following defined in the specification. For error in the header document:

- ❑ UnableToParse
- ❑ ValueNotRecognized
- ❑ NotSupported
- ❑ Inconsistent
- ❑ OtherXML

Or for problems that are not related to XML documents:

- ❑ MessageTooLarge
- ❑ MimeProblem
- ❑ Unknown

The actual error code should be one of the above with a narrative description appended to it. This should be localized when practical to make use of the language identified in the `Description` element. Severity can take one of two values:

- ❑ Warning
- ❑ Error

`ErrorLocation` identifies where the error occurred. Since it may be an error in the message itself, it can refer to a part of the message. Alternatively (or in addition – multiple locations are permissible), it can refer to something outside the message:

```
<ebXMLError>
   <!-- Mandatory ErrorHeader element removed for clarity --
  <ErrorLocation ID='...'>
    <RefToMessageId> "Unique msg ID" </RefToMessageId>
    <Href> "Reference to message" </Href>
  </ErrorLocation>
</ebXMLError>
```

BizTalk vs. ebXML

It is interesting to compare BizTalk and ebXML. Looking only at message formats, they are really far more similar that they are different. Superficially, the tags have different names, but for the most part, there exist equivalent constructs in both. Furthermore:

- ❑ Both designs emphasize flexibility and extensibility; their use of XML as a header container makes it very simple to add new tags and structures to the basic header

- ❏ Both decouple from transport, and provide the key tags needed to maintain reliable messaging services

- ❏ Both have a flexible means to render exceptions and communicate them to other systems (here, BizTalk uses existing SOAP error reporting mechanisms)

- ❏ Neither explicitly supports transaction hooks, although this could be added easily within the frameworks

The BizTalk `deliveryReceiptRequest` and `commitmentReceiptRequest` headers are particularly detailed and flexible, and have no direct equivalents in ebXML. Furthermore, BizTalk provides rich semantics for message, delivery receipt, and commitment receipt expiries, all of which are very important, and have direct equivalents in JMS.

The ebXML standard explicitly supports a version model for the message framework. The ebXML `RoutingHeader` is nicely separated and distinct, acknowledging the importance of intermediates in global business messaging. The `TPAInfo` header nicely encapsulates the logical concept of business process, the articulation of which is an important goal of the ebXML group, and reflects its larger focus as a horizontal framework for global electronic commerce.

XMSG

XMSG is an XML message format described in a W3C Note published in Oct 2000, residing at http://www.w3.org/TR/xmsg. The goal of XMSG is to define a simple XML container that could be used to transport one or more XML documents, or other data rendered as MIME types. It provides a flexible means of adding metadata about the contained documents as property fields. XMSG is simple, yet still supports a number of the fields necessary to support more advanced messaging.

Unlike BizTalk and ebXML, which define these fields as elements in a header structure, XMSG declares these fields as attributes of the message envelope:

```
<message xmlns="..."
         to="..."
         from="..."
         id="..."
         generated.on="..."
         reply.to="..."
         originator="..."
         originator.id="..."
         priority="..."
         expires="..."
         tracking.code="..."
         action="..."
         manifest="..."
         receipt.required="..."
         for.receipt="...">

<hop received.on="..." received.by="..." transport.used="..."/>
<property name="..." value="..."/>

<document uri="..." version="...">
   ...
</document>
</message>
```

Note the hop element. XMSG explicitly records the message trail across intermediates, as SMTP does. The originator and the originator.id attributes record the original sender of a message and its original unique ID (the from and id attributes record these properties only for the current hop).

Properties are extensible, although the specification does explicitly offer a number of properties mirroring the attributes in the message element. The document element can contain either XML documents, non-XML data encoded as a MIME type, or a reference to external data.

The document element, depicted above, may be replaced by either a failure element or a receipt element. The failure element contains a text description of why the failure occurred:

```
<failure on="..." reason.code="...">
   "Description of cause of failure"
</failure>
```

The receipt elements exist for applications requiring acknowledgements of message receipt:

```
<receipt message.tracking.code="..." timestamp="..."/>
```

XMSG provides a good, simple framework for messages. It is likely that some of these ideas will resurface in the W3C's XP initiative, described below.

W3C XP

The XML Protocol Activity was launched under the W3C to define a standardized XML messaging framework. The activity formally started in September 2000, allocating an 18-month timeframe and a goal to deliver a formal recommendation in the fall of 2001. The XML Protocol Working group will actually define an XML messaging framework. The group intends to incorporate a number of the qualities that made SOAP so popular, but at the same time address its limitations as a generalized messaging framework.

The Activity will attempt to keep the specification simple and very easy to extend. It will include a specification for a messaging envelope, and a specification for serialization of application data. XP (as it has come to be know) primarily targets RPC-style communications, and the framework will describe typical Request/Response message formats.

However, XP will not be limited to this, so it will be appropriate as a message format for applications using paradigms like Publish/Subscribe. XP explicitly decouples transport and message format (that is, everything contained in the XP envelope), although the specification will define a default binding to HTTP.

Outside of the message formatting, the Activity will define XML protocol modules, which provide the additional services needed in messaging applications. These could include security services, interaction with caches, triggering of applications and events, message routing, etc. It acknowledges that messaging goes beyond simple direct connections and will accommodate intermediates in message transfer. The Activity declared repositories and service discovery outside of its scope.

XP has the influence of the W3C behind it, a stellar roster of participants from the XML and messaging community, and the opportunity to address the problems in the current XML message offerings.

A working draft of the XML Protocol Requirements, *published in December 2000, is available on the Activity web site at* http://www.w3.org/2000/xp. *It will be interesting to watch what happens to XP.*

Others

The formats described in this section are certainly not the only ones available. The point of this section was not to review all the formats in existence, but rather to examine a few to illustrate how they solve some typical messaging problems. There are other formats, like RosettaNet, WDDX, RDF, and ICE that could equally have been included. For those interested in exploring other protocols, the W3C keeps an excellent matrix comparing a number of formats at http://www.w3.org/2000/03/29-XML-protocol-matrix.

Service Discovery and Description

Defining messaging APIs is only the first challenge. To do global electronic commerce, businesses need to have to have a systematic way of publishing the API and providing a means of letting others discover that it exists (or, in a worldwide marketplace, even letting potential customers know that the business exists). The goal is to support late, run-time binding of applications to services.

The ebXML repository group is addressing this problem within the context of its own specification; however there are other efforts in the emerging web services community that also try to standardize how this might be implemented. The latter tend to be focused on serving the current HTTP-centric web service model, but the specifications will likely to be extended to support transport infrastructures that would be made accessible using JMS.

UDDI

In September 2000, Ariba, IBM, and Microsoft jointly announced the formation of the **Universal Description, Discovery, and Integration (UDDI)** initiative. The goal was to build broad industry support around a standard for the discovery of businesses and services on the Internet.

To accomplish this, the initiative would seek input from a large number of players both in the Internet space, and from traditional industries such as manufacturing, which will be big consumers of business-to-business solutions. Over an 18-month timeframe, the UDDI community will define standards and APIs that build on existing successful technologies like HTTP, XML, SOAP, DNS, etc. After managing this process, the committee will ultimately transfer the results to an external standards body (not formally identified by press time).

By the end of the year, there were over 130 vendors involved in the group, including most of the key players in the business-to-business infrastructure space. Indeed, even a number of companies with alterative solutions, such as HP with its eSpeak framework, have become involved.

Arguably, UDDI is putting itself in the same space as the ebXML Registry and Repository Team. The difference is really one of scope and focus. Organizations are beginning to deploy SOAP-based web services now, and a solution for service discovery and registration, again with SOAP as a focal point, is urgently required. The ebXML group is taking a more generalized approach to repositories, considering them as placed to register business processes, core components, etc.

UDDI proposes the construction of a centralized, but replicated repository of business information. The repositories will not hunt out services on the net like a web crawler. Rather, businesses will explicitly register with any convenient repository; these entries will be replicated among a global network of cooperating repositories, thus minimizing potential issues around politics and scalability. Thus, the model is more like DNS than a web search engine.

The specification will define the XML-based messages to query the repository to discover information about businesses and the interfaces that they support. The specification will also describe publishing interfaces businesses can use to register and update their entries.

Businesses register themselves in white, yellow, and green pages in the repository. Naturally, all registrations make use of XML documents. White pages contain general information about the business. Name, contact details like phone and address, web site location, registration numbers (such as DUNS codes), key personnel, etc. constitute typical white pages entries. This in itself solves a key business problem. Today, there is no single search engine that is global, comprehensive, and devoted to business. There are, of course, industry-specific databases, sometimes run by professional organizations. However, there is no general, central repository.

Yellow pages group businesses into categories, using a number of standard taxonomies. The North American Industry Classification System (NAICS, see http://www.census.gov/epcd/www/naics.html), which defines a hierarchical series of numeric identifiers that classify businesses into categories like "Book Publishers (code 51113)" is one such taxonomy.

The Universal Standard Products and Services Classification (UNSPSC, see http://www.unspsc.org) is another, with a more global focus. Finally, green pages will incorporate location-based classifications. Additional taxonomies will be introduced as the specification evolves.

Green pages contain information about how an organization conducts business. This includes descriptions of business processes, and descriptions about the services the organization provides as APIs. If a business supports other discovery services, such as its own service discovery repository, a reference to that will be contained here.

The community quickly published a number of specifications: the *UDDI Programmer's API Specification*; the *UDDI Data Structures Reference*; and the *UDDI XML Schema* (all three documents are available at http://www.uddi.org/specification.html). The API defines a simple mechanism for businesses to publish information, and to make inquiries of the repository using simple XML API inside SOAP, and based on a synchronous, request/response call model. Nevertheless, the community does not intend to limit itself to a single API; instead, it anticipates that it will support a number of different APIs for repository access.

By November 2000, a test implementation of the repository became publicly available for beta testing. This will probably be available for at least six months. This first version of the repository is free to access and register. Each of the three founding members hosts a replica of the repository. Businesses can register at any one; replication of the entry among the other systems is automatic. The link http://www.uddi.org/register.html provides access to all of the test systems so that businesses can make basic registrations now.

People interested in experimenting with UDDI (and in particular, WSDL, described in the next section) can download the IBM Web Services Toolkit from http://alphaworks.ibm.com/tech/webservicestoolkit, which supports some publication and interface discovery functions aligned to the current specification. The toolkit contains a web service browser – similar in function to a class browser in an IDE, but used to explore the services registered in a repository. As web services become more commonplace, service browsers will become essential development tools. The toolkit also provides a preview of the work IBM is doing to bind SOAP to MQSeries.

Example

The *UDDI Programmer's API Specification* outlines a relatively simple mechanism for querying a repository for information about a business and the services it offers. We will not cover this in detail here, but instead show some simple examples of UDDI in action.

The following dialogs show some typical requests and responses for queries against IBM's UDDI test installation, using the HTTP binding. First, a query using the UDDI `find_business` function, searching for "IBM". The request:

```
POST /services/uddi/inquiryapi HTTP/1.1
Accept: text/xml
Cache-Control: no-cache
SOAPAction: ""
Content-Length: 216
User-Agent: Mozilla/4.0 (compatible; MSIE 5.01; Windows NT)
Host: www-3.ibm.com
Connection: Keep-Alive

<?xml version='1.0' encoding='UTF-8'?>
<Envelope xmlns='http://schemas.xmlsoap.org/soap/envelope/'>
  <Body>
    <find_business generic='1.0' xmlns='urn:uddi-org:api'>
      <name>IBM</name>
    </find_business>
  </Body>
</Envelope>
```

The response (note that a number of `ServiceInfo` elements have been removed for clarity):

```
HTTP/1.1 200 ok
Date: Wed, 07 Feb 2001 00:15:43 GMT
Server: IBM_HTTP_Server/1.3.6.2 Apache/1.3.7-dev (Unix)
content-length: 2656
Connection: close
Content-Type: text/xml

<?xml version="1.0" encoding="UTF-8" ?>
<Envelope xmlns="http://schemas.xmlsoap.org/soap/envelope/">
<Body>
  <businessList generic="1.0" xmlns="urn:uddi-org:api"
     operator="www.ibm.com/services/uddi" truncated="false">
  <businessInfos>
    <businessInfo businessKey="6827FE60-00E2-F6A9-F6C4-C6113993AA77">
      <name>IBM Corporation</name>
      <description xml:lang="en">At IBM, we strive to lead in the creation,
          development and manufacture of the industry's most advanced
          information technologies, including computer systems, software,
          networking systems, storage devices and microelectronics.
      </description>
      <serviceInfos>
        <serviceInfo serviceKey="6828022E-00E2-E46A-9849-C6113993AA77"
            businessKey="6827FE60-00E2-F6A9-F6C4-C6113993AA77">
          <name>Buy from IBM</name>
```

```
        </serviceInfo>
        <serviceInfo serviceKey="68280790-00E2-E6C8-E8F8-C6113993AA77"
              businessKey="6827FE60-00E2-F6A9-F6C4-C6113993AA77">
          <name>
            Buy from IBM using business-to-business e-commerce applications
          </name>
        </serviceInfo>
        <serviceInfo serviceKey="68280878-00E2-E84B-CCDF-C6113993AA77"
              businessKey="6827FE60-00E2-F6A9-F6C4-C6113993AA77">
          <name>Supply goods and services to IBM</name>
        </serviceInfo>

<!—Removed some serviceInfo elements for clarity -->

        <serviceInfo serviceKey="68280D53-00E2-E6A7-19BD-C6113993AA77"
                    businessKey="6827FE60-00E2-F6A9-F6C4-C6113993AA77">
          <name>UDDI Publish</name>
        </serviceInfo>
        <serviceInfo serviceKey="68280DC6-00E2-F664-135E-C6113993AA77"
                    businessKey="6827FE60-00E2-F6A9-F6C4-C6113993AA77">
          <name>UDDI Inquiry</name>
        </serviceInfo>
      </serviceInfos>
    </businessInfo>
    <businessInfo businessKey="844105EB-00E4-F2B6-38F7-C6113993AA77">
      <name>IBM Webservices Test Area</name>
      <description xml:lang="en">Use this area for investigating visual
          Webservice components
      </description>
      <serviceInfos></serviceInfos>
    </businessInfo>
  </businessInfos>
</businessList>
</Body>
</Envelope>
```

Even this early into the specification, IBM has a number of web services available. Note the businessKey attribute of the businessInfo element. The value of this is IBM's globally unique identification as a business entity. Now let's do try the UDDI find_service interface, searching for IBM's "UDDI Inquiry" service. This time, we will edit the HTTP headers out, as they are not significantly different from the previous example. The request:

```
<?xml.version='1.0'.encoding='UTF-8'?>
<Envelope xmlns='http://schemas.xmlsoap.org/soap/envelope/'>
  <Body>
    <find_service generic='1.0' xmlns='urn:uddi-org:api'
        businessKey='6827FE60-00E2-F6A9-F6C4-C6113993AA77'>
      <name>UDDI Inquiry</name>
    </find_service>
  </Body>
</Envelope>
```

The response:

```
<?xml version="1.0" encoding="UTF-8" ?>
<Envelope xmlns="http://schemas.xmlsoap.org/soap/envelope/">
  <Body>
    <serviceList generic="1.0" xmlns="urn:uddi-org:api"
        operator="www.ibm.com/services/uddi" truncated="false">
      <serviceInfos>
        <serviceInfo serviceKey="68280DC6-00E2-F664-135E-C6113993AA77"
            businessKey="6827FE60-00E2-F6A9-F6C4-C6113993AA77">
          <name>UDDI Inquiry</name>
        </serviceInfo>
      </serviceInfos>
    </serviceList>
  </Body>
</Envelope>
```

Note the serviceKey attribute of the serviceInfo element. We will use this to discover some details about the UDDI Inquiry service (again, dropping the HTTP headers for clarity). The request:

```
<?xml version='1.0' encoding='UTF-8'?>
<Envelope xmlns='http://schemas.xmlsoap.org/soap/envelope/'>
  <Body>
    <get_serviceDetail generic='1.0' xmlns='urn:uddi-org:api'>
      <serviceKey>68280DC6-00E2-F664-135E-C6113993AA77</serviceKey>
    </get_serviceDetail>
  </Body>
</Envelope>
```

The response:

```
<?xml version="1.0" encoding="UTF-8" ?>
<Envelope xmlns="http://schemas.xmlsoap.org/soap/envelope/">
  <Body>
    <serviceDetail generic="1.0" xmlns="urn:uddi-org:api"
        operator="www.ibm.com/services/uddi" truncated="false">
      <businessService businessKey="6827FE60-00E2-F6A9-F6C4-C6113993AA77"
          serviceKey="68280DC6-00E2-F664-135E-C6113993AA77">
        <name>UDDI Inquiry</name>
        <description xml:lang="en">
          Inquire about UDDI registry information
        </description>
        <bindingTemplates>
          <bindingTemplate bindingKey="68280DF5-00E2-EC71-11AF-C6113993AA77"
              serviceKey="68280DC6-00E2-F664-135E-C6113993AA77">
          <description xml:lang="en">UDDI inquiry (servlet)</description>
          <accessPoint URLType="http">
             http://www-3.ibm.com/services/uddi/inquiryapi
          </accessPoint>
            <tModelInstanceDetails>
              <tModelInstanceInfo
                 tModelKey="UUID:4CD7E4BC-648B-426D-9936-443EAAC8AE23">
              </tModelInstanceInfo>
```

```
            </tModelInstanceDetails>
          </bindingTemplate>
          <bindingTemplate bindingKey="68280E20-00E2-F116-0F36-C6113993AA77"
              serviceKey="68280DC6-00E2-F664-135E-C6113993AA77">
          <description xml:lang="en">UDDI Inquiry (web)</description>
          <accessPoint URLType="http">
            http://www.ibm.com/services/uddi/find.htm</accessPoint>
            <tModelInstanceDetails>
              <tModelInstanceInfo
                 tModelKey="UUID:4CD7E4BC-648B-426D-9936-443EAAC8AE23">
              </tModelInstanceInfo>
            </tModelInstanceDetails>
          </bindingTemplate>
        </bindingTemplates>
      </businessService>
    </serviceDetail>
  </Body>
</Envelope>
```

The `bindingTemplate` element describes the service bindings for UDDI Inquiry. Binding templates are one of the fundamental structures defined by UDDI. They provide details about a service entry point, as well as information needed to access the service. There are two `bindingTemplate` elements here: one marked web (with an HTML page as access point) and another servlet (with what we can assume is a URL pointing to a servlet as the access point).

In UDDI, tModels are unique interface identities – the specification calls them fingerprints for services. For example, here one logical service, UDDI Inquiry, has multiple interfaces (web and servlet). Each of these has a unique identification, shown here as the `tModelKey` attribute on the `tModelInstanceInfo` element. Note also that each distinct binding template contains a `serviceKey` attribute referencing back to the service name. Simply by inspecting this structure, we can infer much about what kinds of queries are available in UDDI.

For those interested in exploring this further, Microsoft provides a tool that launches queries against the test repositories at http://msdn.microsoft.com/workshop/xml/articles/12182000-test.htm.

WSDL

The **Web Services Description Language (WSDL)** is a specification for describing the interfaces and deployment of web services in a standardized manner. IBM and Microsoft unveiled it at the end of September 2000 and submitted it to the UDDI initiative, where at press time it resides under the category "Potential Submissions." Copies of the spec are available from http://www.uddi.org/submissions.html.

WSDL evolved from two separate vendor initiatives: IBM's Network Accessible Service Specification Language (NASSL) and Microsoft's SOAP Contract Language (SCL). The specification's goal is to describe the interfaces of a web service without necessary documenting its behavior or the rules governing message exchange (the authors will explore this in later revisions). WDSL approaches this by describing web services as a collection of related endpoints. Endpoints are aggregations of ports, which are the concrete realizations of a message bound to a location and protocol such as HTTP, SOAP, or MIME.

The specification is complex and likely to evolve significantly in the near future, so I will not try to describe it here. It does, however, appear to solve a difficult problem: how does one tie the abstract concept of a service to a concrete description of the actual APIs that implement it. Different transport bindings result in different APIs (which, ultimately, is all the clients of the service are interested in), even though these bindings may package the same underlying abstract message.

At present, the specification only defines bindings to HTTP, SOAP, and MIME, so using it in a JMS implementation would require many assumptions that may ultimately go against the specification. Later revisions of WSDL will offer alternative bindings, and we can probably expect IBM to provide an implementation for its MQSeries MOM product, which of course supports a JMS API. Anybody interested in exploring WSDL now can look at the WSDL Toolkit on IBM's AlphaWorks (http://www.alphaworks.ibm.com).

This package generates Java stubs and skeletons from a WSDL document, using the Apache SOAP implementation for communications. The Web Services Toolkit (described in the UDDI section) also demonstrates how WSDL documents describing interfaces can be stored in a UDDI repository.

JAXR

The Java API for XML Registries is a project to create a client-side Java API that encapsulates the process of interacting with a registry. Like JAXP for parsers, the intention is to create a standard client-side API that provides query and publishing functions for a number of different registry systems.

The initial implementation targets the ebXML registry, but it could also provide access to UDDI registries. JAXR will make use of the messaging abstractions developed as part of JAXM, discussed below. Interestingly, one of the project goals is to enable the adoption of publish/subscribe models for XML messages between businesses.

JAXP is registered as JSR 000093 in the Java Community Process, and can be found at http://java.sun.com/aboutJava/communityprocess/jsr/jsr_093_jaxr.html. The group intends to publish a public draft of its specification by Q2 2001.

Message APIs

Once an XML-based message format definition is available, how should developers access it? They could use DOM, SAX, or even data binding, as described previously. But each one of these requires intimate knowledge of the message formatting details. Developers working in a high-level language like Java should not be concerned with wire formats anymore that they ever consider the format of CORBA, IDL, or JRMP. This section describes some of the standardization efforts underway that address this issue.

JAXM

The **Java API for XML Messaging (JAXM)** is an attempt to define a JAVA API to access the contents of XML messages, without having to concentrate on the actual message format (which as we have seen, can be quite complex). The idea is to provide a consistent API that provides access to a number of the key fields needed in reliable messaging (such as those described in the examples above – common fields like To, From, MessageID, etc.) without concerning the programmer with the details of how these are realized in the message or potentially in the transport.

In fact, JAXM will not attempt to define its own wire protocol – as we have seen, that's already being done elsewhere. Formats like ebXML, W3C XP, and BizTalk could all be accessed consistently through the same JAXM API. JAXM will support access to reliable messaging features, as well as security features like confidentiality, integrity, non-repudiation, authentication, authorization, and audit. Thus, it can effectively abstract away all the issues of whether these are implemented in a message, or delegated to transport. JAXM will be transport agnostic, although implementations over HTTP and SMTP are to be expected.

The Java Community Process governs development of JAXM. The JAXM classification is JSR-000067, http://java.sun.com/aboutJava/communityprocess/jsr/jsr_067_jaxm.html. At the time of writing, there is an early access package available for download. It runs in the Tomcat servlet container, and uses ebXML messages as a wire protocol. This is not production code, but is discussion point for project participants and other interested parties. Download the kit from: http://developer.java.sun.com/developer/earlyAccess/mproject/.

Java APIs for XML-Based RPCs

The goal of the Java APIs for XML-based RPC is to create pure Java APIs that encapsulate XML RPC protocols, like SOAP and the W3C's emerging Xprotocol. The group intends to create tooling that will marshal and unmarshal between Java objects and an XML protocol, and create reverse mappings of an existing class to a particular protocol, and forward mappings to go from an existing XML protocol message schema to Java classes.

This is registered as JSR-000101 under the Java Community Process. At the time of publication, the expert group was just forming. See http://java.sun.com/aboutJava/communityprocess /jsr/jsr_101_xrpc.html.

CMI

In June 1999, IBM announced the **Common Message Interface (CMI)**. The intent of CMI is to abstract away message construction and examination independent of language. The company also announced the Application Messaging Interface (AMI), which will be a cross-language API for messaging systems (including Java).

CMI will handle binary data like C `struct`s, MQIntegrator dictionaries, and tagged data. In particular, it supports XML messages. CMI is not coupled to a transport API, so JMS, AMI, MQI, or any vendor interface could be used. There has been very little publicity about CMI since its announcement, so the project may be dead.

Summary

We have looked at a number of the emerging standards for messaging using XML. At the time of publication, the future is looking very bright for these standards. In particular, the ebXML consortium have just announced that SOAP 1.1 is to become the encoding format used for the ebXML Messaging Specification.

com.sun.jn...
com.sun.jn...
weblogic.jndi.T3Initia...
weblogic.jms.rtl.Fiorar...
fiorano.jms.runtime.na...
ch.softwired.jms.naming.RefSContextFactory
com.sun.jndi.ldap.LdapCtxFactory
com.sun.jndi.WLInitialContextFactory
weblogic.jndi.T3InitialContextFactory
fiorano.jms.rtl.FioranoInitialContextFactory
weblogic.jndi.FioranoInitialContext
fiorano.jms.runtime.naming.FioranoInitialContextFactory
ch.softwired.jms.naming.IBusContextFactory

com.sun.jndi.fscontext.RefFSContextFactory
weblogic.jndi.ldap.LdapCtxFactory
weblogic.jndi.WLInitialContextFactory
fiorano.jms.rtl.FioranoInitialContextFactory
ch.softwired.jms.runtime.naming.FioranoInitialContextFactory
ch.softwired.jms.naming.IBusContextFactory

Index

A Guide to the Index

The index is arranged hierarchically, in alphabetical order, with symbols preceding the letter A. Most second-level entries and many third-level entries also occur as first-level entries. This is to ensure that users will find the information they require however they choose to search for it.

H

Professional JMS Programming

```
com.sun.jn...
com.sun.jn...
weblogic.jndi.T3Initial Fiorar...
weblogic.jms.rtl.fioran...
fiorano.jms.runtime.n...
ch.softwired.jms.naming.RefFSContextFactory
fiorano.jndi.LdapCtxFactory
com.sun.jndi.WLInitialContextFactory
com.sun.jndi.T3InitialContextFactory
weblogic.jndi.FioranoInitialContextFactory
fiorano.jms.rtl.FioranoInitialContextFactory
fiorano.jms.runtime.naming.FioranoInitialContextFactory
ch.softwired.jms.naming.IBusContextFactory
```

p2p.wrox.com
The programmer's resource centre

A unique free service from Wrox Press
with the aim of helping programmers to help each other

Wrox Press aims to provide timely and practical information to today's programmer. P2P is a list server offering a host of targeted mailing lists where you can share knowledge with your fellow programmers and find solutions to your problems. Whatever the level of your programming knowledge, and whatever technology you use, P2P can provide you with the information you need.

ASP — Support for beginners and professionals, including a resource page with hundreds of links, and a popular ASP+ mailing list.

DATABASES — For database programmers, offering support on SQL Server, mySQL, and Oracle.

MOBILE — Software development for the mobile market is growing rapidly. We provide lists for the several current standards, including WAP, WindowsCE, and Symbian.

JAVA — A complete set of Java lists, covering beginners, professionals,and server-side programmers (including JSP, servlets and EJBs)

.NET — Microsoft's new OS platform, covering topics such as ASP+, C#, and general .Net discussion.

VISUAL BASIC — Covers all aspects of VB programming, from programming Office macros to creating components for the .Net platform.

WEB DESIGN — As web page requirements become more complex, programmer sare taking a more important role in creating web sites. For these programmers, we offer lists covering technologies such as Flash, Coldfusion, and JavaScript.

XML — Covering all aspects of XML, including XSLT and schemas.

OPEN SOURCE — Many Open Source topics covered including PHP, Apache, Perl, Linux, Python and more.

FOREIGN LANGUAGE — Several lists dedicated to Spanish and German speaking programmers, categories include .Net, Java, XML, PHP and XML.

How To Subscribe

Simply visit the P2P site, at **http://p2p.wrox.com/**

Select the 'FAQ' option on the side menu bar for more information about the subscription process and our service.

Programmer to Programmer™

wrox
PROGRAMMER TO PROGRAMMER™

Wrox writes books for you. Any suggestions, or ideas about how you want information given in your ideal book will be studied by our team. Your comments are always valued at Wrox.

Free phone in USA 800-USE-WROX
Fax (312) 893 8001

UK Tel. (0121) 687 4100   Fax (0121) 687 4101

wrox
PROGRAMMER TO PROGRAMMER™

NB. If you post the bounce back card below in the UK, please send it to:

Wrox Press Ltd., Arden House, 1102 Warwick Road,
Acocks Green, Birmingham B27 6BH. UK.

——— *Computer Book Publishers* ———